Lecture Notes in Artificial Intelligence   1303

Subseries of Lecture Notes in Computer Science
Edited by J. G. Carbonell and J. Siekmann

Lecture Notes in Computer Science

Edited by G. Goos, J. Hartmanis and J. van Leeuwen

T0223199

Springer
Berlin
Heidelberg
New York
Barcelona
Budapest
Hong Kong
London
Milan
Paris
Santa Clara
Singapore
Tokyo

Gerhard Brewka   Christopher Habel
Bernhard Nebel (Eds.)

KI-97: Advances in Artificial Intelligence

21st Annual German Conference
on Artificial Intelligence
Freiburg, Germany, September 9-12, 1997
Proceedings

Springer

Series Editors
Jaime G. Carbonell, Carnegie Mellon University, Pittsburgh, PA, USA
Jörg Siekmann, University of Saarland, Saarbrücken, Germany

Volume Editors

Gerhard Brewka
Universität Leipzig, Institut für Informatik
Augustusplatz 10/11, D-04109 Leipzig, Germany
E-mail: brewka@informatik.uni-leipzig.de

Christopher Habel
Universität Hamburg, Fachbereich Informatik
Vogt-Kölln-Str. 30, D-22527 Hamburg, Germany
E-mail: habel@informatik.uni-hamburg.de

Bernhard Nebel
Albert-Ludwigs-Universität Freiburg i. Br., Institut für Informatik
Am Flughafen 17, D-79110 Freiburg, Germany
E-mail: nebel@informatik.uni-freiburg.de

Cataloging-in-Publication Data applied for

Die Deutsche Bibliothek - CIP-Einheitsaufnahme

Advances in artificial intelligence : proceedings / KI-97, 21th
**Annual German Conference on Artificial Intelligence, Freiburg,
Germany, September 9 - 12, 1997. Gerhard Brewka ... (ed.). - Berlin ;
Heidelberg ; New York ; Barcelona ; Budapest ; Hong Kong ;
London ; Milan ; Paris ; Santa Clara ; Singapore ; Tokyo : Springer,
1997**
    (Lecture notes in computer science ; Vol. 1303 : Lecture notes in
    artificial intelligence)
    ISBN 3-540-63493-2

CR Subject Classification (1991): I.2

ISBN 3-540-63493-2 Springer-Verlag Berlin Heidelberg New York

© Springer-Verlag Berlin Heidelberg 1997
- Printed in Germany

Typesetting: Camera ready by author
SPIN 10545921   06/3142 – 5 4 3 2 1 0   Printed on acid-free paper

Preface

This volume contains the invited contributions, accepted papers and poster presentations of the 21st German Artificial Intelligence Conference, KI-97, held in Freiburg, Sept. 9–12, 1997.

In recent years the German AI conference has turned from a more local event which remained almost unnoticed outside Germany into a meeting of international character attracting submissions from all over the world. This trend has continued this year: we have received about 70 submissions from many different countries including Austria, Brazil, Finland, France, Hungary, India, Italy, Mexico, the Netherlands, Norway, Spain, Romania, UK, Ukraine, USA, and Yougoslavia. We believe that this is at least partly due to the excellent international reputation of German AI research.

The program comittee selected 26 contributions in the full paper category and 10 contributions in the poster category for presentation at the conference. In addition, three of the leading international researchers in the field were invited to present their recent work. In his contribution *Anthony Cohn* (Leeds) investigates qualitative methods for spatial reasoning. These methods are based on advanced philosophical logics, and the calculi developed by Cohn are highly relevant for a number of applications, such as geographical information systems, to name an example. *Kurt Konolige* (Stanford), well known for his fundamental work on epistemic and nonmonotonic logics, presents new results on multi-agent systems which are particularly relevant for robotics. *Pat Langley* (Palo Alto) discusses machine learning methods for adaptive advisory systems. His work demonstrates how AI methods can successfully be combined with user modeling approaches that have their roots in cognitive psychology.

The invited and accepted contributions cover a large variety of different AI topics: advances in the logical foundations of AI, new deduction methods, reasoning about action, spatial reasoning, diagnosis, search, computational linguistics, robotics, computer vision, and neural networks. Moreover, much of the work contained in this volume clearly demonstrates that different AI methods – which often have been considered as competing – can support each other in an extremely fruitful manner and thus should be integrated. A very good example is the paper

M. Haag, W. Theilmann, K. Schäfer, H.-H. Nagel,
Integration of image sequence evaluation and fuzzy metric temporal logic programming

This paper was selected by the program committee for the Springer best paper award. The authors show that considerable advances in the interpretation of image sequences can be achieved through the integration of techniques fom image processing, logic programming, and fuzzy reasoning. We would like to congratulate the authors for this excellent piece of work.

As usual, there is a large number of people who helped to make the conference a success. First of all, we would like to thank the members of the program committee and the reviewers for the tremendous work they had to do in an extremely short period of time. All reviews arrived in time, many hours were spent discussing difficult cases, and we strongly believe that a fair decision was reached in each case. Of course, there could be no conference without submissions and we also thank all authors – successful or not – for submitting to KI.

Thanks also go to the many people who helped organize the conference, in particular to our excellent organization team headed by Christine Harms and Andrea Hemprich. It was fun to work with them.

We would also like to thank our sponsors Daimler Benz, Sun Microsystems, Infix Verlag, SICK, Valtech-IO, and Springer-Verlag. Springer not only provided the best paper award but also made producing these proceedings a rather easy undertaking. Special thanks to Alfred Hofmann for supporting the editors whenever a problem came up.

Finally, we thank Steffen Lange, Leipzig, for his help in producing the final version of these proceedings.

July 1997

Gerhard Brewka
Christopher Habel
Bernhard Nebel

KI-97

Conference Chair

Bernhard Nebel, Freiburg

Program Committee Chairs

Gerhard Brewka, Leipzig   Christopher Habel, Hamburg

Program Committee Members

Franz Baader, Aachen   Gerhard Lakemeyer, Aachen
Clemens Beckstein, Jena   Bärbel Mertsching, Hamburg
Stephan Busemann, Saarbrücken   Wolfgang Nejdl, Hannover
Jürgen Dix, Koblenz   Uwe Reyle, Stuttgart
Boi Faltings, Lausanne   Helge Ritter, Bielefeld
Uli Furbach, Koblenz   Torsten Schaub, Angers
Daniel Hernandez, München   Ute Schmid, Berlin
Gerhard Jäger, Bern   Gerald Sommer, Kiel
Jana Köhler, Freiburg   Stefan Wrobel, St. Augustin
Rudolf Kruse, Magdeburg

List of Additional Referees

Chandrabose Aravindan
Rainer Bäuerle
Peter Baumgartner
Michael Beetz
Siegfried Bell
Philippe Besnard
Susanne Biundo
Christian Borgelt
Sven Erik Bornscheuer
Thorsten Brants
Stefan Brass
Hans-Jürgen Bürckert
Wolfram Burgard
Diego Calvanese
Jörg Denzinger
Yannis Dimopoulos
Jürgen Eckerle
Stefan Edelkamp
Uwe Egly
Andreas Eisele
Thomas Eiter
Wolfgang Finkler
Peter Fröhlich
Bertram Fronhöfer
Jörg Gebhardt
Ian Gent
Reiner Hähnle
Wolfgang Hatzack
Joachim Hertzberg
Alain Heuerding
Knut Hinkelmann
Wiebe van der Hoek
Juraj Hromcovic
Jörg Hudelmaier
Anthony Jameson
Geert Janssen
Jürgen Kalinski
Manfred Kerber
Joachim Klausner
Frank Klawonn

Thomas Kolbe
Bernd Korn
Hans-Ulrich Krieger
Monika Lundell
John-Jules Meyer
Katharina Morik
Alexander Narejek
Detlef Nauck
Pascal Nicolas
Ilkka Niemelä
Jens Otten
Jochen Renz
Marie-Christine Rousset
Harald Rueß
Ulrike Sattler
Tobias Scheffer
Christoph Schlieder
Peter H. Schmitt
Stephan Schmitt
Ernst G. Schukat-Talamazzini
Stefan Schwendimann
Friedhelm Schwenker
Roberto Sebastini
Giovanni Semeraro
Manfred Stede
Jochen Steil
Igor Stephan
Frieder Stolzenburg
Eva Stopp
Thomas Strahm
Michael Thielscher
Heiko Timm
Carla Umbach
Klaus Voss
Heinrich Wansing
Gerd Wechsung
Gerhard Weiss
Sylvia Wiebrock
Werner Wolff
Ede Zimmermann

Table of Contents

Spatial Reasoning

Computational Linguistics

Computer Perception / Neural Nets

Planning, Diagnosis, and Search

Posters

Qualitative Spatial Representation and Reasoning Techniques

A G Cohn

Division of Artificial Intelligence, School of Computer Studies,
University of Leeds,Leeds LS2 JT, UK.
Email: agc@scs.leeds.ac.uk WWW: http://www.scs.leeds.ac.uk/

Abstract. The field of Qualitative Spatial Reasoning is now an active research area in its own right within AI (and also in Geographical Information Systems) having grown out of earlier work in philosophical logic and more general Qualitative Reasoning in AI. In this paper (which is an updated version of [25]) I will survey the state of the art in Qualitative Spatial Reasoning, covering representation and reasoning issues as well as pointing to some application areas.

1 What is Qualitative Reasoning?

The principal goal of Qualitative Reasoning (QR) [129] is to represent not only our everyday commonsense knowledge about the physical world, but also the underlying abstractions used by engineers and scientists when they create quantitative models. Endowed with such knowledge, and appropriate reasoning methods, a computer could make predictions, diagnoses and explain the behaviour of physical systems in a qualitative manner, even when a precise quantitative description is not available[1] or is computationally intractable. The key to a qualitative representation is not simply that it is symbolic, and utilises discrete quantity spaces, but that the distinctions made in these discretisations are *relevant* to the behaviour being modelled – i.e. distinctions are only introduced if they are *necessary* to model some particular aspect of the domain with respect to the task in hand. Even very simple quantity spaces can be very useful, e.g. the quantity space consisting just of $\{-, 0, +\}$, representing the two semi-open intervals of the real number line, and their dividing point, is widely used in the literature, e.g. [129]. Given such a quantity space, one then wants to be able to compute with it. There is normally a natural ordering (either partial or total) associated with a quantity space, and one form of simple but effective inference

---

[1] Note that although one use for qualitative reasoning is that it allows inferences to be made in the absence of complete knowledge, it does this not by probabilistic or fuzzy techniques (which may rely on arbitrarily assigned probabilities or membership values) but by refusing to differentiate between quantities unless there is sufficient evidence to do so; this is achieved essentially by collapsing 'indistinguishable' values into an equivalence class which becomes a qualitative quantity. (The case where the indistinguishability relation is not an equivalence relation has not been much considered, except by [86, 83].)

is to exploit the transitivity of the ordering relation. More interestingly, one can also devise qualitative arithmetic algebras [129]; for example one can perform addition on the above qualitative quantity space and add '+' to '+' to get '+'; however certain operations will in general yield ambiguous results (e.g. adding '+' and '−' yields no information). This is a recurring feature of Qualitative Reasoning – not surprisingly, reducing the precision of the measuring scale decreases the accuracy of the answer. Much research in the Qualitative Reasoning literature is devoted to overcoming the detrimental effects on the search space resulting from this ambiguity, though there is not space here to delve into this work. However one other aspect of the work in traditional Qualitative Reasoning is worth noting here: a standard assumption is made that change is continuous; thus, for example, in the quantity space mentioned above, a variable cannot transition from − to + without first taking the value 0. We shall see this idea recurring in the work on qualitative spatial reasoning described below.

2 What is Qualitative Spatial Reasoning?

QR has now become a mature subfield of AI as evidenced by its 11th annual international workshop, several books (e.g. [129] [51],[88]) and a wealth of conference and journal publications. Although the field has broadened to become more than just Qualitative Physics (as it was first known), the bulk of the work has dealt with reasoning about scalar quantities, whether they denote the level of a liquid in a tank, the operating region of a transistor or the amount of unemployment in a model of an economy.

Space, which is multidimensional and not adequately represented by single scalar quantities, has only a recently become a significant research area within the field of QR, and, more generally, in the Knowledge Representation community. In part, this may be due to the *Poverty Conjecture* promulgated by Forbus, Nielsen and Faltings [129]: "there is no purely qualitative, general purpose kinematics". Of course, qualitative spatial reasoning (QSR) is more than just kinematics, but it is instructive to recall their third (and strongest) argument for the conjecture – "No total order: quantity spaces don't work in more than one dimension, leaving little hope for concluding much about combining weak information about spatial properties". They correctly identify transitivity of values as a key feature of a qualitative quantity space but doubt that this can be exploited much in higher dimensions and conclude: "we suspect the space of representations in higher dimensions is sparse; that for spatial reasoning almost nothing weaker than numbers will do".

The challenge of QSR then is to provide calculi which allow a machine to represent and reason with spatial entities of higher dimension, without resorting to the traditional quantitative techniques prevalent in, for example, the computer graphics or computer vision communities.

Happily, over the last few years there has been an increasing amount of research which tends to refute, or at least weaken the 'poverty conjecture'. There is a surprisingly rich diversity of qualitative spatial representations addressing many different aspects of space including topology, orientation, shape, size and distance; moreover, these can exploit transitivity as demonstrated by the relatively sparse transitivity tables (cf the well known table for Allen's interval temporal logic [129]) which have been built for these representations (actually 'composition tables' is a better name for these structures, as explained below).

In the remainder of this paper, first I will mention some possible applications of QSR, then I will survey the main aspects of the representation of qualitative spatial knowledge including ontological aspects, topology, distance, orientation, shape and uncertainty. Then I will move on to qualitative spatial reasoning including reasoning about spatial change. The paper concludes with a discussion of theoretical results and a glimpse at future work. This paper is a revised and updated version of [25]. Although I have tried to cover the main areas of QSR, this paper is certainly not a comprehensive survey of the subject and there is much interesting work which unfortunately I have not had space to describe here.

3 Possible applications of qualitative spatial reasoning

Researchers in qualitative spatial reasoning are motivated by a wide variety of possible application areas, including: Geographical Information Systems (GIS), robotic navigation, high level vision, the semantics of spatial prepositions in natural languages, engineering design, commonsense reasoning about physical situations, and specifying visual language syntax and semantics. Below I will briefly discuss each of these areas, arguing the need for some kind qualitative spatial representation. Other application areas include document-type recognition [56] and domains where space is used as a metaphor, e.g. [90], [104].

GIS are now commonplace, but a major problem is how to interact with these systems: typically, gigabytes of information are stored, whether in vector or raster format, but users often want to abstract away from this mass of numerical data, and obtain a high level symbolic description of the data or want to specify a query in a way which is essentially, or at least largely, qualitative. Arguably, the next generation of GIS will be built on concepts arising from *Naive Geography* [47] which requires a theory of qualitative spatial reasoning.

Although robotic navigation ultimately requires numerically specified directions to the robot to move or turn, this is not usually the best way to plan a route or other spatially oriented task: the AI planning literature [123] has long shown the effectiveness of hierarchical planning with detailed decisions (e.g. about how or exactly where to move) being delayed until a high level plan has been achieved; moreover the robot's model of its environment may be imperfect (either because of inaccurate sensors or because of lack of information), leading to an inability to use more standard robot navigation techniques. A qualitative model of space would facilitate planning in such situations. One example of this kind of work is [89]; another, solving the well known 'piano mover's problem' is [50].

While computer vision has made great progress in recent years in developing low level techniques to process image data, there is now a movement back (e.g. [52]) to try to find more symbolic techniques to take the results of these low level computations and produce higher level descriptions of the scene or video input; often (part of) what is required is a description of the spatial relationship between the various objects or regions found in the scene; however the predicates used to describe these relationships must be sufficiently high level, or qualitative, in order to ensure that scenes which are semantically close have identical or at least very similar descriptions.

Perhaps one of the most obvious domains requiring some kind of theory of qualitative spatial representation is the task of finding some formal way of describing the meaning of natural language spatial prepositions such as "inside", "through", "to the left of" etc. This is a difficult task, not least because of the multiple ways in which such prepositions can be used (e.g. [82] cites many different meanings of "in"); however at least having a formal language at the right conceptual level enables these different meanings to be properly distinguished. Examples of research in this area include [4, 128].

Engineering design, like robotic navigation, ultimately normally requires a fully metric description; however, at the early stages of the design process, it is often better to concentrate on the high level design, which can often be expressed qualitatively. The field of qualitative kinematics (e.g. [49]) is largely concerned with supporting this kind of activity.

The fields of qualitative physics and naive physics [129] have concerned themselves with trying to represent and reason about a wide variety of physical situations, given only qualitative information. Much of the motivation for this was given above in the section on qualitative reasoning; however traditionally these fields, in particular qualitative physics, have had a rather impoverished spatial capacity in their representations, typically restricting information to that which can be captured along a single dimension; adding a richer theory of qualitative spatial reasoning to these fields would increase the class of problems they could tackle.

Finally, the study and design of visual languages, either visual programming languages or some kind of representation language, perhaps as part of a user interface, has become rather fashionable; however, many of these languages lack a formal specification of the kind that is normally expected of a textual programming or representation language. Although some of these visual languages make metric distinctions, often they are predominantly qualitative in the sense that the exact shape, size, length etc. of the various components of the diagram or picture are unimportant – rather, what is important is the topological relationship between these components and thus a theory of qualitative spatial representation may be applicable in specifying such languages [65, 64, 77, 78].

4 Aspects of qualitative spatial representation

There are many different aspects to space and therefore to its representation: not only do we have to decide on what kinds of spatial entity we will admit (i.e. commit to a particular ontology of space), but also we can consider developing different kinds of ways of describing the relationship between these kinds of spatial entity; for example we may consider just their topology, or their sizes or the distance between them, or their shape. Of course, these notions are not entirely independent as we shall see below.

4.1 Ontology

In developing a theory of space, one can either decide that one will create a *pure* theory of space, or an *applied* one, situated in the intended domain of application; the question is whether one considers aspects of the domain, such as rigidity of objects, which would prevent certain spatial relationships, such as interpenetration, from holding. In order to simplify matters in this paper, we shall concentrate mainly on pure spatial theories – one could very well argue that such a theory should necessarily precede an applied one which would be obtained by extending a purely spatial theory.

Traditionally, in mathematical theories of space, points are considered as primary primitive spatial entities (or perhaps points and lines), and extended spatial entities such as regions are defined, if necessary, as sets of points. However, within the QSR community, there has been a strong tendency to take regions of space as the primitive spatial entity. There are several reasons for this. If one is interested in using the spatial theory for reasoning about physical objects, then one might argue that the spatial extension of any actual physical object must be region-like rather than a lower dimensional entity. Similarly, most natural language (non mathematical) uses of the word "point" do not refer to a mathematical point: consider sentences such as "the point of pencil is blunt". Moreover, it turns out that one can define points, if required, from regions (e.g. [11] following earlier work [16, 130]). Another reason against taking points as primitive is that many people find it counterintuitive that extended regions can be composed entirely of dimensionless points occupying no space! However, it must be admitted that sometimes it is useful to make an abstraction and view a 3D physical entity such as a potholed road as a 2D or even 1D entity. Of course, once entities of different dimensions are admitted, a further question arises as to whether mixed dimension entities are to be allowed. Further discussion of this issue can be found in [27, 73, 26].

Another ontological question is what is the nature of the embedding space, i.e. the universal spatial entity? Conventionally, one might take this to be R^n for some n, but one can imagine applications where discrete (e.g. [43]), finite (e.g. [72], or non convex (e.g. non connected) universes might be useful.

Once one has decided on these ontological questions, there are further issues: in particular, what primitive "computations" will be allowed? In a logical theory, this amounts to deciding what primitive non logical symbols one will admit without definition, only being constrained by some set of axioms. One could argue that this set of primitives should be small, not only for mathematical elegance and to make it perhaps easier to assess the consistency of the theory, but also because this will simplify the interface of the symbolic system to a perceptual component resulting in fewer primitives to be implemented; the converse argument might be that the resulting symbolic inferences may be more complicated

(and thus perhaps slower) and for the kinds of reasons argued for in [79], i.e.
that rather than just a few primitives it is more natural to have a large and rich
set of concepts which are given meaning by many axioms which connect them
in many different ways.

One final ontological question we will mention here is how to model the
multi dimensionality of space? One approach (which might appear superficially
attractive) is to attempt to model space by considering each dimension separately, projecting each region to each of the dimensions and reasoning along
each dimension separately; however, this is easily seen to be inadequate: e.g. two
individuals may overlap when projected to both the x and y axes individually,
when in fact they do not overlap at all.

4.2 Topology

Topology is perhaps the most fundamental aspect of space and certainly one
that has been studied extensively within the mathematical literature. It is often described informally as "rubber sheet geometry", although this is not quite
accurate. However, it is clear that topology must form a fundamental aspect of
qualitative spatial reasoning since topology certainly can only make qualitative
distinctions; the question then arises: can one not simply import a traditional
mathematical topological theory wholesale into a qualitative spatial representation? Although various qualitative spatial theories have been influenced by
mathematical topology, there are a number of reasons why such a wholesale
importation seems undesirable in general [73]; not only does traditional topology deal with much more abstract spaces that pertain in physical space or the
space to be found in the kinds of applications mentioned above, but also we are
interested in qualitative spatial *reasoning* not just representation, and this has
been paid little attention in mathematics and indeed since typical formulations
involve higher order logic, no reasonable computational mechanism would seem
to be immediately obvious.

One exception to the disregard of earlier topological theories by the QSR
community, is the tradition of work to be found in the philosophical logic literature, e.g. [131, 36, 132, 15, 16, 11]. This work has built axiomatic theories of space which are predominantly topological in nature, and which are
based on taking regions rather than points as primitive – indeed, this tradition has been described as "pointless geometries" [61]. In particular the work
of Clarke [15, 16] has lead to the development of the so called RCC systems
[109, 108, 107, 105, 34, 28, 7, 68, 24, 73, 27, 26] and has also been developed
further by [128, 3].

Clarke took as his primitive notion the idea of two regions x and y being
connected (sharing a point, if one wants to think of regions as consisting of sets
of points): $C(x, y)$. In the RCC system this interpretation[2] is slightly changed to
the closures of the regions sharing a point[3] – this has the effect of collapsing the

---

[2] A formal semantics for RCC has been given by [69, 37, 121].

[3] Actually, given the disdain of the RCC theory as presented in [108] for points, a

distinction between a region, its closure and its interior, which it is argued has no relevance for the kinds of domain with which QSR is concerned (another reason for abandoning traditional mathematical topology). This primitive is surprisingly powerful: it is possible to define many predicates and functions which capture interesting and useful topological distinctions. The set of eight jointly exhaustive and pairwise disjoint (JEPD) relations illustrated in figure 1 are one particularly useful set (often known as the RCC8 calculus) and indeed have been defined in an entirely different way by [42] – see below.

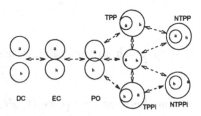

Fig. 1. 2D illustrations of of the relations of the RCC8 calculus and their continuous transitions (*conceptual neighbourhood*).

The work of [128, 3] mentioned above is also based on Clarke's calculus. The original interpretation of $C(x, y)$ is retained though the general fusion operator is discarded, it is made first order and several mistakes are corrected. An additional predicate $WC(x, y)$ is defined in order to try to model the distinction between two bodies being 'joined' and merely touching – consider the left and right halves of a table top compared to the table top and a book resting on it: the former case is modelled by EC(lefthalf,righthalf)[4] whilst the latter by WC(book,tabletop). $WC(x, y)$ is true when x is connected to the closure of the *topological neighbourhood* of y, i.e. the smallest open region the closure of y is part of.

Expressiveness of $C(x, y)$ The predicate $C(x, yy)$ can be used to define many more predicates than simply the RCC8 relations and $WC(x, y)$. For example one could define predicates which counted the number of times two regions touched. In a series of papers, [67, 68, 73, 71], Gotts sets himself the task of distinguishing a 'doughnut' (a solid, one-piece region with a single hole). It is shown how (given certain assumptions about the universe of discourse and the kinds of regions inhabiting it) all the shapes depicted in Fig.2 can be distinguished. In so doing he defines many predicates in terms of the $C(x, y)$ primitive, for example the distinction between being a firm and non firm tangential part (FTPP), i.e. whether the tangential connection is point-like or not. Fig.3 illustrates another

---

better interpretation, given some suitable distance metric, would be that $C(x, y)$ means that the distance between x and y is zero, c.f. [121].

[4] And thus C(lefthalf,righthalf) holds too.

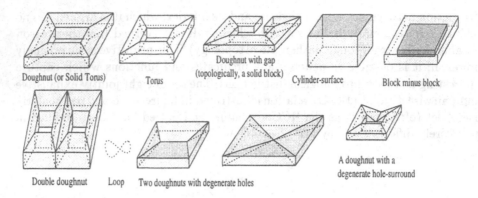

Doughnut (or Solid Torus) Torus Doughnut with gap (topologically, a solid block) Cylinder-surface Block minus block

Double doughnut Loop Two doughnuts with degenerate holes A doughnut with a degenerate hole-surround

Fig. 2. It is possible to distinguish all these shapes using $C(x, y)$ alone.

range of topological distinctions between one-piece (CON) regions that can be made (under certain assumptions) using C. A region, if it is connected, may or may not also be interior-connected (INCON), meaning that the interior of the region is all one piece. It is relatively easy to express this property (or its converse) in RCC terms. However, INCON(r) does not rule out all regions with anomalous boundaries, and in particular does not exclude the region at the right of Fig.3, nor any of the final three cases illustrated in Fig.2, which do have one-piece interiors, but which nevertheless have boundaries which are *not* (respectively) simple curves or surfaces, having 'anomalies' in the form of points which do not have line-like (or disc-like) neighbourhoods within the boundary (i.e. which are *locally Euclidean*.)

It appears possible using $C(x, y)$ to define [68] a predicate (WCON) that will rule out the INCON but anomalous cases of Fig.3, but it is by no means straightforward,[5] and it is not demonstrated conclusively in [68] that the definitions do what is intended. One source of the difficulties arising is the fact that within RCC, since all regions in a particular model of the axioms are of the same dimensionality as the universal region, u , assuming u itself to be of uniform dimensionality (this follows from the fact that all regions have an NTPP), there is no way to refer directly to the boundary of a region or to the dimensionality of the shared boundary of two EC regions, or to any relations between entities of different dimensionalities.

---

[5] Note, however, that this task becomes almost trivial once the conv(x) primitive is introduced in Section 4.3.

Fig. 3. Types of CON Region

In cases where reasoning about dimensionality becomes important, RCC and related systems based on a $C(x, y)$ predicate are not very powerful (and to reason about regions of different dimensionality is impossible with out imposing a sort structure and essentially taking a copy of the theory for each dimension-sort). To remedy this Gotts proposed a new primitive $INCH(x, y)$, whose intended interpretation is that spatial entity x *includes a chunk of* y, where the included chunk is of the same dimension as x. The two entities may be of differing (though uniform) dimension. Thus if x is line crossing a 2D region y, then $INCH(x, y)$ is true, but not vice versa. It is easy to define $C(x, y)$ in terms of INCH, but not vice versa, so the previous RCC system can be defined as a sub theory. An initial exposition of this theory can be found in [70].

Another proposal addressing the problem of representing and reasoning about regions of differing dimensionality (though still not of mixed dimensionality) is [59]. Here, two primitives are proposed, the mereological part relation, $P(x, y)$, and a boundary operator, $B(x, y)$ – x is the boundary of y (being a region of one less dimension). This follows on from other theories which introduce boundaries of regions explicitly (e.g. [119, 120, 125, 109]) but which did not explicitly introduce dimensional reasoning.

Topology via "n-intersections" An alternative approach to representing and reasoning about topological relations has been promulgated via series of papers (e.g.[23, 39, 41, 41, 40, 46, 42]). In the most recent calculus three sets of points are associated with every region – its interior, boundary and complement; the relationship between two regions can be characterized by a 3x3 matrix,[6] called the 9-intersection, each of whose elements denotes whether the intersection of the corresponding sets from each region are empty or not. Although it would seem that there are $2^9 = 512$ possible matrices, after taking into account the physical reality of 2D space and some specific assumptions about the nature of regions, which can then be translated into constraints between the matrix values, it turns out that there are exactly 8 remaining matrices, corresponding to the eight RCC8 relations. One can use this calculus to reason about regions which have holes by classifying the relationship not only between each pair of regions, but also the relationship between each hole of each region and the other region and each of its holes [45]. By changing the underlying assumptions about what a region is, and by allowing the matrix to represent the codimension of the intersection, different calculi with more JEPD relations can be derived. For example, one may derive a calculus for representing and reasoning about regions in Z^2 rather than R^2 [43] – there are 16 possible matrices representing the set of JEPD relations in this case. Alternatively, one can extend the representation by noting in each matrix cell the dimension of the intersection rather than simply whether it exists or not [17]; this allows one to enumerate all the relations between areas, lines and points –

---

[6] Actually, a simpler 2x2 matrix [41], known as the 4-intersection, featuring just the interior and boundary is sufficient to describe the eight RCC relations; however the 3x3 matrix allows more expressive sets of relations to be defined as noted below since it takes into account the relationship between the region and its embedding space.

this extension is known as the "dimension extended method (DEM)". [22] have noted the very large number of possible relationships that may be defined in this way and have proposed a way (which they call the "calculus based method (CBM)", to generate all these from a set of five polymorphic binary relations between a pair of spatial entities x and y: disjoint, touch (a/a, l/l, l/a, p/a, p/l), in, overlap (a/a, l/l), cross (restrictions on the arguments are denoted by the notation α/β, e.g. a/a meaning that both arguments must be areal, p/p that they must be points and l/l that they must both be linear). In addition, operators are introduced to denote the boundary of a region and the two endpoints of a non circular line. A complex relation between x and y may then formed by conjoining atomic propositions formed by using one of the five relations above, whose arguments may be either be x or y or a boundary or endpoint operator applied to x or y. [22] have analysed the number of JEPD relations relations) for each of the techniques mentioned above (4- and 9-intersections, DIM and CBM). For the most expressive calculus (either the CBM or the combination of the 9-intersection and the DIM), there are 9 area/area relations, 31 line/area relations, 3 point/area relations, 33 line/line relations, 3 point/line relations and 2 point/point relations giving a grand total of 81.

Mereology and Topology Although mereology (being the theory of the part-whole relationship) would seem at first sight simply to be a subtheory of topology (and indeed is presented thus in the topological theories mentioned so far in this section), there are arguments against this view. Varzi [126] has discussed the issue and notes that whilst certain mereology is not sufficient by itself, there are three main ways in which theories in the literature have proposed integrating topology and mereology:

1. Generalise mereology by adding a topological primitive. This is the approach taken by, for example, [12] who add the topological primitive $SC(x)$, i.e. x is a self connected (one-piece) spatial entity to the mereological part relation. Alternatively a single primitive can be used to as in [125]: "x and y are connected parts of z. Generally, this approach forces the existence of boundary elements (i.e. spatial entities of lower dimensions). The main advantage of separate theories of mereology and topology is that it allows colocation without sharing parts which is not easily possible in the second two approaches below.

2. Topology is primal and mereology is a sub theory. For example in the topological theories based on $C(x, y)$, such as those mentioned above, one defines $P(x, y)$ from $C(x, y)$. This has the elegance of being a single unified theory, but colocation implies sharing of parts. These theories are normally boundaryless (i.e. without lower dimensional spatial entities) but this is not absolutely necessary [109, 70]. Thus, for example $EC(x, y)$ not necessarily explained by sharing a boundary.

3. The final approach is that taken by [48], i.e. topology is introduced as a specialised domain specific sub theory of mereology. Of course an additional primitive needs to be introduced since mereology alone is not powerful

enough to define topology. The idea is to use restricted quantification by introducing a sortal predicate Region(x). C(x, y) can then be defined thus: C(x, y) $\equiv$ def O(x, y) $\wedge$ Region(x) $\wedge$ Region(y).

4.3 Between Topology and Fully Metric Spatial Representation

Topology can be seen as perhaps the most abstract and most qualitative spatial representation, furthest removed from fully metric representations. However it is clear that although potentially useful there many be many domains where topological information alone is insufficient but it would still be desirable to have a qualitative representation. In the following subsections a selection of different ways of add qualitative non topological information are presented.

Orientation Orientation is a naturally qualitative property: in 2D it is very common to talk about clockwise or anticlockwise orientation for instance. However, unlike most of the topological relations on spatial entities mentioned above, orientation is not a binary relation – at least three elements need to be specified to give an orientation between two of them (and possibly more in dimensions higher than 2D). If we want to specify the orientation of a *primary object* (PO) with respect to a *reference object* (RO), then we need some kind of *frame of reference* (FofR). An *extrinsic* frame of reference imposes an external, immutable orientation: e.g. gravitation, a fixed coordinate system, or an third object (such as the North pole). A *deictic* frame of reference is with respect to the "speaker" or some other internal observer. Finally, an *intrinsic* frame of reference exploits some inherent property of the RO – many objects have a natural "front", e.g. humans, buildings and boats. This categorization manifests itself in the display of qualitative orientation calculi to be found in the literature: certain calculi have an explicit triadic relation while others presuppose an extrinsic frame of reference and, for example, use compass directions [54, 80]. Of those with explicit triadic relations is it especially worth mentioning the work of Schlieder [114] (following earlier work [66]) who develops a calculus based on a function which maps triples of points to one of three qualitative values, + , 0 or -, denoting anticlockwise, colinear and clockwise orientations respectively. This can be used for reasoning about visible locations in qualitative navigation tasks, or for shape description [116] or to develop a calculus for reasoning about the relative orientation of pairs of line segments [115] – see figure 4. Schlieder also notes that the notion of a *permutation sequence* [66] subsumes this framework. In this representation, given a set of points and directed lines connecting them, one chooses a new directed line l, not orthogonal to any existing line and notes the order of all the points projected onto l. One then rotates l counterclockwise until order of projection changes. As l continues to rotate, one will generate further permutations of the set of points.

Another important triadic orientation calculus is that of Roehrig [113]; this calculus is based on a relation CYCORD(x, y, z) which is true (in 2D) when x, y, z are in clockwise orientation. Roehrig shows how a number of qualitative calculi (not only orientation calculi) can be translated into the CYCORD system, whose reasoning system (implemented as a constraint logic program) can then be exploited.

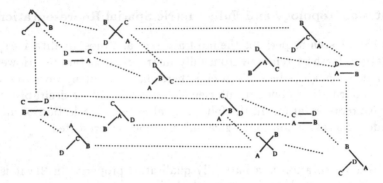

Fig. 4. The 14 JEPD relations of Schlieder's oriented line segment calculus and their *conceptual neighbourhood*.

Distance and size Distance and size are related in the sense that traditionally we use a linear scale to measure each of these aspects, even though distance is normally thought of as being a one dimensional concept, whilst size is usually associated with higher dimensional measurements such as area or volume. The domain can influence distance measurements, as we shall see below, but first I will discuss pure spatial representations. These can be divided into two main groups: those which measure on some "absolute" scale, and those which provide some kind of relative measurement. Of course, since traditional Qualitative Reasoning [129] is primarily concerned with dealing with linear quantity spaces, the qualitative algebras and the transitivity of such quantity spaces mentioned earlier can be used as a distance or size measuring representation.

Also of interest in this context are the order of magnitude calculi [95, 102] developed in the QR community. These calculi introduce measuring scales which allow one quantity to be described as being *much larger* than another, with the consequence that it requires summing many (in some formulations even an infinite number) of the former quantities in order to surpass the second, "much larger" quantity. Most of these "traditional QR" formalisms are of the "absolute" kind of representations mentioned above[7] as is the Delta calculus [134] which introduces a triadic relation, $x(>, d)y$: x is larger/bigger than y by amount d; terms such as $x(>, y)y$ mean that x is more than twice as big as y.

Of the 'relative' representations specifically developed within the spatial reasoning community, perhaps the first is the calculus proposed by de Laguna [36],

---

[7] Actually it is usually straightforward to specify relative measurements given an "absolute" calculus: to say that $x > y$, one may simply write $x - y = +$.

which introduces a triadic CanConnect(x, y, z) primitive, which is true if the body x can connect y and z by simple translation (i.e. without scaling, rotation or shape change). From this primitive it is quite easy to define notions such as equidistance, nearer than, and farther than (as well as the C(x, y) relation). Also note that this primitive allows a simple size metric on regions to be defined: one region is larger than another if it can connect regions that the other cannot. Another technique to determine the relative size of two objects was proposed by Mukerjee and Joe [97] and relies on being able to translate regions (assumed to be shape and size invariant) and then exploit topological relationships – if a translation is possible so that one region becomes a proper part of another, then it must be smaller. Interestingly, these seem to be about the only proposals which are grounded in a region based theory – all the other representations mentioned in this section take points as their primitive spatial entity. An interesting question arises in the case of distances between regions as to where to measure to/from – in the formalisms mentioned above the closest distance is taken, but alternatively one might be interested in the distance between centroids or some other distinguished subregion or point.

Distance is closely related to the notion of orientation: e.g. distances cannot usually be added unless they are in the same direction, and the distance between a point and region may vary depending on the orientation. Thus it is perhaps not surprising that there have been a number of calculi which are based on a primitive which combines distance and orientation information. Arguably, unless both of these aspects are represented then the calculus is not really a calculus of distance, though it might be said that this is a calculus of position rather than mere distance.

One straightforward idea [54] is to combine directions as represented by segments of the compass with a simple distance metric (*far, close*). A slightly more sophisticated idea is to introduce a primitive which defines the position of a third point with respect to a directed line segment between two other points [135] – see figure 5. A calculus which combines the Delta calculus and orientation is presented in [133].

Fig. 5. There are 15 qualitatively different positions a point c (denoted by the shaded circles) can be with respect to a vector from point a to point b. Some distance information is represented, for example the darker shaded circles are in the same orientation but at different distances from ab.

The most sophisticated qualitative distance calculus to date is the framework for representing distances [81] which has been extended to include orientation[21]. In this framework a distance is expressed in a particular *frame of reference* (FofR) between a *primary object* (PO) and a *reference object* (RO). A distance system is composed of an ordered sequence of *distance relations* (between a PO and an RO), and a set of *structure relations* which give additional information about how the distance relations relate to each other (apart from their distance ordering given implicitly by the ordered sequence). Each distance has an *acceptance area* (which in the case of an isotropic space will be a region the same shape as the PO, concentrically located around the PO); the distance between successive acceptance areas defines a sequence of intervals: $\delta_1, \delta_2, \ldots$. The structure relations define relationships between these δ_i. Typical structure relations might specify a monotonicity property (the δ_i are increasing), or that each δ_i is greater than the sum of all the preceding δ_i. The structure relationships can also be used to specify order of magnitude relationships, e.g. that $\delta_i + \delta_j \sim \delta_i$ for $j < i$. The structure relationships are important in refining the *composition tables* (see below). In a *homogeneous* distance system all the distance relations have the same structure relations; however this need not be the case in a *heterogeneous* distance system. The proposed system also allows for the fact that the context may affect the distance relationships; this is handled by having different frames of reference, each with its own distance system and with inferences in different frames of reference being composed using *articulation rules* (cf. [83]). Analogously to orientation calculi, intrinsic, extrinsic and deictic frames of reference can be distinguished.

It is possible that different qualitative distance calculi (or FofR) might be needed for different scale spaces – Montello [96] suggests that there are four main kinds of scale of space, relative to the human body: *figural space* pertains to distances smaller than the human body and which thus can be perceived without movement (e.g. table top space and pictures); *vista space* is similar but pertains to spaces larger than the human body, making distortions more likely; *environmental space* cannot be perceived without moving from one location to another; finally, *geographic space* cannot be properly apprehended by moving – rather it requires indirect perception by a (figural space) map. One obvious effect of moving from one scale, or context to another, is that qualitative distance terms such as "close" will vary greatly; more subtly, distances can behave in various "non mathematical" ways in some contexts or spaces: e.g. distances may not be symmetrical – e.g. because distances are sometimes measured by time taken to travel, and an uphill journey may take longer than the return downhill journey. Distance may easily become non isotropic when time taken to travel is used as a distance measure (i.e. travel in certain directions may take a longer time compared to the actual distance) – e.g. a fast East-West highway will tend to reduce east west travel time[81]. Another "mathematical aberration" is that in some domains the shortest distance between two points may not be a straight line (e.g. because a lake or a building might be in the way,). Human perception of distance can also be distorted – [84] reports experiments which show that cities on the west coast of the USA are viewed as being relatively closer when imagined from the east coast compared to east coast cities and vice versa when the viewpoint is changed to the other coast.

Shape As mentioned above, one can think of theories of space as forming a hierarchy ordered by expressiveness (in terms of the spatial distinctions made possible) with topology at the top and a fully metric/geometric theory at the bottom. Clearly in a purely topological theory only very limited statements can be made about the shape of a region: whether it is has holes (in the sense that a torus has a hole), or interior voids, or whether it is in one piece or not – we have already described this kind of work in section 4.2 above. [60] has observed that one can (weakly) constrain the shape of rigid objects by topological constraints using RCC8: congruent shapes can only ever be DC, EC, PO or EQ; if one shape can just fit inside the other then they can only ever be DC, EC, PO, TPP; if one shape can easily fit inside the other then they can only ever be DC, EC or PO; whilst incommensurate shapes must be DC, EC or PO.

However, if one's application demands finer grained distinctions than these, then some kind of semi-metric information has to be introduced[8]; there is a huge choice of possible primitives for extending topology with some kind of shape primitives whilst still retaining a qualitative representation (i.e. not becoming fully metric). Of course, as [20] note, the mathematical community have developed many different geometries which are less expressive than Euclidean geometry, for example projective and affine geometries, but have not necessarily developed efficient computational reasoning techniques for them[9]. The QSR community has only just started exploring the various possibilities; below we briefly describe some of the approaches.

There are a number of ways to classify these approaches; one distinction is between those techniques which constrain the possible shapes of a region and those that construct a more complex shaped region out of simpler ones (e.g. along the lines of constructive solid geometry [111], but perhaps starting from a more qualitative set of primitives). An alternative dichotomy can be drawn between representations which primarily describe the boundary of an object compared to those which represent its interior (e.g. symmetry based techniques). Arguably [13], the latter techniques are preferable since shape is inherently not a one dimensional concept.

Examples of approaches which work by describing the boundary of an object include those that classify the sequence different types of boundary segments (curving in/out, angle in/out, cusp in/out, straight) [112] or by describing the sequence of different kinds of curvature extrema[91] along its contour. Another related approach would be to pick out distinguished points on the boundary of the object (such as corners) and relate every triple of such points by using the qualitative orientation calculus described in the previous section (i.e. the shape description would consist of a sequence of -/0/+ symbols, one for each triple of distinguished points). Yet another technique is described by [85] who uses a slope projection approach to describe polygonal shape: for each corner, one

---

[8] Of course, the orientation and distance primitives discussed above already add something to pure topology, but as already mentioned these are largely point based and thus not directly applicable to describing region shape.

[9] Though see [5, 6].

describes whether it is convex/concave,obtuse/right-angled/acute together with a qualitative representation of the direction of the corner (chosen from a set of 9 possible values).

One approach of the latter kind is to make use of a shape abstraction primitive such as the bounding box or the convex hull. Both these techniques have been considered briefly within the n-intersection model [19] whilst the latter technique has been investigated extensively within the RCC calculus. The distinction between convex and concave regions seems fundamental to shape description. [10] RCC theory has shown that many interesting predicates can be defined once one takes the notion of a convex hull of a region (or equivalently, a predicate to test convexity) and combines it with the topological representation. By computing the topological relationships between the shape itself and the different components of the difference between the convex hull and the shape, one can distinguish many different kinds of concave shapes [24]. A refinement to this technique exploits the idea of recursive shape description [118] to describe any non convex components of the difference between the convex hull and the shape. One can also develop many sets of JEPD predicates to relate pairs of regions which directly exploit the convex hull function; such predicates give another approach to shape description: one constrains the shape of a region by specifying its relationships to other regions[33].

The convex hull is clearly a powerful primitive and in fact it has recently been shown [35] that this system essentially is equivalent to an affine geometry: any two compact planar shapes not related by an affine transformation can be distinguished by a constraint language of just $EC(x)$, $PP(x)$ and $Conv(x)$.

Various different notions of the inside of a region can be distinguished using a convex hull primitive [24, 33] – these can all be viewed as different kinds of hole. A very interesting line of research [14, 127] has investigated exactly what holes are and proposes an axiomatisation of holes based on a new primitive: $Hosts(x, y)$ – which is true if the *body* x hosts hole y; note that this is not a theory of pure space: holes cannot host other holes, only physical objects can act as hosts.

Another recent proposal [12] is to take the notion of two regions being congruent as primitive; from this it is possible to define the notion of a sphere, and then import Tarski's theory of spheres and related definitions such as 'betweenness' [122]. That this theory is more powerful than one just with convex hull is shown by the fact convexity can now be defined in a congruence based system, whilst the reverse is not the case. Also of interest in this paper is the idea of using a "grain" to eliminate small surface irregularities which might distort the shape description.

The notion of a Voronoi hull has also been used as an approach to qualitative shape description [38]. A set of voronoi regions are computed by drawing lines

---

[10] Note that topology only allows certain rather special kind of non convex regions to be distinguished, and in any case does not allow the concavities to be explicitly referred to – it is a theory of 'holed regions', rather than of holes per se – the distinction between "hole realist" and "irrealist" theories has been made by [14].

equidistant from each pair of closest objects under consideration. Notions such as proximity, betweenness, inside/outside, amidst can all be addressed by this technique.

Finally, before leaving the topic of shape description we should point out the work of [20] on describing shape via properties such as compactness and elongation by using the minimum bounding rectangle of the shape and the order of magnitude calculus of [95]: elongation is computed via the ratio of the sides of the minimum bounding rectangle whilst compactness by comparing the are of the shape and its minimum bounding rectangle.

4.4 Uncertainty and Vagueness

In many applications uncertainty and vagueness, for example because of indeterminate region boundaries are endemic. Such vagueness may arise for a number of reasons, perhaps because of ignorance, i.e. lack of data (e.g. sample oil well drillings) or because of temporal variation (e.g. tidal regions, a flood plain, or a river changing its course), or indeterminacy may arise because of 'field variation' (e.g. the one soil type may gradually change into another) or a region might display what one might term 'intrinsic vagueness' (e.g. 'southern England' might be so regarded since one could never agree as to what determined this region except by some arbitrary process).

Even though any qualitative calculus already makes some attempt to represent and reason about uncertainty because the qualitative abstraction hides some indeterminacy, sometimes some extra mechanism may be required. Of course, it is always possible to glue on some standard numerical technique for reasoning about uncertainty (e.g. [57]), but there has also been some research on extending existing qualitative spatial reasoning techniques to explicitly represent and reason about uncertain information. For example, a GISDATA workshop on representing and reasoning about regions with indeterminate boundaries generated two papers [31, 18] which extended the RCC calculus and the 9-intersection in very similar ways to handle these kind of regions.

The former approach, which is continued in a series of papers [30, 29, 32] postulates the existence of non crisp regions in addition to crisp regions and then adds another binary relation to RCC $-$ x is crisper than region y. A variety of relations are then defined in terms of this primitive and this extended theory is then related to what has become known as the "egg-yolk" calculus which originated in [90] and models regions with indeterminate boundaries as a pair of regions: the 'yolk', which is definitely part of the region and the 'white', which may or may not be part of the region. It turns out that if one generalises RCC8 in this way [32] there are 252 JEPD relations between non crisp regions which can be naturally clustered into 40 sets.

The latter approach looks very similar to the egg-yolk calculus but does not consider such a fine granularity of relations; it postulates 44 JEPD relations, also clustered into groups (18 in their case) but using a more ad hoc technique to achieve this. An interesting extension to this work [19] shows that this calculus of regions with broad boundaries can be used to reason not just about regions with indeterminate boundaries but also can be specialised to cover a number of other kinds of regions including convex hulls of regions, minimum bounding rectangles, buffer zones and rasters (this last specialisation generalises the application of the n-intersection model to rasters previously undertaken by [43]).

Other approaches to spatial uncertainty are to work with an indistinguishability relation which is not transitive and thus fails to generate equivalence classes [124, 86] and the development of nonmonotonic spatial logics [117, 2].

5 Qualitative spatial reasoning

Although much of the work in QSR has concentrated on representational aspects, various computational paradigms are being investigated including constraint based reasoning (e.g. [80]). However, the most prevalent form of qualitative spatial reasoning is based on the composition table (originally known as a transitivity table [1], but now renamed since more than one relation is involved and thus it is relation composition rather than transitivity which is being represented). Given a set of n JEPD relations, the $n \times n$ composition table specifies for each pair of relations R1, and R2 such that $R1(a, b)$ and $R2(b, c)$ hold, what the possible relationships between a and c could be. In general, there will be a disjunction of entries, as a consequence of the qualitative nature of the calculus. Most of the calculi mentioned in this paper have had composition tables constructed for them, though this has sometimes posed something of a challenge [106]. One approach to the automatic generation of composition tables has been to try to reduce each calculus to a simple ordering relation [113]. Another, perhaps more general approach, is to formulate the calculus as a decidable theory (many calculi, e.g. the original RCC system, are presented as first order theories), ideally even as a tractable theory, and then use exhaustive theorem proving techniques to analyze and thus generate each composition table entry. A reformulation of the RCC first order theory in a zero order intuitionistic logic [11] [7] was able to generate the appropriate composition tables automatically; another approach would have been been to use a zero order modal logic [9].

Composition tables provide a very efficient form of reasoning and have certainly been the mostly commonly used form of qualitative spatial inference but they do not necessarily subsume all forms of desired reasoning. For example, reasoning with just three objects at a time will not necessarily determine all inconsistent situations in some calculi. An interesting question then arises: exactly when is composition table reasoning a sufficient inference mechanism (i.e. for which theories is it complete)[10]?

For cases when composition table based reasoning is not sufficient, then other more general constraint based reasoning may be sufficient[80, 76]; more generally one may resort to theorem proving, or preferably, some kind of specialised theorem proving system[7, 113] for example.

---

[11] This reformulation is interesting in that it becomes a true spatial logic, rather than a theory of space: the "logical symbols" have spatial interpretations, e.g. implication is interpreted as parthood and disjunction as the sum of two regions.

5.1 Reasoning about Spatial Change

So far we have been concerned purely with static spatial calculi, so that we can only represent and reason about snapshots of a changing world. It is thus important to develop calculi which combine space and time in an integrated fashion.

There are many kinds of spatial change: individual spatial entities may change their topological structure, their orientation, their position, their size or shape. Such changes are not necessarily independent and of course change in one spatial entity may engender a change in its spatial relationship to other entities.

Topological changes in 'single' spatial entity include: change in dimension (this is usually 'caused' by an abstraction or granularity shift rather than an 'actual' spatial change[12]; change in number of topological components (e.g. breaking a cup, fusing blobs of mercury); change in the number of tunnels (e.g. drilling through a block of wood); change in the number of interior cavities (e.g. putting a lid on a container). Such changes may also simultaneously effect changes in position, size, shape, and orientation as well as in topology (e.g. consider drilling a hole in a block of wood).

In many domains we assume that change is continuous[13], as is the case in traditional qualitative reasoning, and thus there is a requirement to build into the qualitative spatial calculus which changes in value will respect the underlying continuous nature of change, and this requirement is of course common to all the different kinds of spatial change we have mentioned above. It is thus important to know which qualitative values or relations are *neighbours* in the sense that if a value or predicate holds at one time, then there is some continuous change possible such that the next value or predicate to hold will be a neighbour. Continuity networks defining such neighbours are often called *conceptual neighbourhoods* in the literature following the use of the term [55] to describe the of structure Allen's 13 JEPD temporal relations [1] according to their conceptual closeness (e.g. *meets* is a neighbour of both *overlaps* and *before*). Most of the qualitative spatial calculi reported in this paper have had conceptual neighbourhoods constructed for them; see figures 1 and 4 for example[14].

Perhaps the most common form of computation in the traditional QR literature is qualitative simulation; using conceptual neighbourhood diagrams is quite easy to build a qualitative *spatial* simulator [34]. Such a simulator takes a set of ground atomic statements describing an initial state[15] and constructs a tree of

---

[12] E.g. we may view a road as being a 1D line on a map, a 2D entity when we consider whether it is wide enough for an outsize load, and a 3D entity as we consider the range of mountains it passes over, or the potholes and a particularly delicate cargo.

[13] Sometimes changes are discontinuous, e.g. when political fiat moves the boundaries of geopolitical entities in a discontinuous manner.

[14] A close related notion is that of "closest topological distance" [44] – two predicates are neighbours if their respective n-intersection matrices differ by fewer entries than any other predicates; however the resulting neighbourhood graph is not identical to the true conceptual neighbourhood or continuity graph – some links are missing.

[15] The construction of an envisioner [129] rather than a simulator would also be possible of course. See also the transition calculus approach of [63].

future possible states – the branching of the tree results from the ambiguity of the qualitative calculus. Of course, continuity alone does not provide sufficient constraints to restrict the generation of next possible states to a reasonably small set in general – domain specific constraints are required in addition. These may be of two kinds: intra state constraints restrict the spatial relationships that may hold within any state whilst inter state constraints restrict what can hold between adjacent states (or in general, across a sequence of states). Both of these constraint types can be used to prune otherwise acceptable next states from the simulation tree. Additional pruning is required to make sure that each state is consistent with respect to the semantics of the calculus (e.g. that there is no cycle of proper part relationships) – the composition table may be used for this purpose.

A desirable extension, by analogy with earlier QR work, would be to incorporate a proper theory of spatial processes couched in a language of QSR; some work in this direction is reported in: [93] who considers a field based theory of spatial processes such as heat flow; [44] who consider which traversals of their version of the conceptual neighbourhood diagram for an 8 relation topological calculus analogous to RCC8 correspond to processes such as expansion of a region, rotation of region etc; [91] considers how the processes of protrusion and resistance cause changes in his boundary based shape description language mentioned in section 4.3 above – given two shapes he can then infer sequences of processes which could cause one to change into the other. Also worthy of note is the qualitative spatial simulation work of [103] based on the QSIM system [129].

One problem is that the conceptual neighbourhood is usually built manually for each new calculus – a sometimes arduous and error prone operation if there are many relations; techniques to derive these automatically would be very useful. An analysis of the structure of conceptual neighbourhoods is reported by Ligozat [92] goes some way towards this goal. A more foundational approach which exploits the continuity of the underlying semantic spaces has been investigated by [58] – this analysis not only allows the construction of a conceptual neighbourhood for a class of relations from a semantics, but also infers which relations *dominate* other relations: a relation R_1 dominates R_2 if R_2 can hold over an interval followed/preceded by R_1 instantaneously. E.g. in RCC8 TPP dominates NTPP and PO, while EQ dominates all of its neighbouring relations. Dominance is analogous to the equality change law to be found in traditional QR [129] and allows a stricter temporal order to be imposed on events occurring in a qualitative simulation.

5.2 Theoretical results in QSR

There are a number of theoretical questions of interest. Not all calculi have been given a formal semantics by their inventors and even for those that have there is the question of whether it is the best or simplest semantics. Given a semantics one can ask whether the task of showing a set of formulae is consistent or whether one set entails another is decidable, and if it is what is the complexity of the decision procedure. One can ask if a theory is complete, either in the weak sense of every true formula being provable, or the stronger sense of whether every formula is made either true or false in the theory. Obviously, complete first order theories are also decidable. Finally, there is the property of being categorical, i.e. whether all models are isomorphic? Since theories may have both finite and infinite models, a more interesting property is $\aleph_0$ categoricity, i.e. whether all infinite models are isomorphic.

[100] set out to answer the question as to whether there is something special about region based theories from the ontological viewpoint? They believe the answer is in the negative, at least for 2D mereotopology: they show, under certain assumptions, that the standard 2D point based interpretation is simplest model (prime model) proved under assumptions; the only alternative models involve regions with infinitely many pieces. But it may be argued, that it is still useful to have region based theories even if they are always interpretable point set theoretically.

A fundamental result on decidability which has widespread applicability in qualitative spatial theories is that of [75] which shows that although of course Boolean algebra is decidable, adding either a closure operation or an external connection relation results in an undecidable system since one can then encode arbitrary statements of arithmetic. This implies that Clarke's calclus and all the related calculi such as the first order theory of RCC, and the calculi of [3] and [12] are all undecidable.

The question then becomes whether there are any decidable subsystems? [16] The constraint language of RCC8 has been shown to be decidable [7] – this was achieved by encoding each RCC8 relation as a set of formulae in intuitionistic propositional calculus which is a decidable calculus. This language was subsequently shown to be tractable [98] – in fact the satisfaction problem is solvable in polylogarithmic time since it is in the complexity class NC. However the constraint language of 2^{RCC8} (i.e. where constraints may be arbitrary disjunctions of RCC8 relations) is not tractable, though some subsets are tractable – [110] have identified a maximal tractable subset of the constraint language of 2^{RCC8} and furthermore have shown that for path consistency is sufficient for deciding consistency in this case. As in the case of identifying the maximal tractable subset of Allen's interval calculus [99], the analysis relies on an exhaustive computer generated case analysis. Also of interest is the analysis of [74] which considers an RCC8-like calculus and two simpler calculi and determines which of a number of different problem instances of relational consistency and planar realizability are tractable and which are not – the latter is the harder problem. It has also been shown that the constraint language of $EC(x)$, $PP(x)$ and $Conv(x)$ is intractable (it is at least as hard as determining whether a set of algebraic constraints over the reals is consistent) [35].

Clarke's system has been given a semantics (regular sets of Euclidean space

---

[16] Rather in the same manner as the description logic community have sought to find the line dividing decidability from undecidability and tractability from intractability.

are models) and has been shown to be complete in the weak sense [11]. Unfortunately it turns out that contrary to Clarke's intention, only mereological relations are expressible! The theory in fact characterises complete atomless Boolean algebra. The system of [3] which corrects the problems in Clarke as mentioned above, is given a semantics and shown to be complete by the authors but their inclusion of the notion of 'weak connection' forces a non standard model since models must be non dense. [17]

A completeness result (in the strong sense) has been derived by [101] who give a complete 2D topological theory whose elements are 2D finite (polygonal) regions and whose primitives are: the null and universal regions, the Boolean functions (+,*,−), and a predicate to test for a region being one piece. The theory is first order but requires an infinitary rule of inference (which is not surprising in view of the undecidability of first order topology mentioned above [75]. The infinitary rule of inference guarantees the existence of models in which every region is sum of finitely many connected regions. The resulting theory is complete but not decidable.

Notwithstanding the attempt [8] to derive a complete first order topological theory, it is now clear that no first order finite axiomatisation of topology can be complete or categorical because it is not decidable.

6 Final comments

An issue which has not been much addressed yet in the QSR literature is the issue of cognitive validity − claims are often made that qualitative reasoning is akin to human reasoning, but with little or no empirical justification; one exception to this work is the study made of a calculus for representing topological relations between regions and lines [94] where native speakers of several different languages were asked to perform tasks in which they correlated spatial expressions such as "the road goes through the park" with a variety of diagrams which depicted a line and a region which the subjects were told to interpret as as road and a park. Another study is [87] which has investigated the preferred Allen relation (interpreted as a 1D spatial relation) in the case that the composition table entry is a disjunction. Perhaps the fact that humans seem to have a preferred model explains why they are able to reason efficiently in the presence of the kind of ambiguity engendered by qualitative representations.

As in so many other fields of knowledge representation it is unlikely that a single universal spatial representation language will emerge − rather, the best we can hope for is that the field will develop a library of representational and

---

[17] This enforced abandonment of R^n as a model leads one to question whether it is indeed a good idea to try to model the proposed distinction between strong and weak connection topologically in a purely spatial theory, rather than in an applied theory of physical bodies and material substances together with the regions they occupy. It should be pointed out that they do propose an extension to their theory in which they allow the spatial granularity to be varied; as finer and finer granularities are considered, so fewer instances of $WC(x,y)$ are true and in the limit the theory tends to the classical topological model.

reasoning devices and some criteria for their most successful application. Moreover, as in the case of non spatial qualitative reasoning, quantitative knowledge and reasoning must not be ignored – qualitative and quantitative reasoning are complementary techniques and research is needed to ensure they can be integrated, for example by developing reliable ways of translating between the two kinds of formalism[18]. Equally, interfacing symbolic QSR to the techniques being developed by the diagrammatic reasoning community [62] is an interesting and important challenge.

In this paper I have tried to provide an overview of the field of qualitative spatial reasoning; however the field is active and there has not been space to cover everything (for example qualitative kinematics [49]). A European funded *Human Capital and Mobility* Network, Spacenet, links together eleven sites working in the field of qualitative spatial reasoning and the web page (http://www.scs.leeds.ac.uk/spacenet/) provides an entry to point to the ongoing work at these sites and elsewhere. Other relevant web sites include the spatial reasoning home page at http://www.cs.albany.edu/~amit/bib/spatsites.html and the spatio-temporal home page at: http://www.cs.aukland.ac.nz/~hans/spacetime/. An online searchable web bibliographies can be found at http://www.cs.albany.edu/~amit/bib/spatial.html.

7 Acknowledgments

The support of the EPSRC under grants GR/H/78955 and GR/K65041, and also the CEC under the HCM network SPACENET is gratefully acknowledged. In writing this paper I have been greatly influenced not only by my colleagues in the qualitative spatial reasoning group here at Leeds (in particular Brandon Bennett, John Gooday and Nick Gotts and more recently Amar Isli), but also by the many discussions I have participated in at the Spacenet workshops with the participants from the other 10 sites – my sincere thanks to them all. The responsibility for any errors in this paper rests entirely with me of course.

References

1. J F Allen. Maintaining knowledge about temporal intervals. *Communications of the ACM*, 26(11):832–843, 1983.
2. N Asher and J Lang. When nonmonotonicity comes from distance. In L Nebel, B amd Dreschler-Fischer, editor, *KI-94: Advances in Artificial Intelligence*, pages 308–318. Springer-Verlag, 1994.
3. N Asher and L Vieu. Toward a geometry of common sense: A semantics and a complete axiomatization of mereotopology. In *Proceedings of the International Joint Conference on Artificial Intelligence (IJCAI-95), Montreal*, 1995.
4. M Aurnague and L Vieu. A three-level approach to the semantics of space. In C Zelinsky-Wibbelt, editor, *The semantics of prepositions - from mental processing to natural language processing*, Berlin, 1993. Mouton de Gruyter.
5. B Balbiani, V Dugat, L Farninas del Cerro, and A Lopez. *Eléments de géométrie mécanique*. Editions Hermes, 1994.

---

[18] Some existing research on this problem includes [53, 52].

6. P Balbiani, L Del Cerro, T Tinchev, and D Vakarelov. Modal logics for incidence geometries. *J. Logic and Computation*, 1:59 – 78, 1997.

7. B. Bennett. Spatial reasoning with propositional logics. In J Doyle, E Sandewall, and P Torasso, editors, *Principles of Knowledge Representation and Reasoning: Proceedings of the 4th International Conference (KR94)*, San Francisco, CA., 1994. Morgan Kaufmann.

8. B Bennett. Carving up space: steps towards construction of an absolutely complete theory of spatial regions. In L.M. Pereira J.J. Alfres and E. Orlowska, editors, *Proceedings of JELIA '96*, pages 337–353, 1996.

9. B Bennett. Modal logics for qualitative spatial reasoning. *Bulletin of the Interest Group in Pure and Applied Logic (IGPL)*, 1996.

10. B Bennett, A Isli, and A G Cohn. When does a composition table provide a complete and tractable proof procedure for a relational constraint language? In *Proceedings of the IJCAI-97 workshop on Spatial and Temporal Reasoning*, Nagoya, Japan, 1997. to appear.

11. L. Biacino and G. Gerla. Connection structures. *Notre Dame Journal of Formal Logic*, 32(2), 1991.

12. S Borgo, N Guarino, and C Masolo. A pointless theory of space based on strong connecction and congruence. In *Principles of Knowledge Representation and Reasoning, Pro 5th Conference*, pages 220–229, 1996.

13. J M Brady. Criteria for representations of shape. *Human and Machine Vision*, 1993.

14. R Casati and A Varzi. *Holes and Other Superficialities*. MIT Press, Cambridge, MA, 1994.

15. B L Clarke. A calculus of individuals based on 'connection'. *Notre Dame Journal of Formal Logic*, 23(3):204–218, July 1981.

16. B L Clarke. Individuals and points. *Notre Dame Journal of Formal Logic*, 26(1):61–75, 1985.

17. E Clementini and P Di Felice. A comparison of methods for representing topological relationships. *Information Sciences*, 3:149–178, 1995.

18. E Clementini and P Di Felice. An algebraic model for spatial objects with undetermined boundaries. In P Burrough and A M Frank, editors, *Proceedings, GISDATA Specialist Meeting on Geographical Entities with Undetermined Boundaries,*. Taylor Francis, 1996.

19. E Clementini and P Di Felice. Approximate topological relations. *International Journal of Approximate Reasoning*, 1997.

20. E Clementini and P Di Felice. A global framework for qualitative shape description. *GeoInformatica*, 1(1), 1997.

21. E Clementini, P Di Felice, and D Hernández. Qualitative representation of positional information. *Artificial Intelligence*, 1997.

22. E Clementini, P Di Felice, and P Oosterom. A small set of formal topological relationships suitable for end user interatction. In D Abel and B C Ooi, editors, *Proc. 3rd Int. Symp. on Large Spatial Databases, SSD*, number 692 in LNCS, pages 277–295. Springer, 1994.

23. E Clementini, J Sharma, and M J Egenhofer. Modeling topological spatial relations: strategies for query processing. *Computers and Graphics*, 18(6):815–822, 1994.

24. A G Cohn. A hierarchcial representation of qualitative shape based on connection and convexity. In A Frank, editor, *Proc COSIT95*, LNCS, pages 311–326. Springer Verlag, 1995.

25. A G Cohn. Calculi for qualitative spatial reasoning. In J Pfalzgraf J Calmet, J A Campbell, editor, *Artificial Intelligence and Symbolic Mathematical Computation*, volume 1138 of *LNCS*, pages 124–143. Springer Verlag, 1996.

26. A G Cohn, B Bennett, J Gooday, and N Gotts. RCC: a calculus for region based qualitative spatial reasoning. *Geoinformatica*, to appear, 1997.

27. A G Cohn, B Bennett, J Gooday, and N Gotts. Representing and reasoning with qualitative spatial relations about regions. In O Stock, editor, *Temporal and spatial reasoning*. Kluwer, 1997. to appear.

28. A G Cohn, J M Gooday, and B Bennett. A comparison of structures in spatial and temporal logics. In R Casati, B Smith, and G White, editors, *Philosophy and the Cognitive Sciences: Proceedings of the 16th International Wittgenstein Symposium*, Vienna, 1994. Hölder-Pichler-Tempsky.

29. A G Cohn and N M Gotts. Spatial regions with undetermined boundaries. In *Proceedings of Gaithesburg Workshop on GIS*. ACM, December 1994.

30. A G Cohn and N M Gotts. A theory of spatial regions with indeterminate boundaries. In C. Eschenbach, C. Habel, and B. Smith, editors, *Topological Foundations of Cognitive Science*, 1994.

31. A G Cohn and N M Gotts. The 'egg-yolk' representation of regions with indeterminate boundaries. In P Burrough and A M Frank, editors, *Proceedings, GISDATA Specialist Meeting on Geographical Objects with Undetermined Boundaries*, pages 171–187. Francis Taylor, 1996.

32. A G Cohn and N M Gotts. A mereological approach to representing spatial vagueness. In J Doyle L C Aiello and S Shapiro, editors, *Principles of Knowledge Representation and Reasoning, Proc. 5th Conference*, pages 230–241. Morgan Kaufmann, 1996.

33. A G Cohn, D A Randell, and Z Cui. Taxonomies of logically defined qualitative spatial relations. *Int. J of Human-Computer Studies*, 43:831–846, 1995.

34. Z Cui, A G Cohn, and D A Randell. Qualitative simulation based on a logical formalism of space and time. In *Proceedings AAAI-92*, pages 679–684, Menlo Park, California, 1992. AAAI Press.

35. E Davis, N M Gotts, and A G Cohn. Constraint networks of topological relations and convexity. Technical report, Courant Institute, New York University, 1997.

36. T de Laguna. Point, line and surface as sets of solids. *The Journal of Philosophy*, 19:449–461, 1922.

37. C Dornheim. Vergleichende analyse topologischer ansaetze des qualitativen raeuml ichen siessens. Studienarbeit, fachereich informatik, Universitaet Hamburg, 1995.

38. G Edwards. The voronoi model and cultural space: Applications to the social sciences and humanities. In A U Frank and I Campari, editors, *Spatial Information Theory: A Theoretical Basis for GIS*, volume 716 of *Lecture Notes in Computer Science*, pages 202–214, Berlin, 1993. Springer Verlag.

39. M Egenhofer. A formal definition of binary topological relationships. In W. Litwin and H. Schek, editors, *Third International Conference on Foundations of Data Organization and Algorithms (FODO)*,, volume 367 of *LNCS*, pages 457–472. Springer Verlag, 1989.

40. M Egenhofer. Topological similarity. In *Proc FISI workshop on the Toplogical Foundations of Cognitive Science*, volume 37 of *Reports of the Doctoral Series in Cognitive Science*. University of Hamburg, 1994.

41. M Egenhofer and R Franzosa. Point-set topological spatial relations. *International Journal of Geographical Information Systems*, 5(2):161–174, 1991.

42. M Egenhofer and J Herring. Categorizing topological spatial relationships between point, line and area objects. In *The 9-intersection: formalism and its use for natural language spatial predicates, Technical Report 94-1*. National Center for Geographic Information and Analysis, Santa Barbara, 1994.

43. M Egenhofer and J Sharma. Topological relationships between regions in R^2 and Z^2. In D. Abel and B. C. Ooi, editors, *Third International Symposium on Large Spatial Databases*. Springer-Verlag, 1993.

44. M J Egenhofer and K K Al-Taha. Reasoning about gradual changes of topological relationships. In A U Frank, I Campari, and U Formentini, editors, *Theories and Methods of Spatio-temporal Reasoning in Geographic Space*, volume 639 of *Lecture Notes in Computer Science*, pages 196–219. Springer-Verlag, Berlin, 1992.

45. M J Egenhofer, E Clementini, and P Di Felice. Toplogical relations between regions with holes. *Int. Journal of Geographical Information Systems*, 8(2):129–144, 1994.

46. M J Egenhofer and R D Franzosa. On the equivalence of topological relations. *International Journal of Geographical Information Systems*, 9(2):133–152, 1995.

47. M J Egenhofer and D Mark. Naive geography. In A U Frank and W Kuhn, editors, *Spatial Information Theory: a theoretical basis for GIS*, volume 988 of *Lecture Notes in Computer Science*, pages 1–16. Springer-Verlag, Berlin, 1995.

48. C Eschenbach and W Heydrich. Classical mereology and restricted domains. *Int. J. Human-Computer Studies*, 43:723–740, 1995.

49. B. Faltings. A symbolic approach to qualitative kinematics. *Artificial Intelligence*, 56(2), 1992.

50. B Faltings. Qualitative spatial reaoning using algebraic topology. In A U Frank and W Kuhn, editors, *Spatial Information Theory: a theoretical basis for GIS*, volume 988 of *Lecture Notes in Computer Science*, pages 17–30, Berlin, 1995. Springer-Verlag.

51. B. Faltings and P. Struss, editors. *Recent Advances in Qualitative Physics*. MIT Press, Cambridge, Ma, 1992.

52. J Fernyhough, A G Cohn, and D C Hogg. Event recognition using qualitative reasoning on automatically generated spatio-temporal models from visual input. In *Proc. IJCAI97 workshop on Spatial and Temporal Reasoning*, 1997.

53. K Forbus, P Nielsen, and B Faltings. Qualitative kinematics: A framework. In *Proceedings IJCAI-87*, pages 430–436, 1987.

54. A Frank. Qualitative spatial reasoning with cardinal directions. *Journal of Visual Languages and Computing*, 3:343–371, 1992.

55. C Freksa. Temporal reasoning based on semi-intervals. *Artificial Intelligence*, 54:199–227, 1992.

56. H Fujihara and A Mukerjee. Qualitative reasoning about document design. Technical report, Texas A and M University, 1991.

57. M Gahegan. Proximity operators for qualitative spatial reasoning. In W Kuhn A Frank, editor, *Spatial Information Theory: a theoretical basis for GIS*, number 988 in Lecture Notes in Computer Science, pages 31–44, Berlin, 1995. Springer Verlag.

58. A Galton. Towards a qualitative theory of movement. In W Kuhn A Frank, editor, *Spatial Information Theory: a theoretical basis for GIS*, number 988 in Lecture Notes in Computer Science, pages 377–396, Berlin, 1995. Springer Verlag.

59. A Galton. Taking dimension seriously in qualitative spatial reasoning. In W. Wahlster, editor, *Proceedings of the 12th European Conference on Artificial Intelligence*, pages 501–505. John Wiley and Sons, 1996.

60. A P Galton. Towards an integrated logic of space, time and motion. In *Proceedings IJCAI-93*, Chambery, France, September 1993.
61. G. Gerla. Pointless geometries. In F. Buekenhout, editor, *Handbook of Incidence Geometry*, chapter 18, pages 1015–1031. Eslevier Science B.V., 1995.
62. J Glasgow, N H Narayanan, and B Chandrasekara. *Diagrammatic Reasoning*. MIT Press, 1995.
63. J Gooday and A G Cohn. Transition-based qualitative simulation. In *Proceeding of the 10th International Workshop on Qualitative Reasoning*, pages 74 – 82. AAAI press, 1996.
64. J Gooday and A G Cohn. Visual language syntax and semantics: A spatial logic approach. In K Marriott and B Meyer, editors, *Proc Workshop on Theory of Visual Languages*, Gubbio, Italy, 1996.
65. J M Gooday and A G Cohn. Using spatial logic to describe visual languages. *Artificial Intelligence Review*, 10(1-2), 1995. This paper also appears in Integration of Natural Language and Vision Processing (Vol. IV), ed P MckEvitt, Kluwer, 1996.
66. J Goodman and R Pollack. Allowable sequences and order types in discrete and computational geometry. In J Pach, editor, *New trends in discrete and computational geometry*, pages 103–134. Springer Verlag, 1993.
67. N M Gotts. Defining a 'doughnut' made difficult. In C. Eschenbach, C. Habel, and B. Smith, editors, *Topological Foundations of Cognitive Science*, volume 37 of *Reports of the Doctoral programme in Cognitive Science*. University of Hamburg, 1994.
68. N M Gotts. How far can we 'C'? defining a 'doughnut' using connection alone. In J Doyle, E Sandewall, and P Torasso, editors, *Principles of Knowledge Representation and Reasoning: Proceedings of the 4th International Conference (KR94)*. Morgan Kaufmann, 1994.
69. N M Gotts. An axiomatic approach to topology for spatial information systems. Technical report, Report 96.25, School of Computer Studies, University of Leeds, 1996.
70. N M Gotts. Formalising commonsense topology: The inch calculus. In *Proc. Fourth International Symposium on Artificial Intelligence and Mathematics*, 1996.
71. N M Gotts. Toplogy from a single primitive relation: defining topological properties and relations in terms of connection. Technical report, Report 96.23, School of Computer Studies, University of Leeds, 1996.
72. N M Gotts. Using the RCC formalism to describe the topology of spherical regions. Technical report, Report 96.24, School of Computer Studies, University of Leeds, 1996.
73. N M Gotts, J M Gooday, and A G Cohn. A connection based approach to common-sense topological description and reasoning. *The Monist*, 79(1):51–75, 1996.
74. M. Grigni, D. Papadias, and C. Papadimitriou. Topological inference. In *Proc. IJCAI-95*, pages 901–906. Morgan Kaufmann, 1995.
75. A. Grzegorczyk. Undecidability of some topological theories. *Fundamenta Mathematicae*, 38:137–152, 1951.
76. H Guesgen and J Hertzberg. A constraint based approach to spatio-temporal reasoning. *Applied Artificial Intelligence*, 3:71–90, 1992.
77. V Haarslev. Formal semantics of visual languages using spatial reasoning. In *Proceedings of the 11th IEEE Symposium on Visual Languages*, 1995.
78. Volker Haarslev. A fully formalized theory for describing visual notations. In *Proceedings of the AVI'96 post-conference Workshop on Theory of Visual Languages*, Gubbio,Italy, May 1996.

79. P J Hayes. The naive physics manifesto. In D Mitchie, editor, *Expert systems in the micro-electronic age*. Edinburgh University Press, 1979.

80. D Hernández. *Qualitative Representation of Spatial Knowledge*, volume 804 of *Lecture Notes in Artificial Intelligence*. Springer-Verlag, 1994.

81. D Hernández, E Clementini, and P Di Felice. Qualitative distances. In W Kuhn A Frank, editor, *Spatial Information Theory: a theoretical basis for GIS*, number 988 in LNCS, pages 45–58, Berlin, 1995. Springer Verlag.

82. A Herskovits. *Language and Spatial Cognition. An interdisciplinary study of prepositions in English*. Cambridge University Press, 1986.

83. J Hobbs. Granularity. In *Proceedings IJCAI-85*, pages 432–435, 1985.

84. K. J. Holyoak and W. A. Mah. Cognitive reference points in judgments of symbolic magnitude. *Cognitive Psychology*, 14:328–352, 1982.

85. E. Jungert. Symbolic spatial reasoning on object shapes for qualitative matching. In A. U. Frank and L. Campari, editors, *Spatial Information Theory: A Theoretical Basis for GIS*, Lecture Notes in Computer Science No. 716, pages 444–462. COSIT'93, Springer-Verlag, 1993.

86. S Kaufman. A formal theory of spatial reasoning. In *Proc Int. Conf. on Knowledge Representation and Reasoning*, pages 347–356, 1991.

87. M Knauff, R Rauh, and C Schlieder. Preferred mental models in qualitative spatial reasoning: A cognitive assessment of Allen's calculus. In *Proc. 17th Annual Conf. of the Cognitive Science Society*, 1995.

88. B Kuipers. *Qualitative Reasoning*. MIT Press, Cambridge, MA., 1994.

89. B J Kuipers and T S Levitt. Navigating and mapping in large-scale space. *AI Magazine*, 9(2):25–43, 1988.

90. F Lehmann and A G Cohn. The EGG/YOLK reliability hierarchy: Semantic data integration using sorts with prototypes. In *Proc. Conf. on Information Knowledge Management*, pages 272–279. ACM Press, 1994.

91. M Leyton. A process grammar for shape. *Artificial Intelligence*, page 34, 1988.

92. G Ligozat. Towards a general characterization of conceptual neighbourhoods in temporal and spatial reasoning. In F D Anger and R Loganantharah, editors, *Proceedings AAAI-94 Workshop on Spatial and Temporal Reasoning*, 1994.

93. M Lundell. A qualitative model of gradient flow in a spatially distributed parameter. In *Proc 9th Int. Workshop on Qualtiative Reasoning, Amsterdam*, 1995.

94. D Mark, D Comas, M Egenhofer, S Freundschuh, J Gould, and J Nunes. Evaluating and refining computational models of spatial relations through cross-linguistic human-subjects testing. In W Kuhn A Frank, editor, *Spatial Information Theory: a theoretical basis for GIS*, number 988 in Lecture Notes in Computer Science, pages 553–568, Berlin, 1995. Springer Verlag.

95. M Mavrovouniotis and G Stephanopoulos. Formal order-of-magnitude reasoning in process engineering. *Computers and Chemical Engineering*, 12:867–881, 1988.

96. D Montello. Scale and multiple pyschologies of space. In I Campari A Frank, editor, *Spatial Information Theory: a theoretical basis for GIS*, number 716 in Lecture Notes in Computer Science, pages 312–321, Berlin, 1993. Springer Verlag.

97. A Mukerjee and G Joe. A qualitative model for space. In *Proceedings AAAI-90*, pages 721–727, Los Altos, 1990. Morgan Kaufmann.

98. B. Nebel. Computational properties of qualitative spatial reasoning: First results. In *Procedings of the 19th German AI Conference*, 1995.

99. B Nebel. Reasoning about temporal relations: a maximal tractable subset of Allen's interval algebra. *Journal of the Association for Computing Machinery*, 42(1):43–66, January 1995.

100. I Pratt and O Lemon. Ontologies for plane, polygonal mereotopology. Technical Report UMCS-97-1-1, Univ. of Manchester, Dept of Computer Science, 1997.
101. Ian Pratt and Dominik Schoop. A complete axiom system for polygonal mereotopology of the plane. Technical Report UMCS-97-2-2, University of Manchester, 1997.
102. O Raiman. Order of magnitude reasoning. In *AAAI-86: Proceedings of the National Conference on AI*, pages 100–104, 1996.
103. R Rajagopalan. A model for integrated qualitative spatial and dynamic reasoning about physical systems. In *Proc. AAAI*, pages 1411–1417, 1994.
104. C G Ralha. *A Framework for Dynamic Structuring of Information*. PhD thesis, School of Computer Studies, Universities of Leeds, 1996.
105. D A Randell and A G Cohn. Exploiting lattices in a theory of space and time. *Computers and Mathematics with Applications*, 23(6-9):459–476, 1992. Also appears in "Semantic Networks", ed. F. Lehmann, Pergamon Press, Oxford, pp. 459-476, 1992.
106. D A Randell, A G Cohn, and Z Cui. Computing transitivity tables: A challenge for automated theorem provers. In *Proceedings CADE 11*, Berlin, 1992. Springer Verlag.
107. D A Randell, A G Cohn, and Z Cui. Naive topology: Modelling the force pump. In P Struss and B Faltings, editors, *Advances in Qualitative Physics*, pages 177–192. MIT Press, 1992.
108. D A Randell, Z Cui, and A G Cohn. A spatial logic based on regions and connection. In *Proc. 3rd Int. Conf. on Knowledge Representation and Reasoning*, pages 165–176, San Mateo, 1992. Morgan Kaufmann.
109. D.A. Randell and A.G. Cohn. Modelling topological and metrical properties of physical processes. In R Brachman, H Levesque, and R Reiter, editors, *Proceedings 1st International Conference on the Principles of Knowledge Representation and Reasoning*, pages 55–66, Los Altos, 1989. Morgan Kaufmann.
110. Jochen Renz and Bernhard Nebel. On the complexity of qualitative spatial reasoning: a maximal tractable fragment of the Region Connection Calculus. In *Proceedings of IJCAI-97*, 1997.
111. A A G Requicha and H B Boelcke. Solid modelling: a historical summary aand contemporary assessment. *IEEE Computer Graphics and Applications*, 2:9–24, 1992.
112. W Richards and D Hoffman. Codon constraints on closed 2d shapes. *Computer Vision, graphics and impage processing*, 31:265–281, 1985.
113. R Röhrig. A theory for qualitative spatial reasoning based on order relations. In *AAAI-94: Proceedings of the 12th National Conference on AI*, volume 2, pages 1418–1423, Seattle, 1994.
114. C Schlieder. Representing visible locations for qualitative navigation. In N Piera Carreté and M G Singh, editors, *Qualitative Reasoning and Decision Technologies*, pages 523–532, Barcelona, 1993. CIMNE.
115. C Schlieder. Reasoning about ordering. In W Kuhn A Frank, editor, *Spatial Information Theory: a theoretical basis for GIS*, number 988 in Lecture Notes in Computer Science, pages 341–349, Berlin, 1995. Springer Verlag.
116. C Schlieder. Qualitative shape representation. In P Burrough and A M Frank, editors, *Proceedings, GISDATA Specialist Meeting on Geographical Objects with Undetermined Boundaries*. Francis Taylor, 1996.
117. M Shanahan. Default reasoning about spatial occupancy. *Artificial Intelligence*, 1995.

118. J Sklansky. Measuring concavity on a rectangular mosaic. *IEEE Trans. on Computers*, C-21(12):1355–1364, 1972.

119. B Smith. Ontology and the logicistic analysis of reality. In N Guarino and R Poli, editors, *Proceedings International Workshop on Formal Ontology in Conceptual Analysis and Knowledge Representation*, 1993. Revised version forthcoming in G Haefliger and P M Simons, eds, Analytic Phenomenology, Kluwer.

120. B Smith. Mereotopology: A theory of parts and boundaries. *Data and Knowledge Engineering*, 20(3):287–303, November 1996.

121. J. G. Stell and M. F. Worboys. The algebraic structure of sets of regions. In *Proc COSIT97*, LNCS. Springer Verlag, 1997.

122. A. Tarski. Foundations of the geometry of solids. In *Logic, Semantics, Metamathematics*, chapter 2. Oxford Clarendon Press, 1956. trans. J.H. Woodger.

123. A Tate, J Hendler, and M Drummond. A review of AI planning techniques. In J Allen, J Hendler, and A Tate, editors, *Readings in Planning*. Morgan Kaufman, San Mateo, CA, 1990.

124. T Topaloglou. First order theories of approximate space. In F Anger et al., editor, *Working notes of AAAI workshop on spatial and temporal reasoning*, pages 283–296, Seattle, 1994.

125. A Varzi. On the boundary between mereology and topology. In R Casati, B Smith, and G White, editors, *Philosophy and the Cognitive Sciences: Proceedings of the 16th International Wittgenstein Symposium*. Hölder-Pichler-Tempsky, Vienna, 1994.

126. A Varzi. Parts, wholes, and part-whole relations: the prospects of mereotopology. *Data and Knowledge Engineering*, 20(3):259–286, 1996.

127. A C Varzi. Spatial reasoning in a holey world. In *Proceedings of the Spatial and Temporal Reasoning workshop, IJCAI-93*, pages 47–59, 1993.

128. L Vieu. *Sémantique des relations spatiales et inférences spatio-temporelles*. PhD thesis, Université Paul Sabatier, Toulouse, 1991.

129. D S Weld and J De Kleer, editors. *Readings in Qualitative Reasoning About Physical Systems*. Morgan Kaufman, San Mateo, Ca, 1990.

130. A N Whitehead. *Process and Reality*. The MacMillan Company, New York, 1929.

131. A N Whitehead. *Process and reality: corrected edition*. The Free Press, Macmillan Pub. Co., New York, 1978. edited by D.R. Griffin and D.W. Sherburne.

132. J.H. Woodger. *The Axiomatic Method in Biology*. Cambridge University Press, 1937.

133. K Zimmermann. Enhancing qualitative spatial reasoning – combining orientation and distance. In I Campari A Frank, editor, *Spatial Information Theory: a theoretical basis for GIS*, number 716 in Lecture Notes in Computer Science, pages 69–76, Berlin, 1993. Springer Verlag.

134. K Zimmermann. Measuring without distances: the delta calculus. In W Kuhn A Frank, editor, *Spatial Information Theory: a theoretical basis for GIS*, number 988 in Lecture Notes in Computer Science, pages 59–68, Berlin, 1995. Springer Verlag.

135. K Zimmermann and C Freksa. Enhancing spatial reasoning by the concept of motion. In A Sloman, editor, *Prospects for Artificial Intelligence*, pages 140–147. IOS Press, 1993.

COLBERT: A Language for Reactive Control in Sapphira

Kurt Konolige
SRI International
333 Ravenswood Avenue
Menlo Park, CA 94025
konolige@ai.sri.com
http://www.ai.sri.com/~konolige/sapphira

1. Controlling a Robot

What does it mean to write programs to control a robot? Robots can sense the world and act within it; so, in general, a robot control program is one that takes the robot's sensory input, processes it, and decides what motor actions the robot will perform. But the mapping between inputs and outputs is a very complex one, and the control task requires some decomposition into simpler elements to make it workable. In recent years there has been some convergence on an architecture for autonomous mobile robots. In general form it looks something like the diagram in Figure 1-1.

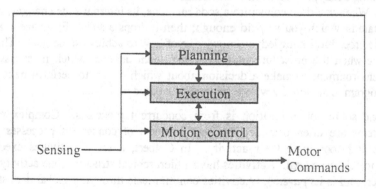

Figure 1-1 A hybrid control architecture

The bottom layer is a controller that implements some form of motion control for the robot. This layer can be quite complex; for example, in the Sapphira architecture it consists of a fuzzy controller that implements a set of behaviors for achieving goals such as corridor following, obstacle avoidance, and the like [Kon97]. The second layer is a *sequencer* that initiates and monitors behaviors, taking care of temporal aspects of coordinating behaviors, such as deciding when they have completed their job, or are no longer contributing to an overall goal, or when environmental conditions have changed enough to warrant different behaviors. The sequencer must complete its computations in a timely manner, although not as quickly as the control layer. In the top layer, long-term deliberative planning takes place, with the results being passed down to the sequencing layer for execution. Generally, the planner is invoked and guided by conditions in the sequencing layer, e.g. a task failing or completing.

There are many different instantiations of this architecture, including Sapphira [Kon97], SSS [Con92], ATLANTIS [Gat92], RAPs [Fir94], AuRA [Ark90], and Payton's reactive planners [Pay90]. In almost all of these, the sequencer plays the role of the main executive, taking advice from the planner and invoking behaviors to accomplish goals. When one thinks of writing robot programs, it is sequencer programs that are the result. In fact, it's possible to think of the planner as an automatic generator of robot programs, which are then executed by the sequencer.

Most of architectures mentioned in the previous paragraph concentrate on the interaction between the layers, how to integrate behaviors, sequencers, and planners. In contrast, in this paper we are concerned with how a user can write sequencer programs to effectively control the robot. Our emphasis is on issues of language and semantics: what is a good language for robot programs, what kind of semantics is appropriate for the sequencer, and how does the language fit the semantics. The result of our inquiries is the sequencer language Colbert, a part of the Sapphira architecture.

Colbert draws on two sources for its concepts. The first is finite state automata (FSAs) [Hop79]. FSAs are ubiquitous in computers and robotics, because they provide a way of defining a mapping between the internal state of a automaton and its operation in the world. When you drop coins into a soda machine, its internal state changes, until it gets to a state in which you've paid enough; then it drops a soda. FSAs are a great way to encode procedural knowledge: knowledge of how to achieve some goal. This is especially true when the procedure includes *conditional actions*, which must test the state of the environment to make a decision about which action to perform next. In Colbert, a program is an *activity* whose semantics is based on FSAs.

The second source of inspiration is from concurrent processes. Complex robot control problems are often best decomposed into sets of concurrent processes that communicate and coordinate their activity. In Colbert, a set of activities executes concurrently to achieve a goal. Activities have a hierarchical structure (one activity can spawn another, and is its *parent*). Activities communicate through a global data store, and by sending each other signals.

Having an adequate semantics doesn't mean that control programs will be easy for a user to write or debug. In fact, writing FSA structures directly is not a pleasant task, and all modern computer languages use implicit sequencing and explicit looping statements to define the flow of execution control. It would be nice to use a language that has familiar control structures, so that users would not have to learn another programming language. With this in mind, we chose for Colbert a subset of the ANSI C language, along with a few extensions for robot control. Surprisingly, even though the semantics is based on FSAs, there is relatively little that a C programmer must learn to begin writing correct robot control programs.

A second user concern is the ability to debug and edit control programs as part of the development cycle. A problem with developing using C is that the compile-load-debug-edit-recompile cycle is tedious, and getting back to where the mistake occurred can be time-consuming or even impossible when dealing with robots operating in a real-world environment. All of these issues indicate that an interpretive development environment is desirable, where errors are signaled, the user can examine the state of the system, make changes to programs, and continue with the changed program. We have implemented a Colbert evaluator that executes source language statements directly, so that programs can be modified during execution. The evaluator also allows the user to probe the state of the system during execution to determine where errors occur, and to load compiled C code for efficient execution of compute-intensive routines as part of an activity.

Finally, we have tried to make Colbert efficient and portable to most operating systems. The evaluator is fast enough to be used for production robot programs; but it is also possible to compile Colbert activities into native C code for even more efficient execution. Since the Colbert executive is written in C, and requires only minimal support from the OS, it can run under most OS's: we have implemented versions on most Unix systems, and on Windows 95/NT.

2. Activity Examples

Activities control the overall behavior of the robot in several ways.

- Sequencing the basic actions that the robot performs.
- Monitoring the execution of basic actions and other activities.
- Executing activity subroutines.
- Checking and setting the values of internal variables.

In this section we'll look at some simple examples of robot behavior. These examples will illustrate the functionality of activities in controlling robot behavior. A more detailed discussion of the syntax and semantics is in subsequent sections.

2.1 Patrol

We want the robot to patrol up and down between two goal points, repeating this activity a specified number of times. The basic actions the robot can perform are (1) turning to a heading, and (2) moving forward a given distance. For this example we won't worry about the problem of *robot localization*, that is, how the robot will maintain registration between its internal map (the two goal points) and the external world.

The simplest way to realize the patrol activity is as a perpetual **while** loop, in which the primitive turn and forward motion actions are executed in sequence. Here is the proposed activity schema:

```
act patrol(int a)
{
    while (a != 0)
    {
        a = a-1;
        Turnto(180);
        Move(1000);
        Turnto(0);
        Move(1000);
    }
}
```

Figure 2-1 A simple patrol activity

This simple example illustrates three of the basic capabilities of the Colbert control language. First, the two basic actions of turning and moving forward are sequenced within the body of the **while** loop. As each action is initiated, an internal monitor takes over, halting the further execution of the **patrol** activity until the action is completed. So, under the guidance of this activity, the robot turns to face the 180° direction, then moves forward 1000 mm, then turns to the 0° direction, then moves forward another 1000 mm. The net effect is to move the robot back and forth between two points 1 meter apart.

The enclosing **while** loop controls how many times the patrol motion is done. The local variable **a** is a parameter to the activity; when the activity is invoked, for example with the call **start patrol(4)**, this value is filled in with an integer. On every iteration, the **while** condition checks whether **a** has been set to zero; if not, the variable is decremented and the loop continues. (Note that, to make this an almost infinite loop, just invoke **patrol** with a negative argument.) Using the variable **a** to keep track of the number of times the movement is done illustrates the capability of checking and setting internal variables, which can be very handy even for simple activities.

The language of activities is based on ANSI C. When an activity schema is defined, the keyword **act** signals the start of the schema. The schema itself looks like a prototyped function definition in C. Constructs such as local variables, iteration, and conditionals are all available. In addition, there are forms that relate specifically to robot action. In this case, the actions are primitive motions available to the robot: turning and moving forward. When the activity schema is invoked, an *activity executive* interprets the statements in the schema according to a finite state semantics. Basic actions cause the executive to wait at a finite state node until the action is completed (or some escape condition holds, such as a timeout). So, while the activity schema looks like a standard C function, its underlying semantics is based on finite state automata for robot control. The user, who typically wants to sequence robot actions in the same way as he or she would sequence computer operations, can write control programs in a familiar operator language; the executive takes care of matching the activity schema statements to the finite state automaton semantics, so that the intended robot behavior is the result.

2.2 Surveillance Robot

While sequencing basic actions is the typical evaluation mode, the language also supports concurrent execution, in which several activities working in parallel coordinate the robot's actions. Suppose we want to program the robot to patrol until it sees some object in front; then it should stop patrolling and approach the object. To accomplish this task, we'll set up two activities: the patrol activity of the previous example, and a supervisory activity that checks if there is something in front of the robot, and if so, approaches it.

```
act approach()
{
    int x;
    start patrol(-1) timeout 300 noblock;
checking:
    if (timedout(patrol) || sfIsStalled()) fail;
    x = sfObjInFront();
    if (x > 2000) goto checking;
    suspend patrol;
    Move(x - 200);
    succeed;
}
```

Figure 2-2 An activity that monitors another

This activity starts off by invoking **patrol** with a negative argument, so it continues indefinitely. However, instead of causing the **approach** to wait for its completion, the **patrol** activity is invoked with two special parameters. The first, **timeout 300**, causes **patrol** to quit after 30 seconds (300 cycles) have elapsed. The second, **noblock**, allows the execution of **approach** to continue in parallel with **patrol**. The former now goes into a monitoring loop, in which it checks for objects in front, for a motor stall, and for the state of the **patrol** activity. If it determines that **patrol** has timed out, or if a motor stalls (indicating the robot ran into something immovable), then **approach** exits in a failure state. The activity executive keeps track of the dependencies among activities; in this case, since **approach** called **patrol**, exiting **approach** automatically exits **patrol**. Thus, if the motor stalls, all activity started by **approach** will be suspended.

If, on the other hand, **approach** determines that there is an object less than 2 meters in front (by calling the perceptual routine **sfObjInFront**, which returns the distance to the nearest object), then it suspends the **patrol** activity, and moves to within 20 cm of the object. The patrol activity must be suspended, otherwise the **Move** action will conflict with the actions being issued by **patrol**. After the robot moves near the object, the **approach** activity exits with the success state.

In this example, two activities execute concurrently, and coordination is achieved by *signals* that are sent between them. Activities can examine each others' state, and take appropriate action. As the monitoring activity, **approach** has the responsibility of checking the state of **patrol** to see if it has timed out, and also checking for other conditions that would cause the suspension of **patrol** and the initiation of new behavior. Finally, if **approach** is itself part of a larger activity, then by exiting with success or failure, it can signal other activities of its result.

The use of a C-like language, together with a concurrent finite state semantics, makes it easy to write complex control routines in a few simple lines. In the next sections we'll examine the semantics of Colbert in more detail, and show how the executive interprets the Colbert language.

3. Language and Semantics

Finite state automata (FSAs) are an ubiquitous paradigm in computer science and electronics engineering. FSAs are used to program logic chips, to design microprocessors, to run soda machines, and to reason about the computational complexity and decidability [Hor89]. They have also been the inspiration for several robot control languages, including the *situated automata* of Kaelbling and Rosenschein [Kae90], and the circuit semantics of ATLANTIS [Gat92]. We combine the basic structure FSAs with ideas from concurrent systems to produce a semantics for Colbert.

3.1 Finite State Automata

A finite state automaton consists of:

- sets S (states), I (inputs), and O (outputs)

- a transition function $f(s, i) \rightarrow s$ from states and inputs to states

- an output function $g(s) \rightarrow o$ from states to outputs

It's convenient to represent FSAs using arcs and nodes: nodes are the states, and arcs are the transitions between states. The arcs are labeled with the transition condition necessary for taking the arc to the next state, and states are tagged with their output function. Figure 3-1 shows the FSA for the **patrol** activity defined in the previous section. The transition function label is in boldface, the output label in italics.

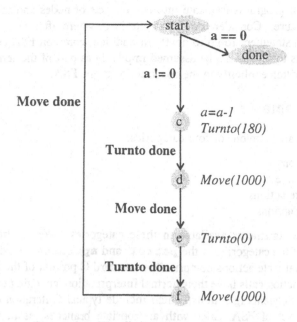

Figure 3-1 The finite state automaton for patrol

The first thing to note about the FSA is that its states don't correspond exactly to the statements in the activity. For example, the **while** statement has been translated into a set of nodes (*start, done, c*) which split the condition of the loop. In general, conditional and looping statements in Colbert will translate to a set of nodes with conditional labels in the FSA.

Actions at the nodes include primitive robot actions and internal state changes. In pure FSAs, all state information is encoded in the states themselves. For Colbert, the nodes represent only the state of the activity; other robot state information is handled separately (and more efficiently) as part of the Sapphira perceptual space.

In the activity schema, no wait conditions for primitive actions were given explicitly. In the FSA, these conditions are given as the conditions for transition to the next state. When an action command is issued, the FSA waits in the issuing state until the action is finished. This default translation can be changed by the addition of the **noblock** and **timeout** parameters in Colbert.

Note that the output function associated with a node is performed only once, when control first arrives at the node. All self-transitions back to the node (which are not explicitly drawn in the figure) do not result in the output function being called again.

The strength of the Colbert language lies in the ability to make an intuitive translation from operator constructs in C to FSAs capable of controlling the robot. FSAs can be tedious to program directly, because straightforward sequences and loops that are typical of most programs translate into lengthy sets of nodes and arcs with a linear or looping structure. Consider trying to write in C, where after each statement you have to say which statement to go to next! In addition, common FSA constructs, like waiting for actions to finish, can be assumed implicitly as part of the semantics of Colbert, rather than written explicitly in the construction of the FSA.

3.2 Colbert Statements

Colbert statements are from one of four categories:

1. Control actions
2. Activity state tests
3. Internal state actions
4. Sequencing actions

Table 3-1 lists the statements available in these categories. We've already seen examples from each of the categories in the **patrol** and **approach** activities. The sequencing and internal state actions comprise the standard C portion of the language. C assignments and function calls have their normal interpretation, changing the state of internal C variables. Sequencing actions, which include typical C iteration operators, are translated into a set of FSA states with appropriate branches, as in the while statement of the patrol activity.

Control Actions	Example	Description
Primitive Action	`Move(1000) timeout 30;`	Start a primitive action
start act	`start patrol noblock;`	Start an activity
<signal> act	`suspend patrol;`	Signal an activity
Activity State Tests		
<state>(act)	`timedout(patrol)`	Test the state of an activity
Internal State		
C assignments and functions	`x = sfObjInFront()+10;`	Test or set the state of the database
Sequencing Actions		
goto	`goto start;`	Go to a state
while, if	`if (a == 0)` `  goto start;`	Iterative and conditional execution
waitfor	`waitfor(timedout(act)` `  ||a<0);`	Conditional suspension

Table 3-1 Colbert statement summary

Control actions translate to a single FSA node for executing the action, and a transition based on the completion of the activity or action. If noblock is asserted, then the transition is taken immediately; if a timeout is asserted, then there is an additional transition based on the timeout value.

Control actions can also change the state of other activities, by sending them signals. Similarly, an activity can accept signals from other activities, changing the state of the underlying FSA.

Activity state tests aren't statements *per se*, but are expressions that can be used where C expressions are normally allowed. They allow conditionals to check for the state of another activity.

Finally, intentions can modify the state of their execution using various sequencing operators: goto, iteration, conditional, and suspension operators.

3.3 Subactivities

Colbert supports an execution model in which activities may be invoked as children of an executing activity. This capability supports hierarchical task decomposition, an important method for robot control [Fir94, Ark90]. Consider the task of moving an object from one place to another (taken from [Fir96]). It's natural to decompose this into three subtasks: picking up the object, going to the destination, and dropping the object. In Colbert, we would write the following activity.

```
act move_object(int dest)
{
    start pickup;
    start goto(dest);
    start drop;
}
```

Figure 3-2 An activity with subactivities

The subactivities **pickup**, **goto**, and **drop** are executed in turn. The **move_object** activity stops at each until it finishes, then goes on to the next. This default execution model is the same as for primitive actions. However, there are cases in which hierarchical decomposition is not the best way to accomplish a task; rather, it is useful to have several activities executing concurrently. This behavior is typical with monitoring tasks, which can stretch over several subactivities. Firby [Fir96] gives the example of monitoring the robot's gripper during the **move_object** activity. If the robot drops the object, it should attempt to pick it up before continuing to the destination. In Colbert, a monitoring activity can be started and run concurrently with the other subactivities, as in the surveillance example of Figure 2-2. In the current example, we start a monitoring activity using the **noblock** option.

```
act move_object(int dest)
{
    start monitor_hand noblock;
    start pickup;
    start goto(dest);
    start drop;
}
```

Figure 3-3 Monitoring the move_object activity

Figure 3-4 shows the execution structure of this activity. The execution of the schema starts at *a*, and invokes the monitoring activity (which starts at node *n*). At *b* the **pickup** subactivity is invoked, and the transition to node *c* doesn't take place until the subactivity finishes. During the execution of pickup, there are three concurrently executing activities: **move_object**, **pickup**, and **monitor_hand**. When the toplevel activity **move_object** is exited, the Colbert executive automatically reaps any subprocesses, so the **monitor_hand** process is terminated.

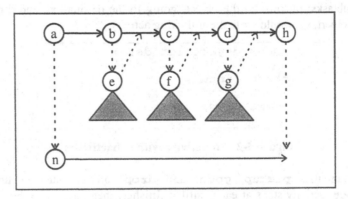

Figure 3-4 Activity execution structures

This example is incomplete, because we haven't shown how the monitoring process interacts with its siblings to achieve the task in the presence of carrying failures. In the next section we look at the coordination mechanisms available to concurrent tasks.

The hierarchical structure of activities is very much like the child process structure of Unix systems. What distinguishes Colbert activities is the FSA nature of their semantics, which makes the coordination process more easily understandable and controllable.

3.4 Concurrent Activities and Synchronization

Often the task of robot control can be decomposed into a set of subtasks that are mostly independent, but require some form of coordination. Colbert's semantics supports a set of concurrent activities that communicate indirectly through a global database, and directly by sending signals. The FSA nature of activities is handy for communicating state information.

Although an activity can be queried to see if it is in any given state, there are some predefined states typically used for signaling. These are listed below in Table 3-2.

State	Meaning
sfINIT	Initial state of an activity
sfSUCCESS sfFAILURE	Termination states: activity succeeded or failed in its goal
SfTIMEOUT	Termination state: activity timed out
sfSUSPEND	Suspended state: the activity is not running
sfINTERRUPT	State for activities after an interrupt signal
sfRESUME	State for activities after a resume signal

Table 3-2 Standard signals for activities

When an activity is first started, it is set to the sfINIT state. Typically this is the first statement of the activity, but an activity can specify a particular start position by using the **onInit** label. For example, the following activity starts in the middle:

```
act aa(int x)
{
  loop:
  if (x == 0) succeed;
  onInit:
  x = x-1;
  goto loop;
}
```

If an activity falls through to the end, it is considered to have succeeded. Otherwise, the activity can terminate itself and signal success or failure by using the special actions **succeed** and **fail**. The activity can also suspend itself by using the **suspend** action. In the suspended state, no further processing takes place until another activity sends a signal, usually the **resume** signal.

Interruption and resumption are the normal way in which activities are requested to stop and start their processing, once invoked. An interrupt signal causes an activity to go to the special **onInterrupt** label. There, the activity should clean up anything that needs it, such as terminating current movement actions, and then suspend itself.

On resumption, the activity should re-establish any state it needs, then continue its processing. Here is an example of making the **patrol** activity interruptable and resumable. When **patrol2** is interrupted, it first waits for any forward motion to be finished (**sfDonePosition()** returns 1 when any **Move** command is finished). Then it suspends itself. This means that the robot finishes up at one of the patrol endpoints. On resumption, the counter is incremented, and the patrol continues. Note that this is not a perfect solution, since the robot could have stopped at either point, and may resume by patrolling ahead of or behind its original path. But it does illustrates the idea of interruptability.

```
act patrol2(int a)
{
  start:
   while (a != 0)
   {
       a = a-1;
       Turnto(180);
       Move(1000);
       Turnto(0);
       Move(1000);
   }
   succeed;
  onInterrupt:
   waitfor (sfDonePosition());
   suspend;
  onResume:
   a = a+1;
   goto start;
}
```

Figure 3-5 An activity that responds to interrupts

Activities can also be coordinated with global variables, which are visible to all activities. For example, the **approach** activity waits for a condition in which there is an object close by. The function **sfObjInFront()** could invoke a perceptual routine, or could just check the value of a variable that another activity was responsible for setting.

One problem that all concurrent systems have is coordinating their accesses to global variables. Several processes may attempt to change the same variable at the same time: for example, a process may be executing the statement **x=x+1**, while another is changing **x**. The result may not be to increment **x**. The same coordination problem exists with signals: one process may attempt to interrupt another when it is executing a statement, and the statement may not be fully executed, leaving the process in an indeterminate state.

In typical concurrent systems, there are coordination mechanisms for dealing with these problems: critical sections, mutexes, and the like. In Colbert, the FSA semantics provides a natural coordination mechanism. Activity transitions are executed *synchronously*, and signaling takes place when all activities are settled at an FSA node.

Synchronous behavior is enforced by the execution model, explained in the next section.

Let's return to the **move_object** example (Figure 3-3) and add coordination signals to the activities. A partial listing is shown in Figure 3-6. As before, the **monitor_hand** activity is started in nonblocking mode, and immediately sent the **suspend** signal so that it isn't active until pickup actually grasps the object, at which point it is sent the **resume** signal. Now monitoring is active throughout the robot's activities, until during **drop** it gets sent a **suspend** signal.

```
act move_object(int dest)
{
    start monitor_hand noblock suspend;
  restart:
    start pickup;
    start goto(dest);
    start drop;
    succeed;
  onInterrupt:
    suspend monitor_hand;
    goto restart;
}

act pickup
{
    gripper down;
    gripper grasp;
    resume monitor_hand;
    gripper up;
}

act drop
{
    suspend monitor_hand;
    gripper ungrasp;
    gripper down;
}
```

Figure 3-6 Signaling in the move_object activity

Note that there is no special processing needed for simple failure recovery. If **monitor_hand** detects a gripper failure, it just sends an interrupt signal to **move_object**. Since all children of **move_object** will also see this signal, whatever subactivity is occurring will also be interrupted. On interrupt, **move_object** resumes by again trying to grasp the object and continue to its drop-off point.

In this example, it was possible to refer to executing activities using their schema names. In more complicated cases, the same schematic activity may be invoked several times, giving rise to an ambiguous reference in signaling. Colbert allows an activity to be given an *instance name* when it is invoked. In this way, multiple invocations of the same schema can be kept separate for signaling purposes. This is not a very sophisticated scheme, however. A more useful but still simple method would be to allow activity instances to be members of user-defined classes, e.g., a *monitor* class, or even a *monitor_gripper* class. The user could create classes and subclasses as needed, and signal an activity based on its name, its name and class, or just its class.

4. Colbert Executive

In this section we describe how the Colbert executive implements the FSA semantics of activities. To start an activity schema, it must be invoked with the **start** command, which puts an instance of the schema onto Colbert's structured list of activities. The Colbert executive has the job of cycling through the activities and executing them incrementally, giving an operational meaning to the underlying FSA semantics.

4.1 Synchronous FSA Cycle

One of the problems faced in implementing the executive is that it must work the same on a number of different OS platforms (MS Windows and different flavors of Unix), all of which have different support for concurrent activity. Another problem is that a Sapphira client can have tens or even hundreds of activities executing concurrently, so the overhead of servicing them must be low. This rules out expensive OS implementations such as separate processes or even threads. Instead, we take advantage of the discrete nature of the FSA to update activities in a round-robin fashion. The executive uses a native timer mechanism to schedule an interrupt every 100 milliseconds, which is its basic cycle time. The cycle time is short enough to ensure timely response to new conditions, while being long enough not to load current processors excessively.

Within this cycle, every executing activity will progress through at least one state of its underlying FSA. The executive cycles through the activity list, and for each activity, it evaluates statements until it reaches a halting condition based on the FSA semantics.

The halting conditions depends on the state of the activity. One of several things may happen.

1. If the current state is waiting for a condition to occur, and that condition is not satisfied, the activity stays in the state and returns. Typically, waiting conditions are issued explicitly with the **waitfor** command, or implicitly by primitive actions or activity calls.

2. If the current state is not waiting, then the current statement is evaluated. Depending on the statement, the executive may halt evaluation and move on to the next activity, or it may continue to evaluate successive statements.

Statements which cause an execution break are:
- **goto**
- the last statement in a **while** body

- the condition of a **while** statement being false
- **waitfor**
- **start**
- any signaling action
- any primitive action

These halting conditions are meant to make ordinary C operations efficient, since they can execute sequentially without causing a break. For example, the following sequence of statements will not cause a break until either the **succeed** or **goto** statement is executed.

```
if (x == 0) succeed;
onInit:
    x = x-1;
    goto loop;
```

By forcing multiple statements to be evaluated in a single execution cycle, the executive preserves the efficiency of sequential execution, while still allowing an activity to break at critical junctures. When the executive has finished with an activity's evaluation cycle, the activity is at an FSA node, with all output functions having been executed.

Because each activity is executed in turn, and execution always finishes at an FSA node, all activities are executed synchronously (and sequentially). Thus, there is no problem of race conditions or competing update among concurrent processes. However, because activities are executed sequentially rather than concurrently, there can be order-dependent phenomena that are unexpected. For example, to propagate a signal sequentially through 4 activities could take 1, 2, 3 or 4 cycles, depending on the execution order of the activities within the cycle.

4.2 Executive Structure

Figure 4-1 shows the structure of the Colbert executive. The main data structure, the activity list, is a structured collection of current activities. One way to think of these activities is as a set of threads in an operating system. Each of the threads is a separate execution module, and all threads share global variables. In addition, there is a hierarchical structure among the threads.

The basic cycle is for the executive to look at each activity in the activity list, check to see if its state can change, invoke the requested actions, and update the state. All of this happens within the 100ms basic cycle time, so the response to new conditions is relatively quick.

For each activity, the executive checks if it is in a waiting or suspended state; if so, it bypasses execution of this activity. If not, it evaluates the activity until its next halting condition, as described in the previous section. In addition, it checks for a timeout condition, and suspends an activity or cancels an action if it exceeds its limit.

An executed action can result in a signal being sent, or a new activity or action being invoked. The executive handles these by issuing the appropriate commands. For activity invocation, the executive looks up the activity schema in its library, instantiates any arguments, and adds the activity to the activity list. In the blocking case, the executive is responsible for checking the blocking and timeout conditions of the subactivity, and resuming the calling activity when appropriate. In the non-blocking case, the executive starts the subactivity as a concurrent activity, and maintains the link to its parent. If the parent is signaled (for example, with an interrupt or resume signal), then the appropriate signal is also passed down to the child. The executive also handles requests from other Sapphira processes for activity invocation or signaling.

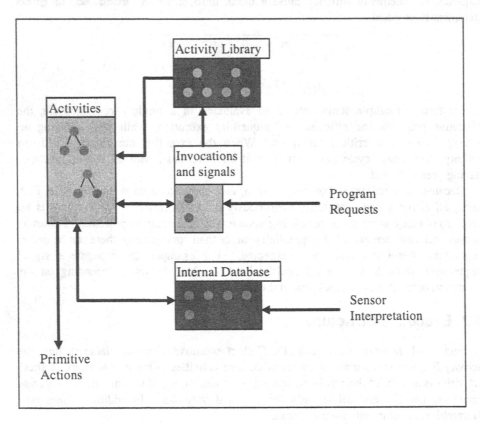

Figure 4-1 Major components of the Colbert executive

In Colbert, there is only one way in which an activity can be invoked, by calling it directly with its arguments. In PRS-Lite, more advanced automatic invocation of activities is possible, through the use of a database of goals and facts [Geo89]. In this mode, environmental conditions or the posting of a goal can trigger the invocation of an activity. It would not be difficult to add this capability to Colbert, and we intend to do so in the future.

When an activity finishes, either explicitly by signaling its success or fail state, or implicitly by falling through its last FSA node, all its children are sent **suspend** signals by the executive. Thus, an activity that finishes has no executing subactivities: the executive enforces the hierarchical nature of subactivities.

4.3 Implementation

The Colbert executive is implemented in C and requires only the services of a 100 ms interrupt. It uses global and local data structures to store activity closures (activities with their variable bindings). Compiled activities use C's native variable storage, so variable access is very fast. For either compiled or evaluated activities, the context switch between activities is also very fast. On typical processors (100 MHz Pentium) we have measured times on the order of 10 μs. A typical Sapphira client will have some 40 compiled activities and 10 interpreted activities running concurrently, all executing within the 100 ms basic cycle. In the normal case these activities use only a small fraction of available CPU resources, on the order of 5% for a 100 MHz Pentium, and less for more powerful processors such as those in current Sparcstations or SGI machines.

The complete Colbert executive has a very small footprint. Although it was not originally intended to run on embedded systems with limited memory, there is no reason it could not do so. For example, we are starting a port of the full Sapphira system to Windows CE processors, which have limited memory (2 - 4 MB).

The compilation of activities takes place in two phases: first, an activity is translated into a C function that implements its underlying FSA, and then the C function is compiled. The translation is relatively straightforward: turning iterations into looping FSA structures, conditionals into branching structures, and so forth. One interesting aspect of the translation is that a static analysis can determine the execution halting points, which can then be incorporated directly into the C procedure. When the executive invokes the procedure, it returns exactly at such a halting point.

Evaluation of activities is more difficult. An activity schema, in text form, is parsed using a YACC front-end and converted into an internal form suitable for evaluation. The parser must recognize a subset of ANSI C expressions and statements; this subset has been simplified to remove complex typing and few other constructs. At this stage all conversion of textual variables to internal pointers is done, as well as linking to internal C functions and variables of Sapphira. There are also some translations to turn iteration constructs into a form that more closely resembles their FSA semantics, as in compilation. The internal form of activities is interpreted by the Colbert evaluator when an activity is invoked.

Because the evaluator is written in YACC, the evaluator itself is a portable C program. We have implemented it on all the systems that Sapphira runs on. The parser program can be large, and may not be suitable for an embedded processor, but we have not yet made any experiments to determine if this is so.

The Colbert evaluator is available to the user at runtime, for examining the state of the system, and for invoking activities and sending them signals from the command line. All Sapphira internal variables and functions are available to the evaluator, as well as any user-defined compiled C functions that are dynamically loaded into the system at runtime. The Colbert executive catches any system errors and suspends the responsible activity, so the user can examine its state and determine the problem. The evaluator makes an effective debugging tool that is portable across all implementations of the Colbert executive. It is also interesting to be able to define and evaluate C functions interactively, something dear to the heart of every LISP programmer.

5. Other Control Languages

There are a large number of languages and systems for robot control, and in this section we look at a few that are directly relevant to Colbert, especially with regard to the issue of language design for user programming.

5.1 PRS-Lite

The immediate predecessor of Colbert is the PRS-Lite executive [Mye96], a reactive controller based loosely on the Procedural Reasoning System [Geo89]. PRS-Lite shares many of the same ideas as Colbert, including a finite state semantics, and concurrent activities. But Colbert differs in some important respects. First, it extends the coordination component of PRS-Lite to include a hierarchical organization among the activities, and a signaling system for interruption, suspension, and resumption. Second, where PRS-Lite takes FSAs as the *language* of activities, Colbert uses C as its language, with FSAs as the underlying *semantics*. While this might not seem like a large difference, conceptually it makes robot control programs much easier to understand and write, especially for programmers used to sequential, conditional, and iterative constructs. Finally, Colbert offers an activity (and C) evaluator, which was not available under PRS-Lite. Interestingly, the full version of PRS, written in LISP, has a graphical and textual language for activities that support the same kind of interactivity as Colbert [Wil95]. But again the language is based on FSAs, and it might be useful to import the Colbert language into PRS as a compact way of specifying activities in that system.

5.2 RAP

RAP [Fir94, Fir96] is a reactive plan execution system that shares many features with PRS and PRS-Lite. A primary emphasis of the RAP system is on modularity and reusability of activity schemas. A RAP method (which corresponds to an activity schema) is a parameterized FSA schema for accomplishing a goal using a sequence of behaviors and other RAPs. The RAP executive manages a hierarchical tree of RAPs, decomposing more difficult tasks into sequences of subtasks. The RAP system also has a facility for concurrent execution of RAPs, along with a signaling system.

RAPs are defined using LISP data structures. There is a limited form of conditionalization, but no iteration operators. Subtasks can be specified as operating in sequence or in parallel; the parallel operator is especially nice for spawning several subtasks that must all complete before continuing. Because it is defined in LISP, the

RAP system has LISP's interactive facilities available for debugging and program development.

5.3 L

L is a commercial language for robot control based on LISP [Bro95]. It is a remarkable language, in that it can run a LISP system in an embedded system with 10 KB of memory, complete with garbage collector. To do so, it makes a number of simplifications of the LISP language. But L also implements a new multithreading facility, to support concurrent execution of multiple threads of execution. And on top of this it defines a set of macros, called MARS, that facilitate interthread coordination.

Because it is a LISP, L lets users examine the executing system for debugging. In a typical configuration, however, L's executive, VENUS, does not include either an evaluator or a compiler, so new or updated programs must be compiled externally and downloaded to the running system. This limitation stems from the use of L in embedded systems with very limited memory; it is conceivable that Colbert could also fit into such systems, but would have to forego the full evaluator with its large parsing program.

Colbert and L, despite their language differences, actually take a similar approach to the robot control problem. Like Colbert, L's multiprocess scheme relies on each process being interruptable at a fine-grained level; in the case of L, it's at every procedure call. And they both define a signaling system for interprocess communication. But Colbert differs in using FSAs as its underlying semantics, in having a hierarchical structure for activities, and in providing support for typical invocations of robot actions. It also appears to be more efficient than L in its multiprocess implementation, since switching threads in L can be expensive.

5.4 MissionLab

MissionLab is a toolset that implements the Societal Agent theory [Mac97]. According to this theory, robot control (including multirobot control) is accomplished by recursive assemblages of behaviors. Temporal sequencing of behaviors is provided by a FSA semantics and language. Like PRS' Act editor, MissionLab provides a graphical interface with which the user can construct and debug FSAs. One of the interesting aspects of MissionLab is that assemblages are defined independent of any particular robot architecture. When an architecture is specified (e.g., SAUSAGES or AuRA [Ark90]), MissionLab generates concurrent procedures for implementing the FSAs using the action methods of the architecture.

MissionLab's strengths are the graphical user interface, the ability to bind to different robot control architectures, and the ability to specify an interaction mode for behaviors: cooperative, competitive, sequential. The use of recursive assemblages of behaviors is similar to the hierarchical structure of activities in Colbert.

5.5 GOLOG

GOLOG is a language for robot control based on the situation calculus [Lev96]. It is unique in robot control languages in having a logic-based semantics. In fact, GOLOG programs look a lot like Prolog programs with added procedural operators, and are interpreted in the same way: by a theorem prover. For example, here are two GOLOG procedures for an elevator control program:

```
proc control
    [while (∃n) on(n) do serve_a_floor endWhile];
    park
endProc

proc park
    if current_floor=0 then open
    else down(0); open
    endIf
endProc
```

Evaluating these procedures, in the presence of initial conditions for the elevator (and some other axioms about actions such as *down*) produces a sequence of primitive actions that can be executed by the elevator controller. Given the truth of the axioms, the sequence is guaranteed to fulfill the conditions of the procedures.

While the GOLOG language uses iterative and conditional constructs similar to those of Colbert, it is much more expressive. For example, there is quantification ($\exists n$) as well as nondeterministic choice. GOLOG programs can be very compact specifications of complex controllers. While theorem proving can be expensive, it takes place offline, generating a executable sequence to be used by a reactive controller.

GOLOG is an interesting experiment in high-level description for robot control. However, it remains to be seen if the rather complicated situation calculus semantics will be suitable for real world controllers. Recently, GOLOG has been extended to deal with prioritized, concurrent programs, as well as exogenous events (those not under the control of the robot) [Lev97].

6. Conclusion

The design criteria for Colbert are:

1. To have a simple language with standard iterative, sequential and conditional constructs.

2. To have a clear and understandable semantics based on FSAs.

3. To have a debugging environment in which the user can check the state of the system and redefine Colbert activities.

4. To have an small, fast, and portable executive.

The current implementation of Colbert fulfills these objectives. Whether Colbert will be successful as a robot control language remains to be seen. Currently it is only available as part of a larger robot architecture, Sapphira, and so is limited to that user community. But it should be possible to adjoin Colbert to other architectures, where it would function as the sequential controller for the system. Given that Colbert programs are compact and easily transferred, we hope to build up a library of useful routines that can be shared in the user community.

References

[Ark90] R. C. Arkin, Integrating behavioral, perceptual and world knowledge in reactive navigation, *Robotics and Autonomous Systems*, **6**:105--122, 1990.

[Bro95] R. A. Brooks and C. Rosenberg, L - A Common Lisp for embedded systems, Association of Lisp Users Meeting and Workshop LUV (1995).

[Con90] J. Connell, SSS: A hybrid architecture applied to robot navigation, in *Proceedings of the IEEE Conference on Robotics and Automation*, pp. 2719-2724, 1992.

[Fir94] R. J. Firby, Task networks for controlling continuous processes, in *Second International Conference on AI Planning Systems*, pp. 49-54, 1994.

[Fir96] R. J. Firby, Modularity issues in reactive planning, in *Third International Conference on AI Planning Systems*, Edinburgh, Scotland, pp. 78-85, 1996.

[Gat92] E. Gat, Integrating planning and reacting in a heterogeneous asynchronous architecture for controlling real-world mobile robots, in *Proceedings of the AAAI Conference*, 1992.

[Geo89] M. P. Georgeff and A. L. Lansky, Reactive reasoning and planning, in *Proceedings AAAI Conference*, pp. 677-682, 1987.

[Hop79] J. E. Hopcroft and J. D. Ullman, *Introduction to Automata Theory, Languages, and Computation*, Addison-Wesley, 1979.

[Hor89] P. Horowitz and W. Hill, *The Art of Electronics*, Cambridge University Press, 1989.

[Kae90] L. Kaelbling and S. Rosenschein, Action and planning in embedded agents, *Robotics and Autonomous Systems*, **6**:35-48, 1990.

[Kon97] K. Konolige, K. Myers, A. Saffiotti and E. Ruspini, The Saphira architecture: a design for autonomy, *Journal of Experimental and Theoretical Artificial Intelligence*, **9** (1997) pp. 215--235.

[Lev96] H. Levesque, R. Reiter, Y. Lespérance, F. Lin, and R, Scherl, GOLOG: A logic programming language for dynamic domains, *Journal of Logic Programming*, 1996.

[Lev97] H. Levesque, Concurrency in the situation calculus, in preparation.

[Mye96] K. L. Myers, A procedural knowledge approach to task-level control, in *Proceedings of the Third International Conference on AI Planning Systems*, AAAI Press, 1996.

[Pay90] D. W. Payton, J. K. Rosenblatt, and D.M. Keirsey, Plan guided reaction, *IEEE Trans. on Systems, Man, and Cybernetics* **20** (6), 1990.

[Wil95] D. E. Wilkins and K. L. Myers, A common knowledge representation for plan generation and reactive execution, Journal of Logic and Computation 5(6), pp. 731-761, 1995.

Machine Learning for Adaptive User Interfaces

Pat Langley

Intelligent Systems Laboratory
Daimler-Benz Research and Technology Center
1510 Page Mill Road, Palo Alto, CA 94304 USA
LANGLEY@RTNA.DAIMLERBENZ.COM

Abstract. In this paper we examine the growing interest in personalized user interfaces and explore the potential of machine learning in meeting that need. We briefly review progress in developing fielded applications of machine learning, then consider some characteristics of adaptive user interfaces that distinguish them from more traditional applications. After this, we consider some examples of adaptive interfaces that use inductive methods to personalize their behavior, and we report some ongoing research that extends these ideas in the automobile environment.

1   The Need for Personalized User Interfaces

Early computer software aimed to solve business and scientific problems in a predetermined way that allowed only very constrained user input, through arguments given to the program at run time. This contrasts sharply with modern-day software, which is much more interactive and supports frequent user input throughout its operation. This shift toward interactive software is reflected in the growing emphasis on interfaces designed to ease communication between software and humans.

Examples of such interactive software abound, and they have even become more common than the earlier, less interactive type, at least for nonspecialists. Most computer users have had experience with WYSIWYG editors for document preparation, with spreadsheets for handling financial data, with interactive computer games, and, most recently, with browsers and search engines for the World Wide Web. Moreover, there is every indication that the number, variety, and importance of such software will increase rather than decrease in years to come.

However, one major drawback of existing interactive systems is that they have little ability to take into account differences in the knowledge, style, and preferences of their users. Systems for document production let one select from a set of default styles and even store his own variations, but the latter process is manual and tedious. Computer games let one specify a difficulty level, but the opponent's strategy cannot reflect the user's strengths or weaknesses. Web browsers let one store bookmarks and preferred layouts, but search engines are only starting to incorporate user preferences to bias the retrieval process.

Clearly, there is a need for increased personalization in many areas of interactive software, not only in the types of flexibility but in the way that personalization occurs. To date, most systems have required that users state their preferences explicitly to the interface, which means the options are either limited in number or tiresome to complete. Moreover, some facets of user styles may be reflected in their behavior but not subject to conscious inspection. This suggests the use of techniques from machine learning to personalize interfaces, based on the observation of user activity.

In the rest of this paper, we explore the potential of machine learning technology for automatic personalization of interactive software. We start by reviewing the state of machine learning and its recent successes in producing fielded applications, then discuss the characteristics of interactive software that differ from other types of learning applications. After this, we consider two broad categories of interactive software – informative and generative – and review some existing systems of each type that draw on machine learning in adapting to individual users. In closing, we consider some new research directions that we are pursuing to aid automobile drivers.

2 The Application of Machine Learning

Research on machine learning has existed since the beginnings of AI, and the past decade has seen considerable developments in this area. For the sake of discussion, we should define the field's object of study:

> A learning algorithm is a software system that improves its performance in some task domain based on partial experience with that domain.

This characterization of learning includes two important features that were absent from early work in the area. First, it states that the goal of learning is to improve performance on some task; the process may involve the creation of knowledge structures, but this is a means to the end of performance improvement. Second, it notes that learning involves *induction* beyond the training data, in that the system must perform after only partial experience with the task. Nearly all recent work on machine learning acknowledges these two requirements, typically reflecting them in their experimental tests of new algorithms.

However, machine learning has done more than evolve into a careful empirical science; it has also developed a successful applications methodology. Induction techniques have aided the construction of many fielded systems in science and industry on a variety of tasks. These include mechanical diagnosis (e.g., Giordana et al., 1993), credit scoring (e.g., Michie, 1989), manufacturing control (e.g., Evans & Fisher, 1994), and scientific classification (e.g., Fayyad, Smyth, Weir, & Djorgovski, 1995). Many of the standard induction algorithms have proven quite robust, and their increasing use for data mining and knowledge discovery promises even more successes in years to come.

The basic development process, although far from entirely automated, does cast machine learning in a central role (Brodley & Smyth, 1997; Langley & Simon, 1995; Rudström, 1995). Briefly, the developer works with a domain expert or user to understand some problem, then reformulates the problem into one solvable by well-established methods for supervised learning. He then selects some likely features to describe training cases and devises an approach to collecting and preparing data, on which he runs some induction method. The developer (and possibly the expert) then evaluate the resulting knowledge base and, if the result seems acceptable, they attempt to deploy the learned knowledge in the field.[1]

Most academic work on machine learning continues to focus on refinements in induction techniques and downplays the steps that must occur before and after their invocation. Indeed, some research groups still emphasize differences between broad classes of induction methods, despite evidence that decision-tree techniques, connectionist algorithms, case-based methods, and other schemes often produce very similar results. In contrast, there is an emerging consensus within the applied community that the steps of problem formulation, representation engineering, and data preparation play a role at least as important as the induction stage itself. Indeed, there is a common belief that, once they are handled, the particular induction method one uses has little effect on the outcome (Langley & Simon, 1995).

We will adopt this viewpoint in our discussion of machine learning's potential for adaptive user interfaces. As a result, we will have little to say about the particular learning methods one might use to personalize an interface, but we will have comments about the nature of the performance task, the source of training data, and similar issues. This bias reflects our belief that adaptive user interfaces are an important application area for machine learning, and that strategies which have proved successful in other areas will also serve us well there.

3   The Nature of Adaptive User Interfaces

We can define adaptive interfaces by direct analogy with our definition for machine learning, using a slightly more specific formulation:

> An adaptive user interface is an interactive software system that improves its ability to interact with a user based on partial experience with that user.

As we suggested above, work on adaptive interfaces has much in common with other applied work on machine learning, including a reliance on careful problem formulation and engineering of useful features. For this reason, we will consider here only those characteristics that are special to this class of problems.

One central feature involves the manner in which the system uses the learned knowledge. Some work in applied machine learning is designed to produce expert systems, that is, knowledge bases (with associated performance elements) intended to replace a human. In contrast, work on adaptive interfaces aims to construct *advisory* systems, in which the knowledge base (through its performance element) only makes recommendations to the user. Rather than replacing

---

[1] Of course, this process is iterative, with problems at any step leading the developer to revisit earlier decisions.

a human, the system suggests information or generates actions that the user can always override. Ideally, the learned knowledge should reflect the preferences of individual users, thus providing personalized services for each one.

However, this focus on advisory systems leads directly to another characteristic – the user's decisions give a ready source of training data to support learning. Every time the interface suggests some choice, the human either accepts that recommendation or rejects it, whether this feedback is explicit or simply reflected in the user's behavior. Either way, the system obtains another datum to drive its search for an improved knowledge base, and each case includes details about the decision-making situation, providing important context for future predictions. This scenario contrasts with the situation for some potential applications of machine learning, where collecting data is a major obstacle.

The embedded nature of the induction process has another implication for the learning task: the system should carry out *online* learning, in which the knowledge base is updated each time an interaction with the interface occurs. This contrasts with most work in data mining, which assumes that all data are available at the outset. Because adaptive user interfaces collect data during their interaction with humans, one naturally expects them to improve during that use, making them 'learning' systems rather than 'learned' systems. This is not a strict requirement, in that the interface could collect data during a session, run the induction method offline, and then incorporate the results into the knowledge base before the next session, but the online approach seems the most natural.

Because adaptive user interfaces must learn from observing their user's behavior, another distinguishing characteristic is their need for *rapid* learning. The issue here in not CPU time, but rather the number of training cases needed to generate good advice. Most work on data mining assumes large amounts of data, typically enough to induce accurate knowledge bases even when the model class includes many parameters. In contrast, adaptive interfaces rely on a precious resource – the user's time – which makes the available data much more limited. This recommends the use of learning methods that achieve high accuracy from small training sets over those with higher asymptotic accuracy but slower learning rates. On the other hand, the advisory nature of these systems makes this desirable but not essential; an interface that learns slowly will be no less useful than one that does not adapt to the user at all. Still, adaptive interfaces that learn rapidly will be more competitive, in the user's eyes, than ones that learn slowly.

We can identify two broad classes of adaptive user interfaces, whose differences have implications for the type of feedback the user must provide. *Informative* interfaces attempt to select or filter information for the user, presenting only those items he will find interesting or useful. The most obvious examples are systems for product recommendation and news filtering, but this category includes any interface that directs the user's attention within a large space of items. Typical user feedback for informative systems includes marking recommended choices as desirable or undesirable, rating them on some scale, or giving some similar form of evaluation. Less obtrusive feedback can sometimes be collected by observing the access process itself, as when one clicks on some items retrieved by a search engine but not others.

The second class, *generative* interfaces, focuses on the generation of some useful knowledge structure. Examples of this category include document preparation and drawing packages, spreadsheet programs, and systems for planning, scheduling, and configuration. These areas support richer types of feedback, in that the user can not only override a recommended action but can replace it with another one entirely.[2] The types of feedback are tied directly to the interaction styles that the interface supports. Some systems require the user to explicitly correct undesirable actions, but others incorporate less obtrusive schemes that collect training data simply by observing the user's normal behavior.

Now that we have considered the characteristics that distinguish adaptive user interfaces from other learning systems and the types of feedback they require, we can consider some examples of systems within both categories.

4 Examples of Informative Interfaces

The growing popularity of the World Wide Web has made informative interfaces the most familiar type of advisory system, and also the most common area for personalization. As their name suggests, such interfaces aim to provide the user with material that he will find informative or useful. Let us examine some existing systems that fall into this category.

One example interface is Pazzani, Muramatsu, and Billsus' (1996) SYSKILL & WEBERT, which recommends web pages on a given topic that the user is likely to find interesting. Starting from a handcrafted page for the topic, the user marks suggested pages as desirable or undesirable, and the system uses these as training data to develop a model of his preferences. SYSKILL & WEBERT incorporates a common scheme, known as *content-based* filtering, as the basis for selection and learning. Briefly, this approach represents each object using a set of descriptors, typically the words that occur in a document. The system uses these descriptors as predictive features when deciding whether to recommend a document to the user, which biases it toward documents that are similar to ones the user has previously ranked highly. Content-based methods also predominate in the older literature on information retrieval.

Another example is FILMFINDER, an interactive system that recommends movies one might enjoy. The user rates a number of sample movies, from which the system (available at www.filmfinder.com) constructs a simple user profile. FILMFINDER then finds other people with similar profiles and suggests films that they liked but that the current user has not yet rated. One can contrast this approach, known as *collaborative filtering*, with content-based methods, since it requires no prespecified descriptions of the objects or products being recommended. In effect, collaborative methods classify users (who are described in

---

[2] The term *learning apprentice* was originally used in the context of such generative systems, although some now use it to describe informative systems as well.

terms of the ratings they provide) rather than classifying the objects being recommended. This makes them well suited for subjective domains like art, where users base their decisions on intangible features that are difficult to measure.

A third system, WISEWIRE, which resides at www.wisewire.com, recommends news stories and web pages to its customers. This interface derives from Lang's (1995) NEWSWEEDER, which used a content-based method, but the new system combines content-based and collaborative filtering to select promising items. The intuition is that content-based methods are best for suggesting topics similar to ones the user has liked in the past, whereas collaborative methods can suggest items outside the user's normal area that he will still find interesting. WISEWIRE users rate the items that it recommends for inspection, but it also lets them note high-level reasons for their evaluation, which constrains the induction process and should improve the rate of learning.

This sample far from exhausts the list of interfaces for information filtering that incorporate machine learning to personalize their interaction with users. Other examples include systems for sorting electronic mail and for matchmaking among users with similar interests, and the number of applications is certain to grow as the Internet and its associated information sources become available to more and more people.

5   Examples of Generative Interfaces

Although informative systems are becoming familiar entities, they are not the only type of adaptive user interfaces. In some domains, one needs more than just information; one needs generative systems that actually construct new knowledge structures to satisfy the user's goals. Let us examine a few systems that address such tasks.

Hinkle and Toomey (1994) describe CLAVIER, an advisory system that recommends loads and layouts for aircraft parts to be cured in an autoclave. The system retrieves previous loads and their layouts from a case library, preferring ones that include more parts that are currently needed and that have cured well in past runs. A graphical interface presents a proposed load and layout to the expert user, who can then replace some parts or rearrange their positions. Each such modification provides a new case for the library, so that CLAVIER's repertoire grows over time. The system has been in continuous use since 1990, generating two to three autoclave loads per day and nearly eliminating problems due to incompatible loads. Although the CLAVIER effort did not focus directly on personalization, the system is a fine example of an adaptive interface of the generative variety.

Another example of an interactive generator comes from Hermens and Schlimmer (1994), who developed an adaptive system for filling out repetitive forms. Their interface suggests values for various fields in the form, but these are defaults that the user can always override. Once the user completes the form, the system interprets the entries as opportunities for learning and uses them to revise its existing rules. Each such rule predicts a default value for a given field based on fields earlier in the form and those in previous forms. Experiments showed that the system reduced keystrokes by 87 percent over an eight-month period. Although this work did not focus on personalization per se, Schlimmer and Hermens (1993) took a very similar approach in their personalizing interface for note taking. This adaptive system learns a grammar that predicts the order and content of a user's notes, aiming to reduce keystrokes and to help them organize their thoughts.

Dent et al.'s (1992) CAP also aims directly at personalization issues, in this case trying to mimic a secretary's expertise at scheduling meetings for a professor. The system includes actions for specifying the day, time, duration, and location of a meeting, for which it offers default values. Again, the user can accept or replace these suggestions, with each decision providing data for the learning process. Induction occurs every night rather than in true online fashion, with CAP learning a separate set of rules for each action that it needs to predict. The system was in use regularly for some years by a departmental secretary to schedule a faculty member's meetings.

Work on *programming by demonstration* also aims to construct personalized generative interfaces by observing the user's behavior. For example, Cypher (1991) describes EAGER, a system that learns iterative procedures from observation in a HyperCard setting, then highlights the actions it anticipates for the user's approval. In general, systems in this paradigm focus on constrained tasks that support online learning from very few training cases, but they carry out induction every bit as much as ones that use less domain-specific learning algorithms. A collection by Cypher (1993) contains a representative sample of work on programming by demonstration.

Some efforts on intelligent tutoring systems also draw on machine learning with the aim of personalizing instruction. For instance, Langley and Ohlsson (1984) adapted methods for learning search-control knowledge to model individual student errors in arithmetic. Also, Anderson's (1984) technique of *model tracing* relies on careful observation of student behavior in the same way as generative user interfaces, giving advice only when the student diverges from acceptable paths. More recently, Baffes and Mooney (1995) have adapted techniques for theory revision to develop personalized student models using similar trace data.

6 Open Issues in Adaptive Interfaces

Although a variety of research and development efforts have shown the potential of adaptive user interfaces, there remains much room for extending their flexibility and their interaction style. In closing, we will consider two ongoing projects designed to address drawbacks in existing systems for personalized interfaces, both carried out at the Daimler-Benz Research and Technology Center and both concerned with improving the automobile environment. [3]

---

[3] Collaborators on these projects include Afsaneh Haddadi, Bryan Johnson, Annabel Liu, Seth Rogers, and Jeff Shrager.

The first effort aims to develop an informative user interface that is more interactive in nature, so that it communicates with the user rather than simply filtering items. The performance task involves recommending places of interest, such as restaurants or theaters, that the user might want as his destination. The system, which we call the *Adaptive Place Advisor*, starts by accepting a query like "Where should I eat?" in a restricted form of natural language. The advisor responds with its own questions, which are designed to refine the user's desires and, eventually, to arrive at a single place that meets his constraints.

The advisor draws on background knowledge, stored in a number of concept hierarchies, to direct this refinement process. For instance, in response to the above query, the system might ask "How about Thai food?" or "Would you like to take something out?". The user can answer these questions in the affirmative or negative, but he can also state a preferred alternative, such as "Let's have Chinese instead" or "I'd like a sit-down meal". The place advisor would continue the process, asking questions such as "Would you like Szechuan?" and using the answer to further narrow the options, until it has jointly agreed with the user on a unique place.

When the Adaptive Place Advisor first interacts with a user, it knows nothing about the person's preferences, so its guesses at each level are poor and the communication process is inefficient. However, as the system gains experience with a user, it collects statistics about his preferences and should come to suggest options he finds attractive, thus reducing the need for interaction. Of course, this is an empirical claim that we must still test with human subjects, but positive results with simpler recommendation systems give us reason for optimism. We must also extend the advisor to generalize beyond individual choices, so that it can predict the user's preferences for new options based on features they share with familiar ones, and improve the system's discourse model, so that its interaction with the user seems as natural as possible.

Generative user interfaces typically support richer interaction with the user than informative systems, but they often require special actions on the user's part. A second project in our group involves a generative interface that draws on special information sources to remain as unobtrusive as possible. Here the performance task is to generate a route between a driver's current and desired location that he will find attractive. This system, which we call the *Adaptive Route Advisor*, uses a Global Positioning System (GPS) to infer the driver's location and constructs routes by searching for paths through a digital map. The system biases this search using learned knowledge about the routes known to the driver, on the assumption that people usually prefer routes with familiar segments over those with unfamiliar segments. This is another empirical claim that we must test in experiments, but it seems plausible enough to use in our prototype software.

We have described the route advisor's learning methods in detail elsewhere (Rogers, Langley, Johnson, & Liu, 1997), so we will not focus on them here. Briefly, the system matches traces of the driver's past trips against segments in the digital map, then transforms them into a constrained context-free grammar that describes his route knowledge at varying levels of resolution. From the driver's perspective, the important point is that the system obtains this personalized route knowledge from GPS traces of his trips, and thus requires no actions on his part other than normal driving behavior. We feel that this approach to unobtrusive data collection can serve as a role model for future work in generative adaptive interfaces, as more sophisticated sensors make similar schemes possible for a wider range of domains.

Clearly, we have only started to explore the space of adaptive user interfaces, and there certainly exist other ways in which we can improve them. But these improvements will only come from designing and implementing prototypes for particular domains, running experimental studies with human subjects, and evaluating their ability to personalize themselves to the user's needs. Although many factors will be important in this process, machine learning seems certain to play a central role.

References

1. Anderson, J. R. (1984). Cognitive psychology and intelligent tutoring. *Proceedings of the Sixth Conference of the Cognitive Science Society* (pp. 37–43). Boulder, CO: Lawrence Erlbaum.

2. Baffes, P. T., & Mooney, R. J. (1995). A novel application of theory refinement to student modeling. *Proceedings of the Thirteenth National Conference of the American Association for Artificial Intelligence* (pp. 403–408). Portland, OR: AAAI Press.

3. Brodley, C. E., & Smyth, P. (1997). Applying classification algorithms in practice. *Statistics and Computing*, *7*, 45–56.

4. Cypher, A. (1991). EAGER: Programming repetitive tasks by example. *Proceedings of CHI* (pp. 33–39). New Orleans: ACM.

5. Cypher, A. (Ed.). (1993). *Watch what I do: Programming by demonstration*. Cambridge, MA: MIT Press.

6. Dent, L., Boticario, J., McDermott, J., Mitchell, T., & Zaborowski, D. (1992). A personal learning apprentice. *Proceedings of the Tenth National Conference on Artificial Intelligence* (pp. 96–103). San Jose, CA: AAAI Press.

7. Evans, B., & Fisher, D. (1994). Overcoming process delays with decision-tree induction. *IEEE Expert*, *9*, 60–66.

8. Fayyad, U. M., Smyth, P., Weir, N., & Djorgovski, S. (1995). Automated analysis and exploration of image databases: Results, progress, and challenges. *Journal of Intelligent Information Systems*, *4*, 1–19.

9. Giordana, A., Saitta, L., Bergadano, F., Brancadori, F., & De Marchi, D. (1993). ENIGMA: A system that learns diagnostic knowledge. *IEEE Transactions on Knowledge and Data Engineering*, *KDE-5*, 15–28.

10. Hermens, L. A., & Schlimmer, J. C. (1994). A machine-learning apprentice for the completion of repetitive forms. *IEEE Expert*, *9*, 28–33.

11. Hinkle, D., & Toomey, C. N. (1994). CLAVIER: Applying case-based reasoning to composite part fabrication. *Proceedings of the Sixth Innovative Applications of Artificial Intelligence Conference* (pp. 55–62). Seattle, WA: AAAI Press.

12. Lang, K. (1995). NEWSWEEDER: Learning to filter news. *Proceedings of the Twelfth International Conference on Machine Learning* (pp. 331–339). Lake Tahoe, CA: Morgan Kaufmann.
13. Langley, P., & Ohlsson, S. (1984). Automated cognitive modeling. *Proceedings of the Fourth National Conference of the American Association for Artificial Intelligence* (pp. 193–197). Austin, TX: Morgan Kaufmann.
14. Langley, P., & Simon, H. A. (1995). Applications of machine learning and rule induction. *Communications of the ACM*, *38*, November, 55–64.
15. Michie, D. (1989). Problems of computer-aided concept formation. In J. R. Quinlan (Ed.), *Applications of expert systems* (Vol. 2). Wokingham, UK: Addison-Wesley.
16. Pazzani, M., Muramatsu, J., & Billsus, D. (1996). SYSKILL & WEBERT: Identifying interesting web sites. *Proceedings of the Thirteenth National Conference of the American Association for Artificial Intelligence* (pp. 54–61). Portland, OR: AAAI Press.
17. Rogers, S., Langley, P., Johnson, B., & Liu, A. (1997). Personalization of the automotive information environment. *Proceedings of the Workshop on Machine Learning in the Real World: Methodological Aspects and Implications* (pp. 28–33). Nashville, TN.
18. Rudström, A. (1995). *Applications of machine learning*. Licentiate thesis, Department of Computer and Systems Sciences, Stockholm University, Sweden.
19. Schlimmer, J. C., & Hermens, L. A. (1993). Software agents: Completing patterns and constructing user interfaces. *Journal of Artificial Intelligence Research*, *1*, 61–89.

Structured Incremental Proof Planning

Stefan Gerberding and Brigitte Pientka

Technical University of Darmstadt
{stefan,pientka}@inferenzsysteme.informatik.th-darmstadt.de

Abstract. We extend our framework of *incremental proof planning*. By employing nested sets of meta-rules the formulation of strategies may be structured. By switching to another meta-rule set the planner can adjust to a new situation within the proof. The new meta-rule set represents a more specialized strategy better suited for the current situation. We define the semantics of our framework by an inference system.

1 Introduction

Automated theorem provers have to cope with tremendous search spaces. Lots of heuristics have been developed to guide the proofs and to prune the search space. We will focus on the domain of automated induction theorem proving, but our method is not limited to this domain. An automated induction theorem prover has various techniques at its disposal. Some are general purpose calculi. Others are specially tailored for certain situations within a proof: Rippling for the rewrite of the conclusion in the step-cases of an induction to make the induction hypothesis applicable [3], generalization, fertilization [1], the computation of induction axioms to choose an appropriate induction relation [5], or symbolic evaluation, case-splits, etc. Those techniques are modeled as *tactics* [4].

Different approaches are known to control the application of tactics. Some systems apply certain tactics in a *fixed order* (waterfall), e.g. NQTHM [1]. Any heuristics to control the application of the different inference mechanisms are hard-coded into the order of application. Other systems leave the control mostly to the user. This is either done implicitly by inserting hints or appropriate lemmata into the problem description or the user explicitly calls the desired tactic.

To overcome the control problem for tactics Bundy proposes the use of *proof plans* [2]. Proof plans can be generated automatically if *meta-reasoning* about tactics is possible. In Bundy's framework the proof plan is computed prior to any proof attempt, i.e. before executing any tactic. The result of the tactics are estimated or simulated for the computation of the new subgoals during proof planning. No information about the history of the proof and previous steps in the proof plan are available to the planner. The planner is *uninformed* apart from the tactics' pre- and postconditions; no further knowledge about the tactics and the domain of application is available. To specify strategy knowledge, the preconditions must be modified to reflect the new strategy. The proof plan is passed to the proof checker to verify that its execution yields a valid proof.

2 Incremental Proof Planning

These drawbacks are obsolete for *incremental proof planning* [6]. The knowledge about the domain of application, i.e. the strategy, and about tactics is declaratively represented by *meta-rules*: triples consisting of a precondition, an action, and a persistence condition. The knowledge about the partial proof and the proof plan is located in the *proof-tree*. Meta-rules can be structured in *meta-rule sets* providing a further level of abstraction and structuring. E.g. techniques for certain proof situations may be collected in some meta-rule sets. If the planner switches to another meta-rule set (as part of an action), it adopts the strategy to the current proof situation. Since the complete strategy information used by the proof planner is declaratively represented by the sets of meta-rules, the user may easily modify the strategy by supplying new sets of meta-rules.

In §2.1 we will briefly explain the framework of *incremental proof planning* introduced in [6]. We will extend our presentation by specifying a set of inference rules defining the semantics of incremental proof planning. In the remainder of this paper we will then focus on incremental proof planning with *meta-rule sets*. To demonstrate the power of the extended framework, we will model a strategy for induction theorem proving similar to lazy induction [11] by meta-rule sets.

2.1 Overview

The partial proof and the proof plan is represented by the *proof-tree*. All information in the proof-tree is available to the planner. A proof-tree is a labeled and-or-tree. The nodes' labels are closed first-order formulae. The root is labeled by the conjecture. A leaf is (*negatively*) *solved* iff its label is the formula **true** (**false**). An and-node resp. or-node is (negatively) solved iff (any) each successor resp. (each) any successor is (negatively) solved. A proof and a successful proof plan has been found for the conjecture iff the root node is solved. If the root node is negatively solved the conjecture is disproved.

Apart from the goal the label of a node N contains the state σ of N (among other information). σ indicates whether the goal G is positively or negatively solved, open, or unprovable by the system, etc. The states of the leaves are propagated through the proof-tree. The edges of a proof-tree are labeled by tactic names, indicating which tactic computed the child nodes, and additional attributes returned by the tactics (e.g. marks for the base and step-case of an induction). Furthermore, the tactics' results determine whether the node corresponding to the current goal becomes an and-node or an or-node.

We use the notation "$\wedge$" for object-level as well as meta-level conjunction; the semantic of the latter is defined by (1) in §2.2. $\equiv$ denotes syntactical equality. We will write lists $o_1, \ldots, o_n$ of variables, terms, etc. as o^*.

The planner's strategy is declaratively implemented by meta-rules. A meta-rule π has the syntactical form $C \Rightarrow A \leftrightarrow P$ where C is the *precondition*, A is the *action*, and P is the *persistence condition*. The precondition C and the persistence condition P are conjunctions of atoms: $C_1(x_1^*) \wedge \ldots \wedge C_n(x_n^*)$. Each atom references a *meta-predicate* on proof-trees. x_i^* is a list of *meta-variables*, which are bound when evaluating the meta-predicate wrt. the proof-tree. The precondition-action pair $C \Rightarrow A$ is similar to a rule of an expert system.

The semantics of a meta-predicate $C_i(x_i^*)$ is given by a PQL-expression. PQL is a *proof-tree query language* developed for our framework to define all bindings to *meta-variables* x_i^*, s.t. $C_i(x_i^*)$ is satisfied for the given proof-tree. A meta-variable may be bound to positions, symbols, terms, formulae, proof-tree nodes, etc. depending on the type[1] of the formal parameter of the corresponding meta-predicate. Using PQL the user is able to specify appropriate meta-predicates, which are needed to express the desired strategy. For details we refer to [6, 9].

The condition $C \equiv C_1(x_1^*) \wedge \ldots \wedge C_n(x_n^*)$ is *satisfiable* (for the given proof-tree representing the current situation) iff a *consistent binding* for the meta-variables $x_1^*, \ldots, x_n^*$ exists, s.t. all meta-predicates are satisfied. A meta-variable binding is *consistent* iff for every x, y identical bindings[2] are implied by $x \equiv y$.

If the precondition C is satisfiable, the meta-rule is applicable and the planner can select the action A for execution. In the most simple case A is a single tactic $T(x^*)$. Since C is satisfiable, bindings for the meta-variables x^* exist. Such a binding is passed as parameter list to T. In general A is a sequence of tactics and calls to meta-rule sets (cf. §2.3) interleaved by optional continuation conditions: $T_1(x_1^*) \leftrightarrow CC_1(y_1^*), T_2(x_2^*) \leftrightarrow CC_2(y_2^*), \ldots, T_m(x_m^*)$: When T_1 completed successfully the satisfiability of the continuation condition CC_1 is checked and T_2 is executed when the condition is satisfied. An action fails explicitly if some T_i returns fail or if a continuation condition is not satisfied. In this case the (partly) executed action is retracted and a different binding for the same meta-rule or another meta-rule is considered. Information about the retracted actions may be stored in the proof-tree and utilized by meta-predicates and the planner.

After the completion of an action A the planner reasons about A's results, provided A did not fail explicitly and a persistence condition P is specified. If P is not satisfied for the proof-tree expanded according to A's results, then the action is retracted as for the explicit failure. Using persistence conditions we are able to identify goals not contributing to the proof.

2.2 Semantics

For the description of the formal semantics of incremental proof planning we need some notation: *Meta-variable bindings* are written like substitutions: v/t. We extend this notation to lists of meta-variables and terms: v^*/t^*. Set notation is used to denote the extension of a binding E: $E \cup v^*/t^*$. For a tactic T with formal parameters x^* and a meta-variable binding $E \ni x^*/t^*$, $T(E)$ denotes the instantiation of the formal parameters by t^*. $\hat{E}$ denotes a stack of meta-variable bindings. The push operation is written by concatenation: $\hat{E}E$. We use the same notation for stacks of meta-rule sets: $\hat{M}M$. Proof-tree expansion is denoted by $\circ$,

---

[1] For brevity we will omit any type information throughout this paper.

[2] This is a simplified description of consistency. Because of the various types a notion of equivalence is employed, which allows bindings of variables of different types to be consistent, e.g. a symbol s and a term whose leading symbol is s.

if cur is a proof-tree or a node cur∘G is the proof-tree obtained by expanding cur by the tree G. P[cur] ambiguously identifies cur as some leaf of the tree P. We use sub-calculi $\vdash_c$ resp. $\vdash_a$ to model the evaluation of conditions resp. actions.

Conditions: The notion of satisfiability of a meta-predicate atom $mp(v^*)$ is defined by PQL [9], see also §2.1. The $\vdash_c$-calculus operates on triples consisting of a proof-tree, a meta-variable binding, and a condition. A c-derivation is a sequence of triples $\ldots, T_{i-1}, T_i, \ldots$, s.t. T_i is derived from T_{i-1} by an application of the inference rule (1). The corresponding inference relation is denoted by $\vdash_c$.

$$\frac{\langle P, E, \text{cond} \rangle}{\langle P, E \cup v^*/t^*, \text{cond} \wedge mp(v^*) \rangle} \quad \begin{array}{l} \text{if } mp(v^*) \text{ is satisfiable for } P, v^*/t^* \text{ is a} \\ \text{meta-variable binding s.t. } mp(t^*) \text{ is sat-} \quad (1) \\ \text{isfied for } P, \text{ and } E, v^*/t^* \text{ are consistent.} \end{array}$$

Lemma 1. *Let P be a proof-tree, E, E' meta-variable bindings, and cond a conjunction of meta-predicate atoms. If $\langle P, E, \emptyset \rangle \vdash_c \langle P, E', \text{cond} \rangle$, then cond is satisfiable for P and E' defines the E-compatible meta-variable binding sufficient to satisfy cond for P.*

Actions: A meta-rule set induces an environment of meta-variable bindings, which is empty for the initial meta-rule set. Meta-rule sets are parameterized like tactics, cf. fig. 2 for an example. When a meta-rule set M is called its parameters define the environment E for M. The preconditions of meta-rules from M are evaluated extending the meta-variable bindings E. There are no restrictions for the hierarchy of calls of meta-rule sets.

Together with $\vdash$ defined later, the semantics of structuring meta-rule sets and the interaction of continuation conditions, persistence conditions, and sequencing is given by $\vdash_a$. The semantics of tactics is not modeled by $\vdash_a$. $\vdash_a$ operates on quintuples: The additional components are $\hat{M}M$ resp. $\hat{E}E$ representing the stack of meta-rule sets resp. the stack of parameter bindings induced by the meta-rule sets. M identifies the active meta-rule set (cf. (5)) and E defines M's parameter bindings. The third component represents the additional meta-variable bindings, s.t. the precondition guarding the action is satisfied.

An action consists of a single tactic or a call to a meta-rule set, or a sequence thereof, optionally interleaved by continuation conditions: $T_1(x_1^*) \leftarrow\!\!\!\!\text{p}$ $CC_1(y_1^*), T_2(x_2^*) \leftarrow\!\!\!\!\text{p} CC_2(y_2^*), \ldots, T_m(x_m^*)$. The parameterization x_i^* of T_i must not depend on meta-variables y_j^*, because CC_j cannot alter the environment (cf. (3): the meta-variable bindings F' satisfying the condition do not alter the environment $E \cup F$). Continuation conditions and persistence conditions are conceptionally identical. So (3) defines both of them.

We assume that a tactic applied to some goal cur either explicitly fails by returning fail or yields a non-empty set G of subgoals, s.t. all of them (and-nodes) resp. one of them (or-nodes) is sufficient for cur. For simplicity we assume that any but the last tactic in a sequence computes only one new subgoal. We refer to §2.3 for the general case.

An a-derivation is a sequence of quintuples $\ldots, Q_{i-1}, Q_i, \ldots$, s.t. Q_i is derived from Q_{i-1} by an application of an inference rule (2)-(4). The corresponding inference relation is denoted by $\vdash_a$.

$$\frac{\langle \hat{M}, \hat{E}E, F, P[\text{cur}], \text{action} \rangle}{\langle \hat{M}, \hat{E}E, F, P[\text{cur} \circ G], \text{action } T \rangle} \quad \begin{array}{l} \text{if cur} \neq \text{fail is a leaf and the applica-} \\ \text{tion of tactic } T(F \cup E) \text{ to cur yields} \\ \text{the subgoals } G \neq \text{fail.} \end{array} \quad (2)$$

$$\frac{\langle \hat{M}, \hat{E}E, F, P[\text{cur}], \text{action} \rangle}{\langle \hat{M}, \hat{E}E, F, P[\text{cur} \circ G], \text{action } T \leftarrow P \rangle} \quad \begin{array}{l} \text{if } \langle P[\text{cur} \circ G], F \cup E, \emptyset \rangle \vdash_c \langle P[\text{cur} \circ \\ G], F', \text{pers} \rangle \text{ plus proviso (2).} \end{array} \quad (3)$$

$$\frac{\langle \hat{M}, \hat{E}, F, P, \text{action} \rangle}{\langle \hat{M}M, \hat{E}E, F, P, \text{action } M \rangle} \quad \begin{array}{l} \text{if } M \text{ is a meta-rule set whose param-} \\ \text{eters are bound according to } E \subseteq F. \end{array} \quad (4)$$

Lemma 2. *Let $P[\text{cur}]$ be a proof-tree with leaf cur, $\hat{M}$, $\hat{M}'$ stacks of sets of meta-rules, $\hat{E}$, $\hat{E}'$ stacks of bindings, F a binding, and action a sequence of tactics and calls to meta-rule sets. If $\langle \hat{M}, \hat{E}, F, P[\text{cur}], \emptyset \rangle \vdash_a \langle \hat{M}', \hat{E}', F, P[\text{cur} \circ P'], \text{action} \rangle$, then no subaction of action failed, each continuation condition and the persistence condition are satisfied, and the proof-tree is expanded by the subtree P'.*

By an induction argument we deduce that the leaves of $P[\text{cur} \circ P']$ are labeled by subgoals sufficient for the formula labeling the root node. Thus the conjecture is verified if a proof-tree is computed, such that each[3] leaf is labeled true. This corollary justifies the definition of *solved* stated in §2.1.

Meta-Rules: The interaction of the calculi $\vdash_c$, $\vdash_a$, and the meta-rule sets is defined by (5) and (6). The inference rules operate on triples consisting of a stack of meta-rule sets, a stack of meta-variable bindings, and the proof-tree. The inference rules treat a meta-rule set M as unordered set. The meta-strategy deciding which meta-rule to apply as well as the backtracking behavior (cf. §2.3 and [10]) is not defined by the inference system. For the implementation of our framework we decided to arrange the meta-rules as totally ordered sequence $M_<$, i.e. applicable meta-rules occurring earlier in $M_<$ are preferred[4].

$$\frac{\begin{array}{c} \langle \hat{M}M, \hat{E}E, P[\text{cur}] \rangle \\ \text{cond} \Rightarrow \text{action} \in M \\ \langle P[\text{cur}], E, \emptyset \rangle \vdash_c \langle P[\text{cur}], E \cup F, \text{cond} \rangle \\ \langle M, E, E \cup F, P[\text{cur}], \emptyset \rangle \vdash_a \langle \hat{M}', \hat{E}', E \cup F, P[\text{cur} \circ G], \text{action} \rangle \\ \langle P[\text{cur}], E, \emptyset \rangle \not\vdash_c \langle P[\text{cur}], F', \text{tc}(M) \rangle \end{array}}{\langle \hat{M}\hat{M}', \hat{E}\hat{E}', P[\text{cur} \circ G] \rangle} \quad (5)$$

$$\frac{\begin{array}{c} \langle \hat{M}M, \hat{E}E, P[\text{cur}] \rangle \\ \langle P[\text{cur}], E, \emptyset \rangle \vdash_c \langle P[\text{cur}], E', \text{tc}(M) \rangle \end{array}}{\langle \hat{M}, \hat{E}, P[\text{cur}] \rangle} \quad (6)$$

---

[3] In the presence of or-nodes in the proof-tree the condition needs to be refined.

[4] Most other strategies, e.g. using the meta-rule with the most specific precondition, can be simulated by ordering the meta-rules appropriately. But our decision allows for maximal flexibility.

The successful application of a meta-rule is described by (5). The optional persistence condition is treated as part of the action. For a meta-rule set M a call to M has the form META-RULE-SET M UNTIL $\text{tc}(M)$, $\text{tc}(M)$ being the optional *termination condition* for this call. The planner returns to the previous meta-rule set, if $\text{tc}(M)$ is satisfied for the active meta-rule set M. Inference rule (6) is applicable in this case: M and E are popped from the stack and planning proceeds using the top of $\hat{M}$ as active meta-rule set.

A proof resp. proof plan for the conjecture ϕ is constructed by computing a derivation $\langle I, \emptyset, P_\phi \rangle \vdash \langle \hat{M}, \hat{E}, P \rangle$ using (5) and (6), where I is the initial meta-rule set, P_ϕ is the proof-tree consisting of a single node labeled by ϕ, and P is proof-tree, s.t. each leaf is labeled true[3].

2.3 Structured Proof Planning

Sequencing: Consider an action $T_1, \ldots, T_n$: If T_{i-1} yields $k > 1$ goals, only the proof-tree node corresponding to one of them is expanded by the $T_i, \ldots, T_n$ according to $\vdash_a$. Hence this case has been ruled out for the presentation of $\vdash_a$ to ease understanding. To generalize $\vdash_a$, the proof-tree component with the current goal as designated node $P[\text{cur}]$ has to be replaced by a proof-tree with k designated nodes $P[\text{cur}_1, \ldots, \text{cur}_k]$, each of which is to be passed to the next tactic T_i. Similarly $P[\text{cur} \circ G]$ in the result needs to be replaced by $P[\text{cur}_1 \circ G_1, \ldots, \text{cur}_k \circ G_k]$ where T_i applied to cur_j yields the goals G_j. Thus the remainder of an action is applied to each leaf of the proof-tree generated as goal in the previous step.

Recovery: The calculus presented in §2.2 defines a successful derivation for a conjecture, i.e. a proof plan and a proof. It does not specify the reaction to a failing subaction or an unsatisfiable continuation condition or persistence condition. The action is retracted in this case, i.e. all effects of subactions are taken back. The planner backtracks over alternative bindings of the retracted meta-rule's precondition and further applicable meta-rules.

Only if the termination condition $\text{tc}(M)$ for the active meta-rule set M is satisfied, the planner returns to the previous meta-rule set. Then the call to M (considering the subaction) is completed and the previous environment is restored, cf. (6). In this case the proof-tree is expanded as if each action, executed while M is the active meta-rule set, were part of the action which contains the call to M. If at least one meta-rule has been applied, no meta-rule is applicable anymore, and the termination condition is not satisfied, the planner backtracks within the meta-rule set M. The call to M fails if no meta-rule is applicable when control enters M. In latter case the proof tree is not expanded.

Ordered (cf. §2.2) meta-rule sets can simulate conditionals. To express an action IF c THEN a_1 ELSE a_2 we use a call to the meta-rule set (7), while specifying the termination condition to apply only one meta-rule: if UNTIL one-step(M). For the remainder of this paper we will use IF c THEN a_1 ELSE a_2 as an abbreviation for a call to a meta-rule set analogous to (7).

$$
\begin{array}{ll}
\multicolumn{2}{l}{\text{META-RULE-SET if}} \\
\text{if-true} : c & \Rightarrow a_1 \qquad (7) \\
\text{else} : & \text{true} \Rightarrow a_2
\end{array}
$$

3 Modeling Strategies

We will present some strategies for automated induction theorem proving, utilizing the additional information available within our framework of *structured incremental proof planning*, thus exemplifying the power of our approach.

3.1 Case-Analysis Using Structured Meta-Rule Sets

Case analysis and induction are competing strategies. Hence it is hard to decide a priori which technique is more appropriate. We view induction as a special case analysis and the decision, whether the case-split is an induction, is postponed. By revising the partial proof we decide, if an induction hypothesis can be applied and which induction hypothesis has to be chosen. Fig. 1 presents the meta-rule set eval, which is the initial meta-rule set for the strategy outlined above. We iterate over eval and apply special techniques for nested cases, symbolic evaluation, and case analysis. This strategy is similar to *lazy induction* [11].

META-RULE-SET eval
nested-case: nested-case(Hyp) ⇒ META-RULE-SET manipulate-hypo(Hyp)
                                              UNTIL solved(Goal) ∨ sym-eval-p(Term)
sym-eval: sym-eval-p(Term)   ⇒   sym-eval(current,Term)
csp: need-case-split(Term) ⇒   case-split(F,current),
              IF base-case(Term) THEN META-RULE-SET eval UNTIL solved(Goal)
              ELSE META-RULE-SET eval-step UNTIL no-meta-rule-applicable(S)

Fig. 1. Meta-rule set eval used as initial meta-rule set.

The meta-rule nested-case is applicable within a nested case-split, which is tested by the meta-predicate nested-case(Hyp). Hyp is bound to the premises of the case corresponding to the current goal. The call manipulate-hypo(Hyp) succeeds, if it is possible to simplify or disprove the hypotheses, or to derive a new condition which enables further symbolic evaluation. This goal is reflected by the termination condition solved(Goal) ∨ sym-eval-p(Term). The parameter Hyp of the meta-rule set manipulate-hypo propagates knowledge from the outer meta-rule set eval into the new meta-rule set. If the known conditions Hyp could be disproved (disprove, fig. 2), then the current subgoal has been solved and the termination condition is satisfied. Hence the planer returns to the surrounding meta-rule set eval and resumes after selecting another unsolved branch of the proof-tree. If a new condition is derived from the hypothesis Hyp (cond-required) or if the known conditions are simplified (simplify), symbolic evaluation should be possible and the planner proceeds with the meta-rule set eval.

The meta-rule sym-eval (fig. 1) checks, if symbolic evaluation is possible and the tactic sym-eval exhaustively applies rewrite rules until no rewrite rule is applicable anymore. If no further symbolic evaluation is possible and a case-split enables further symbolic evaluation, a case-split is performed (csp).

When analyzing proofs by induction one usually concentrates on the step-

META-RULE-SET manipulate-hypo(Hyp)
disprove: hyp-disprovable(Hyp)   ⇒   disprove(Hyp,current)
cond-required: extra-cond-required(Hyp,C) ⇒
                    deduce-cond(Hyp,C,Current) ↤ sym-eval-p(Hyp,C,Term)
simplify: simplify-p(Hyp)   ⇒   simplify(Hyp,current)

Fig. 2. Meta-rule set manipulate-hypo.

cases and applies strategies more cautiously there. The base-cases[5] often can be solved straight forward by applying case analysis and symbolic evaluation. Hence we want to distinguish between strategies applied for the base-cases and strategies applied for the step-cases. This is described by the meta-rule csp. Note that we do not attach a heuristic termination condition, which examines the current goal, to the call of the meta-rule set eval-step (fig. 3). The meta-predicate no-meta-rule-applicable represents a non-heuristic termination condition, because it is independent of the current goal. Using this termination condition, the planner iterates over the given set of meta-rules until no more meta-rule is applicable. If the application of the meta-rule set eval-step does not complete the proof of the step-case a new iteration over the meta-rule set eval is started.

META-RULE-SET eval-step
nested-case-step: nested-case(Hyp)   ⇒   META-RULE-SET manipulate-hypo(Hyp)
                                         UNTIL solved(G) ∨ sym-eval-p(F)
ind: no-sym-eval-p(Term) ∧ induction-split(Split) ∧
                 induction-hyp(Hyp,Split) ∧ hyp-applicable(Hyp,C) ∧
                 ind-base-case-solved(F)   ⇒   fertilize(Hyp,current)
eval-step: sym-eval-p(Subterm)   ⇒   sym-eval-step(current,Subterm)

Fig. 3. Meta-rule set eval-step.

ind captures the central idea of lazy induction: Inspecting the partial proof and deciding, whether an adequate induction hypothesis is applicable. The meta-predicate induction-split(Split) inspects the case-splits on the path from the current goal to the root of the proof-tree if there exists a split which satisfies the induction criterion. The induction criterion is satisfied, if a formula ϕ' is an induction hypothesis for a conjecture ϕ, and if ϕ' is smaller than ϕ wrt. some well-founded relation. If the previous split does not satisfy the induction criterion, the meta-predicate looks for another case-split. If no such case-split satisfies the induction criterion the meta-predicate is not satisfiable. Thus the meta-rule ind is not applicable. The variable Split is bound to the formula which led to the case-split. The meta-predicate induction-hyp(Hyp,Split) binds Hyp to the induction hypothesis for the formula Split, and hyp-applicable(Hyp,C) checks, if the induction hypothesis is applicable for the current goal. If the hypothesis does not match the current goal, Split is bound to another candidate as described above. The meta-predicate ind-base-case-solved(F) ensures that the base-case is verified. By revising case-splits and exploiting the knowledge of the partial proof we are

---

[5] When referring to "base-cases" resp. "step-cases" we also include non-recursive resp. recursive cases of a case-split wrt. a recursively defined function.

able to decide, if an earlier case-split satisfies the induction criterion and if the induction hypothesis is applicable. If symbolic evaluation is possible, the meta-rule eval-step is applied. In contrast to sym-eval the tactic sym-eval-step performs only a single rewrite. Otherwise an applicable induction hypothesis may be lost.

Possible outcomes of a call to the meta-rule set eval-step are: (i) The step-case is solved by the meta-rules eval-step and nested-case-step. Then the goal ψ, which has been the current goal when eval-step was called, is proved. (ii) The meta-rule ind is applied successfully and the goal is solved by eval-step after fertilization. Hence ψ is proved by induction. (iii) The conjecture is evaluated by eval-step, but no earlier case-split satisfies the induction criterion or a possible induction hypothesis is not applicable. (iv) An earlier case-split is revised and an induction hypothesis is applicable, but symbolic evaluation does not suffice to solve the conjecture. For (iii) and (iv) the goal is returned (via the expanded proof-tree) to the meta-rule set eval for further manipulation (case-split).

3.2 Proving Theorems by Revising Case-Splits

To illustrate the planning procedure outlined above, consider the following definitions for ord and ins and the theorem $(8)^6$. ord checks whether l is le-ordered, while ins inserts x into l respecting the le-ordering. The proof starts with an application of csp from the meta-rule set eval, which is illustrated in fig. 4.

$$\forall x : \text{number}, l : \text{list} \quad \text{ord}(l) = \text{ord}(\text{ins}(x, l)) \tag{8}$$

$$
\begin{aligned}
&function \ \text{ord}(l:\text{list}) : \text{bool} \Leftarrow \\
&\quad if \ l = \text{nil} && then \ \text{true} \\
&\quad if \ l = \text{add}(\text{hd}(l), \text{nil}) && then \ \text{true} \\
&\quad if \ l = \text{add}(\text{hd}(l), \text{tl}(l)) \land \text{not}(\text{le}(\text{hd}(l), \text{hd}(\text{tl}(l)))) && then \ \text{false} \\
&\quad if \ l = \text{add}(\text{hd}(l), \text{tl}(l)) \land \text{le}(\text{hd}(l), \text{hd}(\text{tl}(l))) && then \ \text{ord}(\text{tl}(l))
\end{aligned}
\tag{9}
$$

$$
\begin{aligned}
&function \ \text{ins}(x : \text{number}, l : \text{list}) : \text{list} \Leftarrow \\
&\quad if \ l = \text{nil} && then \ \text{add}(x, \text{nil}) \\
&\quad if \ l = \text{add}(\text{hd}(l), \text{tl}(l)) \land \text{le}(x, \text{hd}(l)) && then \ \text{add}(x, l) \\
&\quad if \ l = \text{add}(\text{hd}(l), \text{tl}(l)) \land \text{not}(\text{le}(x, \text{hd}(l))) && then \ \text{add}(\text{hd}(l), \text{ins}(x, \text{tl}(l)))
\end{aligned}
\tag{10}
$$

The base-case $l = $ nil resp. the step-case $\text{le}(x, \text{hd}(l))$ is solved by applying the meta-rule sym-eval from the meta-rule set eval resp. eval-step from the meta-rule set eval-step. The second step-case $\text{not}(\text{le}(x, \text{hd}(l)))$ is evaluated within the meta-rule set eval-step by the meta-rule eval-step. Now the precondition of ind is tested. The first meta-predicate induction-split(Split) is satisfied, as the case-split wrt. the definition of ins also satisfies the induction criterion. But the potential

---

[6] The data structure bool is freely generated by the constructors true and false. list is generated by nil and add, hd and tl are destructor functions for add. We omit the definitions for le ($\leq$) and not. We also omit the quantifier prefix henceforth.

[7] Note that we omitted the literal $l = \text{add}(\text{hd}(l), \text{tl}(l))$ from the condition for lack of space. Obvious structural premises will also be omitted from the remaining figures. The edge labels are premises guarding the cases.

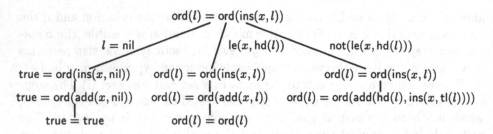

Fig. 4. A case-split of (8) wrt. the definition of ins (10)[7].

induction hypothesis $\text{ord}(\text{tl}(l)) = \text{ord}(\text{ins}(x, \text{tl}(l)))$ is not applicable. Thus the precondition of the meta-rule **ind** is not satisfiable and **ind** is not applicable. Hence the subgoal is returned to the surrounding meta-rule set **eval**.

To prove the conjecture in the step-case another case-split wrt. (10) is performed. The case $\text{tl}(l) = \text{nil}$ is proved by **sym-eval** and **nested-case** from the meta-rule set **eval**. The proof of the step-case $\text{le}(x, \text{hd}(\text{tl}(l)))$ is performed under control of the meta-rule set **eval-step**. First the meta-rule **eval-step** and then **nested-case** succeed. Within the meta-rule set **manipulate-hypo** the meta-rule **cond-required** applies and infers a new condition $\text{le}(\text{hd}(l), \text{hd}(\text{tl}(l)))$, which enables further evaluation. Finally **eval-step** completes the proof, cf. fig. 5.

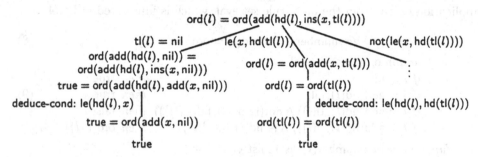

Fig. 5. Two cases of the second step-case from fig. 4.

The proof of the second step-case $\text{not}(\text{le}(x, \text{hd}(\text{tl}(l))))$ is shown in fig. 6. First the meta-rule **eval-step** from the meta-rule set **eval-step** is applicable. However, afterwards no more meta-rule of this set is applicable. Hence the subgoal $\text{ord}(l) = \text{ord}(\text{add}(\text{hd}(l), \text{add}(\text{hd}(\text{tl}(l)), \text{ins}(x, \text{tl}(\text{tl}(l))))))$ is returned to the meta-rule set **eval** again, where the meta-rule **csp** suggests a case-split to symbolically evaluate for ord. The base-case of this conjecture is solved by the meta-rule set **eval** again. The step-case $\text{le}(\text{hd}(l), \text{hd}(\text{tl}(l)))$ is proved by the meta-rule set **eval-step** by applying the meta-rule **eval-step**. The remaining subgoal is the step-case $\text{not}(\text{le}(\text{hd}(l), \text{hd}(\text{tl}(l))))$. The meta-rule set **eval-step** applies first the meta-rule **eval-step**. Afterwards the meta-rule **ind** is tested. Now the precondition is satisfiable. The split satisfying the induction criterion and whose induction hypothesis is applicable is marked by a box in fig. 6. So the original conjecture (8) is verified. (8) cannot be proven merely by induction: A case-split followed by an induction is needed to solve the step-case of the case-split.

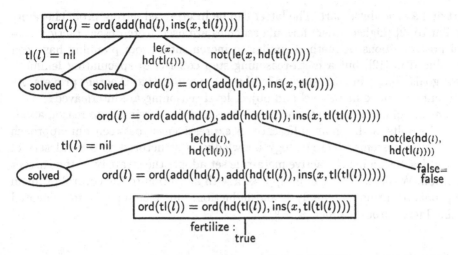

Fig. 6. The proof of the third case $not(le(x, hd(tl(l))))$ from fig. 5.

3.3 Experimental Results

The strategy specified by the meta-rule sets presented in §3.1 also works for proofs by case analysis or proofs by inductions alone. Experimental results are shown in table 1. For some examples (7,8) an induction is needed within the base-case of a case analysis. For other examples a case-split is used first, followed by an induction to verify the step-case. So we combine non-inductive case-splits and induction on demand, which is the key idea of lazy induction.

#	theorem	#	theorem
1	$even(x) = even1(x)$	2	$mem(x, t) \rightarrow mem(x, app(s, t))$
3	$mem(x, t) \rightarrow mem(x, ins(a, t))$	4	$subset(x, y) \rightarrow subset(x, ins(a, y))$
5	$subset(x, delete(a, y)) \rightarrow subset(x, y)$	6	$ord(l) = ord(ins(a, l))$
7	$even(plus(x, y)) \vee odd(plus(y, x))$	8	$mem(x, ins(x, y))$
9	$even(len(app(x, y))) = even(len(app(y, x)))$	10	$len(app(a, b)) = len(app(b, a))$
11	$even(half(x)) \vee odd(half(x))$		

Table 1. Experimental Results.

Examples 7-10 are taken from [8]. We observe that we need less lemmata. In [8] exploiting the failure of an inductive proof is proposed. Lemmata are speculated or an inappropriate induction scheme is revised, in order to succeed. Utilizing the additional information of the partial proof resp. proof plan we are able to prove these theorems merely by case analysis and induction. Other systems cannot reinspect partial proof attempts. User guidance or lemmata are needed in this case to recover from the failure.

4 Conclusion, Related and Future Work

While our technique is forward chaining, a mixed forward/backward chaining technique is presented in [7]. There the tactic knowledge is split into a declarative part and a procedural part. The latter can be interpreted during proof checking. Similar to [2] (higher order) formula schemes are used to represent tactics' pre- and postconditions. A method similar to incremental proof planning has been introduced in [12], but a meta-reasoning step consists of speculating lemmata (new goals) which in turn are verified by other automated theorem provers. As with our technique meta-level and object-level reasoning are interleaved.

The use of meta-predicates on proof-trees and the possibility to reason about tactics' results is the main difference in expressiveness between our approach and similar systems. The strategy knowledge is structured in several sets of meta-rules. Switching the active meta-rule set adopts the strategy to the current situation. We demonstrated our approach with a solution to the control problem for proofs requiring case analysis and induction. Our technique is implemented in the TIGER proof planner [9, 10].

References

1. Robert S. Boyer and J Strother Moore. *A Computational Logic*. ACM Monograph Series. Academic Press, 1979.
2. Alan Bundy. A science of reasoning. In J-L. Lassez and G. Plotkin, editors, *Computational Logic: Essays in Honor of Alan Robinson*, pages 178–198. MIT press, 1991.
3. Alan Bundy, Andrew Stevens, Frank van Harmelen, Alan Smaill, and Andrew Ireland. Rippling: A heuristic for guiding inductive proofs. *Artificial Intelligence*, 62(2):185–253, August 1993.
4. R. L. Constable, T. B. Knoblock, and J. L. Bates. Writing programs that construct proofs. *Journal of Automated Reasoning*, 1:285–326, 1985.
5. Stefan Gerberding and Axel Noltemeier. Choosing induction relations within the INKA system (extended abstract). In *Proceedings of the 19th German Annual Conference on Artificial Intelligence, Bielefeld, Germany*, pages 329–331, 1995.
6. Stefan Gerberding and Axel Noltemeier. Incremental proof planning by meta-rules. In Douglas D. Dankel II, editor, *Proceedings of the 10th FLAIRS Conference, Daytona Beach, Fa.*, pages 171–175. Florida AI Research Society, May 1997.
7. Xiaorong Huang, Manfred Kerber, Jörn Richts, and Arthur Sehn. Planning mathematical proofs with methods. SEKI Report SR-94-08, Universität Kaiserslautern, 1994.
8. Andrew Ireland and Alan Bundy. Productive use of failure in inductive proofs. *Journal of Automated Reasoning*, 16:79–111, 1996.
9. Axel Noltemeier. Inkrementelle Beweisplanung mit Metaregeln. Diploma Thesis, University of Darmstadt, 1996.
10. Brigitte Pientka. Strukturierung der Beweisplanung durch Metaregelmengen. Diploma Thesis, University of Darmstadt, 1997.
11. Martin Protzen. Lazy generation of induction hypotheses. In *Proceedings of the 12th International Conference on Automated Deduction, Nancy, France*, LNAI vol. 814, pages 42–56. Springer, 1994.
12. Inger Sonntag and Jörg Denzinger. Extending automated theorem proving by planning. SEKI Report SR-93-02, Universität Kaiserslautern, 1993.

Many-Sorted Logic in a Learning Theorem Prover

Thomas Kolbe[1]   **Sabine Glesner[2]**

[1] FB Informatik, TH Darmstadt, Alexanderstr. 10, 64283 Darmstadt, Germany
[2] Fakultät für Informatik, Universität Karlsruhe,
Vincenz-Prießnitz-Straße 3, 76128 Karlsruhe, Germany
kolbe@informatik.th-darmstadt.de   glesner@ipd.info.uni-karlsruhe.de

Abstract. In a learning theorem prover, formulas can be verified by reusing proofs of previously verified conjectures. Reuse proceeds by transforming a successful proof into a valid schematic formula which can be instantiated subsequently. In this paper, we show how this reuse approach is extended to many-sorted logic: We first present the logical foundations for reasoning w.r.t. different sortings. Then their operational realization is given by developing a many-sorted proof analysis calculus for extracting the sort constraints imposed by a proof. For guaranteeing the validity of subsequent instantiations, we extend the second-order matching calculi for retrieving and adapting schematic formulas such that the computed sort constraints are satisfied. Finally we demonstrate the relevance of our extensions with several examples of many-sorted reuse.

1 Introduction

The improvement of theorem provers by machine learning techniques has recently been realized successfully in a number of applications, cf. e.g. [2, 3, 10]. The PLAGIATOR-system [9] is a learning theorem prover based on the *reuse* of previously computed proofs by the method of *Kolbe & Walther* [7, 8]: From an abstract point of view, a given proof is transformed into a *valid* formula, which is generalized and instantiated subsequently by certain (second-order) substitutions while preserving its validity. More precisely, a given proof $AX \vdash \varphi$ of a conjecture φ from some axioms AX is analyzed and generalized, yielding a valid formula $C \rightarrow \Phi$ containing function variables instead of function symbols. Now for each new conjecture ψ where some (second-order) matcher π is found such that $\pi(\Phi) = \psi$, the original proof can be reused obtaining a set $\pi(C)$ of proof obligations for ψ, i.e. $\pi(C) \rightarrow \psi$ is valid and the reuse succeeds if $\pi(C)$ is verified.

However, problems arise if this reuse approach for unsorted logic is extended to *many-sorted logic*, where objects of different basic data structures like numbers, lists, trees etc. can be distinguished syntactically by specifying their *sort*, cf. e.g. [4]. A many-sorted logic is an unsorted logic parameterized by a *sorting*, i.e. a mapping which provides the sort information for variables and function symbols. This is commonly used in automated reasoning since more efficient calculi can be built which exploit the given sort information (here we do not consider more general *order-sorted* logics with hierarchical sort relations, cf. [11]).

As terms and formulas are interpreted w.r.t. the sorting of variables and function symbols occurring in them, also the *validity* of formulas depends on the specified sorting: Consider e.g. the formula $\phi := (\forall x \ x \equiv a) \rightarrow b_1 \equiv b_2$ where a, b_1, b_2 are constants and x is a variable. In unsorted logic or in a many-sorted logic where a, b_1, b_2 and x have the same sort, ϕ is valid, while in a many-sorted logic where e.g. a, x have the sort A and b_1, b_2 have the different sort B, ϕ is not valid. Hence a successful proof of ϕ w.r.t. the first sorting cannot be reused without considering the sort information, because otherwise an obviously incorrect "proof" of ϕ w.r.t. the second sorting would be obtained. A simple remedy for this problem would be to admit only those substitutions for reuse where the sorting is exactly retained, but this approach is far too restrictive.

For obtaining a more general criterion concerning admissible substitutions, we must be able to *abstract* from the fixed sorting used in the proof of some conjecture φ: We extract the *sort constraints* a proof imposes on the symbols occurring in it, e.g. the constraint that the (range) sort of b_1, b_2 must be identical to the sort of x in our example above. In this way we obtain the general statement that φ is valid w.r.t. *each* sorting *satisfying* the sort constraints, and therefore the given proof of φ can be reused for verifying some conjecture ψ which is specified w.r.t. some *different* sorting only if the sort constraints are satisfied.[1]

In Section 2 we introduce some formal concepts and show that the validity of formulas w.r.t. sortings or sort constraints is retained when applying sorted (second-order) substitutions. Section 3 shows how a successful proof is analyzed yielding a set of sort constraints whose satisfaction guarantees the validity of instantiations. We further extend the notion of *proof shells* [8], which represent reusable proofs, by a component obtained by generalizing the sort constraints. In Section 4 we deal with the goal-directed instantiation of proof shells for new conjectures respecting the sort constraints and give examples for many-sorted reuse. We summarize in Section 5 and comment on implementational issues.

2 Many-Sorted Logic

We introduce the syntax and semantics of many-sorted logic as we use it throughout this paper. In contrast to common formalizations [4] which assign a priori sorts to (variable and function) symbols, we introduce *sortings* as special syntactic objects for assigning sorts to symbols. This allows us to reason about formulas w.r.t. different sortings without changing the formulas themselves.

2.1 Syntax of Many-Sorted Logic

The many-sorted language is built from the set $\mathcal{X}$ of first-order variables and the set $\Theta = \bigcup_n \Theta_n$ of function symbols which is the union of all function symbols of arity $n \in \mathbb{N}$. The set $\mathcal{T}(\Theta, \mathcal{X})$ of terms and the set $\mathcal{F}(\Theta, \mathcal{X})$ of formulas are built as usual, where only equations $t_1 \equiv t_2$ with $t_1, t_2 \in \mathcal{T}(\Theta, \mathcal{X})$ are used as predicates. For representing second-order substitutions, we introduce a second

---

[1] The usual *relativization* (using unary predicate symbols for each sort) to transform many-sorted into unsorted formulas is not helpful for our application, since we have to reason about the validity of some (unchanged) formula w.r.t. different sortings.

set $W = \{w_i \mid i \in \mathbb{N}\}$ of *parameter* variables. Here $w_i \in W_n = \{w_1, \ldots, w_n\}$ denotes the ith argument position of an n-ary function, i.e. a functional term $t \in T(\Theta, W_n)$ built from function symbols and parameter variables corresponds to the λ-term $\lambda w_1, \ldots, w_n.t$ from the λ-calculus. To obtain a many-sorted logic, we introduce *sortings* for assigning sorts to variables and function symbols:

Definition 1 (sorts, sort variables, sortings). Let S be a set of *sort symbols* and let $S_{\Theta, \mathcal{X}} = S_\Theta \cup S_\mathcal{X}$ be the set of *sort variables*, where $S_\mathcal{X} = \{S(x) \mid x \in \mathcal{X}\}$ and $S_\Theta = \bigcup_n S_{\Theta_n}$ with $S_{\Theta_n} = \{S(f,i) \mid f \in \Theta_n, 0 \leq i \leq n\}$. A sorting δ is a function $\delta : S_{\Theta, \mathcal{X}} \to S$ from sort variables to sort symbols.

Compared to the usual notion of an S-*ranked alphabet* [4], sort variables provide an indirection when assigning sorts: For a fixed sorting δ therefore $\delta(S(f,0))$ denotes the range sort of a function symbol f and $\delta(S(f,i)), 1 \leq i \leq n$, denote the domain sorts of f. This formalization is better suited for dealing with sort constraints subsequently but makes no difference when defining well-sortedness:

The set of all (δ-)sorted terms of sort s consists of variables $x \in \mathcal{X}$ where $\delta(S(x)) = s$ and terms $f(t_1, \ldots, t_n)$ where $f \in \Theta_n$, $\delta(S(f,0)) = s$, and t_i is a δ-sorted term of sort $\delta(S(f,i))$, for $1 \leq i \leq n$. Similarly δ-sorted formulas are built from δ-sorted equations $t_1 \equiv t_2$ where t_1, t_2 are δ-sorted terms of the same sort. Since all sort information is supplied by the sorting δ, we do not need any sort information in formulas, i.e. we use (unsorted looking) quantifiers like $\forall x$ instead of denoting the sort of a quantified variable by $\forall x : s$ for $\delta(S(x)) = s$.

In general, a substitution ξ is a partial function $\xi : \mathcal{X} \cup \Theta \to T(\Theta, \mathcal{X} \cup W)$ whose finite domain is denoted by $\mathrm{dom}(\xi) \subseteq \mathcal{X} \cup \Theta$. A substitution $\sigma : \mathcal{X} \to T(\Theta, \mathcal{X})$ is called a *first-order substitution*. An injective first-order substitution $\gamma : \mathcal{X} \to \mathcal{X}$ is a *variable renaming*. A *second-order substitution* π is a substitution $\pi : \Theta \to T(\Theta, W)$ such that $\pi(f) \in T(\Theta, W_n)$ for each $f \in \Theta_n \cap \mathrm{dom}(\pi)$. We neither admit non-parameter variables from $\mathcal{X}$ occurring in $\pi(f)$ ("π is *closed*") nor variables from $\mathcal{X} \cup W$ occurring in $\mathrm{dom}(\pi)$ ("π is *pure*").

First-order substitutions are applied to terms as usual. Variable renamings can also be applied to formulas, replacing variables in the scope of quantifiers. A second-order substitution π is applied to terms by $\pi(x) = x$ and $\pi(f(t_1, ..., t_n)) = \sigma(\pi(f))$ for the first-order substitution $\sigma = \{w_1/\pi(t_1), ..., w_1/\pi(t_1)\}$ on parameter variables. Applying π to a formula ϕ is done by preserving the structure of ϕ and replacing the terms contained in ϕ as described. The restrictions "closed" and "pure" for second-order substitutions prevent variables from being caught within the scope of quantifiers and preserve the closeness of formulas in applications. E.g. applying the non-closed substitution $\{b/x\}$ to the closed formula $(\forall x \, f(x) \equiv b) \to f(a) \equiv b$ yields the non-closed formula $(\forall x \, f(x) \equiv x) \to f(a) \equiv x$.

As usual, a first-order substitution σ is δ-sorted if $\sigma(x)$ is a δ-sorted term of sort $\delta(S(x))$ for each $x \in \mathrm{dom}(\sigma)$. A second-order substitution π is δ-sorted if for each $f \in \Theta_n \cap \mathrm{dom}(\pi)$, the term $\pi(f)$ is δ_f-sorted of sort $\delta(S(f,0))$ for the modified sorting $\delta_f := \{S(w_1) \mapsto \delta(S(f,1)), \ldots, S(w_n) \mapsto \delta(S(f,n))\} \circ \delta$. It is easy to show (by structural induction) that the δ-sortedness of terms and formulas is retained when applying a first-order substitution σ, variable renaming γ, or second-order substitution π which is δ-sorted, cf. [5].

2.2 Semantics of Many-Sorted Logic

The semantics of a δ-sorted logic is given as usual [4]: A δ-sorted algebra $M = (U, I)$ is a pair of a universe $U = \bigcup_s U_s$, where $U_s \neq \emptyset$ is the universe of sort $s \in S$, and an interpretation I, mapping each function symbol $f \in \Theta$ to a function f_I on U of the appropriate arity and respecting $\delta(S(f, i)), 0 \leq i \leq n$. A δ-sorted variable assignment $V : \mathcal{X} \to U$ maps variables to elements of the universe of the appropriate sort. A formula ϕ is called δ-satisfiable if an algebra M exists such that $(M, V) \models_\delta \phi$ for each variable assignment V, where $\models_\delta$ denotes the meaning w.r.t. fixed M and V. A formula ϕ is δ-valid, written $\models_\delta \phi$, if $M \models_\delta \phi$ for each δ-sorted algebra M.

If a δ-sorted variable renaming γ is applied to a δ-valid, closed formula ϕ, then $\gamma(\phi)$ is also δ-valid because the application of γ results in a bound renaming of quantified variables which is known to be validity preserving. More interesting is the application of a second-order substitution π to a δ-valid formula, which is validity-preserving due to the properties of π being pure and closed, cf. [5]:

Theorem 2 (δ-validity under second-order substitutions). *Let δ be a sorting and let ϕ be a δ-sorted, closed formula. If ϕ is δ-valid, then $\pi(\phi)$ is also δ-valid for each δ-sorted second-order substitution π.*

For reasoning about the validity of a formula w.r.t. different sortings, however, we now replace the *absolute* sorting from Theorem 2 by a *relative* sorting, for which only the satisfaction of some *sort constraints* is required:

Definition 3 (sort constraints, collision sets, satisfy, *col*-valid). A *(sort) collision set* $col \subseteq S_{\Theta, \mathcal{X}}^2$ is a set of pairs of sort variables $(S_1, S_2) \in S_{\Theta, \mathcal{X}}^2$, called *sort constraints*. A sorting δ *satisfies* a collision set col iff it satisfies each contained sort constraint $(S_1, S_2) \in col$ by $\delta(S_1) = \delta(S_2)$. A formula ϕ is called *col-valid* iff ϕ is δ-valid for each sorting δ where col is satisfied and ϕ is δ-sorted.

E.g. the sort constraint $(S(f, 0), S(x))$ represents that the range sort of the function symbol f must be identical to the sort of the variable x, cf. Definition 1, but without committing this sort to a specific $s \in S$. Hence due to Theorem 2, "ϕ is *col*-valid" is a stronger statement w.r.t. instantiations than "ϕ is δ-valid":

Corollary 4 (*col*-validity under second-order substitutions). *Let col be a collision set and ϕ a closed col-valid formula. If the sorting δ satisfies col and ϕ is δ-sorted, then $\pi(\phi)$ is δ-valid for each δ-sorted second-order substitution π.*

Note that the δ-validity of a formula ϕ is *independent* of the part of δ concerning (sort variables for) symbols *not* occurring in ϕ. Hence when considering the δ-validity of ϕ we may modify δ for those new symbols.

Example 5 (*col*-validity vs. δ-validity). *Let δ be a sorting where the constants a_1, a_2, a_3, a_4 and the variables x, y have sort A, the constants b, b_1, b_2 and the variable u have sort B, and the constant c and the variable v have sort C. Consider the following formulas and assume that ϕ is known to be δ-valid.*

$$\phi := (\forall x \; x \equiv a_3) \wedge (\forall y \; y \equiv a_4) \to a_1 \equiv a_2$$
$$\phi' := (\forall u \; u \equiv b) \wedge (\forall v \; v \equiv c) \to b_1 \equiv b_2.$$

Now we cannot apply Theorem 2 for showing the δ-validity of ϕ', because the second-order substitution $\pi := \{a_3/b, a_4/c, a_1/b_1, a_2/b_2\}$ and the variable renaming $\gamma := \{x/u, y/v\}$ with $\pi(\gamma(\phi)) = \phi'$ are both not δ-sorted. However, if we even know ϕ to be col-valid for the collision set $col := \{(S(x), S(a_1, 0))\}$, we can apply Corollary 4 for the modified sorting δ' where a_1, a_2, a_3, x have sort B and a_4, y have sort C, because δ' satisfies col, and ϕ as well as π and γ are δ'-sorted. Thus the δ'-validity and in turn the δ-validity of ϕ' is implied.

Example 5 illustrates that the notion of *col*-validity allows to abstract from the specific sorting concerning the originally proven formula ϕ. Thus our results on the validity of formulas under variable renamings and second-order substitutions which respect a given (absolute or relative) sorting serve as logical basis of extending our reuse procedure to many-sorted logic. However, we must find a way for showing the *col*-validity of formulas for a collision set *col* to be determined.

3 Preparing Proofs for Reuse

For making a proof in many-sorted logic reusable, our goal according to Corollary 4 is to extract the sort collisions *col* the proof imposes on the symbols occurring in it, i.e. to transform the proof into a *col*-valid formula ϕ. As demonstrated in Example 5, reasoning about instantiations is simplified if two disjoint languages are used for specifying the original formula and the one obtained by instantiations, where (first- and second-order) substitutions connect both levels.

Therefore we assume the set $\mathcal{X}$ of variables from Section 2 to be divided into two disjoint subsets $\mathcal{X} =: \mathcal{V} \cup \mathcal{U}$, and the same holds for function symbols $\Theta_n =: \Sigma_n \cup \Omega_n$, $n \in \mathbb{N}$. Then $\mathcal{F}(\Sigma, \mathcal{V})$ denotes the set of formulas built from $\mathcal{V}$ and $\Sigma := \bigcup_n \Sigma_n$ which is used for expressing *specific* formulas, and $\mathcal{F}(\Omega, \mathcal{U})$ built from $\mathcal{U}$ and the set $\Omega := \bigcup_n \Omega_n$ of *function variables* is used for expressing *schematic* formulas.[2] The set of parameter variables $\mathcal{W}$ remains unchanged. We often use (partial) sortings $\delta_1 : S_{\Sigma,\mathcal{V}} \to S$ and $\delta_2 : S_{\Omega,\mathcal{U}} \to S$, where $\delta := \delta_1 \circ \delta_2$ denotes the (total) sorting with $\delta(S) := \delta_1(S)$ for $S \in S_{\Sigma,\mathcal{V}}$ and $\delta(S) := \delta_2(S)$ for $S \in S_{\Omega,\mathcal{U}}$. We let $\mathcal{V}(\phi)$ denote the variables from $\mathcal{V}$ occurring in ϕ etc.

Now we proceed as follows: We first extend the *proof analysis calculus* from [7] by a component for collecting sort constraints, such that a *col*-valid specific formula $\phi \in \mathcal{F}(\Sigma, \mathcal{V})$ is obtained from a proof. Then ϕ and *col* are *generalized* by mapping them to a schematic *Col*-valid formula $\Phi \in \mathcal{F}(\Omega, \mathcal{U})$ with $Col \subseteq S_{\Omega,\mathcal{U}}^2$ which is stored in a *proof shell*, a data structure for representing reusable proofs [8]. Thus new, valid, specific formulas $\phi' = \pi(\gamma(\Phi)) \in \mathcal{F}(\Sigma, \mathcal{V})$ can be obtained by re-instantiating proof shells with substitutions respecting *Col*.

3.1 Many-Sorted Proof Analysis

In this subsection only formulas $\mathcal{F}(\Sigma, \mathcal{V})$ and sortings $\delta : S_{\Sigma,\mathcal{V}} \to S$ are used. We let x^* denote a tuple of variables, $\varphi|_o$ denotes the subterm of φ at position o, and $\varphi[o \leftarrow t]$ denotes subterm replacement at position o.

---

[2] We do *not* perform second-order reasoning by quantifying function variables etc.

In [7] a proof is modeled as a derivation in a simple proof calculus $\vdash_{AX}$, where deriving $\varphi \vdash_{AX}$ TRUE entails that the (conditional) equation φ is provable from the (equational) axioms AX using equational reasoning, i.e. an axiom $\forall x^* l \equiv r \in AX$ can be used for deriving $\varphi[o \leftarrow \sigma(r)]$ from φ if $\varphi|_o = \sigma(l)$ for some (first-order) substitution σ and some position o in φ. In [7], $\vdash_{AX}$ is extended to a proof *analysis* calculus $\vdash^a_{AX}$ by collecting the applied axioms in an *accumulator* component A, i.e. deriving $\langle \varphi, \emptyset \rangle \vdash^a_{AX} \langle$ TRUE, $A \rangle$ entails that also $\varphi \vdash_A$ TRUE can be derived and therefore $\models A \to \varphi$ holds for $A \subseteq AX$ (we use a set of formulas A also as a single formula: the conjunction of the elements of A).[3]

Since (equational) reasoning in many-sorted logic is done like in unsorted logic provided that all objects in the derivation are well-sorted, we can use the unsorted analysis calculus also for many-sorted proofs w.r.t. a fixed sorting δ [5]:

Lemma 6 (proof analysis with fixed sorting). *Let δ be a sorting, let AX be a set of axioms, let φ be a δ-sorted formula, and let $A \subseteq AX$ be δ-sorted. If $\langle \varphi, \emptyset \rangle \vdash^a_{AX} \langle$ TRUE, $A \rangle$ is derived in the unsorted proof analysis calculus and each substitution σ used in this derivation is δ-sorted, then $\models_\delta A \to \varphi$.*

Lemma 6 demands that (rather obviously) the input φ and the output A of a derivation $\langle \varphi, \emptyset \rangle \vdash^a_{AX} \langle$ TRUE, $A \rangle$ must be δ-sorted for guaranteeing $\models_\delta A \to \varphi$. Resuming Example 5, we show that the additional requirement concerning the δ-sortedness of applied substitutions is indeed necessary:

Example 7 (proof analysis and sorts). *The conjecture $\varphi := \mathsf{a}_1 \equiv \mathsf{a}_2$ can be verified from the axioms $AX = \{\forall x\ x \equiv \mathsf{a}_3,\ \forall y\ y \equiv \mathsf{a}_4\}$ in the simple proof analysis calculus obtaining the accumulator $A = \{\forall x\ x \equiv \mathsf{a}_3\}$, i.e. the formula $\phi := A \to \varphi$ is valid w.r.t. the sorting δ from Example 5:*

$$\mathsf{a}_1 \equiv \mathsf{a}_2 \qquad \text{apply axiom } \forall x\ x \equiv \mathsf{a}_3 \text{ to } \mathsf{a}_1 \text{ with } \sigma_1 = \{x/\mathsf{a}_1\}$$
$$\mathsf{a}_3 \equiv \mathsf{a}_2 \qquad \text{apply axiom } \forall x\ x \equiv \mathsf{a}_3 \text{ to } \mathsf{a}_2 \text{ with } \sigma_2 = \{x/\mathsf{a}_2\}$$
$$\mathsf{a}_3 \equiv \mathsf{a}_3 \qquad \text{built-in reflexivity of } \equiv \text{ yields TRUE}$$

But regarding this proof for verifying the same formula ϕ w.r.t. a new sorting δ' where a_3, x have the sort A and $\mathsf{a}_1, \mathsf{a}_2$ have a different sort B would be invalid since ϕ is well-sorted but does not hold w.r.t. δ'. The substitutions σ_1 and σ_2 used in the proof are only well-sorted w.r.t. the original but not the new sorting.

The example reveals the need for inspecting a specific proof and extracting the sort constraints the proof imposes on the symbols occurring in it. We represent this information concerning the well-sortedness of applied substitutions by certain collision sets, cf. Definition 3, which depend on the replaced term l:

Definition 8 (collision set for substitutions). For a (first-order) substitution σ and a term l, the collision set $col(\sigma, l) \subseteq \mathcal{S}^2_{\Sigma, \mathcal{V}}$ for σ w.r.t. l is defined by $col(\sigma, l) := \{(S(l), tls(\sigma(l)))\}$ if $l \in \mathcal{V}$ and $col(\sigma, l) := \emptyset$ if $l \notin \mathcal{V}$.
Here the function $tls : \mathcal{T}(\Sigma, \mathcal{V}) \to \mathcal{S}_{\Sigma, \mathcal{V}}$ yields a designator for the *top level sort* of a term, where $tls(x) := S(x)$ for $x \in \mathcal{V}$ and $tls(f(\ldots)) := S(f, 0)$ for $f \in \Sigma$.

---

[3] The *refined* analysis calculus from [7] additionally distinguishes different occurrences of function symbols (thus increasing the reusability of proofs), and the extension to many-sorted logic is done in the same way as described here.

Now $\vdash^a_{AX}$ is extended to a *many-sorted* proof analysis calculus $\vdash^{ac}_{AX}$ by collecting the collision set for used substitutions in an additional component, i.e. derivations have the form $\langle\varphi,\ \emptyset,\ \emptyset\rangle\ \vdash^{ac}_{AX}\ \langle\text{TRUE},\ A,\ col\rangle$ with $col\subseteq S^2_{\Sigma,\mathcal{V}}$. Here for each application $\varphi[o\leftarrow\sigma(r)]$ of an axiom $\forall x^*l\equiv r\in AX$ using a substitution σ with $\varphi|_o=\sigma(l)$, the sort constraints $col(\sigma,l)$ are added to the col-component. The following theorem proven in [5] states that these collected sort constraints are enough to guarantee the well-sortedness of applied substitutions (note that col-validity of some formula ϕ requires ϕ only to be δ-valid for sortings δ where ϕ is δ-sorted (and col is satisfied), cf. Definition 3):

Theorem 9 (many-sorted proof analysis). *Let AX be a set of axioms, let φ be a formula, let $A\subseteq AX$ be an accumulator, and let col be a collision set such that $\langle\varphi,\ \emptyset,\ \emptyset\rangle\ \vdash^{ac}_{AX}\ \langle\text{TRUE},\ A,\ col\rangle$ is a derivation in the many-sorted proof analysis calculus. Then the formula $A\rightarrow\varphi$ is col-valid.*

Theorem 9 shows how the calculus $\vdash^{ac}_{AX}$ can be used for simultaneously *proving* a conjecture φ from given axioms AX and *analyzing* the constructed proof w.r.t. applied axioms and necessary sort constraints: If φ and AX are specified w.r.t. a fixed sorting δ_0, then $AX\models_{\delta_0}\varphi$ is verified if a derivation $\langle\varphi,\ \emptyset,\ \emptyset\rangle\ \vdash^{ac}_{AX}\ \langle\text{TRUE},\ A,\ col\rangle$ in the many-sorted proof analysis calculus can be established where all applied substitutions are δ_0-sorted. But additionally — by analyzing the proof — the more general statement $\models_\delta A\rightarrow\varphi$ is verified where δ may be *any* sorting such that $A\rightarrow\varphi$ is well-sorted and col is satisfied.[4] For instance the reuse attempt described in Example 7 is prohibited as the sort constraints $\{(S(x),S(\mathbf{a_1},0)),(S(x),S(\mathbf{a_2},0))\}$ which are collected for the substitutions used in the proof are not satisfied by the new sorting δ'.

3.2 Constructing Proof Shells

The improved analysis technique avoids invalid proof reuses when considering conjectures specified for new sortings. For achieving the separation into specific and schematic formulas mentioned in the beginning of this section, we let generalizations map between the signatures Σ and Ω resp. the variable sets $\mathcal{V}$ and $\mathcal{U}$ (schematic objects are denoted by capital symbols):

Definition 10 (generalization). A *generalization* $\mu\circ\beta$ is a substitution built from a second-order substitution $\mu:\Sigma\rightarrow\mathcal{T}(\Omega,\mathcal{W})$, replacing function symbols $f\in\Sigma_n$ by functional terms $\mu(f)=F(w_1,\ldots,w_n)$ for function variables $F\in\Omega_n$, and a variable renaming $\beta:\mathcal{V}\rightarrow\mathcal{U}$.

A generalization $\mu\circ\beta$ can also be applied to sort collision sets by defining $\mu(S(f,i))=S(F,i)$ for $\mu(f)=F(w_1,\ldots,w_n)$ and $\beta(S(x))=S(\beta(x))$. E.g. $\{\mathbf{a_3}/F,\ \mathbf{a_1}/G,\ \mathbf{a_2}/H\}\circ\{x/u\}$ generalizes the specific symbols from Example 7.

We characterize *proof shells* [8] as a data structure for representing the essentials of a proof $\langle\varphi,\ \emptyset,\ \emptyset\rangle\ \vdash^{ac}_{AX}\ \langle\text{TRUE},\ A,\ col\rangle$ in the schematic language $\mathcal{F}(\Omega,\mathcal{U})$, extended by a component for (generalized) sort constraints:

---

[4] Theorem 9 also holds for more general calculi containing unification rules etc. as e.g. used in the PLAGIATOR-system [9] for treating arbitrary formulas, cf. Section 5.

Definition 11 (proof shells). A proof shell $PS = \langle \Phi, C, Col \rangle$ is built from a closed second-order formula $\Phi \in \mathcal{F}(\Omega, \mathcal{U})$ (also called *schematic conjecture*), a set of closed second-order formulas $C \subseteq \mathcal{F}(\Omega, \mathcal{U})$ (also called *schematic catch*), and a collision set $Col \subseteq \mathcal{S}^2_{\Omega, \mathcal{U}}$ such that $C \to \Phi$ is Col-valid.

A proof shell captures the "idea" of a successful proof, viz. that the schematic catch C entails the schematic conjecture Φ for all sortings satisfying Col. E.g. $PS = \langle G \equiv H, \{\forall u\ u \equiv F\}, \{(S(u), S(G, 0)), (S(u), S(H, 0))\} \rangle$ is a proof shell constructed from many-sorted analysis of the proof of φ from Example 7, using the generalization from above.

Theorem 12 (construction of proof shells). *For a derivation $\langle \varphi, \emptyset, \emptyset \rangle \vdash^{ac}_{AX}$ $\langle$ TRUE, A, $col \rangle$ in the many-sorted proof analysis calculus, $PS := \langle \Phi, C, Col \rangle :=$ $\langle \mu(\beta(\varphi)), \mu(\beta(A)), \mu(\beta(col)) \rangle$ is a proof shell, where $\mu \circ \beta$ is a generalization with $\Sigma(A \cup \{\varphi\}) \subseteq \mathrm{dom}(\mu)$ and $\mathcal{V}(A \cup \{\varphi\}) \subseteq \mathrm{dom}(\beta)$.*

Proof. Follows easily from Theorem 9 by showing that the Col-validity of $C \to \Phi$ is implied by the col-validity of $A \to \varphi$: For each sorting $\delta_2 : \mathcal{S}_{\Omega, \mathcal{U}} \to \mathcal{S}$ such that $C \to \Phi$ is δ_2-sorted and Col is δ_2-satisfied, we define a corresponding sorting $\delta_1 : \mathcal{S}_{\Sigma, \mathcal{V}} \to \mathcal{S}$ w.r.t. $\mu \circ \beta$ by stipulating $\delta_1(S(f, i)) := \delta_2(S(F, i))$ for $\mu(f) = F(w_1, \ldots, w_n)$ and $\delta_1(S(x)) := \delta_2(S(u))$ for $\beta(x) = u$. Then Corollary 4 is applicable for col, $A \to \varphi$, $\delta_1 \circ \delta_2$, and μ, yielding the δ_2-validity of $C \to \Phi$. $\square$

So far we have formalized how proof shells are constructed by analyzing and generalizing successfully computed proofs. Now we show how proof shells are re-instantiated for obtaining proofs of new conjectures.

4 Reusing Proofs

In the remainder of this paper we assume that the new conjectures ψ to be proven are δ_1-sorted w.r.t. a fixed sorting $\delta_1 : \mathcal{S}_{\Sigma, \mathcal{V}} \to \mathcal{S}$ for the language defined by $\Sigma \cup \mathcal{V}$. When considering proof reuse, δ_1 must be extended by a sorting $\delta_2 : \mathcal{S}_{\Omega, \mathcal{U}} \to \mathcal{S}$ for the proof shell PS, such that a total sorting $\delta = \delta_1 \circ \delta_2$ is obtained for checking the well-sortedness of substitutions and the sort constraints. To commit these language restrictions, we let "mapper" denote a second-order substitution $\Omega \to \mathcal{T}(\Sigma, \mathcal{W})$, "renaming" denotes a variable renaming $\mathcal{U} \to \mathcal{V}$, and "conjecture" denotes a closed δ_1-sorted first-order formula. The *goal-directed* computation of admissible mappers π and renamings γ for instantiating a proof shell w.r.t. given δ_1 and ψ (guaranteeing the existence of a suited sorting δ_2) is based on an algorithm for *sorted second-order matching* which is presented first. Finally we give examples of many-sorted reuse revealing the gains of our treatment of sorts, as naive approaches would restrict the reusability of proofs.

4.1 Many-Sorted Second-Order Term-Matching

An unsorted second-order matching problem $p \lhd t$ for a *pattern* $p \in \mathcal{T}(\Sigma \cup \Omega, \mathcal{V} \cup \mathcal{U})$ and a *target* $t \in \mathcal{T}(\Sigma, \mathcal{V})$ is solved by computing a mapper $\pi : \Omega \to \mathcal{T}(\Sigma, \mathcal{W})$ with $\pi(p) = t$ (we perform "pure" second-order matching as first-order variables in the pattern are not instantiated). The standard algorithm from [6] uses the operations *decomposition, projection,* and *imitation* for solving a (generally simultaneous) second-order matching problem $R := [p_1 \vartriangleleft t_1, \ldots, p_n \vartriangleleft t_n]$. Since several operations may be applicable, branching leads to multiple solutions, and we let $\Pi := match(R)$ denote the set Π of mappers computed by this calculus.

For extending *match* w.r.t. sorts, we provide a flexible way to express the well-sortedness of objects by defining the well-sortedness of arbitrary collision sets $Q \subseteq S^2_{\Sigma \cup \Omega, \mathcal{V} \cup \mathcal{U}}$, cf. Definition 3, w.r.t. a fixed sorting $\delta_1 : S_{\Sigma, \mathcal{V}} \to S.$[5]

Definition 13 (δ_1-sorted collision sets). A collision set $Q \subseteq S^2_{\Sigma \cup \Omega, \mathcal{V} \cup \mathcal{U}}$ of sort constraints is δ_1-*sorted* iff $S_1 \sim_Q S_2$ for $S_1, S_2 \in S_{\Sigma, \mathcal{V}}$ implies $\delta_1(S_1) = \delta_1(S_2)$, where $\sim_Q \subseteq S^2_{\Sigma \cup \Omega, \mathcal{V} \cup \mathcal{U}}$ is the equivalence relation induced by Q.

Hence a collision set Q is δ_1-sorted iff there is some sorting $\delta_2 : S_{\Omega, \mathcal{U}} \to S$ such that $\delta_1 \circ \delta_2$ satisfies Q. For instance both collision sets $Q_1 := \{(S(F, 1), S(k))\}$ and $Q_2 := \{(S(\text{len}, 1), S(F, 0)), (S(F, 1), S(m)\}$ are δ_1-sorted if k resp. m is a variable of δ_1-sort list resp. nat and len computes the length of a list, but their union $Q_3 := Q_1 \cup Q_2$ is not δ_1-sorted because $S(k) \sim_{Q_3} S(m)$ but $\delta_1(S(k)) =$ list $\neq$ nat $= \delta_1(S(m))$. Now the well-sortedness (w.r.t. *delta_1*) of terms, formulas, and substitutions can be expressed by certain collision sets, viz. *contexts:*

Definition 14 (context of terms). The *context con(p)* of a term $p \in \mathcal{T}(\Sigma \cup \Omega, \mathcal{V} \cup \mathcal{U})$ is the collision set inductively defined by (cf. Definition 8 for *tls*)

$$con(z) := \emptyset, \qquad\qquad\qquad \text{if } z \in \mathcal{V} \cup \mathcal{U}$$
$$con(f(p_1, \ldots, p_n)) := \bigcup_i \{(S(f, i), tls(p_i))\} \cup con(p_i), \quad \text{if } f \in \Sigma_n \cup \Omega_n.$$

The context of a term represents all sort constraints which are implicitly given by the term's structure, i.e. *con(p)* is δ_1-sorted iff there is some sorting $\delta_2 : S_{\Omega, \mathcal{U}} \to S$ such that p is $(\delta_1 \circ \delta_2)$-sorted. For terms $p_1, \ldots, p_n$ we have $\bigcup_i con(p_i)$ δ_1-sorted iff all p_i are $(\delta_1 \circ \delta_2)$-sorted w.r.t. some *same* sorting δ_2. E.g. the terms $p_1 := F(k)$ and $p_2 := \text{len}(F(m))$ are not $(\delta_1 \circ \delta_2)$-sorted w.r.t. any sorting δ_2 because the union Q_3 of the above collision sets $Q_1 = con(p_1)$, $Q_2 = con(p_2)$ obtained as contexts is not δ_1-sorted. Similarly contexts are defined for formulas and substitutions, e.g. $con(\pi) = \{(S(F, 0), S(\text{len}, 0)), (S(\text{len}, 1), S(G, 0)), (S(G, 1), S(F, 2))\}$ for $\pi = \{F/\text{len}(G(w_2))\}$, where the parameter variable w_2 points to $S(F, 2)$.

We extend *match* to an algorithm *sorted_match(R, Q)* yielding the matchers π of R for which $Q \cup con(\pi)$ is δ_1-sorted for an initially given collision set Q, cf. [5]: *During the matching process,* Q *is updated to* Q' *by adding the contexts of the stepwise constructed substitutions, where the actual branch is aborted if* Q' *is not* δ_1-*sorted and otherwise the branch is continued with* $Q := Q'$. Thus parts of the search space are cut by early detecting violations of sort constraints.

---

[5] The algorithm from [6] already assumes that a fixed sort (called "(elementary) type") is given for all symbols, and the matching operations are extended there by conditions checking these sorts. Our sort constraints rather correspond to *polymorphic types* in the typed λ-calculus, e.g. the sort constraint $(S(F, 1), S(F, 0))$ for $F \in \Omega_2$ resembles the typing $F_{\alpha \times \beta} \to \alpha$ where α, β are *type variables* (which can be instantiated by types). We did not follow the way of extending [6] to polymorphic types as our notion of sort constraints allows more compact representations and efficient tests.

4.2 Retrieval and Adaptation of Proof Shells

We formulate our approach to many-sorted reuse using the notion of δ_1-sorted collision sets. Instantiating a proof shell $\langle \Phi, C, Col \rangle$ is split into two phases, resulting in a partially or totally instantiated catch, respectively: For *retrieval* the schematic conjecture Φ is matched with a new conjecture ψ, and during *adaptation* the axioms AX for ψ are used for instantiating the remaining symbols from the schematic catch C such that provable formulas are obtained.

Theorem 15 (reusing proofs by retrieval and adaptation). *If, for a conjecture ψ and a proof shell $PS = \langle \Phi, C, Col \rangle$, there are a mapper π and a renaming γ such that $\pi(\gamma(\Phi)) = \psi$ and $Q_p := Col \cup con(C \cup \{\Phi\}) \cup con(\pi) \cup con(\gamma)$ is δ_1-sorted, then we say PS applies for ψ (via $\pi \circ \gamma$) and we call $C_p := \pi(\gamma(C))$ the partially instantiated catch. If there further are a mapper ρ and a renaming η such that $C_t := \rho(\eta(C_p)) \subseteq \mathcal{F}(\Sigma, \mathcal{V})$ and $Q_t := Q_p \cup con(\rho) \cup con(\eta)$ is δ_1-sorted, then the totally instantiated catch C_t is δ_1-sorted and $\models_{\delta_1} C_t \to \psi$, and we say ψ is reduced to C_t (by PS via $\pi \circ \gamma \circ \rho \circ \eta$).*

Proof. Let π, γ and ρ, η be given as required. Then there is a sorting $\delta_2 : S_{\Omega,\mu} \to S$ such that $C \to \Phi$, $\pi' := \pi \circ \rho$, and $\gamma' := \gamma \circ \eta$ are δ-sorted and δ satisfies Col, for the sorting $\delta := \delta_1 \circ \delta_2$. Therefore $\models_{\delta} \pi'(\gamma'(C)) \to \pi'(\gamma'(\Phi))$ is implied by Corollary 4 and Definition 11. Since $\pi(\gamma(\Phi)) = \psi$ implies $\pi'(\gamma'(\Phi)) = \psi$ and further $\pi'(\gamma'(C)) = C_t \subseteq \mathcal{F}(\Sigma, \mathcal{V})$ holds, we have even $\models_{\delta_1} C_t \to \psi$. $\quad\square$

To treat a *formula*-pair $\langle \Phi, \psi \rangle$ with the algorithm *sorted_match* for *terms*, $\langle R, \gamma \rangle := decompose(\Phi, \psi)$ denotes the preprocessing step of structurally comparing Φ and ψ (up to quantified variables and terms in equations). E.g. $R := [F(u) \lhd a(x), G(v) \lhd b, H(u,v) \lhd f(y), D \lhd c]$ and $\gamma := \{u/x, v/y\}$ results from decomposing $\forall u \forall v\, F(u) \equiv G(v) \wedge H(u,v) \equiv D$ and $\forall x \forall y\, a(x) \equiv b \wedge f(y) \equiv c$. Hence γ is a renaming if *decompose* succeeds, i.e. $PS = \langle \Phi, C, Col \rangle$ applies for ψ via $\pi \circ \gamma$ for each (if any) $\pi \in sorted\_match(\gamma(R), Q)$, if the collision set $Q := Col \cup con(C \cup \{\Phi\}) \cup con(\gamma)$ is δ_1-sorted, cf. Theorem 15. Here $con(C) \subseteq Q$ ensures the sort constraints imposed by the schematic catch C to be checked already during retrieval, i.e. some "mappers" with $\pi(\gamma(\Phi)) = \psi$ are excluded early because there is no δ_1-sorted *total* instantiation of C.

The obtained partially instantiated catch $C_p := \pi(\gamma(C))$ may still contain function variables, stemming from function symbols which appear in the original proof but not in the original conjecture. These *free* function variables are instantiated during the *adaptation* phase: An efficient procedure *solve_catch* incorporates the underlying axioms for ψ by heuristically combining a second-order matching algorithm with the technique of *symbolic evaluation*, cf. [8]. This immediately transfers to many-sorted reuse, where the obtained δ_1-sorted collision set Q_p serves as input for calls of *sorted_match* when further processing C_p.

Hence the presented reuse method reduces the provability of a new conjecture to the provability of a set of speculated conjectures, i.e. for a given underlying set of axioms AX, we have verified $AX \models_{\delta_1} \psi$ if we can show $AX \models_{\delta_1} C_t$. Since the remaining proof obligations C_t can again be proved by reuse, *recursion* is recommendable for the reuse procedure, cf. [8] for controlling termination.

4.3 Examples of Many-Sorted Reuse

We consider some examples from the viewpoint of many-sorted reuse, i.e. we analyze how our techniques for extracting, generalizing and instantiating sort constraints enable proof reuses which were excluded by naive approaches. In some examples we exploit that the applicability of proof shells is increased if one requirement of Theorem 15 is relaxed by demanding only $\pi(\gamma(\varPhi)) \cong \psi$, where $\cong$ allows several equivalence preserving transformations. Transformations like swapping equations or reordering subformulas can be built into the calculus for matching formulas, cf. [1] for recent improvements. Our examples stem from the domain of theorem proving by mathematical induction, cf. Table 1: The proof shell computed from the given proof of the step formula for φ_0 (in the first row) is reused for proving the step formulas for the remaining statements φ_1, φ_2, etc.[6]

The last column shows how the soundness of the many-sorted reuse in the respective row is guaranteed. Here (a) denotes that in the proof by reuse for each symbol exactly the same sorts as in the original proof are used, and (b) denotes that in the proof by reuse only one overall sort is used, i.e. in these cases the soundness of the many-sorted reuse is obvious and our extensions are not necessary. But in the remaining cases (c) only our construction of sort constraints guarantees the validity of instantiations, because e.g. different function symbols in the original proof with the *same* (range and domain) sorts are mapped to different function symbols in the proof by reuse with *different* sorts, however respecting the computed sort constraints. This situation is repeated for other source proofs, i.e. our techniques count for a significant increase of reusability.

φ_0	$\sum k + \sum l \equiv \sum(k <> l)$	
No.	Conjectures proved by reuse	Sorting
φ_1	$\prod k \times \prod l \equiv \prod(k <> l)$	(a)
φ_2	$\mid k \mid + \mid l \mid \equiv \mid k <> l \mid$	(a)
φ_3	$m \times i + n \times i \equiv (m + n) \times i$	(b)
φ_4	$m + (n + i) \equiv (m + n) + i$	(b)
φ_5	$\mid k <> l \mid \equiv \mid l <> k \mid$	(c)
φ_6	$\mid k <> n :: \text{empty} \mid \equiv \text{succ}(\mid k \mid)$	(c)
φ_7	$\mid k <> n :: l \mid \equiv \text{succ}(\mid k <> l \mid)$	(c)
φ_8	$\text{incr}(m, k) <> \text{incr}(m, l) \equiv \text{incr}(m, k <> l)$	(c)
φ_9	$\text{nthcut}(m, \text{nthcut}(n, k)) \equiv \text{nthcut}(m + n, k)$	(c)
φ_{10}	$\text{reverse}(\text{reverse}(k)) \equiv k$	(c)
φ_{11}	$\mid \text{reverse}(k) \mid \equiv \mid k \mid$	(c)
φ_{12}	$\text{reverse}(k <> n :: \text{empty}) \equiv n :: \text{reverse}(k)$	(c)
φ_{13}	$\text{or}(\text{member}(m, k), \text{member}(m, l)) \equiv \text{member}(m, k <> l)$	(c)

Table 1. Conjectures proved by reusing the proof of φ_0

---

[6] The following functions operate on lists: $\sum$ sums up all elements, $<>$ denotes concatenation, $\prod$ multiplies all elements, $\mid . \mid$ yields the length, $::$ adds an element, incr increments each element, nthcut cuts elements from the back end, reverse reverses the order of elements, and member tests for occurrence of elements.

5 Conclusion

We have shown that a learning theorem prover specified for unsorted logic cannot be used for many-sorted logic without further extensions. Learning of proofs is based on their reuse, i.e. from a logical perspective a given proof is transformed into a *valid* formula which can be generalized and instantiated subsequently by certain substitutions while preserving its validity. For many-sorted reuse we have shown that it is necessary to also learn the sort information contained in a formula and its proof to ensure the soundness of instantiations. This allows us to abstract from a specific sorting and reason about the validity of (instantiated) formulas w.r.t. different sortings for the contained symbols.

It turned out that the learning theorem prover can be extended to many-sorted logic with moderate effort as the overall architecture of the reuse procedure remains unchanged. The described extensions for many-sorted logic are implemented in the PLAGIATOR-system [9], the prototype of a learning theorem prover which formerly performed unsorted reuse. The examples given here reveal that using the developed approach to many-sorted reuse increases the reusability of proofs compared to a naive treatment of sorts. An extension to order-sorted logic [11] by interpreting sort constraints as subsort-relations seems possible.

Acknowledgments: We would like to thank Jürgen Giesl and Wolf Zimmermann for many helpful discussions and comments on earlier drafts of this paper.

References

1. R. Curien, Z. Qian, and H. Shi. Efficient Second-Order Matching. In *Proceedings of the 7th International Conference on Rewriting Techniques and Applications (RTA-96)*, pages 317 – 331, New Brunswick, NJ, USA, 1996. Springer LNCS 1103.
2. J. Denzinger and S. Schulz. Learning Domain Knowledge to Improve Theorem Proving. In *Proceedings CADE-13*, pages 62 – 76. Springer LNAI 1104, 1996.
3. M. Fuchs. Experiments in the Heuristic Use of Past Proof Experience. In *Proceedings CADE-13*, pages 523 – 537. Springer LNAI 1104, 1996.
4. J. H. Gallier. *Logic for Computer Science*. John Wiley & Sons, 1987.
5. S. Glesner. Many-Sorted Logic in a Learning Prover. Diploma Thesis (in German), TH Darmstadt, 1996.
6. G. Huet and B. Lang. Proving and Applying Program Transformations Expressed with Second-Order Patterns. *Acta Informatica*, 11:31–55, 1978.
7. T. Kolbe and C. Walther. Reusing Proofs. In A. Cohn, editor, *Proceedings of the 11th European Conference on Artificial Intelligence (ECAI-94)*, Amsterdam, The Netherlands, pages 80–84. John Wiley & Sons, Ltd., 1994.
8. T. Kolbe and C. Walther. Termination of Theorem Proving by Reuse. In *Proceedings CADE-13*, pages 106 – 120. Springer LNAI 1104, 1996.
9. T. Kolbe and J. Brauburger. PLAGIATOR – A Learning Prover. In *Proceedings CADE-14*. Springer LNAI 1249, 1997.
10. E. Melis and J. Whittle. Internal Analogy in Theorem Proving. In *Proceedings CADE-13*, pages 92 – 105. Springer LNAI 1104, 1996.
11. M. Schmidt-Schauß. *Computational Aspects of an Order-Sorted Logic with Term Declarations*. Springer LNAI 395, 1989.

Rigid Hypertableaux

Michael Kühn

Universität Koblenz
Institut für Informatik
Rheinau 1, 56075 Koblenz, Germany
E-mail: kuehn@informatik.uni-koblenz.de

Abstract. This paper extends a calculus for first-order logic that combines the inference mechanism of *hyperresolution* with the more informative structure of *analytic tableaux* and that has been introduced as *hyper tableaux* by Baumgartner et al. (1996). This clausal tableau calculus is proof confluent, but suffers from the need of partial ground instantiations.

I will develop an improvement of hyper tableaux which avoids this by using full unification with rigid variables, but keeps desirable features like proof confluence and a partially universal treatment of variables in a clausal tableau. The resulting calculus can be seen as a refined hyperresolution calculus that deals properly with an arbitrary literal selection function without loss of completeness.

For this calculus, I have implemented and evaluated a proof procedure which takes advantage of proof confluence and addresses the *fairness* problem of tableau caluli with a redundancy criterion based upon literal subsumption.

1 Introduction

This paper extends a calculus for first-order logic that combines the inference mechanism of *hyperresolution* with the more informative structure of *analytic tableaux* and that has been introduced as *hyper tableaux* by Baumgartner et al. (1996). This clausal tableau calculus is proof confluent, but suffers from the need of partial ground instantiations.

I will develop an improvement of hyper tableaux which avoids this by using full unification with rigid variables, but keeps desirable features like proof confluence and a partially universal treatment of variables in a clausal tableau. The resulting calculus can be seen as a refined hyperresolution calculus that deals properly with an arbitrary literal selection function without loss of completeness.

For this calculus, I have implemented and evaluated a proof procedure which takes advantage of proof confluence and addresses the *fairness* problem of tableau caluli with a redundancy criterion based upon literal subsumption.

1.1 Overview

The paper is organized as follows:

In the rest of this section, related work in the area of hyperresolution and clausal tableaux as well as basic notions are presented.

In Section 2, I will repeat the original hypertableau calculus as described in Baumgartner et al. (1996) and define a calculus variant that uses unification of rigid variables instead of purifying substitutions and show the advantages of this approach. Soundness and completeness proofs are sketched.

Section 3 documents the proof procedure of a hyper tableau theorem prover which is based on the results of the previous sections and has been implemented in Prolog. The fairness problem and its chosen solution for this implementation is discussed. Some experimental results are given.

Finally, I will summarize my work and and classify it with respect to related approaches. Some conclusions are drawn and an outlook for future work is given.

1.2 Related work

Hyperresolution: The *hyperresolution* calculus is a refinement of the resolution calculus that restricts the number of derived clauses by generating only purely positive (or only purely negative) clauses. Hyperresolution was introduced by Robinson (1965) in the same year he had developed the resolution principle; Slagle (1967) recognized hyperresolution to be a special case of *semantic resolution*.

For automated theorem proving, hyperresolution has the advantage that it is a more restrictive calculus than resolution and that the splitting interpretation is syntactically fixed, in contrast to the more general semantic resolution. Therefore, it is successfully used in efficient theorem proving systems (e.g. McCune, 1990).

Although hyperresolution can be restricted by a literal ordering (cf. Chang and Lee, 1973), completeness is lost when using an arbitrary literal selection function in an unrestricted way. Rigid hypertableaux can be seen as a refinement of hyperresolution putting constraints on the use of an arbitrary selection function such that completeness is preserved.

Further, the structure of clausal tableaux allows a more efficient storage of a derivation, a strong redundancy check based upon literal subsumption and a controlled splitting of derived clauses.

Disconnection method: Billon (1996) presents an approach how to guide the search for clause instances that are needed in a clause matrix by transferring the underlying idea of the *hyper-linking strategy* by Lee and Plaisted (1992) into the tableaux world. In his *disconnection method*, unification is used to instantiate extending clauses such that the clauses contain a complementary literal in the path if every variable is substituted by a same constant $. A refutation is found, if in every path there are complementary literals after substituting every variable by $. Since no substitutions are applied to the matrix, the guidance of unification is used without losing proof confluence.

One significance of the disconnection method is, that — in contrast to other proof-confluent tableau calculi — there is a fair proof procedure for the disconnection method that does not have to enumerate instances of the input clauses in an unguided manner but uses unification to determine which instances are really needed..

As Billon states, his approach cannot be combined with the clashes of hyperresolution. The reason for this is that he does not instantiate the matrix and therefore does not explicitly compute resolvents, as it is done by rigid hypertableaux.

1.3 Preliminaries

In the following, I assume the reader to be familiar with the basic concepts of first order logic. For an exhaustive introduction, I refer the reader to the textbook of Chang and Lee (1973).

The *complement* of a literal L is defined by $\overline{L} = \neg K$ if $L = K$ and $\overline{L} = K$ if $L = \neg K$ for an atomic literal K. There are also two distinguished and complementary predicates $\top$ and $\bot$ which are assumed to be interpreted by *true* and *false*, respectively.

Two literals L and K are *unifiable*, if there is a substitution σ such that $L\sigma = K\sigma$ and *complementary unifiable*, if $\overline{L}\sigma = K\sigma$. A literal L *subsumes* a literal K, if there is a substitution σ such that $L\sigma = K$.

A *clause* C is a disjunction of literals $C = B_1 \vee \cdots \vee B_n \vee \neg A_1 \vee \cdots \vee \neg A_m$, where $B_1, \ldots, B_n, A_1, \ldots, A_m$ are atoms and every occuring variable is read universally quantified. Mostly, I will represent clauses by $C = B \leftarrow A$, where $B = B_1 \vee \cdots \vee B_n$ and $A = A_1 \wedge \cdots \wedge A_m$. Further, I will sometimes abuse the element relation $\in$ by writing $B_i \in B$ for $B_i \in \{B_1, \ldots, B_n\}$ as well as $A_i \in A$ for $A_i \in \{A_1, \ldots, A_m\}$.

A *renaming* ρ for a clause C is a substitution that maps every variable x in C to a new, unused variable x^ρ. $C\rho$ is called a *clause copy* of C.

An *ordered clause* $D = \underline{L} \vee C$ is a tuple (L, C), where L is said to be *selected* in D.

A *tree* is a tupel $\Theta = (\mathcal{N}, \mathcal{E}, N_0)$ where $\mathcal{N}$ is a finite set of nodes with $N_0 \in \mathcal{N}$ and $\mathcal{E}$ is a relation on $\mathcal{N} \times \mathcal{N} \setminus \{N_0\}$ such that for every node $N \in \mathcal{N} \setminus \{N_0\}$ there is exactly one node $N' \in \mathcal{N}$ with $(N', N) \in \mathcal{E}$. N_0 is called the *root node* of Θ.

A node $N' \in \mathcal{N}$ is called *predecessor node* of a node $N \in \mathcal{N}$, iff $(N', N) \in \mathcal{E}$. N' is called *ancestor node* of N iff (N', N) is in the transitive closure of $\mathcal{E}$. A *leaf* is a node $N \in \mathcal{N}$ that is not a predecessor node. A node $N' \in \mathcal{N}$ is called a *neighbour node* of N, iff there is an ancestor node M of N such that $(M, N') \in \mathcal{E}$.

A *labelled tree* is a tupel $(\mathcal{N}, \mathcal{E}, N_0, \lambda)$ such that $(\mathcal{N}, \mathcal{E}, N_0)$ is a tree and λ is a function that assigns to every node in N a value of a given domain.

2 Hypertableau calculus

The original hypertableau calculus has been developed by Baumgartner et al. (1996) and performs hyperresolution steps with literal selection in a clausal tableau. It uses universal variables and purifying substitutions with the effect that the tableaux never get instantiated and there is a strong redundancy criterion based on literal subsumption. On the other hand, purification of input clauses leads to at least partial ground instantiations such that the advantages mentioned are partially lost again.

Therefore, I develop an improved variant that makes use of unification for rigid variables instead and thus avoids purification of input clauses. This calculus is a real extension of the original approach and thus still proof confluent. Since there is no need to ground instantiate any variables in an input clause, this calculus often behaves better for first order clauses than the purifying version. For ground, horn and pure clause sets, the two calculi coincide.

But first, let me give some basic definitions for clausal tableaux.

2.1 Clausal tableaux

Definition 1 Clausal tableau. A *clausal tableau* for a set of clauses Σ is a 4-tuple $\Theta = (\mathcal{N}, \mathcal{E}, N_0, \lambda)$ where $(\mathcal{N}, \mathcal{E}, N_0)$ is a tree and λ a labelling function that assigns a literal to every node $N \in \mathcal{N}$.

A *branch* of a clausal tableau $\Theta = (\mathcal{N}, \mathcal{E}, N_0, \lambda)$ is a set $\beta = \{N_0, \ldots, N_n\}$ of nodes in $\mathcal{N}$ such that N_0 is the root, N_n is a leaf and N_{i-1} is a predecessor node of N_i for $0 < i \leq n$.

The literals of a branch $\beta = \{N_0, \ldots, N_n\}$ are denoted by the set $\lambda_\beta = \{\lambda(N_0), \ldots, \lambda(N_n)\}$.

A branch β is called *closed*, iff there are two complementary literals L and $\overline{L}$ in λ_β; otherwise β is called *open*.

A clausal tableau Θ is *closed* iff each of its branches is closed; otherwise it is *open*.

From now on, I will often represent a clausal tableau by the set of its branches $\Theta = \{\beta_0, \ldots, \beta_n\}$ and let the labelling function λ be implicitly given, as well as the edge relation $\mathcal{E}$.

The node set $\mathcal{N}$ and the root node N_0 are definitely determinable from this branch representation. For a longer discussion of different clausal tableau representations, see (Baumgartner, 1996).

Definition 2 Extension of a branch. The *extension of a branch* β with a clause $L_1 \vee \cdots \vee L_n$ is the set of branches $\Theta'_\beta = \{\beta'_1, \ldots, \beta'_n\}$ where $\beta'_i = \beta \cup \{N'_i\}$ for a new, unique node N'_i and $\lambda' = \lambda \cup \{(N'_i, L_i)\}$ with $1 \leq i \leq n$.

A clausal tableau Θ' is said to be an *extension* of a clausal tableau Θ on a branch $\beta \in \Theta$ with a clause C, iff $\Theta' = \Theta \backslash \{\beta\} \cup \Theta'_\beta$ where Θ'_β is the extension of β with C.

Of course, the node set $\mathcal{N}$ and the edge relation $\mathcal{E}$ have to be updated for an extension of a tableau Θ with a clause of size n as follows: $\mathcal{N}' = \mathcal{N} \cup \{N'_1, \ldots, N'_n\}$ and $\mathcal{E}' = \mathcal{E} \cup \{(N'_i, N_m) : 1 \leq i \leq n\}$, where N_m is the leaf of the extended branch β.

2.2 Purified hypertableaux

Purification is the application of a substitution to a set of literals, such that the substituted literals get variable-disjunct: A clause $B \leftarrow A$ is called *pure* iff $\mathrm{Var}(K) \cap \mathrm{Var}(L) = \emptyset$ for $K, L \in B$ and $K \neq L$. A substitution π is a *purifying substitution* for a clause C iff $C\pi$ is pure (Baumgartner et al., 1996).

Since it holds that $\forall(A \vee B) \equiv \forall A \vee \forall B$ iff A and B are variable-disjunct, purification allows an universally quantifying treatment of the variables in a clausal tableau.

Thus, the *purified hypertableaux* for a clause set Σ are defined as follows (cf. Baumgartner et al., 1996):

1. The clausal tableau that consists only of the root node labelled with $\top$ is a purified hypertableau for Σ.
2. If Θ is a purified hypertableau for Σ, β is an open branch in Θ, $B \leftarrow A$ is a clause of Σ and σ is a most general substitution such that for every literal $L \in A$ there is a literal $K \in \lambda_\beta$ such that K subsumes $L\sigma$, then the extension of Θ on β with $B\sigma\pi$ is a purified hypertableau for Σ, too, where π is a purifying substitution for $(B \leftarrow A)\sigma$.

Example 1 (Baumgartner et al., 1996). Let Σ consist of the two clauses $Rfx \leftarrow \top$ and $Px \vee Qxy \leftarrow Rx$. Then the clausal tableau with the root labelled $\top$ and its only leaf labelled Rfx is a purified hypertableau for Σ and the clausal tableau depicted in in figure 1, too, since it is an extension with $Px \vee Qxy \leftarrow Rx$ where $\sigma = \{x \backslash fx'\}$ and $\pi = \{x' \backslash a\}$.

Fig. 1. Purified hypertableau for Rfx and $Px \vee Qxy \leftarrow Rx$

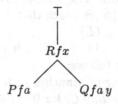

Note that the variables in the tableau do *not* get instantiated and that x and y are read universally quantified. This would be unsound without purification of the extending clause. Further, there are only positive literals in the tableau, since the negative literals are resolved away (Baumgartner et al., 1996, extend with the negative body literals too, but the branches are closed immediately).

Still there is a problem with the purification of input clauses. Consider example 1 with the additional clause $\bot \leftarrow Pf^3a$. Then it might be the case, that several wrong purifying substitutions are guessed for the second clause, until the branch is closed with the new clause.

This guessing of purifying substitutions can be avoided if we use unification of rigid literals in the tableau.

2.3 Rigid hypertableaux

The idea of my rigid hypertableau calculus is to view a clausal tableau as a set of (universally quantified) clauses where every branch corresponds to a literal selection function on a subset of these clauses (cf. Billon, 1996).

Now, instead of deriving new variants of the same clause in a branch, we allow to extend a hypertableau with copies of these branch clauses before a branch is extended with an input clause. Thereby, it can be determined how many clause variants are needed to apply the next input clause.

For the special case that the branch clauses are unit clauses (e.g. if the input clauses are horn-clauses), a universally quantified treatment of the branch literals is gained with all advantages exhibited by purified hypertableaux (cf. Baumgartner et al., 1996).

Definition 3 Branch clause. Let $\beta = \{N_0, \ldots, N_n\}$ be an open branch in a clausal tableau Θ. For $0 \leq i \leq n$ let $L_i = \lambda(N_i)$ and C_i denote the clause $\{\lambda(N') : N' \in \beta'$ is a neighbour of N_i for an open branch $\beta'\}$.

Then the *branch clauses* of β are the ordered clauses defined by $\Pi_\beta = \{\underline{L_i} \vee C_i : 0 \leq i \leq n\}$.

To make use of these branch clauses in an extension step quite similar to the *clash* of hyperresolution, I define a macro operation that extends a branch with some ordered clauses, such that one of the resulting branches contains all selected literals.

Definition 4 Multi-extension. The *ordered extension* of a branch β with an ordered clause $\underline{L} \vee C$ is a tuple (β', Θ') such that $\beta' \notin \Theta'$, $\{\beta'\} \cup \Theta'$ is an extension of β with $L \vee C$ and $\lambda_{\beta'} = \lambda_\beta \cup \{L\}$.

Now, a *multi-extension* of a branch β with a set of ordered clauses $\{\underline{L_1} \vee C_1, \ldots, \underline{L_n} \vee C_n\}$ is defined as follows:

Let $\beta_0, \ldots, \beta_n$ be a sequence of branches such that $\beta_0 = \beta$ and (β_i, Θ_i) is an ordered extension of β_{i-1} with $\underline{L_i} \vee C_i$ for $0 < i \leq n$.

Then the tuple $(\beta_n, \Theta_1 \cup \cdots \cup \Theta_n)$ is a *multi-extension* of β with $\underline{L_1} \vee C_1, \ldots, \underline{L_n} \vee C_n$.

The augmented branch of a multi-extension now is used in a *hyperextension* inference step to resolve the negative literals of an extending clause.

Definition 5 Hyperextension. Let β be an open branch in a clausal tableau Θ, $B \leftarrow A$ a clause and (β', Θ') a multi-extension of β with some clauses $\underline{L_1} \vee C_1, \ldots, \underline{L_n} \vee C_n$.

If σ is a most general unifier such that $\{L_1, \ldots, L_n\}\sigma \subseteq A\sigma \subseteq \lambda_{\beta'}\sigma$, then $(\Theta \setminus \{\beta\} \cup \Theta' \cup \Theta_{\beta'})\sigma$ is a hyperextension of Θ on β with $B \leftarrow A$ for some clauses $\underline{L_1} \vee C_1, \ldots, \underline{L_n} \vee C_n$, where $\Theta_{\beta'}$ is the extension of β' with $B \leftarrow A$.

Note that by the condition $\{L_1, \ldots, L_n\}\sigma \subseteq A\sigma$ it is assured that every selected literals of the multi-extension is actually needed for resolving with the extending clause, i.e. there is no multi-extension with clauses which are irrelevant for the hyperextension.

Example 2. Let β be the open branch in the clausal tableau Θ depicted in Figure 2.a) that contains Px'. The single branch clause of β is $\underline{Px'} \vee Qx'$. The tableau of Figure 2.b) is a multi-extension of β with a new branch clause copy $\underline{Px''} \vee Qx''$ where the branch with Px' and Px'' is selected.

Then the tableau in Figure 2.c) is a hyperextension of Θ on β with the clause $Ry \leftarrow Pa \wedge Pfx$ for a branch clause copy $\underline{Px''} \vee Qx''$.

Fig. 2. Hyperextension with $Ry \leftarrow Pa \wedge Pfx$

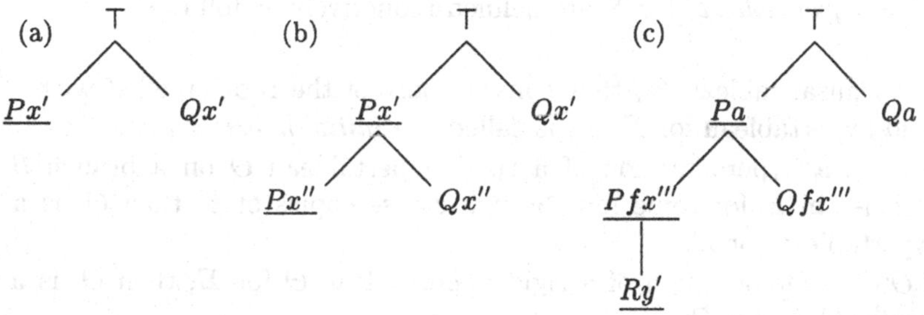

Some important observations can be made at this point:

- Obviously, it is never necessary to use a branch clause copy in a multi-extension where the selected literal is ground like in $\underline{Pa} \vee Qa$ (Figure 2.c), since this does not augment the set of branch literals.
- Previously derived clauses in the tableau may become instantiated. This restricts the local search space, but also leads to longer derivations. For unit branch clauses, it will be advantageous not to become instantiated. This is achieved by using a copy that is instantiated in a hyperextension step.
- In contrast to a hyperresolution clash, only selected literals of the branch clauses may be resolved upon. This is an essential point, as hyperresolution is *not* compatible with arbitrary literal selection: Consider the ordered positive clauses $\{\underline{A} \vee B, \underline{B} \vee C, \underline{C} \vee A\}$ with the negative clauses $\{\neg A \vee \neg B, \neg B \vee \neg C, \neg C \vee \neg A\}$. Then the positive hyperresolvents $\{B \vee C, C \vee A, A \vee B\}$ may be ordered like the original positive clauses and there will be no refutation.

– The branch literal selection enables us to perform a splitting for branch clauses: Since $\forall(A \vee B) \equiv (\forall A) \vee (\forall B)$, iff A and B are variable disjunct, we may restrict a branch clause to its subclause which contains the selected branch literal together with all sibling literals that share variables. Therefore, the literal Ry in the selected branch of Figure 2.c) can be used as unit clause and therefore read universally quantified.

Like in resolution calculi, an inference rule corresponding to factorization is needed. Otherwise, we may construct an infinite derivation for $Px \vee Py$ and $\neg Pz$ by always using a branch clause copy of $\underline{Px} \vee Py$ in a hyperextension with $\neg Pz$. Letz et al. (1994) describe the need for acyclic factorizations in clausal tableaux, which is achieved here by factorizing only between literals of *open* branches.

Definition 6 Factorization of a clausal tableau. Let Θ be a clausal tableau. A clausal tableau $\Theta'\sigma$ is a *factorization* of Θ, iff Θ' is an extension of Θ on an open branch β with $\perp$ and there is a node $N \in \beta$ and a sibling node N' of N with $N' \in \beta'$ for an open branch β', such that $\lambda(N)\sigma = \lambda(N')\sigma$ for a most general unifier σ.

Definition 7 Rigid hypertableaux. Let Σ be a finite set of input clauses. The *rigid hypertableaux* for Σ are defined inductively as follows:

1. The clausal tableau Θ_0 that consists only of the root labelled with $\top$ is a rigid hypertableau for Σ; Θ_0 is called the *initial hypertableau*.
2. If Θ' is a hyperextension of a rigid hypertableau Θ on a branch β with a clause in Σ for some new branch clause copies of β, then Θ' is a rigid hypertableau for Σ.
3. If Θ' is a factorization of a rigid hypertableau Θ for Σ, then Θ' is a rigid hypertableau for Σ.

A *hypertableau derivation* for a set of clauses Σ is a possibly infinite sequence $\hat{\Theta} = \Theta_0, \ldots, \Theta_{i-1}, \Theta_i, \ldots$ of hypertableaux for Σ such that Θ_0 is the initial tableau and for every $i > 0$ holds: Θ_i has been derived from Θ_{i-1}.

A hypertableau derivation is called a *hypertableau refutation* iff it contains a closed tableau.

Soundness of rigid hypertableaux is shown by techniques used also for other clausal tableau calculi (e.g. Baumgartner, 1996, for theory model elimination). The interesting point in our case is to prove that a multi-extension with branch clause copies does not destroy the satisfiability of a hypertableau with an interpretation for the input clause set.

Completeness is a more difficult matter, since I additionally state the confluence of the hypertableau calculus, i.e. *any* hypertableau derivation must lead to a refutation if the input clause set is unsatisfiable and inference steps have been applied in a fair way.

The basic idea of the completeness proof is to assign an interpretation to every open branch in a hypertableau and to prove that this interpretation approximates a model of a satisfiable input clause set, if the branch is never closed and every possible inference is eventually applied to it.

The question, how this model construction exactly looks like, is not yet completely answered.

3 An implementation

In this section, I will describe the basics of my automated theorem prover *Hyper, hyper!* which implements the hypertableau calculus developed in the previous sections. I will present the main proof procedure and address the *fairness* problem. Some experimental results are given.

3.1 Proof procedure

The representation I have chosen for a clausal tableau restricts the hypertableaux derivation to a left-most depth-first computation, i.e. always the left-most open branch is selected. Therefore, it suffices to store only one branch with its branch clauses.

The main prover loop is called initially with one initial branch. There are three cases that have to be distinguished:

1. The closed tableau has been computed and the clause set has been refuted. The proof procedure is terminated successfully.
2. The selected branch has been closed. Then remove the last literal of the selected branch and try to prove the tableau with the next branch selected after removing unused tableau clauses (*tableau condensation*, cf. Oppacher and Suen, 1988).
3. Neither the tableau nor the selected branch has been closed. Then derive the next hypertableau by hyperextension that passes fairness and redundancy checks and prove this. If there is no next hypertableau, the input clauses are satisfiable and the proof procedure can be aborted.

Note that by virtue of proof-confluence it is never necessary to take back a hypertableau that has been derived in step 3 and to try another inference at this point.

3.2 Fairness and redundancy

Fairness is a central and difficult issue for an efficient proof procedure of logical calculi. This question has not yet been theoretically solved for rigid hypertableaux.

The experimental redundancy check mentioned in the proof procedure works as follows: A branch is called *irregular* for rigid hypertableaux iff there is an ancestor literal K of a branch literal L that *rigidly subsumes* L, i.e. there is a substitution σ such that $K\varphi\sigma = L\varphi$ where φ is a freezing substitution for the variables in L, and there is no sibling literal $K' \in \beta'$ of K such that $\beta'\varphi\sigma$ is irregular by itself. Then every hypertableaux containing an irregular branch can be rejected for further derivation.

Example 3. Consider the selected branch β in Figure 3.a) with $\lambda_\beta = \{Qa, Px\}$. Then an extension on β with a literal Py would yield an irregular branch β' with $\lambda'_\beta = \{Qa, Px, Py\}$, since $Px\varphi\sigma = Py\varphi$ for $\varphi = \{y/c_y\}$ and $\sigma = \{x/c_y\}$, while the branch containing Qx does *not* become irregular by applying the substitutions $\varphi\sigma$.

On the other hand, an extension on β with Pa or with Pfx is not irregular, since in the first case (Figure 3.b), applying the most general unifier $\sigma = \{x/a\}$ to the tableau would yield an irregular branch α with $\lambda_\alpha = \{Qa, Qa\}$, and in the second case (Figure 3.c) there is no most general unifier σ such that $Px\varphi\sigma = Pfx\varphi$ for the freezing substitution $\varphi = \{x/c_x\}$.

Fig. 3. Irregularity based upon rigid literal subsumption

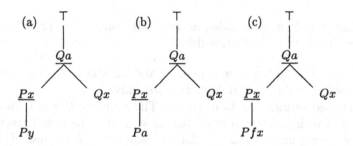

The assumptions I have used for my implementation is that for a given maximal term depth there are only finitely many literals such that a branch is not irregular in terms of the described redundancy check and that this check preserves completeness of rigid hypertableaux.

Then, by iterating the allowable term depth of branch literals, it is guaranteed that every possible inference step is eventually applied in a fix term depth and the *fairness* requirements would be fulfilled.

Note that for fairness, it is not needed to enumerate clause copies as it is necessary in other tableau calculi, since the clause copies that are needed for a hyperextension with an input clause are generated on the fly. E.g. in the free variable tableau calculus (Fitting, 1990), it would be necessary for the selected branch depicted in Figure 2.a) to become extended with arbitrarily many copies $Px' \vee Qx', Px'' \vee Qx'', \ldots$ of the input clause $Px \vee Qx$. This is not the case for rigid hypertableaux.

Therefore, it is promising that the fairness matter may be answered in a more efficient and reasonable way for rigid hypertableaux as it is the case for other proof-confluent tableau calculi with exception of the disconnection calculus by Billon (1996).

3.3 Experimental results

I have tested my hypertableaux therorem prover which is written in ECLiPSe Prolog with the 2759 problems of the TPTP-library (Sutcliffe et al., 1994) on a SPARC 10 restricting the runtime to 90 seconds. In this time, 513 problems have been solved, where for 303 problems runtime has been below 1 second and for 114 problems below 10 seconds.

In contrast to other automated theorem provers, *Hyper, hyper!* detected 29 from the 59 satisfiable problems and never failed because of memory consumption. The longest proof for a logical puzzle PUZ019-1 needed 482 inferences; for this problem, the hyperresolution prover *Otter* (McCune, 1990) could not find a refutation since it ran out of memory.

Table 1. Some runtime comparisons with *Otter*

Problem	Hyper, hyper!		Otter	
	Seconds	Length	Seconds	Length
GEO002-1	20.10	37	*out of time*	
GRP001-1	0.43	9	0.11	4
MSC006-1	0.14	15	1.86	11
MSC007-1.005	2.34	261	0.53	142
PUZ019-1	78.08	482	*out of mem.*	
SYN036-1	23.79	77	*out of time*	
SYN037-1	35.17	279	9.77	83

4   Conclusions

I have presented a new clausal tableau calculus that improves the purified hypertableaux of Baumgartner et al. (1996) by using full unification and avoiding unguided ground instantiation of input clauses.

This rigid hypertableau calculus uses arbitrary clause literal selection in an admissible way and thereby refines hyperresolution which is incompatible with unrestricted literal selection. The structure of clausal tableaux is exploited by a redundancy check based upon literal subsumption, a compact storage of derivations and by the possibility of clause splitting.

Like the disconnection method of Billon (1996) this clausal tableau calculus is proof-confluent as sketched in section 2, but uses hyperresolution inference steps instead of binary resolution in a clausal tableau setting.

I have addressed the difficult fairness problem of proof-confluent tableau calculi in section 3 and offered a possible solution by term-depth iterating together with a redundancy check based upon rigid literal subsumption.

With this fairness criterion a proof procedure for rigid hypertableaux has been implemented and evaluated with the TPTP problem library (Sutcliffe et al., 1994). Although the implementation is non-optimized Prolog code, there are encouraging experimental results, especially concerning satisfiability detection and memory consumption.

Remaining task is to finish the model construction approach mentioned in section 2 and to establish theoretically the fairness criterion experimentally used in my implementation.

References

P. Baumgartner. *Theory Reasoning in Connection Calculi and the Linearizing Completion Approach.* PhD thesis, Universität Koblenz-Landau, 1996.

P. Baumgartner, U. Furbach, and I. Niemelä. Hyper Tableaux. In *Proc. JELIA '96*, volume 1126 of *LNAI.* Springer, 1996.

J.-P. Billon. The Disconnection Method. In P. Moscato, U. Moscato, D. Mundici, and M. Ornaghi, editors, *Proc. TABLEAUX '96*, volume 1071 of *LNAI.* Springer, 1996.

C. Chang and R. Lee. *Symbolic Logic and Mechanical Theorem Proving.* Academic Press, 1973.

M. Fitting. *First-Order Logic and Automated Theorem Proving.* Springer-Verlag, 1990.

S.-J. Lee and D. Plaisted. Eliminating Duplicates with the Hyper-Linking Strategy. *Journal of Automated Reasoning*, 9:25–42, 1992.

R. Letz, K. Mayr, and C. Goller. Controlled Integrations of the Cut Rule into Connection Tableau Calculi. *Journal of Automated Reasoning*, 13, 1994.

W. McCune. Otter 2.0 Users Guide. Technical Report ANL-90/9, Argonne National Laboratory, 1990.

F. Oppacher and E. Suen. HARP: A Tableau-Based Theorem Prover. *Journal of Automated Reasoning*, 4:69–100, 1988.

J. A. Robinson. Automated deduction with hyper-resolution. *Internat. J. Comput. Math.*, 1:227–234, 1965.

J. R. Slagle. Automatic theorem proving with renamable and semantic resolution. *J. ACM*, 17(3):535–542, 1967.

G. Sutcliffe, C. Suttner, and T. Yemenis. The TPTP problem library. In A. Bundy, editor, *Proc. CADE-12*, volume 814 of *LNAI.* Springer, 1994.

Minimal Model Generation Based on E-hyper Tableaux

Wenjin Lu*

Department of Computer Science
University of Koblenz-Landau
Rheinau 1, D-56075 Koblenz, Germany
lue@informatik.uni-koblenz.de

Abstract. Minimal model generation has received great attention as people have deeper and deeper understanding in the semantics of the logic programming, deductive database, non monotonic reasoning and the relationships among them. But most proposed minimal model generation procedures in the literature are inappropriate in the sense that while generating minimal model, they also generate non-minimal models. This means that an explicit minimization has to be employed to obtain minimal models. This may be a great factor of inefficiency. In this paper we develop an approach to generate the minimal models, without explicit minimization process, based on E-hyper tableau which is a variant of hyper tableaux. The soundness and completeness of the procedure is shonw.

1 Introduction

Minimal model generation has received great attention as people have deeper and deeper understanding in the semantics of the logic programming, deductive database, non monotonic reasoning and the relationships among them. Every proposed semantics seems in some extent to be dependent on the minimal models, such as GCWA[10] for disjunctive logic program, static semantics[15] and D-WFS[6] for disjunctive normal logic program.

Several minimal model reasoning approaches have been proposed in the literature [13,11,9,8,14,1]. Among them the tableaux method seems to offer a promising basis for minimal model reasoning[12]. But as a minimal model generation procedure, most of them seem to be inappropriate in that while generating minimal model, they also generate non-minimal models. This means that an explicit minimization process has to be employed to obtain minimal model. It can be a great factor of inefficiency. This deficiency lead us to consider new minimal model generation procedures. In this paper we describe such a method based on E-hyper tableau which is a variant of hyper tableaux introduced in [3]. It generates all minimal models without explicit minimization process. This procedure is sound and complete in the sense that when the procedure terminates,

---

* Financially supported by Graduate Scholarship of University Koblenz-Landau

the generated E-hyper tableau is such that each open branch in it corresponds to a minimal model and each minimal model is represented by a unique open branch.

Hyper tableau[3] is a variant of clause normal form tableaux. It combines the idea from hyper resolution and analytic tableaux. Since the forward-chaining way of proving theorems, as it is employed by hyper tableaux, can be seen as a model generation procedure, it is very obvious to relate hyper-tableaux calculus to work done in semantics of disjunctive logic program and in disjunctive deductive database. Indeed, in [3] some basic relationships between hyper tableaux and fixpoint iteration techniques from work done in semantics of disjunctive logic program have been established. But directly taking it as a minimal model generation procedure would share the same deficiency, that is, too many redundant models are generated and an explicit minimization process has to be employed to get minimal models.

The key problem in generating minimal models of clause theories based on tableaux method is to deal with the positive literals in clause. In hyper tableau, there is almost no restriction on the extending step which results in great redundancy. To overcome this problem, we introduce the concept of E-hyper tableau. The basic idea comes from a fixpoint characterization of minimal model. In hyper tableau language, it says if an open branch corresponds to a minimal model and the branch contains more than one head atoms of one extending clause, then there is another open branch which corresponds to the same minimal model. Based on this characterization in each extending step, instead of attaching just one atom to an extending node, we attach an atom with related "evidence" which consists of other head atoms in the current extending clause. The evidence is used to test if a branch contains more than one head atom from one extending clause. By closing these branches, we can get a sound hyper tableau calculus about minimal model. Unfortunately, it is not complete. To get a sound and complete minimal model generation procedure, a committing procedure is developed. The whole minimal model generation procedure consists of a series of extending and committing.

The rest of the paper is organised as follows. In section 2 we give definitions and background material related to disjunctive logic programming and hyper tableau. In section 3 we present a fixpoint characterization of minimal models, which provides a basis for our minimal model generation procedure. Section 4 defines E-hyper tableau, some properties about E-hyper tableau are also discussed therein. Minimal model generation procedure based on E-hyper tableau and its soundness and completeness are given in section 5. Section 6 concludes this paper and discuss some further work.

2 Preliminaries

In what follows, we assume that the reader is familiar with the basic concepts of first-order logic. Given a first order language, a disjunctive logic program P consists of logical clauses of the form

$$A_1 \vee ... \vee A_n \leftarrow B_1 \wedge ... \wedge B_m$$

where A_i $(1 \leq i \leq n)$ and B_j $(1 \leq j \leq m)$ are atoms in the language. A clause is called a fact if $m = 0$. In this paper we only consider those program in the language without function symbol. Each clause of disjunctive logic program represents the following first order formula:

$$A_1 \vee ... \vee A_n \vee \neg B_1 \vee ... \vee \neg B_m$$

If $n = 1$ for all clauses in P, then P is called a *Horn Program*.

Definition 1. Given a disjunctive logic program P, the Herbrand base of P, HB_P, is the set of all ground atoms that can be formed using the predicate symbols and constants in the first order language. A *Herbrand interpretation* is any subset of HB_P. A Herbrand interpretation is called a Herbrand model of P if every clause in P is true in the interpretation. A model M is called minimal if no proper subset of M is a model of P.

A literal tree T is a pair (t, λ) consisting of a finite, ordered tree t and a labelling function λ that assigns a literal to every non-root node of t. A branch of T is a path from root to a leaf. Let b be a branch in T, we denote the set of positive literals by $lit(b)$, Note that $lit(b)$ can be regarded as an Herbrand interpretation. A hyper tableau[3] for a disjunctive logic program P is a special literal tree in which branches can be marked as open or closed. In our case it is inductively defined as follows.

Definition 2. Let P be a disjunctive logic program and f be a selection function.

- Initialization: A one node tree is a basic hyper tableau of P, whose unique branch is marked as "open".
- Extending: Let T be an hyper tableau for P with some open branches.
  - if $f(T) = b$ with leaf node N and
  - $C = A_1 \vee ... \vee A_n \leftarrow B_1 \wedge ... \wedge B_m$ is a clause from P such that $B_1 \wedge ... \wedge B_m$ is true but $A_1 \vee ... \vee A_n$ is false in $lit(b)$.

  Then the literal tree T' is a hyper tableau for P, where T' is obtained from T by attaching $m + n$ child nodes $M_1, ... M_n, N_1, ..., N_m$ to b with respective labels

$$A_1, .., A_n, \neg B_1, ..., \neg B_m$$

Marking every new branch $(b, M_1), ... (b, M_m)$ with positive leaf as "open" and Marking every new branch $(b, N_1), ... (b, N_n)$ with negative leaf as "closed"

Nodes $M_1, ... M_n, N_1, ..., N_m$ are also called successor sequence of a node N in T'.

Note that we depart from the original definition of hyper tableau in[3], in that we require the extending clause not to be redundant because we are only interested in minimal models. It is clear that this requirement has no effect on minimal model of disjunctive logic program. We say a hyper tableau T is finished if for any open branch in T no extending step can be carried out. The following proposition is from [9].

Proposition 3. *Let P be a disjunctive logic program, T be a finished hyper tableau for P. Then for every minimal model M of P there is an open branch b in T such that $M = lit(b)$.*

The open branches corresponding to minimal models are called minimal branches. In the following discussion we always assume that the given program is instantiated, that is, all caluses in the progrm are ground.

3 A Characterization of Minimal Models

In this section, we present a characterization of minimal model which provides the basis for our approach to minimal model generation. The characterization is based on the following program transformation.

Definition 4. Given a disjunctive logic program P, let I be an interpretation of P and $C = A_1 \lor ... \lor A_n \leftarrow B_1 \land ... \land B_m$. Then the Horn transformation of C wrt I, denoted by $Horn(C, I)$, is the set of Horn clauses.

$$Horn(C, I) = \begin{cases} \emptyset: & \text{if } B_1 \land ... \land B_m \text{ is false} \\ \{A \leftarrow B_1 \land ... \land B_m \mid A \in I \cap \{A_1, ..., A_n\}\}: & \text{otherwise} \end{cases}$$

The Horn transformation of P wrt I, denoted by $Horn(P, I)$, is the set of Horn programs defined by

$$Horn(P, I) = \{P' \mid P' \subseteq \bigcup_{C \in P} Horn(C, I) \quad \text{and} \quad |P' \cap Horn(C, I)| = 1$$
$$\text{for all} \quad C \in P, Horn(C, I) \neq \emptyset\}$$

Let P be an Horn logic program and T_P be the immediate consequence operator of P. Then it is well known that T_P is monotonic and has the least fixpont $T_P \uparrow \omega$ which is the smallest model of P [16].

Lemma 5. *For any interpretation I and any $P' \in Horn(P, I)$, $T_{P'} \uparrow \omega \subseteq I$.*

Proof. It follows from the fact that the head of any clause in P' is in I.

The following is the least fixpoint characterization of minimal model of disjunctive logic program.

Theorem 6. *Let M be a model of disjunctive logic program P, then M is a minimal model of P iff for any $P' \in Horn(P, M)$, $M = T_{P'} \uparrow \omega$.*

Below we translate this characterization of minimal model into hyper tableau language, to provides a basis for our minimal model generation procedure.

Definition 7. Let P be a disjunctive logic program and T be a hyper tableau for P. For a given open branch b of T, the branch transformation of P w.r.t. b, denoted by $Branch(P, b)$, is a disjunctive program defined as follows. For any $C = A_1 \vee ... \vee A_n \leftarrow B_1 \wedge ... \wedge B_m \in P$,

- If in some extending step of T, a prefix b' of b is selected as the extended branch with the extending clause C and $b' \circ A_i$ is a prefix of b, then $A_i \leftarrow B_1 \wedge ... \wedge B_m \in Branch(P, b)$. Otherwise
- $C \in Branch(P, b)$

Nothing else is in $Branch(P, b)$.

Lemma 8. *Let P be a disjunctive logic program and T be a finished hyper tableau for P and let b be a open branch in T. If in some extending step of T, a prefix b' of b is selected as the extended branch with the extending clause*

$$C = A_1 \vee ... \vee A_n \leftarrow B_1 \wedge ... \wedge B_m$$

and b contains more than one head atom of C, say, $A_1, ..., A_k$ and b first goes through node N_1 labelled with A_1. Then there exist $k - 1$ branches $b_2, ..., b_k$ in T which go through nodes $N_2, ..., N_k$ (resp.) such that $lit(b_i) \subseteq lit(b)$ $(i = 2, ..., k)$, where $N_2, ..., N_k$ are brother nodes of N_1 and are labelled with $A_2, ..., A_k$, respectively, in T.

Proof. For N_i $(2 \leq i \leq k)$ let $P_{N_i} = Branch(P, b' \circ A_i)$. Then the subtree T_{N_i} obtained from T by cutting all branches not going through node N_i is a hyper tableau for P_{N_i}. $lit(b)$ is a model of P_{N_i} and therefore it contains a minimal model of P_{N_i} which should correspond to a minimal branch b_i in T_{N_i} by Proposition 3. This means $lit(b_i) \subseteq lit(b)$.

Theorem 9. *In addition to the assumption of Lemma 8, if b is a minimal branch of T, then $lit(b) = lit(b_i)$ $(i = 1, ..., k)$.*

Proof. It follows from Lemma 8 and the fact that every open branch is a model of P.

4 E-hyper Tableaux

In this section, we introduce E-hyper tableau, which is a variant of hyper tableau introduced in [3]. The purpose is to make it easy to test if a branch contains more than one head atom from same extending clause. We do it in a natural way: at extending step, instead of attaching a single head atom to the extended branch we attach the head atom with an "evidence" which consists of the rest of head atoms. To distinguish this tableau from hyper tableau we call it E-hyper tableau.

Definition 10. Let P be a disjunctive logic program and let C be a clause of the form

$$A_1 \vee ... \vee A_i \vee ... \vee A_n \leftarrow B_1 \wedge ... \wedge B_m$$

in P. Then an evidential head of C is a triple

$$(A, E^-, E^+)$$

where $A \in \{A_1, ..., A_n\}$ is called evidenced atom, $E^- \subset \{A_1, ..., A_n\}$, $E^+ \subseteq \{A_1, ..., A_n\}$ and satisfy $E^- \cap E^+ = \emptyset$, $E^- \cup E^+ = \{A_1, ..., A_n\}$, $A \notin E^-$.

Especially, the evidential head of the form

$$(A_i, \{A_1, ... A_{i-1}, A_{i+1}, ... A_n\}, \{A_i\})$$

$(i = 1, 2, ..., n)$ is called a initial evidential head of C.

Definition 11. A evidential tree T is a pair (t, λ) consisting of a finite, ordered tree t and a labelling function λ that assigns an evidential atom or a negative literal to every non-root node of t. A branch of T is a path $N_0, ..., N_n$ $(n \geq 0)$ from root N_0 to leaf N_n in t and each node N_i is with respective label. Sometimes for convenience we also think a branch as a set of labels in it. Given branch $b = N_0, ..., N_n$, the branch literals $lit(b)$ is defined as below:

$$lit(b) = \bigcup_{(A, E^-, E^+) \in b} \{A\}$$

For a given branch b, when we regard b as an Herbrand interpretation we mean that the interpretation consists of the atoms in $lit(b)$. When we say a formula F is true(false) in b we always means that F is true(false) in the Herbrand interpretation determined by $lit(b)$.

A branch in T can be marked as open, closed or pseudo-closed. T is called closed if each branch of T is marked as closed or pseudo-closed, otherwise it is open. A selection function is a total function which maps an open evidential tree to one of its open branches. If $f(T) = b$ we also say b is selected by f.

Let P be a disjunctive logic program, then the E-hyper tableau for P is a special evidential tree which is defined inductively as follows.

Definition 12. Let P be a disjunctive logic program and f be a selection function.

Initialization: A one node evidential tree is a basic E-hyper tableau of P, whose unique branch is marked as "open".

Extending and Marking: Let T be an open hyper tableau for P. If $f(T) = b$ with leaf node N and $C = A_1 \vee ... \vee A_n \leftarrow B_1 \wedge ... \wedge B_m$ is a clause from P such that $B_1 \wedge ... \wedge B_m$ is true but $A_1 \vee ... \vee A_n$ is false in $lit(b)$. Then the evidential tree T' is hyper tableau for P, where T' is obtained from T as follows:

- Extending: attaching n successor nodes $N_1, ... N_n$ with n initial evidential head $(A_i, \{A_1, ..., A_{i-1}, ... A_{i+1}, A_n\}, \{A_i\})$ $(i = 1, ..., n)$ of C, respectively, to N.

– Marking: for each new branch $b \circ N_i$, if there exists a label $(A, E^-, E^+) \in b$ such that $A_i \in E^-$, then marking this new branch as "pseudo-closed", otherwise "open"

Committing: Let T be a E-hyper tabeleau. Let $b_1 = bN_1 b_1' N_2$ and $b_2 = bN_3 b_2' N_4$ be two pseudo-closed branches in T and N_i is labelled with (A_i, E_i^-, E_i^+) ($i = 1, 2, 3, 4$), $A_2 = A_3$ and for any label (A, E^-, E^+) in b_1' $A_2 \notin E^-$. Then the evidential tree T' is a E-hyper Tableau for P, where T' is obtained from T as follows:

– Marking b_1 closed and
– Labelling node N_3 with $(A_3, E_3'^-, E_3'^+)$, where $E_3'^- = E_3^- \setminus E_1^+$ and $E_3'^+ = E_3^+ \cup E_1^+$. If there exists a label $(A, E^-, E^+) \in b$ such that $A_4 \in E^-$, then marking b_2 pseudo-closed, otherwise open.

In the above definition, at extending step b is called extended branch of T and C extending clause, we say C is applicable to b in this context and at committing step b_1 is said to be committed to b_2 and we say b_1 is committable to b_2.

Example 13. Given program $P = \{A \vee B, \quad B \vee C \leftarrow A, \quad A \leftarrow B, \quad C \vee D \leftarrow A \wedge B\}$.

A E-hyper tableau for P without involving any committing step is shown in Fig. 1. In Fig. 1 there are two pseudo-closed branches $b_1 = N_1 N_2$ and $b_2 = N_3 N_4$(marked with $\heartsuit$), where N_i ($i = 1, 2, 3, 4$) is labelled with $(A, \{B\}, \{A\})$, $(B, \{C\}, \{B\})$, $(B, \{A\}, \{B\})$ and $(A, \emptyset, \{A\})$, respectively. Then b_1 is committable to b_2. After committing we get Fig. 2 in which b_1 is closed(marked with $\spadesuit$) and node N_3 is relabelled with $(B, \emptyset, \{B, A\})$ and b_2 is remarked as open.

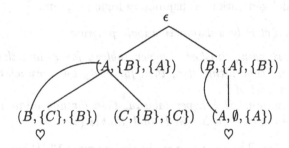

Fig. 1. A E-hyper tableau for P without involving any commtting step

Definition 14. A branch in a E-hyper tableau is called extending finished iff either b is marked "closed" or "pseudo-closed" or no clause in P is applicable to b. A E-hyper tableau T is called extending finished iff all branches in T are extending finished. If T is extending finished and has no commitable branch, then T is called finished.

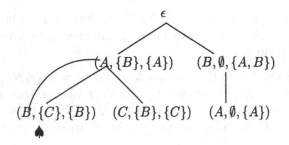

Fig. 2. The E-hyper tableau for P after committing b_1 to b_2

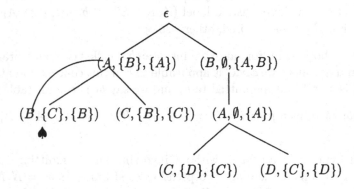

Fig. 3. The E-hyper tableau for P after extending b_2 with clause $C \vee D \leftarrow A \wedge B$

The following lemma states some basic properties of E-hyper tableau for the minimal model generation of disjunctive logic program.

Lemma 15. *Let P be a disjunctive logic program.*

1. *If T is extending finished E-hyper tableau for P and the generation of T involves no committing step, then for every open branch b in T, $lit(b)$ is a minimal model of P.*
2. *If T be the finished E-hyper tableau, then for any minimal model M of P, there is an open branch b in T such that $lit(b) = M$.*

Example 16. Let P be the program in the example 13. P has two minimal models: $M_1 = \{A, \quad C\}$ and $M_2 = \{A, \quad B, \quad D\}$.

Fig. 1 is a extending finished E-Hyper tableau for P without involving any committing step. Its unique open branch $b = (A, \{B\}, \{A\}) \circ (C, \{B\}, \{C\})$ corresponds to a minimal model M_1 of P.

Fig. 3 is a finished E-hyper tableau for P in which there are three open branches:

$b_1 = (A, \{B\}, \{A\}) \circ (C, \{B\}, \{C\})$,
$b_2 = (B, \emptyset, \{A, B\}) \circ (A, \emptyset, \{A\}) \circ (C, \{D\}, \{C\}$,
$b_3 = (B, \emptyset, \{A, B\}) \circ (A, \emptyset, \{A\}) \circ (D, \{C\}, \{D\})$.

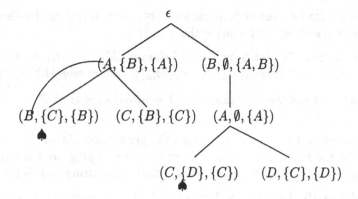

Fig. 4. A finished E-hyper tableau generated by the minimal model generation procedure

But only b_1 and b_3 correspond to minimal models M_1 and M_2, respectively. b_2 corresponds to no minimal model of P because $lit(b_1) \subset lit(b_2)$.

5 Minimal Model Generation

The example in the last section indicates that E-hyper tableau can not be directly used as a minimal model generation procedure because it also generates non minimal model while generating all minimal models. For a given disjunctive logic program P, by lemma 15, all open branches in the E-hyper tableau for P without involving any committing step are minimal models. This means the non-minimal models in a E-hyper tableau are introduced by committing. To obtain a sound and complete minimal model generation procedure we have to put some restriction on the application of committing.

Let P be a disjunctive logic program, T be E-hyper tableau and N be a node, then $branch(N)$ denotes the set of all open branches through N in T.

Lemma 17. *Let P be a disjunctive logic program and T be a E-hyper tableau for P. Let N be a node with label (A_N, E_N^-, E_N^+) and N' a brother of N with label $(A_{N'}, E_{N'}^-, E_{N'}^+)$ and $A_{N'} \in E_N^-$. Then for any $b' \in branch(N')$ there is no $b \in branch(N)$ such that $lit(b') \subseteq lit(b)$*

Proof. Notice that $A_{N'} \in lit(b')$. If $lit(b') \subseteq lit(b)$, then $A_{N'} \in lit(b)$ but $A_{N'} \in E_N^-$. It contradicts that b is an open branch.

In other words, if $lit(b') \subseteq lit(b)$, then the evidenced head $A_{N'}$ must occur in E_N^+. But notice that, in the E-hyper tableau T for P without involving any committing step all nodes are labelled with initial evidential head in which E^+ only contains the evidenced head. Only committing can change E^- and E^+. This suggests that we can avoid the generation of non-minimal model by carefully using committing. Fortunately, the idea presented in [17] can be also used in our case. It is based on the following theorem [17].

Theorem 18. *[17] Let S be a set of clauses, M_1, ..., M_m be minimal models of S. Let $S' = S \cup \{neg(M_1), ..., neg(M_m)\}$, where $neg(M_i) = \bigvee_{A \in M_i} \neg A$ ($i = 1, ..., m$). Then S' has the same set of minimal models as S except for the M_i ($i = 1, ..., m$).*

As a result it is possible to restrict the generation of non minimal branch by retaining the found minimal models and adding to program the negation clause corresponding to each of these models when committing step is used.

Definition 19. Let P be a disjunctive logic program and T be an extending finished-hyper tableau for P. For any node N of T. we denote T_N the subtree with root N. T_N is called ripe iff there is no branch is committable in T_N.

Intuitively, the subtree T_N is ripe if as a part of whole E-hyper tableau of P, it is "local" finished in the sense that no extending step and committing step can be carried out in T_N.

Definition 20. (Minimal Model Generation Procedure) Let P be a disjunctive logic program, then the minimal model generation procedure for P is defined as follows.

1. Initialize E-hyper tableau T for P.
2. Extend T until T is extending finished.
3. If there are pseudo-closed branches $b_1 = bN_1 b'_1 N_2$ and $b_2 = bN_3 b'_2 N_4$ and N_i is labelled with (A_i, E_i^-, E_i^+) ($i = 1, 2, 3, 4$), $A_2 = A_3$ and T_{N_1} is ripe, then for each $b \in branch(N_1)$, add $neg(lit(b))$ to P, then committing b_1 to b_2, goto 2. If no branch is committable then stop.

Note 21. To prevent the found minimal model M from being closed by the $neg(M)$, in the step 2 some special mark have to be given to the open branch corresponding to M. But this is not explicitly stated in the definition for simplicity.

Example 22. Considering the program P in example 13. Fig. 1 is a extending finished E-hyper tableau. b_1 and b_2 are two pseudo-closed branches. By the step 3, before committing b_1 to b_2, clause $\leftarrow A \wedge C$ is added to P. Then Fig. 3 can be further extended with this clause, which results in the E-hyper tableau in Fig. 4. This E-hyper tableau is finished. The two open branches just correspond to the two minimal models of P.

Based on the observations presented at the beginning of this section, we can conclude that the procedure is sound and complete in generating the minimal models of disjunctive logic program, that is,

Theorem 23. (Soundness and Completeness) *Let P be a disjunctive logic program and T be a finished E-hyper tableau for P generated by the minimal model generation procedure. Then M is a minimal model of P iff there is open branch b in T such that $M = lit(b)$.*

6   Conclusion and Further Work

We conclude this paper by comparing the minimal model generation procedure reported here with related works and discuss some further topics related to this paper.

The minimal model generation procedure presented here is based on E-hyper tableau which is a variant of hyper tableau. The theorem 6 provides a basis of our approach. This procedure consists of three basic operators: initialization, extending and restricted committing and without explicit minimalization process. The minimalization process is implicitly done during the building of the E-hyper tableau by putting a restrication on the committing procedure.

There are other tableau methods for minimal model generation reported in literature. But most of them need an explicit minimalization process, which seems to cost too much. However, after writing this paper, we find the idea for minimal model generation in [7] is very similar to us. We both are using "complement splitting" as a means to reduce the generation of non-minimal model. But the complement splitting used in [7] could be regard as a "partial complement splitting" because for a disjunction of the form $A_1 \vee A_2 \vee ... \vee A_n$, the complement splitting in [7] will produce $A_1 \wedge \neg A_2 \wedge ... \wedge \neg A_n$, $A_2 \wedge \neg A_3 \wedge ... \wedge A_n$, ..., A_n. In this sense, our complement splitting could be regarded as a "complete complement splitting" because for $A_1 \vee A_2 \vee ... \vee A_n$ we produce n evidenced heads, semantically, they are equivalent to the n formulas: $A_1 \wedge \neg A_2 \wedge ... \wedge \neg A_n$, ..., $A_n \wedge \neg A_2 \wedge ... \wedge \neg A_{n-1}$. As a result, we do not generate minimal models one by one and no special search order is needed. In addition, we augment P with the negation of minimal model "by need", for example, if no committing step is used, then no negation of minimal model need to be added to P.

We have implemented a prototype for the minimal model generation procedure reported here. The initial test result shows that in most cases it works well. A deficiency in our method is that we have to keep the pseudo-closed branches for committing. To overcome this problem we are working out a new procedure for minimal model generation based on hyper tableau refined with factoization and groundness test[12]. It can be implemented in polynomial space and with less groundness tests than in the procedure in[12] Further, we plan to compare our procedure with other related methods in more detail. We also plan to use the basic method reported in this paper to compute semantics of disjunctive logic porgrams and disscuss its aplication in real-world problems such as diagonosis[4,5] and database updates [2].

Acknowledgements

The author would like to thank all the members of Artificial Intelligence Research Group at the University Koblenz.Landau for their support and useful comments. Special thanks to Prof. U.Furbach for his advice and encouragement.

References

1. Chandrabose Aravindan. An abductive framework for negation in disjunctive logic programming. In J. J. Alferes, L. M. Pereira and E. Orlowska, editors, Proceednigs of Joint European workshop on Logics in AI, Lecture Notes in Artificial Intelligence 1126, pages 252-267, Springer-Verlag, 1996.
2. Chandrabose Aravindan and Peter Baumgarter. A rational and effecient algorithm for view deletion in database. Technical Report RR-10-97,Fachbericht Informatik, Universität Koblenz-Landa, Germany.
3. P. Baumgartner and U. Furbach and I. Niemelä. Hyper Tableaux. In Proc. JELIA 96, number 1129 in LNAI. European Workshop on Logic in AI, Springer, 1996.
4. P. Baumgartner, Peter Fröhlich, U. Furbach and Wofgang Nejdel. Semantically Guided Theorem Proving for Diagnosis Application. In Proc. of IJCAI'97. IJCAI. 1997. To appear.
5. P. Baumgartner, Peter Fröhlich, U. Furbach and Wofgang Nejdel. Tableaux for Diagnosis Application. In Tableaux '97, LNAI. Springer, 1997. To appear.
6. S. Brass and J. Dix. A Disjunctive Semantics Based on Bottom-Up Evaluation and Unfolding. Proceedings of the 13th World Computer Congress '94, IFIP, GI-Workshop W2 (Disjunctive Logic Programs and Disjunctive Databases). 1994
7. Bry, F. and Yahya, A. Minimal Model Generation with Positive Unit Hyper-Resolution Tableaux Proceedings of the Fifth Workshop on Theorem Proving with Analytic Tableaux and Related Methods 1996, 143–159. Springer-Verlag.
8. M.L. Ginsberg. A Circumscriptive Theorem Prover. Artificial intelligence, 39:209-230, 1989.
9. K. Inoue and M. Koshimura and R. Hasegawa. Embedding Negation as Failure into a Model Generation Theorem Prover. The 11th International Conference on Automated Deduction, 400–415, Saratoga Springs, NY, USA, June 1992, LNAI 607.
10. J. Minker. On indefinite databases and the closed world assumption. In Lecture Notes in Computer Science 138, pages 292-308, Springer-Verlag, 1982.
11. A. Nerode, R.T. Ng and V.S. Subrahmanina. Computing circumscriptive databases: I. theory and algorithms. Information and Computation, 116:58-80, 1995.
12. I. Niemelä. A Tableau Calculus for Minimal Model Reasoning. Proceedings of the Fifth Workshop on Theorem Proving with Analytic Tableaux and Related Methods, 278–294, Springer-Verlag, May 1996.
13. N. Olivetti. A tableaux and sequent calculus for minimal modelentailment. Journal of Automated Reasoning, 9:99-139, 1992.
14. T. C. Przymusinski. An Algorithm to Compute Circumscription. Artificial intelligence, 38: 49-73, 1989.
15. T.C. Przymusinski. Static Semantics for Normal and Disjunctive Logic Programs. Annals of Mathematics and Artificial Intelligence, Special Issue on Disjunctive Programs, 1995.
16. J. W. Lloyd. *Foundations of Logic Programming*, Springer-Verlag, second extended edtion, 1987.
17. A. Yahya, J. A. Fernandez, and J. Minker. Ordered model tree: A normal form for disjunctive deductive databases. J. Automated Reasoning, 13(1):117-144, 1994.

External Analogy in Inductive Theorem Proving

Erica Melis[1] and Jon Whittle*[2]

[1] Universität des Saarlandes, FB Informatik
D-66041 Saarbrücken, Germany. melis@cs.uni-sb.de.
[2] Dept. of Artificial Intelligence, University of Edinburgh
80 South Bridge, Edinburgh EH1 1HN, UK. jonathw@dai.ed.ac.uk.

Abstract. This paper investigates analogy-driven proof plan construction in inductive theorem proving. Given a proof plan of a *source* theorem, we identify constraints of second-order mappings that enable a replay of the source plan to produce a similar plan for the *target* theorem. In addition, the analogical replay is controlled by justifications that have to be satisfied in the target. Our analogy procedure, ABALONE, is implemented on top of the proof planner, CI^AM. Employing analogy has extended the problem solving horizon of CI^AM: with analogy, some theorems could be proved that CI^AM could not prove automatically.

1 Introduction

Theorem proving by analogy is a process in which the experience of proving a *source* theorem guides the search for a proof of a similar *target* theorem. Several attempts to employ analogy have been made, but these have failed to influence automated theorem proving. Early approaches, e.g. Munyer's [15], have been shown to be insufficient by Owen [16]. Approaches based on second-order matching such as [10, 6] have advanced the state of the art. They deal, however, with relatively restricted modifications of proofs only. Melis [11] describes analogy-driven proof plan construction, where proof plans are abstractions of proofs. By making analogies at the proof plan level, the potential for using analogy is extended because at the proof plan level, the analogical transfer breaks down less frequently. Furthermore, [11] introduces reformulations that map proof plans to proof plans enabling a replay between source and target plans that are significantly different in some respect.

The main issue of this paper is: how can the model of analogy-driven proof plan construction be applied to inductive theorem proving? This problem gives rise to more specific questions addressed in this paper, for instance:

- Which constraints ensure that the plan for the target theorem is similar to the source plan in inductive theorem proving?
- How can we ensure that the analogical replay yields correct planning steps in the target?

---

* The first author was supported by the HC&M grant CHBICT930806 whilst visiting Edinburgh and the SFB 378 and the second author by an EPSRC studentship. Computing facilities were in part provided by EPSRC grant GR/J/80702

As a basis for these investigations, we use the proof planner $CIAM$ [4]. Our analogy procedure, ABALONE, is implemented as an extension to $CIAM$.

In contrast to [13] that addresses internal analogy, this paper investigates the more general external analogy. For internal analogy, source and target problems belong to the same theorem proving process, whereas for external analogy source and target are independent problems. In internal analogy, the source and target problems are very similar. In external analogy, complex mappings are needed to match source and target, and advanced features are needed to replay the source plan.

In the remainder of this paper we first briefly review proof planning in $CIAM$ (§2) as a background for the analogy. §3 introduces the analogy procedure including the mappings implemented (§3.1) and the analogical replay (§3.2). A section on our results follows.

2 Background

A proof plan for a conjecture g is an abstract representation of a proof that consists of trees of method nodes. A *method* is a (partial) specification of a tactic, represented in a meta-level language, where a tactic executes a number of logical inferences [7]. Backward proof planning as introduced by [2] starts with the conjecture as an open goal g. It *searches* for a method M applicable to g and introduces a node with M into the proof plan. The subgoals g_i produced by the application of M become the new *open* subgoals and g now has status *closed*. The planner continues to search for a method applicable to one of the open subgoals and terminates if there are no more open goals. The Edinburgh proof planner $CIAM$ [4] has been applied successfully to inductive theorem proving.

The main idea in $CIAM$ is to use a heuristic known as rippling [8, 3] to guide the search for methods. Rippling is used in the step-cases of inductive proofs. We briefly explain rippling in the following because the abstraction underlying rippling plays a major role in restricting analogical mappings and reformulations.

The major aim of step-cases in inductive proofs is to reduce the differences between the induction conclusion and the induction hypothesis so the latter can be used in the proof. To that end, $CIAM$ employs rippling which involves annotating the induction conclusion with *wave fronts* and *wave holes*: Wave fronts mark the differences between induction hypothesis and conclusion. Waves annotate the smallest terms containing wave fronts. Wave holes represent the parts of waves that also appear in the induction hypothesis. For example, in planning the theorem, lenapp:[3]

$$\forall a, b. \, len(a <> b) = len(b <> a) \tag{1}$$

the induction hypothesis is

$$len(a <> b) = len(b <> a) \tag{2}$$

and the annotated conclusion is

$$len(\boxed{h :: \underline{a}} <> b) = len(b <> \boxed{h :: \underline{a}}). \tag{3}$$

---

[3] $len, <>, ::$ denote the list functions length, append, and cons respectively. Typewriter font is chosen for names of conjectures.

The boxes denote the waves. Wave holes are underlined and wave fronts are the non-underlined parts within the boxes. The *skeleton* of an annotated term is constructed from wave holes and the parts of the term that do not belong to a wave. *Wave-rules* are annotated, skeleton preserving rules. E.g. a wave-rule for the function $<>$ is

$$\boxed{(X :: \underline{Y})} <> Z \Rightarrow \boxed{X :: (\underline{Y <> Z})} \tag{4}$$

where the skeleton on each side of the implication is $Y <> Z$.

Wave-rules are applied to the induction conclusion and to successive goals in the planning process. In this way, rippling moves or removes waves in the induction conclusion to a point where the induction hypothesis, represented by the skeleton of the conclusion, can be used. In our example, the waves are moved outwards. Hence, rippling provides guidance as to which wave-rules should be applied.

3 Analogy-Driven Proof Plan Construction in *CIAM*

In the following, we first explain the analogy procedure ABALONE in a nutshell. Then we go into more detail accompanied by an example.

ABALONE analogically transfers a source plan produced by *CIAM* to a plan for a target problem. The transfer is done on the basis of basic and extended mappings. These are second-order mappings which work like second-order matching but handle source constants as if they were variables. Additional induction-specific constraints restrict the mappings. The replay of the source plan is made node by node. At each node in the source we store *justifications* or reasons why a planning decision was taken. In *CIAM* these justifications tell us why a particular method was applied. During the analogy process, these justifications are also replayed. A source node is only replayed if its justifications still hold in the target. This serves two purposes. First, it guarantees the correctness of target method applications. Second, it provides a way of transferring only part of the source plan in some cases. If justifications cannot be established in the target, a gap is left in the target plan. In this way, it is only this part of the source that is not transferred, whereas the replay of the rest of the source plan can still be attempted.

Sometimes a node by node replay as described above is insufficient because the source and target plans differ in a significant respect. An example might be if the source and target plans have different induction schemes at a certain point. Rather than failing, ABALONE is equipped with a number of *reformulations* which can resolve these differences by making additional changes in the target plan. Space precludes us from describing the reformulations available in ABALONE. In this paper, we only describe the *1to2* reformulation – see §3.2. The main steps in the analogy-driven proof plan construction can be summarised as:

- Find a second-order mapping m_b from the source theorem to the target theorem.
- Extend m_b to a mapping m_e from source rules to target rules.
- Decide about the reformulations to be applied. The need for a reformulation is triggered by patterns in m_b or m_e.

- Following the source plan, analogically replay the methods. This includes
  - Apply reformulations
  - **if** method justifications hold, **then** apply method in target,
    else try to establish justification.
  - **if** justification not establishable, **then** leave gap in target plan.

Throughout the rest of this paper details of the procedure are explained and the following example illustrates the techniques.

Source theorem: `lenapp` $len(a <> b) = len(b <> a)$

Target theorem: `halfplus` $half(a + b) = half(b + a)$[4]

Source wave-rules[5]:

`app2:` $\boxed{(X :: \underline{Y})} <> Z \Rightarrow \boxed{X :: (Y <> Z)}$

`len2:` $len(\boxed{X :: \underline{Y}}) \Rightarrow \boxed{s(len(Y))}$

`lenapp2:` $len(X <> (\boxed{Y :: \underline{Z}})) \Rightarrow \boxed{s(len(X <> Z))}$

Target wave-rules:

`plus2:` $\boxed{s(\underline{Y})} + Z \Rightarrow \boxed{s(Y + Z)}$

`half3:` $half(\boxed{s(s(\underline{Y}))}) \Rightarrow \boxed{s(half(Y))}$.

The `lenapp` proof plan generated by CI^AM does not rely on the commutativity of $+$. The plan's step-case branch is displayed in Figure 1. The method WAVE applies a wave-rule, EVAL evaluates a term by applying a definition. FERTILIZE applies the induction hypothesis once rippling is completed and ELEMENTARY resolves goals that are trivially true (such as $x = x$).

Justifications Stored in the Source Plan

During the planning of the source theorem, justifications, i.e. reasons for the application of a method, are stored at each source plan node. These justifications are used later, in the analogical replay, where instead of blindly replaying the source plan, we actually replay the decisions that were taken in the source, provided the justifications for the decisions hold again in the target.

In CI^AM, each method has preconditions for its application. Legal preconditions are stored as justifications - they *must* be satisfied for the method to be applicable. The WAVE method, e.g., has preconditions that require the existence of a wave-rule that matches the current goal. Other preconditions just encode heuristics and these are not stored as justifications. In this way, our analogy procedure can override some heuristics. Overriding heuristics, without guidance from analogy, is unwise, however.

We also consider a kind of justification that is due to the use of indexed functions. ABALONE is able to send a function symbol at different positions in the source to different target images. For this reason, source function symbols at different positions are differentiated by indices. During the source planning, constraints may be placed on

---

[4] $half$ and $+$ denote the usual functions on natural numbers.

these indices, yielding a set of *C(onstraint)-equations* of the form $f_i = f_j$ (see Figure 1). These C-equations form an additional source justification that must be satisfied in the target for a successful replay. Since wave-rules have to be skeleton preserving, the functions that belong to the skeleton of a wave-rule have the same index on both sides of the wave-rule.

Figure 1 shows the step-case of the plan of **lenapp** with indexed functions.[5] The induction hypothesis is $len(a <> b) = len(b <> a)$. Note how the C-equations arise. When WAVE(**app2**) is applied, the lhs of **app2** matches with the lhs of the current goal - i.e. $(X ::_1 Y) <> Z$ matches with $(h ::_5 a) <> b$ which requires that $::_5 = ::_1$.

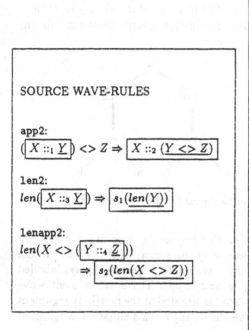

SOURCE WAVE-RULES

app2:
$$\boxed{(X ::_1 \underline{Y}}) <> Z \Rightarrow \boxed{X ::_2 (\underline{Y <> Z})}$$

len2:
$$len(\boxed{X ::_3 \underline{Y}}) \Rightarrow \boxed{s_1(len(Y))}$$

lenapp2:
$$len(X <> \boxed{Y ::_4 \underline{Z}})$$
$$\Rightarrow \boxed{s_2(len(X <> Z))}$$

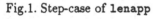

Fig.1. Step-case of **lenapp**

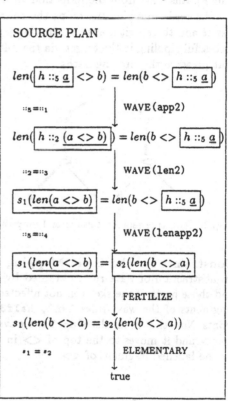

SOURCE PLAN

$$len(\boxed{h ::_5 \underline{a}} <> b) = len(b <> \boxed{h ::_5 \underline{a}})$$

$::_5 = ::_1$ WAVE(app2)

$$len(\boxed{h ::_2 (\underline{a <> b})}) = len(b <> \boxed{h ::_5 \underline{a}})$$

$::_2 = ::_3$ WAVE(len2)

$$s_1(\boxed{len(a <> b)}) = len(b <> \boxed{h ::_5 \underline{a}})$$

$::_5 = ::_4$ WAVE(lenapp2)

$$s_1(\boxed{len(a <> b)}) = \boxed{s_2(len(b <> a))}$$

FERTILIZE

$$s_1(len(b <> a)) = s_2(len(b <> a))$$

$s_1 = s_2$ ELEMENTARY

true

3.1 Mappings

We use second-order mappings, that is, mappings that send function constants to function terms, to map the source theorem to the target theorem and source rules to target rules. First, a constrained basic mapping m_b is constructed that maps the source theorem with indexed function symbols to the given target theorem. m_b is then augmented by an extended mapping m_e which maps the source rules to the target

---

[5] The index 5 of :: is introduced by the INDUCTION method. We have omitted indices from the statement of the source theorem for the sake of clarity because they are irrelevant in our example. In general, however, all function symbols are indexed.

rules. In addition to the most essential constraints of the basic mapping presented below, the mappings are designed to favour maps that preserve the term structure. Space prevents us from giving all the heuristics here (see [18]) but an example is biasing against projection mappings because they alter the term structure.

Basic Mapping The term tree representation of a theorem is called the *theorem tree*. The *rippling paths* in the theorem tree – indicated in bold in Figure 2 – are the paths on which the wave-fronts are moved through the theorem tree by rippling. These paths start from the induction variables.

The basic mapping m_b maps the source theorem tree ts to the target theorem tree tt and thereby it maps the rippling paths of ts to paths of tt. We try to achieve successful rippling in the target via the following induction-specific constraints for m_b that preserve the rippling paths.

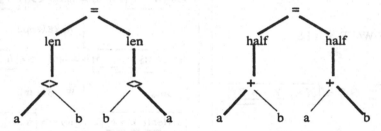

Fig. 2. Term tree representations of lenapp and halfplus2 with the rippling paths in bold

Constraints for the Basic Mapping *Labelled fragments*, introduced in [9], are an abstraction of wave-rules obtained by removing the structure of the wave fronts and those parts of the skeleton not affected by wave fronts. Figure 3 displays labelled fragments of the wave-rules len2, half3, plus2, app2. The dots represent wave fronts. Note that in the lhs of app2 the wave-front is situated at the first(left) argument of <> and it moves to the top of <> in the rhs of app2. This situation is reflected by the labelled fragment of <>.

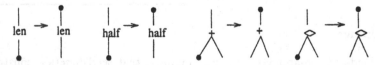

Fig. 3. Labelled fragments

The labelled fragments of function/relation nodes in a theorem tree determine the rippling paths [9]. The rippling paths in a theorem tree abstractly encode the consecutive application of the WAVE method relying on the wave-rules the labelled fragments are built from. Therefore, we require the mapping m_b to **preserve labelled fragments** or to change labelled fragments in a controlled way. The "controlled way" gives rise to the reformulations that are beyond the focus of this paper. By this constraint, we preserve the method applications in the step-case of the source and target plans.

This constraint reduces the search space for sources and mappings. In our example, we obtain $m_b : len \mapsto half$, and $m_b :<> \mapsto +$ because the labelled fragments for len and $half$ are identical as are those for $<>$ and $+$.

Extended Mapping The extended mapping m_e provides images terms for function symbols occurring in the source plan but not occurring in the source theorem. It maps source rules to target rules. In general, function symbols in the source may have different image function terms. To some extent m_e is restricted by C-equations and by m_b. Different extended mappings are constructed for the target step-cases and for the target base-cases because different sets of C-equations belong to the step- and base-cases and different rules are used. The indexing of the rules enables different applications of the same source rule to map to different target rules.

Consider our example again. For the indexed source wave-rules refer to Figure 1 and for the target rules to §3. Since $m_b(<>) = +$, app2 can be partially mapped. The mapping is completed by mapping the source wave-rules to available target wave rules. In this way, app2 maps to plus2 with $m_e(::_1) = \lambda w_1 \lambda w_2.s(w_2)$ and $m_e(::_2) = \lambda w_1 \lambda w_2.s(w_2)$. Similarly, len2 maps to half3 because of $m_b(len) = half$, giving $m_e(s_1) = \lambda w_1.s(w_1)$ and $m_e(::_3) = \lambda w_1.w_2.s(s(w_2))$. The latter violates the C-equation $::_3 = ::_2$, because $::_2$, $::_3$ have different target images. This violation tells us that we need to add extra methods in the target. This is taken care of by the *1to2* reformulation described in §3.2. The source rule lenapp2 cannot be mapped to plus2 or half3 by extending m_b.

3.2 Analogical Replay

As already described briefly, the main body of the analogical procedure replays the source plan node by node checking justifications at each stage. There are two occasions when ABALONE deviates from this simple node by node replay.

First, there is the case that a justification does not hold in the target. In this instance, ABALONE will try to establish the justification. Its exact action will depend on the type of justification:

- If the failed justification is associated with a WAVE method, and the situation is such that a source wave-rule has no corresponding rule in the target, then ABALONE speculates a target wave-rule. It does this by applying m_b and m_e to the source rule.
- A justification may fail because some side-condition does not hold. Whereas the side-condition may trivially hold in the source, the mapped version in the target may not hold trivially. Hence, ABALONE will set up the target side-condition as a lemma.
- Certain justifications cannot be established by ABALONE, so the source method is not replayed.

If a justification does not hold and cannot be established, then ABALONE produces a target plan node that has an empty method slot and a conclusion that contains special meta-variables, *gap variables* $?_i$. The gap variable is a place holder for the unknown subexpression of the sequent in the (current) target node that corresponds to the source subexpression that was changed by the source method which could not be transferred. Sometimes these variables can be instantiated when subsequent methods are replayed. If no subexpression other than a gap variable occurs in the current target goal, the replay stops here and proceeds to the next open target goal.

Secondly, reformulations of the source plan are needed because sometimes the mappings alone are not sufficient to produce a plan proving the target theorem. Reformulations do more than just map symbols. In general, reformulations may insert, replace or delete methods or may change methods, sequents and justifications of proof plan nodes in a substantiated rather than in an ad hoc way. We have come up with a number of reformulations. Each is triggered by peculiarities of the mappings or by failed justifications. We only explain the reformulation *1to2* in this paper.

In our example, the image of the source justification $::_3 = ::_2$ does not hold in the target but exposes a certain pattern triggering the reformulation *1to2*. The frequently occurring pattern consists in a combination $f_i = f_j$ with $m_e(f_i)(m_e(f_i)) = m_e(f_j)$ that indicates the need for a change of the induction scheme. *1to2* changes a one-step induction in the source to a two-step in the target. In doing this, an extra constructor function is introduced into the target step-case. This means that certain source methods need to be doubled in the target. This is also taken care of by *1to2*, see Figure 4. In addition, an extra base-case in the target is introduced.

Let us consider the replay of the step-case of our example in Figure 4. At the INDUCTION node, ABALONE suggests the induction variable a and replays the one-step INDUCTION to a two-step INDUCTION because of *1to2*. Then WAVE(app2) is replayed, where app2 was mapped to plus2 already. *1to2* doubles the method in the target. This gives *two* applications of WAVE(plus2). ABALONE does not double methods other than WAVE(app2) because once half3 has been applied, the extra constructor function has vanished. The next node, WAVE(len2), is replayed easily. At the WAVE(lenapp2) node the justification fails because there is no target image for the source wave-rule lenapp2. The appropriate action is to suggest a target wave-rule lemma by using the mappings and the C-equations to suggest a target rule. It uses the mappings plus C-equations $s_2 = s_1$ with $s_1 \mapsto s(w_1)$, and $::_4 = ::_5$ with $::_5 \mapsto s(s(w_2))$ to come up with the image wave-rule:

$$half(X + \boxed{s(s(\underline{Z}))}) \Rightarrow \boxed{s(\underline{half(X + Z)})}$$ [6] As the next steps of the replay, the methods FERTILIZE and ELEMENTARY are replayed easily.

The source base-case is replayed to the first target base-case ($a = s(0)$): The first method in the base-case is EVAL(app1), for app1 $:= nil <> X \Rightarrow X$. app1 maps to the incorrect rule $s(0) + X \Rightarrow X$ because $m_e(nil) = s(0)$. ABALONE's lemma disprover spots the incorrectness, so a gap variable $?_1$ is inserted in place of $s(0) + a$ on the rhs of the target subgoal.

---

[6] All lemma suggestions are accompanied by a simple disprover that finds very simple false conjectures such as $x > x, F \wedge \neg F$ and which avoids unnecessary effort by rejecting some false lemmas.

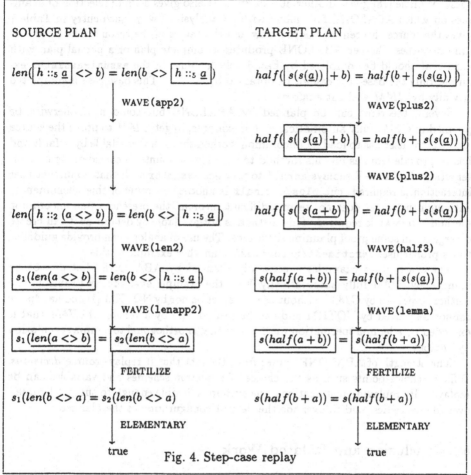

Fig. 4. Step-case replay

The replay of the base-case continues as the next method, INDUCTION, is applicable in the target. Again, the step-case of this induction is replayed with a *1to2* reformulation. WAVE(app2) is replayed and is doubled and WAVE(len2) is also replayed. The next replay of WAVE(len2) fails because of the presence of the gap variable where the image of len2 would have been applied. Hence, another gap variable $?_2$ is inserted. The next method is FERTILIZE which is applied to the lhs of the target but because the induction hypothesis has $?_1$ in it, there is now a gap on both sides of the equality and so the replay stops. In this way, ABALONE has produced an incomplete proof plan (sketch) of this base-case which can be completed by base-level planning, that is, proof planning that is not guided by analogy. The other base-case is replayed by ABALONE in a similar way. Space precludes us from illustrating the base-case replay by a figure.

4 Results

ABALONE is implemented in Quintus Prolog as an extension to *CIAM*. It has been tested on a wide range of examples. We include a selection in Table 1. In addition to these, Whittle [18] gives another 30 examples. It also gives a small selection of examples on which ABALONE fails along with an analysis of why. Each entry in Table 1 gives the source theorem in the first row and the target in the second. The third column describes whether ABALONE produces a complete plan or a partial plan with gaps that should be completed by base-level planning. In the assuni-assinter example, only the base-case cannot be obtained by analogy. This base-case is completed trivially by CI^AM without analogy.

Several theorems can be planned by ABALONE but could not otherwise be planned in CI^AM fully automatically. For example, to get CI^AM to prove the source assuni, the user has to load an uncommon method that is not available by default and has to provide lemmas for this method to use. This amounts to considerable user interaction. ABALONE replays assuni to produce assinter such that no further user interaction is required. cnc_plus/cnc_half is another example of this phenomenon. Although the target does not seem a difficult theorem, the presence of an uncommon method, NORMAL is required. This method is not available by default as it can create divergence in some proof planning situations. The use of analogy can provide guidance to its proper use. zerotimes1/zerotimes3 is another example of this.

There are other examples successfully planned by ABALONE that cannot be planned by CI^AM fully automatically. E.g., the example evensumrev (Table 1) can neither be proved by CI^AM without user interaction nor by NQTHM [1] and halfplus cannot be proved by NQTHM and can be proved only by a version of CI^AM that is extended by a lemma speculation mechanism that is orthogonal to lemma speculation by analogy.

The strength of ABALONE comes from the fact that it replays source *decisions*. Difficult choice-points such as the choice of induction schemes and variables can be replayed. By replaying justifications, the system is flexible enough to suggest lemmas, override heuristics, and to override the default configuration of the planner.

5   Conclusion and Related Work

In this paper, we have described analogy-driven proof-plan construction in inductive theorem proving that is incorporated into a generic proof planner. As a bottom line, ABALONE can prove theorems that could not be proved by CI^AM or NQTHM.

The mapping and reformulation components of the system ABALONE systematically aim at providing a justified target plan that is similar to the source plan by preserving the abstractions underlying rippling or by tightly controlled changes. This paper focused on the mappings and on the role of justifications in the replay. Firstly, second-order mappings are found that satisfy certain constraints in order to have similar source and target plans. Our restriction of mappings differs considerably from other approaches, e.g., in [10]. Secondly, a node by node replay of the (reformulated) source plan produces a structured plan for the target theorem rather than just yielding the lemmas that are needed to carry out the proof as in [10]. Checking the justifications stored in the source plan ensures that the replay yields only correct planning steps in the target. Certain reactions to failed justifications try to establish justifications in the second place. Ignoring heuristic preconditions helps to speculate

lenapp	$len(a <> b) = len(b <> a)$	partial
halfplus	$half(a + b) = half(b + a)$	
zerotimes1	$x = 0 \rightarrow x * y = 0$	complete
zerotimes3	$x * y = 0 \rightarrow (x * y) * y = 0$	
sumrev	$sum(rev(x)) = sum(x)$	complete
evensumrev	$even(sum(rev(x))) = even(sum(x))$	
assuni	$x \cup (y \cup z) = (x \cup y) \cup z$	partial
assinter	$x \cap (y \cap z) = (x \cap y) \cap z$	
assp2	$(y + x) + z = (x + y) + z$	complete
lenapp	$len(a <> b) = len(b <> a)$	
plussum	$sum(x) + sum(y) = sum(x <> y)$	complete
apprev	$rev(x) <> rev(y) = rev(y <> x)$	
cnc_plus	$x = y \rightarrow x + z = y + z$	complete
cnc_half	$x = y \rightarrow half(x) = half(y)$	
plussum	$sum(x) + sum(y) = sum(x <> y)$	complete
assapp	$x <> (y <> z) = (x <> y) <> z$	
sumapp	$sum(x <> y) = sum(y <> x)$	complete
prodapp	$prod(x <> y) = prod(y <> x)$	
lenapp	$len(x <> y) = len(y <> x)$	complete
doubleplus	$double(x + y) = double(y + x)$	

Table 1. Some examples run by ABALONE

lemmas and to override heuristic default control and default configurations. The latter changes of the control as well as the characterization of analogy as a control strategy are discussed in more detail in [14]. As outlined in §3.2, our procedure sometimes produces a proof plan with gaps in it that has to be completed by usual planning methods. We consider this an improvement on the alternative of experiencing failure in these cases. In many cases, the gaps in the plan can be filled by base-level planning.

These features as well as the elaborate reformulations (that are discussed very briefly only) are new compared to other approaches to theorem proving by analogy, e.g. in PLAGIATOR [10] and Mural [17]. Including the replay of induction schemes and suggestion of induction variables is also new. A further comparison with [10] shows that ABALONE works at the proof plan level and aims at transferring the proof structure rather the relevant lemmas only. Its suggestion of target lemmas is justified by mappings that preserve labelled fragments. Thereby the speculation of lemmas becomes more targeted. The main advantage of ABALONE over Mural is that it works at the plan-level rather than at the calculus-level. Thereby the analogy does not break down as quickly as the analogical transfer of calculus-level proofs. The target proofs provided by Mural are incorrect in many respects and have to be ad-hoc amended by the user, whereas our use of a justified transfer ensures that our target plan is correct.

The analogy between different source and target problems as described in this paper differs from the internal analogy presented in [13]: First of all, internal analogy works inside of planning for one theorem, where the subgoals are very similar, i.e., no reformulation and extremely simple mappings are needed. Furthermore, the current paper describes how the problem solving capabilities of a theorem prover can be extended whereas in [13] internal analogy is used for efficiency gains by replaying very specific search-intensive subprocedures in planning. The internal analogy replays at INDUCTION nodes only and has specific justifications. External analogy is a far more difficult problem. [12] contains a comparison between experiences and goals of analogical reasoning in different theorem proving settings.

References

1. R.S. Boyer and J.S. Moore. *A Computational Logic*. Academic Press, London, 1979.
2. A. Bundy, 'The use of explicit plans to guide inductive proofs', in *Proc. 9th International Conference on Automated Deduction (CADE)*, eds., E. Lusk and R. Overbeek, volume 310 of *Lecture Notes in Computer Science*, pp. 111–120, Argonne, (1988). Springer.
3. A. Bundy, Stevens A, F. Van Harmelen, A. Ireland, and A. Smaill, 'A heuristic for guiding inductive proofs', *Artificial Intelligence*, **63**, 185–253, (1993).
4. A. Bundy, F. van Harmelen, J. Hesketh, and A. Smaill, 'Experiments with proof plans for induction', *Journal of Automated Reasoning*, **7**, 303–324, (1991).
5. J.G. Carbonell, 'Derivational analogy: A theory of reconstructive problem solving and expertise acquisition', in *Machine Learning: An Artificial Intelligence Approach*, eds., R.S. Michalsky, J.G. Carbonell, and T.M. Mitchell, 371–392, Morgan Kaufmann Publ., Los Altos, (1986).
6. R. Curien, *Outils pour la Preuve par Analogie*, Ph.D. dissertation, Universite Henri Poincare - Nancy, January 1995.
7. M. Gordon, R. Milner, and C.P. Wadsworth, *Edinburgh LCF: A Mechanized Logic of Computation*, Lecture Notes in Computer Science 78, Springer, Berlin, 1979.
8. D. Hutter, 'Guiding inductive proofs', in *Proc. of 10th International Conference on Automated Deduction (CADE)*, ed., M.E. Stickel, volume Lecture Notes in Artificial Intelligence 449. Springer, (1990).
9. D. Hutter, 'Synthesis of induction orderings for existence proofs', in *Proc. of 12th International Conference on Automated Deduction (CADE)*, ed., A. Bundy, Lecture Notes in Artificial Intelligence 814, pp. 29–41. Springer, (1994).
10. Th. Kolbe and Ch. Walther, 'Reusing proofs', in *Proceedings of ECAI-94*, Amsterdam, (1994).
11. E. Melis, 'A model of analogy-driven proof-plan construction', in *Proceedings of the 14th International Joint Conference on Artificial Intelligence*, pp. 182–189, Montreal, (1995).
12. E. Melis, 'When to Prove Theorems by Analogy?', in *KI-96: Advances in Artificial Intelligence. 20th Annual German Conference on Artificial Intelligence*, pp. 259–271, Lecture Notes in Artificial Intelligence 1137, Springer, (1996).
13. E. Melis and J. Whittle, 'Internal Analogy in Inductive Theorem Proving', in *Proceedings of the 13th Conference on Automated Deduction (CADE-96)*, eds., M.A. McRobbie and J.K. Slaney, Lecture Notes in Artificial Intelligence, 1104, pp. 92–105. Springer, (1996).
14. E. Melis and J. Whittle, 'Analogy as a Control Strategy in Theorem Proving', in *Proceedings of the 10th Florida International AI Conference (FLAIRS-97)*, (1997).
15. J.C. Munyer, *Analogy as a Means of Discovery in Problem Solving and Learning*, Ph.D. dissertation, University of California, Santa Cruz, 1981.
16. S. Owen, *Analogy for Automated Reasoning*, Academic Press, 1990.
17. S. Vadera, 'Proof by analogy in Mural', *Formal Aspects of Computing*, **7**, 183–206, (1995).
18. J. Whittle, 'Analogy in CL^AM', MSc.thesis, University of Edinburgh, Dept. of AI, Edinburgh, (1995). Also available at http://www.dai.ed.ac.uk/daidb/students/jonathw/publications.html

Mechanising Partiality
Without Re-implementation

Manfred Kerber[1] and Michael Kohlhase[2]

[1] The University of Birmingham, School of Computer Science
Birmingham, B15 2TT, England
e-mail: M.Kerber@cs.bham.ac.uk
WWW: http://www.cs.bham.ac.uk/~mmk

[2] Universität des Saarlandes, FB Informatik
D-66041 Saarbrücken, Germany
e-mail: kohlhase@cs.uni-sb.de
WWW: http://jswww.cs.uni-sb.de/~kohlhase

Abstract. Even though it is not very often admitted, partial functions do play a significant role in many practical applications of deduction systems. Kleene has already given a semantic account of partial functions using a three-valued logic decades ago. This approach allows rejecting certain unwanted formulae as faulty, which the simpler two-valued ones accept. We have developed resolution and tableau calculi for automated theorem proving that take the restrictions of the three-valued logic into account, which however have the severe drawback that existing theorem provers cannot directly be adapted to the technique. Even recently implemented calculi for many-valued logics are not well-suited, since in those the quantification does not exclude the undefined element. In this work we show, that it is possible to enhance a two-valued theorem prover by a simple strategy so that it can be used to generate proofs for the theorems of the three-valued setting. By this we are able to use an existing theorem prover for a large fragment of the language.

1 Introduction

Many practical applications of deduction systems in mathematics, philosophical logic and computer science rely on the correct and efficient treatment of partiality. For instance, in order to describe formally the semantics of computer programs, the logic has to be able to model that real programs may crash (i.e, are only partial functions from inputs to outputs). For example, one would like to distinguish the faulty type description of the tail function "$l: list \Rightarrow \mathsf{tail}(l): list$" from the correct one "$l: list\ l \neq [] \Rightarrow \mathsf{tail}(l): list$". Such differences can be made formal in the VDM language (see for instance [Jon90, p.68ff] or [BFL*94, p.3]). Unfortunately up to now there is no efficient mechanisation of reasoning with partiality in VDM.

There are different approaches – ranging from workarounds for concrete situations to a proper general treatment – to model partiality. For an overview[i], we

---

[i] For a more detailed discussion of the different approaches compare [Far90].

will introduce the main approaches and exemplify their advantages and disadvantages by some trivial examples from arithmetic. We have chosen this domain for its clarity, even though for mathematics a logical treatment of partiality might successfully be replaced by a workaround.

We will recall the four main options of treating partiality and then advocate the fourth one. In the first approach, undefined expressions like $1/0$ are syntactically excluded, for instance by using a sorted logic. In the second approach, partiality is either disregarded or bypassed, for instance, a value is assigned to $1/0$, either a fixed value (e.g. 0) or an undetermined one. In both cases it is necessary to tolerate undesired theorems, in the first case, for instance, $1/0 = 0$, or in the second case from $0 \cdot x = 0$ the instance $0 \cdot 1/0 = 0$. This approach is not satisfying if such theorems are unwanted and that is normally the case in mathematics.

In the third and fourth, partiality is taken seriously and this is reflected in the semantics and the calculus. While the third considers undefined terms only, but atomic formulae are evaluated either to false or true, in the fourth, atomic formulae can be undefined too, that is, be evaluated to a third truth value "undefined". Concretely, in the third approach terms of the form $1/0$ are treated as undefined and all atomic formulae containing such a meaningless term are evaluated to false. This has the advantage that partial functions can be handled within the classical two-valued framework. However, the serious drawback is that the results of these logic systems can be un-intuitive to the working mathematician. For instance in elementary arithmetic the following sentence

$$\forall x_{\mathbb{R}}, y_{\mathbb{R}}, z_{\mathbb{R}}.\ z = \frac{x}{y} \Rightarrow x = y * z$$

is a theorem of such systems since the scope is true for the case $y \neq 0$ and for the case $y = 0$, the formula $z = x/0$ obtains the truth value f which in turn makes the implication true, too. However, it is mathematical consensus that the equation should only hold provided that y is not 0. In the fourth approach, which has, in particular, been investigated by Kleene in [Kle52], this is not a theorem. In this approach atomic formulae containing meaningless terms are evaluated to undefined. In particular, the example above is not a theorem in the three-valued approach, since for the instantiation $y = 0$ the formula evaluates to undefined.

Now we address the question which price has to be paid for the proper treatment in the three-valued approach. Indeed in unsorted mechanisations of Kleene's approach by Tichy [Tic82], Lucio-Carrasco and Gavilanes-Franco [LG89], it is necessary to pay a high computational price. In [KK94,KK96] we have developed a sorted three-valued logic $\mathcal{SKL}^3$ and corresponding resolution and tableau calculi $\mathcal{RPF}^3$ and $\mathcal{TPF}^3$ carefully integrating ideas from sorted dynamic logics as introduced by Weidenbach [WO90,Wei95] and from many-valued truth-functional logics as mechanised by Hähnle [Häh94] as well as by Baaz and Fermüller [BF95]. In these logics the additional computations are relatively modest and in many cases proofs in the two-valued logic can be the structurally isomorphically transformed into proofs in the three-valued logic.

The main contribution of this paper is the result that for a large class of $\mathcal{SKL}^3$-theorems (which are also classical theorems by construction) the $\mathcal{TPF}^3$

and $\mathcal{RPF}^3$ proofs can be transformed into classical sorted tableau and resolution proofs and vice versa conserving the structure and size of the proofs. Furthermore we can show that by adding a simple strategy in proof search for two-valued theorems, it is possible to use a two-valued theorem prover for proving $\mathcal{SKL}^3$-theorems. However, unlike to the first of the four above-mentioned approaches, ours does not trivialise undefinedness information in a way that it would become decidable.

2 Strong Sorted Kleene Logic ($\mathcal{SKL}^3$)

In [Kle52] Kleene presents a logic, which he calls *strong three-valued logic* for reasoning about partial recursive predicates[ii] on the set of natural numbers. He argues that the intuitive meaning of the third truth value should be "undefined" or "unknown" and introduces the truth tables shown in Definition 1. Similarly Kleene enlarges the universe of discourse by an element $\perp$ denoting the undefined number. In his exposition the quantifiers only range over natural numbers, in particular he does not quantify over the undefined individual (number).

In [KK94] we have made Kleene's meta-level discussion of defined and undefined individuals explicit and presented a formal syntax and semantics that we will now present informally.

The universe of discourse is structured into the sort Δ for all defined individuals and an error element $\perp$; all functions and predicates are strict, that is, if one of the arguments of a compound term or an atom evaluates to $\perp$, then the term evaluates to $\perp$ or the truth value of the atom is u respectively. Just as in Kleene's system, our quantifiers only range over individuals in Δ, that is, individuals that are not undefined. Since $\mathcal{SKL}^3$ needs the sort Δ for bounded quantification anyway, it is no further effort to give the full sorted system. The further use of sorts gives the well-known advantages of sorted logics for the conciseness of the representation and the reduction of search spaces.

Terms in $\mathcal{SKL}^3$ are ordinary first-order terms. Atomic formulae are defined as usual, in addition, there are atomic formulae of the kind $t \triangleleft S$, where t is a term and S a sort symbol. Here, $t \triangleleft S$ stands for "t has sort S". Formulae are built up from atomic formulae by the usual connectives, and a unary connective ! with the intended meaning that $!A$ is true, whenever the value of A is not u. Furthermore, all quantifications are bound by a sort S (i.e., are of the form $\forall x_S. A$ or $\exists x_S. A$).

The three-valued semantics for $\mathcal{SKL}^3$ has a "undefined individual" $\perp$ in the universe of discourse. Note that this is similar to the classical flat CPO construction [Sco70], but Kleene's interpretation of truth values does not make u

---

[ii] Most logic-based accounts of partiality only treat partiality for functions corresponding to the mathematical notion of a partial function, defined as a right-unique relation opposed to a total function which is left-total *and* right-unique. Indeed, at first glance there seems to be no need for having partial relations as well, since relations are defined as subsets of Cartesian products. However, most mathematicians would agree that the relation $x > y$ does not make much sense for arbitrary complex numbers (rather than saying that it is false for most complex numbers), while $x > y$ is perfectly well-defined for real numbers.

minimal. The standard notion of value function, Σ-algebra and assignments directly carry over to the partial-function case. The only interesting part is the non-classical truth functions for the connectives and quantifiers.

Definition 1. The value of a formula dominated by a connective is obtained from the value(s) of the subformula(e) in a truth-functional way. Therefore it suffices to define the truth tables for the connectives:

$\wedge$	f	u	t
f	f	f	f
u	f	u	u
t	f	u	t

$\vee$	f	u	t
f	f	u	t
u	u	u	t
t	t	t	t

$\Rightarrow$	f	u	t
f	t	t	t
u	u	u	t
t	f	u	t

$\neg$	
f	t
u	u
t	f

$!$	
f	t
u	f
t	t

As usual the semantics of formulae with respect to an interpretation $\mathcal{I}$ and an assignment φ is defined recursively. The atomic formulae of the form $t \prec S$ are treated like expressions of the form $S(t)$. For the quantifiers it is defined with the help of function $\widetilde{\forall}$ and $\widetilde{\exists}$ from the non-empty subsets of the truth values in the truth values. We define

$$\mathcal{I}_\varphi(Qx_S.\,A) := \widetilde{Q}(\{\mathcal{I}_{\varphi,[a/x]}(A) \mid \mathcal{I}(S)(a) = t\}),$$

where $Q \in \{\forall, \exists\}$ and $\varphi, [a/x]$ coincides with φ away from x and maps x to a. Furthermore we define

$$\widetilde{\forall}(T) := \begin{cases} t & \text{for } T = \{t\} \text{ or } T = \emptyset \\ u & \text{for } T = \{t, u\} \text{ or } \{u\} \\ f & \text{for } f \in T \end{cases} \qquad \widetilde{\exists}(T) := \begin{cases} t & \text{for } t \in T \\ u & \text{for } T = \{f, u\} \text{ or } \{u\} \\ f & \text{for } T = \{f\} \text{ or } T = \emptyset \end{cases}$$

Note that with this definition quantification is separated into a truth-functional part $\widetilde{Q}$ and an instantiation part that considers members of the universe according to the sort S (that is, those members for which $\mathcal{I}(S)(a) = t$). Note furthermore, that although there is no semantical difference between sorts and unary predicates, by the definition of the semantics of the quantifiers, only those elements are considered where the sort is defined and evaluates to t. According to this semantics, the relativisation $\Re(\forall x_S.\,A)$ is $\forall x.\ S(x) \wedge !S(x) \Rightarrow \Re(A)$ and not just $\forall x.\ S(x) \Rightarrow \Re(A)$.

Finally, quantification never considers undefined values and therefore cannot be truth-functional even for the unsorted case. As a consequence, we cannot directly use the methods developed for truth-functional many-valued logics from [Häh94,BF95].

Finally, the "tertium non datur" principle of classical logic is no longer valid, since formulae can be undefined, in which case they are neither true nor false. We do, however, have a "quartum non datur" principle, that is, formulae are either true, false, or undefined, which allows us to derive the validity of a formula by refuting that it is false or undefined. We will use this observation in our calculi.

While in classical logic, the consequence relation is directly connected to the implication by the deduction theorem, in $\mathcal{SKL}^3$ things are a little bit more difficult, since the classical deduction theorem is not valid. In particular, when proving mathematical theorems, it is quite usual to do this with respect to some background theory (axioms and definitions), which can no longer simply be taken in the antecedent of an implication. Actually, the $\mathcal{SKL}^3$ deduction theorem has the form $\Phi \cup \{A\} \models B$ iff $\Phi \models A \wedge !A \Rightarrow B$.

Now, the definedness connective ! for formulae does not have an explicit counterpart in informal mathematical practice, instead definedness assumptions are implicitly made in the assumptions. Hence for mathematical applications we will consider so-called *consequents*, that is, pairs consisting of a set of formulae Φ and a formula A, in which all formulae in Φ are assumed to be defined. We call a consequent $\Phi \models A$ valid if A is entailed by Φ in all Σ-models.

In fact the tautologies in the !-free fragment of $\mathcal{SKL}^3$, i.e., valid consequents of the form $\emptyset \models A$, where A does not contain any !, are very limited. The only atoms that are defined in an empty context are of the form $t \lessdot \Delta$. Therefore the set of tautologies can be generated by adding disturbances to classical propositional tautologies, where the propositional variables have been replaced by such atoms, for instance $(t \lessdot \Delta \Rightarrow t \lessdot \Delta) \vee A$ for arbitrary formulae A.

Now we can come back to the example from the exposition. The assertion is not a theorem of $\mathcal{SKL}^3$, since the instance $1 = \frac{1}{0} \Rightarrow 1 = 0 \cdot 1$ is not a valid formula (in any reasonable axiomatisation of elementary arithmetic). While the antecedent of the implication evaluates to u, the succedent evaluates to f, hence the whole expression to u.

Example 2 (Extended Example). We will formalise an extended example from elementary algebra that shows the basic features of $\mathcal{SKL}^3$. Here the sort $\mathbb{R}^*$ denotes the real numbers without zero. Note that we use the sort information to encode definedness information for inversion: $\frac{1}{x}$ is defined for all $x \in \mathbb{R}^*$, since the formula A2 is taken as an axiom. Naturally, we give only a reduced formalisation of real number arithmetic that is sufficient for our example. Consider the consequent $\{A1, A2, A3, A4, A5\} \models T$ with

A1 $\forall x_{\mathbb{R}}.\ x \neq 0 \Rightarrow x \lessdot \mathbb{R}^*$ A4 $\forall x_{\mathbb{R}}.\ \forall y_{\mathbb{R}}.\ x - y \lessdot \mathbb{R}$

A2 $\forall x_{\mathbb{R}^*}.\ \frac{1}{x} \lessdot \mathbb{R}^*$ A5 $\forall x_{\mathbb{R}}.\ \forall y_{\mathbb{R}}.\ x - y = 0 \Rightarrow x = y$

A3 $\forall x_{\mathbb{R}^*}.\ x^2 > 0$ T $\forall x_{\mathbb{R}}.\ \forall y_{\mathbb{R}}.\ x \neq y \Rightarrow \left(\frac{1}{x-y}\right)^2 > 0$

In an informal mathematical argumentation why T is entailed by $\{A1, \ldots, A5\}$, the Ai are assumed to be true, that is, neither false nor undefined. Let x and y be arbitrary elements of $\mathbb{R}$. If $x = y$, the premise of T is false, hence the whole expression true (in this case the conclusion evaluates to u). For $x \neq y$ the conclusion $\left(\frac{1}{x-y}\right)^2 > 0$ can be derived from A1 through A5.

3   Tableau

In our tableau calculus, a labeled formula A^α means that A has the truth value α. For the purposes of this paper, it is essential to make use of multi-indices [Häh94] (semantically $A^{\alpha\beta}$ is equivalent to $A^\alpha \vee A^\beta$, however syntactically, on the calculus level it is treated specially.). This not only gives us notational conciseness, but also drastically improves our calculus over a single-index variant, since we can introduce special rules for their treatment. So in general we think of the labels α

as truth value sets, which may be singletons. Note that we normally do not have to treat triple-indices as in A^{fut}, since that would correspond to a three-valued tautology, which cannot contribute to a refutation.

Definition 3 (Tableau Rules). The tableau rules consist of the traditional tableau rules for the propositional connectives, augmented by the case of the label u.

$$
\frac{(A \vee B)^{\text{t}}}{A^{\text{t}} \mid B^{\text{t}}}
\qquad
\frac{(A \vee B)^{\text{u}}}{\begin{array}{c} A^{\text{fu}} \\ B^{\text{fu}} \\ A^{\text{u}} \mid B^{\text{u}} \end{array}}
\qquad
\frac{(A \vee B)^{\text{f}}}{\begin{array}{c} A^{\text{f}} \\ B^{\text{f}} \end{array}}
\qquad
\frac{(A \vee B)^{\text{ut}}}{A^{\text{ut}} \mid B^{\text{ut}}}
\qquad
\frac{(A \vee B)^{\text{fu}}}{\begin{array}{c} A^{\text{fu}} \\ B^{\text{fu}} \end{array}}
$$

The negation rules just flip the labels in the intuitive way.

$$
\frac{(\neg A)^{\text{t}}}{A^{\text{f}}}
\qquad
\frac{(\neg A)^{\text{u}}}{A^{\text{u}}}
\qquad
\frac{(\neg A)^{\text{f}}}{A^{\text{t}}}
\qquad
\frac{(\neg A)^{\text{ut}}}{A^{\text{fu}}}
\qquad
\frac{(\neg A)^{\text{fu}}}{A^{\text{ut}}}
$$

The ! rule for the u case closes the branch (we use an explicit symbol $*$ for that), since $(!A)^{\text{u}}$ is unsatisfiable in $\mathcal{SKL}^3$.

$$
\frac{(!A)^{\text{t}}}{A^{\text{ft}}}
\qquad
\frac{(!A)^{\text{u}}}{*}
\qquad
\frac{(!A)^{\text{f}}}{A^{\text{u}}}
\qquad
\frac{(!A)^{\text{ut}}}{A^{\text{ft}}}
\qquad
\frac{(!A)^{\text{fu}}}{A^{\text{u}}}
\qquad
\frac{A^{\text{ft}}}{A^{\text{f}} \mid A^{\text{t}}}
$$

The last rule is a splitting[iii] rule reflecting the definition of multi-index ft as a disjunction. We only need this one splitting rule, since we have treated the multi-indices ut and fu explicitly in the rules.

The quantifier rules for the classical truth values and multi-indices are very similar to the standard rules ($\{x_S, y^1, \ldots, y^n\}$ are the free variables of A and f is a new function symbol of arity n), with the exception that the sort of the Skolem function has to be specified. The rule for the case u has a mixed existential and universal character: for y_S the value of A is undefined or true (that is there is no instance, which makes the formula false) *and* there is at least one defined witness for the undefinedness.

$$
\frac{(\forall x_S.\, A)^{\text{t}}}{[y_S/x_S]A^{\text{t}}}
\qquad
\frac{(\forall x_S.\, A)^{\text{u}}}{\begin{array}{c} [f(y^1, \ldots, y^n)/x_S]A^{\text{u}} \\ (f(y^1, \ldots, y^n){<}S)^{\text{t}} \\ [y_S/x_S]A^{\text{ut}} \end{array}}
\qquad
\frac{(\forall x_S.\, A)^{\text{f}}}{\begin{array}{c} [f(y^1, \ldots, y^n)/x_S]A^{\text{f}} \\ (f(y^1, \ldots, y^n){<}S)^{\text{t}} \end{array}}
$$

$$
\frac{(\forall x_S.\, A)^{\text{ut}}}{[y_S/x_S]A^{\text{ut}}}
\qquad
\frac{(\forall x_S.\, A)^{\text{fu}}}{\begin{array}{c} [f(y^1, \ldots, y^n)/x_S]A^{\text{fu}} \\ (f(y^1, \ldots, y^n){<}S)^{\text{t}} \end{array}}
$$

[iii] Note that the inverse rule that merges literals A^{α} and A^{β} into a multi-literal $A^{\alpha \cup \beta}$ is not present in the calculus and merging is also not carried out implicitly.

The rules for connectives and quantifiers above can now be used to reduce complex labeled formulae to literals.

Now we only need tableau closure[iv] rules: Undefined definedness literals can be used to close the tableau due to the fact that the predicate Δ is defined everywhere. In the rules *total*, *cut* and *strict*

$$\frac{(t<\Delta)^{u\alpha}}{(t<\Delta)^{\alpha}} \qquad \frac{A^{\alpha} \qquad B^{\beta}}{A^{\alpha\cap\beta} \mid \mathscr{SC}(\sigma)}\,\sigma \qquad \frac{C^{\gamma} \qquad (t<\Delta)^{f}}{* \mid \mathscr{SC}(\sigma)}\,\sigma$$

we require that $\gamma \subseteq \{\mathrm{ft}\}$ and $\sigma = [t_1/x^1_{S_1}], \ldots, [t_n/x^n_{S_n}]$ is the most general unifier of A and B or the most general unifier of the term t and a subterm s of C, respectively. Note that the *cut* rule is only non-redundant if $\alpha \cap \beta$ is a proper subset of both α and β; we will assume this in the following.

In both cases the *sort constraint* $\mathscr{SC}(\sigma) = ((t_1 < S_1) \wedge \ldots \wedge (t_n < S_n))^{\mathrm{fu}}$ insures the correctness of the instantiations. We have employed the notation of writing the substitution σ next to the tableau schema, to indicate that the whole tableau is instantiated by σ during the application of the rule.

A tableau is built up by constructing a tree with the tableau rules starting with an initial tree without branchings. We call a tableau *closed* iff all of its branches end in $*$. Note that the disjunct $*$ in the succedent of the rules above is only needed if the set of sort constraints is empty. Then this rule closes the branch without residuating.

Definition 4 (Tableau Proof). A *tableau proof for a formula* A is a closed tableau constructed from the initial tree consisting of the labeled formula A^{fu}. A *tableau proof for a consequent* $\Phi \models A$ is a closed tableau constructed from $\Phi^{\mathrm{t}} \cup \{A^{\mathrm{fu}}\}$.

The tableau proof of a consequent $\Phi \models A$ essentially refutes the possibility that A can be undefined or false under the assumption that all formulae in Φ are true. By the quartum non datur rule, we can then conclude that A is entailed by Φ. The soundness of the $\mathcal{TPF}^3$ rules can be verified by a tedious recourse to the semantics of the quantifiers and connectives. Completeness is proved by the standard argument using a model existence theorem for $\mathcal{SKL}^3$. For details see [KK96].

Example 5 (continuing Example 2). Taking the above example we give a proof for $\{A1, A2, A3, A4, A5\} \models T$ using the above tableau rules. The proof is shown in Fig. 1. Applying the closure rule in the case of non-empty sort constraints, we omit the $*$ branch for simplicity reasons. Note that the unsorted unifiers $[c - d/u_{\mathbb{R}}]$, $[c/x_{\mathbb{R}}]$, and $[d/y_{\mathbb{R}}]$ have to be applied to the whole tableau. For display reasons, however, we only add the relevant formulae to the tableau instead of replacing them, that is, correctly (F8) and (F13) have to replace (F3) and (F9) respectively.

[iv] We define that a literal $A^{\emptyset}$ closes a branch of the tableau and denote it with $*$.

The proof in Fig. 1 shows an interesting feature, namely it corresponds in length and structure to a proof of the theorem in a two-valued variant of $\mathcal{TPF}^3$. This observation has a more general background: [Häh94] shows that for so-called regular truth functional logics (all our connectives and quantifiers except for ! are regular), the sets-of-signs method allows a presentation of the tableau system in Smullyan's universal notation, varying only the closure conditions, i.e., the structure is isomorphic to the classical tableau system. However, this result is not directly applicable, since $\mathcal{SKL}^3$ is not truth-functional (we have to consider bounded quantifiers) and we assume strictness.

Definition 6 ($\mathcal{TPF}^2$). Formally this proof system (we will call it $\mathcal{TPF}^2$) can be obtained from $\mathcal{TPF}^3$ by removing all inference rules for the ! connective, the *total* rule and all connective and quantifier rules that contain the label u. This is essentially a tableau variant of [WO90] in the style of [Wei95].

(A1) $\forall x_{\mathbb{R}}.\ x \neq 0 \Rightarrow x \triangleleft \mathbf{R}^*)^{\mathrm{t}}$	
(A5) $(\forall x_{\mathbb{R}}.\ \forall y_{\mathbb{R}}.\ x - y = 0 \Rightarrow x = y)^{\mathrm{t}}$	
(T) $(\forall x_{\mathbb{R}}.\ \forall y_{\mathbb{R}}.\ x \neq y \Rightarrow \left(\frac{1}{x-y}\right)^2 > 0)^{\mathrm{fu}}$	
(A1') $(u_{\mathbb{R}} \neq 0 \Rightarrow u_{\mathbb{R}} \triangleleft \mathbf{R}^*)^{\mathrm{t}}$	$\forall^{\mathrm{t}}$(A1)
(A2') $(\frac{1}{v_{\mathbb{R}^*}} \triangleleft \mathbf{R}^*)^{\mathrm{t}}$	$\forall^{\mathrm{t}}$(A2)
(A3') $(w_{\mathbb{R}^*}^2 > 0)^{\mathrm{t}}$	$\forall^{\mathrm{t}}$(A3)
(A4') $(s_{\mathbb{R}} - t_{\mathbb{R}} \triangleleft \mathbf{R})^{\mathrm{t}}$	$\forall^{\mathrm{t}}$(A4) (2 times)
(A5') $(x_{\mathbb{R}} - y_{\mathbb{R}} = 0 \Rightarrow x_{\mathbb{R}} = y_{\mathbb{R}})^{\mathrm{t}}$	$\forall^{\mathrm{t}}$(A5) (2 times)
(T1) $(c \triangleleft \mathbf{R})^{\mathrm{t}}$	$\forall^{\mathrm{fu}}$(T) (2 times)
(T2) $(d \triangleleft \mathbf{R})^{\mathrm{t}}$	$\forall^{\mathrm{fu}}$(T) (2 times)
(T3) $(c = d \vee \left(\frac{1}{c-d}\right)^2 > 0)^{\mathrm{fu}}$	$\forall^{\mathrm{fu}}$(T) (2 times)
(T3') $(c = d)^{\mathrm{fu}}$	$\vee^{\mathrm{fu}}$(T3)
(T3'') $(\left(\frac{1}{c-d}\right)^2 > 0)^{\mathrm{fu}}$	$\vee^{\mathrm{fu}}$(T3)
(F1) $(\frac{1}{c-d} \triangleleft \mathbf{R}^*)^{\mathrm{fu}}$	*(T3'',A3')
(F2) $(c - d \triangleleft \mathbf{R}^*)^{\mathrm{fu}}$	*(F1,A2')

(F3) $(u_{\mathbb{R}} = 0)^{\mathrm{t}}$	(F4) $(u_{\mathbb{R}} \triangleleft \mathbf{R}^*)^{\mathrm{t}}$	$\vee^{\mathrm{t}}$(A1')
	(F5) $((c - d) \triangleleft \mathbf{R})^{\mathrm{fu}}$	*(F4,F2)
	(F6) $(c \triangleleft \mathbf{R})^{\mathrm{fu}}$ (F7) $(d \triangleleft \mathbf{R})^{\mathrm{fu}}$	*(F5,A4')
	* *	*(F6,T1), *(F7,T2)
(F8) $(c - d = 0)^{\mathrm{t}}$		σ(F3,[c − d/u])
(F9) $(x_{\mathbb{R}} - y_{\mathbb{R}} = 0)^{\mathrm{t}}$	(F10) $(x_{\mathbb{R}} = y_{\mathbb{R}})^{\mathrm{t}}$	$\vee^{\mathrm{t}}$(A5')
	(F11) $(c \triangleleft \mathbf{R})^{\mathrm{fu}}$ (F12) $(d \triangleleft \mathbf{R})^{\mathrm{fu}}$	*(F10,T3')
	* *	*(F11,T1), *(F12,T2)
(F13) $(c - d = 0)^{\mathrm{f}}$		σ(F9,[c/x], [d/y])
*		*(F13,F8)

Fig. 1 Tableau proof sketch

The correspondence mentioned above can be realised by replacing all multi-indices fu in $\mathcal{TPF}^3$ by the truth value f in $\mathcal{TPF}^2$. The formal reason that this is possible, lies in the fact that in $\mathcal{TPF}^3$ the tableau rules for R^α and $R^{\alpha u}$ have exactly the same structure for $\alpha \in \{f, t\}$ and $R \in \{\vee, \neg, \forall\}$.

In other words the simple measure of using rules for truth-value sets provides proofs that are as short as in the two-valued case. If, however, truth-value sets are not used, certain parts of the proofs must be duplicated. This relationship can only hold for so-called *normal problems* of course, that is, problems which do not contain any ! connective, since formulae containing a ! do not make any sense in classical two-valued logic. Let now $\mathcal{SFL}^2$ be a two-valued sorted logic, that is, the same logic as $\mathcal{SKL}^3$ with two truth values and without the ! connective.

Theorem 7 (Conservativity). *Each $\mathcal{TPF}^3$-tableau proof for a normal problem $\Phi \models A$ in $\mathcal{SKL}^3$ can be transformed into a $\mathcal{TPF}^2$-tableau proof in $\mathcal{SFL}^2$.*

Remark 8. Obviously, the converse of the above theorem does not hold. Not each $\mathcal{TPF}^2$ proof can be transformed into an $\mathcal{TPF}^3$ proof even if there is a $\mathcal{TPF}^3$ proof. Consider for example the relation $\{A\} \models A \vee (B \vee \neg B)$ which holds in $\mathcal{SKL}^3$ as well as in $\mathcal{SFL}^2$. An $\mathcal{TPF}^2$-proof is given in Fig. 2.

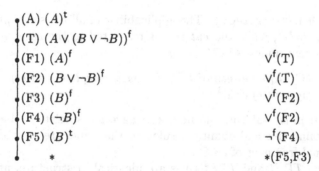

Fig. 2. Counterexample to the converse conservativity

This proof cannot be transferred since in $\mathcal{SKL}^3$ (T), (F1), (F2), (F3), (F4), and (F5) are labeled by the truth value u in addition, hence applying the closure to (F5) and (F3) leaves a label u in $\mathcal{SKL}^3$ and does not lead to *. This comes from the fact that $B \vee \neg B$ is not a tautology in $\mathcal{SKL}^3$. However, the other straightforward closure of the tableau by applying the closure rule to (A) and (F1) can be applied in $\mathcal{SFL}^2$ as well as in $\mathcal{SKL}^3$.

Certainly it would be nice to have the property that for each classical $\mathcal{SFL}^2$ proof there exists an $\mathcal{SKL}^3$ proof which is as short as the classical (of course only if the classical theorem is also an $\mathcal{SKL}^3$ theorem). The example above shows that this property does not hold in general, for instance, replace the assumption set $\{A\}$ by a set from which A can be derived in 20 steps only. On the other hand this example is rather artificial insofar as the theorem would normally not be stated in this form in mathematics, because mathematical theorems are normally not redundant in the way that two true statements are linked by an "$\vee$", on the contrary *usual* mathematical theorems employ preconditions as weak as possible and consequences as strong as possible. For instance, in a mathematical context we would expect theorems like A, $B \vee \neg B$, $A \wedge (B \vee \neg B)$. While a proof for the first (from the assumptions A) can be transferred from $\mathcal{SFL}^2$ to $\mathcal{SKL}^3$, the latter two are not theorems in $\mathcal{SKL}^3$. Hence we expect that for usual mathematical theorems the proof effort in $\mathcal{SKL}^3$ will not be bigger then in $\mathcal{SFL}^2$.

If we look again at the counterexample above, we see a general principle, how it is possible to generate a classical proof that cannot be lifted to a $\mathcal{TPF}^3$ proof, essentially closing the tableau by two complementary formulae, which both stem from the theorem. In such a case the branch can be closed on two formulae, labeled t and f in the two-valued setting, but in the three-valued setting they are labeled by tu and uf, so the closure results in a formula labeled by u only.

In the following, we want to give a formal definition of a control strategy for $\mathcal{TPF}^3$ that avoids these pitfalls. For this, we mark theorem nodes with $\mathcal{U}$ and leave assumption nodes unmarked. Marking the nodes generated by the application of a $\mathcal{TPF}^3$ rule Φ is carried out as follows: Add the truth value u to the labels of the premises and apply Φ, then mark the new nodes with $\mathcal{U}$, iff their formulae contain the truth value u. It is a simple exercise to check, that the labeling of a node in a $\mathcal{TPF}^3$ tableau only depends on its origin (i.e., whether it descends from the theorem or not).

Definition 9 ($\mathcal{U}^3$-Strategy). The applicability of all rules except *cut* remains unrestricted by $\mathcal{U}^3$, while the *cut* rule is restricted to the case, where at most one of the parent nodes is in $\mathcal{U}$.

Lemma 10 (Completeness of $\mathcal{U}^3$). *$\mathcal{U}^3$ is a complete strategy for $\mathcal{TPF}^3$ on the normal fragment of $\mathcal{SKL}^3$.*

Note that in $\mathcal{U}^3$-tableaux no node can have the singleton label u, and that hence the connective and quantifier rules for that label are redundant in $\mathcal{TPF}^3$ for the normal fragment of $\mathcal{SKL}^3$.

Since, the $\mathcal{TPF}^3$ and $\mathcal{TPF}^2$ rules are identical in structure, and the marks $\mathcal{U}$ only depend on the origin of formulae, they can also be computed for $\mathcal{TPF}^2$-tableaux, if we leave formulae of the form $t \triangleleft \Delta$ unmarked, irrespective of their origin. This move imitates an application of the *total* rule that does not exist in $\mathcal{TPF}^2$. Let $\mathcal{U}^2$ be that strategy for $\mathcal{TPF}^2$-tableaux that forbids *cut* on formulae marked with $\mathcal{U}$.

Theorem 11 (Lifting). *Each $\mathcal{U}^2$-tableau can be lifted to an isomorphic $\mathcal{U}^3$-tableau.*

Obviously, the strategy $\mathcal{U}^2$ is not complete for $\mathcal{SFL}^2$, and indeed we do not want it to be, since $\mathcal{SKL}^3$ was developed to eliminate formulae from the set of formulae that are provable in $\mathcal{SFL}^2$ and thus in classical first-order logic, but that are generally not considered as *mathematical* theorems (like $1/0 = 0 \vee 1/0 \neq 0$).

Actually, we show the adequacy of $\mathcal{U}^2$-tableau for the normal fragment of $\mathcal{SKL}^3$. To see that $\mathcal{U}^2$ is sound let $\mathcal{T}$ be a closed $\mathcal{U}^2$-tableau for a consequent $\Phi \models A$, then it can be lifted to a closed $\mathcal{U}^3$-tableau by Theorem 11, by the soundness of $\mathcal{TPF}^3$ the consequent must be unsatisfiable. The completeness of $\mathcal{U}^3$-tableau, Lemma 10, for the normal fragment of $\mathcal{SKL}^3$, directly entails the completeness of $\mathcal{U}^2$ with respect to the three-valued (mathematical) semantics by conservativity, Theorem 7.

Theorem 12. *The $\mathcal{TPF}^2$ calculus with the $\mathcal{U}^2$ restriction strategy is an adequate calculus for the normal fragment of $\mathcal{SKL}^3$.*

Now, we can ask, what is lost by restricting ourselves to the normal fragment of $\mathcal{SKL}^3$. It is not that we cannot specify definedness assumptions for the mathematical objects. This is always possible in the assumption part of consequents, even without an explicit !-connective since $(!A)^t$ is equivalent to $(A \vee \neg A)^t$. In the theorem part, this is not possible, since the presence of the label u blocks the equivalence. Thus it is not possible to prove theorems about the undefinedness of formulae such as $1/0 \not\lessdot \Delta \models \neg! P(1/0)$. Note that we can still prove assertions about the definedness of terms, like in $1/0 \not\lessdot \Delta \models f(1/0) \not\lessdot \Delta$. So in fact $\mathcal{SFL}^2$ with $\mathcal{U}^2$-tableau is a very good approximation of $\mathcal{SKL}^3$.

As discussed in Remark 8 proofs in $\mathcal{SKL}^3$ may be inevitably longer than proofs in $\mathcal{SFL}^2$. This, however, does not mean that short proofs are excluded by the $\mathcal{U}^2$-strategy if they exist in the three-valued calculus, since the truth value set tf in $\mathcal{TPF}^3$ proofs does not occur for the normal fragment of $\mathcal{SKL}^3$.

In the resolution calculus $\mathcal{RPF}^3$ [KK94], we have a similar conservativity and strategy result. One reason for that is that the clause normal form transformations directly correspond to the analytic tableau rules for connectives and quantifiers. For details see [KK97].

4 Conclusion

In this paper we have refuted the common assumption, that a three-valued treatment of partial functions following the ideas of Kleene is impractical, since it requires a fundamental redesign of the current theorem proving technology. This tacit assumption has led to a practical preference of the simpler (but less adequate) two-valued treatment of partial functions. The results in this paper show a simple way towards a practical implementation: In an existing theorem prover for dynamic sorts like SPASS [WGR96], only the strategy $\mathcal{U}^2$ has to be imposed[v].

As we have stated in Remark 8, for most mathematical theorems, this does not even result in a loss of efficiency (proof length). However, the experiment in SPASS should not be regarded as a full-blown implementation of the normal fragment of $\mathcal{SKL}^3$, since the interaction with equality and the interaction of the $\mathcal{U}^3$-strategy with the other strategies (e.g. reduction) has not been addressed in this paper. We leave this problem to future work.

From another perspective, the $\mathcal{U}^3$ strategy can be seen as a substitute (that is easier to implement) for the third truth value, whose presence is adequately represented by marking a two-valued literal by $\mathcal{U}$. Note that this underlines the intuition, that strong Kleene logic is a variant of classical first-order logic that only adds a definedness check for the application of partial functions to the logic without changing the logic proper. In particular, it is plausible that results as those presented in this paper will not in general hold for multi-valued logics.

---

[v] Christoph Weidenbach has added the necessary extensions to the pure resolution part of SPASS [WGR96] in a matter of a few hours.

Note that it is essential for the theorem prover to be able to treat dynamic sorts, for the conservativity results break down with most relativisation techniques. The only counterexample is the technique of term relativisation [Sti86], where in the case of static tree-ordered sorts a conservativity theorem holds. If this could be extended to dynamic sorts, then any existing theorem prover could (without loss of efficiency) be augmented by partial functions by a term relativisation pre-process and $\mathcal{U}^2$.

References

[BF95]   Matthias Baaz and Christian G. Fermüller. Resolution-based theorem proving for many-valued logics. *Journal of Symbolic Computation*, 19(4):353–391, April 1995.

[BFL*94]   Juan C. Bicarregui, John S. Fitzgerald, Peter A. Lindsay, Richard Moore, and Brian Ritchie. *Proof in VDM: A Practitioner's Guide*. Springer, London, United Kingdom, 1994.

[Far90]   William M. Farmer. A partial functions version of Church's simple theory of types. *The Journal of Symbolic Logic*, 55(3):1269–1291, 1990.

[Häh94]   Reiner Hähnle. Automated Deduction in Multiple-Valued Logics, Oxford University Press, 1994.

[Jon90]   Cliff B. Jones. *Systematic Software Development using VDM*. Prentice Hall, New York, USA, second edition, 1990.

[KK94]   Manfred Kerber and Michael Kohlhase. A mechanization of strong Kleene logic for partial functions. In *Proc. CADE-12*, pp. 371–385, 1994. Springer LNAI 814.

[KK96]   Manfred Kerber and Michael Kohlhase. A tableau calculus for partial functions. *Collegium Logicum – Annals of the Kurt Gödel Society*, 2:21–49, 1996.

[KK97]   Manfred Kerber and Michael Kohlhase. Mechanising Partiality without Re-Implementation. Technical Report CSRP-97-10, School of Computer Science, The University of Birmingham, Birmingham, England, 1997 `ftp://ftp.cs.bham.ac.uk/pub/tech-reports/1997/CSRP-97-10.ps.gz`.

[Kle52]   Stephen C. Kleene. *Introduction to Metamathematics*. Van Nostrand, 1952.

[LG89]   Francisca Lucio-Carrasco and Antonio Gavilanes-Franco. A first order logic for partial functions. In *Proceedings STACS'89*, pages 47–58. Springer, LNCS 349, 1989.

[Sco70]   Dana Scott. Outline of a mathematical theory of computation. In *Proc. Fourth Annual Princeton Conference on Information Sciences and Systems*, pages 169–176. Princeton University, 1970.

[Sti86]   Mark E. Stickel Schubert's Steamroller Problem: Formulations and Solutions, *Journal of Automated Reasoning*, 2:89–101, 1986.

[Tic82]   Pawel Tichy. Foundations of partial type theory. *Reports on Mathematical Logic*, 14:59–72, 1982.

[WO90]   Christoph Weidenbach and Hans Jürgen Ohlbach. A resolution calculus with dynamic sort structures and partial functions. *Proceedings of the 9th ECAI*, pages 688–693, 1990. Pitman.

[Wei95]   Christoph Weidenbach. First-order tableaux with sorts. *Journal of the Interest Group in Pure and Applied Logics, IGPL*, 3(6):887–906, 1995.

[WGR96]   Christoph Weidenbach, Bernd Gaede and Georg Rock. Spass & Flotter, Version 0.42, In *Proc. CADE-13* pages 141–145, 1996. Springer LNAI 1104.

From Linear Proofs to Direct Logic with Exponentials

Enno Sandner

Fachgebiet Wissensverarbeitung, Fakultät Informatik
Technische Universität Dresden
enno@inf.tu-dresden.de

Abstract. Following the idea of *Linear Proofs* presented in [4] we introduce the Direct Logic [14] with exponentials (DLE). The logic combines Direct Logic with the exponentials of Linear Logic. For a well-chosen subclass of formulas of this logic we provide a matrix-characterization which can be used as a foundation for proof-search methods based on the connection calculus.

1 Introduction

The last years have shown a growing interest in the computer science community concerning non-classical logics [8]. Besides well-known approaches like Girard's Linear Logic [12] the linear connection method (LCM) proposed by Bibel [4] and its underlying notion of the *Linear Proof* have so far not gained the deserved attention. Bibel aimed at overcoming the frame-problem [18] in deductive planning tasks, which were defined by an initial situation, situation-transform rules, called *actions rules* for short, and a goal situation. Formulas were used to represent (consumable) resources. To avoid frame axioms the applicability of formulas was restricted to at most once during a proof. This restriction reflects to the consumption of the resource represented by the formula but preserves the liberty to let some resources *unconsumed*. Action rules, intended to be *reusable*, could be copied arbitrarily often in the proof. Instead of developing a completely new method to perform planning in this setting, Bibel used a variation of the connection method [2]. There the spanning set of connections has additionally to fulfill the linearity constraint, which claims that a literal must not to be connected more than once. Unfortunately the presentation in [4] lacks a precise definition of the underlying logic, i.e. it remains unclear what is proved by the LCM. Though a lot of work has been done in relating the Linear Proofs concept with standard presentations of logics [3, 9] we think that they fail in introducing a reasonable counterpart for the reusability of action-rules. This is in our opinion mainly caused by the demand to stay as close as possible to the original presentation, which allows an easy distinction between action-rules and the formulas describing the initial (goal) situation. The approach of this paper is different. We consider the formulas used in [4] as being a specific subclass of formulas of a logic – in rough analogy like horn-formulas being part of the first-order formulas. The aim of this paper is to present this logic and identify the appropriate subclass of formulas.

The central idea is simple: Combine Direct Logic (i.e. $\mathcal{L}_K$ without contraction) [1, 14] with the exponentials of Linear Logic, to reintroduce contraction. Because contraction is not available in general, no formula (resource) can be reused in a proof unless it is marked as *reusable*. In contrast to Linear Logic weakening is still present and therefore formulas need not necessarily be used in a proof, i.e. they can remain unconsumed. The resulting logic is called *Direct Logic with exponentials*, DLE for short, and is a fragment of Affine Logic, i.e. Linear Logic with weakening. We provide a matrix-characterization for a subclass of the DLE-formulas and outline the relation to the LCM.

The paper is organized as follows. In the next section we introduce DLE, its syntax, an appropriate sequent calculus, and its semantics. Then we present a matrix-characterization for a subclass of DLE formulas. Afterwards we sketch the proof of the correspondence between the DLE and the given matrix-characterization and outline the relation between the LCM and the DLE. We conclude with a comparison of related work and some notes about future extensions.

2 DLE – Direct Logic with exponentials

In this section we introduce the DLE. We begin with the syntax and proof-theory and then provide possible world semantics.

2.1 Syntax and proof-theory

The language of DLE is an extension of the first-order language with two unary modalities !, ?, named the *exponentials*. More precisely we assume a countable infinite set of variables V, functions O and relation symbols Rel. Nullary function symbols are called constants. Atomic formulas, denoted by F_0 and composite formulas (F) based on the logical connectives $\neg, !, ?, \wedge, \vee$ and the quantifiers $\forall, \exists$ ($\neg, !, ?$ are considered as unary and $\wedge, \vee$ as binary) are build as usual. Terms (T), subformulas, free and bound occurrences of variables are also defined in the usual way. The set of ground terms, i.e. terms without variables is denoted by T^g. A sentence is a formula without free-variables. A formula is said to be in negation-normal form (short: NNF) if no non-atomic formula is in the scope of some negation. The set of all formulas in NNF is denoted by F^{nnf}. A formula is $\approx$-*prenex* if it is in NNF and no universal-quantifier is in the scope of some conjunction. We use $A_{t_1,\ldots t_n}^{x_1,\ldots x_n}$ for some $n \in \mathbb{N}$ to denote the simultaneous substitution of the variables $x_1, \ldots x_n$ by the terms $t_1, \ldots t_n$. For arbitrary formulas $\phi, \psi \in F$ we introduce the implication $\phi \rightarrow \psi$ as an abbreviation for $\neg \phi \vee \psi$.

The meaning of the connectives are defined by a sequent-calculus which is a combination of *Direct Logic* [1, 14] ($\mathcal{L}_K$ without the contraction rule) and the exponentials of *Linear Logic* [12]. Because weakening is already present, we can drop the explicit weakening rules for the exponentials. In the following possible indexed occurrences of Γ and Δ denote finite (possible empty) multi-sets of formulas, A, B arbitrary formulas, x, a variables and t a (compound) term.

$$\frac{}{A \Rightarrow A}\ Id \qquad \frac{\Gamma_1 \Rightarrow A, \Delta_1 \quad \Gamma_2, A \Rightarrow \Delta_2}{\Gamma_1, \Gamma_2 \Rightarrow \Delta_1, \Delta_2}\ Cut$$

$$\frac{\Gamma \Rightarrow \Delta}{\Gamma, A \Rightarrow \Delta}\ WL \qquad \frac{\Gamma \Rightarrow \Delta}{\Gamma \Rightarrow A, \Delta}\ WR \qquad \frac{\Gamma \Rightarrow A, \Delta}{\Gamma, \neg A \Rightarrow \Delta}\ \neg L \qquad \frac{\Gamma, A \Rightarrow \Delta}{\Gamma \Rightarrow \neg A, \Delta}\ \neg R$$

$$\frac{\Gamma, A, B \Rightarrow \Delta}{\Gamma, A \wedge B \Rightarrow \Delta}\ \wedge L \qquad \frac{\Gamma_1 \Rightarrow A, \Delta_1 \quad \Gamma_2 \Rightarrow B, \Delta_2}{\Gamma_1, \Gamma_2 \Rightarrow A \wedge B, \Delta_1, \Delta_2}\ \wedge R$$

$$\frac{\Gamma_1, A \Rightarrow \Delta_1 \quad \Gamma_2, B \Rightarrow \Delta_2}{\Gamma_1, \Gamma_2, A \vee B \Rightarrow \Delta_1, \Delta_2}\ \vee L \qquad \frac{\Gamma \Rightarrow A, B, \Delta}{\Gamma \Rightarrow A \vee B, \Delta}\ \vee R$$

$$\frac{\Gamma, A_t^x \Rightarrow \Delta}{\Gamma, \forall x. A \Rightarrow \Delta}\ \forall L \qquad \frac{\Gamma \Rightarrow A_a^x, \Delta}{\Gamma \Rightarrow \forall x. A, \Delta}\ \forall R \qquad \frac{\Gamma, A_a^x \Rightarrow \Delta}{\Gamma, \exists x. A \Rightarrow \Delta}\ \exists L \qquad \frac{\Gamma \Rightarrow A_t^x, \Delta}{\Gamma \Rightarrow \exists x. A, \Delta}\ \exists R$$

$$\frac{\Gamma, !A, !A \Rightarrow \Delta}{\Gamma, !A \Rightarrow \Delta}\ !C \qquad \frac{\Gamma, A \Rightarrow \Delta}{\Gamma, !A \Rightarrow \Delta}\ !D \qquad \frac{!\Gamma \Rightarrow A, ?\Delta}{!\Gamma \Rightarrow !A, ?\Delta}\ !E$$

$$\frac{\Gamma \Rightarrow ?A, ?A, \Delta}{\Gamma \Rightarrow ?A, \Delta}\ ?C \qquad \frac{\Gamma \Rightarrow A, \Delta}{\Gamma \Rightarrow ?A, \Delta}\ ?D \qquad \frac{!\Gamma, A \Rightarrow ?\Delta}{!\Gamma, ?A \Rightarrow ?\Delta}\ ?E$$

with the usual restrictions for the quantifier rules and $!\Gamma = !A_1, !A_2, \ldots, !A_n$ ($?\Delta = ?A_1, ?A_2, \ldots, ?A_n$) for $n \in \mathbb{N}$, $\Gamma = \Delta = A_1, A_2, \ldots, A_n$. We name the sequent-calculus $\mathcal{L}_{DLE}$. The fragment without exponentials and quantifier rules is called $\mathcal{L}_{DLE}^{qe}$. Its formulas are said to be *simple*.

Direct Logic is known to be decidable [1, 14]. Therefore the exponential-free fragment is indeed weaker as classical first order logic (short: classical logic). Due to the exponentials we can reobtain the power of classical logic, i.e. for every formula in classical logic there exists a formula in the DLE which is provable iff the DLE formula is provable. In addition the DLE is a fragment of Affine Logic. From [15] we know that the propositional fragment of Affine Logic (with exponentials) is decidable. By this the propositional fragment of the DLE is also decidable.

The following results are the foundation for the matrix-characterization presented in the next section. The first theorem states that the cut-rule is superfluous with regard to provability. The rather longish proof is omitted.

Theorem 1. *Cut-elimination for $\mathcal{L}_{DLE}$.*
Every proof in $\mathcal{L}_{DLE}$ can be transformed to a proof with the same end-sequent but without an application of the cut rule. □

Let us call two formulas $\phi, \psi \in F$ *weakly-equivalent* if whenever $\Rightarrow \phi$ then $\Rightarrow \psi$ and vice versa. It is easy to see, that given a $\phi \in F$ we can always find a weakly-equivalent sentence $\psi \in F^{nnf}$ in NNF eliminating double negations, use the dualities between $\wedge, \vee, \forall, \exists$ and $!, ?$ to propagate the negations to subformulas and finally close the formula with universal quantifiers. Therefore from the point of provability regarding only sentences in NNF is no restriction. We will make use of this to simplify the presentation.

The following theorems could be summarized as an attempt to *approximate* the provability of formulas by simple sentences. We start with a theorem which can be seen as the counterpart of the Skolem-Herbrand theorem for exponentials. For this we need some additional notation.

Definition 2. $\wedge, \vee$-Expansion, $!,?$-Instance.

Let $\phi \in F^{nnf}$ be a formula and ψ a designated subformula of ϕ. We call a substitution of ψ by $\overbrace{\psi \wedge \ldots \wedge \psi}^{n-times}$ $(\overbrace{\psi \vee \ldots \vee \psi}^{n-times})$ for $n \in \mathbb{N}_1$ ($\mathbb{N}_1 := \mathbb{N} \setminus \{0\}$) a $\wedge$-*expansion* ($\vee$-*expansion*). A $!$-instance ($?$-instance) of ϕ is the result of substituting every subformula $!\psi$ ($?\psi$) by a $\wedge$-expansion ($\vee$-expansion) of ψ. $\qquad\square$

For example $\neg\phi \vee \phi$ and $\neg\phi \vee (\phi \wedge \phi)$ are both $!$-instances of $\neg\phi\vee!\phi$ for $\phi \in F_0$. The next theorem shows that exponentials can be *approximated* by exponential free formulas.

Theorem 3. *Approximation-theorem for exponentials.*
Let $\phi \in F^{nnf}$ be a formula.

1. *If ϕ is provable, then for each $!$-instance of ϕ there is a provable $?$-instance.*
2. *Let ϕ exponential free with designated subformulas $\psi_1^\wedge, \ldots \psi_n^\wedge, \psi_1^\vee, \ldots \psi_m^\vee$ for $n, m \in \mathbb{N}$. If for each $\wedge$-expansion of $\psi_1^\wedge, \ldots \psi_n^\wedge$ there is a $\vee$-expansion of $\psi_1^\vee, \ldots \psi_m^\vee$ and the resulting formula is provable then the formula obtained by substituting $\psi_i^\wedge$ with $!\psi_i^\wedge$ and $\psi_j^\wedge$ with $?\psi_j^\wedge$ for $1 \le i \le n$ and $1 \le j \le m$ is also provable.* $\qquad\square$

Note, though the $!$-instance $\neg\phi \vee \phi$ of $\neg\phi\vee!\phi$ is provable, according to theorem 3 $\neg\phi\vee!\phi$ correctly fails to be provable, because its $!$-instance $\neg\phi \vee (\phi \wedge \phi)$ is not provable.

Next we relate the provability of a formula with quantifiers with the provability of quantifier-free formulas. We begin with Herbrand's theorem that turns out to be trivial for an exponential free formula, because in a proof of such a formula no contraction can be applied. Therefore the Herbrand disjunction is of length 1. For this let us call a simple sentence $\hat\phi \in F^{nnf}$ obtained from an exponential and universal quantifier free sentence $\phi \in F^{nnf}$ by substituting every subformula $\exists x.\psi$ of ϕ with ψ_t^x for some $t \in T^g$ a *ground instance* of ϕ.

Corollary 4. *Herbrand theorem for Direct Logic.*
Let $\phi \in F^{nnf}$ be an exponential and universal quantifier free sentence. Then ϕ is provable iff there exists a ground instance $\hat\phi \in F^{nnf}$ of ϕ which is provable. $\qquad\square$

To get rid of universal quantifiers but keep close to the presentation of [4] we try to remove the universal quantifiers *before* proof-search.[1] In classical logic the standard approach is to use skolemization for this task. In non-classical logics, like the DLE this quite often turns out to be non-practicable. Consider e.g. the classical but DLE unprovable sequent $\Rightarrow \exists x.(\neg p(x) \vee \neg q), q \wedge \forall y.p(y)$ for some sentence q. Applying classical skolemization leads to $\Rightarrow \exists x.(\neg p(x) \vee \neg q), q \wedge p(c)$ for some new constant c, which is a derivable sequent in the DLE, i.e. classical skolemization turns out to be unsound in the DLE. A closer examination

---

[1] Another approach is to perform skolemization *during* the proof search [7, 20].

of the sequent-rules shows that this behavior is caused by the inpermutabil-
ities (see e.g. [11]) of the DLE, i.e. constraints on the order of the rule application. Here the two inpermutable pairs $\wedge R, \vee R$ and $\forall R, \exists R$ cause a *dead-
lock* in reducing the sequent. In general the skolem-function have to record
exactly the a-priori detected violations against the preferred reduction ordering, concerning the universal quantifier. Without going into details one might
get an idea that there is no simple substitution for the universal quantifier, if
one realizes that $\Rightarrow \exists x.(\neg p(x) \vee \neg q), q \wedge \forall y.p(y), \neg q$ is a provable sequent while
$\Rightarrow \exists x.(\neg p(x) \vee \neg q), q \wedge \forall y.p(y), a$ is not. If we restrict ourself to $\approx$-prenex formulas things turn out to be more friendly, because the $\wedge R, \vee R$ inpermutability
has no longer an impact on the elimination of the universal quantifier. To obtain
a reasonable proof-procedure we further narrow the class of $\approx$-prenex sentences
to those without the !-exponential. These formulas will be called *regular* and
are denoted by F°. For regular formulas classical skolemization is sound (and
complete). The following theorem restates the previous results for this restricted
formula class.

Corollary 5. *Approximation for regular-formulas.*
*Any regular $\phi \in F^\circ$ is provable iff there is an ?-instance and ground-instance
such that the resulting formula is also provable.* $\qquad\qquad\square$

Let us demonstrate the applicability of the DLE for planning tasks by a
simple example. We borrow the *getting a drink* example from [13]. We have five
50 Pfennig coins and want to get two cokes for one *Mark* from an automaton
that only accepts one Mark coins. Assuming that there is an action to exchange
two 50 Pfennig coins in a one Mark coin, the resulting planning problem (which
could be rewritten as a regular formula) reads as:

$$!(m \to c) \wedge \,!(p \wedge p \to m) \wedge p \wedge p \wedge p \wedge p \wedge p \to c \wedge c$$

whereby the exponentials are used to mark the reusability of the action rules
and m, c, p represent a Mark, a coke, respectively a 50 Pfennig coin. We omit
the easy proof of this formula. Note that, following the ideas of [4] we may use
unification to collect the appropriate actions.

2.2 Semantics

An appealing feature of classical logic is its simple model-theoretic semantics.
In general non-classical logics do not have such simple semantics and the DLE
forms no exception. In this section we present algebraic semantics related to
those of [10, 19]).

The semantics are defined in two steps. Firstly corresponding structures, so
called *DLE-structures* for simple formulas are introduced. In contrast to [10, 19]
we do not use additional operators and interpret exponentials and quantifiers
purely in DLE-structures. Exponentials and quantifiers are treated as *modalities*
and we use *accessibility relations* to encode their typical properties. In this way
our semantics could be seen as an extension of possible world semantics, whereby

classical truth, i.e. boolean algebras are exchanged by algebraic structures suitable to reflect truth of simple formulas. Let us begin with the definition of the underlying algebraic structures.

Definition 6. DLE-structure.
A DLE-structure $\mathcal{D} = (D, \leq, \circ, +, -)$ consists of a complete ortho-lattice [5] $(D, \leq, -)$, a commutative semi-group $(D, \circ)$ with $\circ$ order-preserving, residuated and monotone on $(D, \leq)$, i.e. $a \leq b \Rightarrow a \circ c \leq b \circ c, a \circ b \leq c \iff a \leq -b + c$ and $a \circ b \leq a$ for $a, b, c \in D$. $+$ is defined dual to $\circ$, i.e. $a + b = -(-a \circ -b)$. $\quad\square$

It is helpful to note that DLE-structures reflect the properties *spanning, linear and acyclic* introduced in the next section.

The key for understanding the following definition is to recognize that classical logic can be considered as a multi-modal logic, whereby the family of quantifiers $(\forall x)_{x \in V}$ and $(\exists x)_{x \in V}$ play the role of modalities. The *worlds* are all possible variable assignments and the *accessibility relation* R_x for $\forall x$ and $\exists x$ relates variable assignments that are equal up to variable x. Adapting this idea to our needs we obtain:

Definition 7. Semantics of the DLE.
Let $\mathcal{J} = (J, (f)_{f \in O})$ a term-algebra and $\mathcal{D}$ a DLE-structure. We denote the set of all variable-assignments into $\mathcal{J}$ by J^V. A 6-tuple $\mathcal{R} = (\mathcal{J}, \mathcal{D}, (\rho_r)_{r \in Rel}, W, R, d)$ is called a *realization in a DLE-structure* provided $\rho_r : J^k \to D$ is a mapping associated with each k-ary atomic relation symbol $r \in Rel$, named the *r-realizer*, W is a non-empty set of *worlds*, $R \subseteq W \times W$ a reflexive and transitive relation on W and $d : W \to 2^{J^V}$ a mapping, assigning to each world a non-empty set of *applicable* variable assignments. d fulfills the following hereditary condition: For every $w, \hat{w} \in W$: if $(w, \hat{w}) \in R$ then $d(w) \subseteq d(\hat{w})$. Intuitively this condition states that every variable assignment applicable in a world is also applicable in all other reachable worlds. Assume $v \in d(w)$. For each formula $\phi \in F$ the realization $\mathcal{R}$ induces a mapping $\phi_{\mathcal{R}} : W \times J^V \to D$ defined as:

- For an n-ary relation symbol $r \in Rel$ ($n \in \mathbb{N}$) and $t_1, t_2, \ldots t_n \in T$ we have $r(t_1, t_2, \ldots t_n)_{\mathcal{R}}(w, v) = \rho_r(v(t_1), v(t_2), \ldots v(t_n))$ (we do not distinguish v and its homomorphic extension to J^T).
- The logical connectives are homomorphicly extended, e.g.

$$(\phi \wedge \psi)_{\mathcal{R}}(w, v) = \phi_{\mathcal{R}}(w, v) \circ \psi_{\mathcal{R}}(w, v)$$

- The exponentials and the quantifiers are denotated using the infinite join $\bigvee$ and meet $\bigwedge$ in $\mathcal{D}$:

$$(\forall x.\phi)_{\mathcal{R}}(w, v) = \bigwedge \{\phi_{\mathcal{R}}(w, \hat{v}) \mid v =_x \hat{v} \text{ and } \hat{v} \in d(w)\}$$

$$(!\phi)_{\mathcal{R}}(w, v) = \bigwedge \{\phi_{\mathcal{R}}(\hat{w}, v) \mid (w, \hat{w}) \in R\}$$

whereby $v =_x \hat{v}$ holds, if $v, \hat{v} \in J^V$ are equal up to the assignment of variable x. We further require that

$$(!\phi \wedge !\psi)_{\mathcal{R}}(w, v) = \bigwedge \{(!\phi)_{\mathcal{R}}(w, v), (!\psi)_{\mathcal{R}}(w, v)\}$$

to reflect the contractability of !. The remaining exponential and quantifier is defined dual.

A formula $\phi \in F$ is *satisfiable* in a realization $\mathcal{R}$, if there is a world w and an applicable variable assignment v with $\phi_{\mathcal{R}}(w, v) = 1$. $\mathcal{R}$ is a *model* of ϕ if every world with its applicable variable assignments satisfies ϕ in $\mathcal{R}$. ϕ is *valid*, if every realization is a model of ϕ. □

We can show soundness and completeness of this semantics versus provability in the sequent calculus, i.e. a formula $\phi \in F$ is provable iff ϕ is valid. It is noteworthy that exchanging DLE-structures by boolean algebras leads to a semantic of first-order modal logic S4 with cumulative domains [21]. People familiar with [21, 16] may recognize that our semantics could be helpful to obtain a Wallen style matrix-characterization of the DLE, whereby the accessibility relations reflect the conditions imposed on the substitutions.

3   Linear Proofs revisited

We turn to an appropriate matrix-characterization for regular formulas. For a logic with a consequence relation definable by a sequent-calculus, a *matrix-characterization* consists of a description of the *well-formed matrices* (short: matrices), a concept defining which matrices are considered as *complementary* and two functions relating formulas with matrices and vice versa. In our example a matrix represents some weakly-equivalent regular formulas. The complementarity of this representation guarantees the existence of a class of sequent proofs for the corresponding formulas. Thus a complementary matrix is a compact evidence for provability in a sequent calculus.

It has already been mentioned [9] that the representation of matrices as a set of sets [2] turn out to be not directly applicable in the setting of non-classical logics. In this paper we represent matrices as terms over some basic building blocks, called *literals*. A literal consists of a *polarity* and a *label*. The polarity can take two values: 0 or 1. For simplicity we assume that the labels are just the atomic formulas of the DLE. We define the set of literals or *atomic matrices* M_0 by $M_0 = \{(p, \phi_0) \mid p \in \{0, 1\} \text{ and } \phi_0 \in F_0\}$ and use the unary $\sqcap, \sqcup, \bigvee, \nabla$ to build composite matrices. The set of matrices M is defined as the smallest set fulfilling 1-3 below:

1. $M_0 \subseteq M$
2. If $m \in M$ and $v \in V$ then $\nabla m, \bigvee v.m \in M$
3. If $m_1, m_2 \in M$ then $m_1 \sqcap m_2, m_1 \sqcup m_2 \in M$

The polarity represents formulas in the succedent respectively antecedent. $\bigvee$ corresponds to the existential quantifier and ∇ to the ?-exponential. By this definition every non-atomic matrix can be decomposed in its submatrices, e.g. m_1 and m_2 are submatrices of $m_1 \sqcap m_2$. We use $m_1 \sqsubseteq m$ to denote that either $m_1 = m$ or m_1 is a submatrix of m. A matrix is called *simple* if it does not contain any variables and no occurrences of ∇ and $\bigvee$. The set of all simple matrices is denoted by M^S. We call a variable $v \in V$ *bound* in a submatrix m_1 of m, if m has submatrix of the form $\bigvee v.m_2$ and $m_1 \sqsubseteq m_2$. Otherwise v is said to be *free* in m_1. Two matrices m_1 and m_2 are $\sqcup$ ($\sqcap$) *related* in a matrix m, if there is a submatrix $\hat{m}_1 \sqcup \hat{m}_2$ ($\hat{m}_1 \sqcap \hat{m}_2$) of m and $m_1 \sqsubseteq \hat{m}_1$ and $m_2 \sqsubseteq \hat{m}_2$. A *closed matrix* is a matrix without free variables. We denote the set of all closed matrices with M°.

We associate with each submatrix a unique *position* represented as a finite string over $\{0,1\}$. The root position is denoted by ϵ and the set of all positions by $\{0,1\}^*$. For a position $n \in \{0,1\}^*$ and $i \in \{0,1\}$, $i.n$ denotes a subposition of n. The *principal type* of a non-atomic matrix is its uppermost connective. We use the function $\text{PTYPE} : M \times \{0,1\}^* \rightarrow \{atomic, \nabla, \sqcup, \sqcap, \bigvee\}$ to denote the principal type of a submatrix or *atomic* in the case that the matrix is atomic. A position n in a matrix m is called *atomic* if $\text{PTYPE}(m,n) = atomic$. Due to the definition of matrices every atomic position has an associated label and a polarity.

Having clarified the syntax of matrices we turn to the complementarity concept, which is defined in two steps. First the notion of *basic-linear complementarity* for simple matrices is introduced. Based upon this definition we define the *linear complementarity* for closed matrices. This reflects the results of the previous section concerning the approximation of regular formulas by simple formulas.

Definition 8. Path of a simple matrix.
A path of $m \in M^S$ is a set of positions constructed in the following way (with $n, m \in \{0,1\}^*$ being positions):

1. $\{\epsilon\}$ is a path.
2. If $P \mathbin{\dot{\cup}} \{n\}$ ($\dot{\cup}$ denotes the disjoint union) is a path and $\text{PTYPE}(m,n) = \sqcap$ then $P \cup \{0.n\}$ and $P \cup \{1.n\}$ are both paths.
3. If $P \mathbin{\dot{\cup}} \{n\}$ is a path and $\text{PTYPE}(m,n) = \sqcup$ then $P \cup \{0.n, 1.n\}$ is also a path.

A path is *atomic* if all positions are atomic. □

Besides paths a central concept for defining basic-linear complementarity is the *connection*.

Definition 9. Connection of a simple matrix.
Let $m \in M^S$ be a simple matrix. A *connection* of m is a set of two $\sqcup$-related atomic positions with identical labels but different polarities. If $\{l, k\}$ is a connection of m (l, k) is called a *connection-pair* of m. The *connection-pairs induced by a connection* $\{l, k\}$ are (l, k) and (k, l). A *connection chain* is a finite sequence of connections-pairs $((l_i, k_i))_{1 \leq i \leq n}$ for some $n \in \mathbb{N}$ with the l_i and k_i pairwise distinct, k_i and l_{i+1} $\sqcap$-related, l_i (k_i) $\sqcup$-related to all other positions of the connection-chain but l_i and $k_{i-1 \bmod n}$ (k_i and $l_{i+1 \bmod n}$). A connection chain is called *cyclic* when in addition l_1 is $\sqcap$-related to k_n. Otherwise it is called *acyclic*.

A set of connections S of m is called *spanning* if every atomic path through m contains at least one connection. S is called *linear* if no two different connections share a common position. Because every connection induces a set of connection-pairs, every subset of S induces a (possible empty) set of connection-chains. The set of induced connection-chains of S is just the union of all induced connection-chains of subsets of S. S is said to be *acyclic* if every induced connection chain of S is acyclic. □

The acyclicity condition necessitates some further explanation. In the next section provability of DLE formulas is associated with the complementarity of the corresponding matrices. Roughly, the acyclicity condition reflects the tree-like structure of sequent-proofs and is necessary to ensure soundness of the matrix-characterization (see e.g. [9] for a more detailed discussion).

The next definition relates simple matrices with closed matrices. It is the key to lift basic linear complementarity to linear complementarity.

Definition 10. ∇- and simple instances.
Let $m \in M^\circ$ be a closed matrix. A matrix $\bar{m} \in M$ obtained from m by replacing every submatrix $\nabla \hat{m}$, ($\bigvee v.\hat{m}$ for $v \in V$) with $\overbrace{\hat{m} \sqcup \ldots \sqcup \hat{m}}^{n-times}$ for $n \in \mathbb{N}_1$ ($\hat{m}_t^v$ for some ground term $t \in T^g$) is called a ∇ (simple) instance. □

We are now in the position to define linear complementarity.

Definition 11. Linear complementarity.
A simple matrix $m \in M^S$ is said to be *basic linear complementary* ($\vdash_b m$) if there is a linear, acyclic and spanning set of connections of m. A closed matrix $m \in M^\circ$ is *linear complementary* ($\vdash m$) if there is a ∇-instance and a variable-instance $\hat{m}$ of m such that $\hat{m}$ is basic linear complementary. □

The reader familiar with [2] or [9] might be confused by the rather complicated representation of matrices. To keep our approach extendable we have decided to separate the way matrices are displayed, briefly called the *display-form* from their representation as mathematical objects, its *mathematical representation*. The display-form is just an appealing graphical notation of mathematical representation exploiting some equivalences induced by the complementarity concept, while the mathematical representation should provide some uniformity in the representation and proofs related to the representation. In our example connections can been drawn without taking care of the structure of matrices. So we will at least identify matrices up to commutativity and associativity. Employing the linearity constraint, multisets seem to be the right choice to represent matrices. If literals could be connected arbitrarily often, matrices would be identified up to idempotency and would end up with the set representation of matrices proposed for classical logic in [2].

4 Returning to DLE

It remains to clarify that the matrix-characterization reflects the provability of DLE-formulas. For this we firstly relate formulas and matrices. Let $(F^\circ)^s$ be obtained from F° by eliminating universal quantifiers using skolemization.

Definition 12. Let $i : (F^\circ)^s \to M^\circ$ and $j : M^\circ \to (F^\circ)^s$ be mappings from formulas to matrices and vice versa defined as:

$$i(\phi_0) = (0, \phi) \qquad i(\neg\phi_0) = (1, \phi) \qquad i(\phi \wedge \psi) = i(\phi) \sqcap i(\psi)$$
$$i(\phi \vee \psi) = i(\phi) \sqcup i(\psi) \qquad i(?\phi) = \nabla i(\phi) \qquad i(\exists x.\phi) = \bigvee x.i(\phi)$$

whereby $\phi_0 \in F_0$, $\phi, \psi \in (F^\circ)^s$ and $x \in V$. j is defined as $j = i^{-1}$. $\qquad\square$

Given this, the correspondence result reads as:

Theorem 13. *Completeness and Soundness.*
Let $\phi \in (F^\circ)^s$ and $m \in M^\circ$. For every provable sequent $\Rightarrow \phi$ the matrix $i(\phi)$ is linear complementary and for every linear complementary matrix m the sequent $\Rightarrow j(m)$ is provable.
Proof-sketch: *For completeness assume $\Rightarrow \phi$ is a provable sequent. Using corollary 5 and definition 11 it is enough to show that for every provable simple formula $\hat\phi$ obtained from ϕ, $i(\hat\phi)$ is basic linear complementary. This can be proved by induction on the length of the sequent-proof in $\mathcal{L}_{DLE}^{qe}$.*

For soundness assume $\vdash m$. Thus there is a ∇- and a variable-instance such that the resulting matrix $\hat m$ is basic linear complementary. Using the properties of spanning, linear and acyclicity the existence of a sequent proof in $\mathcal{L}_{DLE}^{qe}$ for $\Rightarrow j(\hat m)$ can be shown. Applying corollary 5 allows us to conclude that $\Rightarrow j(m)$ is provable. $\qquad\square$

In general one need additionally $\Rightarrow \phi$ provable if $\Rightarrow j(i(\phi))$ provable and $\vdash m$ if $\vdash i(j(m))$. Otherwise two non-equivalent formulas $\phi, \psi \in F$ with ϕ provable and ψ not provable could be handled similar in their matrix-representation (choose e.g. $i(\phi) = i(\psi) = m$ and $j(m) = \phi$). Due to our previous assumptions i, j are injective and such problems cannot occur.

Bearing the discussion of the previous section in mind we return to the *getting a drink* example and represent the following proof in a 2-dimensional way. To mark *expandable* parts of the matrix we use dashed boxes. The indices represent the multiplicity of the box, i.e. how often the box has to be copied to perform the proof. In addition we use the negation sign to mark literals with polarity 1. Note that a reasonable proof-procedure based on this matrix-characterization

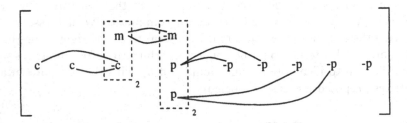

Fig. 1. Connection proof of the getting-a-drink example

would perform the expansion of the ∇ matrices *by need*.

5 The correspondence between the LCM and the DLE

The language used in [4] for representing planning tasks is best described by introducing three classes of formulas. Every planning problem considered in [4] consists of a description of an initial situation, several action rules and a goal situation. We use the term I-,A- and G-formulas to denote the appropriate formula classes. Let us abbreviate a conjunction of atomic formulas by an *a-conjunction*. An I-formula is a closed universally quantified a-conjunction of formulas. An A-formula is a closed universally or/and existential quantified implication of two a-conjunctions. Finally a G-formula is a closed existential quantified a-conjunction. Given that $I, A_1, \ldots A_n$ for $n \in \mathbb{N}$ and G are respectively I-,A- and G-formulas $I \wedge \bigwedge_{1 \leq i \leq n} \underline{A_i} \rightarrow G$ is a description of a planning problem. In contrast to I- and G-formulas which can be used at most once, A-formulas can be used arbitrarily often in a proof, which is represented by the underline. The classical formula $I \wedge \bigwedge_{1 \leq i \leq n} \underline{A_i} \rightarrow G$ is translated into the DLE formula $I \wedge \bigwedge_{1 \leq i \leq n} !A_i \rightarrow G$. The !-exponential reflects the reusability of the action rules. It is easy to show that $I \wedge \bigwedge_{1 \leq i \leq n} \underline{A_i} \rightarrow G$ is valid according to the LCM iff $I \wedge \bigwedge_{1 \leq i \leq n} !A_i \rightarrow G$ is a provable DLE formula. Thus there is a direct correspondence between classical first order formulas valid according to the LCM and a subclass of provable regular DLE-formulas.

6 Conclusion

We have presented a logic that nicely reflects the concept of Linear Proofs and offers the possibility to *locally relax* this concept in a controlled manner. By this we extend the results of [9] concerning a calculus for the LCM in a reasonable way. In our opinion the existence of Linear Logic's exponentials allow us to explore new formula classes that might be practicable for planning tasks. For instance in full DLE reasoning about actions becomes possible.

There are similarities to the work done by [17]. However in the DLE reusability is expressible at the object-level. Consider for instance $\Rightarrow \phi$ should be proved by using an action rule ψ. Instead of adding $\Rightarrow \psi$ as new axiom to the sequent calculus to represent the reusability of the action rule, we simply show the provability of $\Rightarrow !\psi \rightarrow \phi$. Our conviction is that the approach presented here is better suited for automated proof search, because adding new axioms in general prevents cut-elimination.

A careful reader might have some problems with the applicability of the non-idempotent disjunction of the DLE. Indeed it has already been observed that planning tasks use a multiplicative conjunction but an additive disjunction [17, 6] (in the terminology of [12]). This is in our opinion mainly caused by the fact that disjunction used in natural language is rather different from the multiplicative disjunction and planning is mainly triggered by real-world problems. Although it is possible to solve this problem for Horn-like formulas making use of the exponentials, we might add new connectives to the DLE representing an idempotent disjunction and its dual. In this case we end up with Affine Logic, which might be a good candidate for representing planning tasks, but so far no reasonable proof-methods have been developed for this logic. Our next step will be a matrix-characterization for the full DLE based on the results of [21, 16]. We plan to extend these results to full Affine Logic in the future.

References

1. G. BELLIN, J. KETONEN. A decision procedure revisited: Notes on Direct Logic, Linear Logic and its implementation. *Theoretical Computer Science*, 95:115–142, 1992.
2. W. BIBEL. On matrices with connections. *Journal of the ACM*, 28:633–645, 1981.
3. W. BIBEL, L. FARINAS DEL CERRO, B. FRONHÖFER, A. HERZIG. Plan Generation by Linear Proofs: On Semantics. In *GWAI'89 13th German Workshop on Artificial Intelligence* ed. D. Metzing, 49-62. Informatik-Fachberichte 216, Springer.
4. W. BIBEL. A deductive solution for plan generation. *New Generation Computing*, 4:115-132, 1986.
5. G. BIRKHOFF. Lattice Theory. American Mathematical Society, New York, 1967.
6. S. BRÜNING, S. HÖLLDOBLER, J. SCHNEEBERGER, U. SIGMUND, M. THIELSCHER. Disjunction in Resource-Oriented Deductive Planning. Technical Report AIDA-93-03, Intellektik, Informatik, TH-Darmstadt, 1994.
7. S. CERRITO. Herbrand Methods in Sequent Calculi: Unification in LL. *Proceedings of the Joint International Conference and Symposium on Logic Programming*, 607–621, 1992.
8. K. DOSEN. A Historical Introduction to Substructural logics. In *Substructural Logics* ed. by K. Dosen and P. Schroeder-Heister. Oxford University Press, 1993.
9. B. FRONHÖFER. The Action-as-Implication Paradigm. CS Press, München, 1996.
10. J. GALLIER. Constructive Logics. Part II: Linear Logic and Proof Nets. Research Report PR2-RR-9, Digital Equipment Corporation, Paris, May 1991.
11. D. GALMICHE, G. PERRIER. On Proof Normalization in Linear Logic. *Theoretical Computer Science*, 135:67–110, 1994.
12. J.-Y. GIRARD. Linear Logic. *Theoretical Computer Science*, 50:1–102, 1987.
13. G. GROSSE, S. HÖLLDOBLER, J. SCHNEEBERGER. Linear deductive planning. *Journal of Logic and Computation*, 6: 233-262, 1996.
14. J. KETONEN, R. WEYHRAUCH. A decidable fragment of predicate calculus. *Theoretical Computer Science*, 32:297-307, 1984.
15. A.P. KOPYLOV. Decidability of Linear Affine Logic. In *Tenth Annual IEEE Symposium on Logic in Computer Science* ed. by D. Kozen, 496-504, 1995.
16. C. KREITZ, H. MANTEL, J. OTTEN, S. SCHMITT. Connection-based proof construction in Linear Logic. *CADE-14*, 1997.
17. M. MASSERON, C. TOLLU, J. VAUZILLES. Generating Plans in Linear Logic I: Actions as Proofs. *Theoretical Computer Science*, 113: 349-370, 1993.
18. J. MCCARTHY, P.J. HAYES. Some Philosophical Problems from the Standpoint of Artificial Intelligence. *Machine Intelligence*, 4:463–502, 1969.
19. H. ONO. Semantics for Substructural Logics. In *Substructural Logics* ed. by K. Dosen and P. Schroeder-Heister. Oxford University Press, 1993.
20. N. SHANKAR. Proof Search in intuitionistic sequent calculus. *CADE-11*, 1992.
21. L. WALLEN. *Automated deduction in nonclassical logics*. MIT Press, 1990.

Integrating an Equality Prover into a Software Development System Based on Type Theory *

Martin Strecker, Maria Sorea

Universität Ulm
D-89069 Ulm, Germany

Abstract. This paper reports on the integration of an untyped equational prover into a proof system based on an expressive constructive type theory. The proofs returned by the equational prover are effectively verified for type correctness, a proof term can be constructed. The scheme of proof translation described here is illustrated by the integration of the DISCOUNT prover into the software development system TYPELAB.

1 Introduction

In recent years, most effort in automated reasoning research has been expended on improving the performance of systems that support deduction in classical first order logic or fragments thereof. The advances that have been achieved in this area permit to successfully apply automated theorem proving in some branches of mathematics or for problems such as diagnosis.

Because the (practical) expressiveness of first-order logic is quite restricted, most systems that are routinely used in software development or for large-scale hardware verification tasks [OSR93, Pau94, Bar96] are based on a higher-order logic with a more or less elaborate type system. The automation provided by these systems has to a great extent been directly coded into specialized tactics and mostly relies on other techniques than those employed by dedicated proof systems, such as congruence closure for equality reasoning with ground terms in PVS.

The work presented here is part of a larger research programme aiming at making traditional first-order theorem proving techniques available for fragments of more expressive logics. This paper discusses an integration of an untyped first-order equality prover into a software development system based on constructive type theory with dependent types (see Section 2). By the "propositions as types" paradigm, a proposition in type theory can be interpreted as a type whose elements are the proofs of the proposition. A proof problem can then be understood as the problem of constructing a term prf such that the typing judgement $\Gamma \vdash prf : P$ holds, where P is the type corresponding to the proposition to be proved, and Γ is a context containing the hypotheses. The approach taken for integrating an equality prover into a proof assistant for type theory is roughly the following: Given a set of hypotheses Γ and an equality P to be proved, transfer the relevant information to the equality prover (see Section 4), invoke it on the proof problem and read in the trace of the

---

* This research has partly been supported by the "Deutsche Forschungsgemeinschaft" within the "Schwerpunktprogramm Deduktion"

equality proof. The trace should permit to construct the proof object *prf*. The details of the steps carried out to obtain the proof object are spelled out in Section 5. The procedure described here has been implemented in the software development system TYPELAB [vHLS97], using DISCOUNT [DKS97] as equality prover.

There are several examples of cooperation between proof systems, most of which, however, are instances of a "black box" paradigm where results returned from the cooperating prover are not checked for validity: KIV [HRS88] uses 3TAP [BHG+96] for automating proof search in predicate logic; ILF [DGH+95] provides an interface to several proof engines (among them Discount , KoMeT, Otter, Setheo and Spass), which are called depending on the problem at hand. PVS [OSR93] invokes an external BDD package for Boolean simplification and a model checker for CTL formulas. There are only few examples of a cooperation in which results are effectively verified: Harrison [HT93] describes an interface between the HOL theorem prover and a computer algebra system, in which the result returned by the computer algebra system, such as a factorization of a polynomial, is checked for validity. Recently, there are efforts to integrate a proof search procedure for intuitionistic predicate logic [KOS96], based on an extension of the connection method, into the NuPRL system [Con86].

A careful analysis of the proof returned by the equality prover is necessary to ensure that the proof carried out in an untyped logic is valid in a typed logic. Section 6 will provide arguments why a proof returned by the equality prover is typecorrect in most interesting cases. The typing rules presented in Section 5 describe how proof objects can be constructed that permit to verify the validity of every instance of an equality proof. Since proof objects tend to become very large, their construction may not always be desirable. The typing rules can then be understood as safeguards that have to be built in to ensure the correctness of proofs.

Due to lack of space, this paper has to remain cursory. A more detailed description, in particular of implementation aspects, can be found in [Sor96]. An extended version of this paper, containing proofs of some of the statements made below, will be made available on the Web page of the TYPELAB project:

http://www.informatik.uni-ulm.de/ki/Forschung/Deduktion/index-e.html

2 Languages

In this section, the language of type theory and the language of the equality prover will be contrasted. Since the language of type theory contains expressions which cannot sensibly be mapped to a first-order equality prover, a sublanguage will be identified which is suitable for stating equality proof problems.

2.1 Typed Language

The type theory this work is based on is the *Extended Calculus of Constructions (ECC)* [Luo90], an expressive logic whose language comprises:

- Term constructors such as:
  - Lambda-abstraction $\lambda x : T.\ M$ and function application $(M\ N)$
  - Tuple formation $\langle M, N \rangle$ and projection $P.1, P.2$
- Type constructors such as:

- Type constants *Prop* (the collection of propositions) and *Type* (the collection of types)
- Dependent function type $\forall x : A.B$. The non-dependent function type $A \rightarrow B$ is an abbreviation for the dependent function type $\forall x : A.B$, where x does not occur in B.
- Dependent record types $\Sigma x : M. N$

Details of the structure of the terms of *ECC* are not relevant for the purposes of this paper. Further below we will only make precise what the fragment of the language looks like that is used for stating equality problems.

A typing judgement $\Gamma \vdash t : T$ expresses that term t is of type T in context Γ. A context is a finite sequence of variable declarations of the form $x : A$, where x is a variable and A a type. By the "propositions as types" paradigm, propositions are interpreted as types. Informally, a variable declaration such as $h : t_1 =_T t_2$ can then be understood as a hypothesis labelled with h.

Typing judgements are defined inductively on the structure of terms. Again, the whole set of typing rules is not relevant in our case. We just cite the rules for Lambda abstraction and application:

$$\frac{\Gamma, x : A \vdash M : B}{\Gamma \vdash \lambda x : A.M : \forall x : A.B} \; (\lambda)$$

$$\frac{\Gamma \vdash M : \forall x : A.B \quad \Gamma \vdash N : A}{\Gamma \vdash (M \; N) : B[x := N]} \; (\text{app})$$

Definition 1 Bound and free variables. Suppose t is a term which is well-typed in a context Γ. An occurrence of a variable x will be called *bound* in t if x occurs in the scope of an abstraction in t. It will be called *free* otherwise (then x occurs in Γ).

The notion of a variable being bound or free is relative: In the premiss of the (λ) rule, x occurs free in M (if it occurs in M), but bound in $\lambda x : A.M$.

The equality $t_1 =_T t_2$ we will be using in the sequel (t_1 equals t_2, where both terms have type T) is not predefined, but can be encoded by means of Leibniz' principle which says that two terms are equal if they agree in all properties expressible in the language:

$$x =_T y := \forall P : T \rightarrow Prop.(P \; x) \leftrightarrow (P \; y)$$

Leibniz equality is weaker than syntactic equality or convertibility in the sense that convertible terms can be shown to be Leibniz equal, but not vice versa. As a consequence, two terms which are Leibniz equal cannot be arbitrarily substituted for one another without endangering type correctness. For example, if type T contains a term n_1 of type *Nat*, $n_1 =_{Nat} n_2$ and $\lambda x : T[n_1].(f \; x)$ is typecorrect, then $\lambda x : T[n_2].(f \; x)$ is usually not typecorrect.

In order to exclude problematic cases like this one already on the language level, we will in the following identify a sublanguage $\mathcal{L}_T$ of *ECC* in which equality problems will be stated. We will consider *generalized equations* $\forall x_1 : T_1, \ldots x_n : T_n.l =_T r$, which are built up from the type constants, a set of variables $\mathcal{V}_T$, and from function application. The grammar for generalized equations is given by production $\mathcal{E}_T$, defined as follows:

$$\mathcal{T}_T ::= Prop \mid Type \mid \mathcal{V}_T \mid (\mathcal{T}_T \, \mathcal{T}_T)$$

$$\mathcal{E}_T ::= (\mathcal{T}_T = \mathcal{T}_T) \mid \forall \mathcal{V}_T : \mathcal{GT}_T . \mathcal{E}_T$$

Here, $\mathcal{GT}_T$ denotes the set of general terms of the logic ECC. Note that function application is in curried form, i.e. an application $f(a_1, a_2)$ is here written as $((f \, a_1) \, a_2)$, but will often be abbreviated to $(f \, a_1 \, a_2)$.

The following semantic constraints are imposed on the equations that we will consider:

Definition 2 Valid Generalized Equation. A generalized equation E is *valid* in a context Γ if it fulfills the following requirements:

- E is well-typed in context Γ, that is, $\Gamma \vdash E : Prop$ is derivable.
- Each element of $\mathcal{V}_T$ has associated with it a fixed arity, which is the number of arguments which are applied to it.
- Every x_i occurs in l or in r.
- In an application $(f \, a)$, f is not a bound variable.

Remarks:

The arity of a variable is related to, but not completely determined by its type. For example, a function symbol $f : A \to B$ might have arity 0 (if only used as a functional constant) or 1 (in applications like $(f \, a)$). The restriction stated in the definition ensures that variable symbols are used in a uniform manner.

In a typed logic, it is not generally valid to conclude from $\forall x : A, z : C.(f \, x) = b_1$ and $(f \, a) = b_2$ that $b_1 = b_2$, because no element of type C is given which would permit a correct instantiation of the universal quantifier. The third condition of the definition is thought to prevent such conclusions.

The fourth condition of the definition prohibits generalized equations of the form $\forall f : A \to B.(f \, a) = b$, which would lead to problems during a translation to a first-order prover.

Note that higher-order abstractions are not disallowed altogether:

$$\forall f : A \to B, a : A, l : (List \, A).$$
$$(map \, f \, (cons \, a \, l)) =_{List \, B} (cons \, (apply \, f \, a) \, (map \, f \, l))$$

is a valid equation, however not the (more natural)

$$\forall f : A \to B, a : A, l : (List \, A).$$
$$(map \, f \, (cons \, a \, l)) =_{List \, B} (cons \, (f \, a) \, (map \, f \, l))$$

because the bound function symbol f is then used with different arities and in addition occurs in a functional position. In this example, map is assumed to be of type $(A \to B) \to A \to (List \, A) \to (List \, B)$, where A and B are fixed types. In the fragment of the logic considered here, we could also use a version of the map function with parametric polymorphism. map would then have type $\forall X, Y : Type. (X \to Y) \to \dots$, and applications of map would be written as: $(map \, A \, B \, f \, l)$.

Definition 3 Valid Proof Problem. A valid proof problem (with respect to a context Γ) consists of a set of *hypotheses* $\{E_1, \ldots E_n\}$, which are generalized equations valid in Γ, and a quantifier-free *goal* equation E_g which is valid in Γ.

The requirement that E_g is a quantifier-free equation is not a genuine restriction, since any universally quantified goal equation can be converted into a quantifier-free one by moving universally quantified variables into the context, thus converting them to constants.

2.2 Language of the Equality Prover

We assume a usual untyped first-order language $\mathcal{L}_E$, whose terms $\mathcal{T}_E$ and equations $\mathcal{E}_E$ are built up from a set of functions and constants $\mathcal{FC}_E$ and a set of variables $\mathcal{V}_E$, according to the following grammar:

$$\mathcal{T}_E ::= \mathcal{V}_E \mid \mathcal{FC}_E(\mathcal{T}_E \ldots \mathcal{T}_E) \qquad \mathcal{E}_E ::= (\mathcal{T}_E = \mathcal{T}_E)$$

Again, each symbol of $\mathcal{FC}_E$ has associated with it an arity which determines the number of arguments it takes. Functions are here written in the usual un-Curried form.

3 An Example Proof

Before giving a formal presentation of the translation of proof problems and the resulting proofs, the interaction of TYPELAB and DISCOUNT will be illustrated by a standard example from group theory, the problem of showing that $x + (-x) = 0$. The problem to be solved in TYPELAB is displayed in Figure 1.

```
T:Type
op:T->T->T
unit:T
inv:T->T
unit_ax_r:all(x:T) op x unit = x
unit_ax_l:all(x:T) op unit x = x
left_inv_ax:all(x:T) op (inv x) x = unit
assoc_ax:all(x,y,z:T) op (op x y) z = op x (op y z)
x:T
|-------------------------------------------
?2:op x (inv x) = unit
```

Fig. 1. TYPELAB proof problem

The declarations of free variables and the hypotheses are listed above the stylized turnstile, the goal formula below. ?2 is a *metavariable* representing the proof term to be constructed. This proof problem is written on file in a format appropriate for DISCOUNT (see Section 4). Upon successful completion of the proof, a trace is returned by DISCOUNT (see Figure 2), which is then interpreted by TYPELAB and ultimately yields the proof term shown in Figure 3. Its structure closely reflects the structure of the proof translation, which will be further discussed in Section 5. In order to avoid name clashes, the variable x occuring free in the TYPELAB goal has been renamed to x4 in DISCOUNT.

```
Consider the following set of axioms:
  Axiom 1: op(x,unit()) = x
  Axiom 2: op(unit(),x) = x
  Axiom 3: op(inv(x),x) = unit()
  Axiom 4: op(op(x,y),z) = op(x,op(y,z))

Proof:
  Lemma 1: y = op(inv(inv(y)),unit())
    y = op(unit(),y) by Axiom 2 RL at e with {x <- y}
      = ...
      = op(inv(inv(y)),unit()) by Axiom 3 LR at 2 with {x <- y}

  Theorem 1: op(x4(),inv(x4())) = unit()
  op(x4(),inv(x4())) = op(op(inv(inv(x4())),unit()),inv(x4()))
                       by Lemma 1 LR at 1 with {y <- x4()}
      = ...
      = unit() by Axiom 3 LR ..
```

Fig. 2. DISCOUNT proof (shortened)

```
let (lemma_1:=
 fun(y:T) equal_transitive T y (op unit y) (op (inv (inv y)) unit)
            (equal_symmetric T (op unit y) y (unit_ax_1 y))
            (equal_transitive T (op unit y) ...))
in
equal_transitive T (op x (inv x)) (op ... (inv x)) unit
 (lemma_1 x (fun(v:T) op x (inv x) = op v (inv x)) (..))
 (equal_transitive T (op (op (inv (inv x)) unit) (inv x)) ...
   (unit_ax_r (inv (inv x)) ..))
```

Fig. 3. Proof Term (shortened)

4 Translations to the Equality Prover

The translation of *terms and equations* from the typed language $\mathcal{L}_T$ to the untyped language $\mathcal{L}_E$ of the equality prover is carried out as follows:

- The quantifier prefix is discarded.

- Variables of $\mathcal{L}_T$ which are free in the context under consideration are mapped to function symbols or constants, that is, elements of $\mathcal{F}C_E$.
- Variables of $\mathcal{L}_T$ which are bound in the context under consideration are mapped to variables, that is, elements of $\mathcal{V}_E$.
- Function applications are written in un-curried form.

Since only valid equations in the sense of Definition 2 are translated, it can be shown that only correct terms of $\mathcal{L}_E$ are produced by the translation.

As to the translation of an entire *proof problem*, we assume that in the equality prover, proof problems are stated as a list of axioms together with the goal formula to be proved, possibly with some additional information. A proof problem $\Gamma, h_1 : E_1, \ldots h_n : E_n \vdash ?n : E_g$ can then be transferred to the equality prover simply by translating every equation $E_1, \ldots E_n, E_g$.

5 Translations from the Equality Prover

5.1 Translating Terms

The translation from the untyped language $\mathcal{L}_E$ to the typed language $\mathcal{L}_T$ requires the reconstruction of type information. We assume that untyped terms are translated by a function *trTerm* and untyped equations by *trEquation*. These functions roughly work as follows:

- Since no new constants are generated during an equality proof, elements of $\mathcal{F}C_E$ are contained in the current context, their type can therefore be looked up.
- The type of variables (elements of $\mathcal{V}_E$) is not generally known and therefore has to be inferred. For example, the type of the variable y of the proof in Figure 2 is inferred to be T. Variables can only occur in argument position, so the method for infering argument types, described below, applies.
- An application $f(a_1, \ldots a_n)$ is first represented in Curried form. We thus only have to deal with the problem of translating terms $(f\ a)$. Noting that the head term of f can only be a function constant, it can be shown by an inductive argument that the type of f can be completely determined. If f is of type $\forall x : A.B$, the argument a has to be evaluated. If a is a variable which has not been assigned a type before, its type is set to be A. Otherwise, evaluation of a returns a type A'. If A and A' are the same, $(f\ a)$ can be typed to $B[x := a]$, otherwise the term is not correctly typed.
- The function *trEquation* evaluates the left and right sides of an equation, compares their types and universally abstracts over all the variables occuring free in the equation.

Type reconstruction works for all terms except for "pure" variables not occurring embedded in terms. In an equation $l = x$ or $x = r$, the type of the pure variable x can be determined, respectively, by the type of l or r, unless both sides of an equation are variables. We have here a situation in which a valid equality proof cannot be translated back because type inference fails. Note that this situation can only arise in the case of an equation $x = x$, which is trivial, or an equation $x = y$, which indicates that the equational theory is inconsistent.

5.2 Translating Proofs

The translation of proofs serves the double purpose of checking that the proof found by the equational prover is typecorrect and constructing a proof term. In order to obtain an independent certification that the proof is correct, the proof term can be evaluated and its type can be compared to the theorem it is supposed to prove. Construction of a proof term is not an essential part of the procedure presented below. Since proof terms tend to become quite large, they will usually not be constructed in a realistic scenario.

We make the following assumptions about the representation of equality proofs, which are reasonable for completion-based equality provers:

- An equational proof is a sequence of *lemmas*, where each lemma consists of a statement of the lemma of the form $l = r$ and a subsequent proof of this lemma. The sequence of lemmas may just have a length of one, in which case the main theorem can be proved directly. Otherwise, some intermediate lemmas are used to prove the main theorem. They usually result from critical pairs which are generated during completion.
- The proof of each lemma $l = r$ is in turn composed of a sequence of equations $l \equiv t_0 = t_1 \ldots t_n \equiv r$. Each such equation $t_i = t_{i+1}$, together with its justification, is called a *subproof*.
- A *justification* provides evidence for the correctness of an equation $t_i = t_{i+1}$. The justification has to state which axiom or preceding lemma has been applied, at which position of term t_i it is applied, and in which direction and with which instantiations it is applied.

For the constructs cited above, translation functions $tr\ldots$ will be given. The behaviour of these translation functions will be specified by inference rules

$$\frac{trfun_1(\ldots) \Rightarrow \Gamma_1 \vdash t_1 : T_1 \quad \cdots \quad trfun_n(\ldots) \Rightarrow \Gamma_n \vdash t_n : T_n}{trfun_0(\ldots) \Rightarrow \Gamma_0 \vdash t_0 : T_0}$$

which have to be read as: If after evaluation of $trfun_i(\ldots)$ the judgement $\Gamma_i \vdash t_i : T_i$ holds ($i = 1 \ldots n$), it can be concluded that after evaluation of $trfun_0(\ldots)$, the judgement $\Gamma_0 \vdash t_0 : T_0$ holds. The correctness of these inference rules can be verified by checking that the corresponding typing rules

$$\frac{\Gamma_1 \vdash t_1 : T_1 \quad \cdots \quad \Gamma_n \vdash t_n : T_n}{\Gamma_0 \vdash t_0 : T_0}$$

are derivable.

Notational convention: Untyped terms resp. equations are primed (such as $l' = r'$), the corresponding typed terms resp. equations have not primes (such as $l =_T r$). For lack of space, we only present the most interesting rules. The reader is invited to compare the translation as suggested by the rules below with the example of Figures 2 and 3.

Translating a proof: A proof is a sequence of lemmas.

$$\frac{trLemma(\Gamma;\ AxiomMap;\ lemma) \Rightarrow \Gamma \vdash lmp : LM \qquad trProof(\Gamma, d := lmp : LM;\ NewAxiomMap;\ lemlist) \Rightarrow \Gamma, d := lmp : LM \vdash thp : TH}{trProof(\Gamma;\ AxiomMap;\ lemma :: lemlist) \Rightarrow \Gamma \vdash \text{let } d := lmp : LM \text{ in } thp :\ TH}$$

With $d := lmp : LM$, the name d can be introduced in a context as a definition of term lmp of type LM. Similarly, d can be bound locally within a term by a let-abstraction. Note that d can occur in thp, but not in TH, the theorem to be proved. $AxiomMap$ is a function mapping equations $l' = r'$ to a pair

$$\langle p, \forall x_1 : T_1, \dots x_n : T_n . l =_T r \rangle$$

consisting of the generalized equation corresponding to $l' = r'$ and its proof object p. $NewAxiomMap$ is the obvious extension of $AxiomMap$ by the lemma just proved. For example, referring back to Figure 3, the abstraction `let lemma_1:= fun(y:T)` `equal_transitive ... in ...` is the result of translating the entire equality proof, by first translating Lemma 1 and binding its result to the identifier `lemma_1` before translating the main theorem.

Translating a lemma: A lemma consists of the statement of an equality and a subproof of the validity of this equality.

$$\frac{trEquation(\Gamma; \; l' = r') \Rightarrow \Gamma \vdash \forall x_1 : T_1, \dots x_n : T_n . l =_T r \; : \; Prop \\ trSubProof(\Gamma, x_1 : T_1, \dots x_n : T_n; \; AxiomMap; \; subprf) \Rightarrow \\ \Gamma, x_1 : T_1, \dots x_n : T_n \vdash p : l =_T r}{trLemma(\Gamma; \; AxiomMap; \; \langle l' = r', subprf \rangle) \Rightarrow \\ \Gamma \vdash \lambda x_1 : T_1, \dots x_n : T_n . p \; : \; \forall x_1 : T_1, \dots x_n : T_n . l =_T r}$$

Note that the subproof is evaluated in a context in which the bound variables of the equation corresponding to the lemma have been moved into the context. Thus, the terms occuring in the subproof are actually ground. For the proof of correctness of this rule, compare with typing rule (λ) of Section 2.1.

Translating a subproof: A subproof of an equation $l =_T r$ consists of a sequence of steps $l \equiv t_0 =_T t_1 \dots =_T t_n \equiv r$, where each step $t_i =_T t_{i+1}$ is provided with a justification $just_i$ explicating how the equation $t_i =_T t_{i+1}$ can be derived. Essentially, the transitivity of equality is used to concatenate the proof steps.

$$\frac{trJust(\Gamma; \; AxiomMap; \; t'_0 = t'_1; \; just) \Rightarrow \Gamma \vdash p_0 : t_0 =_T t_1 \\ trSubProof(\Gamma; \; AxiomMap; \; splist) \Rightarrow \Gamma \vdash p_1 : t_1 =_T t_2}{trSubProof(\Gamma; \; AxiomMap; \; \langle t'_0 = t'_1, just \rangle :: splist) \Rightarrow \\ \Gamma \vdash (equal\_transitive \; T \; t_0 \; t_1 \; t_2 \; p_0 \; p_1) \; : \; t_0 =_T t_2}$$

For example, when translating Lemma 1 in Figure 3, the equality `y = op(unit(),y)` is translated first, then (by a repeated application of the transitivity rule) the equality `op(unit(),y) = op(inv(inv(y)),unit())`. Finally, both proof steps are joined to yield the term `equal_transitive T y (op unit y) (op (inv (inv y))` `unit) ... ....`

Translating a justification: A justification is translated by first instantiating the referenced axiom or lemma as given by the instantiation list $instlist$, then orienting the resulting equation in the direction specified by dir and finally carrying out the replacement at the term position indicated by $poslist$.

$$\frac{trInst(\Gamma; \; AxiomMap; \; l' = r'; \; instlist) \Rightarrow \Gamma \vdash p_i : l_i =_{T_i} r_i \\ trDir(\Gamma; \; dir; \; p_i; \; l_i =_{T_i} r_i) \Rightarrow \Gamma \vdash p_d : l_d =_{T_d} r_d \\ trCong(\Gamma; \; l' = r'; \; poslist; \; p_d; \; l_d =_{T_d} r_d) \Rightarrow \Gamma_c : l_c =_{T_c} r_c}{trJust(\Gamma; \; AxiomMap; \; l' = r'; \; \langle poslist, dir, \langle axiom, instlist \rangle \rangle) \Rightarrow \Gamma \vdash p_c : l_c =_{T_c} r_c}$$

6 Type preservation

One might object against using an untyped logic for carrying out proofs in a typed logic that the untyped proofs will too often include inferences which are not type-correct, thus making the cooperation between a typed and an untyped prover practically useless. This section provides some evidence which invalidates this objection and shows that, under some reasonable assumptions about the inference mechanisms used by the equality prover, types are preserved in a rewrite proof. Due to lack of space, the arguments have to remain on an informal level.

We assume that the equality prover is initialized with a proof problem which is the result of translating a valid typed problem (in the sense of Def. 3). Thus, the terms and equations the equality prover starts with are typeable, and the question that has to be examined is whether inferences of the equality prover can produce terms or equations that are not typeable. We further assume that the basic inference mechanisms of an equality prover are rewriting a term (resp. an equation) and completion, i.e. the generation of lemmas from critical pairs. Under this assumption, the above question can be restated:

- Does rewriting a typeable term t (a typeable equation $t_l = t_r$) with a typecorrect rule $l \rightarrow r$ always produce a term t' (an equation $t'_l = t'_r$) which is typeable?
- Does the completion procedure always introduce rewrite rules as lemmas which are typeable?

If these questions can be affirmed, a simple inductive argument shows that the untyped equality proof retains its validity in a typed framework. Unfortunately, this is not so in general. Consider the problem of proving from the equation $\forall x : A.x =_A a$ that $b_1 =_B b_2$, where b_1, b_2 are constants of type $B \neq A$. If type information is discarded, the proof succeeds by showing that $b_1 = a = b_2$. Of course, the resulting equations cannot be typed any more. In a dependently typed calculus, still more arcane effects can arise due to the interaction between the value of one term and the type of another term.

We will argue that, with "interesting" equations as defined in the following, a kind of proof as in the above example cannot be carried out in a simply-typed framework. This argument can be extended to a polymorphic calculus under the assumption that there are only equations between values and no equations between types.

Definition 4 Interesting equation.
A valid equation $\forall x_1 : T_1, \ldots x_n : T_n.l =_T r$ is defined to be *interesting* if l being a variable x implies that r is a term unequal x, but containing x.

All equations of the form $\forall x_1 : T_1, \ldots x_n : T_n.f(t_1, \ldots, t_k) =_T r$ (with $k \geq 0$) are interesting in this sense, also equations of the form $\forall x_1 : T_1, \ldots x_n : T_n.x =_T f(\ldots, x, \ldots)$. Under usual variable assumptions ($Var(r) \subseteq Var(l)$ or vice versa) only equations of the form $\forall x : A.x =_A a$ are excluded, which express that type A consists of just a single element. Note that any reasonable equality prover based on rewriting applies an equality $x = f(\ldots, x, \ldots)$ in the direction $f(\ldots, x, \ldots) \rightarrow x$.

The important feature of interesting equations is that the outermost function symbol provides a cover which ensures that the equation is only applied at a term of the same type. More precisely, assume that the term $t := f(t_1, \ldots t_n)$ can be typed with type T_1 and equation $f(l_1, \ldots l_n) = r$ can be typed with type T_2. T_1 and T_2 then have to agree. If t and $f(l_1, \ldots l_n)$ can be matched, that is, there is a substitution σ such that $t \equiv f(l_1, \ldots l_n)\sigma$, then both $f(l_1, \ldots l_n)\sigma$ and $r\sigma$ are typeable with T_1, so that the inference $t = r\sigma$ is typecorrect. A similar argument holds for critical pairs generated during completion.

Summarizing the above argument, it can be shown that an untyped equality prover produces a proof which is typeable under the following assumptions:

- The initial set of equations consists of "interesting" equations, in the above sense.
- During completion, only interesting equations are generated.
- The basic inferences of the equational prover consist of replacing equal terms for equals, subject to usual variable requirements, and of generating lemmas from critical pairs.

7 Conclusions

This paper has described the integration of an untyped equality prover into a system based on a constructive type theory. As opposed to most other examples of prover cooperation, a rigorous verification of the proof returned by the equality prover is carried out. This verification comprises the reconstruction of necessary type information and, if desired, also the construction of a proof term which, through typechecking, permits the direct validation of the proof.

It has been shown that proof verification fails for valid equational proofs only in rare cases. In a similar vein, it has been argued that for equational problems which are "interesting" (in a precise sense), omitting type information does not lead to type-incorrect proofs.

A sublanguage of type theory in which proof problems can be stated has been identified. In some applications involving refinements between abstract data types or theory morphisms, a more expressive language is required. In this case, the translation between the typed and untyped language could assign uninterpreted symbols to terms not forming part of the language identified in Section 2 (such as Lambda-abstractions, tuples or projections). It remains a topic of future research to precisely define these abstracting translations and to clarify their semantics and pragmatics. Also, the role of weaker equalities than Leibniz equality, for example the congruence relations often employed in specifications of abstract data types, has to be investigated. In principle, the verification that congruence properties of function symbols have been used correctly could be carried out in an *a posteriori* fashion, as described above for Leibniz equality. However, it may be wondered whether it is possible to show, in analogy to the results of Section 6, that there is no perceptible mismatch between the actual outcome of an equality proof and the expected result, as defined by the semantics of the equality relation involved.

Acknowledgments

The TYPELAB system is a joint development by the first author and Marko Luther. Suggestions by Friedrich von Henke, Holger Pfeifer, Harald Rueß, Detlef Schwier and Matthias Wagner have influenced the system design. We are grateful to Jörg

Denzinger and Matthias Fuchs for making the DISCOUNT system available and for providing assistance with the installation. Wolfgang Reif and Gerhard Schellhorn have patiently answered our questions about the integration between KIV and 3TAP.

References

[Bar96]   Bruno Barras et al. *The Coq Proof Assistant Reference Manual, Version 6.1.* INRIA Rocquencourt and CNRS-ENS Lyon, November 1996.

[BHG+96]   Bernhard Beckert, Reiner Hähnle, Karla Geiß, Peter Oel, Christian Pape, and Martin Sulzmann. The many-valued tableau-based theorem prover $_3T^AP$, version 4.0. Interner Bericht 3/96, Universität Karlsruhe, Fakultät für Informatik, 1996.

[Con86]   R.L. Constable et al. *Implementing Mathematics with the Nuprl Proof Development System.* Prentice-Hall, 1986.

[DGH+95]   Bernd I. Dahn, Jürgen Gehne, Thomas Honigmann, Lutz Walther, and Andreas Wolf. *Integrating Logical Functions with ILF.* Humboldt-Universität Berlin, 1995.

[DKS97]   J. Denzinger, M. Kronenburg, and S. Schulz. Discount - a distributed and learning equational prover. *Journal of Automated Reasoning*, 1997. To appear.

[HRS88]   M. Heisel, W. Reif, and W. Stephan. Implementing verification strategies in the KIV-System. In *Proc. 9th CADE*, pages 131–140. Springer LNCS 310, 1988.

[HT93]   John Harrison and Laurent Théry. Extending the HOL theorem prover with a computer algebra system to reason about the reals. In Jeffrey J. Joyce and Carl Seger, editors, *Proceedings of the 1993 International Workshop on the HOL theorem proving system and its applications*, volume 780 of *Lecture Notes in Computer Science*, pages 174–184, UBC, Vancouver, Canada, 1993. Springer-Verlag.

[KOS96]   Christoph Kreitz, Jens Otten, and Stephan Schmitt. Guiding program development systems by a connection based proof strategy. In *LoPSTr'95: Proceedings of the 5th International Workshop on Logic Program Synthesis and Transformation*, pages 137–151. Springer LNCS 1048, 1996.

[Luo90]   Zhaohui Luo. *An Extended Calculus of Constructions.* PhD thesis, University of Edinburgh, July 1990.

[OSR93]   S. Owre, N. Shankar, and J.M. Rushby. *The PVS Specification Language.* Computer Science Lab, SRI International, Menlo Park CA 94025, March 1993.

[Pau94]   Larry Paulson. *Isabelle - a generic theorem prover.* Springer LNCS 828, 1994.

[Sor96]   Maria Sorea. Integration von Gleichheitsbeweisen in einen typentheoretischen Beweiser. Master's thesis, Universität Ulm, 1996.

[vHLS97]   F.W. von Henke, M. Luther, and M. Strecker. TYPELAB: An environment for modular program development. In M. Dauchet M. Bidoit, editor, *Proceedings TAPSOFT'97*, pages 851–854. Springer LNCS 1214, 1997.

Causation and Nonmonotonic Temporal Reasoning

Peter Grünwald
E-mail: pdg@cwi.nl

CWI, P.O. Box 4079, 1009 AB AMSTERDAM, The Netherlands

Abstract. We introduce a new approach to reasoning about action and change using nonmonotonic logic. The approach is arrived at by applying Pearl's theory of causal networks to logical formalizations of temporal reasoning domains. It comes in two versions: version S_0 that works for logical theories in which causal knowledge is represented explicitly, and version I_0 that works for logical theories in which this is not the case. It turns out that various restrictions of S_0 are equivalent to various existing approaches that are explicitly based on causation. Similarly, two of the most well-known non-causal approaches, namely Baker's account and 'chronological minimization with filter preferential entailment', can be reinterpreted as approximations of I_0. We thus provide a reinterpretation in terms of causal network theory of much of the work done in nonmonotonic temporal reasoning.

1 Introduction

Any approach to common-sense temporal reasoning must address the notorious *frame problem* [14]: how can one properly model the common sense intuition that most facts about the world tend not to change over time? There have been numerous proposals to formalize this notion of *inertia* or *persistence*. In many of these, causal knowledge is represented explicitly; we will call these approaches the *causal* ones (as opposed to the other, *non-causal* approaches).

Now in recent years there has been a lot of work, mainly by J.Pearl, on the use of graphs for modeling causal relations; the theory of these 'causal networks' is successfully applied in several domains [12, 4]. In our work, we connect common-sense temporal reasoning to Pearl's account of causation. We apply Pearl's theory to arrive at a nonmonotonic logic that formalizes persistence. It comes in two versions: the first, *model selection criterion* S_0, works for causal logical theories (i.e. theories in which causal knowledge is axiomatized explicitly). It selects only those models of a theory that are subject to persistence, and it does so the way Pearl's theory prescribes that it should be done. The second version, model selection criterion I_0, first infers – again by applying Pearl's ideas – *what causes what* in a non-causal theory. It then uses the causal relations it found to select the models subject to persistence. Now S_0 can be formally compared to the existing causal approaches to formalizing persistence, and I_0 can be compared to the non-causal ones. We have been able to prove that some recent causal and 'action description language'-based[1] approaches are equivalent to various restrictions of S_0; for most other causal approaches we have examples of reasoning domains where our approach gives better results than they do. For some of the non-causal approaches, we argue that they can be interpreted as implementing an approximation of I_0. For one of the most well-known of these, namely Baker's [1, 8, 3], we actually prove this; and again, for some non-causal approaches we have examples that I_0 handles differently (and better) than they do. Summarizing, *Our approach to nonmonotonic temporal reasoning can be seen as a generalization and/or correction of many existing ones* .

This paper first introduces our formalism and discusses how Pearl's approach leads to I_0 and S_0. It then compares I_0 to other non-causal approaches. Our comparisons of S_0 to other approaches are only summarized here; we extensively treat them in the technical report [6]; there we also treat some of the issues of this paper in more detail.

2 Our Formalism

We use a many-sorted first order logic. The sorts in our logic are *generalized fluents* (variables of the sort will be denoted by g) and *timepoints* (t). There are two 'subsorts' to generalized fluents: *regular fluents* (f) and *event fluents* (e). A regular fluent denotes a property of the world that may be subject to persistence; an event fluent stands for an event or action. The set of regular fluent constants for our language will be called FC; it will always be finite: $FC = \{F_1, \ldots, F_{|FC|}\}$. Similarly, the set $EC = \{E_1, \ldots, E_{|EC|}\}$ contains our event fluent constants. Time-points will be equated to the integers. The predicate $Ho(g, t)$ will denote that generalized fluent g is the case ('*Holds*') at time t. $\mathbf{e}, \mathbf{f}, \mathbf{g}$ and $\mathbf{t}$ will be used as meta-variables that can stand for any ground term of the sort indicated by the letter.

We formalize our domain knowledge in two different manners: non-causal theories T_{NC} , which are intended to formalize knowledge essentially in the same way as most existing non-causal approaches do, and causal theories T_C , which are intended to do this essentially in the same way as most existing causal approaches do. We will use a variation of the Yale Shooting Domain [14] to illustrate both of them. In this domain there is a person that can be alive or not; there is a gun that can be loaded or not; there is an action 'load' which loads the gun, an action 'wait' which has no effects at all and an action 'shoot', which, if performed when the gun is loaded, causes the person not to be alive anymore. We further suppose that the person is alive and that the gun is unloaded at time $t = 0$, and that, starting at time $t = 0$, someone first loads the gun, then waits and then shoots. We will first show our non-causal formalization T_{YSP-NC} of this domain. It contains axioms (1)-(8) :

$$Ho(Load, t) \supset Ho(Loaded, t + 1) \tag{1}$$

$$Ho(Loaded, t) \land Ho(Shoot, t) \supset \neg Ho(Alive, t + 1) \tag{2}$$

---

[1] Indeed, from our point of view these approaches simply belong to the causal ones.

$$Ho(Alive, 0) \wedge \neg Ho(Loaded, 0) \qquad (3)$$

$$Ho(Load, 0) \wedge Ho(Wait, 1) \wedge Ho(Shoot, 2) \qquad (4)$$

Here *Alive* and *Loaded* are regular fluents, while *Load*, *Wait* and *Shoot* are event fluents. (1) and (2) are the *effect axioms* which describe the 'action laws' of our domain. (3) and (4) are our *observation axioms* which are always propositional combinations of *fluent facts*. The latter are defined to be instances of *Ho* that contain no variables. Our language further contains a function *Not* mapping event fluents to event fluents and regular fluents to regular fluents. It occurs in the following two *domain independent axioms* that will be included in any T_{NC} :

$$Ho(g, t) \equiv \neg Ho(Not(g), t) \qquad (5)$$

$$Not(Not(g)) = g \qquad (6)$$

The restriction of a T_{NC} to its domain independent axioms will be called $T_{NC} \rfloor_{IND}$ The effect axioms together with $T_{NC} \rfloor_{IND}$ will be called $T_{NC} \rfloor_{GEN}$ (the *general axioms* of a T_{NC}). For each T_{NC} , $T_{NC} \rfloor_{IND}$ further contains unique-names axioms: for all $F_1, F_2 \in FC$, $F_1 \neq F_2$ we have: $\qquad F_1 \neq F_2$ (7)
For all $E_1, E_2 \in EC$, $E_1 \neq E_2$ we have: $\qquad\qquad\qquad E_1 \neq E_2$ (8)

And what about step 1 of I_0? Causal and non-causal theories share the same domain-independent axioms: $T_C \rfloor_{IND} = T_{NC} \rfloor_{IND} = $ (5)-(8). Thus they are also part of our causal formalization of the shooting domain, T_{YSP-C}. T_{YSP-C} also contains observation axioms (3) and (4). General axioms (1) and (2) however will be replaced by the following two axioms that make use of an additional predicate $Ca(g, t)$ denoting that g is *Ca*used to hold at time t:

$$Ho(Load, t) \supset Ca(Loaded, t + 1) \qquad (9)$$

$$Ho(Loaded, t) \wedge Ho(Shoot, t) \supset Ca(Not(Alive), t + 1) \qquad (10)$$

We denote by $Mod(T)$ the class of those classical models for any T in which *timepoints* are interpreted as the integers. If two models $\mathcal{M}_1$ and $\mathcal{M}_2$ share the same interpretation of *Ho* - which means that they model exactly the same 'history' or 'development' of the domain under consideration - we will say $\mathcal{M}_1$ and $\mathcal{M}_2$ *correspond in terms of Ho*, written as $\mathcal{M}_1 \equiv_{Ho} \mathcal{M}_2$. Formally, $\mathcal{M}_1 \equiv_{Ho} \mathcal{M}_2$ iff for all $\mathbf{g}, \mathbf{t}$ we have $\mathcal{M}_1 \models Ho(\mathbf{g}, \mathbf{t}) \Leftrightarrow \mathcal{M}_2 \models Ho(\mathbf{g}, \mathbf{t})$

3 Our Two Basic Ideas

All existing causal approaches to formalizing persistence [5, 7, 9, 10, 11, 16] are based on variations of the same idea: prefer those models of a theory in which there is a *cause* for all changes of fluent values. We will refine this idea by connecting causation to explanation: informally, if A causes B, then A also provides an explanation for B. But in domains subject to persistence, we may also say that if we have $Ho(f, t)$ for some regular fluent f and nothing happens between t and $t + 1$, then this explains $Ho(f, t + 1)$ just as well. This leads us to the two key ideas behind our approach:

Basic Principle *From among the classical models, select those with the least* unexplained *fluent facts.*

Preliminary Work *We must correctly determine for* each *fluent fact in* each *model whether it is explained or not.*

Intuitively, something is 'explained' in a model if it is normally ('by default') the case given the rest of the model. Thus nonmonotonic model selection becomes an abductive 'search for explanations' consisting of two stages: first, the 'preliminary work' is done to find out what is explained in each model; second, this is used to find the models in which as much as possible is explained, i.e. the models which are the *least surprising*. Now the first stage is where Pearl's account of causation comes in – we use it to do our 'preliminary work'.

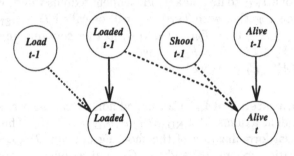

Fig. 1. A Yale Shooting Causal Graph

4 Pearl's Account of Causation

Here we will only treat Pearl's theory in a very informal manner, specifically geared to enable us to quickly introduce I_0 and S_0. Given a domain with some variables, Pearl's theory uses 'causal graphs' to depict which variables have causal relationships to each other and which *direction* these relationships take. A causal graph G together with a description D of the functional relations between its variables is called a *causal network* (G, D). In order to give a rough idea of how this works, fig. 1 gives a causal graph of the YSP domain. For example, it shows that (performing) a *Load*-action at time $t - 1$ has a *causal influence* on (whether we have) *Loaded* at time t. Also, *Loaded* at time $t - 1$ has a causal influence, but of a different kind, on *Loaded* at time t. The parents of a node (connected by either dashed or solid arrows) in the network are called its 'direct causes'. Here is the fundamental idea of Pearl's theory:

The Sufficient Cause Principle If an *action* that sets the truth value of a proposition P is performed successfully, then the truth values of all propositions in the causal network that are not descendants of P become independent of P.

In graphical terms this means that we *delete* all arrows of variables going into the node that represents P. In our example: *normally*, $Ho(Loaded, t)$ implies $Ho(Loaded, t - 1)$. But if a *Load*-action takes place at $t - 1$, then $Ho(Loaded, t)$ does not tell us anything anymore on whether we had $Ho(Loaded, t - 1)$. Pearl's theory also tells us that for every causal network (G, D) the functions in D must be such that the following principle holds, which for example makes sure that there are no dependencies between variables which are not connected by any path in the graph:

The Causal Independence Principle Once all unexplainable facts and the direct causes of a proposition P are known, the truth value of P becomes independent of all propositions in the causal network that are not descendants of P.

5 Model Selection Criteria I_0 and S_0

In the following, we assume that T_{NC}'s are defined for a language that also contains the Ca-predicate and a new predicate JE ('*Just Explained*' - the name will become clear later). But T_{NC}'s themselves never contain axioms about either Ca or JE.

I_0 is defined on the next page as a five-step procedure that receives as input a theory T_{NC} and that outputs a set of models $I_0(T_{NC}) \subset Mod(T_{NC})$. Steps 1-4 of I_0 implement our 'preliminary work' (section 3). Step 5 uses the results of steps 1-4 to apply our 'basic principle' (section 3). The 'preliminary work' can further be decomposed into two stages: in the first stage (steps 1-3 in definition 1), I_0 will *build a complete causal network for* T_{NC}. It will do this by using Pearl's theory and some precisely stated additional assumptions about the 'physics' of the domain under consideration. This is meant in the following sense: given theory T_{NC} and the additional assumptions, there is only one specific causal network for T_{NC} which does not contradict the properties that causal networks must have according to Pearl's theory. In the second stage (step 4 in the definition), I_0 will apply Pearl's semantics to the causal network found to determine for each fluent fact in each model whether it is explained or not.

This means that steps 1-3 (i.e. the first stage) should not rule out any particular interpretation of Ho; rather, they will determine for each interpretation of Ho a single interpretation of Ca and JE belonging to it. This interpretation of Ca and JE *encodes* a causal graph in the following sense: if, after performing the first stage of I_0, we have $Ca(\mathbf{g}, \mathbf{t})$ in a model this will mean that there is a *sufficient* cause for the fluent $\mathbf{g}$ to hold at time $\mathbf{t}$ in the model (i.e. there is an *action* that successfully makes $\mathbf{g}$ true); in graphical terms, there is a *dashed* arrow pointing into node $(\mathbf{g}, \mathbf{t})$. $JE(\mathbf{g}, \mathbf{t})$ in a model will mean that there is a causal influence on $\mathbf{g}$ which, *if no intervention takes place* would *normally* make it hold at time t; graphically, a solid arrow points into $(\mathbf{g}, \mathbf{t})$. We will now go through the five steps of definition 1 in detail, using the YSP as an example as we go along .

Definition 1. The model selection criterion I_0 from theories T_{NC} to sets of models $M \subseteq Mod(T_{NC})$ is defined by the following procedure:

Step 1 *Perform the following two sub-steps:*
1. *First derive 'what causes what' in T_{NC} using the procedure of definition 2 (next page).*
2. *Now select a model $\mathcal{M} \in Mod(T_{NC})$ iff for all ϕ, ψ, Φ (as in def. 2) we have that*

   if $\quad \mathcal{M} \models \Phi \wedge \phi$

   and $\quad \phi$ **s–causes** ψ **under circumstances** Φ

   then $\quad \mathcal{M} \models Ca(\mathbf{g}_\psi, \mathbf{t}_\psi)$

   Let $I_{0,1}$ be the set of models thus selected.

Step 2 *Among the remaining models $\mathcal{M} \in I_{0,1}$, we select exactly those $\mathcal{M}$ with*
1) $\mathcal{M} \models \forall f, t.\ Ho(f, t-1) \supset JE(f, t)$ *and*
2) $\mathcal{M} \models \forall e, t.\ JE(Not(e), t)$.

   Let the set of resulting $\mathcal{M}$ be $I_{0,2}$.

Step 3 *Further select any $\mathcal{M} \in I_{0,2}$ iff $\mathcal{M}$ has a minimal extension of Ca within*
$$\{\mathcal{M}' \mid \mathcal{M}' \in I_{0,2} \text{ and } \mathcal{M} \equiv_{Ho} \mathcal{M}'\}$$
and $\mathcal{M}$ has a minimal extension of JE within
$$\{\mathcal{M}' \mid \mathcal{M}' \in I_{0,2} \text{ and } \mathcal{M} \equiv_{Ho} \mathcal{M}'\}$$
Let the set of remaining models be $I_{0,3}$.

Step 4 *We determine for each model $\mathcal{M} \in I_{0,3}$ the set of unexplained fluent facts:*
$$\mathbf{Ab}_g^1(\mathcal{M}) = \{(\mathbf{g}, t) | \mathcal{M} \models \neg Ho(\mathbf{g}, t) \wedge Ca(\mathbf{g}, t)\}$$
$$\mathbf{Ab}_f^2(\mathcal{M}) = \{(\mathbf{f}, t) | \mathcal{M} \models JE(Not(\mathbf{f}), t) \wedge Ho(\mathbf{f}, t) \wedge \neg Ca(\mathbf{f}, t)\}$$
$$\mathbf{Ab}_e^2(\mathcal{M}) = \{(\mathbf{e}, t) | \mathcal{M} \models JE(Not(\mathbf{e}), t) \wedge Ho(\mathbf{e}, t) \wedge \neg Ca(\mathbf{e}, t)\}$$

Step 5 *Perform the following steps in order:*

1. *Select any $\mathcal{M} \in I_{0,3}$ iff $\mathbf{Ab}_g^1(\mathcal{M})$ is minimal over $I_{0,3}$, i.e.. for no $\mathcal{M}' \in I_{0,3}$, $\mathbf{Ab}_g^1(\mathcal{M}')$ is a proper subset of $\mathbf{Ab}_g^1(\mathcal{M})$. Let the set of remaining models be $I_{0,4}$.*
2. *Select any $\mathcal{M} \in I_{0,4}$ iff $\mathbf{Ab}_f^2(\mathcal{M})$ is minimal over $I_{0,4}$. Let the set of remaining $\mathcal{M}$ be $I_{0,5}$.*
3. *Select any $\mathcal{M} \in I_{0,5}$ iff $\mathbf{Ab}_e^2(\mathcal{M})$ is minimal over $I_{0,5}$.*

$I_0(T_{NC})$ is now defined to be the set of models remaining after step 5.3.

Definition 2. Suppose a theory T_{NC} is given. Let $M_{GEN} = Mod(T_{NC}\rfloor_{GEN})$. Let $\phi = Ho(\mathbf{e}_\phi, \mathbf{t}_\phi)$, $\psi = Ho(\mathbf{g}_\psi, \mathbf{t}_\psi)$ be any (event and generalized, respectively) fluent facts, and Φ be any propositional combination of fluent facts. We say that ϕ **s–causes** ψ **under circumstances** Φ iff all of the following hold:

1. For all $\mathcal{M} \in M_{GEN}$: $\quad \mathcal{M} \models \Phi \Rightarrow \mathcal{M} \models \phi \supset \psi$.
2. There is an $\mathcal{M} \in M_{GEN}$ with $\mathcal{M} \models \Phi \wedge \phi$. There also exists a 'counterfactual model' $\mathcal{M}_c \in M_{GEN}$ of $\mathcal{M}$ w.r.t. ϕ, ψ and Φ, i.e. $\mathcal{M}_c \models \Phi \wedge \neg \phi \wedge \neg \psi$.
3. There exists an $\mathcal{M} \in M_{GEN}$ with $\mathcal{M} \models \Phi \wedge \neg \phi \wedge \psi$.
4. For all time points $\mathbf{t}_\Phi$ occurring in Φ: $\mathbf{t}_\Phi \le \mathbf{t}_\phi < \mathbf{t}_\psi$.

Step 1 Here we determine the causal relations that hold in T_{NC} . This is the most complicated step by far, and for the time being we will content ourselves by explaining the *outcome* of this step: after step 1, a model $\mathcal{M}$ with $\mathcal{M} \models Ca(\mathbf{g}, \mathbf{t})$ will be selected if there is a sufficient cause within the model for $\mathbf{g}$ to hold at $\mathbf{t}$. For example, for $T_{\text{YSP-NC}}$, all models remaining after step 1 will have $Ca(Loaded, 1)$. Also, among all models for $T_{\text{YSP-NC}}$ with $Ho(Loaded, 2)$ all those selected in step 1 will also have $Ca(Not(Alive), 3)$.

Step 2 introduces persistence; if something holds at time t, there will be an explanation for it to hold at time $t+1$. It also makes sure that 'normally we do not expect events to happen'. For example, in $T_{\text{YSP-NC}}$, all models further selected will have $JE(Not(Shoot), 2)$. Among all models for $T_{\text{YSP-NC}}$ with $Ho(Alive, 2)$, those further selected will also have $JE(Alive, 3)$.

Step 3 We have determined in step 1-2 all places in the causal graph where there *must* be a causal influence and we *must* have an arrow. Step 3 embodies a *domain closure* of Ca and JE. It effectively minimizes the interpretations of Ca and JE for every interpretation of Ho, while it does not rule out any interpretation of Ho itself. This closure follows from the *physical assumption* that $T_{\text{NC}}\rfloor_{\text{GEN}}$ and the persistence assumption of step 2 of $\mathbf{I}_0$ are *all* the laws of nature to which our domain is subjected. Also, this step forces the functional relations between the variables in the domain to obey Pearl's *principle of causal independence* (sec.4)!

In $T_{\text{YSP-NC}}$, all models further selected will have $\forall t. \neg Ca(Alive, t)$. Also, among those models in $\mathbf{I}_{0,2}$ that have $Ho(Alive, 2)$, all those further selected will also have $\neg JE\, (Not(Alive)), 3)$.

Step 4 We now use Pearl's *sufficient cause principle* to determine for each model $\mathcal{M}$ the set of unexplained fluent facts $\mathbf{Ab}_g^1(\mathcal{M}), \mathbf{Ab}_f^2(\mathcal{M}), \mathbf{Ab}_e^2(\mathcal{M})$ - first, a fluent fact $(\mathbf{g}, \mathbf{t})$ in a model $\mathcal{M}$ is unexplained (i.e. $(\mathbf{g}, \mathbf{t}) \in \mathbf{Ab}_g^1(\mathcal{M})$) iff there is a sufficient cause for $(\mathbf{g}, \mathbf{t})$ in the model, while $(\mathbf{g}, \mathbf{t})$ does not hold; i.e. an action has not had its regular effect. *Regular* fluent fact $(\mathbf{f}, \mathbf{t})$ is in $\mathbf{Ab}_f^2(\mathcal{M})$ if a) there is an explanation for it not to hold, b) there is no *sufficient* cause for it to hold (i.e. the sufficient cause principle does not apply), but c) in fact, it does hold. This means there is an unexplained *breach of persistence*. *Event* fluent fact $(\mathbf{e}, \mathbf{t})$ is in $\mathbf{Ab}_e^2(\mathcal{M})$ if event $\mathbf{e}$ takes place at time $\mathbf{t}$ without being caused by something else in the model. Ca always overrules JE: if we have $JE(Alive, 3)$ but $Ca(Not(Alive), 3)$ in all models, we prefer models with $Ho(Not(Alive), 3)$: *Alive* was 'just' explained, $Not(Alive)$ had a *sufficient* cause.

The intended model $\mathcal{M}$ of $T_{\text{YSP-NC}}$ will have empty $\mathbf{Ab}_g^1(\mathcal{M})$ and empty $\mathbf{Ab}_f^2(\mathcal{M})$, while $\mathbf{Ab}_e^2(\mathcal{M}) = \{(Load, 0), (Wait, 1), (Shoot, 2)\}$. The models $\mathcal{M}'$ in which the gun gets unloaded at $t = 1$ will all have $(Not(Loaded), 2) \in \mathbf{Ab}_f^2(\mathcal{M}')$.

Step 5 We first select the models with the least violations of causal laws; we then further select those with the least breaches of persistence. Finally, we rule out as many unexplained events as possible. We perform this step as the latest because we regard unexplained events as less 'surprising' than unexplained breaches of persistence. In all selected models for T_{YSP-NC}, we have $\neg Ho(Alive, 3)$, so we solve the YSP.

And what about S_0? Reconsider a causal theory such as our T_{YSP-C}. From a Pearlian viewpoint, we can see that what is actually formalized by axioms like (9) and (10) are the *sufficient causes* for fluents to hold at some time. This means that what S_0 really must do is to perform steps 2, 3, 4 and 5 of I_0 as step 1 has already been done by the person who formalized the domain knowledge! Formally, we define S_0 to be the procedure that results from setting $I_{0,1} := Mod(T_C)$ and jumping into the procedure of I_0 at the beginning of step 2.

And what about step 1 of I_0? In step 1 we need to find out for each (g, t) in each model whether there is a sufficient cause for it in the same model. We will do this by first generating the *causal laws* that must minimally hold in all models of our theory T_{NC}. To find them, we need to temporarily restrict it to $T_{NC} \rfloor_{GEN}$ – we will see that we must not let our *general* causal relations be influenced by *contingent* observations! We see in definition 2 that we can infer ϕ **s−causes** ψ **under circumstances** Φ (**s-causes** is to be read as 'is a sufficient cause of') if, given that Φ holds, ϕ *always* implies ψ (step 1 of definition 2) and (step 2), that ψ is actually *brought about* by ϕ. Step 3 in definition 2 tells us that the causal influence only goes one way. Steps 1, 2 and 3 are necessary if we want our causal relations to stand for causal networks in Pearl's sense – steps 1 and 2 follow from the sufficient cause principle, step 3 from the directedness of the causal graph! We can never be sure that ϕ is a sufficient cause for ψ by step 1 alone; ϕ could then still 'cause' ψ in the models with Ψ if Ψ implied both ϕ and ψ. Step 2 rules out this possibility. Step 4 adds another assumption about the physics of our domains, which simply says that performing an action at time t can never change anything about the world at an earlier point in time t'.

For example, in T_{YSP-NC} we will get '$Ho(Shoot, 2)$ **s-causes** $Ho(Not(Alive), 3)$ **u.c.** $Ho(Loaded, 2)$'. Now consider what would have happened if we had not restricted ourselves to $T_{NC} \rfloor_{GEN}$: we would have had $Ho(Shoot, 2)$ in *all* models; therefore we could never have checked whether it is really the *shooting* that brought about $Not(Alive)$. For this, we need to be able to look at a counterfactual model $\mathcal{M}_c$ where *no* shooting takes place at time 2! We must then check whether a) we can have $Ho(Alive, 3)$ in $\mathcal{M}_c$ (step 2), and b) whether, in *all* models with $Ho(Shoot, 2)$ and $Ho(Loaded, 2)$, we must have $Ho(Not(Alive), 3)$ (step 1) .

6 Validation of S_0 and I_0 - the Harvest

We will now see that two popular non-causal approaches, namely Baker's [1, 8, 3] and 'Chronological Minimization' [15, 13, 14] can be reinterpreted as an approximation of I_0 - specifically, they try to generate sufficient causes, but sometimes fail to do so. Constraints on the length of this paper force us to be very brief here; a much more detailed discussion can be found in [6].

I_0 and Baker Baker's approach is based on the situation calculus [14] where time is represented by *situations* s rather than timepoints; there still is a finite set of regular fluent constants FC and of events EC, but Ho is now defined only for regular fluents f and situations s. For any e and s, $Result(e, s)$ stands for the situation that results when performing e in s. Theories T_B for Baker's approach all contain domain independent axioms (5), (6) (with g replaced by f and t by s) and (8). Furthermore they contain the fluent domain-closure axiom (11) and the *frame axiom* (12) :

$$f = F_1 \vee \ldots \vee F_{|FC|} \tag{11}$$

$$\neg Ab(f, e, s) \supset (Ho(f, Result(a, s)) \equiv Ho(f, s)) \tag{12}$$

Finally, there are *existence of situations* ('EOS') axioms (the precise form of which is given in def. 4, next page) that make sure that for each set of fluents $F \subseteq FC$ there is at least one situation in which they hold. Baker's method consists of circumscribing [14] the Ab-predicate in a T_B with Ho fixed and *Result* allowed to vary. Roughly, this means that we select those models of T_B in which we have $Ab(f, e, s)$ (and thus, by (12), no persistence) only if f is *forced* to take on another value if e is performed in s.

If we reinterpret $Ab(f, e, s)$ as saying 'e is a sufficient cause for f in situation s', we see that circumscribing Ab is very similar to the inference of s – causes in step 1 of I_0: we have $Ab(f, e, s)$ only if there is an *event* e, that, when performed in *circumstances* s, *brings about* a new value of f. The EOS- axioms can now be interpreted as making sure that, in determining the instances of Ab, one looks at all possible situations, including *counterfactual* ones in which the contingent observations do not hold! But EOS only creates counterfactual situations for all possible combinations of *regular* fluent values, while step 1 of I_0 takes into account *all* counterfactual *models* consistent with the effect axioms. This means that in Baker's approach, contingent observations can sometimes still influence the sufficient causes found. We illustrate this by a new variation of the YSP, in which a new action *Point* is introduced: we suppose that if we *Shoot*, we have to *Point* first in order not to miss. We formalize this in a T_B containing axioms (5),(6),(8) & (11)-(14) :

$$Ho(Loaded, Result(Point, s)) \supset$$
$$[\neg Ho(Alive, Result(Shoot, Result(Point, s)))] \tag{13}$$
$$Ho(Alive, S_0) \wedge Ho(Loaded, S_0) \tag{14}$$

Suppose $s = Result(Shoot, Result(Point, S_0))$. It is easy to show by the technique used in [1] that models with $\neg Ho(Alive, s)$ are not preferred above models with $Ho(Alive, s)$; this is because no counterfactual situation exists in which the *Point*-action does not take place. All other problems with Baker's approach we are aware of, like the 'extended stolen car problem', the 'two-tank problem' [3] and the general problem of handling actions with nondeterministic effects [8] can be seen to stem from either this narrow definition of counterfactual situations or from the fact that Baker uses a single predicate Ab to denote both causation (our Ca) and surprise (our $\mathbf{Ab}_g^1$ and $\mathbf{Ab}_f^2$).

If one restricts $\mathbf{I}_0$ such that our 'circumstances' (in def.2) coincide with Baker's 'situations', and furthermore one allows only theories for which there are models without surprises about regular fluents, then the two methods become the same! Formally, we define $\mathbf{I}_0^B$ to be the same as $\mathbf{I}_0$ except that a) in definition 2, Φ must only contain fluent facts of the form $Ho(\mathbf{f}, \mathbf{t}_\phi)$, and b), step 5.3 is changed such that only models in which exactly one event happens at a time are selected.

In def. 4 (next page) we define $T_{NC} \sim T_B$ to hold for theories T_{NC} of our approach and theories T_B of Baker's approach which intuitively encode the same domain knowledge. The class of T_{NC} for which $T_{NC} \sim T_B$ is defined seems rather restricted; still, most specific examples of reasoning problems given in the literature on Baker's approach fit in this format. We want to prove that Baker's method and $\mathbf{I}_0^B$ select the same models in terms of what holds at what time. However, one model for a theory in situation calculus corresponds to a whole *set* of models in our language, namely, one specific model for each possible sequence of events. We call such a set of models a 'b.t. model set' (def. 4). In def. 5 we define $\mathcal{M}_B \cong M_{bt}$ for models $\mathcal{M}_B \in Mod(T_B)$ and b.t. model sets $M_{bt} \subset Mod(T_{NC})$ to hold iff $\mathcal{M}_B$ models exactly the same fluent histories as the elements of M_{bt}.

Theorem 3. *If we have any T_{NC} and T_B such that a) $T_{NC} \sim T_B$, and b) there is a b.t. model set $M_{bt} \subseteq \mathbf{I}_0^B(T_{NC})$ with for all $\mathcal{M}_{NC} \in M_{bt}$, $\mathbf{Ab}_f^2(\mathcal{M}_{NC}) = \emptyset$ then for all $\mathcal{M}_B$ and M_{bt} :*

1. *Baker's procedure selects $\mathcal{M}_B$ $\Rightarrow$ There exists an M_{bt} with $M_{bt} \cong \mathcal{M}_B$ and $M_{bt} \subseteq \mathbf{I}_0^B(T_{NC})$.*
2. *$M_{bt} \subseteq \mathbf{I}_0^B(T_{NC})$ $\Rightarrow$ There exists an $\mathcal{M}_B$ preferred by Baker's procedure with $M_{bt} \cong \mathcal{M}_B$.*

$\mathbf{I}_0$ and Chronological Minimization *chronological minimization* (CM) selects a model with a change of fluent value at time t only if there is no model which is the same up until time t but in which no fluent changes value at time t. Again, this can be reinterpreted as approximating step 1 of $\mathbf{I}_0$: we seek those changes which are forced to happen (step 1 in def. 2) given the fact that the past cannot be altered by any event (step 4). It should then come as no surprise that CM does not work very well unless enhanced by *filter preferential entailment* [13, 14] which modifies CM by first removing all regular fluent facts from a theory, then performing CM on the models of this 'general' theory and only then further select those models in which the regular fluent facts hold .

Comparisons to $\mathbf{S}_0$ Elsewhere we have proved [6] equivalences between a restriction of $\mathbf{S}_0$ and the theory of ramifications and qualifications of [11] and

We call a vector $\mathbf{f} = (\mathbf{f}_1, \ldots, \mathbf{f}_{|FC|})$ where each $\mathbf{f}_i \in \{F_i, Not(F_i)\}$) a *full fluent vector*. We abbreviate '$Ho(\mathbf{f}_1, t) \wedge \ldots \wedge Ho(\mathbf{f}_{|FC|})$' to '$Ho(\mathbf{f}, t)$'.

Definition 4. For any two theories T_{NC} for our language and T_B for a language of Baker's approach, we define $T_{NC} \sim T_B$ to hold iff all of the following hold:

1. The two languages share the same FC and EC .
2. $T_{NC}\rfloor_{IND}$ consists of all domain independent axioms (5)-(8). T_B contains axioms *(5),(6),(8),(11),(12)* .
3. $T_{NC}\rfloor_{GEN}$ contains an axiom of form
   $$Ho(\mathbf{f}_1, t) \wedge \ldots Ho(\mathbf{f}_n, t) \wedge Ho(\mathbf{e}, t) \supset Ho(\mathbf{f}_r, t+1)$$
   iff T_B contains the axiom
   $$Ho(\mathbf{f}_1, s) \wedge \ldots Ho(\mathbf{f}_n, s) \supset Ho(\mathbf{f}_r, Result(\mathbf{e}, s)) \quad (B0)$$
4. $T_{NC}\rfloor_{GEN}$ contains an axiom of form
   $$Ho(\mathbf{f}, t) \supset Ho(\mathbf{f}', t) \qquad\qquad (B1)$$
   iff T_B contains the same axiom (where t is taken to be a situation constant) .
5. T_B contains a propositional combination of fluent facts, each of the form $Ho(\mathbf{f}, s)$, with
   $$s = Result(\mathbf{e}_t, Result(\mathbf{e}_{t-1}, \ldots, Result(\mathbf{e}_0, S_0)\ldots))$$
   iff T_{NC} contains the corresponding propositional combination where each $Ho(\mathbf{f}, s)$ is replaced by $[Ho(\mathbf{e}_0, 0) \wedge \ldots \wedge Ho(\mathbf{e}_t, t) \supset Ho(\mathbf{f}, t+1)]$.
6. T_B contains *existence of situations*-axioms of the form $\exists s Ho(\mathbf{f}, s)$ for all $\mathbf{f}$ whose existence is consistent with all axioms in T_B of the form *(B0)* and *(B1)* (i.e. $Ho(\mathbf{f}, s) \nvdash \neg(\bigwedge (B0) \wedge \bigwedge (B1))$).
7. Each axiom in T_B is of one of the forms occurring in conditions 2-6 above. Each axiom in T_{NC} is of one of the forms occurring in conditions 2-5 above.

between a restriction of $\mathbf{S}_0$ and the approach based on Baral & Gelfond's action-description language $\mathcal{L}_3$ (an extension of Lifschitz' $\mathcal{A}$) [2]. For the causal approaches of Morgenstern & Stein, Geffner and Lifschitz, Haugh and Rabinov [5, 7, 9, 16] we give examples of reasoning domains where our approach gives better results than they do. We take this as evidence that $\mathbf{S}_0$ works well for wide classes of causal theories. Note that $\mathbf{S}_0$ can handle a much wider class of reasoning domains than $\mathbf{I}_0$, since, using the Ca-predicate, in causal theories T_C we can express many kinds of interesting causal relations that cannot be generated by $\mathbf{I}_0$ from *any* non-causal theory whatsoever [6].

References

1. A.B. Baker. Nonmonotonic reasoning in the framework of situation calculus. *Artificial Intelligence*, 49:5–23, 1991.
2. C. Baral, M. Gelfond, and A. Provetti. Reasoning about actual and hypothetical occurrences of concurrent and non-deterministic actions. In *Proceedings AAAI Spring Symposium*, 1995.
3. J.M. Crawford and D.W. Etherington. Formalizing reasoning about change: a qualitative reasoning approach. In *Proceedings AAAI-92*, pages 577–583, 1992.

In the following $Ho!(e,t)$ will be an abbreviation for

$$Ho(e,t) \wedge \left[\bigwedge_{1 \le i \le |EC|, E_i \neq e} \neg Ho(E_i, t) \right].$$

Definition 5. A *branching time (b.t.) model set* M_{bt} is any set of models for a theory T_{NC} such that :

1. For all finite sequences of events $[e_0, \ldots, e_t]$ $(t \ge 0)$
   - M_{bt} contains an $\mathcal{M}$ with $\mathcal{M} \models Ho!(e_0, 0) \wedge \ldots \wedge Ho!(e_t, t)$.
   - There is a sequence of full fluent vectors $[f_0, \ldots f_{t+1}]$ such that for all $\mathcal{M}$ in
     $$M_{bt}: \mathcal{M} \models \left[\bigwedge_{0 \le i \le t} Ho!(e_i, i) \right] \supset \left[\bigwedge_{0 \le i \le t+1} Ho(f_i, i) \right]$$
2. For all $\mathcal{M}$ in M_{bt}, $\mathcal{M} \models \forall t \exists e \, . \, Ho!(e, t)$

Definition 6. Given an $\mathcal{M}_B$ for a T_B and a b.t. model set M_{bt} of models for a T_{NC} with $T_{NC} \sim T_B$ we write $\mathcal{M}_B \cong M_{bt}$ iff for all finite sequences of events $[e_0, \ldots, e_t]$ $(t \ge 0)$ and for all f:

$$\mathcal{M}_B \models Ho(f, Result(e_t, \ldots, Result(e_0, S_0) \ldots))$$

iff for all $\mathcal{M} \in M_{bt}$ we have

$$\mathcal{M} \models [\bigwedge_{0 \le i \le t} Ho!(e_i, i)] \supset Ho(f, t+1)$$

4. A. Darwiche and J. Pearl. Symbolic causal networks. In *Proceedings AAAI-94*, 1994.
5. H. Geffner. Causal theories for nonmonotonic reasoning. In *Proceedings AAAI-90*, pages 524–530, 1990.
6. P.D. Grünwald. Causation, explanation and nonmonotonic temporal reasoning. Technical Report INS-R9701, CWI, jan 1997. Available at ftp://ftp.cwi.nl/pub/pdg/R9701.ps.Z.
7. B.A. Haugh. Simple causal mimimizations for temporal persistence and projection. In *Proceedings AAAI-87*, pages 218–223, 1987.
8. G.N. Kartha. Two counterexamples related to Baker's approach to the frame problem. *Artificial Intelligence*, 69:379–391, 1994.
9. V.L. Lifschitz and A. Rabinov. Miracles in formal theories of action. *Artificial Intelligence*, 38:225–237, 1989.
10. F. Lin. Embracing causality in specifying the indeterminate effects of actions. In *Proceedings AAAI-96*, 1996.
11. N. McCain and H. Turner. A causal theory of ramifications and qualifications. In *Proceedings IJCAI-95*, 1995.
12. J. Pearl. Causation, action and counterfactuals. In Y. Shoham, editor, *Proceedings TARK-VI*, pages 51–73. Morgan Kaufmann, 1996.
13. E.J. Sandewall. *Features and Fluents*. Oxford University Press, 1994.
14. E.J. Sandewall and Y. Shoham. Nonmonotonic temporal reasoning. In *Handbook of Logic in Artificial Intelligence and Logic Programming*, volume 4. Oxford University Press, 1995.
15. Y. Shoham. Chronological ignorance: experiments in nonmonotonic temporal reasoning. *Artificial Intelligence*, 36:279–331, 1988.
16. L.A. Stein and L. Morgenstern. Motivated action theory: A formal theory of causal reasoning. *Artificial Intelligence*, 71(1):1–42, nov 1994.

Labelled Quantified Modal Logics

David Basin[1], Seán Matthews[2], Luca Viganò[2]

[1] Institut für Informatik, Universität Freiburg
Am Flughafen 17, D-79110 Freiburg, Germany
basin@informatik.uni-freiburg.de
[2] Max-Planck-Institut für Informatik
Im Stadtwald, D-66123 Saarbrücken, Germany
sean@mpi-sb.mpg.de, luca@mpi-sb.mpg.de

Abstract. We present an approach to providing natural deduction style proof systems for a large class of quantified modal logics with varying, increasing, decreasing or constant domains of quantification. The systems we develop are modular both in the behavior of the accessibility relation and quantification relative to the semantics, and in the proofs of soundness and completeness relative to that semantics. Our systems also provide the basis of simple implementations of quantified modal logics in a standard logical framework theorem prover.

1 Introduction

Modal logic is an active area of research in computer science and artificial intelligence, as a language for formalizing and reasoning about, e.g., knowledge, belief, time, space, and other dynamic 'state oriented' properties. The principles of propositional modal logics (PMLs) are well understood, and the relationship between semantics and proof theory captured in general metatheorems which we can exploit in developing new systems. The situation is not, however, so well understood in the more complex case of quantified modal logics (QMLs), where arbitrary ingenuity may be needed to establish standard metatheoretic results for a new system [7,9,11].

The problems are the result of the new semantic possibilities introduced by quantifiers: in a QML we have to decide not only the properties of the accessibility relation between worlds in the Kripke frame but also how quantification in these worlds behaves. As we move from world to world, the domain of quantification might vary arbitrarily (varying domains), remain constant (constant domains), or expand (increasing domains) or shrink (decreasing domains). These two parts of the semantics are essentially independent of each other and define a two-dimensional space[1] which, in the past, has been explored piecemeal; i.e. there is no uniformity in the presentation of proof systems and the way metatheoretic results are proved.

---

[1] Even more complexity is possible, e.g. non-rigid designators [7,9], where the meaning of a name varies from world to world; we consider here only the rigid case.

There are several difficulties for a uniform approach. First, it may be difficult to find a suitable proof system for an intended semantics: QMLs are (like PMLs) usually presented as Hilbert systems. But the usual quantifier rules for Hilbert systems work only for increasing domains [7, p. 426]. This problem can sometimes be solved by adopting a more complex proof system (e.g. adopted from free logic) or even by redefining the principles of the semantics (e.g. by introducing truth value gaps). However these solutions are imperfect in that they are not uniform: different strategies for proving completeness are needed for different conditions on the domains [9,11]. Second, the relationship between the Kripke semantics of a PML and its quantified extension may not be simple. Just because a PML is complete with respect to a semantics it does not follow that the corresponding QML is complete with respect to the corresponding extension of the semantics. Moreover, minor changes to a complete QML, e.g. modifying the conditions on the domains, can produce incompleteness.[2]

Context and Contribution This paper is a companion to [4]; we extend and generalize the results given there for PMLs to the quantified case and thereby provide solutions to the above problems. Let us first briefly summarize the approach and some of the results that we previously developed. In [4] we formalized natural deduction proof systems for PMLs, based on the view of a logic as a Labelled Deductive System [8]. We decomposed a modal logic into two interacting parts: a *base logic*, fixed for all modal logics, and a *relational theory*, different for each modal logic. In the base logic, we reason about formulae paired with labels; instead of $\vdash A$, we prove $\vdash w{:}A$, where $w{:}A$ is a *labelled formula*, w is an element of the set of possible worlds W in the Kripke frame, and $\vdash A$ iff $\forall w \in W(\vdash w{:}A)$. In the relational theory, we formalize the behavior of the accessibility relation R in the Kripke frame. *Relational formulae* $w\,R\,w'$ state that w accesses w'. This allows us, for instance, to formulate the behavior of modal operators like $\square$ independent of the properties of R in the frame taken as providing the semantics, i.e. $\vdash w{:}\square A$ iff $\vdash w'{:}A$ for all $w' \in W$ such that $\vdash w\,R\,w'$. As a consequence, we are able to give natural deduction introduction and elimination rules for $\square$ that are fixed for all the logics we consider. The main results that we established can be summarized as follows.

Soundness and completeness: we uniformly showed that all PMLs formalizable in our framework are sound and complete with respect to the corresponding Kripke semantics.

Proof theory: we explored tradeoffs in formulating the base logic and the relational theory. We showed, for example, that when the relational theory can be formulated as a set of Horn clauses (as opposed to a set of first or second-order axioms), then proofs are normalizing and there is a strict separation between the base logic and the relational theory, i.e. derivations in the base logic may depend on derivations in the relational theory, but not vice versa.

---

[2] There are, e.g., QMLs without the *Barcan Formula* (BF, $\forall x.\square A \to \square \forall x.A$) which are complete, where the introduction of BF produces incompleteness, or vice versa. For example QS4.2 + BF is incomplete even though QS4.2 is complete [11].

Implementation: we showed that the resulting proof systems can be implemented in a standard logical framework such as Isabelle [14] or the Edinburgh LF [10]. We implemented our approach in Isabelle and the result is a simple and natural environment for interactive proof development that supports hierarchical structuring: logics are structured by extension (enrichment with new rules) and theorems are inherited in extensions.

We give a natural deduction presentation of QMLs that is modular in two dimensions, reflecting the two degrees of freedom described above. As before, it is based on a fixed base logic (now QK, for quantified K) where extensions are made by independently instantiating two separate theories: a relational theory (as before), and a *domain theory*, which formalizes the behavior of the domains of quantification. This second theory requires the introduction of *labelled terms*, $w{:}t$, expressing the existence of term t at world w. Thus $\vdash w{:}\forall x.A$ iff $\vdash w{:}A[t/x]$ for all t such that $\vdash w{:}t$. This formulation naturally suggests adopting the quantifier rules of free logic [5], and we show later that the previously mentioned problems for Hilbert-style QMLs based on free logic do not apply in our approach. By appropriate instantiation of these two theories, it is possible to present the predicate extensions (with varying, increasing, decreasing, or constant domains) of the PMLs belonging to a large class, which includes the Geach hierarchy and hence contains logics like K, D, T, B, S4, S4.2, KD45, and S5.

The metatheory of our QMLs is also modular. The use of explicit labels leads to a modular and uniform proof of soundness and completeness for all the logics we consider, which differs from the standard one: we provide a new kind of canonical model construction that accounts for the explicit formalization of labels, of the accessibility relation, and of the properties of the domains of quantification. This means that our presentations are sound and complete with respect to the appropriate Kripke semantics, and are thus equivalent to the corresponding Hilbert systems only when these are themselves complete with respect to the same semantics.

Due to lack of space, discussions and proofs have been omitted or considerably shortened; a detailed account is given in our technical report [3]. Furthermore, here we do not discuss proof theoretic results and implementational aspects, but point out that (i) the proof theoretic results for labelled PMLs carry over to QMLs, so that proof search may be restricted (normal proofs have the subformula property) and the effectiveness of theorem proving can be improved; (ii) our approach to implementing labelled modal logics in a logical framework carries over directly to the quantified case. In fact, all the proofs of modal theorems given in this paper (e.g., at the end of § 2) have been machine checked in our implementation of QMLs in the Isabelle logical framework.

2 A modular presentation of QMLs

We introduce a labelled natural deduction presentation of QMLs, where we use labels to associate possible worlds with terms and formulae. Let W be a set of *labels* and R a binary relation over W. If w and w' are labels, then $w\,R\,w'$

$$\frac{\begin{array}{c}[w_i:A \to \bot]\\ \vdots\\ w_j:\bot\end{array}}{w_i:A} \perp E \qquad \frac{\begin{array}{c}[w:A]\\ \vdots\\ w:B\end{array}}{w:A \to B} \to I \qquad \frac{w:A \to B \quad w:A}{w:B} \to E$$

$$\frac{\begin{array}{c}[w_i \ R \ w_j]\\ \vdots\\ w_j:A\end{array}}{w_i:\Box A} \ \Box I \qquad \frac{w_i:\Box A \quad w_i \ R \ w_j}{w_j:A} \ \Box E \qquad \frac{\begin{array}{c}[w:t]\\ \vdots\\ w:A[t/x]\end{array}}{w:\forall x.A} \ \forall I \qquad \frac{w:\forall x.A \quad w:t}{w:A[t/x]} \ \forall E$$

In $\Box I$, w_j is different from w_i and does not occur in any assumption on which $w_j:A$ depends other than $w_i \ R \ w_j$. In $\forall I$, t does not occur in any assumption on which $w:A[t/x]$ depends other than $w:t$.

Fig. 1. The rules of QK

is a *relational formula* (*rwff*). If t is a constant c or a variable x, then $w:t$ is *labelled term* (*lterm*). If A is a modal formula built from atomic propositions (i.e. predicates applied to terms) and the connectives and quantifiers $\bot$, $\to$, $\Box$, $\forall$, then $w:A$ is a *labelled formula* (*lwff*). We can define the other connectives and quantifiers in the usual manner, e.g. $\neg A$ as $A \to \bot$, $\Diamond A$ as $\neg\Box\neg A$, and $\exists x.A$ as $\neg\forall x.\neg A$. Henceforth, we assume that the variable w ranges over labels, t ranges over terms, and A, B range over modal formulae. Further, let $\Gamma = \{w_1:A_1,\ldots,w_n:A_n\}$, $\Delta = \{w_1 \ R \ w_2,\ldots,w_l \ R \ w_m\}$ and $\Theta = \{w_1:t_1,\ldots,w_j:t_j\}$ be arbitrary sets of lwffs, rwffs and lterms, respectively. All metavariables may be annotated with subscripts or superscripts.

The rules given in Fig. 1 determine QK, the base natural deduction system formalizing quantified K. The rules for $\forall$ are a labelled version of the rules of free logic [5], and, as in free logic, $w:\forall x.A \to \exists x.A$ is provable only under the assumption $w:t$, stating that the domain of quantification of w is non-empty. Note the symmetry between the rules for $\Box$ and those for $\forall$; this reinforces the role of $\Box$, and of modal logics in general, "as a replacement for the more powerful machinery of quantified classical logic, at least in some cases" [7, p. 377].

Relational theories

Different QMLs are obtained from the base logic QK by placing conditions on the accessibility relation R in the Kripke frame; e.g. we get the logic QT from QK by adding that R is reflexive, and then QS4 from QT by further adding transitivity. We formalize particular QMLs by extending QK with relational theories, which axiomatize properties of R. However, not all modal axioms can be axiomatized in a first-order setting (e.g. the McKinsey axiom $\Box\Diamond A \to \Diamond\Box A$, or the Löb axiom $\Box(\Box A \to A) \to \Box A$) and hence there is an important decision that we must make: Should our relational theories be axiomatized in higher-order logic (and

$$\text{Transitivity, 4: } \Box A \rightarrow \Box\Box A \qquad\qquad \text{Euclideaness, 5: } \Diamond A \rightarrow \Box\Diamond A$$

$$\frac{w_i \; R \; w_j \quad w_j \; R \; w_k}{w_i \; R \; w_k} \; trans \qquad\qquad \frac{w_i \; R \; w_j \quad w_i \; R \; w_k}{w_j \; R \; w_k} \; eucl$$

$$\text{Reflexivity, T: } \Box A \rightarrow A \qquad\qquad \text{Convergency, 2: } \Diamond\Box A \rightarrow \Box\Diamond A$$

$$\frac{}{w_i \; R \; w_i} \; refl \qquad \frac{w_i \; R \; w_j \quad w_i \; R \; w_k}{w_j \; R \; g(w_i, w_j, w_k)} \; conv1 \qquad \frac{w_i \; R \; w_j \quad w_i \; R \; w_k}{w_k \; R \; g(w_i, w_j, w_k)} \; conv2$$

Fig. 2. Some properties of R, axioms, and relational rules (g is a Skolem function)

thus allow the formalization of all quantified modal logics), first-order logic, or some subset thereof? We showed in [4] that there are tradeoffs in formalization: different choices require different formalizations of the base modal logic and have different metatheoretic properties (see also [3]). In [4] we settled on those logics with an accessibility relation axiomatizable in terms of Horn clauses, a choice we repeat here. We choose to admit precisely those properties of R that can be formulated by a collection of *relational rules*, i.e. (Horn) rules of the form

$$\frac{p_1 \; R \; q_1 \quad \cdots \quad p_m \; R \; q_m}{p_0 \; R \; q_0}$$

where $m \geq 0$, and p_i and q_i are terms built from labels $w_1, \ldots, w_n$ and function symbols.[3] A *relational theory* $\mathcal{T}$ is a theory generated by a set of such rules.

Relational rules suffice to formalize the predicate extensions of the most common PMLs, for example those in the Geach hierarchy. Examples of some common characteristic axioms and the corresponding relational rules are given in Fig. 2. The QML $L = \text{QK} + \mathcal{T}$ is obtained by extending QK with a given relational theory $\mathcal{T}$; this extension is represented by the horizontal arrows in Fig. 3(a). We adopt the convention of naming the logic QK$+\mathcal{T}$ as QKAx, where Ax is a string consisting of the standard names of the characteristic axioms corresponding to the relational rules generating $\mathcal{T}$; e.g. QKT4 identifies the logic also known as QS4. Various combinations of relational rules define therefore different QMLs, including QK, QD, QT, QB, QS4, QS4.2, QKD45 and QS5.

Domain theories

So far, we have made no commitments to the relationship between the domains of quantification in the different worlds, i.e. the domains of QK$+\mathcal{T}$ are *varying*. We can impose semantic conditions on them by, e.g., requiring that, when moving to

---

[3] Some properties of R, e.g. seriality and convergency, can be expressed as relational rules only after the introduction of Skolem function constants. By the theorem on functional extensions [15, p. 55], the introduction of such constants is a conservative extension; see [3,4].

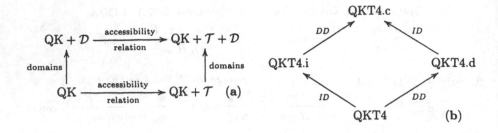

Fig. 3. A hierarchy of labelled QMLs (a); QKT4.*l* (b)

an accessible world, objects persist (the domains are *increasing*), are not created (and possibly deleted, i.e. the domains are *decreasing*), or stay the same (the domains are *constant*). The conditions for increasing and decreasing domains are formalized by the (Horn) rules *ID* and *DD* respectively:

$$\frac{w_i \ R \ w_j \quad w_i{:}t}{w_j{:}t} \ ID \qquad \frac{w_i \ R \ w_j \quad w_j{:}t}{w_i{:}t} \ DD$$

Different combinations of these rules define different QMLs: the logic $L = \mathrm{QK} + \mathcal{T} + \mathcal{D}$ is obtained by extending $\mathrm{QK} + \mathcal{T}$ with a given theory $\mathcal{D}$ of the domains of quantification (or *domain theory*, for short), generated by a subset of $\{ID, DD\}$; this extension is represented by the vertical arrows in Fig. 3(a). This yields the two-dimensional uniformity of the proof system motivated in the introduction. (Uniform proofs of soundness and completeness are given in § 3.) We extend the above convention and name the logic $\mathrm{QK} + \mathcal{T} + \mathcal{D}$ as QK$Ax.l$, where l represents the conditions imposed on the domains. We write QKAx when $\mathcal{D}$ is empty, as done above; QKAx.i (respectively QKAx.d) when $\mathcal{D}$ is generated by *ID* (respectively *DD*); QKAx.c when $\mathcal{D}$ is generated by *ID* and *DD*. We can thus specify one of four related QMLs simply by instantiating $\mathcal{D}$; as shown in Fig. 3(b), we can specify QKT4 (QS4) with domains that are varying (QKT4), increasing (QKT4.i), decreasing (QKT4.d), or constant (QKT4.c).

This is *not* the case in Hilbert systems for QMLs, where the domains are committed to being increasing, since the classical rules for ∀ automatically enforce the *Converse Barcan Formula* (CBF), $\Box \forall x.A \to \forall x.\Box A$, which corresponds to the increasing domains condition [7, p. 426]. Constant domains are then obtained by further adding as an axiom the *Barcan Formula* (BF), $\forall x.\Box A \to \Box \forall x.A$, which corresponds to the decreasing domains condition. Hilbert-style proof systems for QMLs with varying domains can be given by substituting the classical quantifier rules with the rules of free logic, as done by Garson in [9]. However, Garson also shows that his completeness proof is not general, and fails for some QMLs, e.g. QB; we return to this at the end of § 3.

Definition 1. An *L-derivation* of an lwff, rwff or lterm φ from Γ, Δ, Θ, is a tree formed using the rules in L, ending with φ and depending only on Γ, Δ, Θ. We write $\Gamma, \Delta, \Theta \vdash_L \varphi$ when φ can be so derived. φ is a *theorem* of L, $\vdash_L \varphi$, if it is L-derivable when Γ, Δ, Θ are all empty.

Fact 2. *Due to the separations enforced between the base logic, the relational theory, and the domain theory, we have (i)* $\Gamma, \Delta, \Theta \vdash_L w_i \ R \ w_j$ *iff* $\Delta \vdash_L w_i \ R \ w_j$, *and (ii)* $\Gamma, \Delta, \Theta \vdash_L w{:}t$ *iff* $\Delta, \Theta \vdash_L w{:}t$.

That is, while lwffs are derived from lwffs, rwffs *and* lterms, i.e. $\Gamma, \Delta, \Theta \vdash_L w{:}A$, (i) rwffs are derived from rwffs *alone*, and (ii) lterms are derived from rwffs and lterms *but not* from lwffs. In comparison, note that in approaches based on *semantic embedding*, also called *semantics-based translations*, e.g. [1,13], a formula of quantified modal logic is translated into a formula in first-order predicate logic and shown to be true (or false) in a first-order theory formalizing the semantics of the modalities and quantification domains. However, with these translations all structure is lost as relations, predicates and terms are flattened into formulae of first-order logic, and derivations of lwffs are mingled with derivations of rwffs and lterms.

As an example of a derivation, we show that CBF is a theorem of (any extension of) QK.i:

$$
\cfrac{\cfrac{\cfrac{[w{:}\Box\forall x.A]^3 \quad [w \ R \ w_1]^1}{w_1{:}\forall x.A} \Box E \quad \cfrac{[w \ R \ w_1]^1 \quad [w{:}t]^2}{w_1{:}t} ID}{\cfrac{w_1{:}A[t/x]}{\cfrac{w{:}\Box A[t/x]}{\cfrac{w{:}\forall x.\Box A}{w{:}\Box\forall x.A \to \forall x.\Box A} \to I^3} \forall I^2} \Box I^1} \forall E}{}
$$

Note that we associate discharged assumptions with rule applications.[4] In a similar manner, we can prove BF in QK.d, (1) below, and other common examples:

(1) $\vdash_{\text{QK.d}} w{:}\forall x.\Box A \to \Box\forall x.A$ \quad (2) $\vdash_{\text{QKB.i}} w{:}\forall x.\Box A \to \Box\forall x.A$

(3) $\vdash_{\text{QK.d}} w{:}\Diamond\exists x.A \to \exists x.\Diamond A$ \quad (4) $\vdash_{\text{QK.i}} w{:}\exists x.\Diamond A \to \Diamond\exists x.A$

Some remarks are in order. *ID* and *DD* are interderivable when the rule $\dfrac{w_i \ R \ w_j}{w_j \ R \ w_i}$ is present, i.e. when the accessibility relation is *symmetric* (symmetry corresponds to the modal axiom B: $A \to \Box\Diamond A$). (2) shows that a QML with a symmetric accessibility relation and with increasing domains (QKB.i) validates BF, and has therefore constant domains; similarly we can show that CBF is a theorem of QKB.d. By (3) and (4), $\Diamond\exists x.A$ and $\exists x.\Diamond A$ are equivalent in QK.c.

3 Soundness and completeness of labelled QMLs

Definition 3. A *model* for a QML L is a tuple $\mathfrak{M} = (\mathfrak{W}, \mathfrak{R}, \mathfrak{D}, \mathfrak{q}, \mathfrak{a})$, where $\mathfrak{W}$ is a non-empty set of worlds; $\mathfrak{R} \subseteq \mathfrak{W} \times \mathfrak{W}$; $\mathfrak{D}$ is a set of objects; $\mathfrak{q}$ is a mapping

---

[4] CBF is not a theorem of QK, because *ID* is missing and the application of $\forall I$ at world w cannot discharge $w_1{:}t$. A formal proof of this can be given by exploiting the results on proof normalization discussed in [3], to show that there is no normal proof (and, a fortiori, no proof at all) of CBF in QK.

assigning to each member w of $\mathfrak{W}$ some subset of $\mathfrak{D}$, the *domain of quantification* of w; $\mathfrak{a}$ is function interpreting the terms and predicate letters by assigning them the corresponding kind of intensions with respect to $\mathfrak{W}$ and $\mathfrak{D}$. $\mathfrak{a}(w,t)$ is an element of $\mathfrak{D}$, and for an n-ary predicate letter P, $\mathfrak{a}(w,P)$ is a set of ordered n-tuples, $\langle a_1, \ldots, a_n \rangle$, where each $a_i \in \mathfrak{D}$. Moreover, for every $w_i, w_j \in \mathfrak{W}$ such that $(w_i, w_j) \in \mathfrak{R}$, the domains of $\mathfrak{M}$ are: *increasing* iff $\mathfrak{q}(w_i) \subseteq \mathfrak{q}(w_j)$; *decreasing* iff $\mathfrak{q}(w_i) \supseteq \mathfrak{q}(w_j)$; *constant* iff $\mathfrak{q}(w_i) = \mathfrak{q}(w_j)$. Otherwise, the domains are *varying*.

Note that we only consider rigid designators [7,9], where $\mathfrak{a}$ is such that $\mathfrak{a}(w_i, t) = \mathfrak{a}(w_j, t)$ for all $w_i, w_j \in \mathfrak{W}$. Moreover, our models do not contain functions corresponding to possible Skolem functions in the signature; when such constants are present, the appropriate Skolem expansion of the model is required [16, p. 137].

Call the ordered triple (Γ, Δ, Θ) a *proof context* (pc). We write $w{:}A \in (\Gamma, \Delta, \Theta)$ when $w{:}A \in \Gamma$; $w \; R \; w' \in (\Gamma, \Delta, \Theta)$ when $w \; R \; w' \in \Delta$; and $w{:}t \in (\Gamma, \Delta, \Theta)$ when $w{:}t \in \Theta$. We say that a label w *occurs in* (Γ, Δ, Θ), and, continuing our slight notational abuse, write $w \in (\Gamma, \Delta, \Theta)$, if there exists an A such that $w{:}A \in \Gamma$, or a w' such that $w \; R \; w' \in \Delta$ or $w \; R \; w' \in \Delta$, or a t such that $w{:}t \in \Theta$. $t \in (\Gamma, \Delta, \Theta)$ is defined analogously. We now define truth for ground lterms, rwffs and lwffs, where truth for lterms indicates definedness, truth for rwffs indicates accessibility, and quantifiers are treated in each world as ranging over the domain of that world only.

Definition 4. We define a ground lterm, rwff or lwff φ to be *true* in a model $\mathfrak{M}$, in symbols $\models^{\mathfrak{M}} \varphi$, as follows. First, we ensure that we have a name for each object in the domain $\mathfrak{D}$ of $\mathfrak{M}$ by extending, if necessary, the class of terms with a new constant c_o for each $o \in \mathfrak{D}$, and then extending $\mathfrak{a}$ so that $\mathfrak{a}(w, c_o) = o$, as is standard [12,15]. Then, we define $\models^{\mathfrak{M}}$ to be the smallest relation satisfying:

$$
\begin{aligned}
&\models^{\mathfrak{M}} w{:}t && \text{iff } \mathfrak{a}(w,t) \in \mathfrak{q}(w) \\
&\models^{\mathfrak{M}} w_i \; R \; w_j && \text{iff } (w_i, w_j) \in \mathfrak{R} \\
&\models^{\mathfrak{M}} w{:}P(t_1, \ldots, t_n) && \text{iff } \langle \mathfrak{a}(w, t_1), \ldots, \mathfrak{a}(w, t_n) \rangle \in \mathfrak{a}(w, P) \\
&\models^{\mathfrak{M}} w{:}A \to B && \text{iff } \models^{\mathfrak{M}} w{:}A \text{ implies } \models^{\mathfrak{M}} w{:}B \\
&\models^{\mathfrak{M}} w{:}\Box A && \text{iff for all } w_i, \models^{\mathfrak{M}} w \; R \; w_i \text{ implies } \models^{\mathfrak{M}} w_i{:}A \\
&\models^{\mathfrak{M}} w{:}\forall x.A && \text{iff for all } t, \models^{\mathfrak{M}} w{:}t \text{ implies } \models^{\mathfrak{M}} w{:}A[t/x]
\end{aligned}
$$

By extension, $\models^{\mathfrak{M}} (\Gamma, \Delta, \Theta)$ means that $\models^{\mathfrak{M}} \varphi$ for all $\varphi \in (\Gamma, \Delta, \Theta)$; $\Gamma, \Delta, \Theta \models^{\mathfrak{M}} \varphi$ means that $\models^{\mathfrak{M}} (\Gamma, \Delta, \Theta)$ implies $\models^{\mathfrak{M}} \varphi$ in the model $\mathfrak{M}$; and $\Gamma, \Delta, \Theta \models \varphi$ means that $\Gamma, \Delta, \Theta \models^{\mathfrak{M}} \varphi$ for all models $\mathfrak{M}$.

Truth for lwffs containing other connectives and quantifiers can be defined in the usual manner, e.g. $\models^{\mathfrak{M}} w{:}\exists x.A$ iff $\not\models^{\mathfrak{M}} w{:}\forall x.\neg A$, since $\not\models^{\mathfrak{M}} w{:}\bot$ for every w. The explicit embedding of properties of the models, and the possibility of explicitly reasoning about them, via lterms and rwffs, require us to consider soundness and completeness results also for lterms and rwffs. We define:

Definition 5. The QML $L = QK + \mathcal{T} + \mathcal{D}$ is *sound* iff (i) $\Delta \vdash_L w_i \; R \; w_j$ implies $\Delta \models w_i \; R \; w_j$, (ii) $\Delta, \Theta \vdash_L w{:}t$ implies $\Delta, \Theta \models w{:}t$, and (iii) $\Gamma, \Delta, \Theta \vdash_L w{:}A$ implies $\Gamma, \Delta, \Theta \models w{:}A$. L is *complete* iff the converses hold.

Theorem 6. $L = \mathrm{QK} + \mathcal{T} + \mathcal{D}$ *is sound and complete.*

We only sketch the main proof ideas; see [3] for a full account. Soundness follows by induction on the structure of the L-derivations. The base cases, e.g. $w{:}A \in (\Gamma, \Delta, \Theta)$, are trivial, and there is a step case for each inference rule of L. As an example, we give the case for $\Box I$; the cases for the other rules follow analogously. Let $\mathfrak{M}_L$ be an arbitrary model for L and consider an application of $\Box I$

$$
\begin{array}{c}
[w \; R \; w_i] \\
\Pi \\
\dfrac{w_i{:}A}{w{:}\Box A} \; \Box I
\end{array}
$$

where Π is the L-derivation $\Gamma, \Delta_1, \Theta \vdash_L w_i{:}A$, with $\Delta_1 = \Delta \cup \{w \; R \; w_i\}$. By the induction hypothesis, $\Gamma, \Delta_1, \Theta \vdash_L w_i{:}A$ implies $\Gamma, \Delta_1, \Theta \models w_i{:}A$. Assume $\models^{\mathfrak{M}_L} (\Gamma, \Delta, \Theta)$. By the restriction on the application of $\Box I$, we can extend Δ to $\Delta' = \Delta \cup \{w \; R \; w'\}$ for an arbitrary $w' \notin (\Gamma, \Delta, \Theta)$, and assume $\models^{\mathfrak{M}_L} \Delta'$. Since $\models^{\mathfrak{M}_L} \Delta'$ implies $\models^{\mathfrak{M}_L} \Delta_1$, the induction hypothesis yields $\models^{\mathfrak{M}_L} w_i{:}A$, i.e. $\models^{\mathfrak{M}_L} w'{:}A$ for an arbitrary $w' \notin (\Gamma, \Delta, \Theta)$ such that $\models^{\mathfrak{M}_L} w \; R \; w'$. We conclude $\models^{\mathfrak{M}_L} w{:}\Box A$ by Definition 4.

Completeness follows by a Henkin-style proof, where a canonical model $\mathfrak{M}_L^C = (\mathfrak{W}_L^C, \mathfrak{R}_L^C, \mathfrak{D}_L^C, \mathsf{q}_L^C, \mathsf{a}_L^C)$ is built to show the contrapositives of the conditions in Definition 5, i.e. (i') $\Delta \nvdash_L w_i \; R \; w_j$ implies $\Delta \not\models^{\mathfrak{M}_L^C} w_i \; R \; w_j$, (ii') $\Delta, \Theta \nvdash_L w{:}t$ implies $\Delta, \Theta \not\models^{\mathfrak{M}_L^C} w{:}t$, and (iii') $\Gamma, \Delta, \Theta \nvdash_L w{:}A$ implies $\Gamma, \Delta, \Theta \not\models^{\mathfrak{M}_i^C} w{:}A$. In particular, given the presence of labelled formulae and explicit assumptions on the relations between the labels and their domains of quantification (i.e. Δ and Θ), in our version of the Lindenbaum lemma (Lemma 8 below) we consider a 'global' saturated set of labelled formulae, where consistency is also checked against the additional assumptions in Δ and Θ, instead of the usual saturated sets of unlabelled formulae. Moreover, given a logic $L = \mathrm{QK} + \mathcal{T} + \mathcal{D}$ and a proof context (Γ, Δ, Θ), we consider the deductive closure Δ_L of Δ under L, and the deductive closure $\Theta_{L,\Delta}$ of Θ under L with respect to Δ, i.e.

$$\Delta_L =_{def} \{w_i \; R \; w_j \mid \Delta \vdash_L w_i \; R \; w_j\} \quad \text{and} \quad \Theta_{L,\Delta} =_{def} \{w{:}t \mid \Delta, \Theta \vdash_L w{:}t\}.$$

Definition 7. (Γ, Δ, Θ) is *saturated* iff (i) (Γ, Δ, Θ) is consistent, i.e. $\Gamma, \Delta, \Theta \nvdash_L w{:}\bot$ for every w; (ii) $\Delta = \Delta_L$ and $\Theta = \Theta_{L,\Delta}$; (iii) for every lwff $w{:}A$, either $w{:}A \in \Gamma$ or $w{:}\neg A \in \Gamma$; (iv) for every w, if $\Gamma, \Delta, \Theta \vdash_L w{:}t$ implies $\Gamma, \Delta, \Theta \vdash_L w{:}A[t/x]$ for every t, then $\Gamma, \Delta, \Theta \vdash_L w{:}\forall x.A$; and (v) for every w, if $\Gamma, \Delta, \Theta \vdash_L w \; R \; w_i$ implies $\Gamma, \Delta, \Theta \vdash_L w_i{:}B$ for every w_i, then $\Gamma, \Delta, \Theta \vdash_L w{:}\Box B$.

In the Lindenbaum lemma for first-order logic, a saturated set of formulae is inductively built by adding for every formula $\neg \forall x.A$ a *witness* to its truth, namely a formula $\neg A[c/x]$ for some new individual constant c. This ensures that the set is ω-complete, a property equivalent to condition (iv) in Definition 7. A similar procedure applies here not only for every lwff $w{:}\neg \forall x.A$, but also for every lwff $w{:}\neg \Box A$ (cf. (v) in Definition 7); i.e. together with $w{:}\neg \Box A$, we consistently add $v{:}\neg A$ and $w \; R \; v$ for some new v, which acts as a 'witness world' to the truth of $w:\neg\Box A$. This ensures that the saturated pc (Γ, Δ, Θ) is such that $w:\Box B \in \Gamma$ iff $w\ R\ w_i \in \Delta$ implies $w_i:B \in \Gamma$ for every w_i, as shown in Lemma 9 below.[5]

Lemma 8. *Every consistent pc* (Γ, Δ, Θ) *can be extended to a saturated pc.*

Proof (Sketch). We first extend the language of the logic L with infinitely many new constants for witness terms and witness worlds. Let s range over the new constants for witness terms, and r range over the original terms and over the new constants. Analogously, let v range over the new constants for witness worlds, and u range over labels and over the new constants. All these may be subscripted. Let $l_1, l_2, \ldots$ be an enumeration of all lwffs in the extended language. Starting from $(\Gamma_0, \Delta_0, \Theta_0) = (\Gamma, \Delta, \Theta)$, we inductively build a sequence of consistent pcs by defining $(\Gamma_{i+1}, \Delta_{i+1}, \Theta_{i+1})$ to be:

- $(\Gamma_i, \Delta_i, \Theta_i)$, if $(\Gamma_i \cup \{l_{i+1}\}, \Delta_i, \Theta_i)$ is inconsistent; else
- $(\Gamma_i \cup \{l_{i+1}\}, \Delta_i, \Theta_i)$, if l_{i+1} is neither $u:\neg\Box A$ nor $u:\neg\forall x.A$; else
- $(\Gamma_i \cup \{u:\neg\forall x.A, u:\neg A[s/x]\}, \Delta_i, \Theta_i \cup \{u:s\})$, for an $s \notin (\Gamma_i \cup \{u:\neg\forall x.A\}, \Delta_i, \Theta_i)$, if l_{i+1} is $u:\neg\forall x.A$; else
- $(\Gamma_i \cup \{u:\neg\Box A, v:\neg A\}, \Delta_i \cup \{u\ R\ v\}, \Theta_i)$, for a $v \notin (\Gamma_i \cup \{u:\neg\Box A\}, \Delta_i, \Theta_i)$, if l_{i+1} is $u:\neg\Box A$.

A saturated pc is then $(\Gamma^*, \Delta^*, \Theta^*) =_{def} (\bigcup_{i\geq 0} \Gamma_i, (\bigcup_{i\geq 0} \Delta_i)_L, (\bigcup_{i\geq 0} \Theta_i)_{L,\Delta})$.

Lemma 9. *Let* $(\Gamma^*, \Delta^*, \Theta^*)$ *be a saturated pc.*

(i) $\Gamma^*, \Delta^*, \Theta^* \vdash_L \varphi$ *iff* $\varphi \in (\Gamma^*, \Delta^*, \Theta^*)$, *where* φ *is an lterm, rwff or lwff.*
(ii) $u:A \to B \in \Gamma^*$ *iff* $u:A \in \Gamma^*$ *implies* $u:B \in \Gamma^*$.
(iii) $u_i:\Box B \in \Gamma^*$ *iff for all* u_j, $u_i\ R\ u_j \in \Delta^*$ *implies* $u_j:B \in \Gamma^*$.
(iv) $u:\forall x.A \in \Gamma^*$ *iff for all* r, $u:r \in \Theta^*$ *implies* $u:A[r/x] \in \Gamma^*$.

Definition 10. Given a saturated pc $(\Gamma^*, \Delta^*, \Theta^*)$, we define the *canonical model* $\mathfrak{M}_L^C$ for the logic L as follows: $\mathfrak{W}_L^C = \{u \mid u \in (\Gamma^*, \Delta^*, \Theta^*)\}$; $(u_i, u_j) \in \mathfrak{R}_L^C$ iff $u_i\ R\ u_j \in \Delta^*$; $\mathfrak{a}(u, r) = r$, and $\langle r_1, \ldots, r_n \rangle \in \mathfrak{a}(u, P)$ iff $u:P(r_1, \ldots, r_n) \in \Gamma^*$, for P an n-ary predicate; $\mathfrak{q}(u) = \{\mathfrak{a}(u, r) \mid u:r \in \Theta^*\}$; $\mathfrak{D} = \bigcup_{u \in (\Gamma^*, \Delta^*, \Theta^*)} \mathfrak{q}(u)$.

The standard definition of $\mathfrak{R}_L^C$, i.e. $(u_i, u_j) \in \mathfrak{R}_L^C$ iff $\{A \mid \Box A \in u_i\} \subseteq u_j$, is not applicable in our setting, since $\{A \mid \Box A \in u_i\} \subseteq u_j$ does *not* imply $\vdash_L u_i\ R\ u_j$. We would therefore lose completeness for rwffs, since there would be cases, e.g. if $L = QK$ and $\Delta = \{\}$, where $\nvdash_L u_i\ R\ u_j$ but $(u_i, u_j) \in \mathfrak{R}_L^C$ and thus $\models^{\mathfrak{M}_L^C} u_i\ R\ u_j$. Hence, we instead define $(u_i, u_j) \in \mathfrak{R}_L^C$ iff $u_i\ R\ u_j \in \Delta^*$; note that therefore $u_i\ R\ u_j \in \Delta^*$ implies $\{A \mid \Box A \in u_i\} \subseteq u_j$. The deductive closures of Δ^* and Θ^* ensure not only completeness for rwffs and lterms, but also that the conditions on $\mathfrak{R}_L^C$ and $\mathfrak{D}_L^C$ are satisfied, so that $\mathfrak{M}_L^C$ is really a model for L.

We immediately have (i) $u_i\ R\ u_j \in \Delta^*$ iff $\Delta^* \models^{\mathfrak{M}_L^C} u_i\ R\ u_j$, and (ii) $u:r \in \Theta^*$ iff $\Delta^*, \Theta^* \models^{\mathfrak{M}_L^C} u:r$. By induction on the size of $u:A$, we can then prove that

---

[5] In the standard completeness proof for unlabelled modal logics, $\mathfrak{W}_L^C$ is defined to be the set of all saturated sets, and it is possible to show that if $w \in \mathfrak{W}_L^C$ and $\neg\Box A \in w$, then there is a $w' \in \mathfrak{W}_L^C$ accessible from w such that $\neg A \in w'$.

$u{:}A \in \Gamma^*$ iff $\Gamma^*, \Delta^*, \Theta^* \models^{\mathfrak{M}^C_L} u{:}A$, and thus conclude the proof of completeness, by showing (i'), (ii') and (iii') above.

Some remarks and comparisons are in order. Our proof is modular: the same method applies uniformly to every logic L. As explained previously, this is *not* the case for the completeness proof of unlabelled QMLs based on free logic [9,11]. Garson himself points out that his proof "lacks generality" [9, pp. 280-281], since (i) it does not work for systems with constant domains, and (ii) it is not general with respect to the underlying PML (although there are tricks one can use to overcome the difficulties for particular systems). As we have shown, none of these problems applies in our approach. Most importantly, being complete, our QMLs are adequate presentations of the Kripke semantics, and are thus equivalent to the corresponding Hilbert systems only when these are themselves complete with respect to the same semantics. For example, by the incompleteness results in [11], QKT42.i is equivalent to the Hilbert system for QS4.2 since they are both complete with respect to reflexive, transitive and convergent Kripke models with increasing domains; on the other hand, QKT42.c is not equivalent to the Hilbert system for QS4.2 + BF, since the latter is incomplete.

4 Related Work

In the introduction we described various problems that arise in traditional approaches to QMLs based upon Hilbert formalizations, and throughout the paper we have argued how these problems are solved in our approach. We now compare our work with approaches based on sequent or tableau systems, and on embeddings of modal logics in first-order logic.

Fitting introduces cut-free sequent systems for QMLs in [6,7], giving 'standard' systems for non-symmetric logics with increasing domains, and then, to capture the other conditions, introducing *prefixes*. These allow him to formulate sequent systems for a class of QMLs (including symmetric logics like S5) with varying, increasing, or constant domains. In prefixed systems, the different properties of the domains are expressed by imposing different side conditions on the applicability of the quantifier rules; analogously, the properties of the accessibility relation require different side conditions on the rules for the modalities. The main disadvantage of these systems, apart from the fact that they do not capture decreasing domains, is that their formalizations often requires considerable ingenuity, and the rules for the modalities and quantifiers can be awkward, carrying side conditions on the complete set of assumptions.[6] Thus, unlike our approach, which leads to simple implementations, these systems cannot be easily formalized in standard logical frameworks such as Isabelle or the Edinburgh LF.

Our work is closely related to approaches based on semantic embeddings, e.g. [1,8,13], where a formula of quantified modal logic is translated into a for-

---

[6] See Avron's discussion of degrees of impurity of natural deduction systems in [2, §5.5]. Note also that prefixed sequent systems and prefixed tableau systems could be modified to cover decreasing domains. To do so, however, one would need to replace the standard quantifier rules with rules similar to ours.

mula in first-order predicate logic and shown to be true (or false) in a first-order theory formalizing the semantics of the modalities and domains of quantification. For example, $\Box(A \wedge B)$ is translated into some first-order formula like $\forall w.\, R(0, w) \to (A(w) \wedge B(w))$, and there may be additional axioms characterizing the accessibility relation R and the domains of quantification. Ohlbach [13], for example, provides a general framework for carrying out such translations and reasoning about their soundness and completeness; translations are defined by morphisms on formulae and these are shown sound and complete by providing morphisms on interpretations. Our work differs from embedding based approaches in the nature of the translations, the metatheoretic properties that hold, and how they are proved. First, we separate, rather than combine, reasoning about relations, predicates and terms (cf. Fact 2). With semantic embedding there is no formal distinction between lwffs, rwffs and lterms or separation between relational and first-order reasoning. Second, rather than using interpretation morphisms and building on top of the semantics of first-order logic, we directly define deductive systems for QMLs and show their completeness by a parameterized canonical model construction. Finally, as shown in [3], the normal form of a derivation in our approach preserves important extra structure compared to the normal form of a derivation in the translation approach.

References

1. Y. Auffray and P. Enjalbert. Modal theorem proving: An equational viewpoint. *Journal of Logic and Computation*, 2(3):247–297, 1992.
2. A. Avron. Simple consequence relations. *Inf. and Comp.*, 92:105–139, 1991.
3. D. Basin, S. Matthews, and L. Viganò. Labelled modal logics: quantifiers. Technical Report MPI-I-97-2-001, MPI für Informatik, Saarbrücken, 1997.
4. D. Basin, S. Matthews, and L. Viganò. Labelled propositional modal logics: theory and practice. *Journal of Logic and Computation*, 1997. To appear.
5. E. Bencivenga. Free logics. In D. Gabbay and F. Guenthner, editors, *Handbook of Philosophical Logic, Vol. III*, pages 373–426. Reidel, Dordrecht, 1986.
6. M. Fitting. *Proof methods for modal and intuitionistic logics*. Kluwer, Dordrecht, 1983.
7. M. Fitting. Basic modal logic. In D. Gabbay et al., editors, *Handbook of Logic in AI and Logic Programming, Vol. I*, pages 365–448. Clarendon Press, Oxford, 1993.
8. D. Gabbay. *Labelled deductive systems*. Clarendon Press, Oxford, 1996.
9. J. Garson. Quantification in modal logic. In D. Gabbay and F. Guenthner, editors, *Handbook of Philosophical Logic, Vol. II*, pages 249–307. Reidel, Dordrecht, 1984.
10. R. Harper, F. Honsell, and G. Plotkin. A framework for defining logics. *Journal of the ACM*, 40(1):143–184, 1993.
11. G. Hughes and M. Cresswell. *A new introduction to modal logic*. Routledge, 1996.
12. A. Nerode and R. Shore. *Logic for applications*. Springer, Berlin, 1993.
13. H. J. Ohlbach. Semantics based translation methods for modal logics. *Journal of Logic and Computation*, 1(5):691–746, 1991.
14. L. C. Paulson. *Isabelle: a generic theorem prover*. Springer, Berlin, 1994.
15. J. R. Shoenfield. *Mathematical logic*. Addison Wesley, Reading, 1967.
16. D. van Dalen. *Logic and structure*. Springer, Berlin, 1994.

Defining Decision Rules in Signed Horn Clauses

Barbara Messing
Department of Computer Science
University of Karlsruhe
D - 76128 Karlsruhe
E-Mail: messing@ira.uka.de
URL: http://liinwww.ira.uka.de/~messing/

Abstract. Making decisions is one of the central problems in knowledge based and expert systems. It is in particular a fundamental issue of Distributed AI. In this paper we define some well-known, rather simple rules from decision theory within a framework of many-valued logic programming. We show how these rules can also be generalized using partially ordered preference functions and how they can apply to multi-agent systems.

1 Introduction

Making decisions is one of the central problems in knowledge based and expert systems. It is in particular a fundamental issue of Distributed Artificial Intelligence (DAI). Therefore many topics of DAI are related to decision theory [5, 21, 22]. On the other hand, multiple-valued logics have been more and more adapted to applications in the context of representing and combining knowledge [10, 11, 14, 16, 17, 20, 24]. Handling inconsistent and conflicting information is one of the merits of multiple-valued formalisms. But up to now, semantically motivated conflict handling strategies have not been developed within such a framework. In this contribution, we apply some well-known, rather simple decision rules within a framework of many-valued logic programming.

The basic idea here is to *express preferences in many-valued Horn clauses*. This means, literals in Horn clauses are attached with truth values that attribute the literals to be true, false or something between true and false. In [3], Dubois and Prade summarize three interpretations of such a *graded membership*: The degree of uncertainty, the degree of similarity and the degree of preference. The degree of uncertainty refers to the probability that an element x belongs to a set M; the degree of similarity refers to the distance of an element x to a prototype element y. The third interpretation is closely related to decision theory. If the membership function expresses preferences, it can be thought as an utility function. In this paper we adopt this way of interpretation. The decision strategies make use of the utility functions. But within the presented approach we are not only able to formulate the existing strategies, we can even generalize them to partially ordered preference functions.

This paper is organized as follows: In section 2 we briefly summarize signed Horn clauses and MSLD-resolution as proposed in [15, 16, 17]. In section 3 we formulate decision rules within this framework: In 3.1 some decision rules are described; the idea of how to define such rules in signed Horn clauses is presented in 3.2. In this section we show an MSLD-proof tree for an example of a simple decision rule and point out how the search space can be restricted according to Birkhoff's representation theorem. In 3.3 we consider a partially ordered set of utility values and propose corresponding decision rules. In 3.4 we sketch how the approach can be applied to a multiple-agent environment. Section 4 reports related work. In section 5 we conclude the work and discuss future directions.

2 Signed Horn Clauses and MSLD - Resolution

Horn clauses are commonly used for knowledge representation on an implementation level. It is a simple matter to generalize them to the many-valued case. The basic idea is to attach literals A with sets of truth values S, called *signs*, and to transform the query "Does A hold" to the query "Does A evaluate to an element of S?". To distinguish positive and negative literals, *directed subsets* of partially ordered sets are employed. With Δ we refer to the set of truth values. In the following we assume Δ to be a *complete lattice*. We refer to its bottom element with the symbol $\perp$.

We define many-valued Horn clauses in an informal way, hoping that the close relationship to classical Horn clauses and the examples make things clear. For technical details, the reader is referred to [8, 9, 10, 15, 16, 20].

Definition 1 (Syntax) Let Δ be a complete lattice. A Δ -*valued Horn clause* is a rule of the form $P<\uparrow f(\mu_1,..., \mu_n)> \leftarrow P_1<\uparrow\mu_1>,..., P_n<\uparrow\mu_n>$ where

(i) $P, P_1,...,P_n$ are first-order literals and

(ii) $\mu_1,..., \mu_n$ are elements of Δ, or variables, and f refers to a function with values in Δ. $\uparrow f(\mu_1,..., \mu_n)$ and $\uparrow\mu_1, ..., \uparrow\mu_n$ are the *signs* of the clause.

The set $\uparrow\mu := \{x \in \Delta | \mu \leq x\}$ is called the *upset* of μ. A set of Δ-valued Horn clauses is called a Δ-*valued program*, denoted by (P, Δ). *Facts* and *rules* are defined as usual.

Definition 2 (Semantics) A *sign - instance* of a Δ-valued Horn clause C results from substituting the variables occurring in the signs of C by elements of Δ. The notation $[X_1/s_1,...,X_n/s_n]$ means that X_i is replaced by s_i (i = 1, ..., n). An interpretation I from the ground atoms to Δ *satisfies* a signed ground atom $P<\uparrow\mu>$ (P being ground, $\mu \in \Delta$) if $I(P) \in \uparrow\mu$ (that is, $I(P) \geq \mu$).
An interpretation is a *model* of a rule $P<\uparrow f(\mu_1,..., \mu_n)> \leftarrow P_1<\uparrow\mu_1>,..., P_n<\uparrow\mu_n>$ if $I(P_1) \in \uparrow\mu_1,..., I(P_n) \in \uparrow\mu_n$ implies $I(P) \in \uparrow f(\mu_1,..., \mu_n)$[1]. An interpretation is a *model of a* Δ-*valued program* if I is a model of each clause.

Example 1 Consider the program P_1 (see [12]) with values in the well-known lattice FOUR (Figure 1) of four-valued logic [1]:

(1) $p<\uparrow V> \leftarrow q(X)<\uparrow V>$
(2) $q(a)<\uparrow true> \leftarrow$
(3) $q(b)<\uparrow false> \leftarrow$

The first rule can be read as the *union* of the following rules:

---

1. If all variables have been replaced by elements of Δ, f can be evaluated and hence $f(\mu_1,...,\mu_n)$ is an element of Δ.

(1a) p<↑true> ← q(X)<↑true>
(1b) p<↑false>← q(X)<↑false>
(1c) p<↑both> ← q(X)<↑both>

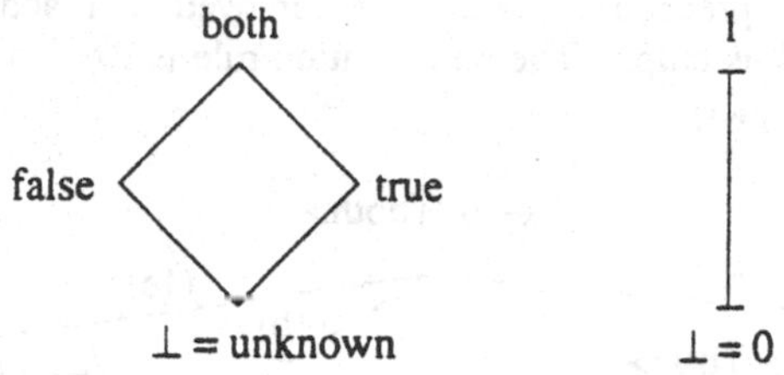

Fig. 1. The Truth Value Sets FOUR and [0,1]

Instantiating X with "unknown" is superfluous, because the resulting rule is tautologic.

It is easy to see that p<↑both> follows from the program: From (2) combined with (1a) (X = a) follows p<↑true>, and from (3) combined with (1b) (X = b) follows p<↑false>, so each interpretation must map p to a value equal to or greater than false *and* true, such that the only possibility is I(p) = both. In other words, we conclude I(p) ∈ ↑true and I(p) ∈ ↑false and hence I(p)∈ ↑true ∩ ↑false = {both}.

Example 2 Consider the following program P_2:

(A) p<↑0>←

(B) p<↑((1+X)/2)>←p<↑X>

where Δ = [0,1]. It is easy to see that a model of P_2 must evaluate p to 1, because for any other value there is an instance of (B) being not satisfied. But to compute p<↑1> from P_2, the second rule must be applied *infinitely often*.

In the following we assume that each program has the fixpoint reachability property [10]. Briefly put, this means that a fixpoint can be reached in a finite number of steps and hence programs like P_2 are not allowed. Notice that a clause like (B) looks, carefully considered, not very meaningful, because the truth value increases "out of nothing". This should not be confused with induction steps, which refer to functions (in first-order literals), not to truth values.

Signed resolution [8, 11, 12, 15, 16, 19] is based on *set-intersection*. For example, {p<S>, q<T>} and {p<U>, r<V>} resolve to {p<S∩U>, q<T>, r<V>}. Literals with empty signs can be removed from the resolvent. It has been shown that signed resolution is correct and complete, that is, the empty clause can be deduced from M by signed resolution if and only if M is an unsatisfiable set of signed clauses [19]. We introduce here MSLD-resolution, a specialization of signed resolution for Horn clauses.

Before we give the complete definition, we show example 1(see Figure 2). MSLD-resolution always starts with the query. Each resolution step performs a set intersection. The sign of p in the query ←p<↑both> is (↑both)^c= {false, true, unknown}. It is first intersected with the sign of p in the head of (1a), the result is intersected with the head of (1b). Applying then the third and second rule yields the empty clause. Starting with the clause (1c) leads to a failure (see paths in Figure 2).

MSLD-resolution is "SLD-style", that is, a proof starts with a query and treats it like a stack: During the proof procedure literals are removed and added. The proof has succeeded when the stack is empty. The computation rule is fixed such that the leftmost literal is chosen from the query.

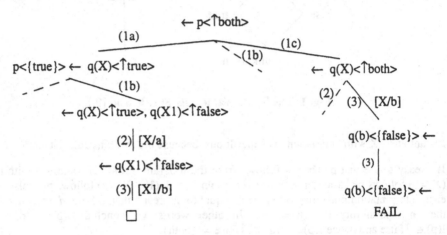

Fig. 2. The Proof Tree of an MSLD-Resolution (Example 1)

The exact definition of MSLD-resolution is a bit clumsy. The reason for this is, that we deal with two types of queries, such with empty head (resulting from an empty intersection of signs) and such with non-empty head (resulting from a non-empty intersection of signs). Therefore we have to distinguish four cases.

Definition 3 (MSLD - Resolution) Let (**P** , Δ) be a many-valued program. A clause ← Q_1<↑μ_1>,...,Q_n<↑μ_n> where no sign is a variable is called a *query*. A clause Q<σ> ← Q_1<↑μ_1>,...,Q_n<↑μ_n>, where σ is an arbitrary *set of truth values* and no sign is a variable is called a *proof query*.
M^c denotes the complement of a set M.

1. Let Q = ← Q_1<↑μ_1>,...,Q_n<↑μ_n> be a query and
   C_S = P<↑f(v_1,..., v_m)> ← P_1<↑v_1>,...,P_m<↑v_m> be a sign-instance of a program clause that does not share any first-order variables with Q. Suppose P and Q_1 are unifiable via (first - order) mgu Θ.

   (i) If ↑f(v_1,..., v_m) ∩ (↑μ_1)^c = ∅, the query
      (←Q_2<↑μ_2>,...,Q_n<↑μ_n>, P_1<↑v_1>,..., P_m<↑v_m>) Θ
      is the *MSLD-resolvent* of C_S and Q.

(ii) If $\uparrow f(v_1,..., v_m) \cap (\uparrow\mu_1)^c = \sigma \neq \varnothing$, the proof query

$(Q_1<\sigma> \leftarrow Q_2<\uparrow\mu_2>,...,Q_n<\uparrow\mu_n>, P_1<\uparrow v_1>,..., P_m<\uparrow v_m>) \Theta$ is the *MSLD-resolvent* of C_S and Q.

2. Let $Q^P = Q<\sigma> \leftarrow Q_1<\uparrow\mu_1>,...,Q_n<\uparrow\mu_n>$ be a proof query and $C_S = P<\uparrow f(v_1,..., v_m)> \leftarrow P_1<\uparrow v_1>,..., P_m<\uparrow v_m>$ be a sign-instance of a program clause that does not share any variables with Q. Suppose P and Q are unifiable via (first-order) mgu Θ.

   (i) If $\sigma \cap (\uparrow f(v_1,..., v_m)) = \varnothing$, the query

   $(\leftarrow Q_1<\uparrow\mu_1>,...,Q_n<\uparrow\mu_n>, P_1<\uparrow v_1>,..., P_m<\uparrow v_m>) \Theta$

   is the *MSLD-resolvent* of C_S and Q^P.

   (ii) If $\sigma \cap \uparrow f(v_1,..., v_m) = \tau \neq \varnothing$, the proof query

   $(Q<\tau> \leftarrow Q_1<\uparrow\mu_1>, ...,Q_n<\uparrow\mu_n>, P_1<\uparrow v_1>,..., P_m<\uparrow v_m>) \Theta$

   is the *MSLD-resolvent* of C_S and Q^P.

The complement of an upset $\uparrow\mu$ is not to be confused with a "downset" $\downarrow\mu := \{\delta \in \Delta ; \mu > \delta\}$ (e.g., $(\uparrow false)^c = \{unknown, true\}$ but $\downarrow false = \{unknown\}$).

If the head of any signed Horn clause contains the sign $\uparrow\perp$, the clause can be removed from the program (such a clause is always satisfied). If the body of a signed Horn clause contains a literal signed with $\uparrow\perp$, this literal can be removed without changing the semantics (such a literal is never satisfied).

The completeness of MSLD-resolution for signed Horn-clauses that fulfill the fixpoint reachability property follows from the results of [13] and is shown in [15, 16].

The search space of MSLD-resolution can be reduced by exploiting the structure of the underlying truth value space applying Birkhoff's representation theorem (see, for example, [2]). Then the functions in the heads of the clauses must be continuous lattice-operations on Δ^1. Decomposing a distributive lattice due to Birkhoff's representation theorem leads to an essential reduction [15, 16]. MSLD-Resolution has been implemented in the prototype system REGULA, which supports the selection of various truth value spaces and applies Birkhoff's theorem.

The definition of MSLD-Resolution as given here does not allow variables in signs. However, in the implementation they are possible for Δ being finite. REGULA then selects all possible instantiations and puts the successful values together (for example, if it succeed to proof p<$\uparrow$true> and p<$\uparrow$false>, REGULA will return p<$\uparrow$both>). For an efficient selection of the instantiations the structure of Δ is again exploited.

3 Decision Rules

We consider here decision rules for one-step individual decisions under uncertainty [5, 22]. This is, an individual is confronted with several alternatives one of which has to be selected and several situations that may arise after the alternative has been chosen. The outcomes, depending on the decision and the actual situation, is assessed with the values

---

1. That is, $f((\cup x_i)_{i \in I}) = \cup(f(x_i))_{i \in I}$ for arbitrary index sets I.

of a utility function. Such a decision problem is represented in a table of possible alternatives a_i, situations s_j (which may be uncertain) and possible outcomes e_{ij} depending on a_i and s_j. Figure 3 shows an example of a decision matrix (cf. [22], p.81).

	s_1	s_2	s_3	s_4
a_1	6	9	-7	-1
a_2	-4	0	8	4
a_3	-1	1	2	3
a_4	0	6	1	0

Fig. 3. Decision Matrix

In the following sections we introduce some decision rules (section 3.1), give examples how to formulate one of them in many-valued Horn clauses (section 3.2), how to generalize it to a partial ordering (section 3.3) and how to apply it in a multiple-agent environment (section 3.4).

3.1 Decision rules: Some Examples

The decision rule is defined by a goal-function ϕ which is maximized or, sometimes, minimized. We restrict here to very simple rules. Examples are the following:

Hurvicz-rule: Maximize $\phi(a_i) := \lambda \max_j(e_{ij}) + (1-\lambda) \min_j(e_{ij})$ with $0 \leq \lambda \leq 1$

In the above example, for $\lambda = 0.9$, we have $\phi(a_1) = 7.4$, $\phi(a_2) = 6.8$, $\phi(a_3) = 2.6$ and $\phi(a_4) = 5.4$, therefore we would chose a_1.

For $\lambda = 0$ we have the *Maximin -rule: Maximize* $\phi(a_i) := \min_j (e_{ij})$.

In our example, the choice would be a_4 (0 is the maximum of the minimal outcomes).

Laplace-rule: Maximize $\phi(a_i) := \dfrac{1}{n}\sum_1^n e_{ij}$

Following this rule, the choice would be a_2 (the maximum of the average outcomes is $\frac{8}{4}$).

Savage-Niehans-rule: Let $\bar{e}_{ij} = \max_k(e_{ik}) - e_{ij}$ and *minimize* $\phi(a_i) := \max_j \{\bar{e}_{ij}\}$

This would lead to alternative a_3 or a_4 (the deviation of the maximal outcome of each situation is minimized).

We can see that in our example every rule leads to a different result. The Maximin-rule (called "pessimistic") maximizes the minimal outcome of each alternative. The Laplace-rule maximizes the average outcome, where any situation is supposed to have the same probability. The idea behind the Savage-Niehans-rule is the following: Each situation has a maximal outcome. The "disappointment" connected with an outcome can be measured as the difference between the actual and the maximal possible outcome. The maximal possible disappointment is minimized by this rule.

3.2 Decision Rules Defined in Signed Horn Clauses

A decision rule, defined in signed Horn clauses, has essentially the following form:

$$\text{aggregated\_value}(A){<}{\uparrow}f(v_1,...,v_n){>} \leftarrow \text{value}(A,s_1){<}{\uparrow}v_1{>},...,\text{value}(A,s_n){<}{\uparrow}v_n{>}$$

where A refers to an alternative and s_1, ..., s_n to the possible situations. "value$(A,s_i){<}{\uparrow}v_i{>}$" reads "The outcome of s_i after choosing A is assessed with v_i".

For example, the Maximin-rule is computed in two steps:

(1) $\text{min\_value}(A){<}{\uparrow}\min\{v_1,...,v_n\}{>} \leftarrow \text{value}(A,s_1){<}{\uparrow}v_1{>},...,\text{value}(A,s_n){<}{\uparrow}v_n{>}$

(2) $\text{min\_max\_value}(a_1,...,a_n){<}{\uparrow}\max\{w_1,...,w_n\}{>} \leftarrow$
$$\text{min\_value}(a_1){<}{\uparrow}w_1{>},..., \text{min\_value}(a_n){<}{\uparrow}w_n{>}$$

Here $\Delta = \{-N, ..., 0, 1,...,N\}$ for an upper bound N. For MSLD-resolution it is essential that Δ forms a complete lattice; for an efficient search Δ should be a discrete ordering.

Figure 4 shows a proof tree for the program P_3 defined as follows:

(1) $\text{min\_value}(A){<}{\uparrow}\min\{v_1,...,v_4\}{>} \leftarrow \text{value}(A,s_1){<}{\uparrow}v_1{>},...,\text{value}(A,s_4){<}{\uparrow}v_4{>}$

(2) $\text{min\_max\_value}(a_1,...,a_4){<}{\uparrow}\max\{w_1,...,w_4\}{>} \leftarrow$
$$\text{min\_value}(a_1){<}{\uparrow}w_1{>},..., \text{min\_value}(a_4){<}{\uparrow}w_4{>}$$

(E_{ij}) value$(a_i,s_j){<}{\uparrow}e_{ij}{>} \leftarrow$ *where i, j =1,...,4; e_{ij} from Figure 3*

Computing the Maximin-Rule now means to proof the query

$\leftarrow\text{min\_max\_value}(a_1,...,a_4){<}{\uparrow}X{>}$, $\text{min\_value}(A){<}{\uparrow}X{>}$, which reads "What is the maximum of ϕ and for which alternatives is $\phi(a_i) = \max_i: \phi(a_i)$?". The variable X here has to be replaced by an element of Δ to start MSLD-resolution. Generally we must try all elements; but we can choose the sequence skillfully.

A second problem here is to "guess" the values $v_1,...,v_n$ such that $X = \min\{v_1,...,v_n\}$. As mentioned above, essential reduction of the search follows from Birkhoff's representation theorem. In this example it can be reduced to the following two observations:

1. If a query $\leftarrow q{<}{\uparrow} MAX{>}$ has a solution resulting from an MSLD-resolution with the program clause $q{<}{\uparrow}\max\{w_1,...,w_n\}{>} \leftarrow$ *body* then it suffices to consider the instantiations $[w_1/\perp,..., w_{i-1}/\perp, w_i/MAX, w_{i+1}/\perp, w_3/\perp, w_n/\perp]$ for i = 1, ..., n.

2. If a query $\leftarrow q{<}{\uparrow} MIN{>}$ has a solution resulting from a MSLD-resolution with the program clause $q{<}{\uparrow}\min\{w_1,...,w_n\}{>} \leftarrow$ *body* then it suffices to consider the instantiation $[w_1/MIN, ..., w_n/MIN]$.

One can show for 1. and 2. that other resolutions can be subsumed by the above [16, p. 63] which are "minimal". In case of Δ being a totally ordered set no proof queries occur.

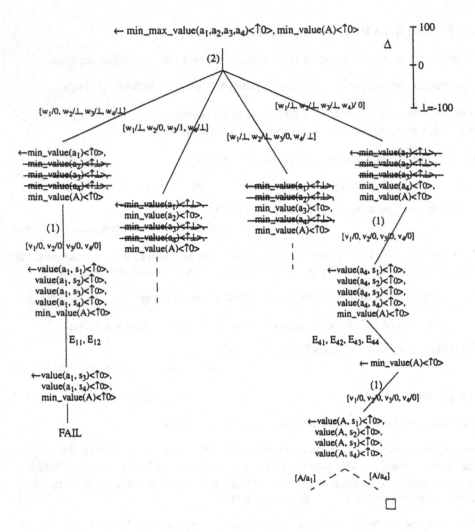

Fig. 4. MSLD-Resolution for the Maximin-Rule

3.3 A Generalization of the Maximin-rule: Utility vs. Costs

Using *pairs* of values makes it possible to split the outcomes into positive and negative aspects. This can be useful if, for example, utilities versus costs are considered.

For example, we replace the values e_{ij} of the above decision matrix by values (u_{ij}, c_{ij}) such that $e_{ij} = u_{ij} - c_{ij}$. u_{ij} then stands for "utility" and c_{ij} for "costs". For example, $e_{21} = -4$ is replaced by $(u_{21}, c_{21}) = (6,10)$ which means that the utility of the outcome is assessed with

6 items and the costs with 10. The overall outcome remains the same because 6 - 10 = -4. Figure 5 shows such a split-up.

	s_1	s_2	s_3	s_4
a_1	(7,1)	(10,1)	(3,10)	(1,2)
a_2	(6,10)	(3,3)	(10,2)	(4,0)
a_3	(1,2)	(1,0)	(2,0)	(6,3)
a_4	(10,10)	(12,6)	(9,8)	(2,2)

Fig. 5. Splitting up the Outcomes

We define a modified Maximin-rule:

$u\_min_i := min_j(u_{ij})$

$c\_max_i := max_j(c_{ij})$

Maximize $\phi(a_i) = u\_min_i - c\_max_i$

For the above example we have $\phi(a_1) = 1 - 10 = -9$, $\phi(a_2) = 3 - 10 = -7$, $\phi(a_3) = 1 - 3 = -2$ and $\phi(a_4) = 2 - 10 = -8$. So the choice is a_3. This strategy is even more pessimistic than the original Maximin-rule.

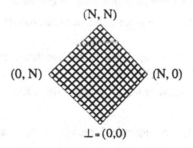

Fig. 6. $\Delta = [0, N] \times [0, N]$

In signed Horn clauses, we have

(1) $u\_min\_c\_max(A) < \uparrow(min\{U1,...,U4\}, max\{C1,...,C4\})> \leftarrow$
$\qquad\qquad\qquad value(A,s_1) < \uparrow(U1,C1)>,..., value(A,s_4) < \uparrow(U4,C4)>$

Figure 6 shows Δ for this application. $[0,N]^2$ is taken as a lattice with the ordering defined pointwise. The MSLD-search can be reduced by considering that (x,y) is the union of (x,0) and (0,y)[1].

---

1. The notion "union" refers to the lattice operation on Δ. The lattice operations have not been explicitly introduced here because they can be mixed up with set intersection as performed by MSLD-resolution.

3.4 Another Generalization: Multiple Agents

We consider a group decision problem. Every agent assesses the outcome of a situation separately and a joint decision has to be made. So instead of the values e_{ij} we have tuples of values. With e_{kij} we refer to the assessment of agent k, given alternative i and situation j. For example we assume three agents to be involved. The following decision matrix is constructed from the example given in Figure 3 such that $e_{ij} = e_{1ij} + \ldots + e_{4ij}$.

	s_1	s_2	s_3	s_4
a_1	(2,2,2)	(3,3,3)	(-7,0,0)	(-1,0,0)
a_2	(-2,-2,0)	(0,-3,3)	(4,2,2)	(10,-6,0)
a_3	(7,-8,0)	(8,-7,0)	(0,2,0)	(-7,0,10)
a_4	(0,0,0)	(9,-12,9)	(-1,5,-3)	(11,-6,-5)

Fig. 7. Decision Matrix for Multiple Agents

We can apply various decision rules in such a multi-agent scenario. An example for a decision strategy that is performed in more than one step (and regarding that alternatives may be incomparable) is

1. Reject those alternatives that have possible outcomes below -8 for any agent.

2a. If more than one alternative is left, choose that promising the maximal output for any agent.

2b. If no alternative is left after applying 1., choose that alternative promising the maximal output for any agent without applying 1.

3. If more than one alternative is left after applying 1. and 2., choose that with the smallest loss for any agent.

For the above example, applying rule 1 means to reject a_4; the result of rule 2. is that alternatives $\{a_2, a_3\}$ are left, and the final result is a_2. Δ is then $[-N,N]^3$.

4   Related Work

Integrating information from diverse sources and formalizing mediators as proposed by Wiederhold [25] is the aim of the project HERMES [23]. It is essentially based on the theory of *Hybrid Knowledge Bases* [14, 24]. The notion of a hybrid knowledge base refers to a deductive database that is able to deal with temporal and uncertain information as well as numerical constraints and non-monotonous reasoning. The theory of hybrid knowledge bases extends the results of *Generalized Annotated Logic Programming* [10]. Methods of conflict resolution provided in [23] are preferences of latest data, special predicates or valuation-based preferences. This contribution shows how decision strategies based on utility functions can be applied in such a framework.

5 Concluding Remarks and Future Directions

In this paper we have presented a connection of many-valued logic programming and decision making in multi-agent systems. The central idea is to take the values of a preference function as truth values. This raises the option to apply decision strategies to diverse knowledge sources. This extends the possibilities of many-valued formalisms, which have already proved to be appropriate for integrating distributed knowledge.

The above decision rules evolve from a prescriptive way of view, that is, they express how decisions *should* be made, not how they *are* usually made. So they seem to be appropriate for *rational agents*; human's behavior is, as it is well-known, in general not rational. It cannot be described in such simple rules as the above. Using these rules is not a kind of cognitive modeling of decisions but guided by the idea of what rational decisions are. The construction of utility functions is not elaborated here.

A severe problem of computing signed Horn clauses as described above are arithmetic functions on the signs. For example, in section 3.3 we compute the difference between minimal utility and maximal costs. But adding the program clause

(3) u_min_c_max(A)<↑(U-C)> ← min_utility(A)<↑U>, max_costs(A)<↑C>

raises severe problems if a query like

← u_min_c_max(A)<↑X>

is to be computed. A decomposition of U-C is not efficiently possible. MSLD-resolution is very close to common SLD-resolution but for computing arithmetical functions on signs a simple top-down evaluation is not sufficient. There are two possibilities of further development: First, MSLD-resolution could be combined with a bottom-up evaluation such that the instantiation of variables in signs is guided by the values that are available. Second, constraints can be used to deal with variables in signs as already done in annotated logic programs [10].

The flexibility of signed Horn clauses lies in the variety of truth value spaces. Bilattices [4, 6, 7, 18] have been extensively used in this context [15, 16, 17]. They enable to model gradual, preliminary and inconsistent knowledge. This contribution shows how decision rules can be defined in such a framework ($[0,N]^2$, for example, is a bilattice). Future work includes defining more complex decision strategies, for example, incremental decision processes.

References

1. N. D. Belnap. A useful four-valued Logic. J.M. Dunn and G. epstein (Hrsg.). *Modern Uses of Multiple-valued Logics*, 8-37. Reidel, 1977.

2. B. A. Davey, H.A. Priestley. Introduction to lattices and order. Cambridge University Press, 1994.

3. D. Dubois, H. Prade. Approximate and Commonsense reasoning: From Theory to Practice. Proceedings of the 9th International Symposium ISMIS 96. LNAI 1079, Springer, 1996.

4. M.Fitting. Bilattices and the semantics of logic programming. *J. Logic Programming* 11 (2), 91-116, 1991.

5. S. French. Decision Theory: An Introduction to the Mathematics of rationality. Ellis Horwood Limited, John Wiley & Sons, 1986.

6. M.Ginsberg. Multivalued logics. *Computational Intelligence* 4(3), 1988.

7. M.Ginsberg. Bilattices and modal operators. *J. Logic and Computation*, 1991.

8. R.Hähnle. *Automated deduction in multiple-valued logics.* International series of monographs on computer science 10. Oxford science publications, 1992.

9. R.Hähnle. Exploiting Data Dependencies in Many-Valued Logics. *Journal of Applied Non-Classical Logics*, Vol 6, Number 1, 49-69, 1996.

10. Michael Kifer, V.S. Subrahmanian.Theory of Generalized Annotated Logic Programming and its Applications. *Journal of Logic Programming* 1992:12:335-367.

11. J.J. Lu. Logic Programming with Signs and Annotations. Journal of Logic and Computation, Vol. 6, No 6, Oxford Univ. Press, Dec 1996.

12. S.M.Leach, J.J.Lu. Computing Annotated Logic. *Proceedings of the Eleventh International Conference on Logic Programming.* MIT Press, Massachusetts, 257-271, 1994.

13. J.J. Lu, N.M. Murray, E. Rosenthal. Signed Formulas and Annotated Logics. *Proceedings of the 23th International Symposium on Multiple-valued Logics* 1993, 48 - 53.

14. J.J. Lu, A. Nerode, V.S. Subrahmanian. Hybrid Knowledge Bases. To appear in *IEEE Transactions on Knowledge and Data Engineering.*

15. B. Messing. REGULA: Knowledge Representation and Processing in Many-valued Logics. Research Report No 320 of the Institut für Angewandte Informatik und Formale Beschreibungsverfahren, University of Karlsruhe

16. B. Messing. Darstellung und Integration von Wissen in verbandsbasierten signierten Logik-programmen (in german). DISKI 132, infix-Verlag, St. Augustin, 1996.

17. Messing, B. Combining Knowledge with Many-Valued Logics. To appear in: *Data & Knowledge Engineering.*

18. B. Mobasher, D. Pigozzi, G. Slutzki. Multi-valued Logic Programming Semantics: An Algebraic Approach. *Theoretical Computer Science* 171 (1-2):77-109, 1997.

19. N.M. Murray, E. Rosenthal. Signed formulas: A liftable Meta-Logic for Multiple-Valued Logic. *Proc. of the International Symposium on Methodologies for Intelligent Systems.* Springer, 275-284, 1993.

20. J.J. Lu, N.M. Murray, E. Rosenthal. A Framework for Automated Reasoning in Multiple Valued Logics. To appear in *Journal of Automated Reasoning.*

21. J. Rosenschein, G. Zlotkin. Rules of Encounter: Designing Conventions for Automated Negotiation among Agents. MIT press, 1994.

22. Saliger. E. Betriebswirtschaftliche Entscheidungstheorie. R. Oldenbourg Verlag, München, Wien, 1993.

23. V.S. Subrahmanian, S. Adali, A. Brink, R. Emery, J.J Lu, A. Rajput, T. Rogers, R. Ross, C. Ward. HERMES: A Heterogeneous reasoning and Mediator System. Draft manuscript (URL: http://www.cs.umd.edu/projects/hermes/index.html).

24. V.S. Subrahmanian. Amalgamating Knowledge Bases. *ACM Transactions on Database Systems*, 19 (2), 291-331, 1994.

25. G. Wiederhold. Mediators in the Architecture of Future Information Systems. *IEEE Computer*, 38 - 49, March 1992.

Modelling Subjective Distances*

Bettina Berendt

University of Hamburg, Department of Computer Science, WSV,
Vogt-Kölln-Str. 30, D-22527 Hamburg, Germany
berendt@informatik.uni-hamburg.de

Abstract. Theories of subjective distance cognition in different scientific fields seem to deal with incomparable subject matters. It is shown in this paper, however, that psychophysical descriptions of subjective distances as power functions of objective distances and the modelling of Qualitative Distances in artificial intelligence can be related to one another from a representation-theoretic perspective. Both claim that subjective distances represent an aspect of objective distances – the difference is which aspect, ratios or order. However, aspects of objective distances alone can neither incorporate the influence of environmental features or hierarchies on subjective distances, nor can they explain memory structures or processes involved in distance cognition. A processing model of knowledge about distances is described, which integrates these considerations. The model explains existing empirical data, and it generates further predictions. The model shows distance estimates as produced by two representations, in which subjective distances *and* other subjective spatial relations represent objective distances *and* other objective spatial relations.

1   What's in a Distance?

Within the study of spatial cognition, the development of formal descriptions has received a lot of attention recently. This must often be based, however, on an abundance of empirical and modelling results, which seem to stand in no relation to or even to contradict one another. This is shown, maybe most clearly of all spatial relations, in the study of knowledge about distances:

Knowledge about distances: a paradox? There has been growing emphasis in recent years on the importance of *qualitative* concepts of space throughout cognitive psychology and artificial intelligence. 'Qualitative' has different meanings (and even different names!), but always implies 'knowledge that is in some way metrically underspecified'. Now first, distances appear to be the prime example of 'non-qualitative' concepts, in the sense that they are usually described as numerical, with the corresponding operations defined. Second, it is often found that distances, by theory the defining elements of a metric, violate all crucial axioms of a metric [11]. At first glance, the observations 'people have mainly qualitative knowledge' and 'subjective distances violate the

---

* The author's work was supported by the Deutsche Forschungsgemeinschaft through a scholarship in the doctoral program in cognitive science (*Graduiertenkolleg Kognitionswissenschaft*) and through a project of the priority program on spatial cognition (*Raumkognition*) (AZ Fr806/8-1).

metrical axioms' versus 'people have non-arbitrary, useful knowledge about distances' appear to be a contradiction, although there is empirical evidence for all three of them. So if there is knowledge about distances at all, it seems advisable to model subjective distances as 'qualitative' and/or as 'non-metric'. So *what kind of knowledge* do people have about distances?

Isolated approaches in different disciplines This 'imperfect' knowledge about distances is investigated from different perspectives in different disciplines. Psychology describes subjective distances as psychophysical power functions of objective distances, and artificial intelligence formalises Qualitative Distances. At first glance, these approaches seem to be incomparable. However, there is empirical evidence for both: Power functions are fitted to empirically obtained data, i.e. the relation between subjective distances e and objective distances d is described as $e = a\, d^b$, with the parameters a, b to be determined empirically. But there is the evidence for the general pervasiveness of qualitative knowledge (see above). How can these approaches be compared at all? This question is addressed in section 2, which proposes a representation-theoretic framework.

Isolated approaches in psychological work Empirical work has not only concentrated on possible 'underlying' power function relations, but also on 'superimposed' or 'distorting' influences. In particular, distance estimates (subjective distances) are sensitive to changes in the structure of the space created by hierarchical organisation and 'features'.

Research on distance cognition has also often neglected the distinction between *spaces* (e.g. [13]): what scale a space has and how we interact with it may affect our representations of that space. Here, two spaces are relevant: *Vista spaces* are larger than the human body, but can be perceived from a single vantage point (e.g. rooms, route stretches). *Environmental spaces* cannot be perceived from a single vantage point, the acquisition of knowledge about them requires locomotion and integration of consecutive perceptions (e.g. buildings, routes). Therefore, knowledge about vista spaces needs to be represented and inference performed on it to derive knowledge about environmental spaces. To model this, one needs to describe **memory** structures and processes involved in inference.

How can these effects and observations be integrated into one model, and what are the testable predictions arising from this? These questions are addressed in section 3, which describes FEATURE, a new processing model of subjective distances. FEATURE is then analysed with the help of the representation-theoretic framework proposed in section 2. It is argued that the model is also a way of addressing the paradox of knowledge about distances. The paper concludes by outlining the contribution of the model and the unifying framework to the study of spatial cognition in general.

2 A Unifying Framework: Subjective Distances as Representations

This section argues that existing approaches to subjective distances can be viewed as a statement about which aspects of distances are (a) relevant and (b) possible given knowledge acquisition, representation, and processing constraints. In all approaches, an underlying assumption is that objective distances are numerical, and the space has a Euclidean metric.[2]

2.1 What is a Representation?

A representation is a structure S_2 standing for another structure S_1 such that S_1 and S_2 behave in a similar way in the sense that – relevant – relations are preserved when passing from S_1 to S_2. Formally: the represented structure S_1 contains an n-ary relation R_1 on its elements x_i. The representing structure S_2 contains an n-ary relation R_2 on its elements y_i. The function ϕ maps elements of S_1 onto elements of S_2. For all n-tupels $\langle x_1, ..., x_n \rangle$, if $R_1(x_1, ..., x_n)$ holds in S_1, then $R_2(\phi(x_1), ..., \phi(x_n))$ holds in S_2 (a homomorphism; for a related definiton, see [8]). So the representation only 'respects' certain relations or aspects R_1. With respect to other relations, the representing world may behave differently than the represented world. Therefore, we always need to ask: Which aspects are represented?

2.2 Psychophysical Power Functions as Representations of Ratios

Empirically obtained distance estimates e are usually fitted by a power function to objective distances d. This reflects the assumption that internal psychological dimensions are ratio scaled. Representationally, being ratio scaled means that there is a true zero, and the subjective distances e_i together with ratio relations on them represent objective distances d_i and the ratio relations on them: Let $e_1 = \phi(d_1)$ and $e_2 = \phi(d_2)$. Let $R_1(d_1, d_2)$ iff $\frac{d_1}{d_2} = r$ and $R_2(e_1, e_2)$ iff $\frac{e_1}{e_2} = s$, where s functionally depends on r. Then (for all d_1, d_2, r: if $R_1(d_1, d_2)$, then $R_2(e_1, e_2)$) if the following conditions hold: (1) The estimates are numerical, and they can be described as a power function of objective distances: $e = \phi(d) = a\, d^b$ with some scaling factor a and some exponent $b > 0$. (2) People 'use their estimates like numbers', i.e. when they rate one distance as 1 unit, a second as 2 units, and a third as 4 units, they mean that the ratio between the first and the second is the same as that between the second and the third. Then $s = f_\phi(r) = r^b$. This representation of the aspect 'ratio' also implies knowledge about other relations, e.g. of the order of distances. It is *not* represented or assumed (a) that people are able to handle culturally given measurement units – otherwise a would be 1 – and (b) that people are able to mentally simulate 'putting a distance behind itself or another one' (= inference via addition) – otherwise b would be 1. Apart from this, inferential capabilities are not discussed.

---

[2] Sometimes, it is argued that this kind of model is only one possibility. However, to make approaches comparable, and in the absence of evidence for other candidates, I shall assume that this is the intended model.

2.3 Qualitative Distance Calculi as Partial Representations of Order Relations and of how Order and Addition Work

Based on the assumption that qualitative knowledge is superior to numerically-based methods in robustness, tractability, and employability in user interfaces, Qualitative Distance calculi investigate the consequences of different ways in which knowledge about distances can be ordinal, meaning that distances can only be compared with other distances. There are various calculi (e.g. [7, 21, 6]), and the following formalisation does not claim to describe them in all detail, but is restricted to the description of what I see as their main, shared idea. This restriction makes it possible to give a formal framework for all these calculi, which has been lacking up until now. All calculi require the metrical axioms to be satisfied, possibly with some modifications [6].

In all calculi, there are, as subjective distances, *path-distances* e_i. These represent *ordinary-distances* d_i, which are objective distances 'in the scene' (i.e. between entities one talks about, such as landmarks): $e_i = \phi(d_i)$. In all calculi, it is assumed that there is an order relation ($\leq$ or $<$) in which every objective distance is comparable to every other objective distance. However, this order relation is only partially known. It is reflected in a corresponding order relation in the calculus, which is axiomatised like $\leq$ ($<$). Details of possible choices for this order relation are explicated below. For those tuples for which the order relation is known, the definition of representation given above is satisfied. I call this a partial representation of order relations. A basic difference between calculi lies in whether or not different kinds of objective and subjective distances are distinguished, and in the restrictions as to *what* distances are ordered.

(1) Path-distances e_i are ordered with respect to each other (e.g. [21]). Together with this order relation ($\prec$ or $\preceq$), the e_is represent the d_is and order on a subset of them: a partial representation of order relations.

(2) Path-distances e_i are categorised (e.g. [7, 6]). For example, *small* distances could be those up to 100 metres. These 100 metres are a *special-distance* λ_k. Atomic categories like *small* are called q_k; categorisation is expressed as $q_k(e_i)$. There is a total order $\prec$ on the q_k: for all k, $q_k \prec q_{k+1}$. Consecutive atomic categories form further categories: Let $(k...l)$ be a sequence of successive indices. Then $q_{\{k,...,l\}}$ is also a category. The categories and $\prec$ represent the special-distances and order on them: For all k, $\lambda_{k-1} < \lambda_k$. Categorisation represents order on ordinary-distances and special-distances: If $q_k(\phi(d_i))$ then $\lambda_{k-1} \leq d_i < \lambda_k$.[3] The highest category K extends into infinity: If $q_K(\phi(d_i))$ then $\lambda_{K-1} \leq d_i$. If $q_{\{k,...,l\}}(\phi(d_i))$ then $\lambda_{k-1} \leq d_i < \lambda_l$. Comparable to (1) above, categorisation represents order only on a subset of (d, λ) pairs: a partial representation of order relations. In this scheme relying on categorisation, path-distances are not directly ordered with respect to one another, but only via their categorisations.[4]

---

[3] The statements about order must be slightly modified (1) if categories are non-exhaustive: Each category q_k needs a lower bound λ_k^b and an upper bound λ_k^t, and $\lambda_k^b < \lambda_k^t \leq \lambda_{k+1}^b < \lambda_{k+1}^t \cdots$; and (2) if categories overlap (but are still linearised): The total order on the λs is lost and replaced by the constraint $\forall k, l : \lambda_k^b < \lambda_l^b \Leftrightarrow \lambda_k^t < \lambda_l^t$. However, this does not change the central argument concerning the order on ordinary-distances and special-distances.

[4] A related interpretation of categories in terms of intervals and their lengths is proposed by Clementini, Di Felice and Hernández [6]. In the present study, start- and endpoints were needed to compare a wider range of approaches.

Using the axioms of the order relation, further order relations between distances can be inferred. This models the assumption that 'agents know how orders work'.

A focus of the calculi is on inference via *qualitative addition* $\oplus$. The basic assumption is: 'agents know how addition works': $\oplus$ is axiomatised as commutative, associative and having a neutral element (but no inverse element[5], since there are no negative distances). A monotonicity axiom governs the relation between order and addition: $e_1 \leq e_2 \rightarrow e_1 \oplus e_3 \leq e_2 \oplus e_3$. To see how qualitative addition works, consider a system with 4 categories as an example. Let $q_1(e_1)$ and $q_3(e_2)$. This means that $\lambda_0 \leq d_1 < \lambda_1$ and $\lambda_2 \leq d_2 < \lambda_3$. If we have no further knowledge about the λs, all we can infer from this is that $\lambda_2 < d_3 = d_1 + d_2$, and that the class containing the sum d_3 can contain values smaller than λ_3 and values equal to or larger than λ_3. Therefore the inference rule must be: $q_1(e_1) \wedge q_2(e_2) \rightarrow q_{3,4}(e_1 \oplus e_2)$. So knowledge is *coarsened* by addition: This restricts the set of represented order relations. (The same coarsening happens when path-distances are added.)

An inference rule working in the opposite direction, *refining* knowledge, is: if $q_{\{k,...,l\}}(\phi(d_i))$ and $q_{\{m,...,n\}}(\phi(d_i))$ then infer $q_{\{k,...,l\}\cap\{m,...,n\}}(\phi(d_i))$, which reflects that if $\lambda_{k-1} \leq d_i < \lambda_l$ and $\lambda_{m-1} \leq d_i < \lambda_n$, then $max(\lambda_{k-1}, \lambda_{m-1}) \leq d_i < min(\lambda_l, \lambda_n)$. This can be regarded as another aspect of the underlying assumption 'agents know how orders work'.[6]

2.4 Problems: Hierarchical Structure and Features

There are some problems with both of these kinds of accounts, however. In their pure form, both assume that subjective distances – and only they – represent objective distances – and only them.[7] This may not always be the case. The distorting influence of a hierarchical organisation of knowledge, e.g. into states or neighbourhoods, is well known (e.g. [11]). Distances are exaggerated across the boundaries of such containers, and directions are derived from the containers' directions.

Distance estimates usually increase with the number of features of the route or environment retrieved (see however [12]): Montello [14] calls this *feature accumulation* (e.g. [19, 18, 17]). Allen and his colleagues [1, 2] found that if routes are structured

---

[5] Note, however, that in [21] differences between distances can be described.

[6] In many calculi, one can identify a third kind of distances, which represent sums, differences, integer multiples or even arbitrary multiples of ordinary-distances (e.g. [21]). I call these *generated-distances* g representing *extra-distances* c. For example, one may know that "e_i is more than twice as long as e_j". Expressed as an order relation, this is $\prec (g_k, e_i)$, where g_k is a generated-distance representing the extra-distance $c_k = 2e_j$. Similarly, there may be knowledge about sums or differences of special-distances (e.g. category width $\lambda_k - \lambda_{k-1}$ is assumed to be constant), and in addition, metrical prototypes of categories can be introduced [7, 6]. The representation of order relations is partial in the same sense as above. 'Metrical measurements' are a limiting case of refinement. Assuming generated-distances necessitates assuming the availability of the corresponding operation, e.g. integer multiplication.

[7] Clementini et al. [6] introduce *frames of reference* for Qualitative Distances. These do allow differentiation by / representation of, e.g., density of features considered as context properties. However, process details pertaining to this are not discussed.

into stretches, distances across a stretch boundary are overestimated relative to distances within stretches, and knowledge about what stretches lie between two landmarks (and not the metrical distance between them) may be sufficient to predict the distance estimate. I call this *route structuring*. On the one hand, this is related to hierarchical effects – stretches are containers of landmarks. On the other hand, it may be considered a feature effect – structure is in some way or other induced by features (e.g. if features segment the route into stretches).

3 FEATURE: a new Model of Subjective Route Distances in Environmental Space

The main purpose of this model (see also [5]) was to give a unified, computational explanation for two effects empirically observed in route distance estimation, which had not been related to one another before (*feature accumulation, route structuring*) [14], integrating the considerations discussed in the preceding sections:

(1) Subjective distances increase with objective distances, but at a decreasing rate (often described by a *power function*).

(2) The difference between *spaces* described in section 1 requires a distinction between two kinds of subjective distances: *Vista distances* (distance estimates in vista space) can be perceived, stored and directly retrieved. *Cognitive distances* (distance estimates in environmental space) always have to be inferred. Also, cognitive distances increase more slowly than vista distances with objective distances in the sense that when described by a power function, the cognitive distance function has a lower exponent than the vista distance function [20]. I propose a more detailed investigation of what causes these two 'power function relations' – while vista distances reflect a perceptual, psychophysical phenomenon, cognitive distances reflect the way these estimates are constructed/inferred from separate, sequentially perceived components. The outcome of these construction processes can be *described* by a power function, but this is different in nature from the vista distance power function.

(3) The necessity of inference in the generation of cognitive distances requires the specification of *memory* structures and processes.

(4) Qualitative relations are important determinants of subjective distances. Order and containment relations are important determinants of subjective distances. This is expressed by the distorting influence of retrieved *features* and *route structure*. *Order on distances* should be reflected in the model where such knowledge can plausibly be assumed.

3.1 Memory Structures

FEATURE contains a long-term memory (LTM) representation of the route which is a labelled graph with three hierarchical levels: There are the *route*, the *stretch*, and the *landmark* level. The route is the whole route and therefore the root node; a stretch is a 'subdivision' as identified by [1]; a landmarks is "any distinct object or feature that is noticed and remembered" [16] (for related models, see [10, 15]). The levels are linked by immediate-containment links between nodes. Landmark nodes are linked by immediate-successor links, labelled with a distance value. This is taken to be a vista distance, reflecting the simplifying assumption that from one landmark, one sees the next one and remembers the distance [10]. Stretch nodes too are linked by immediate-successor links with an distance value label (derivation of this value is discussed below).

Cognitive distance are inferred. This involves the construction of a **working memory** (WM) representation based on the retrieval of parts of the LTM representation, and the evaluation of this representation as a value, the subjective distance. The central question of this construction is to specify what parts of the LTM representation are employed, when they are employed, and how they are transformed.

A second question is whether the construction process also involves the construction of a separate WM representation of the relevant and retrieved parts of the route. The assumption of such a representation can motivate the way the proposed construction process operates (see below). To see why, consider WM to be a visuo-spatial sketchpad [3]. A WM like this is usually assumed to be size- and number-of-items-limited, and to hold positional, metrically specified representations. The construction process distorts the distances between two items considered: the later during construction they are considered, the more the distance between them gets shrunk. This makes sense if 'space runs out', and this can happen in a metrically specified, size-limited medium. Also, this assumption can motivate why often, hierarchically chunked items are considered, and that items considered at any time of construction probably remain represented. This makes sense if 'the number of free places runs out', and this can happen in a number-of-items-limited medium.

However, it is also possible that the WM representation is simply a numerical value which gets incremented during retrieval of the relevant parts of the LTM representation. The 'shrinking' must then be explained by different processes. Additional research to try to determine what kind(s) of WM representation(s) are involved is the generation of cognitive distances is needed.

The evaluation of the WM representation as a subjective distance value reflects what kind of representation this is. A positional representation needs to be scanned from beginning to end to obtain a value. A numerical value already *is* the required value when construction is finished.

3.2 Different Distances, and Processes Generating Cognitive Distances

Distance values Distance values are assumed as labels of immediate-successor links. There are two reasons for not using the weaker assumption that there is knowledge about order on distances only. First: The set of distances that can be directly compared with one another is limited. They need to be aligned with one another and start at the same point, because then we have an easy procedure to compare them: follow them in their common direction, and the one whose end is encountered first is the shorter one.[8] In the following, these will be called *ordinal distances*: If along some route one encounters A, then B and then C, C is a successor of B, i.e. the distance AC is larger

---

[8] Equivalently: from the common starting point, one endpoint is seen in front of the other one. In a two-dimensional world, three distances forming a triangle allow some further inferences (e.g. [21]).

than AB, i.e. there is a (positive) distance BC. But in other cases, distances have to be represented before they can be compared with one another. And distances can only be represented if they are given a value first. This may be derived from 'measurement standards' of the human body (stride length, subjective time, ...), or in other ways (e.g. the average length of a block of buildings). This value may be regarded as a category. However (and this is the second reason), it can be argued that categorisation is not only an ordinal comparison with special-distances (categories with sharp boundaries), but also knowledge of the kind 'about as long as', corresponding to metrical prototypes of a category [7, 4] – this produces empirically observed *one*-valued results and simplifies processing. In a calculus based on order, this would require additional, other kinds of information. The processing model in principle allows both symbolic distance values interpreted as prototypes and numerical values, but the assumption of a metrically specified WM representation as well as the extension of the model to a simulation model require numerical values.

Stored distances: specificity of knowledge Stored distances are distances between landmarks which are successors on the route (vista distances) and distances between stretches which are successors on the route. In FEATURE, ordinal distances are the least specific kind of knowledge about distances that can be expressed. Ordinal distances reflect succession. Assigning a prototype s to the metrically underspecified relation 'immediate-successor', i.e. s as the distance value on all immediate-successor links, can express a particular form of ordinal distances. Any labelling of the immediate-successor links with values that differ from one another reflects more specific knowledge about distances. The values should depend on objective distances. Where vista distances must be specified (in particular in the simulation model, see below), values given by a psychophysical power function have been chosen. This decision, i.e. the assumption that subjective vista distances are ratio scaled, is a strong form of dependency. However, this is based on empirical evidence. It also illustrates the range of specificity of knowledge about distances that can be modelled in FEATURE.

How are distances between stretches determined? The simplest possibility would be: They aren't, they are ordinal distances. This would be a formalisation of what Allen and Kirasic [2] suggest based on their data. Constraints on that metrical prototype would be that it is large enough to be larger than within-stretch distances, otherwise we would not obtain the overestimation of between-stretch distances relative to within-stretch distances as observed by Allen [1] and Allen and Kirasic [2]. Another possibility would be that there is some rough estimate of the distance between, say, the middle of the first and the middle of the second stretch, based on distances between landmarks. Cognitive distances based on this would, on average, be larger than a 'locally based' within-stretch distance, giving the observed relative over-estimation.[9]

Cognitive distances Cognitive distances are inferred from stored distances in a procedure based on addition of transformed retrieved distance values. The process consists of repeating the following steps:

---

[9] It is possible that the values of stretch distances are from a different distance system [6] than those of landmark distances.

(1) Activate an item I (landmark or stretch) from the LTM representation of the route. The choice of I is described below.

(2) Retrieve the distance e associated with I, the distance label on the immediate-successor link leading to I.

(3) Transform e according to the current stage of processing, shrinking it the more the later during construction I is considered. Let the obtained value be e'.

(4) Insert I into the WM representation at the transformed distance (if the representation is positional) or add e' (if the representation is a numerical value).

The items chosen by step (1) are found during a traversal of the LTM representation. Traversal can be undirected 'spreading activation' (which reaches more or fewer features depending on how many are stored and/or retrieved: feature accumulation), or directed 'search' (which may use 'shortcuts' through the graph: route structuring). The strategy reflects the task (estimation of the whole route, or between a start and a goal landmark).

3.3 Modelling Known Effects and Making New Predictions

The functional relation between cognitive distances and objective distances may be described as follows: $d_e(i, j) = \Sigma_{k \in M\text{-set}} f(d_{succ}[k], k)$. d_{succ} is the vector of remembered immediate-successor distances. Usually, these are landmark distances. These vista distances can be described as a function of objective distances (a power function). If they are stretch distances, the distance estimate is based on the stretches i and j belong to (*route structuring*). M-set is the index set of the retrieved features (*feature accumulation*) – these can be landmarks or stretches, depending on whether d_{succ} concerns landmarks or stretches.

In the following, it will be shown how the expression for $d_e(i, j)$ and further constraints on its constituents produce the empirical effects described above.

The *feature accumulation* effect is produced by this function because if there are more features along the same objective length of a route, and the stored length of each individual part (the distance between a landmark and its immediate successor) is related to its objective value by a function growing at a decreasing rate, then this partitioning of the same objective length into more parts and their addition will produce a larger value than partitioning that length into fewer parts and then adding these would ('scaling hypothesis', see e.g. [17]). It should be expected that if the total length of a route is kept constant and the number of retrieved stretches increases, this will also increase the estimate.

The *route structuring* effect is produced because using stretch distances in the generation of a cognitive distance between landmarks in different stretches leads to an overestimation of these distances relative to estimates of distances between landmarks in the same stretch, which use landmark distances.

Cognitive distances increase with objective distances, but at a decreasing rate, if f increases with distance – f's first argument –, but decreases with how far away the considered distance is from the reference point of the estimation (operationalised as the stage k at which item k and its associated route piece, the distance between it and its immediate predecessor, are considered) – f's second argument.

Cognitive distances increase more slowly with objective distances than vista distances do (in the sense described above): This is guaranteed if there are upper bounds on the ratio of successive increases of $d_e(i, j)$. These can be expressed as functions of the stage of processing, the exponent of the vista distances power function, and the way the route is partitioned. Where needed, the simplest possibility has been assumed, a partition into pieces of the same length, i.e. $d_{succ}[k]$ constant. This construction shows that the description of $d_e(i, j)$ as a power function is not well-defined in the sense that for an identical total distance, the value of $d_e(i, j)$ depends on which pieces are added and in which order. This is the sense in which I regard a power function description of cognitive distances as an approximation – that larger objective distances are underestimated relative to smaller objective distances is the result of a process.

Transforming this model into a **simulation model** requires more specifications about f. A very simple functional form for f produced successful fits for a number of experiments from the literature, and some of the new predictions generated were corroborated by an experiment recently carried out [5].

3.4 FEATURE as a System of Representations of Containment, Order, and Ratios

In the LTM representation, there are immediate-successor links representing *immediate succession* and immediate-containment links representing *immediate containment*. The successor links together with a transitivity axiom (i.e. one that allows the chaining of immediate-successor links to a non-immediate successor relation) also represent *ordinal distance* (see the definition above). The labels of the immediate-successor links *between landmarks* represent *ratios of distances*. What stretch distance labels represent depends on how they are derived.

If inference proceeds along the successor links, it cannot change the order of landmarks and stretches. Therefore, if the WM representation is a positional representation, it preserves order and therefore ordinal distances. In this sense, FEATURE too assumes that 'people know how orders work'. If the inference process uses only containment links, however (as may well be the case in typical feature accumulation tasks), the order of items is not preserved, WM does not represent any aspect of distance locally – though it may represent ordinal distance globally (for the whole route): If it were true that route r_1 is longer than route r_2 if and only if it has more (retrievable) features, then a WM representation with an extension determined by the number of retrievable features would also be longer if and only if this corresponds to greater length in reality. This may well be the heuristic behind this strategy of estimating the length of a route. However, since in inference (transformed) power function estimates are added, *distance in WM does not represent distance in the world, or if it does, it is only in a very coarse way (possibly amounting to a categorisation)*. In fact, *distance in WM mainly represents non-spatial relations*: Entities comparatively far from the reference point of an estimation, but close to each other, share the property of being reachable from the reference point with a comparable amount of effort, time, money, etc., and the property of being relatively unimportant for the present stage of behaviour and/or planning. However, reflecting these properties' correlation with spatial distance, cognitive distance does represent spatial relations: comparability as implied by containment in the same super-structure (a stretch). This leads to a 'rationality argument' for this distorting way of constructing the WM representation: elaborate immediately relevant portions, neglect others (for a similar point, see [9]). This may be an explanation for the most important difference between FEATURE and the other approaches discussed here: in FEATURE, 'people know what addition means, but they add the wrong things'!

A second way in which people 'add the wrong things' is the choice of stretch distances instead of landmark distances. However, this can also be reframed as a rational heuristic: the 'shortcut' taken will save time in estimation, but still yield an approximately correct result (given the correlation between order and distance also found in the real world).

The construction performed by FEATURE also addresses the paradox mentioned in the beginning: There is knowledge about distances representing aspects of objective distances, but different, constructed subjective distances – taken together – need not satisfy the metrical axioms. Concerning the question of what may be 'qualitative' in knowledge about distances, this model takes a different perspective than the Qualitative Distances approaches described above. While these give a central role to qualitativeness characterised as knowledge about the order between distances, FEATURE focusses on qualitativeness characterised by distance estimates being *constructed* from a representation determined by qualitative relations of succession and containment. FEATURE also addresses questions of general importance for spatial cognition (order effects, metrical prototypes, strategies). The model could be extended and used to model human performance in other spatial tasks. The representation-theoretic framework can be applied to the study of other spatial relations. In particular, other cognitive spatial relations too might require a more process-oriented analysis, both for modelling performance and for answering questions concerning what aspects are represented.

Acknowledgements

I wish to thank Stefan Haar, Petra Jansen-Osmann, and Simone Pribbenow for discussion and comments, and three anonymous referees for comments.

References

1. Allen, G.L. (1981). A developmental perspective on the effects of "subdividing" macrospatial experience. *Journal of Experimental Psychology: Human Learning and Memory, 7*. 120–132.
2. Allen, G.L. & Kirasic, K.C. (1985). Effects of the cognitive organization of route knowledge on judgments of macrospatial distance.*Memory & Cognition,13*.218–227.
3. Baddeley, A.D. & Lieberman, K. (1980). Spatial working memory. In R. Nickerson (Ed.), *Attention and Performance VIII* (pp. 521–539). Hillsdale, NJ: Lawrence Erlbaum.
4. Berendt, B. (1996). Explaining preferred mental models in Allen inferences with a metrical model of imagery. In *Proc. CogSci'96*. 489–494.
5. Berendt, B. & Jansen-Osmann, P. (1997). *Feature accumulation and route structuring in distance estimations – an interdisciplinary approach*. To appear in *Proc. COSIT'97*.

6. Clementini, E., Di Felice, P. & Hernández, D. (1995). *Qualitative Representation of Positional Information*. Report FKI-208-95. TU München, Inst. f. Informatik (H2). July 1995. (revised March 1997: http://www7.informatik.tu-muenchen.de-/mitarbeiter/danher/node3.html).

7. Frank, A.U. (1992). Qualitative Spatial Reasoning about Distances and Directions in Geographic Space. *Journal of Visual Languages and Computing, 3*. 343–371.

8. Gurr, C.A. (1996). On the Isomorphism (or Otherwise) of Representations. *CAVI'96 Post-Conference Workshop*. Gubbio, Italy, May 1996.

9. Holyoak & Mah (1982). Cognitive reference points in judgments of symbolic magnitude. *Cognitive Psychology, 14*. 328–352.

10. Kuipers, B.J. (1978). Modeling Spatial Knowledge. *Cognitive Science, 2*. 129–153.

11. McNamara, T.P. (1991). Memory's view of space. In G.H. Bower (Ed.), *The psychology of learning and motivation: Advances in research and theory* (Vol. 27, pp. 147–186). New York: Academic Press.

12. Montello, D.R. (1988). *Route information and travel time as bases for the perception and cognition of environmental distance.* Unpublished Ph.D. thesis, Arizona State University, Tempe, AZ.

13. Montello, D.R. (1993). Scale and multiple psychologies of space. In A. U. Frank & I. Campari (Eds.), *Proc. COSIT'93* (pp. 312–321). Berlin etc.: Springer.

14. Montello, D. (1995). *The perception and cognition of environmental distance: Processes and knowledge sources.* Unpublished manuscript. University of California at Santa Barbara, Departments of Geography and Psychology.

15. Muller, P. (1996). Representing route networks for some cases of motion description. In *ECAI'96: Proceedings of the Workshop on Representations and Processes between Vision and NL.* (pp. 51–58). Budapest, Hungary.

16. Presson, C.C. & Montello, D.R. (1988). Points of reference in spatial cognition: Stalking the elusive landmark. *British Journal of Developmental Psychology, 6*, 378–381.

17. Sadalla, E.K. & Magel, S.G. (1980). The Perception of Traversed Distance. *Environment and Behavior, 12*. 65–79.

18. Sadalla, E.K. & Staplin, L.J. (1980). An information storage model for distance cognition. *Environment and Behavior, 12*. 183–193

19. Sadalla, E.K., Staplin, L.J. & Burroughs, W.J. (1979). Retrieval processes in distance cognition. *Memory & Cognition, 7*. 291–296.

20. Wiest, W.M. & Bell, B. (1985). Steven's Exponent for Psychophysical Scaling of Perceived, Remembered, and Inferred Distance. *Psychological Bulletin, 98*. 457–470.

21. Zimmermann, K. (1995). Measuring without measures. The Δ-Calculus In A. U. Frank & W. Kuhn (Eds.), *Proc. COSIT'95* (pp. 59–67). Berlin etc.: Springer.

An Axiomatic Approach to the Spatial Relations Underlying *Left–Right* and *in Front of–Behind*

Carola Eschenbach & Lars Kulik
University of Hamburg
{eschenbach, kulik}@informatik.uni-hamburg.de

Abstract
This paper presents an axiomatic characterization of spatial orderings in the plane and of concepts underlying intrinsic and deictic uses of spatial terms such as *in front of, behind, left* and *right*. This characterization differs in several aspects from existing theories that either employ systems of coordinate axes or systems of regions to specify the meaning of such expressions. We argue that the relations given by *in front of* and *behind* can be modeled on the basis of linear orders and on the basis of axes, whereas the relations given by *left* and *right* can be modeled as planar and on the basis of regions. The explicit characterization of the means necessary to specify the intrinsic and deictic uses thereby sheds light on the structures contributed by different frames of reference and therefore contributes to understanding the deictic/intrinsic-distinction.

1 Introduction

The representation and processing of spatial language and spatial concepts plays an important role in several tasks performed by humans and to be performed by artificial intelligence systems. The most obvious ones are communication about space (as in the context of configuration or navigation) and the use of spatial representations for non-spatial problems (as in diagrammatic reasoning and visualization of information).

Several disciplines contribute to the study of spatial concepts. Geometry is concerned with formal means of representing space and studies formal spatial concepts with respect to their expressive power and interrelations. Linguistic semantics analyzes natural language expressions relating to space with respect to the applicability, semantic interrelations and their diversity of uses. In computer science internal models of space are assumed to be some kind of geometric representation. Therefore, one task of specifying the meaning of spatial terms for use in an artificial intelligence system is to map such terms to geometric descriptions (cf., e.g., Retz-Schmidt 1988).

The relation between spatial terms and geometric concepts has not been neglected by linguistic semantics, but the relation is mostly either rather vague or based on a specific geometric framework, namely, on coordinates. The aim of this paper is to specify the information contributed by some spatial terms on the basis of geometric concepts that are sufficient for this task and–thereby–as unspecific as possible.

*   The research reported in this paper was supported by the Deutsche Forschungsgemeinschaft (DFG) in the project 'Axiomatik räumlicher Konzepte' (Ha 1237/7) that is part of the research initiative on "Spatial Cognition". We would like to thank Christopher Habel, Annette Leßmöllmann, Hedda Rahel Schmidtke and three anonymous referees for their helpful comments and criticism. Due to space constraints we were not able to react to all their points. Author's address: FB Informatik (AB WSV) und Graduiertenkolleg *Kognitionswissenschaft*, Universität Hamburg, Vogt-Kölln-Str. 30, D-22527 Hamburg, Germany.

The natural language terms *in front of*, *behind*, *left* and *right* (called 'projective prepositions' by Herskovits (1986)) specify the location of two objects relative to each other. The information contributed can be characterized as two dimensional ordering information.

Different views about how ordering information (in the plane) shall be specified and about the structure and contribution of the underlying frame of reference are exemplified by the following approaches. Tversky (1996) assumes that persons construct a mental spatial framework consisting of body axes that are used in interpreting the terms. Hernández (1992) models the ordering relations of objects by separating the local neighborhood of the objects into eight sectors labeled as 'front', 'right-front', 'right' and so forth. In contrast to these descriptions Freksa (1992) and Schlieder (1995) describe spatial ordering by specifying relations between three points. Whereas Freksa (1992) employs three axes and six regions generated by them in the specification, Schlieder (1995) only distinguishes two orientations of the triangles constituted by the points.

Instead of modeling the four relations on the basis of axes like Tversky (1996) or on the basis of regions like Hernández (1992) we present an approach that is closer to Freksa's (1992). We show that it is possible to distinguish four directions in the plane on the basis of just one line or axis. In our proposal the linear structure is used to characterize *in front of/behind* and the planar structure is used to describe *left/right*.

The question which aspects of the semantics of so-called 'spatial terms' of natural language can be characterized on a purely spatial basis is tackled in this paper in the following way. The analysis is developed on a purely geometric basis, i.e., using concepts and relations that have an obvious geometric interpretation and are (or can be) easily embedded in a geometry as specified by Euclid or Hilbert (1956). The geometric concepts are formally characterized and used in the specification of the meaning of the natural language terms. Since we aim at modeling four terms of ordering or direction only, the geometric language we employ is not rich. Notions of metric or orthogonality are omitted.

To develop the geometric framework we employ the axiomatic method. An axiomatic system does not define basic terms like 'point' and 'lines' or 'incidence.' Instead, it constitutes a system of constraints that determines the properties of these basic terms by specifying their interrelations. Therefore, an axiomatic specification of spatial relations has at least two advantages. Firstly, it provides an exact characterization of the structure of a spatial relation. Secondly, axiomatic systems can be compared as to how restrictive they are.

Our geometric description is meant as a formal basis to model empirical findings such as the specific uses of natural language in specifying the location of objects. Therefore, it is not restricted to the assumption that spatially extended entities are represented as points. Geometric points are rather taken as spatial objects that are most easily and uniquely described with respect to their position. Whether and in which cases extended entities are represented as points, lines or regions has to be a matter of further study. Additionally, the question whether the localization of an extended (and possibly scattered) entity is in accordance with the localization of all or just some points that it occupies should be a matter of empirical investigations.

The generality of the theories developed using the axiomatic method is sometimes seen as a disadvantage, since they cannot be restricted to the one (intended) model the analysis is based on. But in the context of the analysis of natural language expressions, this property turns out to be an advantage again, since the variability of expressions with respect to their domain of application is a well known feature of natural languages (cf. Habel & Eschenbach 1995).

2 Projective Prepositions and Spatial Reference Frames

Projective prepositions such as *in front of, behind, left* and *right* are (superficially) binary, i.e., they relate two entities. If, e.g., Y is in front of X, then we refer to X as the 'reference object' of the relation *in front of* and to Y as the 'target.'

As is well known, different uses of projective prepositions can be identified (cf. the survey of Retz-Schmidt (1988)). Miller and Johnson-Laird (1976) introduce the terms 'deictic' and 'intrinsic' to distinguish between two characteristic spatial reference systems. The deictic system employs 'the speaker's egocentric origin and coordinate axes' for specifying spatial relations. The projective prepositions to be used can vary relative to the speaker's position and orientation in the scene.

The intrinsic system is independent of the speaker's position or orientation. It refers to intrinsic parts of the reference object, such as its distinguished front, top or right side. It is available, if the reference object induces an appropriate labeling of its sides. Therefore, as Levelt (1984) points out, the intrinsic system depends on a more detailed spatial interpretation of the reference objects than the deictic system.

The reference systems described differ with respect to inferences they justify. Levelt (1984) shows that transitivity and converseness hold in deictic systems, whereas it is not guaranteed in the intrinsic case.[1] If, e.g., two people X and Y face each other, then X is in front of Y, and Y is in front of but not behind X. Some differences between the deictic and the intrinsic systems are according to the fact that the spatial reference frame in different deictic uses can be kept constant, while it has to differ across different intrinsic uses.

The spatial frame of reference as employed in the deictic system is determined not on the basis of geometric aspects but on the basis of pragmatic or communicative factors. Therefore, we specify the geometric relation expressed by the deictic uses of the terms as a ternary relation between the two explicitly given relata and the implicitly given spatial reference frame. Since in the intrinsic uses the reference object determines the spatial reference frame, they are assumed to lead to binary relations. One aim of the analysis proposed here is to specify explicitly which spatial information is contributed by a spatial reference frame in the case of deictic uses and what is, in the case of intrinsic uses, contributed by the reference object.

We specify the meaning of the four projective terms on the basis of one axis in the plane and labels on the half-planes defined by this axis. We suggest that it is appropriate to use the linear concepts as a basis to model the expressions *in front of* and *behind*, while *left* and *right* are modeled by the induced planar concepts.[2] Before we concentrate on the geometric problems and formalization, we give some points supporting this claim.

The possibility of intrinsic uses of projective prepositions depends on the categorization of the object sides in accordance with directions. Symmetric and arbitrarily

---

[1] Let X and Y denote two arbitrary objects. Converseness of $\langle relation_1 \rangle$ and $\langle relation_2 \rangle$ means that:
$X \langle relation_1 \rangle Y \Leftrightarrow Y \langle relation_2 \rangle X$, e.g., X is *in front of* $Y \Leftrightarrow Y$ is *behind* X.

[2] This claim is in accordance with, e.g., Clark (1973), who calls *in front of* and *in back of* ' one-dimensional intrinsic prepositions' and *to the left of* and *to the right of* 'two-dimensional prepositions.' This analysis also gives a formal basis to categorizing the *in front of/behind* distinction as on 'the primary horizontal dimension' and the *left/right* distinction as on 'the secondary horizontal dimension' (cf. Clark (1973), Grabowski and Weiß (1996)).

formed objects like balls, cubes or stones do not exhibit such intrinsic sides, while persons and many artifacts do. The assignment of intrinsic sides to bounded objects obeys the following rule: if an object has intrinsic left and right sides, then it has an intrinsic front, back, top and bottom as well (cf. Wunderlich 1984). That is to say, *left* and *right* presuppose a knowledge of *front* and *back* Spears, rockets and books are objects with fronts and backs that lack left and right sides. Spears can be considered as linear objects. The possibility to ascribe fronts and backs to them supports the thesis that linear spatial constellations are geometrically rich enough to support the use of *in front of* and *behind*.

In addition, the *front/behind* distinction is applicable with reference to paths, i.e., linear structures that are induced by (the possibility of) movement. Using a person's trip route as reference frame, the spatial relation between any entities on the route, e.g., cities that are encountered one after the other can be specified using *before* or *behind*. X is behind Y (with respect to the trip route) if X is encountered after Y is. The route does not need to be straight but may be arbitrarily curved. Additionally, reference to a path (e.g., street or river) and picking out one end as the start can serve as a basis for using such prepositions (cf. Habel (1990) for a similar argument concerning *between*).

Although this is not the place to discuss the criteria underlying the assignment of the intrinsic sides, it is important to notice that non-geometric aspects are involved. There are two alternatives to assign *left/right* relative to the assignment of *front/back*. The choice usually depends on whether people assume a characteristic position inside or outside the reference object. The intrinsic right side of a car corresponds to the right side of a person sitting inside, whereas the intrinsic right side of a desk corresponds to the right side of a person sitting in front of it. This variation is taken care of in the formalization.

One goal is to work out the similarities and differences between intrinsic and deictic uses of the preposition to develop a geometric understanding of the notion of 'reference system' or 'frame of reference' often employed in their informal characterization. To emphasize the difference between directions in linear and planar structures, we develop the framework in two parts.

3 Order and Directions on Linear Structures

The axiomatic system given here is structured similarly to the system presented in Hilbert (1956), which is divided into different groups of axioms that describe incidence, order, congruence, parallelism and continuity. To characterize the terms *in front of/behind* and *left/right* we employ only parts of the first two groups of the whole system, i.e., axioms of incidence and ordering. However, we diverge from Hilbert's account that expresses order by the primitive relation of betweenness. Since we need a simple notion of direction, we enrich the basic inventory by assuming oriented lines in addition to straight lines and points (cf. Aurnague & Vieu 1993). Oriented lines can be considered lines supplied with an orientation. We do not assume that straight lines or oriented lines are sets of points. Points, straight lines and oriented lines are rather assumed to constitute three independent systems of entities and the axioms determine the relations between these entities.

Thus, in the description of spatial constellations we employ the following fundamental mathematical concepts:

(a) 'Points', '(straight) lines' and 'oriented lines.' Let Π denote the set of points, Λ the set of lines and Ω the set of oriented lines. Capitals in italics like P, P', P_1, ...,

Q and R denote points, lower case italics like l, l', l_1, ... denote (straight) lines and lower case italics like o, o', o_1, ... denote oriented lines.

(b) A binary relation of 'incidence' (symbolized by ι), whose domain is Π and whose range is $\Lambda \cup \Omega$. This relation characterizes the fact that a point lies on a straight line or an oriented line and that a line or an oriented line goes through a point.

(c) A ternary relation of 'precedence' (symbolized by $\prec$). It combines oriented lines and two points. With this relation, ordering of points on oriented lines can be described.

3.1 Ordering on Linear Structures

We develop the axiomatic system in several steps. First, we need axioms that set up the incidence relation between points and straight lines. Then we relate points and oriented lines using the ternary relation of precedence. Finally, we establish a link between lines and oriented lines. According to the explanations given in the introduction the following axioms do not define the primitive concepts 'point', 'line' and 'oriented line' but characterize their relationships.

3.1.1 Axioms of Incidence

Three axioms relate points and straight lines using incidence.

(I1) $\forall l \; \exists P \; \exists Q \qquad [P \neq Q \wedge P \iota l \wedge Q \iota l]$

(I2) $\forall P \; \forall Q \qquad [P \neq Q \Rightarrow \exists l \, [P \iota l \wedge Q \iota l]]$

(I3) $\forall P \; \forall Q \; \forall l_1 \; \forall l_2 \qquad [(P \iota l_1 \wedge Q \iota l_1 \wedge P \iota l_2 \wedge Q \iota l_2) \Rightarrow (P = Q \vee l_1 = l_2)]$

According to (I1) for every straight line there are at least two different points that are incident with this line. Axiom (I2) states that for two points there is at least one straight line such that both points are incident with it. And (I3) says that two different lines do not have more than one point (on them) in common and two different points do not have more than one straight line (through them) in common.

Based on incidence between points and straight lines, incidence between points and oriented lines can be sufficiently characterized by condition (I4), saying that for every oriented line there is a straight line such that they have exactly the same points incident with them.

(I4) $\forall o \; \exists l \; \forall P \qquad [P \iota o \Leftrightarrow P \iota l]$

3.1.2 Axioms of Ordering

The next group of axioms characterizes the relation of precedence that holds between an oriented line and two points. It is the basis of the ordering of points in linear structures. The relation $\prec(o, P, Q)$ is read as *the point P precedes the point Q with respect to the oriented line o*.

(O1) $\forall o \; \forall P \; \forall Q \qquad [\prec(o, P, Q) \Rightarrow P \iota o \wedge Q \iota o]$

(O2) $\forall o \; \forall P \; \forall Q \qquad [P \neq Q \wedge P \iota o \wedge Q \iota o \Rightarrow \prec(o, P, Q) \vee \prec(o, Q, P)]$

(O3) $\forall o \; \forall P \; \forall Q \qquad [\prec(o, P, Q) \Rightarrow \neg(\prec(o, Q, P))]$

(O4) $\forall o \; \forall P \; \forall Q \; \forall R \qquad [\prec(o, P, Q) \wedge \prec(o, Q, R) \Rightarrow \prec(o, P, R)]$

Axiom (O1) ensures that if P precedes Q with respect to o then P and Q are incident with o. Axiom (O2) states that of two different points incident with an oriented line o one precedes the other relative to o. According to axiom (O3), only one of the two options is valid. Therefore, no point precedes itself on any oriented line: $\neg(\prec(o, P, P))$. Axiom (O4) says that precedence relative to an oriented line is transitive. To sum up, the set of points that are incident with a fixed oriented line constitutes a strictly and linearly ordered set according to $\prec$.

We conclude this section by defining the ternary relation of betweenness that relates points on a straight line. This definition enables us to give the characterizations in section 4 in a more compact form.

Definition (β)

$$\beta(P, Q, R) \quad \Leftrightarrow_{def} \quad \exists o \, [\prec(o, P, Q) \wedge \prec(o, Q, R)]$$

If $\beta(P, Q, R)$ holds, then we say: Q is *between P and R* or *P and R are on different sides of Q*. Some properties of betweenness that are provable from the axioms of ordering and are used in the following are: If Q is between P and R, then Q is between R and P, the three points are pairwise distinct and incident with one straight line. If P, Q and R are pairwise distinct and incident with the same line, then one and only one of them is between the other two.

To ensure the existence of oriented lines we further assume that for any pair of different points there is an oriented line that orders them (I5), and (I6) states that for a given pair of points there is at most one oriented line that orders them in the same way. These axioms together with (I1) establish that every straight line can be oriented in exactly two ways.

(I5) $\forall P \, \forall Q \qquad [P \neq Q \Rightarrow \exists o[\prec(o, P, Q)]]$

(I6) $\forall o_1 \, \forall o_2 \qquad [\exists P \, \exists Q \, [\prec(o_1, P, Q) \wedge \prec(o_2, P, Q)] \Rightarrow o_1 = o_2]$

According to axiom (I6) and (O2) two different oriented lines that are coincident with the same straight line order the points in opposite manners.

3.2 *In front of* and *behind* in the Intrinsic Reference System

Oriented lines and the ordering of points on them is the geometric basis to character-ize the conditions under which statements using *in front of* and *behind* apply. They can be used intrinsically, only if the reference object has a front and a corresponding back side (cf. Levelt 1984). Therefore, a point and an oriented line through it are an appropriate representation of the reference object on the geometric level. The point characterizes the location of a reference object and the oriented line its front-back axis.

Characterization (front$_i$, behind$_i$)

Let P_X denote the location of the reference object X and o_X its oriented front-back axis. Moreover, let P_Y denote the location of the target Y.

front$_i$(Y, X) $\qquad \Leftrightarrow \qquad \prec(o_X, P_Y, P_X)$

behind$_i$(Y, X) $\qquad \Leftrightarrow \qquad \prec(o_X, P_X, P_Y)$

That is to say, the target Y is in front of the reference object X in an intrinsic reference system, if the position of the target P_Y precedes that of the reference object P_X with respect to its front-back axis (o_X). We emphasize that the axiom (O1) implies that both positions P_X and P_Y are incident with the axis o_X. In agreement with the analysis of Levelt (1984), converseness as well as transitivity can be violated, due to the use of different orientations of the objects involved.

3.3 *In front of* and *behind* in the Deictic Reference System

The deictic reference system is independent of the spatial structure of the relata but employs an independent spatial reference frame. Therefore we use points to represent the reference object as well as the target and employ a ternary rather than binary rela-tion symbol in the characterization.

Using a deictic reference system means–intuitively–that an externally given perspective, direction, or point of view is employed that might be related to a person who describes a spatial scene or a person whom the description is addressed to. Directions, perspectives and points of view are important concepts that require a more detailed analysis than we can give here. Still, those aspects important for the current task can be given a first geometric characterization. Furthermore, we can distinguish these notions as three different specifications of spatial reference frames.

Characterization (front$_d$, behind$_d$)

Let P_D denote the origin of a deictic reference system (D) and o_D a distinguished orientation of this system. Both may be supplied by the position and line of vision of a person. Moreover, let P_Y denote the location of the target (Y) and P_X the location of the reference object (X).

$$\text{front}_d(Y, X, D) \quad \Leftrightarrow \quad \prec(o_D, P_D, P_X) \wedge \prec(o_D, P_D, P_Y) \wedge \prec(o_D, P_Y, P_X)$$
$$\text{behind}_d(Y, X, D) \quad \Leftrightarrow \quad \prec(o_D, P_D, P_X) \wedge \prec(o_D, P_D, P_Y) \wedge \prec(o_D, P_X, P_Y)$$

That is to say, the target is in front of the reference object from a person located at P_D and looking into direction o_D, if P_D precedes P_Y with respect to o_D and P_Y precedes P_X with respect to o_D. In this characterization of front$_d$, the first clause is not necessary as well as the second clause in the characterization of behind$_d$, since both are derivable from the remaining clauses and (O4). They are both specified to highlight the similarity of the two relations. Consequently we obtain converseness (cf. Levelt 1984).

$$\text{behind}_d(Y, X, D) \quad \Leftrightarrow \quad \text{front}_d(X, Y, D)$$

To put it another way, with regard to a fixed deictic reference system, Y is behind X, if and only if X is in front of Y. The transitivity of *in front of/behind* in a deictic reference system can also be deduced from this characterization using the axiom (O4).

The symbol D introduced in the characterization is used to indicate that the objects X and Y are related with respect to a deictic reference system. This notion enables us to make the contributions of the deictic reference system explicit. In the variant proposed above, D specifies the origin P_D and a distinguished orientation o_D. In two slightly less restrictive variants the deictic reference system characterizes a distinguished direction or a point of view only. The first only employs the notion of a direction (in the sense of a specific oriented line).

Alternative Characterization (front$_d$, behind$_d$)

Let o_D denote a distinguished orientation in a deictic reference system (D), and let P_Y denote the location of the target (Y) and P_X the location of the reference object (X).

$$\text{front}_d(Y, X, D) \quad \Leftrightarrow \quad \prec(o_D, P_Y, P_X)$$
$$\text{behind}_d(Y, X, D) \quad \Leftrightarrow \quad \prec(o_D, P_X, P_Y)$$

The similarity of this characterization with the one given for the intrinsic system is obvious, since they only differ in the way the oriented line is specified. In contrast to the first characterization of the deictic use, an origin of the reference system (or point of view) is not employed. Since this description is compatible with any origin on the oriented line, it is less restrictive than the former.

The second alternative, in contrast, only uses the notion of a point of view.

Alternative Characterization (front$_d$, behind$_d$)

Let P_D denote the origin of a deictic reference system (D) (i.e., a point of view), P_Y and P_X the locations of the target (Y) and of the reference object (X), respectively.

$$\text{front}_d(Y, X, D) \quad \Leftrightarrow \quad \exists o \, [\prec(o, P_D, P_X) \wedge \prec(o, P_D, P_Y) \wedge \prec(o, P_Y, P_X)]$$
$$\text{behind}_d(Y, X, D) \quad \Leftrightarrow \quad \exists o \, [\prec(o, P_D, P_X) \wedge \prec(o, P_D, P_Y) \wedge \prec(o, P_X, P_Y)]$$

In this case, the origin of the frame of reference is fixed, while the orientation is not specified. This characterization is therefore compatible with any orientation of the source of the deictic perspective. The three characterizations presented have a wide range of cases in which they all apply. To determine which is the most appropriate for capturing deictic uses of *in front of* and *behind* a thorough empirical investigation is needed.

3.4 Oriented Lines in Intrinsic and Deictic Reference Systems

Comparing the characterizations of front_i and front_d we observe an important asymmetry with respect to the conception of oriented lines and their role in modeling deictic and intrinsic uses of projective prepositions. In order to emphasize the similarity of the distinguished uses, we included a condition of the form $\prec(o, P_Y, P_X)$ in both of them. In case of the intrinsic use, the front-back axis of the reference object specifies the oriented line o. In case of the deictic use, o is specified by the distinguished axis of the deictic reference system, such as the line of vision of some person.

On this basis, we can formulate the condition $\prec(o, P_Y, P_X)$ by 'Following o, P_Y is encountered before P_X is.' Thus, the orientation on the front-back axis employed in the intrinsic case must also be understood in the same way: Following X's front-back axis, X's front is encountered before its back is. The table is in front of John (intrinsically) if, following John's front-back axis, the table is encountered before John is. Thus, the front-back axis of a person needed in the intrinsic case is oppositely oriented to the oriented line needed in the specification of the deictic reference system, which we described as the line of vision of a person.

4 Order and Directions in Planar Structures

The axioms presented in section 3.1 deal with linear structures only. Before we can give the characterizations for the spatial relations described by *left/right*, we have to introduce further geometric concepts that enable us to talk about objects in the plane.

4.1 Ordering in the Plane

A planar structure is only available if not all points are incident with one straight line. The transition from a linear structure to a planar structure, therefore, is done by another axiom of incidence that for any straight line guarantees the existence of at least one point not incident with the line.

4.1.1 Axiom of Incidence (planar case)

(I7) $\quad \forall l \, \exists P \quad\quad [\neg (P \, \iota \, l)]$

By (I7) it is not possible to show that the resulting structure is really planar since it could be as well higher-dimensional. In order to exclude the latter we require a axiom which we introduce below.

Points that are not incident with a given line can be on the same side or on different sides of the line.

Definition (σ, δ)

$$\delta(l, P, Q) \quad\quad \Leftrightarrow_{\text{def}} \quad \neg(P \, \iota \, l \vee Q \, \iota \, l) \wedge \exists R \, [R \, \iota \, l \wedge \beta(P, R, Q)]$$
$$\sigma(l, P, Q) \quad\quad \Leftrightarrow_{\text{def}} \quad \neg(P \, \iota \, l \vee Q \, \iota \, l) \wedge \forall R \, [R \, \iota \, l \Rightarrow \neg\beta(P, R, Q)]$$

P and Q are on different sides of l (in symbols: $\delta(l, P, Q)$), if neither P nor Q is incident with l and a point R between P and Q is incident with l. If no point is on l and between P and Q then we say that P and Q are on the same side of l (in symbols: $\sigma(l, P, Q)$). We summarize some basic properties:

Lemma

(a) $\forall l \, \forall P \, \forall Q \quad [\neg(P \iota l \vee Q \iota l) \Rightarrow (\delta(l, P, Q) \Leftrightarrow \neg(\sigma(l, P, Q)))]$

(b) $\forall l \, \forall P \quad [\neg(P \iota l) \Leftrightarrow \sigma(l, P, P)]$

(c) $\forall l \, \forall P \, \forall Q \quad [(\delta(l, P, Q) \Leftrightarrow \delta(l, Q, P)) \wedge (\sigma(l, P, Q) \Leftrightarrow \sigma(l, Q, P))]$

Formula (a) says that if P and Q are not incident with a line l, then they are either on the same or on different sides of l. According to (b) any point not on a line is on the same side of it as itself. And (c) states that P and Q are on different sides of l, if and only if Q and P are on different sides of l. The same applies to the relation σ.

The collection of axioms specified can be fulfilled by geometric spaces of higher dimension than the plane. In order to restrict the system to the plane, as we intent here, we include the axiom of separation. The axiom of separation says (informally spoken) that any straight line separates all the points not incident with it in at most two groups, i.e., it divides the universe into two half-planes. In other geometric systems, it can be derived with the aid of the so-called 'axiom of Pasch' (for details see for instance Hilbert (1956)).

4.1.2 Axiom of Separation

(S) $\forall l \, \forall P \, \forall Q \, \forall R$

$[\neg(R \iota l) \wedge \delta(l, P, Q) \Rightarrow ((\delta(l, P, R) \wedge \sigma(l, Q, R)) \vee (\delta(l, Q, R) \wedge \sigma(l, P, R)))]$

The axiom of separation states: Given a straight line l and three points P, Q, R such that R is not on l and P and Q are on different sides of l. Then R is on the same side of l as exactly one of P and Q, and on a different side of l from the other one. From axiom (S) we can derive the following statements:

- If P and Q are on different sides of l and Q and R are on the same side of l, then P and R are on different sides of l.
- If P and Q are on different sides of l and Q and R are on different sides of l, then P and R are on the same side of l.
- And finally, if P and Q are on the same side of l and Q and R are on the same side of l, then P and R are also on the same side of l.

The last statement expresses transitivity of the relation σ. In conjunction with the above lemma we obtain that the relation σ together with a straight line defines an equivalence relation of the points not on the line.

4.2 To *the left of* and *to the right of* in the Intrinsic Reference System

Intrinsic uses of *to the left of* and *to the right of* are based on an assignment of a left side and a right side to the reference object. On the geometric level we reflect the front-back axis by employing an oriented line. Since the straight line coincident with it separates the plane in two half planes, labeling one of the sides as the right side (and the other one as the left side) is sufficient. As indicated in section 2, the assignment of left and right sides does not follow a single scheme. Therefore, the oriented front-back axis is not sufficient to label the sides, as would be the case, if we would assume the plane to be canonically oriented. Consequently, we need an additional means on the geometric level to distinguish the two sides, independent of the orientation of the front-back axis.

In the case of *left/right*, we do not employ another axis but a point. I.e., on the geometric level, we describe the property of an object X having an intrinsic left and right side by assigning a so-called *right point* R_X to this object. The right point R_X of an object is just a geometric proxy that locates the right side of the object relative to its front-back axis. Therefore, the right point is not incident with the front-back axis. It is obvious that we could ascribe a *left-point* in exactly the same way. If a symmetrical representation is desired, it is possible to introduce both points. Since the order of the front-back axis of the object as well as its position is irrelevant for the assignment of left and right, we only refer to the underlying straight line in this description.

Characterization (left$_i$, right$_i$)

Let R_X denote the right point of the reference object (X) and l_X its front-back axis. Moreover, let P_Y denote the location of the target (Y).

$$\text{right}_i(Y, X) \quad \Leftrightarrow \quad \sigma(l_X, R_X, P_Y)$$
$$\text{left}_i(Y, X) \quad \Leftrightarrow \quad \delta(l_X, R_X, P_Y)$$

If right$_i(Y, X)$ holds, then the position of Y is on the same side of the front-back axis of X as the right point of X. And, if left$_i(Y, X)$ holds, then the position of Y is on the other side of this axis. Converseness as well as transitivity does not have to be valid since the front-back axis varies according to the variation of the reference object. These conclusions are in accordance with the analysis of Levelt (1984).

This characterization is independent of the assignment of one specific point as the location of the reference object. Therefore, unbounded entities whose locations are linear structures rather than points (such as rivers or streets) and that allow the assignment of a right point can be a basis for intrinsic uses of *left* and *right*, even if they do not have intrinsic fronts and backs.

4.3 *To the left of* and *to the right of* in the Deictic Reference System

There are different possibilities to describe the use of *to the left of* and *to the right of* in a deictic reference system. Since we rely on a weak geometric structure in which parallels and translations are not available, the characterization below is generally applicable but based on a disjunction. The complexity of this description reflects the well known problems of the acquisition and use of *left* and *right* (cf. Clark 1973).

The benefit of this procedure is that we are able to show that this weak axiomatic system is strong enough to characterize *left* and *right* in a deictic reference system. As a result, we can give an upper limit of the maximally necessary axioms.

We present five figures in order to indicate in which cases the use of *to right of* is justified in a deictic reference system.

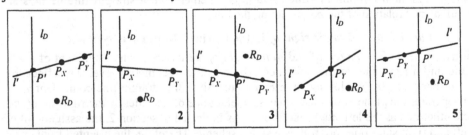

Figure 1–5: All cases of *to the right of* in a deictic reference system.

In all five cases, it should be possible to say that Y is to the right of X relative to D. R_D denotes the right point of the reference frame specified by D. The line l_D characterizes its orientation and the line l' is an auxiliary line that is uniquely determined by P_X and P_Y according to axiom (I3).

Characterization (left$_d$, right$_d$)

Let the line l_D characterize an axis and R_D denote the right point of a deictically given spatial reference frame D. Moreover, let P_X denote the location of the reference object (X) and P_Y denote the location of the target (Y). If we designate the line that is uniquely determined by P_X and P_Y with l', then

$$\text{right}_d(Y, X, D) \Leftrightarrow P_X \neq P_Y \wedge \exists P' \, [P' \iota \, l_D \wedge \exists l' \, [P_X \iota \, l' \wedge P_Y \iota \, l' \wedge P' \iota \, l'] \wedge$$
$$((\sigma(l_D, R_D, P_Y) \wedge \neg\beta(P', P_Y, P_X)) \vee (\delta(l_D, R_D, P_X) \wedge \neg\beta(P', P_X, P_Y)))]$$

$$\text{left}_d(Y, X, D) \Leftrightarrow P_X \neq P_Y \wedge \exists P' \, [P' \iota \, l_D \wedge \exists l' \, [P_X \iota \, l' \wedge P_Y \iota \, l' \wedge P' \iota \, l'] \wedge$$
$$((\delta(l_D, R_D, P_X) \wedge \neg\beta(P', P_Y, P_X)) \vee (\sigma(l_D, R_D, P_X) \wedge \neg\beta(P', P_X, P_Y)))]$$

I.e., Y is to the right of X relative to the spatial reference frame D, if they are at different locations, the line through their positions meet the axis supplied by D, Y is on the right side of this axis and not between X and the point of intersection, or X is on the left side of the axis and not between Y and the point of intersection. The first condition subsumes the first three figures, the second condition the last three figures. The middle figure is integrated in both conditions and defines the most uncontroversial case: X is to the left of D and Y to the right of D.

If the location of a person and its alignment remains constant then the relation left$_d$ and right$_d$ fulfill converseness and transitivity. We omit the proof.

4.4 A Comparison of the Intrinsic and Deictic Reference System

The characterizations of right$_i$ and right$_d$ essentially agree, even though they differ in complexity. In the intrinsic case as well as in the deictic case right-constellations are characterized based on a linear structure: the front-back axis of X and the axis supplied by D (e.g., the line of vision), respectively. Figure 2 demonstrates the connections of the intrinsic and deictic reference systems: the intrinsic case corresponds to the deictic case if the respective lines coincide. Therefore we find that

$$\text{right}_i(Y, X) \Leftrightarrow \text{right}_d(Y, X, X).$$

5 Conclusion

The formal description of the purely spatial aspects of the meaning of the projective prepositions *in front of, behind, left* and *right* has led us to a better understanding of the role of so-called 'spatial frames of reference.' Spatial frames of reference are derived from the reference object (intrinsic uses) or the context, e.g., the speaker or hearer of an utterance (deictic uses).

In contrast to some informal characterizations that equated the frame of reference with a 'point of view' (cf., Retz-Schmidt 1988) we saw that, geometrically speaking, one point (or location) is only sufficient in the case of deictic uses of the linear *in front of* and *behind*. To characterize the common core in their deictic and intrinsic uses the assumption that the spatial reference frame contributes a direction (i.e., and oriented line in our description) is preferable. Assuming a 'point of view' is less useful for the characterization of the role of the spatial frame of reference in the planar case of *left* and *right*. In this case, a straight line separating two half-planes and a label on one of the planes (modeled as the 'right point') are needed. Of course, persons are the ideal source of deictic perspectives, since they can contribute any kind of spatial structure by their front-back axes, lines of vision, locations and right hands (just to name the few we need).

A final remark shall be devoted to the vertical dimension ignored so far. If the third dimension is added to the geometric framework, then our argument concerning *left/right* would be based on planes dividing the space in two half-spaces. As far as we see now, the prepositions of the vertical dimension (*over/under*) could be analyzed according to the linear *front/behind* as well as according to *left/right* (assuming the plane of the ground to be a fundamentally available vertically separating plane for the horizontal dimension.) Which analysis is to be preferred and its consequences for the general notion of spatial reference frame has to be discussed at some other place.

6 References

Aurnague, M. & Vieu, L. (1993). A three-level approach to the semantics of space. In: C. Zelinsky-Wibbelt (ed.), *The Semantics of Prepositions: From Mental Processing to Natural Language Processing,* Mouton de Gruyter, Berlin.

Clark, H.H. (1973). Space, semantics, and the child. In: T.E. Moore (ed.): *Cognitive development and the acquisition of language.* (pp. 27–63). New York, Academic Press.

Freksa, C. (1992). Using orientation information for qualitative spatial reasoning, *Proceedings of the International Conference GIS – From Space to Territory: Theories and Methods of Spatio-Temporal Reasoning,* LNCS, 1992.

Grabowski, J. & Weiß, P. (1996). Das Präpositionsinventar als Determinante des Verstehens von Raumpräpositionen: *vor* und *hinter* in fünf Sprachen. In: E. Lang & G. Zifonun (eds.), *Deutsch–typologisch* (pp. 289–311). Berlin: Walter de Gruyter.

Habel, Ch. (1990). Propositional and depictorial representations of spatial knowledge: The case of path concepts. In: R. Studer (ed.): *Natural Language and Logic* (pp. 94–117). Berlin: Springer.

Habel, Ch. & Eschenbach, C.: (1995). Abstrakte Räumlichkeit in der Kognition, *Kognitionswissenschaft, 4,* 171–176.

Hernández, D. (1992). *Qualitative Representation of Spatial Knowledge.* Doctoral Dissertation, Technische Universität München.

Herskovits, A. (1986). *Language and Spatial Cognition. An Interdisciplinary Study of the Prepositions in English.* Cambridge, England: Cambridge University Press.

Hilbert, D. (1956). *Grundlagen der Geometrie.* Stuttgart: Teubner.

Levelt, W.J.M. (1984). Some perceptual limitations on talking about space. In: A.J. van Doorn, W.A. van der Grind & J.J. Koenderink (eds.): *Limits in Perception* (pp. 323–358). Utrecht: VNU Science Press.

Miller, G.A. & Johnson-Laird, Ph.N. (1976). *Language and Perception* Cambridge: Cambridge UP.

Retz-Schmidt, G. (1988). Various views on spatial prepositions. *AI Magazine, 9,* 95–105.

Schlieder, Ch. (1995). Reasoning about ordering. In: A. Frank & W. Kuhn (eds.): *Spatial Information Theory. A Theoretical Basis for GIS. Proceedings of the International Conference COSIT'95, Semmering, Austria, September 1995* (pp. 341–349). Berlin: Springer-Verlag.

Tversky, B. (1996). Spatial perspective in descriptions. In: P. Bloom, M.A. Peterson, L. Nadel & M.F. Garrett (eds.): *Language and Space* (pp. 463–491). Cambridge, MA: MIT-Press.

Wunderlich, D. (1986). Raum und die Struktur des Lexikons. In: H.G. Bosshardt (ed.), *Perspektiven auf Sprache* (pp. 213–231).

Representation and Processing of Qualitative Orientation Knowledge

Ralf Röhrig

Universität Hamburg, Vogt-Kölln-Str. 30, 22527 Hamburg
email: roehrig@informatik.uni-hamburg.de

Abstract. Several approaches have been proposed to the representation of qualitative spatial knowledge that address various aspects of the spatial domain. In this paper the potential of mutual reconstruction of the employed concepts and the integration of the applied inference calculi are examined. In order to find a common basis for the investigation of the various spatial concepts, we restrict ourselves to approaches addressing orientation knowledge. An extended version of the CYCORD theory serves as a tool for both the problem of mutual reconstruction and the question of integration. The notion of orientation knowledge is based on points and directions. The basic relation in CYCORDs is the cyclic order of directions, *cycord*. The concepts used in the other approaches to the representation and processing of qualitative orientation knowledge can be defined in terms of this *cycord* relation. This approach gives us an opportunity to see how essential parts of knowledge represented in one formalism can be translated into another language. Furthermore, the formal treatment of CYCORDs provides us with an integrated inference calculus, though in general at higher cost than the specialized calculi of the other approaches.

Introduction

Various approaches to the representation and processing of qualitative orientation knowledge have been developed recently. Their applications cover domains like natural language understanding, geographical information systems, cognitive modelling, and robot navigation. A geometric approach handling triangle orientations over configuration of points in the plane is taken in [16]. Systems of cone shaped sectors as positional reference for orientation relations are used in [4], [5], [9], and [13]. Qualitative descriptions of angles between triple of points in the plane are used in [11]. Order relations between projections of objects to one-dimensional axes are examined in [4], [8], [10], and [13]. An overview of selected references is given in [6]. In order to understand the basic notion of orientation we examine the various approaches with the two following questions in mind:

(1) Can the different concepts in the various systems be integrated in a single inference calculus?

(2) Which type of information given in one formal system can be expressed in one of the other systems?

In order to answer those two questions, we provide in the next section an axiomatisation of a calculus based on directions and points. The calculus is a formal treatment of the CYCORD theory introduced informally in [15]. In section 3 we will show how the different concepts of orientation in selected approaches to qualitative spatial reasoning translate into cyclic orders of directions. Rather than providing the whole list of formal proofs we give some evidence showing that the inference rules and composition tables from the orientation approaches become theorems in CYCORD theory. This provides an answer to the first question: the CYCORD theory serves as an inference calculus that handles most of the different orientation concepts used in the approaches to the representation of qualitative orientation knowledge. In section 4 we show that the CYCORD theory also provides an answer to the second question: by treating the reference orientations as entities in the CYCORD calculus, we can formally combine orientation calculi that use different reference systems. In the final section we consider the connection of CYCORDs to permutation sequences as used in computational geometry and provide some complexity results originating from the theory of cyclic orders.

CYCORDs

The basic type of entities in the CYCORD calculus is the direction. A direction can be characterized in several ways:

a) as a vector ignoring the length,

b) as an oriented line ignoring the location in space,

c) as a point on a circle for graphical purposes.

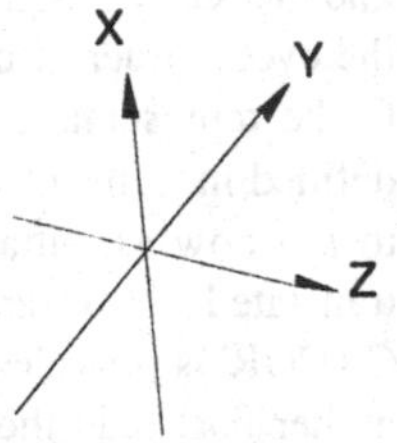

Since both terms, *orientation* and *direction* are used in the literature on orientation approaches, we use them as synonyms throughout this text. The basic relation in the CYCORD calculus is the cyclic order of directions in the plane represented by the ternary predicate *cycord*. If three directions X, Y, and Z are embedded in the same plane and are ordered in a clockwise manner we represent this fact as *cycord(X,Y,Z)*, or X-Y-Z as an abbreviation (cf. Fig. 1).

Fig. 1: Orientations X, Y, and Z are cyclically ordered clockwise. This is denoted by a CYCORD as X-Y-Z.

The second type of entity in the CYCORD theory is the point. The connection between points and directions is established by the function *direction* which takes an ordered pair of points as argument and results in the direction of the oriented line connecting the two points.

Some of the approaches to qualitative orientation knowledge use equidistant rasterings of the circle in order to define orientation relations. Since this results in numeric angles such as 45° or 90° between the reference orientations there is an ongoing discussion whether to call these approaches qualitative or not. In spite of this argument we show how the corresponding orientation concepts can be handled by the CYCORD calculus by augmenting it with a function rot_α which takes a direction as argument and gives a new direction resulting from the argument by rotating it by the angle α. The angle α will be different for different orientation calculi, but will be fixed within one system. Instead of allowing full arithmetic on angles we shall provide the CYCORD calculus with a set of axioms characterizing the function rot_α.

In the following we give an overview of the CYCORD calculus before we start to explain the axioms in detail:

Types
     Direction, Point
Functions
     rot_α: Direction a Direction;   X a $rot_\alpha(X)$
     direction: Point × Point a Direction;   A,B a AB
Predicate
     cycord: Direction × Direction × Direction;
                  cycord(X,Y,Z) ≡ X-Y-Z
Axioms
     axioms of cyclic order: $\forall$ X,Y,Z,U: Direction,

     (1a) X-Y-Z $\Rightarrow$ Y-Z-X   (rotation)

     (1b) X-Y-Z $\Rightarrow$ ¬(Y=Z)   (irreflixivity)

     (1c) X-Y-Z $\Rightarrow$ ¬(X-Z-Y)   (asymmetry)

     (1d) X-Y-Z, X-Z-U $\Rightarrow$ X-Y-U   (bounded transitivity)

     (1e) X-Y-Z $\lor$ X-Z-Y   (saturatedness)

     axioms of rotation: $\forall$ X,Y,Z: Direction, $\forall$ i,j,k $\in$ N$_0$, $\forall$ α $\in$ R,

     (2a) X-Y-Z $\Rightarrow$ $rot_\alpha(X)$- $rot_\alpha(Y)$- $rot_\alpha(Z)$ (splicing)

     (2b) 0≤i<j<k<360/α $\Rightarrow$ $rot_\alpha^i(X)$-$rot_\alpha^j(X)$-$rot_\alpha^k(X)$
                                                        (system of directions)

     (2c) $rot_\alpha^i(rot_\alpha^j(X))$ = $rot_\alpha^{i+j}(X)$ (composition)
     (2d) $rot_{360}(X)$=X   (circularity)

     axioms of direction: $\forall$ A,B,C: Point,

     (3a) AB-AC-BC-BA-CA-CB $\lor$ CB-CA-BA-BC-AC-AB   (triangle condition)
     (3b) AB = $rot_{180}(BA)$ (opposite direction)

The axioms of the CYCORD calculus are presented in three blocks: the first block of axioms describes a general saturated partial cyclic order. Axiom (1a) makes an ordered triple a cyclic list: three elements are ordered clockwise, no matter at which element we start to count. Axiom (1b) makes it an irreflexive cyclic order, because comparing two elements in one CYCORD contains no information: two elements are necessarily cyclically ordered both clockwise and counter-clockwise. The asymmetry axiom (1c) ensures that the circle is only traversed once when picking up the arguments of a CYCORD. The utilization of transitivity may seem to be restricted to the scheme presented in axiom (1d), but together with axiom (1a) more schemes become applicable. For example, X-Y-Z, Y-W-Z $\Rightarrow$ X-W-Z is also valid. Nevertheless, the intuitive scheme X-Y-Z, Y-Z-$W$$\Rightarrow$ X-Y-W is not valid in general. Given, for example, the cyclic order a-b-c-d; a partial cyclic order containing a-c-d, c-d-b, and a-b-c can be derived. Due to asymmetry, since a-b-c is true, a-c-b cannot be true, and so, the intuitive transitivity scheme is not valid. The saturatedness axiom (1e) reflects the fact that in the plane all directions are ordered in a total way, i.e. any three directions are either ordered clockwise or counter-clockwise. This is a very intuitive axiom, but it is also one of those that make the CYCORD calculus computationally expensive (see section 5). Even though (1e) definitely holds for directions in the plane, as shown in the next section the inferences of other orientation approaches can be drawn by the CYCORD calculus without the utilization of this axiom.

The second block of axioms characterizes the rotation function. Axiom (2a) states that cyclic orders stay invariant under rotation. From (2a) we can derive directly $rot_\alpha^i(X)$-$rot_\alpha^j(Y)$-$rot_\alpha^k(X) \Rightarrow rot_\alpha^{i+l}(X)$-$rot_\alpha^{j+l}(Y)$-$rot_\alpha^{k+l}(X)$, which means that, if we know any relation between two systems of rotated axes, then we can derive all other such relations. This is the main rule for the combination of different systems of reference axes in section 3 and 4. Axiom (2b) ensures the cyclic order of successive applications of a rotation by some fixed angle, as long as the overall angle of rotation is less than 360°. Axiom (2c) shows how to handle multiple applications of a fixed rotation without allowing for full arithmetic on angles. Axiom (2d) states that a rotation by 360° is the *identity* function.

The triangle property (3a) is best demonstrated in Fig. 2, where the order of the orientations can be read off the outer circles. A triangle formed by three non collinear points A, B and C is oriented either clockwise or counter-clockwise. In the case of clockwise orientation the cyclic order of the six orientations originating from these three points can be read off Fig. 2a. In the case of counter-clockwise the cyclic order can be read off Fig. 2b. No other orderings of the six orientations are possible. For the case that a direction originates from a pair of points, axiom (3b) shows the relation between the functions *rotation* and *opposite direction*.

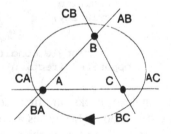

Fig. 2

a) A, B, and C form a clockwise oriented triangle. The CYCORD of the six orientations is AB-AC-BC-BA-CA-CB

b) A, B, and C form a counter-clockwise oriented triangle. The CYCORD of the six orientations is AB-CB-CA-BA-BC-AC

Integration

In this section we show how the basic notions of some other approaches to the representation of qualitative orientation knowledge can be encoded in the CYCORD theory. Instead of full proofs some evidence for the theorems is given in that it is shown that the basic inference rules of these approaches are theorems of the CYCORD theory.

The existing approaches can be classified whether they allow two or three points be related in a single fact. Typical relations comparing two points are *A is in front of B*, *A is north of B, the projection of A on the X-axis comes before the projection of B*. In these cases, a system of fixed reference orientations is used to determine the relative position of two points. A common way to model this type of relation is to use a sector model. One point is the reference point of the relation, and the fixed reference orientations impose a system of oriented lines through this point. This results in a cone shaped partition of the plane. The orientation relation is associated with the sector where the second point is located. The number of sectors varies with the level of granularity. In [9], for example, a 4-sector model is proposed using the orientation

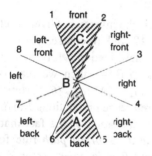
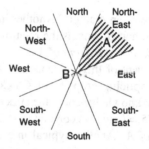

Fig. 3

a) A is in the back of B, C is in front of B   b) A is north-east of B

relations *front*, *back*, *left*, and *right*, and an 8-sector model is proposed using additional relations *left-front, left-back, right-front*, and *right-back* (cf. Fig. 3a). A system of cardinal directions *North, South, East, West*, together with the intermediate directions *North-West, North-East, South-East*, and *South-West* is used in [4] (cf. Fig. 3b). This type of information can be expressed in terms of a cyclic order of orientations in that the direction of the bounds of the sectors become fixed reference orientations (1 to 8 in Fig. 3a). The direction of the oriented line from the reference point of the relation to the second point is then compared with theses newly defined reference orientations. For example, the fact that *A is in the back of B* can be expressed by the CYCORD *5-BA-6*, and the fact that *C is in front of B* as *1-BC-2* (see Fig. 3a). This works because the orientation of the bounds is the same in every reference point (remember we are ordering orientations rather than oriented lines). This informally introduced way of translating sector model relations to CYCORDs generalizes to the following theorem:

Theorem 1

Binary orientation relations based on fixed sector systems can be encoded in the CYCORD theory.

In order to verify this proposition, we look at some of the inferences in [4] and in [9]. Composition of orientation relations is the major inference scheme in both systems: Given a relation between A and B, another relation between B and C, what is the

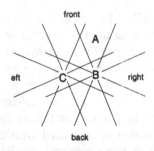

Fig. 4 If A is in front of B, and B is to the right of C, then A is in front of, right-front, or right of C

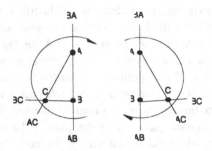

Fig. 5: AC is always on the shortest path between AB and BC.

relation between A and C? Another inference scheme is the inversion: Given a relation between A and B, what is the relation between B and A? And, of course, *if A is in the back of B, then B in front of A* is one of the inferences described in [9]. If we translate the antecedent of this inference rule to CYCORDs as *5-BA-6*, then we may deduce from the splicing property of CYCORDs $rot_{45°}{}^4(5)$-$rot_{45°}{}^4(BA)$-$rot_{45°}{}^4(6)$. From some additional knowledge about the structure of the fixed reference orientations *1* to *8*, such as $rot_{45°}{}^4(5)=1$ etc., we conclude *1-AB-2*, which is the translation of the fact that *B is in front of A*. Another typical inference rule in [9] is the *shortest path* rule for the composition scheme: *if A is in some sector X of B, and B is in some sector Y of C, then A is in one of the following sectors of C: X, Y, or any sector intersecting the shortest path between any point from X and any point from Y*. For example, if *A is in front of B*, and *B is to the right of C*, then
A is in front of, right-front, or right of C (cf. Fig. 4). In terms of CYCORDs this rule corresponds to the triangle property. Depending on the angle between AB and BC, whether it is less or more then 180°, we get *AB-BC-BA* or *BA-BC-AB* (cf. Fig. 5). Now, the triangle property gives us *AB-AC-BC* or *BC-AC-AB*, which means that AC is always on the shortest path between AB and BC.

Approaches that represent knowledge about the ordering of projections of objects along certain axes can be seen as a special case of the sector model (cf. Fig. 6). On an axis X, the projection of point A lies before the

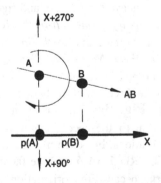

Fig. 6 The fact that the projection of A comes before the projection of B on some axis X corresponds to the circular order $rot_{90}{}^3(X)$-AB-$rot_{90}(X)$.

projection of point B iff the orientations $X+270°$, AB, and $X+90°$ are cyclically ordered clockwise, which is expressed in terms of CYCORDs as $rot_{90°}{}^3(X)\text{-}AB\text{-}rot_{90°}(X)$. These considerations lead to the following theorem:

Theorem 2

A binary order relation on an axis can be encoded in the CYCORD theory.

Orderings of projections are used in [8], [10], and [13]. Projections of connected objects result in intervals, and the inference calculus consists of a composition table for interval relations as it was first introduced in [1]. For a special class of these relations, the so called continuous endpoint relations (cf. [2]), these relations are expressible by conjunctions of linear end point orderings, and therefore, also by CYCORDs. The driving inference rule for linear orders is transitivity: *If A < B, and B < C, then A < C.* As in the general case of sector models, the antecedents of this inference rule translate to CYCORD as $rot_{90°}{}^3(X)\text{-}AB\text{-}rot_{90°}(X)$ and $rot_{90°}{}^3(X)\text{-}BC\text{-}rot_{90°}(X)$, i.e. we either have $rot_{90°}{}^3(X)\text{-}AB\text{-}BC\text{-}rot_{90°}(X)$ or $rot_{90°}{}^3(X)\text{-}BC\text{-}AB\text{-}rot_{90°}(X)$. From the triangle condition we deduce either $rot_{90°}{}^3(X)\text{-}AB\text{-}CA\text{-}BC\text{-}rot_{90°}(X)$ or $rot_{90°}{}^3(X)\text{-}BC\text{-}CA\text{-}AB\text{-}rot_{90°}(X)$, which in both cases reduces to $rot_{90°}{}^3(X)\text{-}CA\text{-}rot_{90°}(X)$. This is the translation of the consequence that *A is in front of C.*

Typical orientation relations comparing three points are *A, B, and C form a clockwise oriented triangle, A is to the left of the line BC,* or *A is front-left w.r.t. the vector AB.* Knowledge expressed by triangle orientation is of the same type as knowledge whose facts relate a point and an oriented line originating from two other points. Qualitatively, an oriented line separates the plane into three disjoint areas, a left and a right semi-plane and the line itself. A point A is to the left of the line CB iff the points A, B, and C form a clockwise oriented triangle (cf. Fig. 2a). As was shown for the triangle property of CYCORDs, all the orientations originating from any two of the three points are cyclically ordered in a characteristic way: $AB\text{-}AC\text{-}BC\text{-}BA\text{-}CA\text{-}CB$. As can be seen from Fig. 2b, if *A is to the right of the line CB*, then the corresponding orientations are ordered in a totally different way: $AB\text{-}CB\text{-}CA\text{-}BA\text{-}BC\text{-}AC$. There is no special notion for the collinear case in the CYCORD theory. Collinearity of three points A, B, and C is divided into three subclasses where either $AB=BC$, or $BA=AC$, or $BC=CA$ holds.

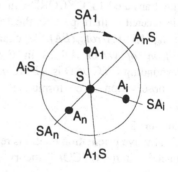

Fig. 7: The location of A_1, A_2, and A_3 around S is described by CYCORDs as $SA_1\text{-}A_3S\text{-}SA_2\text{-}A_1S\text{-}SA_3\text{-}A_2S$.

Theorem 3

The fact that a point lies to the left or the right of an oriented line can be uniquely encoded in the CYCORD theory.

The notion of a *panorama* of reference points $A_1,...,A_n$ as seen from a point S introduced in [16] is the total cyclic order of the oriented lines SA_i and A_iS. Since the common intersection of all these lines in S is trivially given, the panorama can informationally equivalently be represented by the total cyclic order of their orientations, i.e. by a CYCORD containing all orientations SA_i and A_iS (cf. Fig. 7).

Theorem 4

Panoramas can be encoded in the CYCORD theory.

The basic inference in [16] is based on the fact that the *panorama* of reference points $A_1,...,A_n$ as seen from a point S uniquely determines the location of S with respect to any oriented line A_iA_j in the configuration. Now, suppose, from point S we can see A_1 and A_2, and from the panorama around S we get the total cyclic order SA_1-SA_2-A_1S-A_2S. From the triangle rule we conclude SA_1-SA_2-A_1A_2-A_1S-A_2S-A_2A_1 which encodes the fact *that S is to the right of the line A_2A_1.* Thus we have shown how a panorama of a point encoded in terms of CYCORDs determines its qualitative location w.r.t. a line of the configuration. We claim without proof that the following is also a theorem of CYCORD theory: given the qualitative location of a point with respect to all oriented lines in a configuration, the panorama can be derived.

In [5] and in [11] a local quadrant model is used to define a relation between an oriented line AB and an additional point C (cf. Fig. 8). *left-front, right-front, right-back,* and *left-back* is used in [5], while [11] takes a more geometric approach naming the quadrants by a pair of 1) a *left/right* distinction concerning the location of point C, and 2) an *acute/obtuse* distinction concerning the angle (A,B,C). Since all lines meet in B, these relations can be translated to CYCORDs in that orientation BC is ordered with respect to the total cyclic order AB-$rot_{90}(AB)$-BA-$rot_{90}(BA)$. For example, if C *is in right-front of vector AB* as in Fig. 8, then the corresponding CYCORD is AB-BC-$rot_{90}(AB)$. From this observation we formulate the following theorem:

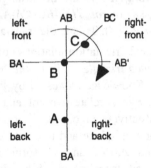

Fig. 8 The fact that C is right-front of some vector AB is represented in terms of CYCORDs as AB-BC-AB'.

Theorem 5

Qualitative orientation relations referring to a local quadrant model can be encoded in the CYCORD theory.

Inferences in [5] are compositions of a relation comparing line AB with C and a relation between BC and D to a relation between the line AB and D. All compositions are collected in a composition table. Each entry from this table can be seen as a single inference rule. Instead of showing, that all 15×15 inference rules are theorems in the CYCORD theory, we restrict ourselves here to one example. All other proofs follow the same scheme. *If C is right-front of AB, and D is right-front of BC, then*, following the composition table in [5], we can conclude that D *is to the right of AB.* In terms of CYCORDs the first antecedent translates to AB-BC-$rot_{90}(AB)$ and we can infer from the splicing condition order AB-BC-$rot_{90}(AB)$-$rot_{90}(BC)$-BA (cf. Fig. 9).

Analogously, the second antecedent translates to CD-CD-$rot_{90^\circ}(BC)$. By the triangle property we infer BC-BD-CD-$rot_{90^\circ}(BC)$, and by transitivity we can conclude AB-BC-BD-CD-$rot_{90^\circ}(BC)$-BA which contains AB-BD-BA. This is the translation of the fact that D *is to the right of* AB, the conclusion of the first inference rule in [5].

Spatial Information Pipes

In the last section, we showed for a selection of existing approaches that the concepts for the representation of qualitative orientation knowledge

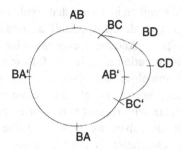

Fig. 9: From AB-BC-AB' and BC-CD-BC' follows AB-BD-BA (AB' is short for $rot_{90^\circ}(AB)$)

can be expressed in terms of CYCORDs, and that the corresponding inferences become theorems in the CYCORD theory. For that reason, the axiomatization of CYCORDs provides us with an integrated inference calculus. The transformation of spatial concepts into CYCORDs is not necessarily reversible, i.e. not every fact given in terms of CYCORDs can be expressed in terms of every other approach. For example, the CYCORD AB-CD-BA represents the fact that the orientation formed by the points C and D points to the right of the orientation formed by A and B. This type of information is not expressible in a sector model like in [4] and [9]. Nor is this type of knowledge expressible in terms of orientation relations as defined in [5], since there only oriented lines with one point in common are compared.

Nevertheless, in general, some of the information from one system can be represented in another system. For example, if A *is behind* B in terms of [9], and C *is in front of* B, then C must be above the perpendicular line crossing the AB in B. While this is graphically clear from Fig. 10, CYCORDs provide us with a formal instrument to verify this sort of inference: A *back* B translates to 5-BA-6; from the angle addition property we get the complete circular order 5-BA-6-7-$rot_{90^\circ}(BA)$-8-1-AB-2-3-$rot_{90^\circ}(AB)$-4; C *front* B translates to 1-BC-2, and from transitivity we can conclude $rot_{90^\circ}(BA)$-BC-$rot_{90^\circ}(AB)$, which corresponds to the resulting fact.

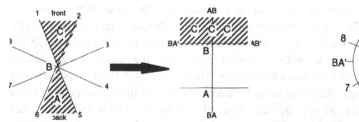

Fig. 10: Spatial Information Pipe

The information that A is in the back of B and C is in the front of B can be used to conclude that C must be above the perpendicular line crossing the line(A,B) in B. In terms of CYCORDs: 5-BA-6 and 1-BC-2 then BA'-BC-AB'. (AB' is short for $rot_{90^\circ}(AB)$)

We call an inference that combines the concepts of two different calculi a *spatial information pipe*. Another example for an spatial information pipe is the following: Given that some object is to the right of us with respect to an 8-sector model, and we are heading north, again with respect to the corresponding 8-sector model, then we know that the object under consideration is north-east, east, or south-east of us (cf. Fig. 11). In terms of CYCORDs the first fact could be represented as *1-nose-2-3-object-4* and the second fact would yield *11-nose-12*. From the splicing property we get for the first fact *1-nose-2-rot$_{45°}$(nose)-3-object-4-rot$_{45°}^3$(nose)-5* and for the second we get *12-rot$_{45°}$(nose)-13-14-rot$_{45°}^3$(nose)-15*.   Now,

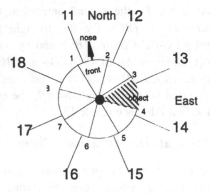

Fig. 11: If we are heading north, than an object to our right is north-east, east, or south-east of us.

from transitivity we can deduce *12-rot$_{45°}$(nose)-3-object-4-rot$_{45°}^3$(nose)-15*, which reduces to *12-object-15* and is the representation of the fact that the object is *north-east, east, or south-east*.

Utilizing spatial information pipes is an alternative to the integration of the inference calculi to the more powerful, but also more expensive CYCORD calculus (see discussion below). Instead of integrating the systems, the results of the single inference processes are combined. The CYCORD theory is only used off-line to verify the validity of the Spatial Information Pipe.

Spatial information pipes allow us to use different orientation concepts in one and the same application. The reasons for doing so can be manifold. For example, information may come from different sources such as vision and natural language understanding or different levels of granularity are used at the same time. Or again, as in the last example, different systems of orientation relations have to be used in one application.

Discussion

CYCORDs have not been developed for their own sake. On the one hand, they provide us with a common semantics for existing approaches to qualitative orientation knowledge. CYCORDs in turn can be expressed in Tarski's elementary geometry [18], which provides us with a logically complete axiomatisation for CYCORDs. On the other hand, they provide us with a powerful tool for the analysis of existing approaches to qualitative orientation knowledge. Their formally defined properties give us an inference calculus which can be compared with respect to logical completeness and complexity to the more specific calculi mentioned above. First results show that for several approaches the CYCORD theory allows for strictly more inferences even though their current properties do not form a complete axiomatisation in a logical sense. A consequence of this result is that the examined approaches are not complete either, which was, of course, commonly known before. An illustrative example is the so called *Indian tent*, where *A*, *B* and *C* form a clockwise oriented triangle, and *D* lies to the left of the line AB and to the right of the line CB (cf. Fig. 12). Geometrically and intuitively, from these facts follows that D is above (or, formally, to the left of) line AC. But even though in most systems it is possible to express the single facts as well as the result, none of the examined inference calculi is able to compute this simple inference.

In the CYCORD theory, this inference is a theorem, but the costs for additional inferences are high. We extended the NP-completeness result for general cyclic orders from [7] to the more specific CYCORD calculus while for some of the existing approaches better results are known.

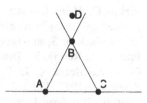

Fig. 12: Indian tent
A, B, and C form a clockwise oriented triangle, and D lies to the left of the line AB and to the right of the line CB. It follows from CYCORDs that D is to the left of AC

With CYCORDs, we can distinguish the same configurations of points in the plane as we can with permutation sequences familiar from combinatorial geometry. For a review of the role of permutation sequences in qualitative spatial reasoning see [17]. Permutation sequences are designed as a data structure to store complete orientation knowledge about a configuration of points in the plane. Algorithms in combinatorial geometry are concerned with the costs for deriving this type of knowledge from a set of points given by their coordinates [3]. Qualitative spatial reasoning, on the other hand, is concerned with the representation and processing of partial knowledge. CYCORDs are designed for expressing partial knowledge about configurations of points in the plane, and for reasoning about sets of facts on the basis of a structural description.

Acknowledgment

I would like to thank Christina Freksa for guiding this work as director of the DFG project *Rauminferenz (Spatial Inference)*. The Grant FR-806/7-1 from DFG supporting this project is gratefully appreciated. Also many thanks to Longin Jan Latecki, Lars Kulik and Christoph Dornheim for their help with the formalisation of the technical material and for proof reading the text.

References

[1] Allen, J.F.: Maintaining knowledge about temporal intervals. in CACM 26 (11) (1983) 832-843.

[2] Nebel, B., Bürckert, H.-J.: Reasoning about Temporal Relations: A Maximal Tractable Subclass of Allen's Interval Algebra. In Proceedings of AAAI-94, AAAI Press, 1994.

[3] Edelsbrunner, H.: Algorithms in Combinatorial Geometry, (EETCS Monographs on Theoretical Computer Science) Brauer, Rozenberg, Salomaa (eds.), Springer, 1987.

[4] Frank, A.: Qualitative Spatial Reasoning with Cardinal Directions. In the Proceedings of the Seventh Austrian Conference on Artificial Intelligence, Wienna, pp. 157-167, Springer, Berlin, 1992.

[5] Freksa, C.: Using Orientation Information for Qualitative Spatial Reasoning. In the Proceedings of the International Conference on GIS - From Space to Territory: Theory and Methods of Spatio-Temporal Reasoning, LNCS; Pisa, September 21-23, 1992

[6] Freksa, C., Röhrig, R.: Dimensions of Qualitative Spatial Reasoning. In [14], 1993.

[7] Galil, Z., Megiddo, N.: Cyclic ordering is NP-complete. In Theoretical Computer Science 5 (1977) 179-182. © North-Holland Publishing Company

[8] Güsgen, H.: Spatial reasoning based on Allen's temporal logic. TR-89-049, International Computer Science Institute, Berkley, 1989.

[9] Hernández, D: Relative representation of spatial knowledge: the 2-D case. In Mark, D.M., Frank, A.U., editors, Cognitive and Linguistic Aspects of Geographic Space, NATO Advanced Studies Institute, pp. 373-385. Kluver, Dotrecht, 1991.

[10] Jungert, E. The observers point of view: An extension to symbolic projections. In A. Frank, I. Campari & U. Formentini (Eds.), Theory and Methods of Spatio-Temporal Reasoning in Geographic Space (pp. 179-195). Berlin: Springer, 1992.

[11] Latecki, L.J., Röhrig, R.: Orientation and Qualitative Angles for Spatial Reasoning. In Proc. of the 13th International Joint Conference on Artificial Intelligence, (pp. 1544-1549), Chambery, France, 1993.

[12] Meggido, M.: Partial and Complete cyclic Orders. In Bulletin of the Am. Math. Soc., Vol. 82, No. 2, March 1976.

[13] Muckerjee, A., Joe, G.: A qualitative model for space. In Proceedings of AAAI-90, AAAI Press, 1990.

[14] N. Piera Carreté and M.G. Singh (Eds.): QUALITATIVE REASONING AND DECISION TECHNOLOGIES, ©CIMNE, Barcelona 1993.

[15]   Röhrig, R. (1994): A Theory for Qualitative Spatial Reasoning Based on Order Relations. In Proceedings of AAAI-94, AAAI Press, 1994.

[16]   Schlieder, C.: Representing Visible Locations for Qualitative Navigation In [14], 1993.

[17]   Schlieder, C.: Ordering information and symbolic projection. In Chang et. al. (eds), Intelligent image database systems, pp.115-140, 1996.

[18]   Tarski, A.: What is elementary geometry. In J. Hintikka (1969, ed.): The Philosophy of Mathematics. OUP: Oxford.

A Contribution to the Question of Authenticity of *Rhesus* Using Part-of-Speech Tagging

Bernd Ludwig

University of Erlangen-Nuremberg, Germany
Department of Artifical Intelligence (IMMD 8)
bdludwig@cip.informatik.uni-erlangen.de

Abstract. This paper presents the results of an experiment to decide the question of authenticity of the supposedly spurious *Rhesus*—a attic tragedy sometimes credited to EURIPIDES. The experiment involves the use of statistics in order to test whether significant deviations in the distribution of word categories between *Rhesus* and the other works of EURIPIDES can or cannot be found. To count frequencies of word categories in the corpus, a part-of-speech tagger for Greek has been implemented. Some special techniques for reducing the problem of sparse data are used resulting in an accuracy of ca. 96.6%.

1 Introduction

1.1 The Philological Problem

In the tradition of ancient Greek texts it sometimes happens that, due to a number of different reasons a text is credited incorrectly to a certain author. It is the—sometimes very difficult—task of classical philology to detect these erroneous assignments and, if possible, to correct them. The methods used for this task and the results achieved by them are often the subject of strong criticism either because the methods are considered inadequate or because the results are doubted for some reason.

One of the methods commonly used consists in searching for special stylistic properties of a given text and comparing them with the personal style of possible Greek authors of the text in question. By these means researchers aim at matching properties of the text with the characteristics of a given writer in order to declare him the author for whom they have searched or, conversely, at finding enough contradictions between the text's and the writer's stylistic properties to be able to negate the authorship of the writer.

One special technique is called "stylometry"[1]. It makes use of several methods from mathematical statistics. More specifically, it uses statistical tests to reject a proposed hypothesis by arguing with quantitative data gained from the text and writer's work.

---

[1] The relation between syntax, vocabulary and style is explained by Hockey ([8]) and Muller ([15])

The first time statistics were used to enlighten the authenticity of *Rhesus* was in 1891[2] and another publication followed in 1893[3].

Although there are many publications[4] reporting empirical results of statistical studies, the debate upon the appropriate methods for stylometry is continuing. What seems to be part of the *comunis opinio* not only among classical philologists is the following:

– The collected data should be independent from content and genre of the text and
– should give quantitative analysis of unconscious effects of writing in order to obtain some type of genetic fingerprint.
– One should not mix up the genre of the texts included in the investigation, because genre-dependent effects can cancel the individual behaviour of a certain author.

The main hypothesis of stylometry is that a typical distribution of certain observations (e.g. frequency of function words) can be assigned to every author, and any text written by him follows this distribution up to a deviation which is statistically irrelevant.

Experiments have shown that two different authors differ in their very own way to distribute word categories in their text[5]. They consequently can be distinguished by computing a distribution of word categories that is typical of their works. Furthermore, the typical distribution for a single author is especially influenced by two facts:

– the literary type of the text ([13], pp. 1–4)
– the author's age and changes in writing style throughout his lifetime

From this observation it follows that there is no typical distribution in EU-RIPIDES' entire works, but only for texts from several limited temporal periods of his total production time.

To address the question of authenticity of *Rhesus* we compute the distribution of word categories in EURIPIDES' works. Doing this we want to try and find the different stylistic periods in his work and then to compare the distribution found in *Rhesus* with the distribution characterizing each period.

The corpus of EURPIDES is available on the *Thesaurus Linguae Graecae* CD-ROM developed by the University of California at Irvine. We have implemented a part-of-speech tagger for attic Greek to determine the needed word categories.

---

[2] L. Eysert, *Rhesus im Lichte des euripideischen Sprachgebrauchs*, Progr. Böhm-Leipa I (1891)

[3] J. C. Rolfe, *The Tragedy of Rhesus*, Harvard Studies in Classical Philology IV (1893)

[4] http://www.ceth.rutgers.edu/info/biblio/index.html gives an extensive bibliography on this topic.

[5] Another study that uses word categories as discriminator among different authors is reported by Gurney ([7])

2 Part-of-Speech Tagging

2.1 Mathematical Foundations

In order to count categories of any text, we need to solve the problem of assigning a sequence of categories to a given sequence of words, i.e. to the sequence of words forming the text actually under investigation.

Using a part-of-speech tagger, for any given sequence $W := (w_1, \ldots, w_K)$ one can estimate the probability of all possible sequences $C := (c_1, \ldots, c_K)$ of categories for W. In part-of-speech tagging a special sequence C^{opt} is a solution for W if and only if it maximizes for all possible C the probability

$$P(C_1 \ldots C_K | w_1 \ldots w_K) = \frac{P(w_1 \ldots w_K | C_1 \ldots C_K) \cdot P(C_1 \ldots C_K)}{P(w_1 \ldots w_K)} \qquad (1)$$

This says that we search for the sequence $(c_1, \ldots, c_K)$ that it most probable when the sequence of words $(w_1, \ldots, w_K)$ is considered. In other words, (1) is an optimal approximation to the grammatically correct sequence of categories valid for W. Due to the enormous amount of data necessary for the computation of the probabilities involved in the term described above, it is impossible to compute a solution directly via this formula. But to get this complexity under control, we may assume (see e.g. [2]) that

1. for any i in $(c_1, \ldots, c_K)$ only the $n+1$ next categories are dependent of each other, which means that

$$P(c_i | c_{i-1} \ldots c_1) \approx P(c_i | c_{i-1} \ldots c_{i-n}) \qquad (2)$$

2. for any i in $(w_1, \ldots, w_K)$, the category c_i assigned to w_i is not dependent of the preceeding and succeeding categories. So we have

$$P(w_1 \ldots w_i \ldots w_K | c_1 \ldots c_K) \approx P(w_1 \ldots w_{i-1} | c_1 \ldots c_{i-1}) \cdot P(w_i | c_i) \cdot$$
$$\cdot P(w_{i+1} \ldots w_K | c_{i+1} \ldots c_K)$$
$$\approx \prod_{i=1}^{K} P(w_i | c_i) \qquad (3)$$

Using (2) and (3), we now can approximate $P(w_1 \ldots w_K | C_1 \ldots C_K)$:

$$P(w_1 \ldots w_K | C_1 \ldots C_K) \approx \prod_{i=1}^{K} P(C_i | C_{i-1} \ldots C_{i-n}) \cdot P(w_i | C_i) \qquad (4)$$

As it is known from probability theory, (4) is the defining equation for a Hidden Markov Model (HMM)[6]. For HMMs there exist algorithms for an efficient solution for (4). All data we need, are the following two tables:

---

[6] From the viewpoint of automata theory, one can understand a HMM as a stochastic finite state automaton (FSA).

- one table for $P(c_i|c_{i-1} \ldots c_{i-n})$ (*n-gram probabilities*)
- and one for $P(w_i|c_i)$ (lexical probabilities)

These probabilities have to be computed before the tagger is used for the disambiguation of text. The process of computing the probabilities is called training.

To train part-of-speech taggers for modern languages such as English people normally use manually annotated corpora containing about two million words. By using corpora of this size which are accessible easily it is possible to approximate very closely the true distribution of part-of-speech tags in the training set. This follows from elementary probability theory. The technique used widely for achieving such an approximation is maximum likelihood estimation (see Cutting et al. ([4]) for more detailed information of how to use and implement MLE for part-of-speech tagging).

The problem with EURIPIDES' corpus—as far as part-of-speech tagging is concerned—is its size. For it contains only about 10% of the two million words mentioned above. This fact leads to very low n-gram and lexical frequencies producing unreliable results when the necessary probabilities discussed earlier in this paper (and in any paper about part-of-speech tagging) are calculated. Gale and Church ([3]) give a very precise and detailed discussion of problems caused by low frequencies. Another analysis of the tagging error rate and of how to increase a tagger's accuracy is presented by Kempe ([10]).

Another problem arising from small corpora is more particular to Greek and—from a more general point of view—to any (highly) inflected language. Inflected or morphologically constructed forms can decrease dramatically the frequency of surface forms with respect to the frequency of their stems or lemmata, especially if surface forms are counted as if they were different words instead of being lemmatized. And besides of inflection there are other morphological elements that are characteristic for certain word categories and can be combined with different stems to form new words. For example, in German, English, and Italian there exist among others the following suffixes:

German	English	Italian
-ig	-ness	-ista
-ung	-ize	-tore
-heit	-ate	-trice
-en	-tion	-tá
-er	-ing	-ndo
-el	-ed	-bile
-erin	-ly	-mente

This observation illustrates that the approach to part-of-speech tagging outlined in this paper is not restricted to Greek, but can be adapted to any other language. In ancient Greek morphology is worth a lot of attention, as the following example shows: one single verb can appear in more than a hundred morphologically different surface forms that can be discriminated by analysing them in its prefix, stem and suffix part. If one used a full-form-lexicon for part-of-speech tagging, all of these forms could appear in the text to be tagged. But in a small corpus the probability of each form is very low even if the probability of the associated lemma is fairly high. So tagging texts written in an inflected language means to cope with morphology. But as morphology normally is a phenomenon with a considerable degree of regularity it should be possible to take advantage of it (at least while part-of-speech tagging the language, not while studying it) in order to resolve the problems posed by a full-form lexicon.

When tagging an unknown word the tagger must make some reasonable guess as to what tags are possible for the word currently under consideration, as it is obliged to substitute the lexical probability by some other value. Normally, this is done by gaining evidence for a possible set of tags from an analysis of the surface form (for example, in German one could use the fact that nouns have an uppercase letter at the beginning). This means that one uses the probability for a class of words instead of the probability for the word itself hoping to have a good approximation. An empirical study of the influence of unknown words upon the average error rate can be found in the paper by Elworthy ([5]). For German, this topic is discussed by Feldweg ([6]). As word categories are influenced strongly by morphological elements. its analysis should provide the desired close approximation for the lexical probability of an unknown word.

Small corpora also conflict with large tag sets. As we intended to count the frequency of word categories in the work of EURIPIDES, we used the categories existing in Greek grammar as possible tags. A large tag set leads to the effect of combinatorial explosion: the number of possible n-grams is enormous, even if not all combinations make sense linguistically (see [11] for trigram statistics in French corpora). But it is clear that many n-grams need a large training corpus for exact approximation. Kempe ([11]) has presented an approach for making the approximation of n-grams better even in the case of a small corpus by splitting each tag into parts that contain linguistically important information.

3 Tagging with Feature Value Pairs

Words do not only carry information about their own category, but also about gender, number, case, person, etc. This linguistic information plays an important role in the solution to our category problem. Therefore, if we could devise a tagging algorithm that uses this information, we certainly could improve the tagger's precision. As an example, consider the word

$$\pi\alpha\iota\delta\epsilon\acute{\upsilon}o\mu\epsilon\nu.$$

It contains the following information:

- first person
- plural
- indicative
- present tense
- active

"Part-of-Speech Tagging" is defined as a process that assigns tags denoting a word's part-of-speech to the considered word. Up to now, the notion of "part of speech" has been equal to "word category". From now on, we do not simply consider tags which represent the word's category only, but tags which encode a list of so called feature value pairs as well. These pairs represent all linguistic and syntactic information contained in a given word.

In the example above we can recode the linguistic information in a list of feature-value pairs (i.e. a tag) as follows:

PER:first NUM:plural MOD:indicative TEN:present VOI:active

Generalising this we write a tag formally as

$$t_i := \bigoplus_{k=1}^{l_i} f_{i,k}, \quad (l_i \text{ is the number of feature value pairs of } t_i) \tag{5}$$

If $(t_1 \ldots t_i \ldots t_n)$ is a sequence of such tags, the probability $P(t_i|t_{i-1} t_{i-2})$ is computed in the following way:

$$
\begin{aligned}
P(t_i|t_{i-1} t_{i-2}) &= P\left(\bigoplus_{k=1}^{l_i} f_{i,k} | t_{i-1} t_{i-2}\right) \\
&= \frac{P\left(\bigoplus_{k=1}^{l_i} f_{i,k} \wedge t_{i-1} t_{i-2}\right)}{P(t_{i-1} t_{i-2})} \\
&= P\left(f_{i,1}|t_{i-1} t_{i-2}\right) \cdot \prod_{k=2}^{l_i} P\left(f_{i,k} | \bigoplus_{m=1}^{k-1} f_{i,m} \wedge t_{i-1} t_{i-2}\right)
\end{aligned} \tag{6}
$$

For lexical probabilities we now write:

$$P\left(w_i | \bigoplus_{k=1}^{l_i} f_{i,k}\right) \tag{7}$$

There are two major advantages to this approach. First of all the sparse data in the case of n-gram probabilities are more dense now. In addition, we can save a lot of storage space and execution time during tagging. For further information, the reader is referred to [11].

4 Tagging with Morphological Analysis

Kempe's idea is very well suited for improving the tagger's precision in the case of trigram probabilities. Unfortunately there are many inflected forms in Greek which induce low frequencies for any lexical entry being an inflection. Feature value pairs do not provide a solution to this problem. Therefore, another idea is to be found, when the frequencies of lexicon entries are to be increased.

Analogously to Kempe's approach additional information should be easily retrievable from the words in the text to be tagged. But with this consideration in mind, a straightforward solution can be found: The inflections themselves carry all information necessary for determining which word form they represent. Thus, we only need to split every word into its three defining parts:

prefix – stem – suffix

The prefix appears in the Greek past tenses only. It must be split from the stem, but carries no information not already contained in stem and suffix. This idea of splitting surface forms leads to a change in the representation of our lexicon. As the stem is the only characteristic part of a word (prefix and suffix are both exchangeable by the rules of inflection which the Greek grammar defines), our idea is to store the word's stem alone in the lexicon. Prefix and suffix are then to be stored in two different tables.

All words that are not inflections, but have categories such as preposition or particle, are stored in the lexicon unchanged as full forms. Thus, in this case, there is no difference between tagging with or without morphological analysis.

The fact that in most cases lexicon entries are stems only – except for full forms – has a severe impact on the computation of lexical probabilities. Since words are split into stem and suffix their lexical probabilities cannot be computed in the same way as before. The lexicon now only contains the lexical probability of the stems that can be valid for a given word. On the other hand, as shown above, an additional table is required which contains the lexical probabilities of all suffixes. The probabilities for the entries in these tables can be determined by MLE from the training corpus. By table lookup we can determine the lexical probabilities of the suffixes valid for a given word. Consequently, given the word w with stem s and suffix u ($w = su$) we have two probabilities now:

- $P(\text{stem} = s|t_i)$, where $1 \leq i \leq n_s$ and n_s is the number of tags t_i for stem s
- $P(\text{suffix} = u|t_j)$, where $1 \leq j \leq n_u$ and n_u is the number of tags t_j for suffix u.

Assuming independence of these two probabilities, we write:

$$P(\text{stem} = s|t_i) \cdot P(\text{suffix} = u|t_j) = P(\text{stem} = s \wedge \text{suffix} = u|t_i \wedge t_j)$$
$$= P(w|t_j) \tag{8}$$

The last step is due to the fact that t_j subsumes t_i. In this context subsumption means that all feature value pairs of t_i occur in t_j, too[7]. Of course, step 2 is valid if and only if suffix and stem form a correct combination with respect to Greek morphosyntax. For example, $\pi\alpha\iota\delta\epsilon\acute{v} - \sigma\alpha\nu\tau\sigma\varsigma$ is correct, while $\pi\alpha\iota\delta\epsilon\acute{v}\sigma\alpha\nu\tau - \sigma\varsigma$

---

[7] [10] shows that in the case of part-of-speech tagging for unknown words $P(w|t_j) \approx P(t_j|w)$. With Bayes' rule a consequence is $P(w) \approx P(t_j)$. So the probability of an unknown word is approximately determined by the probability of valid morphological analysis. This seems quite reasonable.

is not. But in both cases the suffixes are correct. Therefore, during the computation of lexical probabilities there must be a check to determine whether the computed probability is valid at all.

There are some advantages with this approach concerning the computation of lexical probabilities:

- Frequencies for stems and suffixes are higher when considered separately. Thus, tagging precision can be further increased.
- In the case of unknown words, enough information can be extracted from the suffix to significantly limit the number of tags possible for the given word compared to the total number of tags. Taggers often assign the whole tag set to an unknown word before disambiguating. Thus, morphological analysis vastly increases the precision of lexical probabilities during tagging.
- No lexicon for full forms is necessary. For highly inflected languages, this means an enormous decrease of resources needed for lexicon storage and access.

5 Implementation

For our task of tagging the corpus of EURIPIDES we implemented the morphological analysis using regular expressions which describe almost all of the suffixes of the Greek language and the associated tags. On the basis of these regular expressions we implemented a parser that precedes the tagging process and annotates all words with their possible tags and respective lexical probabilities.

More precisely, during the pre-tagging-phase the parser uses two final state automata to recognise sets of possible suffixes and prefixes. Kay and Kaplan [9] have shown that regular expressions suffice for modelling almost all phenomena of morphology. A finite state automaton can be implemented efficiently, as is known from the theory of automata (for a constructive proof see for example [1]).

In particular, the following list of feature value pairs has been used:

```
NUM:dual   NUM:pl      GEN:fem   GEN:mask POS:adjk POS:adjp
NUM:sg                 GEN:neutr          POS:adjs POS:adva
TEM:aor    TEM:fut     GEV:akt   GEV:med  POS:advs POS:arti
GEV:pass               POS:depn  POS:idpn POS:verf POS:veri
TEM:impf   TEM:perf    KAS:akk   KAS:dat  POS:intj POS:irpn
TEM:plperf TEM:praes   KAS:gen   KAS:nom  POS:konj POS:name
PER:drei   PER:eins    KAS:vok            POS:nega POS:nume
PER:zwei               MOD:imp   MOD:ind  POS:parl POS:part
                       MOD:kon   MOD:opt  POS:pepn POS:popn
                                          POS:prae POS:prfx
                                          POS:repn POS:rlpn
                                          POS:subs POS:vera
```

The tag set consists of all syntactically correct combinations of these pairs. The parser is implemented in C and computes hypotheses of such fv-pairs-lists for each word to be tagged.

6 Application to the Corpus of EURIPIDES

6.1 Training

To obtain a training set we have tagged manually three texts out of the corpus of EURIPIDES, namely *Medea* (431), *Electra* (413), and *Orestes* (408), in order to cover the entire production time of EURIPIDES still available to us. Therefore, including one early, one out of his middle period, and one late tragedy, we have been able to compute trigram-probabilities for EURIPIDES from a sample large enough to get reliable estimations, and which, on average, should be typical for the overall style EURIPIDES used in his plays.

Our tagging system has been trained with ca. 17,000 words (see above) and works with an average accuracy of about 96,6%. The lexicon has about 5,900 entries. Due to different accentuation marks possible for the same stem, some of these entries actually occur twice. So the number of different Greek words stored in the lexicon is even lower.

After training the tagger we tagged all the other texts. Therefore, the training set and the working set are definitely distinct. The error rate has been calculated from a large random sample drawn out of the working set which has been checked manually for tagging errors.

An analysis of the errors produced by the tagger has shown that almost all errors have been confusions of proper names with nouns or have been caused by syntactic ambiguities that can only be resolved by a complete comprehension of the whole text.

A morphological analysis (as is available now through the Perseus Project[8]) that could cover the whole vocabulary of ancient Greek and therefore avoid most of the errors just described would have further decreased the error rate.

6.2 Statistics

First we use our tagger to create tables which count the number of words in each category for all eighteen works by EURIPIDES that are not lost during their tradition including the critical *Rhesus*.

On the basis of these data we try to give answers on the questions posed in section 1. To measure the extent to which a certain work deviates from the distribution of several others, we perform the χ^2-test with two classes:

$$\chi^2 := \sum_{1 \le i \le 2} \frac{(M_{i,j} - E_{i,j})^2}{E_{i,j}} \qquad (9)$$

---

[8] for one of the most fascinating WWW-sites about the Greek and Roman world see http://www.perseus.edu.

$E_{i,j}$ is the expected frequency for category j to appear $(i = 1)$ or to not appear $(i = 2)$, while $M_{i,j}$ is the number of words of category j $(i = 1)$ or the number of words of category different from j $(i = 2)$.

Calculating these values for each text we can determine whether the deviation of an observed frequency of a category in a certain text from the expected mean value is significant or not.

Taking into account the fact mentioned in Sect. 1 that one can not expect the whole work of EURIPIDES to be homogeneous, we form groups consisting of texts written in a strictly defined period of several years. When texts out of different groups are mixed this should result in significant changes in the computed χ^2-values.

We have computed a large series of such χ^2-tables in order to characterise precisely the different periods of EURIPIDES' work. An example is $(\sum_i [a_i > b]$ is the number of elements $a_i > b)$[9]:

	Alcestis	Medea	Heraclidae	Hippolytos	Hecuba	Rhesus
adjk	0.0909	1.79	1.28	0.911	0.0500	0.922
adjp	21.7	15.7	9.48	0.846	6.57	0.188
adjs	3.37	5.77	0.270	0.647	4.31	3.67
adva	0.117	2.60	1.63	4.98	0.273	0.0796
advs	0.862	0.00389	0.918	0.101	0.171	4.76
arti	0.383	4.97	4.25	4.30	2.72	11.1
depn	0.567	0.0849	20.1	1.52	1.59	7.17
idpn	0.0684	0.00189	0.154	0.0707	0.957	0.558
intj	4.98	0.176	0.122	13.9	3.93	21.3
irpn	2.48	0.0970	0.600	0.174	1.11	0.292
konj	1.22	2.70	0.165	3.63	2.96	0.0217
name	8.06	31.9	2.07	11.9	14.7	69.0
nega	3.66	0.257	0.171	2.10	4.65	1.29
nume	0.0149	0.0132	0.000453	5.49	1.48	1.40
parl	3.78	0.629	7.44	3.58	7.69	10.8
part	4.67	5.51	0.278	7.47	0.0921	13.3
pepn	3.94	0.801	0.00385	0.357	0.193	3.76
popn	0.252	2.59	2.84	0.371	1.18	7.18
prae	0.459	5.07	2.07	0.233	0.0918	8.72
repn	0.110	0.346	0.482	0.00170	0.00852	1.51
rlpn	0.0156	2.56	3.01	0.165	0.987	0.775
subs	1.96	1.04	11.2	5.11	3.92	13.3
verf	5.17	0.168	0.0111	0.00109	0.853	0.542
veri	0.693	0.00435	5.10	2.26	5.02	1.20

$$\delta_j := \sum_{i=1}^{24} [\hat{\chi}^2 > \chi_\alpha^2] \qquad 2 \quad\quad 2 \quad\quad 4 \quad\quad 3 \quad\quad 2 \quad\quad 8 \qquad \alpha = 0.05$$

$$\delta_j := \sum_{i=1}^{24} [\hat{\chi}^2 > \chi_\alpha^2] \qquad 1 \quad\quad 2 \quad\quad 2 \quad\quad 2 \quad\quad 1 \quad\quad 7 \qquad \alpha = 0.005$$

[9] This notation used in Graham, Knuth, Patashnik, *Concrete Mathematics*, Addison-Wesley 1994 (2nd edition)

The last column shows the χ^2-values for *Rhesus*. As one can see easily, the number of deviating categories is larger here than with the other texts included in the test. Is this number significantly larger? If it were, we would have to reject the hypothesis that all texts are drawn out of the same population—in stylometry this fact is considered as evidence for more than one author.

To clarify this, we perform the Kolmogorov-Smirnov-test on the number of deviations δ_j $(1 \leq j \leq 6)$ and obtain the following:

	Kolmogorov-Smirnov Z	error probability
$\chi^2_\alpha = 3.8 \; (\alpha = 0.05)$	1.225	0.1
$\chi^2_\alpha = 7.9 \; (\alpha = 0.005)$	1.633	0.01

So in the case of $\chi^2 = 3.8$ we can claim that the six tested texts do not obey the same distribution of word-category frequencies with a probability of 90%, whereas in the case of $\chi^2 = 7.9$ this probability is about 99%. From this result we conclude that *Rhesus* has not been written at the same time as the other five plays or by a different author.

To verify the results obtained as described above we have computed the χ^2-value for a $k \times m$-contingency-table (k is the number of texts included in the current test and m denotes the number of categories under investigation) using the well-known formula

$$\chi^2 := \sum_{i=1}^{k} \sum_{j=1}^{m} \frac{(M_{i,j} - E_{i,j})^2}{E_{i,j}}$$

where $M_{i,j}$ denotes the frequency of category j in text i and $E_{i,j}$ the expected value for this frequency which has been determined by MLE.

This second and independent test has always confirmed the results just obtained.

6.3 Results

The comparison of the distribution of word categories as described above has established three periods in the corpus of EURIPIDES, which coincide quite well with the dates when the texts were written.

Some of the texts don't deviate significantly from any group, but none deviates from every group. This means that no text has been rejected completely. Such a rejection would have to be interpreted as if the text had not been written by EURIPIDES. So the method we have proposed has proved to be useful for the goal of determining different stylistic phases in EURIPIDES' work.

As far as *Rhesus* is concerned, we have found a significant deviation from the early period. The same result has been obtained when testing the middle period only and both early and middle periods. Only when compared with the late period, does *Rhesus* show no significant deviation at all.

We therefore conclude that the hypothesis of *Rhesus* being a early or middle-period-work can be rejected. However, EURIPIDES could still have written *Rhesus* in his late period. Therefore, the question of its authenticity still remains open.

7 Acknowledgements

I want to thank the reviewers of this paper for their numerous comments that have been very helpful in producing the final version of the paper.

References

1. **Alfred V. Aho, Ravi Sethi, Jeffrey D. Ullman**, *Compilers—Principles, Techniques and Tools*, Addison-Wesley 1986
2. **James Allen**, *Natural Language Understanding*, The Benjamin/Cummings Publishing Company, Inc. ²1995
3. **W. A. Church, K. W. Gale**, *What's wrong with adding one?*, Statistical Research Reports, No. 90, AT&T Bell Laboratories, Murray Hill
4. **Doung Cutting, Julina Kupiec, Jan Pedersen, and Penelope Sibun**, *A practical part-of-speech tagger*, Proceedings of the Third Conference on Applied Natural Language Processing, Trento 1992
5. **David Elworthy**, *Tagset Design and Inflected Languages*, Sharp Laboratories of Europe, Oxford 1994
6. **Helmut Feldweg**, *Implementation and evaluation of a German HMM for POS disambiguation*, Tübingen 1995
7. **Penelope J. Gurney, Lyman W. Gurney**, *Disputed Authorship: 30 Biographies and Six Reputed Authors. A New Analysis by Full-Text Lemmatization of the "Historia Augusta"*, in: Proceedings of the 1996 Joint International Conference ALLC/ACH '96
8. **S. Hockey**, *L'uso del computer nella letteratura e nella linguistica: strumenti e techniche per la ricerca*, in: **Luciano Gallino**, *Informatica e scienze umane – lo stato dell' arte*, Milano 1991, S. 17–27
9. **Ronald Kaplan, Martin Kay**, *Regular Models of Phonological Rule Systems*, Computational Linguistics 20:3, 1994
10. **André Kempe**, *A Probabilistic Tagger and an Analysis of Tagging Errors*, Technical Report, IMS, Universität Stuttgart 1993
11. **André Kempe**, *Probabilistic Tagging with feature structures*, Technical Report, IMS, Universität Stuttgart 1994
12. **André Kempe**, *Handhabung des N-Gramm-Taggers*, Interner Bericht, Universität Stuttgart (IMS) 1994
13. **Burkhard Meißner**, *Computergestützte Untersuchungen zur stilistischen Einheit der Historia Augusta*, Halle 1992
14. **Charles Muller, Lothar Hoffmann**, *Einführung in die Sprachstatistik*, München Hueber 1972
15. **Charles Muller**, *Perchè si contano le parole. La statistica lessicale e i suoi impieghi.*, in: **Luciano Gallino**, *Informatica e scienze umane – lo stato dell' arte*, Milano 1991, S. 201ff.
16. **Barbara H. Partee, Alice G. ter Meulen, Alice G. TerMeulen, Robert E. Wall**, *Mathematical methods in linguistics*, Dordrecht u.a., Kluwer Acad. Pr. 1990

Making Objects More Knowledgeable

Susanne Schacht & Udo Hahn

㏒ Linguistische Informatik / Computerlinguistik
Universität Freiburg, Werthmannplatz 1, D-79085 Freiburg
http://www.coling.uni-freiburg.de/

Abstract. Despite their common roots, the paradigms of object-oriented programming and object-based knowledge representation techniques could not really be joined again. A synthesis of both worlds would allow for the description of complex knowledge-based systems with dynamic behavior in a unified framework. We propose a corresponding model that extends object-oriented programming into the classification-based paradigm of terminological reasoning and consider a natural language understanding task to demonstrate its application.

1 Introduction

Although the paradigms of object-oriented programming *(OOP)* and of object-centered knowledge representation *(OCKR)* have common roots, they took diverging paths over the past years. While knowledge representation formalisms such as terminological or description logics [31] feature clear and elegant semantics and provide powerful subsumption and classification-based inference algorithms operating on purely declarative databases, object-oriented programming [29] has its strengths in flexible control structures utilizing message passing and in software-engineering issues like modularization and reuse. Several attempts at combining OCKR with programming facilities have been made, but the procedural aspects of knowledge representation systems are often only tacitly dealt with in terms of production rules or side effects. On the other hand, practically all attempts at incorporating classification-based reasoning facilities into an OOP environment have been mainly concerned with implementational issues and failed to provide a tighter coupling with the respective object-oriented computation model.

A synthesis of both approaches seems rewarding, as it would provide a unified framework for the description and implementation of knowledge-based systems in which reasoning about state changes, dynamic environments, i.e., accounting for behavioral aspects, are crucial issues (e.g., adaptive systems, artificial life, multi-agent systems). Our motivation for dealing with an integration of both paradigms comes from the need to provide a formal framework for natural language *performance* grammars, i.e., grammars which combine declarative <u>and</u> procedural aspects of the description of language structures and patterns of language usage, respectively [7]. In this paper we, first, outline a formal foundation for OOP as well as OCKR. Then we propose a denotational semantics that combines their strengths, in that we extend OOP into the subsumption and classification-based paradigm of terminological reasoning. For illustration purposes, we finally consider a natural language processing task that not only relies heavily on object-centered knowledge representation techniques but also requires considering a great amount of procedural specifications. This cannot be dealt with adequately neither in a purely terminological nor in a purely object-oriented framework.

OCKR models are designed for accounting for common-sense-oriented, contextually embedded reasoning in hierarchically organized concept systems. Hence, the support for structurally "complex", mostly networked concept descriptions, defaults, and inheritance mechanisms. On the application side, a family of mostly inheritance-based terminological languages and systems have emerged [31]. They usually do not allow exceptions in the inheritance hierarchies. Rather, their strength lies in the support of the insertion of new items into an existing concept hierarchy by classification (if the new item is an instance) or by subsumption (if it is a concept itself). Consistency checks ensure that the system's knowledge base never becomes contradictory. Despite a brief, yet vivid discussion in the early days of the evolution of knowledge representation models on whether to take a procedural or a declarative approach [30], today's systems are strikingly *static*. They usually have an operational layer built on top of a purely declarative kernel or incorporate calls to the host language they are implemented in. These procedural enhancements are, nevertheless, not explicitly anchored in their formal specifications (cf. LOOM's CLASP architecture [32]).

Object-oriented programming languages, on the other hand, originally were developed for simulations of dynamic systems (cf. Simula [11]) and, hence, always stressed a tight coupling between data and operations. Encapsulation ensures that an object's internal data are only accessed via its defined interface, while message passing allows for a flexible control flow. Inheritance is usually considered from an implementational perspective only. It serves as a mechanism for software reuse of already available data structures, properties, and procedures, and eases the structuring of definitions. Method inheritance is often procedurally implemented as in the method-lookup algorithm of Smalltalk [16]. Contrary to knowledge representation systems, the inheritance relation between classes is *coded* into the system, not *inferred*. Overriding the default behavior is usually encouraged but there is no built-in consistency checking mechanism.

In our integrated model the basic property of objects as containers for data and procedures is preserved. We stipulate that the corresponding language allow the definition of classes and the creation of instances of these classes to transfer the structure and behavior defined by the class, that new classes be derivable from existing ones by adding or overriding methods or instance variables (*class-based* inheritance), and that instances be accessible by message sending. The major extension we argue for relates to moving inheritance from the code to the inference level, i.e., allowing for the computation of implicit inheritance relations among classes and instances, as a supplement to coding that knowledge explicitly. The gain of flexibility and increase in expressibility should be beneficial for the AI as well as for the OOP community.

2 Object-centered Knowledge Representation

OCKR languages, description logics (DL) in particular, are usually based on a model-theoretic semantics [31]. They allow for the definition of *concepts* and *individuals*, as well as *conceptual roles* between individuals. Concepts can be defined either as being primitive or by a combination of existing concepts, and by constraints on their instances' roles and role fillers. Accordingly, concepts are either explicitly defined to be subconcepts of a superconcept, or their superconcept can be implicitly derived by computing the subsumption relation on the basis of restrictions on role definitions. Similarly, individuals can be explicitly defined to be an instance of a concept, or can be implicitly classified by taking their role assignments into account, thus inheriting additional features, if available.

Let us now turn to the natural language processing scenario. For the proper understanding of an utterance like *"In our copying test, the Quantum hard-disk showed excellent results. It is certainly a good buy."*, several kinds of knowledge must be provided – syntactic knowledge (e.g., about parts of speech and their valid combination in terms of correct sentences), semantic knowledge (e.g., about the composition of meaning descriptions of single constituents), and conceptual knowledge (about the domain the utterance is about). Procedural knowledge is also necessary, e.g., relating to adequate parsing strategies, to the resolution of ambiguities, or, more concretely, to determining the valid reference object for a pronoun like *"it"*. Some of the knowledge required for the example above will first be informally described and then rephrased in terms of DL expressions (for the syntax and semantics of the DL notation, cf. [31]):

1. *"excellent"* is an adjective and can be a modifier of a noun like *"results"*.
2. A noun phrase is the subject of a sentence if its grammatical case is nominative and if it has the same number as the governing verb.
3. A pronoun can be used at any occasion where a noun phrase is allowed.
4. The subject of a sentence (in the active voice) is the agent of the communicated action.
5. *"Quantum"* is the name of a hardware manufacturer.
6. In order to resolve a pronoun, its reference object *(antecedent)* is to be found in the same sentence or it is the most recently occurring noun in preceding sentences with which it agrees in gender and number (for more details, cf. [28]).

1. NOUN $\sqsubseteq$ $\forall$modifier:ADJECTIVE , *excellent* : ADJECTIVE , *results* : NOUN
2. SENTENCE $\sqsubseteq$ ($\forall$subject:NOMNOUNPHRASE $\sqcap$ $\forall$predicate:VERBALPHRASE) , NOMNOUNPHRASE $\doteq$ (NOUNPHRASE $\sqcap$ $\forall$case: *nominative*)
3. PRONOUN $\sqsubseteq$ NOUNPHRASE
4. PROPOSITION $\doteq$ ($\forall$agent:NOUNPHRASE $\sqcap$ $\forall$action:VERBALPHRASE) , agent $\sqsubseteq$ subject , action $\sqsubseteq$ predicate
5. *quantum* : MANUFACTURER

The advantages we gain from the terminological description are the convenient expression of concept hierarchies and the ease of defining new concepts by the combination of already given ones. Note that the specification of statement (2) is still incomplete, since we have not yet accounted for the number agreement property required for the subject and the predicate. In order to appropriately capture this constraint, one would have to introduce an additional terminological operator [23]. Statement (6) also requires the specification of feature agreement. Even worse, this expression would tend to become rather cumbersome, since DL formalisms fail to provide means for explicitly dealing with the quantification of individual variables. Anaphora resolution faces the additional problem that individuals – in this case, representational correlates of the antecedent and the pronoun – cannot be merged into one object in order to properly represent the reference identity between the antecedent and the anaphor. Also, the control structure behind the terminological reasoning processes is a hidden part of the implementation of the inference engine. This is particularly unfavorable, as linguistically plausible strategies (e.g., sentence-internal anaphora resolution always precedes sentence-external probings [28]) constitute part of the linguistic knowledge *proper* that, nevertheless, is hard to express in this formalism (provided this is possible at all).

3 Object-oriented Programming Languages

For object-oriented programming languages, untyped languages with denotational semantics as presented in [9,18] are a widely accepted specification standard. Accordingly, we introduce an object-oriented reference language (cf. Fig. 1), which includes expressions for variables x, a let-expression for local variable binding, assignment of an expression e to a variable x, classes c, objects o, and message sendings $o.k(\bar{e})$.

Classes c can be defined directly by giving their instance variable names $(\bar{x})$ and method definitions $(k(\bar{y}) : e)$ consisting of a key k, the formal parameters $\bar{y}$ and the method body e, or by refining a superclass c (in terms of adding fur-

$$e ::= x \mid \text{let } x = e_1 \text{ in } e_2 \mid x := e \mid c \mid o \mid o.k(\bar{e})$$
$$c ::= \text{class } (\bar{x}; \overline{k(\bar{y}) : e}) \mid \text{subOf } c (\bar{x}; \overline{k(\bar{y}) : e})$$
$$o ::= \text{self} \mid \text{super} \mid \text{new } c$$

Fig. 1. Syntax of an object-oriented language

ther instance variables, and adding or modifying method definitions). Objects o can be created as new instances of classes c; also, in method definitions, the (pseudo) variables self or super, as in Smalltalk, can be used to refer to the message environment of the object itself, or of one that is defined by its superclass.

In the language just defined, the description of a grammatically well-formed sentence turns out to become quite complicated (as in all programming languages except for logical ones). This is mainly due to the fact that explicit tests have to be performed as to whether two items may combine or not. Also, some Boolean operators and constants have to be added to the object-oriented description in order to allow for a more readable specification. The complex anaphora resolution procedure is not explicitly spelled out, though this becomes highly feasible in this framework (cf. Section 4). Although quite verbose, an object-oriented description of the grammatical knowledge from Section 2 can be given in a straightforward way. However, it lacks the desired formal rigor, and the specifications are somewhat bizarre, i.e., they hide grammatical generalizations linguists are usually striving for.

1. Adjective := class ((); (isAdjective : *true*));
   Noun := class ((modifier); (canBeModifier(y) : y.isAdjective));
   excellent := new Adjective; *results* := new Noun;
2. Sentence := class ((subject, predicate);
   (canBeSubject(y) : y.isNounphrase ∧ y.isNominative
                    ∧ y.getNumber == predicate.getNumber))
3. Pronoun := subOf NounPhrase

4. Sentence := class ((subject, predicate); ());
   Proposition := subOf Sentence ((agent, action) ;
   (setAgent : agent := subject, setAction : action := predicate))
5. *quantum* := new Manufacturer
6. Pronoun := subOf NounPhrase (antecedent ;
   resolveAnaphor:"search for antecedent within the current sentence; else look backwards")

4 The View from a Bridge

An intriguing feature of OCKR is its potential for automatic classification based on "static" concept descriptions. As the OOP paradigm coherently combines data and procedures, an apparent specification gap concerns the unsettled treatment of method descriptions, i.e., the procedural element of OOP, from a classification viewpoint. There have already been some debates on how classification of methods might be achieved, though they were not conclusive. Borgida [4], e.g., states conditions according to which a procedure should be considered a subordinate to another one. The first of the criteria he proposes is contradictory to our approach, as it requires the more general procedure to be applicable in all situations where the more special one is applicable, too. This might be reasonable for defining a hierarchy of procedures, but it is certainly not when one aims at a hierarchy of objects that contain procedures, as we do. Simple subtyping is also not sufficient for our purposes. Usually, the subtyping rules for function types involve only the domain and the range *types* of a function, not its actual *values*, i.e., its behavior. Therefore, the subtype relation cannot be considered the subsumption relation for functions, since we expect instances of the same concept to behave in a similar way, not only to be of the same type (cf. also [10] for a discussion of the distinction between subtyping and inheritance). *Behavioral* subtyping [2,21], on the other hand, is far too complex for our application, since it is concerned with proving general properties of objects which are preserved under subtyping. The related schemes are very useful for specification and design purposes, but they are not feasible for implementing a classifier. In order to avoid nonmonotonic inheritance and to concentrate on the simpler monotonic case instead, we here restrict the overriding of methods: a function f' is allowed to override f only if it enlarges the domain of f 's external arguments and behaves like f otherwise (this also implies that the range of f is a subset of that of f'; the host object's instance variables are not yet taken into account). As Castagna [8] notes, contravariance (in the functions' domains, A' and A, below) should be used in cases that allow for substitution of the hierarchically higher item by the lower one. On the other hand, covariance (in the functions' ranges, B and B') is more suitable in cases in which the lower item expresses a specialization of the higher ones. In order to incorporate the function's host object we have to consider it a parameter, too. But since we want to restrict the applicability of the function to the elements of the subclass, we have to keep them distinct from the external parameters whose domain we want to be enlarged. Therefore, we define functions as $f : C \times A \rightarrow B$, with C denoting the class at which the function is defined, A the external parameters, and B the range. The *subsumption rule for functions* can then be rephrased as:

$$f' : C' \times A' \to B' \sqsubseteq f : C \times A \to B :\Leftrightarrow$$
$$C' \subseteq C \wedge A \subseteq A' \wedge \forall x \in C', \forall y \in A : f(x,y) = f'(x,y)$$

The combined model we propose is summarized in Figures 2, 3 and 4. Syntactically (cf. Fig. 2), the definition and application of functions (as λ-abstractions) have been included, together with an access method ($o_- x$) for the contents of the objects. In object and class definitions,

$e ::= x \mid \lambda \overline{y}.e \mid e_1(\overline{e}) \mid \text{let } x = e_1 \text{ in } e_2$
$\qquad \mid x := e \mid c \mid o_- x \mid o$
$c ::= \text{class}(x{:}\overline{c}{:}e) \mid \text{subOf } c \ (x{:}\overline{c}{:}e)$
$o ::= \text{self} \mid \text{super} \mid \text{obj}(x{:}\overline{c}{:}e) \mid \text{new } c$

Fig. 2. Syntax of the unifying model

there is only one kind of declaration left instead of the former distinction between variables and methods (we will refer to both of them as the object's *attributes*): the name of the attribute x, followed by a ':', and the *class* c of this variable or this method's parameters followed by another ':', and the attribute expression e itself. This considerably simplifies the handling of instance variables and methods – they can be equally defined (this includes class membership and default values which are both new for instance variables) and easily accessed (selection by name). Sending a message $x(\overline{e})$ to o is therefore written as $o_- x \ (\overline{e})$. Objects still can be created by instantiation of a class (new c), but also by directly stating their attributes (this can be used to infer their class membership by taking value restrictions into account which are defined by the classes). Note that in object-oriented languages, common control structures can be defined by methods of Boolean objects. Therefore, we have no built-in if or while expressions but consider them as implemented in our framework (cf. the ifThenElse method in Fig. 6).

Semantically (cf. Figures 3 and 4), a class is no longer considered a generator of objects. Rather, it is basically a function that maps locations to mappings from identifiers to expressions. These expressions are the default values that the same identifiers map to at the instances of each class. If the expression evaluates to a λ-expression, it will serve as a method. Subclasses are modeled by extending the environment in which the attribute values are interpreted with the pseudo variable super pointing to the superclass's function from attribute

$x, y \in Var$	$\subset Id$	
$\alpha \in Loc$		
$n, b \in Bas$	$= \{\bot\} \cup Int \cup Bool \cup Loc \cup ...$	
$v \in Val$	$= Bas \cup Obj \cup Class \cup SClass \cup Meth$	
$\eta \in Env$	$= Var \to Val$	
$o \in Obj$	$= Loc \times (Var \to Val)$	
$m \in Meth$	$= Val* \to Store \to (Val \times Store)$	
$c \in Class$	$= Loc \to (Var \to Val)$	
$sub \in Trans$	$= Class \times Env \to Class$	
$\sigma \in Store$	$= Loc \to Val$	
	with: $\sigma[x \to v] = \sigma \backslash \{(x, \sigma(x))\} \cup \{(x, v)\}$,	
	$\sigma_\bot$ the empty Store,	
	and $alloc \ \sigma x = \langle \eta, \sigma' \rangle$, an environment and	
	an extension of σ to address the value of x	

Fig. 3. Semantic domains for the unifying model

names to values. Objects are a pair of a location and a mapping from identifiers to expressions, thus making their uniqueness explicit by providing their location. Since we do not distinguish between instance variables and methods any longer (and, therefore, the instance variables do not have to be hidden), the denotations become simpler than for a language with encapsulation.

$$
\begin{aligned}
[\![x]\!]\eta\sigma &= \langle \eta x, \sigma\rangle\\
[\![\text{let } x = e_1 \text{ in } e_2]\!]\eta\sigma &= \text{let } \langle v, \sigma_1\rangle = [\![e_1]\!]\eta\sigma \text{ in } [\![e_2]\!](\eta[x \to v])\sigma_1\\
[\![x := e]\!]\eta\sigma &= \text{let } \alpha = \eta x, \langle v, \sigma_1\rangle = [\![e]\!]\eta\sigma \text{ in } \langle v, \sigma_1[\alpha \to v]\rangle\\
[\![o\_x]\!]\eta\sigma &= \text{let } \langle \rho, \sigma_1\rangle = [\![o]\!]\eta\sigma \text{ in } \rho x \sigma_1\\
[\![\lambda \bar{y}.e(\bar{e})]\!]\eta\sigma &= \text{let } \langle \bar{v}, \sigma'\rangle = \overline{[\![e]\!]}\eta\sigma \text{ in} [\![e]\!](\eta[\bar{y} \to \bar{v}])\sigma'\\
[\![\text{obj}(x : \bar{c} : e)]\!]\eta\sigma &= \text{let } \langle \eta_o, \sigma'\rangle = \textit{alloc } \sigma\bar{x},\\
&\qquad \rho = \textit{fix}(\lambda\rho.\rho\bot[x_i \to [\![e_i]\!]](\eta[\eta_o][\text{self} \to \rho])],\\
&\qquad \langle \alpha \to \rho, \sigma''\rangle = \textit{alloc } \sigma'\rho\\
&\qquad \text{in } \langle\langle \alpha, \rho\rangle, \sigma''\rangle\\
[\![\overline{\text{class}(x : \bar{c} : e)}]\!]\eta\sigma &= \text{let } \langle \eta_o, \sigma'\rangle = \textit{alloc } \sigma\bar{x},\\
&\qquad v_i = [\![e_i]\!](\eta[\eta_o][\text{self} \to \rho]),\\
&\qquad \rho = \textit{fix}(\lambda\rho.\rho\bot[x_i \to v_i])\\
&\qquad \text{in } \langle \lambda\alpha.\rho, \sigma''\rangle\\
[\![\text{subOf } c(x : \bar{c} : e)]\!]\eta\sigma &= \text{let } \langle \lambda\alpha.\rho_c, \sigma_1\rangle = [\![c]\!]\eta\sigma\\
&\qquad \text{in let } \langle \eta_o, \sigma'\rangle = \textit{alloc } \sigma\bar{x},\\
&\qquad v_i = [\![e_i]\!](\eta[\eta_o][\text{self} \to \rho, \text{ super} \to \rho_c]),\\
&\qquad \rho = \textit{fix}(\lambda\rho.\rho\bot[x_i \to v_i])\\
&\qquad \text{in } \langle \lambda\beta.\rho, \sigma''\rangle\\
[\![\text{new } c]\!]\eta\sigma &= \text{let } \langle \lambda\alpha.\rho, \sigma'\rangle = [\![c]\!]\eta\sigma, \langle \beta \to \rho, \sigma''\rangle = \textit{alloc } \sigma'\rho \text{ in } \langle\langle \beta, \rho\rangle, \sigma''\rangle
\end{aligned}
$$

Fig. 4. Denotations in the unifying model

The definition of classes and subclasses resembles the terminological axioms concerning concepts and their role restrictions. There is, however, currently no equivalent of defining roles independently of concepts – therefore, we do not have subroles as a built-in language construct. Another simplification concerns the expression of a role restriction by a class. The definition of objects is equivalent to assertional axioms (also without defining roles independently; only upon creation of an object related to an appropriate role filler does a role become available). In Fig. 5, the most common DL expressions are summarized and translated into our language. The semantics of concept expressions is given as sets of values for which the corresponding first-order formula is satisfied in a structure $\mathcal{K}$, which consists of a domain $\mathcal{D}$ and an interpretation $\mathcal{I}$. $\mathcal{I}$ maps constants and variables to elements of $\mathcal{D}$, concepts to sets of elements of $\mathcal{D}$, and roles to sets of pairs of elements of $\mathcal{D}$. As in standard DL, in our language we require objects to be elements of their classes, i.e. $[\![\text{new } c]\!]\eta\sigma \in [\![c]\!]\eta\sigma$, and, therefore, to be available for classification.

5 A Specification Language Integrating OOP and OCKR

The background for our integration of OOP and OCKR paradigms is a large-scale natural language understanding system for the robust analysis of real-world texts [17]. Its natural language processing kernel consists of a strictly lexicalized dependency grammar and an associated parser that have been fully specified in object-oriented terms [7]. In this framework, declarative specifications (morphosyntactic features, subcategorization and word order constraints, etc.) and procedural ones (i.e., protocols for different grammatical phenomena such as establishing dependency relations [24] or creating referential links among anaphorically related expressions [28]) are expressed in a homo-

DL	semantics	**our model**	(simplified) semantics
C	$\{d \in \mathcal{D} \mid d \in [\![C]\!]^{\mathcal{I}}\}$	C = class()	$[\![C]\!] = \lambda \alpha . \rho \in \text{Loc} \rightarrow (\text{Var} \rightarrow \text{Val})$
$\forall R : C$	$\{d \in \mathcal{D} \mid [\![R]\!]^{\mathcal{I}}(d) \subseteq [\![C]\!]^{\mathcal{I}}\}$	D := class(R:C:y)	$[\![D]\!] = \text{let } \rho = ..[R \rightarrow [\![y]\!]] ..$ $\text{in } \lambda \alpha . \rho; [\![y]\!] \in [\![C]\!]$
$\exists R : C$	$\{d \in \mathcal{D} \mid [\![R]\!]^{\mathcal{I}}(d) \cap [\![C]\!]^{\mathcal{I}} \neq \emptyset\}$	D := class(R:C:y)	$\exists y : [\![D]\!] = \text{let } \rho = ..[R \rightarrow [\![y]\!]] ..$ $\text{in } \lambda \alpha . \rho$
$D \doteq C$	$[\![D]\!]^{\mathcal{I}} = [\![C]\!]^{\mathcal{I}}$	D := subOf C()	$[\![D]\!] = [\![C]\!]$
$D \sqsubseteq C$	$[\![D]\!]^{\mathcal{I}} \subseteq [\![C]\!]^{\mathcal{I}}$	D := subOf C(...)	$[\![D]\!] \subseteq [\![C]\!]$
$a : C$	$[\![a]\!]^{\mathcal{I}} \in [\![C]\!]^{\mathcal{I}}$	a := new C	$[\![a]\!] = \langle \beta, \rho \rangle \in [\![C]\!]$
$a \, R \, b$	$([\![a]\!]^{\mathcal{I}}, [\![b]\!]^{\mathcal{I}}) \in [\![R]\!]^{\mathcal{I}}$	a := obj(R:class():b)	$[\![a]\!] = \text{let } \rho = ..[R \rightarrow [\![b]\!]] ..$ $\text{in } \langle \beta, \rho \rangle; \beta \in [\![\text{class}()]\!]$

Fig. 5. Correspondence between major OCKR/OOP language expressions

geneous OOP framework. The parser, finally, produces a conceptual representation of the content of each text in the format of OCKR structures. As in any strictly lexicalized grammar system, the lexicon is a major source of rapid growth. Hence, inheritance becomes a sheer necessity to keep the increasing volume of data manageable and consistent. We employ several class hierarchies, the most common of which is the word class hierarchy. The linguistic knowledge already discussed in Sections 2 and 3 can be expressed in the integrated framework as stated below. In general, the specifications read more compactly, since we may delegate consistency constraints to the interpreting system (they can, nevertheless, also be implemented in terms of methods).

1. Noun := sub word (modifier: Adjective: , ...);
   excellent := new Adjective ; *results* := new Noun
2. Sentence := class (subject: NomNounPhrase: , agreement: String : 'number', ...)
3. Pronoun := subOf Noun
4. Sentence := class (subject: ..., predicate: ....);
   Proposition := subOf Sentence (agent: : self_ subject, action: : self_ predicate)
5. *quantum* := new Manufacturer
6. Pronoun := subOf Noun (antecedent::,
   resolveAnaphor: : λ . antecedent := ...,)

In Fig. 6, a fragment of the word class hierarchy is shown. Lexical items are modeled as objects, which are instances of word classes organized in this hierarchy. The root node of this hierarchy is the class Word (let Category and Attachment also be classes), a partial definition of which is supplied in the upper box in Fig. 6. In the course of parsing, lexical items incrementally try to combine themselves to establish legitimate structural relations. Possible relations are described as instances of Attachment. The communication among lexical objects is carried out by message passing. In order to establish structural relations, two major criteria have to be evaluated, *viz.* the compatibility of syntactic and semantic properties. The latter condition is embodied in the method checkReference. It sends the message checkSem that takes an instance of Attachment, att, as a parameter and tests whether the instance variable sem of self is conceptually more specialized than that of att (subsumes is a method for all objects and determines whether the receiver's class is a superclass of the parameter's class or not).

While these types of conditions are usually checked with respect to properties that can be determined immediately after the instantiation of a particular lexical object, some

```
Word := class (..., sem: Category: ...,
              checkSem: Attachment: λ att.att_ sem_ subsumes(self_ sem),
              checkReference: Attachment: λ att.self_ checkSem(att),
              testAnaphor: Pronoun: false)

Pronoun:= class (..., sem: Category: nil, ..., ante: Word: nil,
         checkSem: Attachment: λ att.att_ sem_ subsumes(self_ sem),
         resolveAnaphor: :λ. self_searchInternal;
              (self_ante == nil)_ ifTrueThen(self_searchExternal);
              self_ sem := self_ ante_ sem,
         checkReference: Attachment: λ att.self_ resolveAnaphor; self_ checkSem(att))

Pronoun := subOf Word (... , ante:Word: nil,
         resolveAnaphor: : λ. self_searchInternal;
              (self_ante == nil)_ ifTrueThen(self_searchExternal);
              self_ sem := self_ante_sem,
         checkReference: Attachment: λ att.self_ resolveAnaphor; self_ checkSem(att))
```

Fig. 6. Classifying vs. subclassing Pronoun

subclasses of lexical items deviate from the basic policy. Among those exceptions are pronouns – cf. the definition of the class Pronoun in the lower two boxes in Fig. 6 – for which semantical criteria are checked by the corresponding method checkReference only when an agreement relation to an antecedent has already been established. This extra condition is reflected by a method for carrying out the anaphora resolution, resolveAnaphor. The checkReference method of a pronoun then has to evaluate the criteria for the resolution of an anaphoric reference by performing resolveAnaphor and then by proceeding with checkSem, i.e., the message which activates the test on the combinability in the suggested attachment. checkReference not only involves this chronological sequence of events, but faces also state changes via calling resolveAnaphor, i.e., the update of the instance variables ante and sem – a behavior that cannot be appropriately expressed in purely declarative description logics. The actual resolveAnaphor method is concerned with finding the right candidates for possible antecedents of the pronoun under consideration, and with carrying out the test whether the anaphor and the antecedent can combine. Depending on the result of this computation process, the variable sem is set. This search mechanism requires two methods (which are not explicitly defined here and are assumed to assign a value to the variable ante) – searchInternal and searchExternal. Note that only if no intra-sentential antecedent is found (i.e., ante is still nil after having executed searchInternal), searchExternal is triggered. The test for antecedents (testAnaphor) itself boils down to check whether some classes are subsumed by some others (Fig. 7), namely the (morpho-syntactical) features (feature) and the conceptual category (sem) of both, the anaphor and its antecedent. The antecedent's class itself need not be checked, since this is done by the method itself: only instances of Noun perform the test – any words that cannot act as an antecedent (e.g., prepositions) return the default value false for this attribute which is defined at the class Word.

The lower two boxes in Fig. 6 depict two equivalent, yet alternative definitions of the class Pronoun. The middle one contains an independent specification to be *recognized by a classifier*, while the lower one takes advantage of the class inheritance by *explicit coding*. Considering our experience, large-scale lexicon specification becomes much

```
Noun := subOf Word ( ..., feature: FeatureStructure,
              testAnaphor: Pronoun: λ ana. self_feature_subsumes(ana_feature)_and
                                              (self_sem_subsumes(ana_sem))
```

Fig. 7. The method testAnaphor

more convenient with the incorporation of such a classification service. The task left to the grammar engineer is just to describe the *relevant* features of the problem solution, not those additionally required on the basis of formal conventions only.

The proposal we have sketched is a step towards providing a comprehensive formal basis for the specification of declarative as well as procedural knowledge of language as required for performance grammars [7]. The standards for such grammar specification languages have once been set up by PATR-II [25]. In this approach, however, only declarative specification issues are addressed. An extension of PATR to hierarchically structured lexicons, DATR [13,19], introduces an "object flavor" into this lexical specification language by providing multiple inheritance as well as default inheritance mechanisms but still leaves procedural considerations untouched. The lacking account of procedural specifications in these grammar description languages is nevertheless beginning to be recognized even in the declarative camp. For instance, Blackburn & Gardent [3] discuss several ways of incorporating procedural knowledge into their specification language $\mathcal{L}$. One of the ideas they consider, *viz.* the extension of their specification language towards a programming language, has been elaborated in this contribution.

6 Related Work

The relationships between OOP and OCKR are apparent and have also been investigated by other researchers. Möller [22], e.g., suggests an integration of CLASSIC [6] and CLOS by hiding the services of CLASSIC behind a functional layer. In his approach, the semantic models of both modules are kept distinct, while we aim at their unification. Skuce [27] describes an approach to combine OOP and OCKR features that basically extends abstract data types to conceptual descriptions but does not include functions and procedures as we propose. On the other hand, there are also systems that integrate ADTs into OCKR, e.g., KRS [14]. Both directions do not really leave the area of declarative knowledge representation. Borgida provides a type-theoretic semantics for description logics [5]. He shows the similarity between types and concepts but also points out the differences between description logics and statically typed programming languages, in general. Some of these differences do not apply to object-oriented languages, e.g., the missing uniqueness of records. Euzenat [12] argues that a general unification of the two formalisms is infeasible, as a semantic reducibility from one formalism into the complementary one cannot be achieved. He also claims that it would be unlikely to spell out a denotational semantics for OOP languages for a real-world application at the same level of explicitness as can be done for the OCKR languages using a set-theoretical semantics. He nevertheless presents a knowledge representation system, TROPES, implemented in the object-oriented language ICOS. In peaceful coexistence (rather than fully integrated), TROPES objects figure as ICOS *objects* and

ICOS objects constitute *values* for the TROPES system. Thus, he provides two different viewpoints on classes – an ontological and a taxonomic one. Systems designed for deductive and object-oriented databases come quite close to viewing objects in terms of description logics, but also fall short of procedural considerations. For instance, the Fibonacci system [1] offers strong typing and the separation of the objects' interfaces and implementations. Also, it provides a notion of roles which makes it more suitable for knowledge representation than standard object-oriented languages. F-logic [20] is another approach that deals with reasoning in an object-based formalism, but similarly concentrates on declarative issues.

7 Discussion and Outlook

A formal model has been presented that extends standard OOP by some desirable features of description logics. A definition of a subsumption relation between functions has been given that restricts the overriding of methods in subclasses to allow for automatic classification of objects containing methods. Given a class subsumption relation based on this overriding relation, knowledge base operations like consistency checking or classification of new concepts and instances become available for the proposed model. After integrating knowledge representation features into an object-oriented language model, in the next step we compared the achievements of our language definition relative to the original description logic. It turns out that computing classification relations among objects enhances the descriptional power of such an integrated OOP and the ease of generating specifications in such a framework. This is the reason why we stipulate that giving objects a conceptual status renders OOP more knowledgeable. The formal foundations of a specification language for natural language grammars and parsers [26] and the model's applicability to this task are currently under active investigation.

References

1. A. Albano, R. Bergamini, G. Ghelli, and R. Orsini. An object data model with roles. In *Proceedings of the 19th VLDB Conference*, pages 39–51, 1993.
2. Pierre America. Designing an object-oriented programming language with behavioural subtyping. In J.W. de Bakker, W.-P. de Roever, and G. Rozenberg, editors, *Foundations of Object-Oriented Languages*, pages 59–90. Springer, 1990.
3. Patrick Blackburn and Claire Gardent. A specification language for lexical functional grammars. In *Proc. of the 7th Conf. of the European Chapter of the ACL*, pages 39–44, 1995.
4. Alexander Borgida. On the definition of specialization hierarchies for procedures. In *IJCAI '81 – Proc. of the 7th Int'l. Joint Conference on Artificial Intelligence*, pages 254–256, 1981.
5. Alexander Borgida. From type systems to knowledge representation: Natural semantics specifications for description logics. *International Journal of Intelligent and Cooperative Information Systems*, 1(1):93–126, 1992.
6. Alexander Borgida and Peter F. Patel-Schneider. A semantics and complete algorithm for subsumption in the CLASSIC description logic. *Journal of Artificial Intelligence Research*, 1:277–308, 1994.
7. N. Bröker, S. Schacht, P. Neuhaus, and U. Hahn. Performanzorientiertes Parsing und Grammatik-Design: das PARSETALK-System. In C. Habel *et al.*, editors, *Perspektiven der Kognitiven Linguistik. Modelle und Methoden*, pages 79–125. Westdeutscher Verlag, 1996.
8. Giuseppe Castagna. Covariance and contravariance: Conflict without a cause. *ACM Transactions on Programming Languages and Systems*, 17(3):431–447, 1995.

9. William Cook and Jens Palsberg. A denotational semantics of inheritance and its correctness. In *OOPSLA '89 – Proceedings of the Annual Conference on Object-Oriented Programming Systems, Languages and Applications*, pages 433–443, 1989.
10. W. R. Cook, W. L. Hill, and P. S. Canning. Inheritance is not subtyping. In *Conf. Record 17th ACM Symposium on Principles of Programming Languages*, pages 125–135, 1990.
11. Ole-Johan Dahl and Kristen Nygaard. An Algol-based simulation language. *Communications of the ACM*, 9(9):671–678, 1966.
12. Jérôme Euzenat. KR and OOL co-operation based on semantics nonreducibility. In *ECAI-94 Workshop on Integrating Object-Orientation and Knowledge Representation*, 1994.
13. Roger Evans and Gerald Gazdar. Inference in DATR. In *Proc. of the 4th Conference of the European Chapter of the Association for Computational Linguistics*, pages 66–71, 1989.
14. Brian R Gaines. Class library implementation of an open architecture knowledge support system. *International Journal of Human-Computer Studies*, 41(1–2):59–107, 1994.
15. Jérôme Gensel, Pierre Girard, and Olivier Schmeltzer. Integrating constraints, composite objects and tasks in a knowledge representation system. In *Proceedings of the 5th International Conference on Tools with Artificial Intelligence*, pages 127–130, 1993.
16. Adele Goldberg and David Robson. *Smalltalk-80. The Language and its Implementation*. Addison-Wesley, 1983.
17. Udo Hahn and Martin Romacker. Automatische Erzeugung von medizinischen Wissensbasen durch robustes, partielles Textverstehen: Befundtextanalyse im SYNDIKATE-System. *KI – Künstliche Intelligenz*, 11(3), 1997.
18. S. N. Kamin and U. S. Reddy. Two semantic models of object-oriented languages. In C. A. Gunter and J. C. Mitchell, editors, *Theoretical Aspects of Object-Oriented Programming*, pages 463–496. MIT Press, 1994.
19. Bill Keller. DATR theories and DATR models. In *Proceedings of the 33rd Annual Meeting of the Association for Computational Linguistics*, pages 55–62, 1995.
20. Michael Kifer, Georg Lausen, and James Wu. Logical foundations of object-oriented and frame-based languages. *Journal of the ACM*, 42(4):741–843, 1995.
21. B. H. Liskov and J. M. Wing. A behavioral notion of subtyping. *ACM Transactions on Programming Languages and Systems*, 16(6):1811–1841, 1994.
22. Ralf Möller. A functional layer for description logic: Knowledge representation meets object-oriented programming. In *OOPSLA '96 – Proceedings of the Annual Conference on Object-Oriented Programming Systems, Languages and Applications*, pages 198–213, 1996.
23. Bernhard Nebel and Gert Smolka. Attributive description formalisms ... and the rest of the world. In O. Herzog and C.-R. Rollinger, editors, *Text Understanding in LILOG*, pages 439–452. Springer, 1991.
24. Peter Neuhaus and Udo Hahn. Restricted parallelism in object-oriented lexical parsing. In *COLING '96 – Proc. 16th Int'l. Conf. on Computational Linguistics*, pages 502–507, 1996.
25. Fernando Pereira and Stuart Shieber. The semantics of grammar formalisms seen as computer languages. In *COLING '84 – Proceedings of the 10th Int'l. Conference on Computational Linguistics & 22nd Annual Meeting of the ACL*, pages 123–129, 1984.
26. Susanne Schacht and Udo Hahn. Temporal reasoning about actor systems. In *EPIA '97 – Proceedings of the 8th Portuguese Conference on Artificial Intelligence*, Springer, 1997.
27. Douglas Skuce. A frame-like knowledge representation integrating abstract data types and logic. In J. F. Sowa, editor, *Principles of Semantic Networks. Explorations in the Representation of Knowledge*, pages 543–563. Morgan Kaufmann, 1991.
28. Michael Strube and Udo Hahn. PARSETALK about sentence- and text-level anaphora. In *Proc. of the 7th Conference of the European Chapter of the ACL*, pages 237–244, 1995.
29. Ernest R. Tello. *Object-Oriented Programming for Artificial Intelligence. A Guide to Tools and System Design*. Addison-Wesley, 1989.
30. Terry Winograd. Frame representations and the declarative-procedural controversy. In D. G. Bobrow and A. Collins, editors, *Representation and Understanding*, pages 185–210. Academic Press, 1975.
31. W. Woods and J. Schmolze. The KL-ONE family. *Computers and Mathematics with Applications*, 23(2-5):133–177, 1992.
32. J. Yen, R. Neches, and R. MacGregor. CLASP: Integrating term subsumption systems and production systems. *IEEE Trans. on Knowledge and Data Engineering*, 3(1):25–32, 1991.

Constraining the Acquisition of Concepts by the Quality of Heterogeneous Evidence

Klemens Schnattinger & Udo Hahn

⦅ℂⅇ⦆ Linguistische Informatik / Computerlinguistik
Universität Freiburg, Werthmannplatz 1, D-79085 Freiburg
http://www.coling.uni-freiburg.de/

Abstract. A model of concept acquisition is proposed, which combines various forms of linguistic and conceptual evidence that arise in the course of text understanding processes. We use terminological classification for the creation and management of concept hypotheses, for their incremental annotation by assertions which reflect the quality of available evidence, and for their subsequent evaluation and selection.

1 Incremental Learning from Textual Input

Suppose, your knowledge of the information technology domain tells you that *Aquarius* is a company. In addition, you incidentally know that *ASI-168* is a computer system manufactured by Aquarius. By convention, you know absolutely nothing about *Megaline*. Imagine, one day your favorite computer magazine features an article starting with *"The Megaline unit by Aquarius .."*. Has your knowledge increased? If so, what did you learn already from just this phrase?

The problem is graphically restated in Fig. 1. The incremental concept formation process starts upon the reading of the unknown lexical item *"Megaline"*. In this initial step, the corresponding hypothesis space incorporates all the top level concepts available in the ontology for the new lexical item *"Megaline"*. So, the concept MEGALINE may be a kind of an ACTIVITY, OBJECT, etc. Continuing with the processing of the phrase *"The Megaline unit ... "*, the ACTIVITY and other high-level hypotheses are ruled out, while, at the same time, the OBJECT hypothesis is further specialized to HARDWARE; SOFTWARE and COMPANY are also eliminated from further consideration. All these refinements are due to linguistic evidence, *viz.* the co-occurrence of the unknown lexical item *"Megaline"* and *"unit"* within a noun phrase, as well as the selectional constraint that *"unit"*, among others, may denote a piece of HARDWARE, while it may not denote a COMPANY or SOFTWARE, or even an ACTIVITY. Hence, we continue to focus on MEGALINE as a kind of HARDWARE (pruning of hypotheses motivated by linguistic reasons is marked by darkly shaded boxes). The learner then aggressively specializes this single hypothesis to the immediate subordinates of HARDWARE, *viz.* to COMPUTER, PRINTER, etc. in order to test more restricted hypotheses which – according to more specific constraints – are easier falsifiable. Further evidence comes from processing the phrase *"... by Aquarius ... "*. Being left with the PRINTER and COMPUTER hypothesis for MEGALINE, a link between MEGALINE

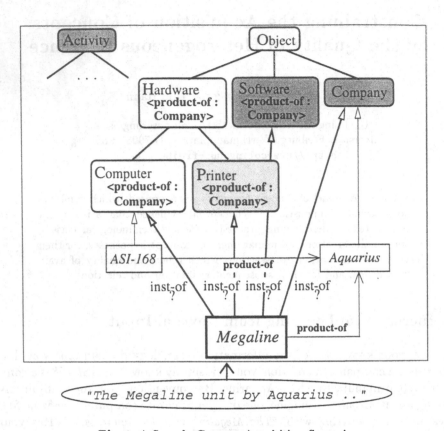

Fig. 1. A Sample Concept Acquisition Scenario

and AQUARIUS via the relation PRODUCT-OF is established based on the occurrence of the preposition *"by"* (other conceptual links emerging from AQUARIUS are also tried). An evaluation heuristic for concept hypotheses indicates that conceptual relations (like PRODUCT-OF) sharing identical or closely related concepts as their domain or range arguments in the *a priori* domain knowledge are inherently more plausible than those which do not. So we conclude that, given *ASI*-168 is a product of *Aquarius* (denoted as *ASI*-168 PRODUCT-OF *Aquarius* in a terminological notation), *ASI*-168 being a COMPUTER (correspondingly denoted as *ASI*-168 : COMPUTER), and *Megaline* is a product of *Aquarius*, it is more plausible to assume that MEGALINE might also be a COMPUTER, rather than being a PRINTER (these preference-based pruning decisions are marked by lightly shaded boxes).

Accordingly, we propose a learning methodology that uses linguistic and conceptual evidence, like the ones just illustrated, to generate, refine, evaluate and, finally, select plausible concept hypotheses on the basis of a continuous stream of textual input. The underlying reasoning mechanism is supplied with knowledge about language, knowledge about the domain of discourse, and metaknowledge about how these two knowledge sources can be combined in terms of deriving and testing reasonable concept hypotheses while reading a text.

2 A Multi-Layered Concept Learning Strategy

The concept acquisition approach we propose consists of four methodological layers. We start with a rich domain model that is encoded in a *terminological knowledge representation* language (cf. [9] for a survey). Since we mainly consider the learning task a problem of reasoning *about* specific linguistic patterns or structural configurations in the domain knowledge base, learning is dependent on the use of various sorts of metaknowledge. The metareasoning devices we employ introduce second-order reasoning power. In order not to run into severe complexity problems, a truth-preserving automatic transformation from second-order to more tractable first-order expressions is achieved by reification and by reasoning on these reified structures in encapsulated first-order knowledge base contexts. The corresponding *translation rules* constitute the second layer of our approach (cf. [13] for more details). The metaknowledge we provide for concept learning from natural language texts consists of various forms of evidence we have for the plausibility, credibility, etc. of emerging concept hypotheses. Any single evidence is assigned a so-called *quality label* which captures the direction (positive or negative) and qualitative degree of support. These labels, in our application context, are either generated as a reflection of patterns of language use (linguistic labels created by the concept hypothesis generator which is closely coupled with the parsing system) or through the inspection and heuristic evaluation of characteristic knowledge base states by qualification rules (according to which conceptual quality labels are issued); cf. [4] for a more detailed account. This specification layer provides the input to the final one. Given various sorts of individual quality judgments in terms of quality labels, a so-called *qualification calculus* [12] contains the rules for evaluating, ranking, and selecting the most plausible hypotheses. A reasoning component (e.g., a terminological classifier) extended by quality-based ranking and selection criteria, the *qualifier*, makes up the fourth layer of our approach. In this paper we will concentrate on methodological issues related to quality labels and the qualifier. Additionally, we present the results from an empirical evaluation of our approach.

2.1 Quality Labels and Qualification Rules

The design of a set of quality labels requires the following steps:

1. *Define the dimensions* from which quality labels can be drawn. In our application, we chose the set $\mathcal{L} := \{l_1, \ldots, l_m\}$ of linguistic quality labels and $\mathcal{C} := \{c_1, \ldots, c_n\}$ of conceptual quality labels. Depending on other application frameworks, alternative choices are equally possible, e.g., replacing linguistic labels by those characteristic of vision or robot data.
2. *Determine a partial ordering among the quality labels from one dimension.* Given the function ρ which yields the quality contribution for each single quality label, this ordering is represented by equations and inequalities comparing different quality labels.[1]

---

[1] Obviously, ρ can be determined by extensive empirical testing.

3. *Determine a total ordering among the dimensions.*[2] In our application, we have empirical evidence to grant linguistic criteria more discrimination power than conceptual ones. As a consequence, we state the following constraint:

$$\forall l \in \mathcal{L}, \forall c \in \mathcal{C} : \rho(l) \; >_\rho \; \rho(c)$$

Linguistic quality labels reflect structural properties of phrasal patterns or discourse contexts in which unknown lexical items occur[3] — we here assume that the type of grammatical construction exercises a particular interpretative force on the unknown item and, at the same time, yields a particular level of credibility for the hypotheses being derived. As concrete examples of high-quality labels, consider the case of APPOSITION or COMPOUND labels which are generated when a construction is encountered such as in *"... the printer @A@ ... "* or *"... the @A@ unit ... "*, respectively, with *"@...@"* denoting the unknown item. Both constructions almost unequivocally determine "@A@" (considered as a potential noun)[4] to denote a *printer* or *unit*, respectively. This assumption is justified independent of further conceptual conditions, simply due to the nature of the linguistic construction being used. Still of good quality but already less constraining are occurrences of the unknown item in a CASEFRAME construction as illustrated by *"... @B@ is equipped with memory ... "*. In this example, case frame specifications of the verb *"equip"* that relate to its PATIENT role carry over to *"@B@"*. So *"@B@"* may be anything that is equipped with memory, e.g., a computer system. Finally, in a PP-ATTACHMENT or GENITIVENP construction the unknown lexical item is still less constrained as, e.g., in *"... @C@ from IBM ... "*, or *"... IBM's @C@ ... "*. Given an attachment of prepositional phrases or relations among nouns in genitive noun phrases, a much wider interpretation space for *"@C@"* is opened. (Almost) any concept that can reasonably be related to the concept "IBM" will be considered a potential hypothesis for *"@C@"*, e.g., its departments, products, Fortune 500 ranking. Hence, at the quality level these latter two labels (just as the first two labels we considered) form an equivalence class the elements of which cannot be further discriminated. So we end up with the following orderings:

$$\rho(\text{COMPOUND}) \quad =_\rho \quad \rho(\text{APPOSITION})$$
$$\rho(\text{COMPOUND}) \quad >_\rho \quad \rho(\text{CASEFRAME})$$
$$\rho(\text{APPOSITION}) \quad >_\rho \quad \rho(\text{CASEFRAME})$$
$$\rho(\text{CASEFRAME}) \quad >_\rho \quad \rho(\text{GENITIVENP})$$
$$\rho(\text{CASEFRAME}) \quad >_\rho \quad \rho(\text{PP-ATTACHMENT})$$
$$\rho(\text{GENITIVENP}) \quad =_\rho \quad \rho(\text{PP-ATTACHMENT})$$

---

[2] This is quite a strong requirement. Though one might conceive of mixed orderings between different dimensions, one should carefully weigh the potential advantages of a mixture with the perspicuity and testability of the constraints being used.

[3] We intend to integrate additional types of constraints, e.g., quality criteria reflecting the degree of completeness *vs.* partiality of the parse. But these experiments have not been conclusive, as yet.

[4] Such a part-of-speech hypothesis can directly be derived from the inventory of valence and word order specifications underlying the dependency grammar model we use [2].

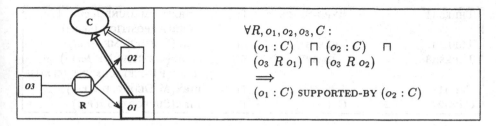

$$\forall R, o_1, o_2, o_3, C:$$
$$(o_1 : C) \quad \sqcap \quad (o_2 : C) \quad \sqcap$$
$$(o_3 \ R \ o_1) \quad \sqcap \quad (o_3 \ R \ o_2)$$
$$\Longrightarrow$$
$$(o_1 : C) \ \text{SUPPORTED-BY} \ (o_2 : C)$$

Table 1. Qualification Rule SUPPORTED

Conceptual quality labels result from comparing the conceptual representation structures of a concept hypothesis with already existing representation structures in the underlying domain knowledge base from the viewpoint of structural similarity, incompatibility, etc. The closer the match, the more credit is lent to a hypothesis.

For instance, a very positive conceptual quality label such as M-DEDUCED is assigned to multiple derivations of the same concept hypothesis in different hypothesis (sub)spaces.[5] Still positive labels are assigned to terminological expressions which share structural similarities in one hypothesis space, though they are not identical. The qualification rule in Table 1[6], e.g., reflects the conceptual proximity a relation R induces on its component fillers, o_1 and o_2,[7] respectively, provided that they share a common concept class C. Accordingly, we may state: $\rho(\text{M-DEDUCED}) >_\rho \rho(\text{SUPPORTED})$.

2.2 Quality-Based Classification

Whenever new evidence for or against a concept hypothesis is brought forth in a simple learning step the entire set of concept hypotheses is reevaluated. First, a selection process is started to eliminate weak or even untenable hypotheses from further consideration. The corresponding quality-based selection among hypothesis spaces is grounded on threshold levels as defined in Table 2 (in Section 3 this selection level will be referred to as **TH**). Their definition takes mostly linguistic evidence into account and evolved in a series of validation experiments. At the first threshold level, all hypothesis spaces with the maximum of COMPOUND or APPOSITION labels are selected. If more than one hypothesis is left to be considered, at the second threshold level only concept hypotheses with the maximum number of CASEFRAME assignments are approved. Finally, if several hypothesis spaces still remain, the ones with the maximum number of GENITIVENP or PP-ATTACHMENT instances are preferred.

---

[5] Note that the entire hypothesis space for a concept yet to be acquired is divided into a hierarchy of conceptually specialized subspaces. Plural usage of this term usually indicates a reference to hypothesis subspaces.

[6] "$\sqcap$" denotes the terminologiscal conjunction, $(o_1 : C)$ stands for "o_1 *is an instance of C*".

[7] o_1 denotes the concept to be learned, o_2's relational linkage to o_3 via R is part of the *a priori* domain knowledge.

THRESH1	$\doteq$	HYPO-SPACE	$\sqcap$	(**max**(COMPOUND *term*) $\sqcup$ **max**(APPOSITION *term*))
THRESH2	$\doteq$	THRESH1	$\sqcap$	**max**(CASEFRAME *term*)
THRESH3	$\doteq$	THRESH2	$\sqcap$	(**max**(GENITIVENP *term*) $\sqcup$ **max**(PP-ATTACHMENT *term*))
CRED1	$\doteq$	THRESH3	$\sqcap$	**max**(M-DEDUCED *term*)
CRED2	$\doteq$	CRED1	$\sqcap$	**max**(SUPPORTED *term*)

Table 2. Selection/Ranking Criteria

Those hypothesis spaces that have fulfilled these threshold criteria will then be classified relative to two different credibility levels (in Section 3 this selection level will be referred to as **CB**). The first level of credibility contains all of the hypothesis spaces which have the maximum of M-DEDUCED labels, while at the second level (again, with more than one hypothesis left to be considered) those are chosen which are assigned the maximum of SUPPORTED labels.

These rankings are formalized in Table 2. The "goodness" of the quality labels as formalized by the inequalities under ρ is realized in terms of corresponding terminological definitions, while terminological disjunction reflects the equations under ρ (cf. Section 2.1). Threshold and credibility criteria make use of composed roles, a specific domain and range restriction on roles (in Table 2 abbreviated as "X *term*"), and a new constructor MAX for the path computation. Their complete terminological specification is given in [12].

3 Evaluation Study

In this section, we present data from an empirical evaluation of the quality-based concept aquisition system. We focus here on the issues of learning accuracy and the learning rate. Due to the given learning environment, the measures we apply deviate from those commonly used in the machine learning community. In concept learning algorithms like IBL [1] there is no hierarchy of concepts. Hence, any prediction of the class membership of a new instance is either true or false. However, as such hierarchies naturally emerge in terminological frameworks, a prediction can be more or less precise, i.e., it may approximate the goal concept at different levels of specificity. This is captured by our measure of *learning accuracy* which takes into account the conceptual distance of a hypothesis to the goal concept of an instance, rather than simply relating the number of correct and false predictions, as in IBL.

In our approach, learning is achieved by the refinement of *multiple* hypotheses about the class membership of an instance. Thus, the measure of *learning rate* we propose is concerned with the reduction of hypotheses as more and more *information* becomes available about one particular new instance. In contrast, IBL-style algorithms consider only one concept hypothesis per learning cycle and their notion of *learning rate* relates to the increase of correct predictions as more and more *instances* are being processed.

Step	Phrase	Semantic Interpretation
1.	*Megaline* from *Aquarius* ...	(PP-Attach,Megaline,product-of,Aquarius)
2.	...in a *mini tower case*	(PP-Attach,Megaline,has-case,MiniTowerCase.1)
3.	*Megaline's CPU* ...	(GenitiveNP,Megaline,has-cpu,CPU.1)
4.	*Megaline* is *equipped with* ...	(CaseFrame,equip.1,patient,Megaline)
5.	...*2 MB working memory*	(CaseFrame,equip.1,co-patient,Memory.1)
		↦ (Megaline,has-memory,Memory.1)
6.	...and two	(CaseFrame,equip.1,co-patient,FloppyDiskDrive.1)
	floppy disk drives	↦ (Megaline,has-drive,FloppyDiskDrive.1))
7.	...the *Megaline unit* ...	(Compound,Megaline,instance-of,Unit.1)

Table 3. Semantic Interpretation of a Text Fragment Featuring *"Megaline"*

We investigated a total of 101 texts from a corpus of information technology magazines. For each of them 5 to 15 learning steps were considered. A learning step is operationalized here by the representation structure that results from the semantic interpretation of an utterance which contains the unknown lexical item. In order to clarify the input data available for the learning system, cf. Table 3. It consists of seven single learning steps for the unknown lexical item *"Megaline"* already introduced in Section 1. Each learning step is associated with a particular natural language phrase in which the unknown lexical item occurs[8] and the corresponding semantic interpretation in the text knowledge base (the data also incorporate the type of syntactic construction in which the unknown item occurs – this indicates the kind of linguistic quality label to be issued; "↦" provides the results from the application of verb interpretation rules).

Learning Accuracy. In a first series of experiments, we investigated the *learning accuracy* of the system, i.e., the degree to which the system correctly predicts the concept class which subsumes the target concept under consideration (the *target* being the new item to be learned). Learning accuracy (LA) is here defined as (n being the number of hypothesis spaces for a single target):

$$LA := \sum_{i \in \{1...n\}} \frac{LA_i}{n} \quad \text{with} \quad LA_i := \begin{cases} \frac{CP_i}{SP_i} & \text{if } FP_i = 0 \\ \frac{CP_i}{FP_i + DP_i} & \text{else} \end{cases}$$

SP_i specifies the length of the *shortest path* (in terms of the number of nodes being traversed) from the TOP node of the concept hierarchy to the maximally specific concept subsuming the instance to be learned in hypothesis space i; CP_i specifies the length of the path from the TOP node to that concept node in hypothesis space i which is *common* both for the shortest path (as defined above) and the actual path to the predicted concept (whether correct or not); FP_i specifies the length of the path from the TOP node to the predicted (in this case *false*) concept and DP_i denotes the node *distance* between the predicted node and the most specific concept correctly subsuming the target in hypothesis

---

[8] Note that our text database consists of German language data. The translations we provide give only rough English correspondences.

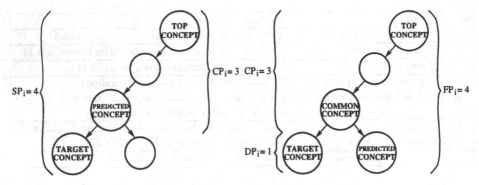

Fig. 2. LA Configuration for an Under-specified Concept Hypothesis

Fig. 3. LA Configuration for a Slightly Incorrect Concept Hypothesis

space i, respectively. Figures 2 and 3 depict sample configurations for concrete LA values involving these parameters. Fig. 2 illustrates a correct, yet too general prediction with $LA_i = .75$, while Fig. 3 contains an incorrect concept hypothesis with $LA_i = .6$.

Given the measure for learning accuracy, Table 4 illustrates how the various learning hypotheses (i.e., hypothesis spaces) for MEGALINE develop in accuracy from one step to the other. The numbers in brackets in the column **Learning Hypotheses** indicate for each hypothesized concept the number of concepts subsumed by it in the underlying knowledge base; **LA CB** gives the accuracy rate for the full qualification calculus including threshold and credibility criteria (cf. Table 2), **LA TH** for threshold criteria only, while **LA -** depicts the accuracy values produced by the terminological reasoning component without incorporating the qualification calculus. It becomes evident from Table 4 that the full qualification calculus produces very early (in step 2) a nearly optimal overall result (85%) and fewer hypothesis spaces (indicated by the number of rows) than the other two approaches.

Generalizing from the learning behavior for a single concept like MEGALINE, Fig. 4 depicts the learning accuracy curve for the entire data set (101 texts). The evaluation starts at LA values in the interval between 48% to 54% for **LA**

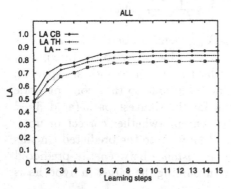

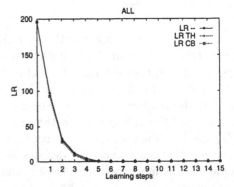

Fig. 4. Learning Accuracy (LA) for the Entire Data Set

Fig. 5. Learning Rate (LR) for the Entire Data Set

Learning Hypotheses	LA -	LA TH	LA CB	Learning Hypotheses	LA -	LA TH	LA CB
Building(0)	0.29	0.29					
Documentation(5)	0.50	0.50	0.50				
User(0)	0.19	0.19		User(0)	0.19	0.19	
Software(26)	0.50	0.50	0.50				
Hardware(101)	0.75	0.75	0.75	PC(0)	1.00	1.00	1.00
				Workstation(0)	0.70	0.70	0.70
				Desktop(0)	0.70		
				Notebook(0)	0.70		
				Portable(0)	0.70		
	ϕ:0.45	ϕ:0.45	ϕ:0.58		ϕ:0.66	ϕ:0.63	ϕ:0.85
Learning step 1				**Learning step 2**			
User(0)	0.19	0.19		User(0)	0.19	0.19	
PC(0)	1.00	1.00	1.00	PC(0)	1.00	1.00	1.00
Workstation(0)	0.70	0.70	0.70	Workstation(0)	0.70	0.70	0.70
Desktop(0)	0.70			Desktop(0)	0.70		
Notebook(0)	0.70			Notebook(0)	0.70		
Portable(0)	0.70			Portable(0)	0.70		
	ϕ:0.66	ϕ:0.63	ϕ:0.85		ϕ:0.66	ϕ:0.63	ϕ:0.85
Learning step 3				**Learning step 4**			
User(0)	0.19	0.19		User(0)	0.19	0.19	
PC(0)	1.00	1.00	1.00	PC(0)	1.00	1.00	1.00
Workstation(0)	0.70	0.70	0.70	Workstation(0)	0.70	0.70	0.70
Desktop(0)	0.70			Desktop(0)	0.70		
Notebook(0)	0.70			Notebook(0)	0.70		
Portable(0)	0.70			Portable(0)	0.70		
	ϕ:0.66	ϕ:0.63	ϕ:0.85		ϕ:0.66	ϕ:0.63	ϕ:0.85
Learning step 5				**Learning step 6**			
PC(0)	1.00	1.00	1.00				
Workstation(0)	0.70	0.70	0.70				
Desktop(0)	0.70						
Notebook(0)	0.70						
Portable(0)	0.70						
	ϕ:0.76	ϕ:0.85	ϕ:0.85				
Learning step 7							

Table 4. Some Concept Learning Results for a Text Featuring *"Megaline"*

-, **LA TH** and **LA CB**, respectively, in the first learning step. In the final step, LA rises up to 79%, 83% and 87% for **LA -**, **LA TH** and **LA CB**, respectively.

The pure terminological reasoning machinery which does not incorporate the qualification calculus always achieves an inferior level of learning accuracy (and also generates more hypothesis spaces) than the learner equipped with the qualification calculus. Furthermore, the inclusion of conceptual criteria (**CB**) supplementing the linguistic criteria (**TH**) helps a lot to focus on the relevant hypothesis spaces and to further discriminate the valid hypotheses (on the range of 4% of precision). Note that an already significant plateau of accuracy is usually

	# texts	steps
LA –	26	4,68
LA TH	31	4,16
LA CB	39	4,15

	# texts	steps
LA –	58	4,69
LA TH	74	4,36
LA CB	85	3,71

Table 5. Learning steps for LA = 1.0   **Table 6.** Learning steps for LA = .8

reached after the third step *viz.* 67%, 73%, and 76% for **LA -**, **LA TH**, and **LA CB**, respectively, in Fig. 4. This indicates that our approach finds the most relevant distinctions in a very early phase of the learning process, i.e., it requires only a *few* examples.

In a concept acquisition application operating on real-world texts, it should be fair to ask what level of precision one is willing to accept as a satisfactory result. We may discuss this issue in terms of degrees of learning accuracy. Under ideal conditions, one might require a 100% learning accuracy. Table 5 gives the number of texts being processed under this constraint and the associated number of learning steps, given the three types of criteria, *viz.* **LA -**, **LA TH**, and **LA CB**. Under the rigid condition that the most specific concept specializing the unknown item is to be learned, the three criteria require almost the same number of learning steps on the average. This is simply due to the fact that the knowledge base we supply has not a full coverage of any domain segment, even in a limited domain such as information technology. (The knowledge base currently comprises 325 concept definitions and 447 conceptual relations.) The picture changes remarkably (cf. Table 6), if we only require a level of precision that does not fall below a learning accuracy of 80%. This also means that more general or slightly incorrect concept descriptions are accepted as a proper learning result, though more specific and entirely correct concept descriptions might have been worked out, at least in principle. About double the number of texts are being processed, but the number of learning steps are decreasing only for the full qualification calculus (*viz.* applying criterion **LA CB**). We may thus conclude that, granted an LA level of 80%, at least for the full qualification calculus only 15% of the learned concepts will be erroneous still. (Note the contrast to the LA values depicted in Fig. 4, which are derived from *averaging* single LA values.)

Summarizing this discussion, we may conclude that lowering the requirements on acceptable precision rates of learning results – within reasonable limits, of course – produces still valid learning hypotheses that are built up in less than four learning steps on the average.

Learning Rate. The learning accuracy focuses on the predictive power of the learning procedure. By considering the *learning rate* (LR), we turn to the stepwise reduction of alternatives of the learning process. Fig. 5 depicts the mean number of transitively included concepts for all considered hypothesis spaces per learning step (each concept hypothesis denotes a concept which transitively subsumes various subconcepts). Note that the most general concept hypothesis in our example denotes OBJECT which currently includes 196 concepts. In general, we observed a strong negative slope of the curve for the learning rate.

After the first step, slightly less than 50% of the included concepts are pruned (with 93, 94 and 97 remaining concepts for **LR CB**, **LR TH** and **LR -**, respectively). Again, learning step 3 is a crucial point for the reduction of the number of included concepts (ranging from 9 to 12 concepts). Summarizing this evaluation experiment, the quality-based learning system yields competitive accuracy rates (a mean of 87%), while at the same time it exhibits significant and valid reductions of the predicted concepts (up to two, on the average).

4 Related Work

Our approach bears a close relationship to the work of [7], [3], [11], [10] [14], [6], and [8], who aim at the automated learning of word meanings from context using a knowledge-intensive approach. But our work differs from theirs in that the need to cope with *several competing* concept hypotheses and to aim at a *reason-based selection* is not an issue in these studies. Learning from real-world textual input usually provides the learner with only sparse, highly fragmentary evidence such that multiple hypotheses are likely to be derived from that input. So, we stress the need for a hypothesis generation and evaluation component as an integral part of large-scale real-world text understanders [5] operating in tandem with concept learning devices.

The work closest to ours has been carried out by Rau *et al.* [10]. As in our approach, concept hypotheses are generated from linguistic and conceptual data. Unlike our approach, the selection of hypotheses depends only on an ongoing discrimination process based on the availability of these data but does not incorporate an inferencing scheme for reasoned hypothesis selection. The difference in learning performance – in the light of our evaluation study in Section 3 – amounts to 8%, considering the difference between **LA -** (plain terminological reasoning) and **LA CB** values (terminological metareasoning based on the qualification calculus). Hence, our claim that we produce competitive results.

5 Conclusion

We have presented a concept acquisition methodology which is based on the incremental assignment and evaluation of the quality of linguistic and conceptual evidence for emerging concept hypotheses. The principles underlying the selection and ordering of quality labels are general, as are most conceptual quality labels. The concrete definition of, e.g., linguistic quality labels, however, introduces a level of application-dependence. Nevertheless, as quality criteria are ubiquitous, one may easily envisage quality labels coming from sources other than linguistic and conceptual knowledge (e.g., a vision system may require quality labels which account for different degrees of signal distortion, 2D vs. 3D representations, etc. in order to interpret visual scenes in the course of learning new gestalts). No specialized learning algorithm is needed, since learning is a (meta)reasoning task carried out by the classifier of a terminological reasoning system. However, heuristic guidance for selecting between plausible hypotheses comes from the different quality criteria. Our experimental data indicate that given these heuristics we achieve a high degree of pruning of the search space for hypotheses in very early phases of the learning cycle.

Acknowledgements. We would like to thank our colleagues in the CLIF group for fruitful discussions and instant support, in particular Joe Bush who polished the text as a native speaker. K. Schnattinger is supported by a grant from DFG (Ha 2097/3-1).

References

1. D. Aha, D. Kibler, and M. Albert. Instance-based learning algorithms. *Machine Learning*, 6:37–66, 1991.
2. N. Bröker, S. Schacht, P. Neuhaus, and U. Hahn. Performanzorientiertes Parsing und Grammatik-Design: das PARSETALK-System. In C. Habel, S. Kanngießer, and G. Rickheit, editors, *Perspektiven der Kognitiven Linguistik. Modelle und Methoden*, pages 79–125. Opladen: Westdeutscher Verlag, 1996.
3. F. Gomez and C. Segami. The recognition and classification of concepts in understanding scientific texts. *Journal of Experimental and Theoretical Artificial Intelligence*, 1:51–77, 1989.
4. U. Hahn, M. Klenner, and K. Schnattinger. Learning from texts: a terminological metareasoning perspective. In S. Wermter, E. Riloff, and G. Scheler, editors, *Connectionist, Statistical and Symbolic Approaches to Learning in Natural Language Processing*, pages 453–468. Berlin: Springer, 1996.
5. U. Hahn, K. Schnattinger, and M. Romacker. Automatic knowledge acquisition from medical texts. In *AMIA'96 - Proc. AMIA Fall Symposium Beyond the Superhighway: Exploiting the Internet with Medical Informatics*, pages 383–387, 1996.
6. P. Hastings. Implications of an automatic lexical acquisition system. In S. Wermter, E. Riloff, and G. Scheler, editors, *Connectionist, Statistical and Symbolic Approaches to Learning in Natural Language Processing*, pages 261–274. Berlin: Springer, 1996.
7. R. Mooney. Integrated learning of words and their underlying concepts. In *CogSci'87 - Proc. 9th Conf. of the Cognitive Science Society*, pages 974–978, 1987.
8. K. Moorman and A. Ram. The role of ontology in creative understanding. In *CogSci'96 - Proc. 18th Conf. of the Cognitive Science Society*, pages 98–103, 1996.
9. B. Nebel. *Reasoning and Revision in Hybrid Representation Systems*. Berlin: Springer, 1990.
10. L. Rau, P. Jacobs, and U. Zernik. Information extraction and text summarization using linguistic knowledge acquisition. *Information Processing & Management*, 25(4):419–428, 1989.
11. E. Riloff. Automatically constructing a dictionary for information extraction tasks. In *AAAI'93 - Proc. 11th National Conf. on Artificial Intelligence*, pages 811–816, 1993.
12. K. Schnattinger and U. Hahn. A terminological qualification calculus for preferential reasoning under uncertainty. In *KI'96 - Proc. 20th Annual German Conf. on Artificial Intelligence*, pages 349–362. Berlin: Springer, 1996.
13. K. Schnattinger, U. Hahn, and M. Klenner. Quality-based terminological reasoning for concept learning. In *KI'95 - Proc. 19th Annual German Conf. on Artificial Intelligence*, pages 113–124. Berlin: Springer, 1995.
14. S. Soderland, D. Fisher, J. Aseltine, and W. Lehnert. CRYSTAL: Inducing a conceptual dictionary. In *IJCAI'95 - Proc. 14th Intl. Joint Conf. on Artificial Intelligence*, pages 1314–1319, 1995.

Conceptualizing Adjectives

Steffen Staab & Udo Hahn

(Qℱ) Linguistische Informatik / Computerlinguistik
Universität Freiburg, Werthmannplatz 1, D-79085 Freiburg
http://www.coling.uni-freiburg.de

Abstract. We specify a model for the conceptual interpretation of relative adjectives (like *"big"*), which covers a crucial aspect of the underlying comprehension process – the comparison to a norm that is associated
with a comparison class. Building on an elaborate domain ontology and
knowledge about intercorrelations, comparison classes are dynamically
created depending on the context in which adjectival utterances occur.

1 Introduction

The conceptual description of relative adjectives[1] differs significantly from those
of other word classes. Unlike concepts denoted by nouns and verbs, such degree
expressions have no canonical, self-contained concept representation. They rather
are dependent on a "reference point" or "class norm" that is associated with a
comparison class. For instance, *"Peter"* in (1b) should not be referred to as *"tall"*
in a general sense, but as *"tall in comparison to the class norm of a comparison
class C"*, where C is constrained by the *context* in which *"tall"* occurs. This
becomes immediately evident in example (1) where the context of the utterance
(1a) crucially determines the valid comparison class for *"tall(Peter,C)"*.

(1) a. Peter is 4 years old.

 b. Peter is tall.

While linguists [8, 1] have already agreed upon modeling relative adjectives
like *"tall"* by a binary predicate that relates a degree to a comparison class
(resp. its class norm), many challenging problems from a natural language understanding perspective are still left open. These fall into two main categories,
viz. representational and computational issues. From the *representational* perspective one may ask:

 – How are comparison classes represented?
 – What kind of knowledge determines comparison classes?
 – What are the conceptual linkages between degree expressions and compari-
 son classes at the knowledge level?

From the *computational* point of view one may ask:

 – How are comparison classes actually determined given a degree expression?

---

[1] Relative adjectives like *"tall"* or *"fast"* are opposed to absolute adjectives such as
 "married" or *"rectangular"*. Though this distinction can be further refined (cf., e.g.,
 [1]), the particular relevance of relative adjectives is commonly agreed upon [10, 8].

– Is there an active, on-the-fly assembly process for comparison classes or are they accessed from a precompiled, enumerable class inventory, just like passive data?
– How are context-dependencies incorporated into the computation of appropriate comparison classes?

We will provide answers to the first set of these questions by developing a formal model of the background knowledge and a representation schema for comparison classes in Sections 2 and 3. These representational foundations are used in an explicit computational model which, at least partially, covers the second set of questions in Section 4. This joint formal model we here propose surpasses entirely descriptive accounts prevailing so far. The constructs we use also incorporate cognitive evidence taken from the relevant literature, if available.

2 Representation of Comparison Classes

A typical (though simplified) sentence from our text corpus on information technology test reports is given by (2).

(2) The picture has a good quality for a picture printed by a laser printer.

The example contains an occurrence of a relative adjective where the comparison class is explicitly given. Hence, its computation boils down to a parsing problem and the associated knowledge base operations for the generation of a conceptual interpretation of the utterance [2]. In our system [5], the representation of a comparison class is *dynamically* created from the utterance and the concepts available in the knowledge base. This view coincides with experimental findings of Rips & Turnbull [13], who let subjects verify sentences with absolute and relative adjectives, given different types of comparison classes. Their results suggest that comparison classes are not predefined, but are computed on the fly.

Following the terminology introduced by Bierwisch [1] and Klein [8], we say that a relative adjective a is related to a *class norm*[2], which is a degree of the same type (e.g., QUALITY) as the one described by the adjective (e.g., *"good"*). The class norm belongs to a *comparison class*[3] (e.g., the set of pictures printed by laser printers), which is a set of individuals or — in terminological terms — a concept C with instances o_i. If the degree of such an instance o_i of C is above the class norm, then one may assert that "o_i is a for C".

The terminological knowledge representation system we use (cf. [18] for a survey) allows to create a comparison class COMP-CLASS-1 for example (2) on the fly. COMP-CLASS-1 is defined by restricting the object class, PICTURE, to pictures printed by a LASER-PRINTER, which is a subconcept of PRINTER (cf. Fig. 1, with COMP-CLASS-1 $\doteq$ PICTURE $\sqcap$ ∀PRINTED-BY.LASER-PRINTER). As a necessary result, the picture O-1 is classified as belonging not only to PICTURE, but also to COMP-CLASS-1. If this were not the case, either the definition of the comparison class or the utterance itself would be invalid. In a metarelation

---

[2] We here abstract from different attributes being associated with different class norms.
[3] Rips & Turnbull [13] use the terms "reference class" and "reference point" instead of "comparison class" and "class norm", respectively.

(CLASS-NORM-OF) the comparison class is associated with the class norm for quality, CLASS-NORM-1, which is related to the quality Q-1 of the picture O-1 by the predicate EXCEEDS-1.

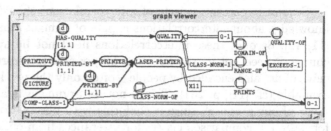

Fig. 1. Representing Comparison Class and Class Norm

3 Knowledge about Intercorrelations

In a discourse setting, a multitude of linguistic possibilities exist to associate a given adjective with a comparison class.

(3) Paul is 4 years old. He is tall.

(4) Paul celebrated his 4th birthday, yesterday. He is tall.

(5) Paul is tall for a 4 year old boy.

These examples indicate that purely linguistic criteria for the restriction of the comparison class of an adjective are not sufficient. Similarly, knowledge-based computations that only rely on static knowledge structures fail to determine the proper interpretations. Our approach contrasts with Bierwisch's proposal [1] that applies to the majority of relative adjectives, which are related to non-generically used nouns. He assumes, that the comparison classes of these adjectives correspond to their directly associated nouns. Cech, Shoben & Love [3] already suggest that such simple processes seem insufficient to account for categorization effects in comparative judgments, an observation to which we subscribe in the case of comparison class formation, too. Instead, they speculate on the possibility to gain more flexibility by the identification of the valid comparison class at a more general, explicitly marked concept level. Still, we do not see how explicit marks could be used to deal with the context phenomena occurring in the examples above. As an alternative, we use *(meta)knowledge about intercorrelations* that describes how a class subhierarchy may influence the relations of class norm instances on a scale *or* how two degrees of a given concept are correlated. As an example, consider the sentences (6) and (7). In both of these the comparison classes are stated explicitly, and, thus, they elucidate the distinction between a proper comparison class restriction and an improper one:

(6) Peter is tall for a gymnast.

(7) ? Peter is tall for a flute player.

The intercorrelation that exists between "hasHeight" and "conductsExercises" describes gymnasts to be usually smaller than the average people. So, being tall for a gymnast does not necessarily imply being tall for the comparison class of all people. It is exactly the absence of corresponding intercorrelations between "hasHeight" and "playsFlute" that renders the restriction of the comparison class to flute players awkward.

Several important aspects of intercorrelations should be noted here. First, knowledge about intercorrelations is part of humans' common-sense knowledge [11, 12]. Second, these intercorrelations need not be symmetrical.[4] Third, of course, it need not be the case that all possible intercorrelations one may conceive of are also encoded by people – often only the particularly salient ones are available (cf. [11], p. 264). This is not an argument against, but rather one in favor of our proposal, since it conforms with observations we made about the formation of comparison classes for utterances from our text corpus. Finally, it is not necessary that knowledge about intercorrelations is overly fine-grained. Only depending on the *strength* of the intercorrelation, the need for constructing a conceptually more specific comparison class arises.[5] As a consequence, the specification of intercorrelations and, thus, the construction of new comparison classes underlie a principle of parsimony, since only the *most relevant* intercorrelations have to be accounted for.

In order to exploit the knowledge about intercorrelations just described we use a specification in terms of description logics. This notation has the advantage that it combines formal explicitness with algorithmic convenience. The intercorrelations have in common that they describe local *restriction classes* which will later be gathered to define the comparison class. We distinguish two basic types of intercorrelations which are illustrated by the examples (8–10) (the relevant comparison classes are underlined). Sentence (8) illustrates a simple case of a degree-hierarchy intercorrelation (for a description of the relevant relations in the knowledge base (KB), cf. Fig. 2). In this example, the relevant comparison class (LASER-PRINTER) is the concept NOISE-LEVEL is *directly* associated with. Therefore, the path from the relevant degree NOISE-LEVEL to the relevant restriction class LASER-PRINTER has the unit length *1* (inheritance links are not counted). (9) refers to the same type of intercorrelation, but differs in the longer distance (two relations have to be passed) that lies between one of the relevant restrictions, 300DPI-LASER-PRINTER, and the degree QUALITY (of picture).

---

[4] Commonsense knowledge tells us that though gymnasts tend to be smaller than the average people, small people do not tend to do gymnastics very much. Assume that a population consists of 50% small and 50% tall people, respectively, 1% being gymnasts, and 90% of the gymnasts being small. Then the probability that a gymnast is a small person is 90%. However, the probability that a small person is a gymnast is only 1.8%. Thus, restricting a comparison class from all people to gymnasts, in fact, decreases the class norm for height considerably, while the reverse is not true.

[5] For instance, for *"a small gymnast"*, it is necessary to define the comparison class GYMNAST (as opposed to the more general class HUMAN) in order to assure that proper assessments about the property HEIGHT can be derived. For *"a small iceskater"*, however, the construction of a corresponding comparison class ICESKATER could possibly be justified, but is not necessary at all. This is due to the fact that iceskaters can still be compared relative to the general class of humans with respect to their height, even though a weak intercorrelation exists between HEIGHT and ICESKATERS, *viz.* a preference for being small. This case of a weak correlation can be further distinguished from one in which actually no intercorrelation seems reasonable as in the case of SPRINTERS, whose average heights do not seem to differ from those of other persons.

(8) Degree-hierarchy intercorrelation (with distance 1):
The noise level of the 300dpi laser printer X11 is high for a <u>laser printer</u>.

(9) Degree-hierarchy intercorrelation (with distance 2):
The picture of the X11 has a good quality for the <u>picture of a 300dpi laser printer</u>.

(10) Degree-degree intercorrelation (with distance 2):
The X11 offers very good quality for a <u>laser printer that costs \$800</u>.

In order to represent the above-mentioned intercorrelations knowledge must be available about which relations (for example (9): QUALITY-OF and PRINTED-BY[6]) lie between the restricting hierarchy (here, the subhierarchy of PRINTER) and

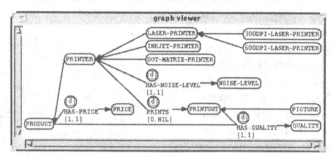

Fig. 2. Hierarchy and Definitory Roles in the KB T-Box

the correlated degree (here, QUALITY). Moreover, it must be known which subclasses of PRINTER have a norm attached for noise level, which is either below or above the class norm associated with their direct superclass.[7] In our example, LASER-PRINTER, INKJET-PRINTER and 600DPI-LASER-PRINTER belong to the set of classes that are associated with class norms above that of their superclass, while DOT-MATRIX-PRINTER and 300DPI-LASER-PRINTER relate to corresponding lower class norms.

For degree-hierarchy intercorrelations we define the operator $\Im_H$ as in Table 1 to represent this sort of knowledge. The operator takes a list of pairs of restriction

$$\Im_H([(\text{RESTRC}_j, \text{R}_j)], \{\text{POS}\text{C}_j\}, \{\text{NEG}\text{C}_j\}) :=$$
$$\{\ i_1 : \text{H-INTERREL},$$
$$\text{R}'_1 \doteq \text{R}_1 \sqcap (\text{TOP} \times \text{RESTRC}_1), i_1 \text{ REL}_1 \text{ R}'_1, \ldots,$$
$$\text{R}'_k \doteq \text{R}_k \sqcap (\text{TOP} \times \text{RESTRC}_k), i_1 \text{ REL}_k \text{ R}'_k,$$
$$i_1 \text{ HAS-POS-CLASS POS}\text{C}_1, \ldots, i_1 \text{ HAS-POS-CLASS POS}\text{C}_n,$$
$$i_1 \text{ HAS-NEG-CLASS NEG}\text{C}_1, \ldots, i_1 \text{ HAS-NEG-CLASS NEG}\text{C}_m\}$$

Table 1. Representing Degree-Hierarchy Intercorrelations

classes (RESTRC_j) and relations (R_j). The relations, R_j, are furthermore restricted to R'_j in order to allow the definition of more specialized intercorrelations. This is especially necessary, if the domain of a relation is not specific enough to ensure an adequate intercorrelation representation (in Fig. 3, e.g., PRINTED-BY is restricted to REL-2-P, such that only pictures are re-

---

[6] For each relation (e.g., HAS-QUALITY, PRINTS) and relation instance we always assume the existence of its inverse, which is then referred to by an intuitively plausible name, like QUALITY-OF, PRINTED-BY.

[7] We here abstract from the consideration of multi-hierarchies.

lated by REL-2-P to their printing source). Furthermore, the operator takes sets of concepts that are associated with class norms above and below the class norm of their direct superclass, $\{PosC_j\}$ and $\{NegC_j\}$, respectively. $\Im_H$ maps them onto assertions of a degree-hierarchy intercorrelation instance $(i_1 : H\text{-}\textsc{Interrel})$. These assertions are propositions *about* the relations in the T-Box, and, thus, they form an independent level of assertional metaknowledge. Our considerations are made more concrete in Fig. 3, which contains a knowledge base fragment for the processing of example (9).

For degree-degree intercorrelations (such as needed for (10)) a similar operator, $\Im_D$, has to be supplied. Just like $\Im_H$ it takes restriction classes and relations, but instead of positive or negative subclass relations (HAS-POS-CLASS, HAS-NEG-CLASS) its specification only requires to indicate whether an intercorrelation is a positive or negative correlation.

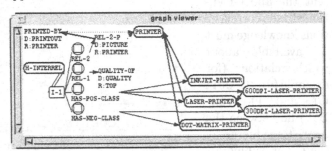

Fig. 3. The Intercorrelation Knowledge Needed for (9).

4 Computing Comparison Classes

Often relative adjectives refer to comparison classes that are only implicitly available (cf. (3) and (4)). Their recognition cannot be considered the task of the parsing mechanism proper, but rather constitutes a task on its own. Accordingly, we here give such an algorithm that computes implicit comparison classes[8] by making use of semantic relations, of the knowledge about intercorrelations as previously described, of text-specific and world knowledge, and of the representation mechanism for comparison classes from Section 2. The algorithm incorporates, to a limited degree, knowledge about the discourse context by way of considering all semantic relations in the current text fragment. At present, this fragment includes the current and the immediately preceding utterance. As a starting condition, we presume the completion of anaphora resolution, verb interpretation and the interpretation of prepositional phrases.

4.1 The Algorithm

The basic idea of the algorithm for computing comparison classes is expressed in Fig. 4: A positive adjective a denotes a degree d in the current text fragment This degree d is related to an object o_1, which itself is related to another object o_p. Of course, there might be no object or several objects related to o_1, and o_p itself might have other relations. Each object o_i has a most specific type $C_{i,1}$.

---

[8] In [17] we consider inferences on degrees and class norms that follow this computation and, thus, complete the understanding process.

The goal of the algorithm is to select all objects o_i that are relevant for the computation of the correct comparison class. Furthermore, for each object o_i it must select its correct intermediate superconcept $C_{i,k(i)}$, which does neither restrict the comparison class too narrowly (as $C_{i,1}$ might do) nor too widely (as

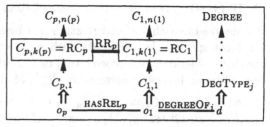

Fig. 4. Basic Structures

$C_{i,n(i)}$ might do, since it yields no restriction at all). This goal is achieved by matching the available knowledge on intercorrelations against the semantic structures of the current text fragment. Finally, a comparison class is (recursively) computed by combining all the gathered restrictions. In Fig. 4 this means that the new comparison class is defined by restricting RC_1 to a new class where the role RR_p is restricted to the range RC_p.

The algorithm starts with a set of relations D_n representing the semantic interpretation of the current text fragment in which the relevant adjective a occurs.

1. Input:
   (a) A positive gradable adjective a which denotes the degree d.
   (b) A set of unary and binary relations representing the meaning of the current text fragment in a Neo-Davidsonian style: $D_n = \{\text{DEGTYPE}_j(d),$ $C_{1,1}(o_1), \text{DEGREEOF}_j(d, o_1), C_{p,1}(o_p), \text{HASREL}_p(o_1, o_p), \dots\}$

Then the comparison class, COMPCLASS, is computed by applying the recursive function *"ComputeRestriction"*.

2. $(\text{COMPCLASS}, RR) := \text{ComputeRestriction}([o_1], [\text{DEGREEOF}_j])$

The main function *"ComputeRestriction"* takes a list of objects $ObjL$ and a list of relations $RelL$. These objects and relations describe the path to the degree under consideration. Thus, in the first call to *"ComputeRestriction"* $ObjL$ will always be $[o_1]$, and $RelL$ will be $[\text{DEGREEOF}_j]$.

1. Parameters given to the function: $ObjL = [o_m, \dots, o_1]$, $RelL = [r_m, \dots, r_1]$

First, *"ComputeRestriction"* tries to match[9] a piece of intercorrelation knowledge against the semantic structures represented by $ObjL$ and $RelL$ (step 2). If the intercorrelation I that has been found is a degree-degree intercorrelation then a singleton concept is returned (step 3).

2. $(I, RR) := \iota(i_k, R_{m,k}) : |RelL| = m \land \text{INSTOF}(i_k, \text{INTERREL}) \land \neg \exists R_{m+1,k}$ $[\text{REL}_{m+1}(i_k, R_{m+1,k})] \land \forall j \in [1, m] : \text{REL}_j(i_k, R_{j,k}) \land \text{INSTOF}(r_j, R_{j,k})$

---

[9] Degree-degree intercorrelations have the type D-INTERREL. INSTOF, ISA, RANGE and HASROLE denote the common terminological relations. As mentioned before, the relevant part of our KB is a simple hierarchy, thus there is only a single path from a concept to the topmost concept and "min" and "max" applied to a (possibly empty) subset of concepts of such a path are, therefore, partial and single-valued.

3. IF INSTOF(I, D-INTERREL) THEN RETURN $(\{o_m\}, R_{m,k})$

If a degree-hierarchy intercorrelation has been found, then it is used to select the most specific class that fits with o_m — that class is either mentioned in the degree-hierarchy intercorrelation or it is the maximal concept which is also defined by an inverse superrelation, R_m^{-1}, of the current relation, r_m (step 4).

4. $RC := \min_{C_k}\{C_k | \text{INSTOF}(o_m, C_k) \wedge C_k \in \{C_l | \text{HAS-POS-CLASS}(i_k, C_l) \vee$ HAS-NEG-CLASS$(i_k, C_l)\} \cup \{\max_{C_l}\{C_l | \text{INSTOF}(o_m, C_l) \wedge \text{HASROLE}(C_l, R_m^{-1}) \wedge$ INSTOF$(r_m, R_m)\}\}\}$

5. IF $RR = \perp$ THEN $RR := \iota R_m : \text{INSTOF}(r_m, R_m) \wedge \text{HASROLE}(RC, R_m^{-1})$

If no intercorrelation could be found, then RC and RR must be defined in a way that renders them neutral up to the point where they themselves might become further restricted (steps 4 and 5). This is necessary, e.g., if there are no known intercorrelations with relation length 1, but intercorrelations with length 2. In this case, RC must be defined "neutrally" first, and is only restricted by $RC := RC \sqcap RR'.RC'$ afterwards. Finally, "*ComputeRestriction*" is applied recursively (step 6a), and each new restriction RC' narrows down the current restriction class RC with the terminological operation (step 6b).

6. $\forall p : \text{HASREL}_p(o_m, o_p) \wedge o_p \notin ObjL$ DO
   (a) $(RC', RR') := \text{ComputeRestriction}([o_p.ObjL], [\text{HASREL}_p.RelL]);$
       (where "[.]" denotes a list constructing operation)
   (b) $RC := RC \sqcap RR'.RC'$

7. RETURN (RC, RR)

The recursion stops when it finds a degree-degree intercorrelation, or when the given semantic structures have been searched exhaustively.

4.2 A Sample Computation

A sample computation of the comparison class is based on example (11):

(11) The picture with the giraffe was printed by the fast laser printer X11. It shows good quality.

1. Input
   (a) "*good*" in conjunction with "*quality*" denotes a quality degree q_1
   (b) The relations conveyed by text fragment (11) are:
       $\{\text{QUALITY}(q_1), \text{PICTURE}(o_1), \text{QUALITY-OF}(q_1, o_1), \text{GIRAFFE}(o_2),$
       DISPLAYS(o_1, o_2), LASER-PRINTER$(X11)$, PRINTED-BY$(o_1, X11)$,
       VELOCITY(o_3), HAS-VELOCITY$(X11, o_3)\}$

2. $(\text{COMPCLASS}, RR) := \text{ComputeRestriction}([o_1], [\text{QUALITY-OF}])$

As can be seen from the following recursion process, the comparison class will be assigned the value "*picture printed by a laser printer*". This result is equivalent to the one for example (2) and, thus, is also summarized by Figure 1. The first recursion of *ComputeRestriction* proceeds as follows:

1. Parameters are: $ObjL = [o_1], RelL = [\text{QUALITY-OF}]$

2. No intercorrelation between PICTURE and QUALITY is found:
   $(I, RR) = (\perp, \perp)$; "$\perp$" denotes that a variable is undefined.
3. IF evaluates to FALSE, since I is undefined.
4. Since I is undefined, the restriction class RC is selected among the concepts that o_1 belongs to and that have "QUALITY-OF^{-1} = HAS-QUALITY" as a role: $RC := $ PICTURE
5. $RR := $ QUALITY-OF
6. Now recursion of depth 2 starts for the relations DISPLAYS and PRINTED-BY:
   HASREL$_p(o_m, o_p) := $ DISPLAYS(o_1, o_2)
   (a) Since no intercorrelation between the objects displayed in a picture and its quality can be found, the most general restriction class and relation is returned: $(RC', RR') := $ ComputeRestriction($[o_2, o_1]$,
   $$[\text{DISPLAYS}, \text{QUALITY-OF}]) = (\text{OBJECT}, \text{DISPLAYS})$$
   (b) Thus, $RC = $ PICTURE is *not* restricted by applying the very general restrictions (RC', RR').
   HASREL$_p(o_m, o_p) := $ PRINTED-BY$(o_1, X11)$
   (a) As the quality of a picture depends on the printer, an intercorrelation is found, and adequate restrictions are returned (cf. Fig. 3 for the relation $R_2' = $ REL-2-P): $(RC', RR') := $ ComputeRestriction($[X11, o_1]$,
   $$[\text{PRINTED-BY}, \text{QUALITY-OF}]) = (\text{LASER-PRINTER}, R_2')$$
   (b) Hence, RC is narrowed down to PICTURE $\sqcap$ R_2'.LASER-PRINTER, a picture printed by a laser printer.
7. RETURN (RC, RR)

While the other two calls to *ComputeRestriction* provide rather obvious results, the one that actually computes the restriction (LASER-PRINTER, R_2' is much more illustrative:

1. $ObjL = [X11, o_1], RelL = [\text{PRINTED-BY}, \text{QUALITY-OF}]$
2. Here, the intercorrelation described in Fig. 3 is found to match:
   $(I, RR) := (i_1, R_2')$
3. IF evaluates to FALSE.
4. The intercorrelation indicates that the most specific known concept (LASER-PRINTER) is relevant: $RC := $ LASER-PRINTER
5. IF evaluates to FALSE.
6. There is one further relation (HAS-VELOCITY$(X11, o_3)$) which yields no restriction, since no intercorrelation exists between the printing velocity and the quality of the picture.
7. Thus, (LASER-PRINTER, R_2') is returned.

5 Empirical Data

In an empirical evaluation we compared the algorithm from Section 4.1 (henceforth, *c3*) against two simpler, more naive approaches. The first of these, *n1*, uses the most specific concept of the object conjoined with the respective degree. The second one, *n2*, which is equivalent to the model used by Rips & Turnbull in their experiments [13], does not select this most specific concept, but its immediate superconcept instead. Both approaches constitute somewhat of a lower bottom line for our approach, since it can switch back to one of these simpler approaches, if it is unable to identify more selective restrictions.

We chose a text which contained 226 sentences with about 4,300 words. 121 positive gradable adjectives were screened, for which a reasonable semantic representation could be determined in 72 cases – and only these were evaluated. The remaining 59 occurrences graded idiomatic expressions, concepts that are hard to model (e.g., *"a good idea"*), or entailed other problems that were not directly related to finding the correct comparison classes. Under the assumption of complete knowledge, *c3* achieved a high success rate (60 cases (83%) were correctly analyzed). *n1* and *n2* performed much worse, as they were only able to properly determine 20 and 15 valid comparison classes (28% *vs.* 21%), respectively.

n1 and *n2* are equivalent to the procedures Bierwisch [1] suggests for adjectives related with generic and non-generic nouns, respectively (e.g., in *"towers are high"* the related noun "towers" is generic, while in *"this tower is high"* it is not). An oracle that tells whether an adjective is related to a generic object and, depending on the result, changes the strategy from *n1* to *n2* would render a mechanism close to the one Bierwisch proposes. However, it would not add much benefit. Since none of the 72 considered adjectives are related to generic nouns, the positive cases of *n2* are not due to any generic use. Our results are interesting still, even though we restricted our approach to *distance-1* and *distance-2* interrelations to keep the modelling problem manageable.

6 Related Work

Though the notion of comparison class has been around for a long time and has been used for many linguistic descriptions [1, 8, 9, 16], no comprehensive theory of comparison class formation exists so far that properly incorporates context information. Following Bierwisch [1], Rips & Turnbull [13] made valuable experiments with generic adjective-noun combinations to shed light on the dynamics of the processes underlying the determination of comparison classes. Their results suggest that comparison classes are not predefined. In general, this approach is too underconstrained to explain context effects. Nevertheless, their results do not rule out more "knowledgeable" approaches (e.g., incorporating a taxonoymy *and* correlations) in order to compute comparison classes.

Further supporting evidence for our proposal is available from researchers that did not consider the comparison class formation problem, but which reported on experiments that indicate that major assumptions underlying our approach can be traced in empirical findings. First, distance and contiguity effects that are observed in comparative judgments suggest that people categorize dynamically for grading processes [14, 3]. Second, several sources (e.g., [11, 12]) sustain the assumption that people encode knowledge about intercorrelations, which lies at the core of the proposed mechanism, and use this information for categorization processes.

The importance of comparison classes for the semantics of relative adjectives might sometimes be underestimated. Relative adjectives are not always used in an attributive way which requires the construction of a comparison class. In an act of reference, a relative adjective such as *"fat"* might be used to distinguish between two objects that are both non-fat. Klein [7] elaborates on this referential/attributive distinction and Kyburg & Morreau [10] present an "extension stretching approach" that can handle such referential cases without the construction of comparison classes. However, they cannot treat the much more often occurring attributive uses of relative adjectives. Moreover, much previous work on the representation of degrees completely abstracts from the problem of comparison class determination. Interval approaches like those in [1] and [16] use class norms to denote the meaning of relative adjectives, but hardly consider the comparison class formation problem. Models of fuzzy logic given by Zadeh [19] and qualitative models from Schwartz [15] or Kamei & Muraki [6] do not mention comparison classes at all. However, this does not mean that they can cope without the representation of comparison classes, rather their models need to be substantially extended. They often take refuge to the simplifying assumption that there is yet another module that maps natural language degree expressions onto the right scale, but then refrain from spelling it out in detail. We claim that this specification will require a comparison class formation mechanism that assigns different comparison classes to different scales on which their models can be applied — exactly the kind of procedure we propose.

7 Conclusion

Surprisingly little evidence has been collected so far concerning the conceptualizations underlying adjectival expressions, relative adjectives in particular — the third major open word class of Western languages. We have introduced a model of adjective interpretation that accounts for some of the intriguing complexities of relating degree expressions to a proper conceptual representation. At the center of the model lie comparison classes and their associated class norms to which degree expressions are related. This is not a static linkage. Rather, contextual indicators together with knowledge about correlations control the process of selecting the appropriate comparison class. The homogeneous formal treatment we give within a terminological specification framework is unique as is the provision of an algorithm for computing complex comparison classes at all.

Still, this is only a first step which leaves several problems open: For instance, a more comprehensive model would have to take into account shared beliefs between participants in the discourse, since these may substantially influence the comparison class formation process. Also, granularity effects in the knowledge base are notoriously difficult, but should be solvable along the lines of path-length neutral computations for textual ellipsis resolution as supplied in [4].

Our model also constitutes an improvement over previous attempts at specifying adjective interpretation from a cognitive perspective. These have focused on the antonymy relation and the linguistic description of polarity properties of adjectives, in particular [1]. The focus of our model, however, is on cognitive explanations and computational issues. Closest to this goal are studies by Rips

& Turnbull [13] who, nevertheless, consider only a lexically fixed set of comparison classes. Hence, our model provides more flexibility and increased empirical coverage compared to these approaches.

Acknowledgements. S. Staab is a member of the Graduate Program *"Human and Machine Intelligence"* at Freiburg University, which is funded by *DFG*. The work of U. Hahn is partially funded by a grant from *DFG* under the account *Ha 2097/5-1*.

References

1. M. Bierwisch. The semantics of gradation. In M. Bierwisch and E. Lang, editors, *Dimensional Adjectives*, pages 71–261. Springer, 1989.

2. N. Bröker, S. Schacht, P. Neuhaus, and U. Hahn. Performanzorientiertes Parsing und Grammatik-Design: das ParseTalk-System. In C. Habel, S. Kanngießer, and G. Rickheit, editors, *Perspektiven der Kognitiven Linguistik. Modelle und Methoden*, pages 79–125. Westdeutscher Verlag, 1996.

3. C.G. Cech, E.J. Shoben, and M. Love. Multiple congruity effects in judgments of magnitude. *Journal of Experimental Psychology: Learning, Memory, and Cognition*, 16(6):1142–1152, 1990.

4. U. Hahn, K. Markert, and M. Strube. A conceptual reasoning approach to textual ellipsis. In *Proc. of the ECAI-96*, pages 572–576. J. Wiley, 1996.

5. U. Hahn and M. Romacker. Automatische Erzeugung von medizinischen Wissensbasen durch robustes, partielles Textverstehen: Befundtextanalyse im SYNDIKATE-System. *KI - Künstliche Intelligenz*, 11(3), 1997.

6. S. Kamei and K. Muraki. A discrete model of degree concept in natural language. In *Proc. of the COLING-94*, pages 775–781, 1994.

7. E. Klein. On formalizing the referential/attributive distinction. *Journal of Philosophical Logic*, 8:333–337, 1979.

8. E. Klein. A semantics for positive and comparative adjectives. *Linguistics & Philosophy*, 4(1):1–45, 1980.

9. E. Klein. Comparatives. In A. von Stechow and D. Wunderlich, editors, *Semantics*, pages 674–691. W. de Gruyter, 1991.

10. A. Kyburg and M. Morreau. Vague utterances and context change. In *Proc. of the 2nd Intern. Workshop on Computational Semantics*, pages 135–155. Tilburg University, The Netherlands, 1997.

11. B.C. Malt and E.E. Smith. Correlated properties in natural categories. *Journal of Verbal Learning and Verbal Behavior*, 23(2):250–269, 1984.

12. K. McRae. Correlated properties in artifact and natural kind concepts. In *Proc. of the 14th Annual Conf. of the Cognitive Science Society*, pages 349–354, 1992.

13. L.J. Rips and W. Turnbull. How big is big? Relative and absolute properties in memory. *Cognition*, 8:145–174, 1980.

14. K.M. Sailor and E.J. Shoben. Effects of category membership on comparative judgment. *Journal of Experimental Psychology: Learning, Memory, and Cognition*, 19(6):1321–1327, 1993.

15. D. G. Schwartz. Outline of a naive semantics for reasoning with qualitative linguistic information. In *Proc. of the IJCAI-89*, pages 1068–1073, 1989.

16. G. Simmons. A tradeoff between compositionality and complexity in the semantics of dimensional adjectives. In *Proc. of the EACL-93*, pages 348–357, 1993.

17. S. Staab and U. Hahn. "Tall", "good", "high" — Compared to what? In *Proc. of the IJCAI-97*, 1997.

18. W. A. Woods and J. G. Schmolze. The KL-ONE family. *Computers & Mathematics with Applications*, 23(2-5):133–177, 1992.

19. L. A. Zadeh. PRUF — a meaning representation language for natural languages. *International Journal of Man-Machine Studies*, 10:395–460, 1978.

Parsing N Best Trees from a Word Lattice

Hans Weber, Jörg Spilker, Günther Görz

University of Erlangen–Nuremberg
IMMD (Computer Science) VIII — AI

Abstract. This article describes a probabilistic context free grammar approximation method for unification grammars. In order to produce good results, the method is combined with an N best parsing extension to chart parsing. The first part of the paper introduces the grammar approximation method, while the second part describes details of an efficient N-best packing and unpacking scheme for chart parsing.

1   Introduction

Recently much attention has been payed to the integration of speech and language technology[1]. The concentration on spontaneous speech understanding led to the definition of a robust interface known as the word graph or word lattice between recognition and understanding. Depending on the application, systems are built to provide a shallow stochastic analysis or a deep linguistic analysis of the word lattice. Using a shallow stochastic approach, a rough template-based analysis can be achieved which makes sense in those cases where a fine grained reconstruction of meanings is not necessary. On the other hand, most applications still require a detailed linguistic analysis. In speech to speech translation of spontaneous negotiation dialogues — the domain of the VERBMOBIL project — speakers' utterances contain a lot of information elements which cannot be captured by a rough paraphrase. Hence, deep syntactic and semantic parsing is necessary to decode the correct meaning, as in example 1.

Example 1. "Yes ... we should meet the fifteenth of July... or... better would be the sixteenth... say... a quarter past three."

2   Word Graphs and Unification Grammars

Deep linguistic analysis based on word lattices is still a difficult problem. There exist a couple of parsing algorithms for context free grammars, as e.g. variants of generalized LR parsing [Tomita 1986], or variants of Earley's parser [Paeseler 1988] and Cocke–Kasami–Younger parsers [Ney 1991] which are of cubic complexity[2]. Some of these have been extended to unification grammars as in

---

[1] This work was funded by the German Federal Ministry for Research and Technology (BMFT) in the framework of the Verbmobil Project under Grant BMFT 01 IV 101 H / 9. The responsibility for the contents of this study lies with the authors.
[2] Tomita's GLRP is exponential in some rare cases.

[Schmid 1994] or [Hauenstein and Weber 1994]. The latter two approaches use unification grammars in conjunction with N-Gram models to search and parse the lattice simultaneously. In [Weber 1994b] and [Görz et al. 1996] a stochastic unification grammar is used for the same task. The lattice is being parsed to prduce deep linguistic descriptions, using a model of the unification grammar's rule and type operations together with a word based N-Gram model, while pruning is performed by a beam search strategy. The work on probabilistic unification grammars was originally inspired by work of [Magerman and Marcus 1991] and [Briscoe and Carroll 1993]. A couple of recent publications present a more fine grained statistical modeling of feature and type operations ([Brew 1995] [Eisele 1994]). Actually, all of these approaches are of exponential complexity and can only be applied to typed input or very shallow word graphs. Cubic complexity has been proven for the intersection of context free and finite state languages[3] in [Bar-Hillel et al. 1991], but parsing of unification grammars is exponential anyway. This still holds for stochastic variants of unification grammars. Unfortunately, word graphs produced from spontaneous speech tend to be very large even for the best word decoders available. So an at most cubic solution had to be developed for a deep unification based analysis on word lattices.

3   Decomposition of Grammar and Context Sensitive Grammar Model

We started with a given unification grammar G for spontaneous speech. The grammar G is a typical HPSG style grammar where syntactic, semantic, and other information is manually encoded in the same complex typed feature structure. Since it contains a lot of rules for spontaneous speech phenomena, as filled pauses, interruptions and repairs, it shows a very high degree of ambiguity due to the required coverage. Tests with directly training the grammar and applying it to word lattices led to parsing times of several minutes on a Sun Ultra Sparc, which was more than unacceptable[4]. In these tests it became obvious that performing unifications during search is prohibitive when input word lattices contain about 1000 word hypotheses.

As a consequence, we built a context free grammar by removing the feature restrictions of the original grammar G and keeping only global type information. This results in G', where $L(G) \subset L(G')$ and even more important Trees$(G) \subset$ Trees(G'), which means there is a one to one mapping of a subset of the trees generated by G' and the set of trees generated by G.

In order to approximate G by G', we trained a model of grammar derivations with the intention that the model prefers trees t, where $t \in$ Trees$(G) \wedge t \in$ Trees(G') to trees t', where $t' \notin$ Trees$(G) \wedge t' \in$ Trees(G'). This task was performed best using a context sensitive variant of Fujisaki's[5] unsupervised PCFG

---

[3] ...which is the formal language metaphor for lattice parsing with context free grammars.

[4] Direct training was carried out in the style of [Weber 1994a].

[5] [Fujisaki et al. 1991]

training procedure. This training procedure is essentially exponential, but on the other hand the well-known inside-outside procedure could not be used since a grammar model with more than one rule of context was needed to characterize a tree set which was essentially not context free. The procedure of building the approximate grammar G' proceeds as follows:

1. Parse a corpus using the original grammar G resulting in an ambiguous tree bank T.
2. Transform the grammar G to G' by removing all features from G.
3. Train the grammar G' unsupervised on T.

4 The Grammar Model

We used a modified top down PCFG model, where the the conditional probability distributions are defined over rules, given the mother rule in a tree and the specific daughter of the mother rule connecting the two rules. Given a tree T which can be written as $S \Rightarrow \ldots X \Rightarrow \alpha\beta\gamma \Rightarrow \alpha\delta\gamma$, and the grammar rule i: $X \rightarrow \alpha\beta\gamma$ and the rule j: $\beta \rightarrow \delta$, where β is the k-th nonterminal in the right hand side of rule i, we say: *rule j occurred, given i and k*. So for each pair i, k we estimate a distribution $P_{i,k} : j \mapsto [0; 1]$. The model was smoothed using absolute discounting [Ney and Essen 1991], redistributing the saved probability mass equally to the unobserved events as a floor value.[6]

5 Parsing a Lattice as a Chart

We parse the lattice using the standard mapping of frame numbers to chart edges. Our parsing schema is the well-known left-to-right active chart parsing with pruning on an agenda in every chart vertex, which results in a beam search. Agendas in each vertex keep pairs of chart edges to be processed next. Those pairs are being scored using a linear combination of the acoustic, N-Gram, and grammar model scores. It is described in more detail in [Weber 1994a] and [Görz et al. 1996].

The grammar trees which are found in that parsing step are passed to a second processing step using the original grammar G. In that step the tree found is re-parsed deterministically using unification.

If the approximation of G by the conjunction of G' and the grammar model would be very close, then strict Viterbi parsing could be used where full structure sharing is employed. Unfortunately this is not the case. Only some of the best trees of G' are in Trees(G), although our context sensitive grammar model is much better than simple PCFG statistics.

A success could be enforced by enumerating all parses in order of quality. Then it would be guaranteed that a tree inside Trees(G) was found. If G' contains no unary recursive rules, this could be achieved in finite time. Anyway,

---

[6] In our experiments a backoff from rule pairs to the standard PCFG statistics did not lead to significant improvements compared to the Laplace distribution.

such a procedure would force us to keep all scores of a partial parse for later unpacking in a bookkeeping mechanism (a list would do it). For a single edge this mechanism had to keep all different derivations leading to that edge. We know that this would cost the same as if we totally abandoned structure sharing. Parsing would be exponential again an we would have gained nothing compared to direct parsing of a probabilistic unification grammar.

On the other hand, in most cases the N best Trees of G' contain at least one in Trees(G) when N is set to 10. Therefore we parse and unpack only the N best trees — a decision which led to a robust and efficient overall parsing behavior.

The following table shows some results of experiments performed on parts of the VERBMOBIL corpus. A HPSG-like grammar was used containing 64 unification grammar rules and 700 lexicon entries. The grammar was used to parse seven dialogs with 150 spontaneous utterances. A set of 61 utterances was used for testing. The N best trees produced by the approximation grammar were re-parsed by the original grammar in order to check whether they are wellformed.

N	correctly parsed utterances
1	12
5	47
10	51

For ten sentences no valid parse tree was found inside the ten best parses of the approximation grammar. In order to apply the method to larger grammars and corpora it should be noted that the important parameters which make the method applicable are the fit between G and G' on the one hand and the power of the stochastic model on the other hand. The looser the fit between the grammars, the more restrictions have to be provided by the stochastic model. For the packing and unpacking procedure described throughout the rest of this article, only a minimal loss in performance could be measured with N set to 100.

6 Parsing of N Best Trees

Our parsing engine is an active chart parser whose initial chart is a word lattice and word boundary hypotheses are mapped to vertices (see [Paeseler 1988], [Thompson 1990], or [Weber 1994a] for examples). The parser is assumed to process all pairs of active and inactive edges in strict best-first order.

Edges, Scores and Bookkeeping

As usual, a chart is an ordered set of vertices $V_1 \dots V_n$.

Definition 1 Edge.
An edge E is a 7-tuple (RNr, RS, LV, RV, F-Pointer, VC, *Unpacked*), which is interpreted as follows:

- RNr and RS are Integers. Each grammar rule has a unique rule number RNr. RS (rule state) is the number of the rule's next daughter to be processed.(zero represents "no more daughter left" and indicates an passive edge).
- LV (left vertex) and RV (right vertex) are the chart vertices which E spans (as usual).
- VC is a simple array of length N of triples (S, AD, PD), where AD (active daughter) and PD (passive daughter) are two edges which led to E with a grammar score S.
- F-Pointer is the fill pointer of VC; it is an integer ranging from 0 to N-1.
- *Unpacked* is a vector of unpacked trees. It is not used during the initial lattice parsing step. In postprocessing it will be filled by the unpacking procedure. The elements of *Unpacked* will be trees represented as nested lists. Every tree node will be a list of the score obtained for the whole tree dominated by that node and the grammar symbol followed by the nested lists for the daughter constituents.

We call the quadruple (RNr, RS, LV, RV) the *edge identifier*, which is uniquely defined[7].

The combination of edges goes almost as usual. The difference to standard chart parsing lies in the redundancy check and packing (structure sharing) mechanism. The best N histories which lead to an edge are stored while all other pairs of edges leading to an edge are discarded. We say an edge is *full* in this case.[8]

Two analyses are shared when the rule and the state of the rule are identical. Only in terminal edges we allow for different lexicon entries leading to the same nonterminal grammar symbol to be shared.

Definition 2 Completer-Operation.
A, B and C are edges.

1. IF A.RV = B.LV
2. AND Cat(A.RNr, A.RS) = LHS(B.RNr)
3. AND B.RS = 0 THEN BEGIN
4. C:= Id(A.RNr, A.RS-1, A.LV, B.RV)
5. IF NOT C THEN
6. C := (A.RNr, A.RS-1, A.LV, B.RV, -1, [ ])
7. IF (C.F-Pointer < N-1) THEN BEGIN
8. Increment C.F-Pointer
9. C.VC[F-Pointer] := (Score(A,B),A,B)
10. END
11. END

---

[7] Id(RNr, RS, LV, RV) returns one edge E with identifier (RNr, RS, LV, RV) or NIL, if such an edge does not exist.

[8] We use some auxiliary function notation here, hoping that it is self-explaining. E.g., Cat(Rule-Number, Rule-State) returns the grammar category of the daughter with the number "Rule-State" of the right hand side of the rule with number "Rule-Number". LHS indicates the same for the left hand side.

The score of C, given A and B, is the product of the best score of A, the best score of B, and the model probability of having the grammar rule of B just below the actual daughter of A's grammar rule when constructing C.

Definition 3 Score.
Score(A,B) := A.VC[0].S × B.VC[0].S × $P_{i,j}(k)$,
where i=A.RNr, j=A.RS, k=B.RNr

Due to lack of space only the completer operation is presented. The same mechanism is used for all edge insertion operations.

On deterministic input, space and time complexity of context free chart parsing is cubic in terms of input words when full packing is employed [Sheil 1976]. We added a constant amount of memory to every edge and a constant amount of processing time to each edge insertion. Consequently the N best packing chart parser is still cubic in time and space.

Lattice parsing is of cubic complexity for that case depending on word graph nodes[9], and the same holds for our modified N best packing parser, since memory and processing steps are multiplied with a constant factor N.

7 Unpacking of N Best Trees

A complete chart of edges as defined above may contain millions of scored derivations in packed format, although it does not contain all of the scored derivations possible according to the grammar. Obviously, the best analysis in the sense of Viterbi parsing can easily be decoded by walking down from the spanning edge representing the grammar's start symbol, using only the first cells of the traversed packing vectors.

In fact, the N best analyses can be unpacked in a time proportional to the number of edges affected in these N best analyses.

First we will have a closer look at edges which are unpacked by definition. Then we present an algorithm to unpack an edge, given all its derivations are already unpacked. We close the section with a strategy which guarantees that only those edges will be unpacked that may contribute to the N best unpacked trees.

7.1 Initial Unpacked Edges

Two kinds of edges are always being unpacked.

- Empty active edges (with zero span) are initialized with an empty vector as the value for VC as well as for *Unpacked*.

---

[9] This follows directly from [Bar-Hillel et al. 1991] and is exemplified in [Noord 1994] and [Weber 1994a].

– Terminal edges which cover all word hypotheses which map to the same grammar category and have an identical span. These edges contain a VC where all word hypotheses w and their scores s are represented as triples (s, NIL, w), where NIL is a dummy component. *Unpacked* contains corresponding tree representations (s w).

For these two kinds of edges the packed and the unpacked representations contain the same elements — namely none in the empty active edge case, and the word hypotheses directly packed together in the case of a terminal edge. A condition we impose is that the tree representations inside the terminal edges are sorted in descending order according to their score. Those edges are the starting point for the recursive unpacking procedure.

7.2 Unpacking other Edges

Unpacking proceeds bottom up. Starting with empty active edges and terminal edges, we build the trees for the resulting edge. If the resulting edge is active, we represent only the list of daughter subtrees contained in that edge. If a resulting edge is passive, we add the mother rule to the nested list representation. We will look at one step in this procedure in detail:

Assume an edge E which fulfills the following conditions: The vector E.VC is filled with n triples, with $1 \leq n \leq N$ and the vector *Unpacked* is empty. This is E's state after parsing has finished, but before unpacking. Assume furthermore that all histories of E, represented as triples in E.VC, are already unpacked. This means that all edges A and P in all triples (s, A, P) in E.VC contain vectors *A.Unpacked* and *P.Unpacked* with corresponding tree representations of at most N best trees contained.

Informally speaking, the following has to be done: Walk along the cells of *E.Unpacked* that are still free and successively fill them with tree representations taken from one of the daughter edges pairs.

For the first cell it is a priori known what to do. Take E.VC[0].A.Unpacked[0] and E.VC[0].P.Unpacked[0] and make a new tree representation out of the two. The result will be the contents of E.Unpacked[0].

For the second element E.Unpacked[1] there are three possible choices from where the second best history is to be taken from. The second best choice is either

– E.VC[1].A.Unpacked[0] and E.VC[1].P.Unpacked[0]
– or E.VC[0].A.Unpacked[1] and E.VC[0].P.Unpacked[0]
– or E.VC[0].A.Unpacked[0] and E.VC[0].P.Unpacked[1]

Depending on the choice the third element has to be taken from VC[0], VC[1] or VC[2], and so on.

Assume for the moment, that the N best trees in E will all come from E.VC[0] — the pair of daughter edges which was responsible for the best tree on top. This slightly easier problem can be characterized as an N out of N^2 maximization which maps to a traversal of a N×N matrix. Only N steps are needed to perform this maximization since some information about a priori orderings can be employed. We know that the value for a subtree for E is the product of the rule application for E on its passive daughter with the values for the active and passive daughters. The first fraction is constant for all histories in E.VC[0], thus we only have to find the maximum for products of the values at two matrix fields.

Assume a maximization matrix M[a,p] with fields M[0,0] to M[N,N] where a is the number of the a-th active subtree, and p is the corresponding number of the p-th passive subtree. Additionally, a control vector C of length N is given initialized with zero in each field. C says for each a with which the corresponding p is to be combined next. To maximize the N best pairs according to the sum of their scores, the vector C is walked along N times:

Definition 4.

1. i:= 0; MaxEl := 0; MaxPos := 0
2. WHILE C[i] $\neq$ 0 AND i $\leq$ N DO BEGIN
3. Increment i;
4. IF MaxEl < M[i,C[i]] THEN BEGIN
5. MaxEl := M[i,C[i]]
6. MaxPos := i; END;
7. Increment C[MaxPos];
8. END;

In fact it is not necessary to create the matrix. The *Unpacked* vectors of the edge pair in E.VC[0] can be used together with a control vector C[10]. Since C is traversed at most one step further in every loop, the maximization costs $O(N \log N)$ steps.

Returning now to the original unpacking problem, the fact is that not all of the N best subtrees are supposed to come from E.VC[0]. In fact we could unpack all of the N E.VC[i], but this would cause a lot of extra work. The solution is to unpack E.VC[0] only one step, then freeze the state of unpacking E.VC[0], and save it, marked with the score of the next element to be picked out of E.VC[0]. We call such a saved object an *Unpack State* S_i. After that we do the same with E.VC[1]. We compare the values of the two states S_0 and S_1. The next unpacked element is taken from the state with the higher score, and the next local unpacking step is executed for that element thereby updating its score. After this operation the score of the element is lower than before. Then S_0 has the score of its second best unpacked element. These scores of S_i can directly be compared to the scores of the triples in VC. If an S_i is created, it has exactly the score of E.VC[i] — namely the best one. If during the search an element of S_i is taken, it receives the score of the second best element contained in it and so on.

The S_i are held in a list which is always kept sorted (a heap) during the search. In the worst case an S_i has to be created for every E.VC[i], which amounts

---

[10] ...and some cells to keep intermediate results.

to the creation of N control vectors and will cost N^2 space and time. In the best case only VC[0] will be unpacked, which will cost $N \mathrm{Log} N$ time and N space, as has already been noted.

7.3 Traversing the Chart

The unpacking procedure starts at a goal edge found, and it is expressed best as a head recursive call. That means one unpacking step first visits its best derivation and then recurs one level down. When unpacking an edge E, some unpacking of edge below E.VC[i] will only be performed then if needed. Unpacking costs the number of edges visited times N^2.

8 Conclusions

The presented parsing and unpacking schema is closely related to well known techniques for processing word lattices and probabilistic grammars. It provides a better solution for the lattice parsing task in speech/language systems than the standard algorithms, since it is only cubic in time compared with a full enumeration of probabilistic grammar trees or unification based parsing. In practice it proved to be appropriate also for huge word lattices, in particular as an approximative first step in a two phase parsing module for HPSG[11].

References

[Bar-Hillel et al. 1991] Bar-Hillel, J., M. Perles and E. Shamir. 1961 On the formal properties of simple phrase structure grammars. In *Zeitschrift für Phonetik, Sprachwissenschaft und Kommunikationsforschung* 14:143-172.

[Brew 1995] Brew, Chris. 1995 Stochastic HPSG. In *Proceedings of EACL-95*.

[Briscoe and Carroll 1993] Briscoe, Ted and John Carroll. 1993. Generalized probabilistic LR parsing of natural language (corpora) with unification-based grammars. *Computational Linguistics*, 19(1):25–59.

[Eisele 1994] Eisele, Andreas. 1994 Towards probabilistic extensions of constraint-based grammars. Technical Report Deliverable R1.2.B, DYANA-2.

[Fujisaki et al. 1991] Fujisaki, T., F. Jelinek, J. Cocke, E. Black, and T. Nishino. 1991. A probabilistic parsing method for sentence disambiguation. In Masura Tomita, editor, *Current Issues in Parsing Technology*, 139–148, Norvell, Mass., Kluver Akademic Publishers.

[Görz et al. 1996] Görz, G., M. Kesseler, J. Spilker, and H. Weber. 1996. Research on Architectures for Integrated Speech/Language Systems in VERBMOBIL. In *Proceedings of COLING-96*, Kopenhagen, August.

[Hauenstein and Weber 1994] Hauenstein, A. and H. Weber. 1994. An investigation of tightly coupled time synchronous speech language interfaces using a unification grammar. In Paul McKevitt, editor, *Proceedings of the Workshop on Integration of Natural Language and Speech Processing at AAAI 94*, 42–49, Seattle, August.

---

[11] The second re-parsing step is described in detail in [Kasper et al. 1996].

[Kasper et al. 1996] Kasper, Walter, Hans-Ulrich Krieger, Jörg Spilker, and Hans Weber. 1996. From word hypotheses to logical form: An efficient interleaved approach. In D. Gibbon, editor, *Natural Language Processing and Speech Technology. Results of the 3rd KONVENS Conference*. Mouton de Gruyter, Berlin, 77–88.

[Magerman and Marcus 1991] Magerman, D.M. and M.P. Marcus. 1991. Pearl: A probabilistic chart parser. In *Proc. of the European ACL*, March.

[Ney 1991] Ney, Hermann. 1991. Dynamic programming parsing for context-free grammars in continuous speech recognition. *IEEE Transactions on Signal Processing*, 39(2):336–340, February.

[Ney and Essen 1991] Ney, Hermann and Essen, Ute. 1991. On smoothing techniques for bigram-based natural language modelling. *IEEE Transactions ASSP*, 39:825–828, February.

[Noord 1994] Noord, G. van. 1994 On the Intersection of Finite State Automata and Definite Clause Grammars. *Proceedings of Twente Workshop on Speech and Language Engeneering*, 107–120, December.

[Paeseler 1988] Paeseler, Annedore. 1988. Modification of Earley's algorithm for speech recognition. *NATO ASI Series: Recent Advances in Speech Understanding*, F46:465–472.

[Schmid 1994] Schmid, Ludwig. 1994. Parsing word graphs using a linguistic grammar and a statistical language model. In *IEEE International Conference on Acoustics, Speech and Signal Processing*, II-41–II- 44.

[Sheil 1976] Sheil, B.A. 1976. Observations on context-free parsing. *Statistical Methods in Linguistics*, 6:71–109.

[Thompson 1990] Thompson, H. 1990. Best-first enumeration of paths through a lattice — An active chart parsing solution. *Computer Speech and Language*, 4:263–274.

[Tomita 1986] Tomita, M. 1986. An efficient word lattice parsing algorithm for continuous speech recognition. *ICASSP, Tokyo*, 1569–1572.

[Weber 1994a] Weber, Hans H. 1994a. LR-inkrementelles probabilistisches Chartparsing von Worthypothesenmengen mit Unifikationsgrammatiken: Eine enge Kopplung von Suche und Analyse. Ph.D. Thesis, Universität Hamburg, FB Informatik, Dezember.

[Weber 1994b] Weber, Hans H. 1994b. Time-synchronous chart parsing of speech integrating unification grammars with statistics. *Proceedings of Twente Workshop on Speech and Language Engineering*, 107–120, December.

Fast Grid-Based Position Tracking for Mobile Robots

Wolfram Burgard, Dieter Fox, and Daniel Hennig

Universität Bonn, Institut für Informatik III, Römerstr. 164, D-53117 Bonn
{wolfram,fox,hennig}@uran.cs.uni-bonn.de

Abstract. One of the fundamental problems in the field of mobile robotics is the estimation of the robot's position in the environment. Position probability grids have been proven to be a robust technique for the estimation of the absolute position of a mobile robot. In this paper we describe an application of position probability grids to position tracking. Given a starting position our approach keeps track of the robot's current position by matching sensor readings against a metric model of the environment. The method is designed to work with noisy sensors and approximative models of the environment. Furthermore, it is able to integrate sensor readings of different types of sensors over time. By using raw sensor data, the method exploits arbitrary features of the environment and, in contrast to many other approaches, is not restricted to a fixed set of predefined features such as doors, openings or corridor junction types. An adaptable sensor model allows a fast integration of new sensings. The results described in this paper illustrate the robustness of our method in the presence of sensor noise and errors in the environmental model.

1 Introduction

In order to autonomously operate in their environments, mobile robots must know their position. The problem of estimating the robot's position can be divided into two sub-problems: the estimation of the *absolute* position in the environment and the tracking of the robot's position *relative* to a given starting point [1]. The task of the tracking techniques is the correction of accumulated dead reckoning errors caused by the inherent inaccuracy of the wheel encoders and other factors such as slipping. Position tracking in fact can be regarded as a special case of estimating the absolute position, because it uses a restricted search space generally centered around the robot's estimated position instead of considering each point in the environment as a possible position. We have the following requirements to such a method:

1. **It must able to deal with uncertain information.** This is important because
    - sensors are generally imperfect. This concerns wheel encoders as well as proximity sensors such as ultrasonic sensors or laser range-finders.
    - models of the environment are generally inaccurate. Possible reasons for deviations of the map from the real world come from imperfect sensors, measuring errors, simplifications, open or closed doors, or even moving objects such as humans or other mobile robots.

2. **It must allow the integration of sensor readings from different types of sensors over time.** Sensor fusion improves reliability while the integration over time compensates noise.

3. **It must be able to exploit arbitrary features of the environment which are visible by the sensors.** Many techniques for position tracking are based on landmarks such as doorways, openings or junction types in corridors. These approaches are therefore not able to exploit geometric features of the environment such as the width of corridors or even the size of rooms and objects.

Our fast grid-based position tracking technique presented in this paper meets all these requirements. The principle of the *position probability grid approach* is to accumulate in each cell of the grid the posterior probability that this cell refers to the current position of the robot. Since each possible state of the robot is defined by a tuple (x, y, θ) representing the position and orientation of the robot, position probability grids have three dimensions. Such a grid provides a discrete approximation of the probability function of the robot's current position. The approximation is adapted by integrating the likelihoods of sensor information over time. These likelihoods are computed by matching the measurements against a given environmental model.

In [3] we showed that this technique allows a mobile robot to determine its absolute position in typical office environments within a short time. In this paper we describe a specialization of the position probability grid approach to the tracking problem. Instead of considering all possible positions of the robot which leads to large state spaces even for environments with a reasonable size, we consider a small cubic state space containing only those positions centered around the currently estimated position of the robot. In addition, we apply a fast sensor model allowing frequent updates of the state space given new sensory input. In different examples we demonstrate the robustness of this tracking technique even if noisy sensors such as ultrasonic sensors are used and if approximative environmental models are given. After discussing related work, Section 3 shows how to build position probability grids for tracking the position of a mobile robot. In Section 4 we describe our fast and adaptable model for proximity sensors. Finally, Section 5 describes different experiments in typical office environments.

2   Related work

Different techniques for the tracking of the position of mobile vehicles by matching sensor readings with maps of the environment have been developed in the past (see [1] for a comprehensive overview). Recently, more and more probabilistic techniques are applied to position estimation problems. These approaches can be distinguished according to the type of maps they rely on.

Techniques based on metric or grid-based representations of the environment generally produce Gaussian distributions representing the estimation of the robot's position. Weiß et al. [18] store angle histograms constructed out of range-finder scans taken at different locations of the environment. The position and orientation of the robot is calculated by maximizing the correlation between histograms of new measurements with the stored histograms. Schiele and Crowley [14] compare different strategies to track the robot's position based on occupancy grid maps. They use two different maps: a local grid computed using the most recent sensor readings, and a global map built during a previous exploration of the environment or by an appropriate CAD-tool. The local map is matched with the global map to produce a position and orientation estimate. This estimate is combined with the previous estimate using a Kalman filter [9], where the uncertainty is represented by the width of the Gaussian distribution. Compared to the approach of Weiß et al., this technique allows the integration of different measurements over time rather than taking the optimum match of the most recent sensing as a guess for the current position.

Other techniques are designed to deal with topological maps. Nourbakhsh et al. [12] apply Markov Models to determine the node of the topological map which refers to the current position of the robot. Different nodes of the topological map are distinguished by walls, doors or hallway openings. Such objects are detected using ultrasonic sensors, and the position of the robot is determined by a "state-set progression technique", where each state represents a node in the topological map. This technique is augmented by certainty factors which are computed out of the likelihoods that the items mentioned above will be detected by the ultrasonic sensors. Hertzberg and Kirchner [6] apply a similar approach for mobile robot navigation in sewerage pipes. Simmons and Koenig [15] additionally utilize metric information coming from the wheel encoders to compute state transition probabilities. This metric information puts additional constraints on the robot's location and results in more reliable position estimates. Kortenkamp and Weymoth [8] combine information obtained from sonar sensors and cameras using a Bayesian network to detect gateways between nodes of the topological map. The integration of sonar and vision information results in a much better place recognition which reduces the number of necessary robot movements respectively transitions between different nodes of the topological map.

Due to the separation of the environment into different nodes the methods based on topological maps, in contrast to the methods based on metric maps, allow to deal with ambiguous situations. Such ambiguities are represented by different nodes having high position probabilities. However, the techniques based on topological maps provide a limited accuracy because of the low granularity of the discretization. This restricted precision is disadvantageously if the robot has to navigate fast through the environment or even perform manipulation tasks.

Position probability grids provide a metric discretization of the environment and thus provide metric estimates of the robot's position. A further advantage is the ability to exploit every sensing instead of only those taken at certain reference points or such sensor readings identifying pre-defined landmarks, such as doors, openings or junction types. By using raw sensory information arbitrary features that are seen by the sensors are exploited. Furthermore, the fast sensor model allows the direct integration of new readings without constructing local maps of the environment. Finally, the increased number of parameters in the discrete state space results in more accurate representations of the position probability density than obtained with Kalman filters.

3   Position tracking with position probability grids

The position probability grid approach [3] initially has been designed to estimate the *global* position of a mobile robot in its environment. The basic idea of this approach is to provide a discrete approximation of the position probability density function for the given environment. A position probability grid is a three-dimensional array containing in each field the probability that this field refers to the current position and orientation of the robot. For a grid field x this value is obtained by repeatedly firing the robot's sensors and accumulating in x the likelihoods of the sensed values supposed the center of x currently is the position of the robot in the environment.

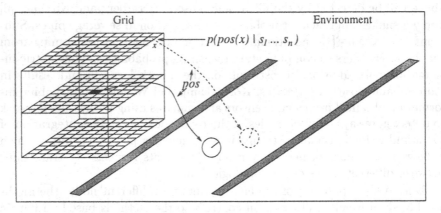

Figure 1. Transformation of grid coordinates into real world coordinates

Whenever the global position of the robot is uniquely determined, the huge state space of the estimation problem can be reduced to a small cube P centered around the robot's estimated position. In this case, tracking the robot's position is equivalent to estimating a function pos transforming the coordinates of the cells x in P to the corresponding coordinates pos(x) in the environment. This mapping is updated whenever new input is obtained from the wheel encoders or the other sensors of the robot:

1. The coordinate transformation pos is updated according to the movements measured by the wheel encoders of the robot since the last update.
2. After each integration of a sensor input, the cell x containing the maximum probability within P is regarded as referring to the current position of the robot. If necessary, the cells in P are shifted such that the cell with the maximum probability becomes the center of P. The transformation pos is adopted accordingly.

3.1 Integrating sensor readings of proximity sensors

To update P given new sensory input s_n we apply the well-known Bayesian update formula. We compute the likelihood $p(s \mid \mathrm{pos}(x) \land m)$ that s is obtained given the robot is in position $\mathrm{pos}(x)$ in the environment, where m is a model of this environment. This likelihood is combined with the probability in x, thus obtaining a new probability that the robot at position $\mathrm{pos}(x)$.

Suppose $p(x \mid s_1 \land \ldots \land s_{n-1} \land m)$ is the (posterior) probability that $\mathrm{pos}(x)$ is the current position of the robot, given m and the sensor readings $s_1, \ldots, s_{n-1}$. Then the probability of x referring to the current position of the robot given new sensory input s_n is defined as

$$p(x \mid s_1 \land \ldots \land s_n \land m) = \frac{p(x \mid s_1 \land \ldots \land s_{n-1} \land m) \cdot p(s_n \mid \mathrm{pos}(x) \land m)}{\alpha} \quad (1)$$

where $\alpha = \sum_{x \in P} p(x \mid s_1 \land \ldots \land s_{n-1} \land m) \cdot p(s_n \mid \mathrm{pos}(x) \land m)$ is a normalizer ensuring that the position probabilities over all x sum up to 1 [13].

For an implementation of this approach Equation (1) defines the update of P given new sensory input s_n. If $P[x]$ is the value of field x in P, then all we have to do is to multiply $P[x]$ by $p(s_n \mid \mathrm{pos}(x) \land m)$ and to store the result in x. After that, we have to normalize P. To initialize $P[x]$ we use the a priori probability $p(\mathrm{pos}(x) \mid m)$ of x referring to the position of the robot given m.

Obviously, the term $p(s_n \mid \mathrm{pos}(x) \land m)$ is the crucial component of the update equation. It specifies the likelihood of observing s_n at location $\mathrm{pos}(x)$, for any choice of s_n and x. In [3,10] $p(s_n \mid \mathrm{pos}(x) \land m)$ is computed at runtime from a metric model of the environment and a model of sonar sensors. [6,7,12,15] use topological representations of the location space and first scan the sensor data for the presence or absence of certain landmarks. In these approaches the probabilities $p(s_n \mid \mathrm{pos}(x) \land m)$ are stored in a lookup table. In Section 4 we show how the sensing probabilities can be computed off-line and compactly stored in a lookup table even for our geometric grid-based approach.

3.2 Integrating the movements of the robot

To integrate the dead-reckoning information of the wheel encoders, we update the coordinate transformation pos according to the measured movement Δ

which is equivalent to shifting P by Δ. In order to deal with possible dead reckoning errors we use a general formula coming from the domain of Markov chains. We regard each cell in P as one possible state of the robot, and determine a state transition probability $p(x \mid \tilde{x} \wedge \Delta)$ for each pair x, $\tilde{x}$ of cells in P, which depends on the trajectory taken by the robot and the time elapsed since the previous update. Then we apply the following update formula:

$$P[x] := \sum_{\tilde{x} \in P} P[\tilde{x}] \cdot p(x \mid \tilde{x} \wedge \Delta) \tag{2}$$

Additionally, we consider how the trajectory taken by the robot fits into the environment. A trajectory leading through free space leads to a higher position probability than a trajectory leading through an obstacle. Therefore, we multiply each field x in P with the a priory position probability $p(\text{pos}(x) \mid m)$. Assuming that the robot does not leave the environmental model m, the update formula is

$$P[x] := \begin{cases} \beta \cdot P[x] \cdot p(\text{pos}(x) \mid m) & \text{if } \text{pos}(x) \in m \\ 0 & \text{otherwise} \end{cases} \tag{3}$$

where β again is a normalizing constant. To estimate the a priori probability $p(\text{pos}(x) \mid m)$ that the robot is at position $\text{pos}(x)$, we use an occupancy probability map o of the environment [11,10], which in our case is computed from m. We assume that $p(\text{pos}(x) \mid m)$ directly depends on the occupancy probability $o(\text{pos}(x))$ of the field $\text{pos}(x)$ in o:

$$p(\text{pos}(x) \mid m) = \frac{1 - o(\text{pos}(x))}{\sum_{\tilde{x} \in o} (1 - o(\tilde{x}))} \tag{4}$$

4 A fast sensor model for proximity sensors

To compute the likelihood $p(s \mid x \wedge m)$ that a sensor reading s is received given a position x we analyze the model m of the environment. Since this likelihood has to be estimated for each possible position x of the robot, the necessary computation time has a high impact on the efficiency of the overall approach.

In [3] we applied an approach similar to Moravec's [10] for estimating the probability that a sensor measures a certain distance. One disadvantage of this approach, however, lies in its computational complexity. For each location x one has to compute a generally not Gaussian probability density function over a discrete set of possible distances measured by the sensor. For an environment of $15 \times 15 m^2$, a discretization of $15 \times 15 cm^2$, and an angular resolution of 1 degree, the state space of the robot contains already 3.600.000 states. Consequently, representing the complete densities for all possible states would by far exceed the memory of typical computers and especially such mobile robots generally are equipped with.

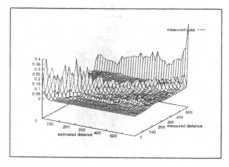 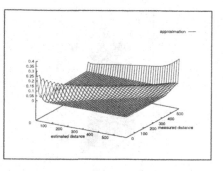

Figure 2. Distances measured by the robot

Figure 3. Approximation of the measured data

The key idea of our approach is to use a simplified sensor model which allows us to compute the likelihood of a proximity sensing solely given the distance to the next obstacle in the sensing direction. This sensor model is based on the following observations. First, if an obstacle is detected by the sensor then the measured distance is generally normally distributed around the exact distance to the object. Second, because of the limited accuracy of the sensors and the world models, there is a small chance for any distance to be perceived by the sensor. Finally, there is an additional probability that the beam is absorbed or completely reflected, which results in a maximum range measurement. Figure 2 shows the probability density of measuring a distance d_1 given an expected distance d_2 and justifies these assumptions. This function was obtained from approximately 190.000 sonar sensings in different environments. Figure 3 shows the density obtained by adapting our model to these data.

Given this model, it suffices to store for each possible state of the robot the distance which is expected to be measured by the sensor. These expected distances can be computed off-line given metric representations of the environment. Because of a compact representation of the expected distances in a table only two lookup operations are necessary to compute the likelihood of a given sensing at runtime. Although this sensor model, in contrast to the original model introduced by Moravec and Elfes [10], has only a small number of parameters, we obtained a significant speed up which results in a better positioning performance for global localization as well as position tracking. In [4] we successfully utilized this model even for active self-localization of mobile robots.

5 Experimental results

The grid-based tracking technique described above has been implemented and extensively tested. The current system is able to interpret sensor readings of ultrasonic sensors and match them with occupancy probability grid maps. The experiments described in this section were carried out with our mobile

Figure 4. The mobile robot *RHINO*   Figure 5. *RHINO's* sister *Amelia*

robot *RHINO* [2,17] (see Figure 4). as well as *Amelia* (see Figure 5) which is one of the mobile robots in the mobile robot laboratory of the computer science department of the Carnegie Mellon University. Both robots are B21 robots manufactured by Real World Interface Inc. They are equipped with a ring of 24 Ultrasonic sensors, each having a cone of 15 deg. Throughout the experiments we used a position probability grid of $15 \times 15 \times 15$ fields, each $15cm \times 15cm \times 1deg$ in size. The integration of a sweep of all 24 sensors takes about 0.2 seconds on a Pentium 120 computer.

5.1 Position tracking in large environments

As a complex example we used a typical run of the mobile robot *Amelia* in the Wean Hall of the Carnegie Mellon University. Figure 6 shows the map of the environment as well as *Amelia's* trajectory as measured by the wheel-encoders. The size of the environment is a about $75 \times 35m^2$, and the length of the trajectory is over $200m$. The starting point is in the northern corridor facing east. As can be seen in the figure the error of the orientation permanently increases up to a value of more than 30 degree. Obviously the model of the environment would be useless after short time if the position tracking would rely on the wheel encoders only.

Figure 7 shows the corrected trajectory of the robot computed with our position probability grid approach based on the information coming from the wheel encoders and the 24 ultrasonic sensors. The likelihoods of the sonar measurements were computed by matching them with the displayed map. At this point it should be noted, that this map is very approximative as it only represents an outline of the environment. For example, the hallway in the south-west of the Wean Hall contains a cafeteria with two bars as well as tables and chairs. Furthermore, the corridors contain several objects not included in the map such as thrash bins, information boards etc. Finally, the state of doors was not represented correctly by the map, and there were many people which walked through the environment and additionally produced unexpected readings. Nevertheless, our approach is able to reliably keep track of the robot's position.

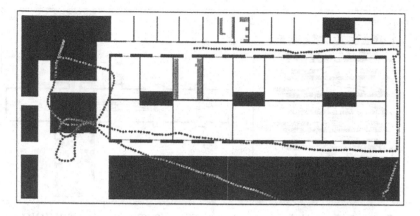

Figure 6. Trajectory measured by the wheel-encoders

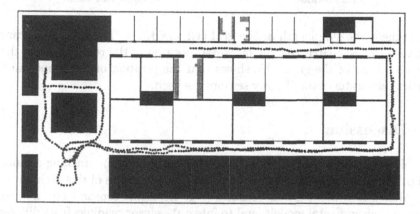

Figure 7. Corrected path

Figure 8 illustrates an example position probability grid. The grid shows the position probability distribution of the robot in a corridor. The different layers represent the position probabilities for 9 orientations. The layers are marked with the deviation of the orientation from the current orientation. Each layer represents a $225 \times 225\,cm^2$ area centered around the currently estimated position of the robot. For simplicity only 9 of the 15 orientations are plotted. Notice that the maximal value lies in the center of the cube.

5.2 Accuracy of the approach

To demonstrate the accuracy of the approach we performed 8 different runs with our mobile robot *RHINO* in a part of our department which has a s size of $20 \times 25m^2$. In all theses runs shown in Figure 9 the robot's starting position was in the southern office. We steered *RHINO* on different trajectories through the corridor and measured the final position in the northern office. In this experiment we used only 12 ultrasonic sensors. As in the previous

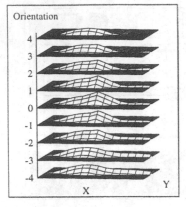

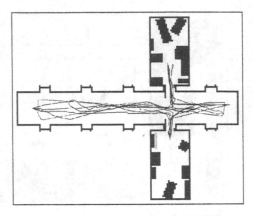

Figure 8. Typical density
in a corridor

Figure 9. Trajectories of *RHINO*
in eight test runs

experiment the side length of one grid cell was $15\,cm$. The average distance between the estimated and the measured position of the robot was less than the resolution of the grid. This shows that the position of the robot can be tracked accurately even if noisy sensors are used.

6 Discussion

In this paper we presented a fast grid-based technique for tracking a mobile robot's position in a known environment. The advantage of this technique is the ability to deal with noisy sensors (e.g. ultrasonic sensors) and approximative environmental models, and to integrate sensor readings from different types of sensors over time. Based on a fast and adaptable sensor model the approach quickly integrates new sensory input. Because it directly uses the proximity information coming from the sensors, it is able to exploit arbitrary features of the environment which are visible by the sensors.

Our technique has been implemented and tested in several complex real-world environments. The experiments presented here demonstrate the robustness of this method in tracking the position of a mobile robot. As the experiment in the over $2000\,m^2$ wide office environment shows, trajectories longer than $200\,m$ are tracked successfully even if only approximative models are given. Due to the fast sensor model, the evaluation of a complete sweep consisting of 24 ultrasonic sensors measurements into a grid consisting of more than 3000 cells takes about 0.2 seconds on a Pentium 120 computer, which turned out to be sufficient for a reliable on-line tracking of the robot's position.

An interesting question concerns the relation of the position probability grid technique to Kalman filters [9,16]. The difference between both approaches lies in the approximation of the position probability density function. Whereas our method provides a discrete approximation of this function,

Kalman filters generally approximate the overall distribution by a Gaussian density function. There are different situations which cannot be represented by single Gaussian distributions. Consider a situation where the robot is close to a wall or another kind of obstacle. In Figure 10, the robot is in corridor and in front of a pillar. This situation leads to a non-Gaussian distribution

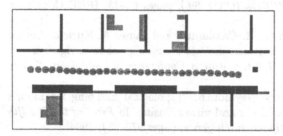

Figure 10. Trajectory of the robot   Figure 11. Resulting density

of the position probability. As illustrated in Figure 11 (more likely positions are darker) our technique adequately represents that the robot cannot be at the same position as the pillar. A similar situation is given when the robot is close to a wall. The resulting density is non-Gaussian, because the robot is more likely in the corridor than in the wall. Thus, a Kalman filter tends to shift the position estimate to the center of the corridor, which is obviously wrong. On the contrary, our approach is able to deal with such situations accordingly (see Figure 11).

Despite these encouraging results, there are further warrants for future research. The most important question concerns the integration of global position estimation and position tracking. In our experiments we sometimes observed a failure of our tracking technique, if the robot was in a large hallway for a long time. In such situations the accumulated dead reckoning errors cannot be corrected due to the lack of features detectable by the proximity sensors. To deal with such cases, we are currently working on a combination of this fast tracking approach with our global position estimation technique described in [3].

References

1. J. Borenstein, B. Everett, and L. Feng. *Navigating Mobile Robots: Systems and Techniques*. A. K. Peters, Ltd., Wellesley, MA, 1996.
2. Joachim Buhmann, Wolfram Burgard, Armin B. Cremers, Dieter Fox, Thomas Hofmann, Frank Schneider, Jiannis Strikos, and Sebastian Thrun. The mobile robot RHINO. *AI Magazine*, 16(2):31–38, Summer 1995.
3. Wolfram Burgard, Dieter Fox, Daniel Hennig, and Timo Schmidt. Estimating the absolute position of a mobile robot using position probability grids. In *Proc. of the Fourteenth National Conference on Artificial Intelligence (AAAI-96)*, pages 896–901, 1996.

4. Wolfram Burgard, Dieter Fox, and Sebastian Thrun. Active mobile robot localization. In *Proc. of the Fifteenth International Conference on Artificial Intelligence (IJCAI-97)*, 1997.

5. I.J. Cox and G.T. Wilfong, editors. *Autonomous Robot Vehicles*. Springer Verlag, 1990.

6. Joachim Hertzberg and Frank Kirchner. Landmark-based autonomous navigation in sewerage pipes. In *Proceedings of the First Euromicro Workshop on Advanced Mobile Robots (EUROMICRO '96)*, pages 68–73. IEEE Computer Society Press, 1996.

7. Leslie Pack Kaelbling, Anthony R. Cassandra, and James A. Kurien. Acting under uncertainty: Discrete bayesian models for mobile-robot navigation. In *Proceedings of the IEEE/RSJ International Conference on Intelligent Robots and Systems*, 1996.

8. David Kortenkamp and Terry Weymouth. Topological mapping for mobile robots using a combination of sonar and vision sensing. In *Proc. of the Twelfth National Conference on Artificial Intelligence*, pages 979–984, 1994.

9. Peter S. Maybeck. The Kalman filter: An introduction to concepts. In Cox and Wilfong [5].

10. Hans P. Moravec. Sensor fusion in certainty grids for mobile robots. *AI Magazine*, pages 61–74, Summer 1988.

11. Hans P. Moravec and A.E. Elfes. High resolution maps from wide angle sonar. In *Proc. IEEE Int. Conf. Robotics and Automation*, pages 116–121, 1985.

12. Illa Nourbakhsh, Rob Powers, and Stan Birchfield. DERVISH an office-navigating robot. *AI Magazine*, 16(2):53–60, Summer 1995.

13. Judea Pearl. *Probabilistic Reasoning in Intelligent Systems: Networks of Plausible Inference*. Morgan Kaufmann Publishers, Inc., 1988.

14. Bernt Schiele and James L. Crowley. A comparison of position estimation techniques using occupancy grids. In *Proc. of the IEEE International Conference on Robotics and Automation*, pages 1628–1634, 1994.

15. Reid Simmons and Sven Koenig. Probabilistic robot navigation in partially observable environments. In *Proc. International Joint Conference on Artificial Intelligence*, 1995.

16. Harold W. Sorensen. *Kalman Filtering: Theroy and Application*. IEEE Press, 1985.

17. S. Thrun, A. Bücken, W. Burgard, D. Fox, T. Fröhlinghaus, D. Hennig, T. Hofmann, M. Krell, and T. Schimdt. Map learning and high-speed navigation in RHINO. In D. Kortenkamp, R.P. Bonasso, and R. Murphy, editors, *AI-based Mobile Robots: Case studies of successful robot systems*. MIT Press, Cambridge, MA, to appear.

18. Gerhard Weiß, Christopher Wetzler, and Ewald von Puttkamer. Keeping track of position and orientation of moving indoor systems by correlation of rangefinder scans. In *Proceedings of the International Conference on Intelligent Robots and Systems*, pages 595–601, 1994.

Integration of Image Sequence Evaluation and Fuzzy Metric Temporal Logic Programming

M. Haag[1], W. Theilmann[1], K. Schäfer[1], H.-H. Nagel[1,2]

[1] Fakultät für Informatik der Universität Karlsruhe (TH)
Postfach 6980, D-76128 Karlsruhe
[2] Fraunhofer-Institut für Informations- und Datenverarbeitung (IITB)
Fraunhoferstr. 1, D-76131 Karlsruhe
Tel. +49 (721) 6091-210 (Fax -413), E-Mail hhn@iitb.fhg.de

Abstract. Advanced image sequence evaluation systems generate a voluminous amount of quantitative data which is increasingly difficult to assess. The challenge consists in abstracting from and reasoning with these data in order to create a more intuitive access to image evaluation results.
This contribution reports about experiences and results gained by connecting an existing advanced image sequence evaluation system with a Fuzzy Metric Temporal Logic (FMTL) system which is able to represent and process uncertain, time–related data. We will explain and demonstrate the advantage of using FMTL in order to automatically analyze traffic situations recorded by a video camera and evaluated by our image evaluation system. In particular, we shall address difficulties arising from feeding a logic inference system with uncertain real world data.

Keywords: Computer Vision, Knowledge Representation, Fuzzy Sets, Temporal Reasoning

1 Introduction and Related Work

Advanced image sequence evaluation systems are able to process large numbers of image frames producing huge amounts of geometric data. For example, the model–based tracking system described in [5, 6] extracts complex driving manoeuvers of vehicles in traffic image sequences and provides (scene domain) estimates for the position, orientation, speed, and angular speed of each moving vehicle at each half–frame time point. Series of several thousand consecutive half–frames of different traffic image sequences have already been processed uninterruptedly. The resulting mass of quantitative data (several 10000 float values) is practically inaccessible to humans. By conceptually abstracting and reasoning, however, vehicle tracking results can be condensed into a small number of natural language statements which can be assessed easily.

We use a system based on the Horn–Logic Fragment of *Fuzzy Metric Temporal Logic* (FMTL) developed by Schäfer [10] which provides a suitable mechanism for processing fuzzy and temporal data. The corresponding logic programming language F–Limette offers the flexibility needed in order to investigate different inference strategies. By describing situation models in an explicit way with FMTL and using the inference mechanisms provided by F–Limette, we are able to explain the behaviours observed in traffic image sequences and even make predictions about temporal evolutions.

A survey of recent publications about gaining symbolic descriptions from image sequences can be found in [1]. We, therefore, only discuss selected recent approaches. [4] and [1] use Bayesian Belief Networks in order to represent sensor values obtained by evaluation of traffic image sequences and to infer more complex descriptions from primitive statements. A network of concept–frames serves [2] for representation of the scene domain. Uncertainty in the results of image evaluation steps is treated by means of the Dempster–Shafer–Theory. Similar to the approach reported here, [2] use a procedural programming language for the image evaluation task and a logic programming language for symbolic reasoning. The aim in [3] consists in incrementally generating natural language descriptions from geometrical scene descriptions of image sequences. [7] exploit Newtonian mechanics for reasoning about interactions between objects in image sequences.

Our approach differs from [1] and [4] in that we represent knowledge in an explicit and hierarchical way, not coded in conditional probabilities. In contradistinction to [2] and [7] we reason in the 3D scene domain. Compared to the approaches cited above, we process much more real world input data. We consider it as a significant achievement to be able to process thousands of automatically estimated quantities with a logic inference system, compared to using a few synthetically provided input data. In extension to [9] where situation analysis is also applied to traffic image sequences, we have now evaluated an order of magnitude more image frames (e. g. over thousand half–frames per object in a gas station scene), a fact which necessitated the integration of more knowledge about objects, about the stationary scene, and about the behaviour of mobile bodies.

2 FMTL and Situation Graphs

The representation of and reasoning with results provided by image sequence evaluation has to consider three special features:

1. Certain statements extracted from image sequences recording time–variant scenes are valid only during certain time intervals.
2. The estimation of quantities from image sequences is uncertain.
3. Additional uncertainty originates from associating conceptual attributes with geometric quantities, for example *low* speed, due to the inherent vagueness of many concepts.

Schäfer [10] extended conventional logic formalisms by a *temporal* and a *fuzzy* component, resulting in *Fuzzy Metric Temporal Logic* (FMTL). While the logic programming language PROLOG is based on resolution calculus and depth search, the FMTL programming language *F-Limette* [10] uses a tableaux calculus and provides several inference strategies (depth search, breadth search, beam search) which can be selected by the user.

The concept *situation* has been introduced by [8] in order to describe the *state* of an agent and of his environment as well as an *action* which can be associated with this state. If two agents find themselves in the same state but have different possibilities to react in this state, then two different situations are associated with the agents. Sequences of situations can be represented by *situation graphs*. They consist of *situation nodes* which generically describe the state and action part of a situation. Each situation node is connected with potential successor nodes by directed labeled edges which define an order for investigation of the successors. Complex situation graphs can be arranged hierarchically into *situation trees* by associating further situation (sub-)graphs to single (parent) situation nodes. All situation nodes in a situation subgraph inherit recursively the descriptions of their parent node, defining a specialization hierarchy. The interpretation of a situation tree attempts to instantiate the most special situation node. If a situation node can be instantiated which owns a subgraph, the subgraph is recursively interpreted (*specialization*). If a subgraph can not be instantiated (for example because no valid successor of the current situation node can be found), interpretation continues with the parent node of this subgraph (*generalization*). The nodes, where the interpretation of a situation (sub-)graph may start or end, can be explicitly specified. Situation trees are described by means of the SIT++ language (see [10]) which is directly translated into FMTL programs. F-Limette processes such situation descriptions as well as conceptual primitives (types and relations) provided by the image evaluation system in order to instantiate appropriate situation nodes.

If one is not interested in *recognizing* a sequence of actions observed, situation trees can conversely be interpreted as hierarchical planning schemata in order to decompose complex tasks. The action description of each situation node can be conceived as a subgoal which has to be solved in order to achieve the overall goal specified in the root node.

Figure 1 shows a section of a situation tree describing situations which can arise at a gas station whose lane model is depicted in Figure 3. The most general graph (**graph_get_gas**) contains just one single node (**get_gas**), whose state description requires only the existence of an agent with an associated trajectory (sequence of estimated vehicle states). The successor node of **get_gas** is the node itself. This node has a specializing situation graph (**graph_tank**) which contains a sequence of three nodes describing the three phases of getting gas: **drive_towards_petrol_pump** (the agent has to be located on a driving lane and must drive; if it stands, it must not stand on a filling place because otherwise the system assumes that the car obtains gas); **fill_up** (the agent must stand on a filling place); **leave_petrol_pump** (the agent drives on a driving lane). The first and the last node contain once more a specializing subgraph. The subgraph for the node **drive_towards_petrol_pump** is shown in Figure 2. This graph interprets the occupation of filling places in order to explain what an agent is actually doing in order to get to a free filling place. The following situations may occur:

1. all filling places are free: the agent will drive to one filling place and stop;
2. at least one filling place is occupied:
   (a) there is a free filling place between the agent and an occupied filling place: the agent will drive onto the free filling place and stop;
   (b) there is a free filling place behind an occupied filling place and the agent can reach this free place: the agent will evade the occupied place via the passing lane (which has to be free) and drive towards the free filling place;
   (c) no free filling place can be reached: the agent will wait in front of an occupied filling place.

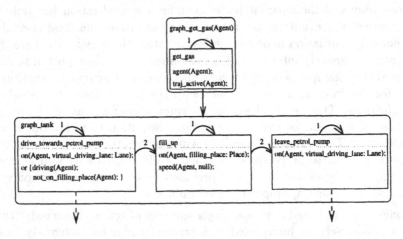

Fig. 1. Section of a hierarchical situation tree describing the situation of getting gas. Action descriptions are omitted for simplicity. The subgraph of the situation node drive_towards_petrol_pump is shown in Figure 2. The label above a dashed line gives the name of the corresponding situation node. Within the predicates describing states, capitalized identifiers denote variables, while identifiers with lower case initial letters denote constants. The directed edges between situation nodes determine the successor nodes, labeled with the priority with which the successor nodes should be evaluated (1 corresponds to highest priority).

3 Results

In order to apply the approach outlined in the preceding section to a real–world scenario, traffic at a gas station has been recorded by a S–VHS video camera and evaluated by a model–based image evaluation system [5, 6]. Based on state estimates for each moving object in the scene and for each half–frame time point,

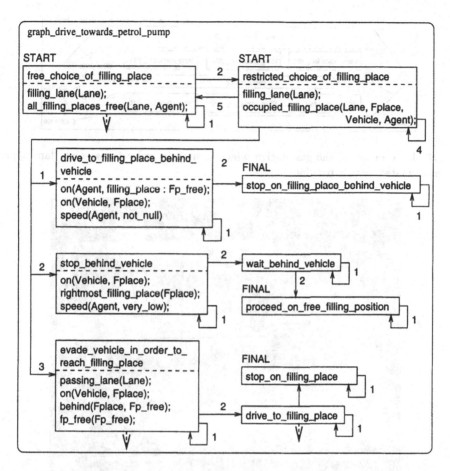

Fig. 2. Situation subgraph of the parent node `drive_towards_petrol_pump` of Figure 1. The variable `Vehicle` represents another object (not the agent), `Fplace` denotes a filling place, `Fp_free` a free filling place. The notation `filling_place : Fp_free` means that the variable `Fp_free` is of the type `filling_place`. The state descriptions of some nodes have been omitted for simplicity. Dashed arrows indicate further subgraphs which have been omitted, too, for the same reason.

symbolic attributes (for example very_low, low, middle, high, very_high for the estimated speed) and spatial relations (e. g. on: agent × lane which associates an estimated vehicle position with a lane) are computed. The latter task is performed by means of a lane model (see Figure 3).

Figure 4 shows an automatically estimated trajectory of object 12 which enters the gas station from the right side, proceeds on the front filling lane to the filling place in front of the middle petrol pump, fills up, and finally drives off leaving the gas station via the left exit.

The sequence of situation nodes visited by applying the situation tree outlined in Figures 1 and 2 is shown in Figure 5. In addition to the corresponding time interval and the situation node name, the participating objects (vehicles

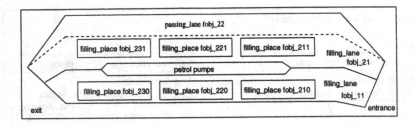

Fig. 3. Lane model of the gas station which is used in order to associate lane types with estimated vehicle positions.

Fig. 4. Image sequence recorded at a gas station with overlaid automatically estimated trajectory for object 12 at half–frame time point #1262.

and lanes) are given. The lane numbers refer to Figure 3. Since the scene contains no further vehicles during the first half–frames (the two vehicles on the back lane in Figure 4 enter the field of view at half–frame time point #300 and #614, respectively), it is assumed that all filling places are unoccupied. So object 12 finds itself in the situation free_choice_of_filling_place driving on filling lane fobj_11. The vehicle stops on the filling place fobj_220 in front of the middle petrol pump. At half–frame time point #1160, the vehicle drives off forward, since no obstacle is located in driving direction.

Figure 6 shows another frame of the gas station sequence with estimated trajectories. First, object 9 enters the gas station from the right side and proceeds behind the middle petrol pump. After that, object 4 also enters the gas station from the right side, evades the standing object 4, proceeds to the left side, stops, backs up and finally stops in front of object 9 behind the leftmost petrol pump.

begin	end	situation node
5 —	111	free_choice_of_filling_place(obj_12, fobj_11)
112 —	114	stop_with_free_choice_of_filling_place(obj_12, fobj_220)
115 —	1159	fill_up(obj_12, fobj_220)
1160 —	1164	drive_forward_after_filling_up_because_no_obstacle_ahead(obj_12)
1165 —	1268	proceed_after_filling_up(obj_12, fobj_11)
1269 —	1270	leave_gas_station(obj_12, fobj_11)

Fig. 5. Sequence of situation nodes visited by applying the situation tree outlined in Figures 1 and 2 on the automatically estimated trajectory of object 12 (see Figure 4). The left column shows the corresponding time interval (half-frame numbers) while the right column shows the situation nodes as well as the participating objects (see Figure 3). Only the most special situation nodes are shown.

Fig. 6. The results of automatically tracking object 4 and 9 at half-frame #1144 of the gas station scene are projected into the image plane.

Figure 7 (top) shows the sequence of situation nodes which have been visited by applying the situation tree introduced in the previous section on the estimated states of object 4 (agent) and object 9. During the time interval #634–#641, the interpretation process assumes that object 4 will stop on the filling place (fobj_211) behind the rightmost petrol pump. This interpretation is plausible, since (1) that filling place is unoccupied and (2) the trajectory of object 4 touches that filling place. However, object 4 actually does not stop at the rightmost filling place. Therefore, the situation node drive_to_filling_place_behind_vehicle

No.	begin	end	situation node
1	614 —	633	restricted_choice_of_filling_place(obj_4, obj_9, fobj_21, fobj_221)
2	634 —	641	drive_to_filling_place_behind_vehicle(obj_4, fobj_211, obj_9)
3	642 —	646	restricted_choice_of_filling_place(obj_4, obj_9, fobj_21, fobj_221)
4	647 —	695	evade_vehicle_in_order_to_reach_filling_place(obj_4, obj_9, fobj_231)
5	696 —	845	pass_vehicle_in_order_to_reach_filling_place(obj_4, obj_9, fobj_231)
6	846 —	860	emerge_behind_vehicle_in_order_to_reach_filling_place(obj_4, obj_9, fobj_231)
7	861 —	973	proceed_in_order_to_reach_filling_place(obj_4, fobj_21, fobj_231)
8	974 —	1016	stop_in_order_to_reach_filling_place(obj_4, fobj_21, fobj_231)
9	1017 —	1064	wait_in_order_to_reach_filling_place(obj_4, fobj_21, fobj_231)
10	1065 —	1071	start_in_order_to_reach_filling_place(obj_4, fobj_21, fobj_231)
11	1072 —	1204	back_up_in_order_to_reach_filling_place(obj_4, fobj_21, fobj_231)
12	1205 —	1245	stop_on_filling_place(obj_4, fobj_231)
13	1246 —	1395	fill_up(obj_4, fobj_231)

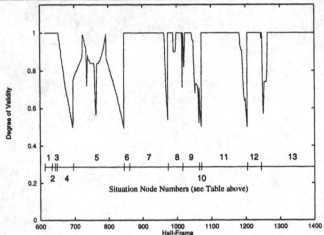

Fig. 7. Top: Sequence of situation nodes visited by applying the situation tree of Figures 1 and 2 on the automatically estimated trajectories of the objects 4 (agent) and 9. Bottom: Temporal development of the resulting fuzzy degree of validity for each situation node in the table above.

has no successor node which can be instantiated. The interpretation process falls back to the more general parent node **drive_towards_petrol_pump** and, since this node can be instantiated, once more enters its subgraph (see Figure 2) and can only instantiate the start node **restricted_choice_of_filling_place** (time interval #642–#646). But as soon as object 4 enters the passing lane (fobj_22 in Figure 3) at time point #647, the interpretation process concludes that object 4 will evade object 9 and drive to the leftmost filling place fobj_231 which is unoccupied.

Originally, the fall–back at time–point #642 had not been admitted by the situation subgraph depicted in Figure 2, since the node `drive_to_filling_place_behind_vehicle` is not marked as a final node. If a non–final node has no valid successor, the interpretation fails. In the case considered, this would mean that the behaviour of object 4 is not compatible with our expectations: although the rightmost filling place is free and object 4 touches this place, it evades object 9 in order to reach the leftmost filling place. In order to avoid a failing interpretation due to an unintuitive behaviour of object 4, the considered situation node has been marked as a final node. A better solution, namely the parallel examination of several alternatives, is presented in Section 4.

In order to illustrate the fuzzy aspect of the interpretation task, Figure 7 (bottom) depicts the temporal development of the degree of validity associated with each situation node visited. For instance, the decreasing degree of validity of the fifth situation node (passing vehicle) decreases when the distance between object 4 and 9 increases. Situation nodes are only valid while their degree of validity exceeds a threshold of 0.5. Therefore, a transition between 'pass vehicle' (see No. 5 in Figure 7) and 'emerge behind vehicle' (see No. 6) takes place as soon as the degree of validity of node 5 drops below 0.5 at time point #846.

The following example shows the results by evaluating spatial relations at a traffic intersection scene (see Figure 8, left). The resulting sequence of situation nodes shown in Figure 9 (top) means that object 4 proceeds on a left–turning lane behind object 5 and that it definitely turns left beginning with half–frame #69. The lane type *left–turning lane* is infered automatically by combining primitives such as lanes and lane markings which have been provided interactively.

Fig. 8. Enlarged sections of two different traffic intersection sequences. Left: First sequence with overlaid estimated trajectories of objects 4 and 5 at half–frame #45. Right: Second sequence with estimated trajectories of objects 1 and 2, the latter having already left the field of view.

begin	end	situation node
5 —	68	proceed_on_left_turning_lane_towards_intersection_behind_vehicle(obj_4,obj_5,fobj_5)
69 —	95	turn_left_behind_vehicle(obj_4,obj_5,fobj_6)

begin	end	situation node
3034 —	3205	proceed_on_intersection(obj_1, fobj_15)
3206 —	3211	wait_on_intersection(obj_1, fobj_15)
3212 —	3215	proceed_on_intersection(obj_1, fobj_15)
3216 —	3228	wait_on_intersection(obj_1, fobj_15)
3229 —	3243	proceed_on_intersection(obj_1, fobj_15)
3244 —	3557	wait_on_intersection(obj_1, fobj_15)
3558 —	3690	give_way(obj_1, fobj_15, obj_2)
3691 —	3709	proceed_despite_of_vehicle(obj_1, fobj_15, obj_2)
3710 —	3720	give_way(obj_1, fobj_15, obj_2)
3721 —	3732	proceed_despite_of_vehicle(obj_1, fobj_15, obj_2)
3733 —	3739	give_way(obj_1, fobj_15, obj_2)
3740 —	3748	proceed_despite_of_vehicle(obj_1, fobj_15, obj_2)
3749 —	3756	give_way(obj_1, fobj_15, obj_2)
3757 —	3761	proceed_despite_of_vehicle(obj_1, fobj_15, obj_2)
3762 —	3762	give_way(obj_1, fobj_15, obj_2)
3763 —	3767	proceed_despite_of_vehicle(obj_1, fobj_15, obj_2)
3768 —	3769	give_way(obj_1, fobj_15, obj_2)
3770 —	3785	proceed_despite_of_vehicle(obj_1, fobj_15, obj_2)
3786 —	3797	give_way(obj_1, fobj_15, obj_2)
3798 —	3798	proceed_despite_of_vehicle(obj_1, fobj_15, obj_2)
3799 —	3985	proceed_on_intersection(obj_1, fobj_15)
3986 —	3993	proceed_on_intersection(obj_1, fobj_26)

Fig. 9. Top: Resulting sequence of situation nodes for the two objects depicted in Figure 8 (left). Bottom: Corresponding sequence of situation nodes for the two trajectories from Figure 8 (right).

The evaluation of give–way situations is demonstrated by means of a second traffic intersection image sequence, see Figure 8 (right). Two objects have been considered in this scene: object 1 enters the field of view from the right side and stops in front of the traffic intersection in order to give way to object 2 which turns left on the lower left lane. The corresponding sequence of situation nodes is shown in Figure 9 (bottom). It can be observed that object 1 waits in front of the traffic intersection and gives way as soon as object 2 enters the field of view in half–frame #3558. After object 2 disappeared (half–frame #3798), object 1 proceeds onto the traffic intersection. The oscillations between the situation nodes proceed_on_intersection and wait_on_intersection as well as between the nodes give_way and proceed_despite_of_vehicle are caused by variations in the estimated vehicle's speed, especially during the time intervals #3200–#3243 and #3691–#3797, see Figure 10.

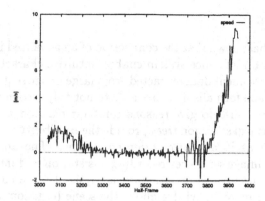

Fig. 10. Estimated speed of object 1 in the second traffic intersection scene (Figure 8, right).

4 Beam Search

Considering only one single path through a situation tree may result in a (at least temporarily) misleading sequence of situation nodes, e. g. due to uncertainties in the estimated geometric data or due to several possible alternative behaviours. We have already seen one example in the preceding section: object 4 in the gas station image sequence (see Figure 6) is expected to stop on the free filling place behind the rightmost petrol pump. Instead, it evades the standing object 9 and drives towards the filling place behind the leftmost petrol pump. At half–frame time point #634 there are two possible alternatives. The path containing the node **drive_to_filling_place_behind_vehicle** can not be continued at half–frame #642, so *a-posteriori* it turned out to be the wrong choice. In this case it would be more appropriate to perform a breadth search, following different paths in parallel, assessing each path, and deleting all paths with a degree of validity below a cut–off threshold.

This strategy is called *beam search*. F–Limette provides a capability to perform beam searches through a graph of situation nodes. Applied to the example outlined above, this interpretation strategy results in the sequence of nodes shown in Figure 11. The two situations **restricted_choice_of_filling_place** and **drive_to_filling_place_behind_vehicle** are now considered in parallel. When there is no instantiable successor for the second situation in half–frame #641, it is rejected and only the first situation is considered to be valid.

begin	end	situation node
614 —	646	restricted_choice_of_filling_place(obj_4, obj_9, fobj_21, fobj_221)
647 —	695	evade_vehicle_in_order_to_reach_filling_place(obj_4, obj_9, fobj_231)

Fig. 11. Sequence of situation nodes visited by interpreting the behaviour of object 4 of the gas station scene (Figure 6), now based on a beam search strategy.

5 Conclusion

Our contribution has shown that the connection of an advanced image evaluation system with a FMTL inference system enables intuitive characterizations of the uncertain, time–dependent data extracted from large image sequences. By means of the situation graph formalism, we are able to not only recognize the behaviour of traffic agents, but also to give reasons for their reaction and to guess their intentions. Hierarchical situation trees provide the possibility to arrange complex situation descriptions in an object–oriented manner. The approach has been applied to several image sequences recording gas station and intersection traffic.

Future work concentrates on situation analysis of more complex image sequences, exploiting more knowledge about the scene (e. g. complete modeling of give–way rules). In addition, the influence of different inference strategies and operator semantics (see [10]) on the interpretation results has to be studied.

References

1. H. Buxton, S. Gong: *Visual Surveillance in a Dynamic and Uncertain World*. Artificial Intelligence **78** (1995) 431–459.
2. S. Dance, T. Caelli, Z.-Q. Liu: *A Concurrent, Hierarchical Approach to Symbolic Scene Interpretation*. Pattern Recognition **29**:11 (1996) 1891–1903.
3. G. Herzog: *From Visual Input to Verbal Output in the Visual Translator*. Working Notes AAAI–95 Fall Symposium Series 'Computational Models for Integrating Language and Vision', R.K. Srihari (ed.), Cambridge/MA, 10–12 November 1995, pp. 9–15.
4. T. Huang, D. Koller, J. Malik, G. Ogasawara, B. Rao, S. Russell, and J. Weber: *Automatic Symbolic Traffic Scene Analysis Using Belief Networks*. Proc. 12th National Conf. on Artificial Intelligence, Seattle/WA, 31 July – 4 August 1994, pp. 966–972.
5. H. Kollnig, H.-H. Nagel: *3D Pose Estimation by Fitting Image Gradients Directly to Polyhedral Models*. Proc. 5th International Conference on Computer Vision ICCV '95, Cambridge/MA, 20–23 June 1995, pp. 569–574.
6. H. Kollnig, H.-H. Nagel: *Matching Objects to Segments from an Optical Flow Field*. Proc. 4th European Conference on Computer Vision (ECCV '96), Vol. II, Cambridge/UK, 15–18 April 1996, Lecture Notes in Computer Science **1065**, Springer–Verlag, Berlin a. o. 1996, pp. 388–399.
7. R. Mann, A. Jepson, J.M. Siskind: *The Computational Perception of Scene Dynamics*. Computer Vision and Image Understanding **65**:2 (1997) 113–128.
8. H.-H. Nagel: *From Image Sequences towards Conceptual Descriptions*. Image and Vision Computing **6**:2 (1988) 59–74.
9. H.-H. Nagel, H. Kollnig, M. Haag, H. Damm: *The Association of Situation Graphs with Temporal Variations in Image Sequences*. Working Notes AAAI–95 Fall Symposium Series 'Computational Models for Integrating Language and Vision', R.K. Srihari (ed.), Cambridge/MA, 10–12 November 1995, pp. 1–8.
10. K. Schäfer: *Unscharfe zeitlogische Modellierung von Situationen und Handlungen in Bildfolgenauswertung und Robotik*. Dissertation, Fakultät für Informatik der Universität Karlsruhe (TH), Juli 1996. Published in: Dissertationen zur Künstlichen Intelligenz (DISKI), Band **135**, infix–Verlag, St. Augustin, 1996.

Designing a Counter: Another Case Study of Dynamics and Activation Landscapes in Recurrent Networks

Steffen Hölldobler, Yvonne Kalinke, Helko Lehmann

TU Dresden, Fakultät Informatik
D–01062 Dresden
{sh,yve,eld}@inf.tu-dresden.de

Abstract. Inspired by the work of Elman and Wiles [15] and based on the notions developed within the theory of dynamical systems it is shown how a simple recurrent connectionist network with a single hidden unit implements a counter. This result is exemplified by showing that such a network can be used to recognize the context–free language $a^n b^n$ consisting of strings of some number n of a's followed by the same number n of b's for $n \leq 250$, whereby the maximum value for n is only restricted by the computing accuracy of the used hardware.

1 Introduction

It is a common hypothesis today that the functionality of the brain and nervous system can be understood within the theory of computation (e.g. [11]), it is widely believed that high–level cognitive tasks require the ability to represent structured objects and to execute structure–sensitive processes on top of these objects (e.g. [3,7]), and it seems that — based on our current data and understanding — connectionist networks in the sense of [2] or [10] are a crude but reasonable model for (real) neural networks [14].

Based on these hypothesis some results have been obtained so far like the result that any computable function can be computed by a connectionist network [6], that networks of binary threshold units are equivalent to finite state automatons [1], that finding a global minimum of the energy function corresponding to a Hopfield network is equivalent to finding a model of an appropriate propositional logic formula [8], or that first–order reasoning can be mapped onto structured connectionist networks [4,12], to mention just a few.

But most of these results are purely theoretical and only very few of them are consistent with biological findings. As neuroscientists are convinced by now that any two neurons are at most four "connections" apart and that there are numerous recurrent "connections" in the (real) brain, an interesting question to ask is how such heavily interconnected and recurrent networks establish high–level cognitive tasks. As our knowledge in this area is quite limited we propose to initiate case studies concerning the dynamics and activation landscapes of simple recurrent connectionist networks.

Such a case study was done by Wiles and Elman [15], who trained two–layer networks, whose hidden units propagate back to themselves, to predict the deterministic elements in sequences of the form $a^n b^n$, where $1 \leq n \leq 12$. Obviously, all that is required for solving such a task is a counter. After extensive training, the networks of Wiles and Elman performed poorly, most of them recognized elements of $a^* b^*$, which is a much simpler task not requiring a counter at all, whereas only a single network was able to generalize to strings of length $n = 21$, and after "making additional small adjustments of recurrent weights by hand" generalized even further to strings of length $n = 85$.

In this paper we formally analyze simple recurrent networks using notions and results from the area of dynamical systems. Based on this analysis we design two types of counters, viz. the non–linear and linear one, the former of which corresponds to the kind of network used by Wiles and Elman. We then applied the latter one to accept sequences of the form $a^n b^n$. The network was able to recognize strings of length $n \leq 250$, where the maximum value of n was only restricted by the computing accuracy of the used hardware. This example is convincing evidence that we have developed a true counter using a two layer network with a single hidden unit having a single recurrent connection.

This paper is organized as follows. After recalling some basic notions and notations concerning dynamical systems in Section 2 simple recurrent connectionist networks are classified wrt their attractors in Section 3. In Section 4 the notions of convergent and divergent intervals of a transformation are introduced as a prerequisite for setting up recurrent connectionist networks as counters (Section 5). The behavior of such a network is exemplified in Section 6, where it is applied to recognize the elements of the context–free language $a^n b^n$. Finally, in Section 7 our results are discussed and some future work is outlined.

2 Notions and Notations

Throughout the paper we will use the metric space $(\mathbb{R}, |x - y|)$, where $|x - y|$ denotes the Euclidean distance between two points x, y in $\mathbb{R}$. Furthermore, $(\mathbb{R}, |x - y|, \sigma)$, where $\sigma : \mathbb{R} \to \mathbb{R}$, will always denote a dynamical system. The *orbit* of a point $x \in M$ is the sequence $\{\sigma^n(x)\}_{n=0}^{\infty}$. $\sigma|_{[l,u]}$ denotes the restriction of σ to the interval $[l, u]$, where $l, u \in \mathbb{R}$ and $l < u$.

Given a dynamical system we are interested in periodic points, i.e. points which are invariant under (possibly repeated) applications of the transformation σ.

Definition 1. $x \in \mathbb{R}$ is an *n–periodic point* of σ iff $\exists n \in \mathbb{N} : \sigma^n(x) = x \wedge (\neg \exists\, m \in \mathbb{N} : m < n \wedge \sigma^m(x) = x)$. The orbit of an n–periodic point of σ is called a *cycle* with *period* n. A *fixed point* is a 1–periodic point.

Periodic points may be attractive or repulsive. Attractive ones are stable with respect to minor perturbations, i.e. the system returns to the periodic point, whereas repulsive ones are unstable, i.e.. perturbations may send the system to another periodic point. The n–periodic attractive points form a class of *attractors*.

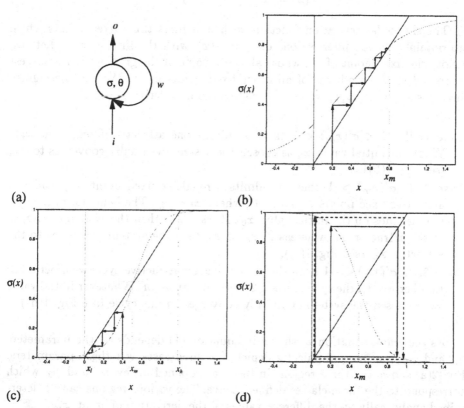

(a)

(b)

(c)

(d)

Fig. 1. (a) A simple recurrent network with threshold θ, sigmoidal activation function σ, input i, output o, and weight w on the recurrent connection. Depending on the parameters $p_1 = -w$ and $p_2 = (\theta + i)/ - w$ the system behavior can be classified by three examples: (b) The case of a single attractor of σ at x_m for the parameter values $p_1 = 3$ and $p_2 = 1/3$. (c) The case of an repulsive fixed point at x_m and two attractors at x_l and x_h of σ for the parameter values $p_1 = 8$ and $p_2 = 1/2$. (d) The case of an attractive cycle with period 2 for the parameter values $p_1 = -8$ and $p_2 = 1/2$.

3　Dynamics in Recurrent Networks

The simplest recurrent network consists of a single unit, whose output is propagated back to itself. Fig. 1(a) shows such a unit with threshold θ, a recurrent connection with weight w, and the sigmoidal activation function $\sigma: \mathbb{R} \to \mathbb{R}:$ $x \mapsto (1 + e^{-wx+\theta})^{-1}$.

Let $p_1 = -w$, $p_2 = (\theta + i)/ - w$, and assume that the input $i \in \mathbb{R}$ is clamped. Then the output behavior of such a simple recurrent network corresponds to a dynamical system $(\mathbb{R}, |x - y|, \sigma)$, where

$$\sigma(x) = (1 + e^{-p_1(x-p_2)})^{-1}. \tag{1}$$

The sigmoidal activation function σ has at most three fixed points which are obtained as the intersections of $y = \sigma(x)$ with the line $y = x$. Let x_m denote the fixed point of σ, whose absolute value of the gradient is the largest compared to the gradients of all other fixed points of σ. We can distinguish three cases wrt $\sigma'(x_m)$, where σ' denotes the first derivative of σ.

Case 1: If $-1 < \sigma'(x_m) < 1$ then σ admits one attractive fixed point x_m. Whatever initial value x_0 is chosen the system eventually converges to x_m (see Fig. 1(b)).

Case 2: If $\sigma'(x_m) > 1$ then σ admits a repulsive fixed point x_m and two attractive fixed points x_l and x_h, where $x_l < x_h$. The behavior of the system depends on the initial value x_0. If $x_0 < x_m$ then the system converges to the attractor x_l, whereas if $x_m < x_0$ then the system converges to the attractor x_h (see Fig. 1(c)).

Case 3: If $\sigma'(x_m) < -1$ then the system has an attractive cycle with period 2. In other words, the system has a 2–periodic attractor. Whatever initial value x_0 is chosen the system eventually converges to this cycle (see Fig. 1(d)).

As the transformation σ shown in equation (1) depends on the parameters p_1 and p_2, we may graphically depict the three cases wrt these parameters. Fig. 2(a) shows the three regions in the space opened up by p_1 and p_2 which correspond to the three classes defined above. The various regions can be determined analytically by the different values of the derivation of σ at x_m,

$$\sigma'(x) = p_1 \sigma(x)(1 - \sigma(x)). \tag{2}$$

Regions 1 and 2 are bounded by $\sigma'(x) = 1$, regions 1 and 3 by $\sigma'(x) = -1$. Using equation (2) we obtain

$$\sigma_{1,2} = \frac{1 \pm \sqrt{1 - \frac{4}{p_1}}}{2} \quad \text{and} \quad \sigma_{3,4} = \frac{1 \pm \sqrt{1 + \frac{4}{p_1}}}{2},$$

and with the fixed point condition $\sigma(x) = x$ we find the borderlines

$$p_2 = \sigma_{1,2} + \frac{\ln(\frac{1}{\sigma_{1,2}} - 1)}{p_1} \quad \text{and} \quad p_2 = \sigma_{3,4} + \frac{\ln(\frac{1}{\sigma_{3,4}} - 1)}{p_1}$$

in the parameter space, respectively.

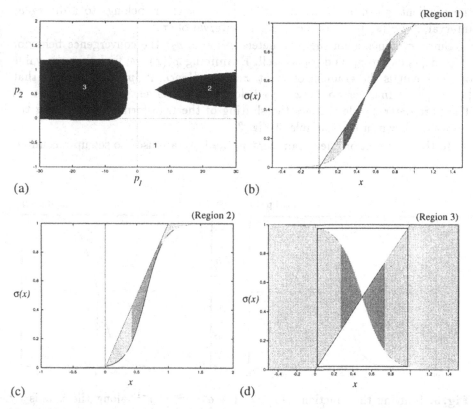

(a)

(b)

(c)

(d)

Fig. 2. (a) Three regions with different dynamical behavior of the activation function depending on the parameters p_1 and p_2 (Shown is a part of the parameter space only.) and corresponding to the cases 1, 2 and 3 defined above. (b)–(d) Convergent (light marking) and divergent (dark marking) intervals of transformations in region 1,2, and 3.

4 Convergence and Divergence

Depending on the gradient the transformation σ shows a different convergence behavior. We distinguish *convergent* and *divergent intervals* of the transformation σ as follows.

Definition 2. Let $l, u \in \mathbb{R}$ with $l < u$. The transformation σ is *convergent in the interval* $[l, u]$ iff $\forall x, y \in [l, u]:\ d(\sigma(x), \sigma(y)) < d(x, y)$. The transformation σ is *divergent in the interval* $[l, u]$ iff $\forall x, y \in [l, u]:\ d(\sigma(x), \sigma(y)) > d(x, y)$.

Fig. 2(b)–(d) shows convergent and divergent intervals for the transformations in each of the regions of the parameter space. To decide whether a point $x \in \mathbb{R}$ belongs to a divergent or convergent interval of σ we have to compute the gradient σ' of σ at x. If $|\sigma'(x)| > 1$ then x belongs to a divergent interval, if $|\sigma'(x)| < 1$ to a convergent interval of σ.

Since σ depends on the parameters p_1 and p_2, the convergence behavior of σ depends on p_1 and p_2 as well. Examining $\sigma'(x)$ we find that the value of $p_1/4$ equals the gradient of σ at $x = p_2$. Hence, if $|p_1| > 4$ we find that $|\sigma'(x)| > 1$. In other words, $x = p_2$ belongs to a divergent interval iff $|p_1| > 4$. The parameter p_2 determines the shifting of the transformation σ along the x–axis as shown in the example of Fig. 3.

In the next section the parameters p_1 and p_2 are used to set up a counter.

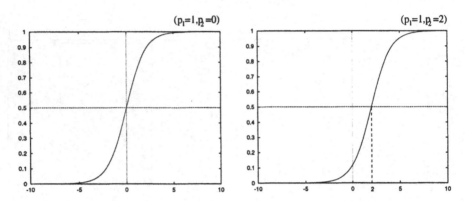

Fig. 3. Shifting the function $\sigma(x) = (1 + e^{-p_1(x-p_2)})^{-1}$ along the x–axis by changing p_2.

5 Setting up a Counter

How can such a simple recurrent network like the one depicted in Fig. 1 be set up such that it acts like a counter, and, in particular, that it increments and decrements? This is the main question to be tackled in this paper. There are basically two possibilities:[1]

1. We may use a divergent interval of a transformation for incrementing and a "complementary" convergent interval for decrementing the counter.
2. We may use convergent intervals for incrementing and decrementing the counter.

Let us call the former possibility the *nonlinear counter* and the latter one the *linear counter*.

---

[1] We may additionally consider the "dual" possibilities, where convergent and divergent transformations are interchanged. But as these dual possibilities share the same properties as the possibilities considered herein we do not discuss them any further.

5.1 The Nonlinear Counter

To construct a nonlinear counter we have to find a transformation with a divergent interval and one with a "complementary" convergent interval. We also have to specify what "complementary" means in this context.

As discussed in Section 4 transformations with divergent intervals can be found if we choose the parameter p_1 such that $|p_1| > 4$. Transformations that fulfill this condition occur in each region of the parameter space (see Fig. 2).

But there is another obvious requirement that has to be satisfied by the activation function such that the above mentioned process specifies indeed a counter: The intervals of the activation functions that are used for the counting process have to be complementary or *symmetric* in the following sense.

Definition 3. Let σ and $\bar{\sigma}$ be transformations. For $x_0 \in [l, u]$ and $\bar{x}_0 \in [\bar{l}, \bar{u}]$ let $\sigma^i(x_0) = x_i \in [l, u]$ and $\bar{\sigma}^i(\bar{x}_0) = \bar{x}_i \in [\bar{l}, \bar{u}]$, respectively, $1 \leq i \leq n$, $n \in \mathbb{N}$. $\bar{\sigma}|_{[\bar{l}, \bar{u}]}$ is *symmetric* to $\sigma|_{[l, u]}$ iff $\forall 1 \leq i \leq n$: $|x_i - x_{i-1}| = c \cdot |\bar{x}_{n-i+1} - \bar{x}_{n-i}|$, where $c \in \mathbb{R}$.

Obviously, this condition can not be met if we take two sigmoidal activation functions, regardless of the choice of the parameters p_1 and p_2. We could use other functions instead of sigmoidal ones but we did not find two transformations meeting the symmetry constraint[2].

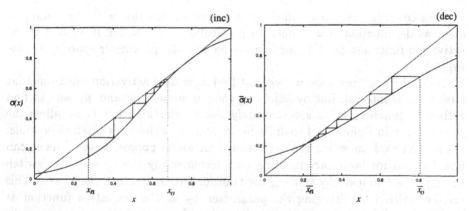

Fig. 4. The principle of a nonlinear counter. Taken an initial value $x_0 \in [l, u]$ the transformation σ is recursively applied until the value $x_n \in [l, u]$ is reached. Each application of σ is divergent and increments the counter (inc). In order to decrement the counter we use the transformation $\bar{\sigma}$ and map x_0 and x_n onto $\bar{x}_n \in [\bar{l}, \bar{u}]$ and $\bar{x}_0 \in [\bar{l}, \bar{u}]$, respectively. Initialized with $\bar{x}_0$ the transformation $\bar{\sigma}$ is now recursively applied until $\bar{x}_n$ is reached. Each application is convergent and decrements the counter (dec).

---

[2] One should observe that the class of functions we examined is restricted by the properties of activation functions.

However, taking two sigmoidal activation functions σ and $\bar{\sigma}$ and adjusting the parameters p_1 and p_2 we can approximate the desired behavior allowing the parameter $c \in \mathbb{R}$ in Definition 3 to differ in an interval, which is as small as possible, that is finding two sigmoidal activation functions σ and $\bar{\sigma}$ that are *approximately symmetric* in the intervals $[\bar{l}, \bar{u}]$ and $[l, u]$ respectively. The resulting nonlinear counter is illustrated in Fig. 4.

The counter can be implemented by a network with two hidden units where one unit uses the sigmoidal activation function σ and the other one the sigmoidal activation function $\bar{\sigma}$. During the incrementing and decrementing process the hidden unit with activation function $\bar{\sigma}$ and σ, respectively, will be suppressed by using appropriate thresholds. Such an architecture was used in [15]. The activation functions used in the implementation in [15] is not symmetric nor approximately symmetric, and this is the reason why the counter does not work appropriate for large sequences $a^n b^n$. In the following section we will design a linear counter whose counting capability is unrestricted in principle.

5.2   The Linear Counter

To construct a linear counter we have to find a transformation σ and an interval such that σ is linear in the interval and the interval itself should be as long as possible.

Definition 4. For $x_0 \in [l, u]$ let $\sigma^i(x_0)) = x_i \in [l, u]$, $1 \le i \le n$, $n \in \mathbb{N}$. $\sigma|_{[l,u]}$ is *linear* iff $\forall 1 \le i \le n$: $x_i = i \cdot s + x_1$, where $s \in \mathbb{R}$.

This condition can be satisfied by an activation function with the same gradient as the function $y = x$ only. In particular, it is satisfied if $p_1 = 4$. Such activation functions can be found in region 1 of the parameter space only (see Fig. 2).

As in the nonlinear case we will not find *sigmoidal* activation functions that have a linear interval. But by adjusting the parameters p_1 and p_2 we can find activation functions with *approximately linear* intervals, that is we allow the parameter s in Definition 4 to differ in an interval, which is as small as possible.

The interval, in which the activation function is approximately linear, can now be used for both, incrementing and decrementing the counter. We switch between the two modi by shifting the transformation σ along the x–axis. This can be realized by changing the parameter p_2 of the activation function as discussed in Section 4 (see Fig. 3). One should notice that we are no longer interested in shifting wrt $x = 0$ but wrt $x = 1/2$, such that we can write $p_2 = 1/2\{+, -\}ds$ where ds denotes the value we use for shifting the activation function wrt $x = 1/2$.

The resulting linear counter is illustrated in Fig. 5. It can be implemented by a network with one hidden unit that uses the sigmoidal activation function σ during the incrementing process and the sigmoidal activation function $\bar{\sigma}$, which is obtained from σ by shifting σ along the x–axis, during the decrementing process. An implementation of such a linear counter will be discussed in the next section.

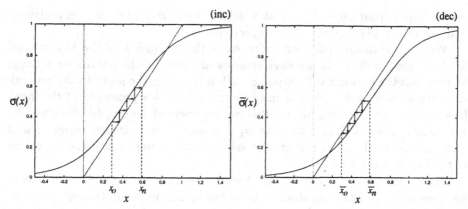

Fig. 5. The principle of a linear counter. Initialized with a value x_0 in the linear interval of the transformation σ, the transformation is recursively applied until the value x_n is reached. Each application increments the counter (inc). In order to decrement the activation function is shifted to the right by changing the parameter p_2 and mapping x_n and x_0 onto $\bar{x}_n$ and $\bar{x}_0$, respectively. Initialized with $\bar{x}_n$ the new transformation $\bar{\sigma}$ is now recursively applied until $\bar{x}_0$ is reached. Each application decrements the counter (dec).

6 An Example

Let us design a network for realizing the task described in [15], that is the recognition of the simple context–free language $a^n b^n$, consisting of strings of some number of a's followed by the same number of b's. We use the network shown in Fig. 6 consisting of one hidden unit h, which receives weighted input from the input unit i, and two output units o_a, o_b, each receiving a weighted input from the hidden unit. The hidden unit h has a self–recurrent connection with weight w_h and uses an activation function σ and the threshold θ_h. The input unit represents the two possible inputs a and b. The output units indicate whether the input sequence consisting of a's and b's, respectively, is acceptable. They

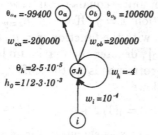

Fig. 6. A network for recognizing strings $a^n b^n$.

receive input from the hidden unit weighted with w_{o_a} and w_{o_b} respectively, and use thresholds θ_{o_a} and θ_{o_b}, respectively.

We start with an initial value for h_0 – the activation of the hidden unit h – at time $t = 0$. If the network receives an input a the parameter settings realize, that the network will output a. While changing the input to the network to b the network will output a until the number of b's presented at the input layer reaches the number of a's that were presented before. In this case the activations of o_a and o_b change to $o_a \approx 0$ and $o_b \approx 1$, the representation of "acceptance" at the output layer. The value of the counter, that is the activation of the hidden unit h is h_0.

To construct the counter we now have to determine the weights of the connections in the net and the thresholds for the hidden unit and the output units. We found the parameters shown in Fig. 6.

Since we chose input values 0.2 for a a and 0.8 for a b the hidden unit h gets different input i from the input unit (Let i_a denote the input for a and i_b the input for b presented to the network.) which results in different values p_{2a}/p_{2b} for the activation function $\sigma_{a,b} = (1 + e^{-p_1(x - p_{2a,b})})^{-1}$.

$$p_1 = -w_h = 4$$
$$i_a = 0.2 \cdot w_i = 2 \cdot 10^{-5}$$
$$i_b = 0.8 \cdot w_i = 8 \cdot 10^{-5}$$
$$p_{2a,b} = (\theta_h + i_{a,b})/ - w_h$$
$$p_{2a} = (2 - 5 \cdot 10^{-5} + 2 \cdot 10^{-5})/4 = 1/2 - 3/4 \cdot 10^{-5}$$
$$p_{2b} = (2 - 5 \cdot 10^{-5} + 8 \cdot 10^{-5})/4 = 1/2 + 3/4 \cdot 10^{-5}$$

Hence, a shifting is obtained by setting $ds_h = 3/4 \cdot 10^{-5}$ for the hidden unit which corresponds to the step width of the counter at $\sigma(1/2)$.

For the output units we found the following parameter settings:

$$o_a : p_1 = -w_{o_a} = 200000$$
$$p_2 = \theta_{o_a}/(-w_{o_a}) + \epsilon = -0.497 + \epsilon = 1/2 - 3 \cdot 10^{-3} + \epsilon$$
$$o_b : p_1 = -w_{o_b} = -200000$$
$$p_2 = \theta_{o_b}/(-w_{o_b}) - \epsilon = -0.503 - \epsilon = 1/2 + 3 \cdot 10^{-3} - \epsilon$$

The shifting for the output units equals $ds_o = 3 \cdot 10^{-3}\{+/-\}\epsilon$, where the ϵ is a small correction term that is used to produce an output smaller or greater than 0.5, respectively, and was chosen to be $\epsilon = 5 \cdot 10^{-6}$. The initial value for h_0 – the activation of the hidden unit – equals the intersection point of the activation function σ_b with the function $x = y$. If we let $h_{x=y}$ denote the intersection of the activation function σ_a with the function $x = y$, the distance between these points, i.e. $dl = |h_{x=y} - h_0|$, denotes the maximum length of the linear interval we use for counting. This corresponds to the shifting of the activation function for the output units as follows:

$$dl = |h_{x=y} - h_0| = |(1/2 + ds_o) - (1/2 - ds_o)| = 2ds_o.$$

Setting the parameter values as shown in Fig. 6 we obtain a counter that is able to recognize strings of the language $a^n b^n$ up to $n = 250$. Obviously, the value decreases with decreasing computing accuracy.

7 Discussion

We have shown how a simple two layer network with a single hidden unit having a single recurrent connection can be used for incrementing and decrementing a counter. The counter outperforms the counter developed in [15] by far and is in fact only limited by the computing accuracy of the underlying hardware. Whereas in [15] notions like divergent or convergent behavior of a transformation are not formally explained and are used in a way which is contrary to our intuition, we have quite rigorously applied notions and results from dynamical systems and have formally defined our counter.

We have also tried to apply learning techniques to our networks and learn the counter. However, we were unable to reach the value $n = 250$ this way. One reason for this failure may be that the system behavior changes dramatically[3] with small changes of the crucial parameters h_0, w_h and θ_h. General learning algorithms as for instance backpropagation do not consider particular dependencies between these parameters. This may also explain why Wiles and Elman [15] couldn't train a counter for a reasonable value of n.

In the past there was a lot of work done to show that recurrent networks are able to realize high–level cognitive tasks as for instance representation of complex structures [9], inference processes [12], unification [13] etc. Since in our opinion it is not only necessary to construct recurrent networks that solve special cognitive tasks but to examine their dynamical behavior, but to understand better why they do fit to this task, we also want to examine more complex recurrent networks that solve more complex tasks than a counter does, in the future.

One step to this direction is the work done in [5] where we have shown that in theory a feedforward neural network with at least one hidden layer can approximate the meaning function T_P for an acceptable logic program P, and thereby the recurrent network (resulting when extending the feedforward net by recurrent connections from the output to the input layer) is able to approximate the semantic of the program P.

References

1. Arbib, M.A. (1987). Brains, Machines, and Mathematics. 2nd edition: Springer–Verlag.
2. Feldman, J.A. & Ballard, D.H. (1982). Connectionist Models and Their Properties. *Cognitive Sciene*, 6(3), 205–254.
3. Fodor, J.A. & Pylyshyn, Z.W. (1988). Connectionism and Cognitive Architecture: A Critical Analysis. In Pinker & Mehler (Eds.), *Connections and Symbols* (pp. 3–71): Springer–Verlag
4. Hölldobler, S. (1993). Automated Inferencing and Connectionist Models. Technical Report AIDA–93–06, Intellektik, Informatik, TH Darmstadt, (Postdoctoral Thesis).
5. Kalinke, Y. & Störr, H.-P. (1996). Rekurrente Neuronale Netze zur Approximation der Semantik akzeptabler logischer Programme. In Bornscheuer, S. & Thielscher, M.

---

[3] Because of its lack of robustness, the represented neural counter implementation is not a good model for a real neural system.

324

(Eds.), *Fortschritte in der Künstlichen Intelligenz* (p. 27), KI-96 Workshop: Dresden University Press.

6. McCulloch, W.S. & Pitts,W. (1943). A logical Calculus and the ideas immanent in nervous activity. *Bulletin of Mathematical Biophysics*, 5,115–133.

7. Newell, A. (1980). Physical Symbol Systems. *Cognitive Science*, 4,135–183.

8. Pinkas, G. (1991). Symmetric Neural Networks and Logic Satisfiability. *Neural Computation*, **3**.

9. Pollack, J.B. (1988). Recursive auto–associative memory: Devising compositional distributed representations. In *Proceedings of the Annual Conference of the Cognitive Science Society*, pp.33–39.

10. Rumelhart, D.E. & Hinton, G.E. & McClelland, J.L. (1986). A General Framework for Parallel Distributed Processing. In *Parallel Distributed Processing*: MIT Press.

11. Sejnowski, T.J. & Churchland, P.S. (1989). Brain and Cognition. In Posner,M.I.(Ed.),*Foundations of Cognitive Science*: MIT Press.

12. Shastri, L. & Ajjanagadde, V. (1993). From Associations to Systematic Reasoning: A Connectionist Representation of Rules, Variables and Dynamic Bindings using Temporal Synchrony. *Behavioural and Brain Sciences*, **16**(3). pp. 417–494.

13. Stolcke, A. (1989). Unification as Constraint Satisfaction in Structured Connectionist Networks. *Neural Computation*, 1(4), pp.559–567.

14. Wiggers, W. & Eurich, C. & Roth, G. & Schwegler, H. (1995). *Salamander und Simulander*. Neuroforum, 1.

15. Wiles, J. & Elman, J. (1995). Learning to Count without a Counter: A case Study of dynamics and activation landscapes in recurrent networks. In *Proceedings of the Seventeenth Annual Conference of the Cognitive Science Society*,Cambridge, MA:MIT Press.

Cooperating Diagnostic Expert Systems to Solve Complex Diagnosis Tasks*

Stefan K. Bamberger

Department of AI and Applied Computer Science
Würzburg University
bambi@informatik.uni-wuerzburg.de

Abstract. Expert systems are already successfully in use for some time. In spite of steadily improved knowledge acquisition techniques and strong problem solving algorithms, very large knowledge bases cannot be managed and maintained reasonably. This article describes the problems and advantages of building expert systems as a consilium of independent agents. The aspects of human teamwork are discussed and an approach is presented to implement it in the diagnostic expert system shell kit D3 with emphasis on distributed knowledge acquisition, competence and problem solving as well as data transfer between agents.

1 Introduction

Diagnostic expert systems are valuable assistants when analyzing abnormal behaviour in technical and medical domains. Due to their inherent inference mechanisms they produce a result which is transparent and understandable. The only risk in developing of expert systems is the dependency on the quality and the scope of the modeled knowledge base. The quality again is dependent on the kind of domain (how well is it understood, how clearly can it be represented, how engaged are the experts and how much time do they have). This decision must be made before the expert system is built and can be influenced on system level only by adequate and customizeable modelling tools to ease the development process. The scope of a knowledge base is also a function of the size of the knowledge base. With sophisticated representation mechanisms it is possible to condense the knowledge to some degree (i.e. expressing any part with one complex rule instead of several simple one) but beyond a certain complexity the increase in size is foreseeable.

The larger a knowledge base grows, the harder it is to keep it consistent, especially when several experts are involved. Problems are inevitable as everybody wants to follow his own structuring technique. Additionally there is a high risk that inconsistent or redundant information will be entered when communication between the experts is insufficient. Problems are further aggravated by geographical seperation, resulting e.g. in long waiting periods for those in need for a common part modeled by absent team members. In consequence not only

---

* The work reported is partially supported by the BMBF (German Ministry of Education, Science, Research and Technology) under grant number 01 HP 844/0.

one integrated expert system has to be developed, but at least one expert system per expert.

The problems of large knowledge base maintenance are especially severe in medicine where knowledge bases tend to be particularly complex because of intrinsic complexity and knowledge overlapping among specialities. Therefore, providing access to other expert systems is often more cost effective than re-modeling common parts in every new system.

The diagnostic experts system shell kit D3 [Puppe *et al.*, 1996] was designed to enable domain experts – usually unfamiliar with computers and AI techniques – to represent their expertise in expert systems. In the reminder of this article we discuss how this shell can be extended to allow to combine existing knowledge bases to build large and more comprehensive ones.

2 Problem Solving by Teamwork

Before a team begins to work, the formation of the team should have been done. The kind of setting-up determines the features of all later members of the team[2]. To work in the team, every agent must have the possibility to get into contact with the other agents. The necessary techniques can be provided either by a centralized service from the team environment or from the agents themselves.

The different kinds of teamwork are very distinct in the medical domain. When a sick patient sees his doctor, he either finds the diagnosis himself or sends the patient to a specialist. This could be either a referral or a clarification.

A special case is the treatment in a hospital. A specialist can cooperate with other specialists to find the correct diagnosis. During the whole process of problem solving they discuss their conclusions until they find a common solution.

As to the language, experts use to communicate, we distinguish two kinds of languages. First, language as a general transmitter (i.e. English or German), second, language as a domain-specific terminology. Whereas different terminology is not easily transformed, the use of different transmitters is even more complicated. In the following text, if we refer to language, we always implicate both kinds. Otherwise we explicitly write transmitter or technical terminology.

2.1 Mechanisms to Cooperate

The above examples demonstrated several aspects relevant to teamwork:
Team Formation

1. centralized: Number and kind of agents are given (typical for a hospital).
2. decentralized: The structure of a team will grow incrementally. The agents themselves can decide when and how they join a team (typical for general practitioners).

---

[2] In the following we will speak of an agent as a member of a team. Therefore an expert system working in a team will be called agent, too.

Determination of Competence

1. static: The competence distribution among team members is known when new agents are admitted. Each team member knows under which circumstances other competence areas have to be activated before the team starts to operate.
2. dynamic: During teamwork, the agents exchange knowledge about their competence to determine which competence area is most appropriate.

How to find a Result

1. autonomous: Each agent decides by himself whether or not his solutions are correct.
2. central: A team control collects the solutions of all agents and selects the final solution according to preset criteria.
3. cooperative: All members of the team discuss the results until they find a common solution. This alternative is preferable among specialists of the same competence area.

Kind of Communication

1. clarification: An agent gets an order and returns control after completion of his work.
2. referral: An agent refers the case completely to another agent.
3. consultation: Two or more agents cooperate and present a common solution.
4. central control: During teamwork, one agent controls the others.

Data Transfer

1. uniform language: Each member of a team uses the same transmitter and technical terminology.
2. central interpreter: The team control provides an interpreter which translates the different languages.
3. decentralized interpreter: Every agent is responsible for being understood by all others.

In the next chapter, the shell kit D3 is described and the extensions are discussed which are necessary to implement teamwork in D3.

3 Diagnostic Shell D3

3.1 D3 at present

D3 consists of four kinds of components: knowledge acquisition, problem solving, dialogue and extensions[3] [Puppe *et al.*, 1994; 1996]. Each component may contain several modules which can be linked dynamically to the shell via an

---

[3] This component subsumes all additional modules, i.e., information system, machine learning modules and so on.

interface and can be registered to become part of the whole system. For example, the problem solving component consists of several problem solving methods including heuristic, categoric, case based, set covering, functional and statistical.

Common to all modules is the basic terminology. Modules are free to extend this basic terminology for their own purpose. This is possible with a descriptive language allowing the definition of objects and their relations on a meta-level [Gappa, 1995].

All modules with user interaction generate their interface during runtime out of the objects' description. Different views on knowledge objects and their relations – via graphical abstraction of knowledge [Bamberger *et al.*, 1997] – allow powerful navigation and intuitive input of complex associations.

Section 2.1 described common constellations in teamwork. To implement teamwork, a compromise has to be found between acceptable effort of realization, simplicity of operation and the most intelligible representation available. The following aspects have priority for the realization within D3:

- Easy integration of already existing independant agents.
- Simulation of human teamwork as closely as possible.

The reuse of already existing agents suggests a decentralized mechanism for team formation. It should be the aim that the individual developer does not have to know anything about the internal structure of other agents for doing his work. That is why a central reference station – an information system – is provided which keeps all necessary data. With it, every developer describes the capabilities and characteristics of his agents.

3.2 D3 Extensions

The realization of a team modul within D3 requires adaptations of the existing knowledge acquisition modules.

Team Formation
Theory. The best of both worlds is a combination of the flexibility of the decentralized approach together with the efficiency of the centralized one. At a central place, in an information system, the data from all sorts of agents and teams are stored. A team is created using those data. For sake of efficiency changes of the team crew is only possible before the team starts to operate. Alteration of team data will force an update of the information system.

Practice. To follow the principle of graphical abstraction, an editor is provided to set up and administer a team graphically. The members of the team can be arranged hierarchically. The root of the hierarchy is the team object itself. The leaves of the tree are agents who work in the team. Knots in the tree represent other teams which are integrated in larger ones. All preferences for the whole team and individual agents will be saved automatically in the information system.

Finding a Result

Theory. During team formation the way how to calculate the final solution is determined. Every alternative has its justification in a given team context. The expert who builds the team has to decide which alternative is best for his team members.

Practice. D3 supports the autonomous and the central alternative. The last alternative (*cooperative*) is very expensive to realize and needs a lot of extra knowledge of the agents to perform it. A special protocol is necessary to allow the agents to discuss their results. We believe that in most cases the simpler alternatives are sufficient. The runtime system of D3 collects the solutions of the individual agents and presents the results at the end of the inference process. With the central alternative the results are first filtered using the characteristics of the agents (see "Determination of Competence") to decide which solution is best. Additionally, case specific values can be taken into consideration, e.g. the certainty of the derived solution.

Determination of Competence

Theory. A necessary feature of an agent in a team is his estimation when to yield control to another agent. This kind of knowledge is complex and often just as hard to realize as the ordinary expert knowledge. A previous self-assessment concerning his competence and the quality of the knowledge in the periphery of his domain is requested.

Self-assessment is difficult. Studies show that experts often tend to overestimate their competence [Kassirer *et al.*, 1982]. There is the risk that experts miss the optimal time for referral. They might consult another competence area too early or too late. Unnecessary examinations happen and the total costs increase.

When an agent realizes that he is no longer competent for a problem, another agent has to be consulted. This decision is complex, because own knowledge and assumptions about the capabilities of the other agents influence it. On the other hand, a wrong decision delays the problem solving process even longer.

Therefore a second knowledge base part must be developed to handle the point of control switching based on self-assessment and the assessments of other agents (competence knowledge).

Practice. Each registered agent has to supply a description of his capabilities and his competence area. The following list gives a survey of possible characteristics:

- Competence area. The agent can provide one or more keywords which stand for his competence area.
- Cost of data capture (number of questions to be asked).
- Costs of additional examinations.
- Quality of the overall used knowledge.

The characteristics are stored in the above mentioned information system.

For each of the items (except the competence area) the expert can specify a qualitative value (i.e. very high, high, normal, low, very low). Based on this information all other experts can make an estimation of their competence. It is of course the expert who has the responsibility to find a useful subdivision so that the whole system will stay functional. For the competence area the expert can define own keywords. Together with a description they are stored in the information system and must be unique. Then, other experts can also use them.

To model the competence knowledge, the same representation language as the one used to model the central knowledge is offered. The built-in language of D3 is powerful enough and can be used without change. The knowledge base of the agent is extended with a sub knowledge base which exclusively deals with the modelling of the competence areas. The object type diagnosis, which is used in the central knowledge to model a solution can be used here to model a competence area.

Establishing of such a diagnosis triggers the switching to an agent who represents the calculated competence area. The derivation of these diagnoses is analogous to conventional diagnosis via rules from all parts of the knowledge base.

The advantage is that the developer of the agent needn't learn a new representation language to enter the competence knowledge.

Above we explained that competence knowledge may be flawed. Seldom the error is in the structure of the knowledge but often in the used weights. That means that the various facts which refer to a certain competence area are well-known to the agent, but the weightings are uncertain. A parameter adaptive learning algorithm [Bamberger et al., 1993] can be used to analyze the path of the case through the team and to adapt the weightings to maximize the overall efficiency of the team.

Data Transfer

Theory. Data transfer subsumes every data exchange between two agents. Submitted data can be divided into those delivered by the user and those inferred from the central knowledge of the agent. The first category can even be subdivided in subjective data based on human perception (i.e. pain), and objective data like readings from technical devices.

Every agent uses a specific terminology. This terminology, however, can differ from agent to agent. Further on, it is possible that two agents use the same term but with a totally different meaning (that happens especially with derived data). In other situations two different terms are used synonymously. In both cases it has to be decided whether the terms are completely, partially or not synonymous.

In order to make a decision feasable, every expert is required to provide a definition for the terms he wants to exchange. The definition can either be formal or informal. A common language must be used to represent them. The definition of subjective or derived data, however, can be very complex, especially when the concepts of the terms differ only marginally.

A formal definition allows automatic transformations. To guarantee a uniform procedure, ontologies have to be defined. Languages like KIF [1992] or Ontolingua [Gruber, 1993] can be used. To achieve an even better understanding of the terms it could be necessary to provide common-sense knowledge [Lenat, 1995]. The Cyc project [Lenat and Guha, 1990] followed this way. To be able to use the concept of formal definitions it is crucial that all participants use the same language primitives.

The disadvantage is that it requires a great deal of energy to provide this formalism. In restricted domains, being the principle range of expert systems, there exists a specific terminology which strongly reduces the possibilities of interpretation. For further verification of various individually applied terms, a good informal definition is sufficient. The remaining amount of discrepancies is compensated by the tolerance of knowledge bases whose inherent quality is their ability to work with fuzzy information. That's why we believe that a formal definition is not necessary in this context.

All terms he wants to share the expert should indicate in the information system which already administers the description of the characteristics and the competence areas of the agents.

All experts who decide to use a shared term after reading the informal definition in the information system have to define a translation to their internal objects. It is advisable to create a special sub knowledge base, similar to the competence knowledge base. That means that along with the central knowledge and the competence knowledge there is a third area – the transformation knowledge.

Practice. There are two situations in which an agent exchanges data with other agents of the team: either the agent himself shares his own data with others or there is public data, which the agent integrates into his knowledge base.

In both cases a number of objects are created in the knowledge base of the agent, which are used as a buffer. In the first case the buffer object has the same structure as the internal object. A copy of the buffer object is placed automatically in the central terminological data base. The terminological data base is inherent to all knowledge bases and – similar to the information system – of indefinite extention. It is used to keep a copy of all public terms and to store their dynamic data during runtime process when team control switches among agents.

In the second case the expert chooses an object of the terminological data base (via the information system). A copy of the object is created in the buffer of the knowledge base. Now the expert can use the whole rule system of D3 to build arbitrary relations between buffer and internal objects (transformation knowledge).

Every expert should provide detailed informal explanations, when publishing own objects. These explanations are made available to other experts in the information system. A reference to the terminological data base allows the transfer of the object to the knowledge base after successful search.

The assignment between objects of two different agents is static and stored during knowledge acquisition. No knowledge is used outside the agents to transfer data from one agent to another.

Communication
Theory. The kind of communication strongly influences teamwork. The most simple one is referral. All public data is forwarded to the next agent. Clarification will create a new context in which the new agent is embedded. After his investigation control automatically falls back to the first agent. Consultation is the most complicated communication and requires a special protocol.

Practice. When modelling the diagnoses for the competence areas, an expert can choose which kind of communication should be established during runtime. He has the choice between clarification and referral. Central control is implicit possible, if there exists a superior agent who uses other agents exclusively for clarification. Consultation is not implemented as we think that its benefit won't justify its expensive realization. The communication itself is executed by the D3 runtime system.

Runtime environment
The biggest change in the runtime environment is that a team case consists of several subcases, spread among a number of agents. Therefore the team modul assists the existing environment to keep track of the team activity and to ensure the right context for every team member.

The team modul stays in background until the inference process establishes a diagnosis referring to another competence area. Now, the team control takes over. The public data are stored in the terminological data base, the new agent is activated and the corresponding buffer objects are preset. Then, the inference process for this agent is started and team control is in the background again.

In principle all agents could act simultaneously. Data being queried or inferred can be spread among all who use them via the terminological data base. No other mechanism needs to be implemented. Only one restriction has to be imposed: to ensure a consistent dialog with the user, only the presently activated agent is allowed to ask him questions.

4 Example

In this chapter we present an example how to use the new approach and its mechanisms to model a cooperation to find a diagnosis typical to a real-world medical team. First, a complete medical case is presented. The numbers in parentheses '()' indicates the expert being active at that time. Second, we'll show how this case can be modeled using our teamwork module.

Case example of a complex diagnosis finding
(1) 44 year-old white female patient (164 cm/72 kg) complains of recuring episodes of colicky pain in the left lower abdominal quadrant radiating to the left loin, associated with fatigue, anorexia, meteorism, constipation and urinary incontinence while coughing and lifting heavy objects. Since start of the symptoms about 6 months ago she has lost 2 kg. Previous medical history: 2 children, no surgery, pyelonephritis at age 32, chronic laxative abuse. Family practitioner's

exam: Puls 76, regular, blood pressure 135/70, pulmonary and cardiac auscultation within normal limits (WNL). In the left lower abdominal quadrant, he palpates localized tenderness and a questionable soft mass. The rectal and pelvic exam are both WNL. Baseline laborartory parameters are all WNL except for mild hypochromic anemia (Hb 11.2 g/dl).

(2) For abdominal ultrasound, the practitioner sends his patient to the ultrsound specialist. This one reports liver, gall-bladder, pancreas, spleen and kidneys to be free, no evidence for bowel obstruction. Especially, he does not notice an intraabdominal mass.

(1) Since the patient starts complaining of nausea/vomiting, the practitioner suspects colonic subileus (bowel obstruction).

(3) For confirmation, he sends her to a radiologist for a barium enema. However, the colonic passage turns out to be free, no evidence for bowel obstruction. In his report, the radiologist mentions calcifications projecting onto the left kidney.

(1) This finding, in combination with the complaint of incontinence and a previous medical history of pyelonephritis makes the practitioner think of ureteric disease and sends the patient for further confirmation to an urologist.

(4) The urologist diagnoses stress incontinence probably secondary to multiparity. However, the i.v. urogram and ureteroscopy do not reveal clear pathologic evidence explaining the patient's other symptoms.

(1) The practitioner adopts this hypothesis which seems all the more plausible since the patient's symptoms have intensified during her intercurrent menstruation, and makes a gynecologic referral.

(5) In his pelvic exam, the gynecologist palpates a questionable mass in the patient's left small pelvis which he cannot unequivocally confirm by ultrasound. However laparoscopy, reveals a benign left adnexal tumor. He recommends operative removal which the patient does not want to be performed before a second opinion and further deliberation.

Modeled with the teamwork module

According to the numbers five specialists are working together to find the correct diagnosis. The first part of the treatment is dominated by expert 1, the family practitioner, who starts the treatment and uses three other experts (2, 3 and 4) for detailed clarification of his suspected diagnoses. Therefore the kind of communication chosen is *clarification*. The first one and the second one are not used for real clarification but to collect more specific data provided by a special examination (radiologist).

The data being exchanged is in direction $(1 \rightarrow 2,3)$ all general data the practitioner possesses so far and in the other direction $(1 \leftarrow 2,3)$ it is the additional examination results of the specialists. In the third case (1) submits (4) a diagnosis to be clarified waiting for the result 'yes' or 'no'. That means, additional to all the general data (1) sends a diagnosis which helps the specialist to start his examinations at a specific point. Otherwise, perhaps he would have done several examinations not necessarily related to the case.

Another speciality could be observed when we look at the data being submitted from (1) to (4). Although (1) has different data for incontinence and coughing and heavy weigthing, (4), the urologist, uses a much more special term, stress incontinence (in difference to urge incontinence). That means, that in the way of transfering the data from one expert to the other there could perfom more complex mapping than only directly from one to the other. The whole D3 rule set can be used to model such mappings (see the practice part in the section 'Data Transfer'). The data sent back is not primarily new case data retrieved by (4), because (1) is a more general expert and cannot process such specific data, but the information whether or not the given diagnoses is excluded.

After the three clarifications (1) decides that with the present symptoms and suspected diagnoses the case is leaving his competence area. That's why he shifts the case completely to another expert (5). This kind of cooperation can be modeled with the communication form *referral*. All data will be submitted from (1) to (5) and no data will come back.

If (5) hadn't find the correct diagnosis, (5) himself and not (1) would have been responsible to find another expert for further treatment.

The five experts are represented in a team by their expert systems (knowledge bases). Starting with (1), the other experts (2, 3, 4, 5 and all the others being in the team but not used for this case) are modeled as diagnoses with additional properties. With this properties, for example, the kind of communication is set and the competence area to which the case should be transmitted. When such a diagnosis is derived, the runtime systems stops the inference process in the actual system, analyzes the properties of the diagnosis to find the next system, transfers all data signed as public to a general available pool and establishes the new system. In case of clarification, the old system state is saved on a stack and resumed automatically by the runtime environment when the new-called system is finished. There is no limit for the stack size.

The first step before a system starts is to look in the pool for data which have a mapping in the own knowledge base (see 'Data Transfer' in the above chapter).

All mechanisms explained in this section and in section 3.2 are implemented in D3 and presently in the process of evaluation in three different projects.

5   Discussion

This paper presents a distributed approach to the setting up and maintaining of large knowledge bases by the experts themselves. It is oriented towards simulating cooperation of specialists in large medical and technical domains. A knowledge base of an agent has three parts: the central, the competence and the terminological knowledge. All parts can be modelled with the same representation language by the expert himself. In an additional step the characteristics of the agent and all shared knowledge objects are published in an information system. The team modul uses this system to manage the communication between all team members.

In contrast, Heller's approach [Heller, 1995] aims to develop and modularize one complex knowledge base with the help of a knowledge engineer. The engineer determines the structure of various knowledge units within the knowledge base out of his mental model of the domain before the bases were built. This approach is realized with an extended KADS architecture [Breuker and Van der Welde, 1980]. Neither an integration of nor a connection to already existing expert systems is not planned.

A more general approach is described in [Neches et al., 1991]. Also driven from the demand to reuse existing knowledge bases, Neches and his group identify four impediments to sharing and reuse: heterogeneous representation, dialects within language families, lack of communication conventions and model mismatch at the knowledge level. Four working groups were initiated to overcome those problems. The general idea is to develop a set of shareable ontologies [Gruber, 1993] and a powerful protocol (KQML) to exchange knowledge and data. Our approach can be understood as a particular instance of this general approach, restricted to the area of diagnoses in the context of the shell kit D3. Therefore we have a *common* knowledge representation language which is powerful enough to make it possible to shift all sensible data for intra-agent communication in the agents' knowledge bases.

Since Minsky wrote his remarkable book [Minsky, 1988] the Distributed Artificial Intelligence [Bond and Gasser, 1988; Müller, 1993] is a fast growing area. Our approach is mainly related to distributed problem solving. Autonomous agents cooperate to achieve a common solution, whereas the agents of a multiagent system are totally independent. Each of them tries to achieve his individual goals which may or may not contribute to a common solution. Although this might be much closer to conflicts in human teams, especially if the agents have the capability of self-adaption by learning systems and can enter into negotiations, we deliberately ommitted these questions in this paper and our current work, because the addressed distributed problem solving issues of team formation, determination of competence, finding a result, kind of communication and data transfer are of sufficient complexity. Efficiency gains when all agents are working simultaneously are not expected, because of the limited options for data gathering. The agents in D3 have to ask their questions sequentially. Systems like DVMT [Lesser and Corkill, 1983] can retrieve their data independently or all data were given in advance (CORTES [Fox and Sycra, 1990]). That's an important difference to the known blackboard architectures where a synchronisation is neither possible nor desired.

Another important aspect of the concept presented is the requirement of a balance between the organizational advantages of independent development of knowledge bases by different experts and the advantages of coherence in a more centralized approach. Our solution is to allow individual expert system developers complete independence while encouraging them to maximise coherence so as to minimize the requirements of provision of additional knowledge necessary for smooth cooperation of independent modules.

References

[Bamberger et al., 1993] Bamberger S., Gappa U., Goos K. and Poeck K.: *Semi-automatical Knowledge Transformation to support Knowledge Acquisition.* in: Puppe F. and Günter A. (Eds.): Expertensysteme-93, Springer, 1993, (in german)

[Bamberger et al., 1997] Bamberger, S., Gappa, U., Klügl, F., Puppe, F.: *Reduction of Complexity via Graphical Knowledge Abstraction.* Proceedings of the 4th German Conference on Expert Systems, Bonn 1997, (in german)

[Bond and Gasser, 1988] Bond, A. and Gasser, L.: *An Analysis of Problems and Research in Distributed Artificial Intelligence.* In Bond, A. and Gasser, L. (Eds.): Readings in Distributed Artificial Intelligence, Morgan Kaufmann, 1988.

[Breuker and Van der Welde, 1980] Breuker, J.A., Van der Welde, W.: *CommonKADS Library for Expertise Modelling.* Amsterdam, IOS Press, 1994.

[Fox and Sycra, 1990] Fox, M. and Sycara, K.: *Overview of CORTES: A Constraint-Based Approach to Production Planning, Scheduling and Control.* In Proc. of Fourth International Conference on Expert Systems in Production and Operations Management, 1990.

[Gappa, 1995] Gappa, U.: *Graphical Knowledge Acquisition Systems and how to generate them.* Infix Verlag 1995, Band 100, (in german).

[Gruber, 1993] Gruber, T.: *A Translation Approach to portable Ontology Specifications,* Knowledge Acquisition, 5, pp.199-220, 1993.

[Heller, 1995] Heller, B.: *Modularization and Focus of extendable complex Knowledge Bases based on Competence Units.* INFIX Verlag, Vo. 120, 1995, (in german)

[Kassirer et al., 1982] Kassirer, J., Kuipers, B., Gorry, G.: *Towards a Theory of Clinical Expertise.* American Journal of Medicine 73, pp. 251-259, 1982

[KIF, 1992] KIF 3.0 Reference Manual, Report Logic-92-1, Stanford University 1992

[Lenat, 1995] Lenat, D.: *Steps to Sharing Knowledge,* in Mars, N.J.I. (ed.): Towards Very Large Knowledge Bases, IOS Press 1995

[Lenat and Guha, 1990] Lenat, D. and Guha, R.: *Building Large Knowledge-Based Systems: Representation and Inference in the Cyc Project,* Addison-Wesley Publishing Company,Inc. CA.1990

[Lesser and Corkill, 1983] Lesser, V. and Corkill, D.: *The Distributed Vehicle Monitoring Testbed.* AI-Magazine 4(3), pp. 15-34, 1983.

[Minsky, 1988] Minsky, M.: *Society of Mind,* Simon&Schuster, 1988.

[Müller, 1993] Müller, J. (Hrsg.): *Distributed Artificial Intelligence,* BI-Wiss.-Verl. 1993, (in german).

[Neches et al., 1991] Neches, R., Fikes, R., Finin, T., Gruber, T., Patil, R., Senator, T., Swartout, W.: *Enabling Technology for Knowledge Sharing.* AI Magazine. Fall 1991, pp. 36-56.

[Puppe et al., 1994] Puppe, F., Poeck, K., Gappa, U., Bamberger, S., Goos, K.: *Reusable Moduls as parts of a configurable Diagnostic Shell.* Special Issue, KI 2/94, (in german).

[Puppe et al., 1996] Puppe, F., Gappa, U., Poeck, K., Bamberger, S.: *Knowledge Based Diagnosis and Information Systems,* Springer 1996, (in german)

Tabu Search vs. Random Walk

Olaf Steinmann[1], Antje Strohmaier[2] and Thomas Stützle[1]

[1] FB Informatik, FG Intellektik, TH Darmstadt
Alexanderstr. 10, D-64283 Darmstadt, Germany
{olaf,tom}@intellektik.informatik.th-darmstadt.de
[2] KI/Wissensverarbeitung, TU Dresden
D-01062 Dresden, Germany
ast@inf.tu-dresden.de

Abstract. We investigate the benefit of Tabu Search for satisfiability (SAT) and constraint satisfaction problems (CSP) and compare it to the more frequently used random walk heuristic. We argue, that a more deterministic direction of search as done with Tabu Search is worth considering also for SAT and CSP. We give experimental evidence that Tabu Search can be used to efficiently guide local search procedures like GSAT and WSAT for SAT and the *min conflicts* heuristic for CSP. The algorithms are tested on randomly generated problems and hard graph coloring instances from the DIMACS benchmark test set. Additionally, we give some explanation on the value of Tabu Search.

1 Introduction

Constraint satisfaction problems (CSPs) and satisfiability (SAT) are central problems in Artificial Intelligence. Many practical problems like machine vision, spatial and temporal reasoning, and scheduling can be represented as CSP. SAT plays a central role in many reasoning applications and in complexity theory. Recently, SAT has also been used for the encoding of many combinatorial problems [10, 8]. These encoded problems then may be solved by general search algorithms for SAT. Traditionally, systematic complete algorithms based on backtracking were used to solve these problems. Only in recent years general local search procedures for SAT and CSPs like GSAT [16] and the *min conflicts* heuristic (MCH) [12], respectively, were proposed. These algorithms typically start with an initial complete assignment s from the set of all possible assignments S and then perform a sequence of moves that lead from one trial solution to another. The possible moves are defined by a neighborhood function. The moves should lead to possibly better assignments satisfying more clauses or constraints. Local search algorithms for SAT or CSP can be seen as operating on an objective function or energy giving the number of unsatisfied clauses or violated constraints. Thus, these algorithms try to globally minimize the corresponding energy via local search.

One major problem of basic local search algorithms is that they can get stuck in a non-global minima of the objective function. Thus, some mechanism is required to allow the local search procedure to escape from local minima.

To this aim in GSAT restart from a new randomly generated solution is used. Another common extension to prevent the local search from getting stuck in local minima is the application of *random walk* that results in a probabilistic modification of the current solution [15]. Random walk modifies the value of a variable involved in a violated constraint or unsatisfied clause randomly by choosing some other value than the current one. This may lead to an increase of the energy function and, thus, helps to leave local minima. Another heuristic that allows to escape from local minima is Tabu Search [7, 6]. Tabu Search is, especially in the Operations Research community, regarded as one of the most powerful heuristics for the solution of hard combinatorial optimization problems. Tabu Search allows the local search heuristics to leave local minima by forbidding moves to recently visited solutions. Additionally for SAT and CSPs it has the advantage of forcing the algorithm to explore new regions of a *plateau*. This is especially helpful as in GSAT the search effort is determined by a plateau phase [5]. On a plateau many neighbored points exist that have the same objective function value. At such a point walk does not help any further, a more directed way, like offered by Tabu Search, to explore this plateau is needed. Although, initially proposed for MAX-SAT [7] and despite some recent work, see e.g. [11], it has not received very much attention for the solution of SAT and CSP compared to other heuristics like random walk. The aim of this paper is to investigate experimentally the application of Tabu Search for SAT and CSP compared to random walk option. We apply Tabu Search not only to GSAT, but also to WSAT [15] and the MCH, extending the work done in [11]. New is also that we investigate hybrid algorithms using both heuristics, Tabu Search and random walk, to see whether these heuristics may be integrated in one. Our experimental results suggest that Tabu Search behaves better than the "celebrated" random walk option on the problem classes tested in this paper.

In the next section we introduce the notion of constraint satisfaction- and SAT-problem. We describe shortly two local search heuristics for SAT and CSP and after that describe Tabu Search as an add-on heuristic to CSP- and SAT-algorithms. Section 3 gives our experimental setting and the obtained results for SAT and CSP together with an interpretation. In Section 4 we discuss some other work and conclude in the last section.

2 Local Search

2.1 CSP and Satisfiability

A discrete CSP is defined by a finite set of Variables $\mathcal{X} = \{X_1, X_2, \ldots, X_n\}$, every variable X_i having an associated finite and discrete domain D_i, and a set of constraints $\mathcal{C}$. A constraint gives the allowed value combinations for the involved variables. A *k-ary constraint* between variables $\{X_{i1}, \ldots, X_{ik}\}$ is a relation $C \subseteq D_{i1} \times \ldots \times D_{ik}$. SAT may be interpreted as a special case of CSP in which the variables only take two values 1 (*true*) and 0 (*false*). We assume that the SAT problem is given in conjunctive clausal form (CNF), i.e. as a conjunction of disjunctions of literals, a literal being a variable or its negation. Usually the clauses in SAT contain more than two variables, thus the constraints are usually of higher arity.[3] We say a constraint is *violated* by a given assignment s if the k-tuple of values of its variables are not contained in the relation. We denote as *conflict set* $\mathcal{K}(s)$ the set of variables that are involved in some constraint violation for the current variable assignment s. Anyway, SAT and CSP are two closely related problems. On the one hand, a CSP can be transformed into SAT [3], on the other hand SAT can be transformed into binary CSP [1]. This is, apart from the similarity of the basic local search procedures, the reason to treat here both problems together.

2.2 GSAT and MCH

GSAT and MCH are two basic greedy local search procedures for SAT and CSP, respectively. In Figure 1 we present an algorithmic frame that applies to both heuristics. Both heuristics start from an initial random assignment and perform hill climbing steps on the current solution. This is done until some upper bound of *maxTries* is reached. In every try, both aim to improve the current assignment *maxLoops* times. If no solution is found, search is restarted from a newly generated random assignment.[4] The two algorithms differ slightly in the *hillClimb*-step they perform and the neighborhood definition. In GSAT all variables are considered for a move and a variable is chosen whose flip decreases most the objective function value. MCH selects in each move one variable $X_i \in \mathcal{K}(s)$ and chooses a value for this variable among those that minimize the number of conflicts. Note that MCH may leave a variable's value unchanged[5] whereas in GSAT always one variable changes its corresponding value.

2.3 Random Walk, WSAT and Tabu Search

One major problem associated with MCH and GSAT is the occurrence of local minima. One common possibility to escape from local minima that is used in GSAT and MCH is to restart the algorithm with another initial random solution. Another possibility is the application of *random walk*, originally introduced in [14] and also used for CSP [20]. Random walk is applied with some fixed probability p_w and usually performs by far better than restart from random solutions. When applied to GSAT with probability p_w a variable appearing in a currently unsatisfied clause is flipped and with probability $1 - p_w$ the usual greedy strategy is followed. For MCH a walk-step consists of picking a variable of the conflict set $\mathcal{K}(s)$ and choosing a random value of the variable's domain. By random walk the number of violated constraints or unsatisfied clauses may increase and local minima may be left. In the following, we always use GSAT with random walk,

---

[3] Note that SAT with clauses containing at most two variables is polynomially solvable.

[4] Initially MCH was presented without restarts to solve one specific problem instance.

[5] In case of MCH we count every variable selection as one move or flip, even if the chosen variable does not change its value.

```
procedure Local Search(X, D, C)
    for i := 1 to maxTries do
        s := random assignment for X ∈ X;
        for j := 1 to maxLoops do
            if s is solution of C then return s
            else
                possFlips := hillClimb(s, C);
                (V, d) := random element of possFlips;
                s := s[V, d];
            end if;
        end for;
    end for;
    return "no solution found";
end Local Search;
```

Fig. 1. General local search procedure applicable for SAT and CSPs.

abbreviated as GWSAT. We also used an extension of this strategy called WSAT [15]. This algorithm differs from GWSAT in making flips by first randomly picking a clause that is not satisfied by the current assignment, and then picking a variable within that clause to flip. The flips are made either at random (with walk probability p_w) or according to a greedy function.[6]

Tabu Search [7, 6] is a heuristic used for the guidance of an underlying local search algorithm. Tabu Search is able to leave local minima, but in contrast to random walk it relies less on probabilistic elements and guides the search in a more deterministic way. Generally, in Tabu Search the best possible move is made, also if the objective function value increases. To avoid revisiting of previously found solutions Tabu Search uses a *tabu list* of length t containing the forbidden moves. The forbidden moves are identified by specific attributes characterizing previously found solutions and usually contains the reverse of the last t moves.[7]

We applied Tabu Search to GWSAT, WSAT, and MCH by imposing the tabu conditions on the set of possible moves.[8] An important design criteria when using Tabu Search are the attributes that may be declared tabu. For GWSAT and WSAT the tabu list consists of the t previously flipped variables, thus for them it is forbidden to flip variables currently in the tabu list. For MCH we considered two possibilities that differ in the tabu attributes used. In one version we declare variable-value pairs (X_i, d_i) as tabu, in the other version complete variables are used as tabu attributes. If variable-value pairs are chosen as tabu attributes, we influence only the value selection for certain variables, when blocking whole

---

[6] For a more detailed description see [10].

[7] The attributes stored in the tabu list may be e.g. specific values for variables.

[8] We used the code for GWSAT and WSAT available from Bart Selman. Note, that this code also offers a Tabu Search option.

variables the selection of the next variable is modified. If we use variables as tabu attributes, this may also lead to a situation in which a variable $X_i \notin \mathcal{K}(s)$ has to be chosen to update its value, in case all variables in $\mathcal{K}(s)$ are tabu.

3 Experimental Results

We now report on our experimental results obtained with versions of Tabu Search. We compare GWSAT, MCH with random walk, and WSAT with extensions of these algorithms involving Tabu Search.[9] We investigate empirically the parameter combinations when random walk and Tabu Search are applied together, giving also an intuitive explanations of the role of these two components.

One part of the tests is based on randomly generated formulae. For SAT we used random 3-SAT formulae from the crossover region and for CSPs we used random binary CSPs generated according to the $< n, k, p, q >$-model [18]. Here n is the number of variables, k the uniform domain size of the variables, p the probability that there is a constraint between a pair of variables, and q is the conditional probability that a pair of values is allowed if a constraint between these variables exists.[10] We used hard binary CSP from the phase transition region [18], unsolvable instances were filtered out by a complete search procedure.

We also applied all algorithms to some graph coloring instances from the DIMACS benchmark problems. Whereas MCH may be used also for very large instances, the size of problems to which GWSAT may be applied is limited by the size of the SAT-encoded formula.

For all algorithms we calculated the number of moves needed to find a solution. Every problem instance was solved for a number of times and then the median number of moves is taken as an estimate of the solution cost. If we do not discuss specific parameter settings for an algorithm, the algorithm was run with the parameters found to be optimal in preliminary runs. New in our investigation is also that we used combinations of both strategies, random walk and Tabu Search. In Figures 2 to 5 we give the median cost surface for different combinations for t and p_w. In all figures, the x-axis shows the tabu list length, the y-axis gives the walk probability and the z-axis shows the number of moves per solution.

3.1 Satisfiability

For SAT we tested random 3-SAT formula of different sizes and investigated empirically the relationship between the tabu list length t and the walk probability for GWSAT and WSAT. This was done for 50 problems of size $n = 50, 100$ with a fixed clause/variable ratio of 4.3 corresponding to the phase transition region [17]. Each problem instance was run 50 times with WSAT and 10 times with

---

[9] We used the versions of GWSAT and WSAT supplied by Kautz and Selman. Note, that in these versions a Tabu Search option is offered.

[10] In the literature usually $p_2 = 1 - q$ is used, where p_2 is the probability that a pair of values is inconsistent.

GWSAT. We chose rather small problems as the experimental burden is very high for larger problems and we are more interested in the mutual influence of the parameter settings. Both heuristics were tested on various combinations of tabu list length t and walk probability p_w. The success rates are omitted, always being near 100%. In Figures 2 and 3 the shape of the cost surface for 100-variable problems is given, for 50-variable problems and SAT-encoded graph coloring the cost surfaces are very similar, see [19].

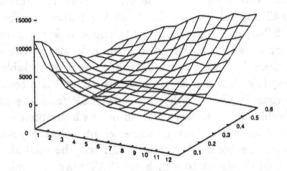

Fig. 2. GWSAT with Tabu Search for 3-SAT, $n = 100$, 430 clauses. The x-axis shows the tabu list length, the y-axis the walk-probability and the z-axis the number of moves per solution.

Several things are remarkable. First of all, the optimal parameter settings can not be determined by evaluating both parameters independently. Whereas for high walk probabilities p_w a lower tabu list length t decreases the solution cost, it is the other way round for low walk probabilities. The cost surfaces in both figures corresponding to the tabu list length and the walk probability suggest that the optimal parameter settings may not be found if one first optimizes e.g. the walk probability and after that tries to find the best parameter for the tabu length. Although this reduces the computational burden, the "best" parameter settings may be missed. This also explains, why — after fixing p_w at the "optimal" value 0.5 — nearly nobody regarded Tabu Search as a valuable heuristics for SAT. There seems to be a strong dependence between the parameter values for which reasonably good results may be achieved – see the valley structure in Figures 2 and 3.

Furthermore one can obtain the optimal parameter settings to use for the solution of the specific problem class. For GWSAT the best parameter settings in the examined region are obtained with no walk and a tabu list length of 12. For WSAT the optimal parameter settings are with a tabu list length of $t = 4$

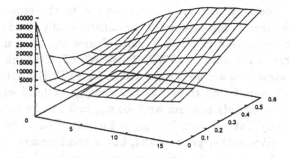

Fig. 3. WSAT with Tabu Search for 3-SAT, $n = 100$, clause/variable ratio 4.3.

and with walk probability $p_w = 0$. The specific parameter settings for both heuristics are qualitatively the same with respect to the effect of Tabu Search. The performance of both heuristics may be improved by adding Tabu Search. Yet, the specific tabu list length for the two heuristics is different, as basically the selection scheme of the variables to be flipped is different. We also tested both heuristics on SAT-encoded graph coloring problems, specifically on the problem instance DSJC125.5 from [9] (also used in [16]). We solved the problem for 18 colors. As the median cost surface has the same shape as shown in Figure 3, we omit it here and only give some landmarks: On this problem, we found for WSAT with the optimal walk probability $p_{opt} = 0.1$ without Tabu Search, i.e. $t = 0$, a median cost of 33219 moves per solution resulting in a 100% success rate. The optimal common parameter setting for this problem was found to be $t_{opt} = 2, p_{opt} = 0.0$ with 100% success rate and a median of 9854 moves per solution — less than one third of the cost when using only random walk!

3.2 Constraint Satisfaction

For MCH we examined both variants of the tabu attributes proposed in Section 2.3. With twmch we denote the variant with walk in which variable-value pairs are declared tabu, with tvwmch we denote the variant with walk that considers variables as tabu attributes. In case only Tabu Search with variable-value tabu attributes is used, we denote this by tmch, wmch denotes MCH with walk but without any form of Tabu Search. We do not present results for tvwmch with $p_w = 0.0$, as this variant does not perform better than pure MCH without tabu lists and random walk.

Random CSPs For the results in Figures 4 and 5 we performed experiments with random binary CSP from the crossover region with 20 variables and domain size 10. The parameter values for p, q correspond to the crossover region. In Figure 4 and 5 the results for parameter combinations of p_w and t are presented for one specific combination of p and q. Both figures exhibit a similar behavior of the cost surfaces as the ones for GWSAT and WSAT, although the differences between the two strategies are not as marked as for SAT. The optimal parameter settings for twmch were found to be $t_{opt} = 2$ and $p_{opt} = 0.025$ with a median of 5868 moves, MCH using only random walk for $p_{opt} = 0.1$ had a cost of 7545 moves and MCH using only Tabu Search for $t_{opt} = 2$ a cost of 6217. For tvwmch using only Tabu Search gives rather poor results, but in combination with the random walk strategy yields considerable improvements over MCH using only random walk. The search cost for the optimal parameter settings $t_{opt} = 4, w_{opt} = 0.075$ yielded a median search effort of 5711, whereas using only walk for $w_{opt} = 0.125$ resulted in a median search cost of 8166.[11]

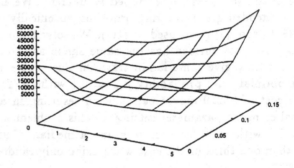

Fig. 4. twmch for random binary CSP, $p = 0.5$, $q = 0.62$.

Other experiments with values for $p \in \{0.1, 0.3, 0.5, 0.7, 0.9\}$, and corresponding values for q, such that the problem instances are from the crossover region, varying q in steps of 0.01, showed that the variants of MCH using elements of Tabu Search performed all better than MCH using only Random Walk.[12]

The same observations as for WSAT and GWSAT on SAT problems also hold for CSP. In general, by adding elements of Tabu Search the search cost can be reduced considerably and the optimal parameter settings for both heuristics may not be determined independently. Additionally it seems that in the version tvwmch elements of Tabu Search and random walk may be integrated successfully.

---

[11] Note, that the number of problem instances used for twmch and tvwmch were not the same.

[12] We also experimented with MCH using other variants of random walk steps than the one presented here. Yet, none of those provided further significant improvements.

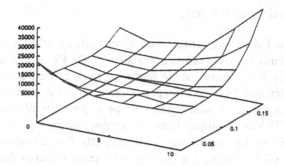

Fig. 5. tvwmch for random binary CSP, $p = 0.5$, $q = 0.62$.

Graph Coloring Problems We also tested MCH on hard graph coloring problems contained in the DIMACS benchmark set[13]. We present some of our results in Table 1. In the experiments for most problems a pure Tabu Search without random walk performed best, always yielding a lower search cost than MCH with random walk. Additionally MCH with random walk has the disadvantage that the optimal walk parameter depends strongly on the problem instance at hand. On the other side for all of the problems a tabu list length of $t = 2$, if variable-value pairs are used as tabu attributes, worked very well.

Table 1. Results for some graph coloring examples. k is the number of used colors. The number of nodes in the problem instance are represented by the first number appearing in the problem instance descriptor. For success rates of 100% , we give the median of the number of moves, otherwise (x%) is the success rate.

Problem / k	tmch	twmch	wmch	tvwmch
DSJC125.1 / 5	33,452	26,243	67,879	43,846
DSJC125.5 / 18	12,980	15,815	25,290	19,773
DSJC125.5 / 17	(72%)	(60%)	(34%)	(24%)
DSJC125.9 / 44	17,026	15,161	18,704	13,770
DSJC250.5 / 30	70,570	84,530	462,421	460,533
DSJC250.5 / 29	(52%)	(36%)	(4%)	(4%)
DSJC500.5 / 48	61,479	74,418	(80%)	191,460
flat300_28_0 / 34	39,699	45,088	90,249	69,920
le450_15c / 22	21,870	22,418	39,139	36,957

---

[13] Available via: ftp://dimacs.rutgers.edu/pub/challenge/graph/benchmarks/color/.

3.3 Interpretation of Results

As we have seen in the experimental results, variants of GSAT using elements of Tabu Search perform better than the variants of GSAT in which only random walk is used. Often Tabu Search alone performs best. In case of random walk for GSAT, Tabu search can best be interpreted as a heuristic that allows GSAT to leave local minima and that additionally helps to pass the plateau phase of the search. It forces GSAT-like algorithms to explore plateaus more systematically and therefore improves the performance significantly. On the other hand, random walk can be best seen as some kind of diversification strategy for Tabu Search, leading it into different regions of the search space. So, if the walk probability is high, Tabu Search is not able to exploit a specific region of the search space any more.

For MCH we used two different kinds of Tabu attributes, on the one side variable-value pairs, on the other whole variables. When considering a Tabu Search variant in which variable-value pairs are used as tabu attributes, our experimental results show that this version behaves better than pure MCH with random walk. Essentially, when combining both heuristics in twmch the walk-probability p_w should be chosen very small, as for larger values, the search cost increases again. Thus, the addition of walk may be interpreted again as the application of a diversification strategy to explore different solutions. If we use variables as tabu attributes in tvwmch, the walk probability should be chosen as a slightly lower value than w_{opt} in wmch. The effect of the tabu list then is to diversify the selection of the variables and to avoid that variables are chosen several times in a row.

4 Related Work

Tabu Search is a general heuristic for optimization problems. One of its first applications has been on MAX-SAT problems [7]. Since then it has not received much attention for the solution of hard SAT-problems, but GSAT and variants of GSAT involving random walk seemed to perform best. We know of only few works in which "memory-based" heuristics like Tabu Search were investigated for SAT and CSP. In [4] a version of GSAT with "memory", called MSAT, is reported to show "improved performance over GSAT ... although the improvement declines as problems grow larger". MSAT essentially equals GSAT with tabu list length 1. Another variant is HSAT which "always picks the (variable) that was flipped longest ago". This can also be best seen as a kind of tie-breaking rule if more than one variable is allowed to flip its value. HSAT is reported to "perform significantly better than GSAT", but has no specific mechanism to leave local minima and, thus, differs from Tabu Search.

In [11] positive results for the application of Tabu Search to SAT are reported. The authors have shown at hand of random 3-SAT instances that Tabu Search applied to GSAT behaves better than GWSAT. Additionally they investigated the dependence of the optimal tabu list length t on the problem size and showed that a linear dependence holds. We extend the results presented in [11] in that we explicitly studied the relationship between the two strategies Tabu Search and random walk and we also show for WSAT that Tabu Search is to be preferred over the random walk option.

In the Constraint Satisfaction community applications of Tabu Search also seem to be rare. An exception here is [21] in which Tabu Search was used for MAX-CSP problems. In this application the selection scheme of the next value is a little bit different and it seems that no systematic investigation of the optimal tabu list length was done, as the authors note that they used usual values given in the literature, i.e. $t = 7$. In contrast to this, when using Tabu Search to solve CSP the tabu list length should be very low, e.g. $l = 2$ showed always a reasonably good performance. Note, that our version of Tabu Search using variables as tabu attributes has some similarity to HSAT [4] in that it also influences the variable selection. Future work will be to compare our variants involving Tabu Search also to some other search methods like the breakout-method [13] as well as to GENET [2], that relies heavily on the breakout method.

5 Conclusion

In this paper we presented the application of Tabu Search as a heuristic for greedy local search procedures used for SAT and CSP. As opposed to probabilistic elements like random walk, Tabu Search offers a more deterministic way of directing an underlying search procedure towards good solutions. We performed extensive tests on random 3-SAT problems at the crossover point, hard binary CSPs and hard graph coloring problems. We considered also hybrids of the two strategies and investigated experimentally the dependency between the tabu list length t and the walk probability p_w. We found that optimal parameter settings may not be determined independently for both heuristics. Thus, both parameters have to be varied to find the best combination of both. Yet, in general we found that the variants using only Tabu Search significantly improve on the variants that rely only on the random walk option.

As we already pointed out, random walk may be interpreted as some special form of diversification of search. We think that by a stronger usage of information gathered during the run of the algorithm we are able to devise more directed diversification strategies improving the performance even more. Further work also will include a more theoretical explanation of the performance of Tabu Search. Obviously, the role of Tabu Search for SAT and CSP has been underestimated. This work aims to be an additional indication that it may be worthwhile to have a closer look at this heuristic that in other fields — e.g. scheduling or quadratic sum assignment problems — is applied with great success.

References

1. H. Bennaceur. The Satisfiability Problem Regarded as a Constraint Satisfaction Problem. In Wolfgang Wahlster, editor, *ECAI'96*, pages 155–160. John Wiley & Sons, Chichester, 1996.

2. A. Davenport, E. Tsang, C.J. Wang, and K. Zhu. GENET: A Connectionist Architecture for Solving Constraint Satisfaction Problems by Iterative Improvement. In *AAAI'94*, 1994.

3. J. de Kleer. A Comparison of ATMS and CSP Techniques. In *IJCAI'89*. Morgan Kaufmann, 1989.

4. I. P. Gent and T. Walsh. Towards an understanding of hill–climbing procedures for SAT. In *AAAI'93*, pages 28–33. MIT press, 1993.

5. I.P. Gent and T. Walsh. An empirical analysis of search in GSAT. *Journal of Artificial Intelligence Research*, 1:47–59, 1993.

6. F. Glover. Tabu Search – Part I. *ORSA Journal on Computing*, 1(3):190–206, 1989.

7. P. Hansen and B. Jaumard. Algorithms for the Maximum Satisfiability Problem. *Computing*, 44:279–303, 1990.

8. H. H. Hoos. Solving hard combinatorial problems with GSAT — a case study. In *KI-96*, volume 1137 of *LNAI*, pages 107–119. Springer Verlag, 1996.

9. D.S. Johnson, C.R. Aragon, L.A. McGeoch, and C. Schevon. Optimization by Simulated Annealing: An Experimental Evaluation; Part II, Graph Coloring and Number Partitioning. *Operations Research*, 39(3):378–406, 1991.

10. H. Kautz and B. Selman. Pushing the Envelope: Planning, Propositional Logic, and Stochastic Search. In *AAAI'96*, volume 2, pages 1194–1201. MIT Press, 1996.

11. B. Mazure, L. Sais, and E. Gregoire. TWSAT: A New Local Search Algorithm for SAT – Performance and Analysis. In *CP'95 Workshop on Solving Hard Problems*, 1995.

12. S. Minton, M.D. Johnston, A.B. Philips, and P. Laird. Minimizing Conflicts: A Heuristic Repair Method for Constraint Satisfaction and Scheduling Problems. *Artificial Intelligence*, 52:161–205, 1992.

13. P. Morris. The Breakout Method for Escaping from Local Minima. In *AAAI'93*, pages 40–45, 1993.

14. B. Selman and Henry A. Kautz. Domain-independent extensions to GSAT: Solving large structured satisfiability problems. In *IJCAI'93*, pages 290–295, 1993.

15. B. Selman, Henry A. Kautz, and Bram Cohen. Noise Strategies for Improving Local Search. In *AAAI'94*, pages 337–343. MIT press, 1994.

16. B. Selman, H. Levesque, and D. Mitchell. A New Method for Solving Hard Satisfiability Problems. In *AAAI'92*, pages 440–446. MIT press, 1992.

17. Bart Selman, David G. Mitchell, and Hector J. Levesque. Generating Hard Satisfiability Problems. *Artificial Intelligence*, 81(1–2):17–30, 1996.

18. B.M. Smith. Phase Transitions and the Mushy Region in Constraint Satisfaction Problems. In *ECAI'94*, pages 100–104, 1994.

19. Olaf Steinmann. Kombinatorische Probleme, Optimierung und Parallelisierung: Eine experimentelle Analyse von Multi–Flip–Netzwerken. Master's thesis, TH Darmstadt, FB Informatik, FG Intellektik, 1997.

20. Richard J. Wallace. Analysis of Heuristic Methods for Partial Constraint Satisfaction Problems. In *Constraint Programming 96*, LNCS, pages 482–496. Springer Verlag, 1996.

21. R.J. Wallace and E. Freuder. Heuristic Methods for Over-Constrained Constraint Satisfaction Problems. In *Over-Constrained Systems*, volume 1106 of *Lecture Notes in Computer Science*. Springer Verlag, 1996.

Multi-flip Networks: Parallelizing GenSAT

Antje Strohmaier[*]

Institut KI, Fakultät Informatik, TU Dresden
D-01602 Dresden, Germany
ast@inf.tu-dresden.de

Abstract. Local hill-climbing algorithms to solve the satisfiability problem have shown to be more efficient than complete systematic methods in many aspects. Many variants and refinements have been developed in the last few years. We present a neural network approach to evaluate such local search algorithms in a parallel manner, i.e. enlarging the neighbourhood of each possible move in the search space. We present an approach which allows the simultaneous change of truth value assignment for more than one variable at a time, such that the theoretical properties of the considered algorithms are preserved, and give experimental evidence that this algorithm is indeed faster than the respective sequential variants.

1 Introduction

Existing complete procedures for the satisfiability problem (SAT) are not practically applicable for more than 400 or 500 variable random problems and take too much time to find a solution for smaller problems. A very fast, though incomplete procedure is the model generating algorithm GSAT together with its variants, first described in [11].

To our knowledge, the parallelizability of GSAT-like algorithms has not been investigated so far, although they contain many computations per variable that can be done simultaneously. Further on, they contain certain aspects very well suited for a less straight forward way of parallelization by enlarging the neighbourhood structure of the search space. By means of the approach presented in this paper, we can exploit this form of parallelism for GSAT-like algorithms. We describe how this parallel GSAT-variant can be implmented on a new type of neural network architecture and show experimentally that the parallelized local search algorithm has a speed up of up to 59.32 compared to GSAT.

In the following, we will give a short introduction to GSAT-like local search and point out the possibilities for parallelization. In Section 3, we show the relationship between SAT-problems, energy functions and neural networks. Section 4 gives the neural architecture for parallel versions of hill-climbing algorithms. Section 5 describes our experimental results obtained and Section 6 points out further approaches, which are discussed in the last section.

---

[*] This work was supported by DFG Grant HO 1294/3-3. The author is also affiliated with TH Darmstadt, FG Intellektik

2   Parallelizing GenSAT

Local hill-climbing methods can be formalized by means of a very general algorithmic frame called GenSAT. The algorithm's input is a propositional formula ϕ in conjunctive normal form (CNF). The algorithm measures the quality of a given truth assignment for the variables in ϕ by counting the number of clauses left unsatisfied by the assignment. The GenSAT-frame given below was first introduced in [4]:

```
procedure GenSAT(φ)
  for i := 1 to maxTries do
    A := random assignment for all V ∈ φ;
    for j := 1 to maxLoops do
      if A satisfies φ then return A
      else
        possFlips := hillClimb(φ, A);
        V := pick(possFlips);
        flip assignment of V in A;
      end if;
    end for;
  end for;
  return ''no satisfying assignment found'';
end GenSAT;
```

A *flip* of a variable means a change of its truth value from "false" to "true" or vice versa. *hillClimb* determines the set possflips of variables whose truth assignment may be changed in order to improve (i.e. decrease) the number of unsatisfied clauses, and *pick* selects one (or some) of these variables.

Different variants of this algorithm differ mainly in the function *hillClimb* building the set possflips. For basic GSAT, possflips consists of the variables whose flip causes a maximal decrease of the number of unsatisfied clauses, for indifferent variants it may contain all variables causing *any* decrease of this number. The basic GSAT algorithm has proven to be less successful than probabilistic variants. The most successful GSAT variants reported in literature are always those using *random walk* [10]: With a given probability p, the function *hillClimb* consists of all variables, that occur in a currently unsatisfied clause, independent of the change of energy caused by their flip. We therefore always used variants with random walk

In our experiments, we used an indifferent GenSAT-variant called I$_2$SAT [6] for comparison, that prefers any energy-reducing flips over those that increase or do not change the energy. As this variant needs only local information, it is better suited for parallelization, but performs similar to GSAT.[2] We give its function *hillClimb* below. $A[V]$ is the assignment A with only the value for variable V flipped, $C_{unsat}(A)$ is the set of clauses unsatisfied by assignment A.

---

[2] This is in contrast to the very similar variant ISAT in [4], which prefers improving and non-changing flips equally.

```
function hillClimb(φ, A) % for I₂SAT
  flips = ∅;
  for V ∈ φ do
    if random walk and V ∈ C ∈ Cₐₐₐₐₐ(A) then
      flips = flips ∪ {V};
    else if |Cₐₐₐₐₐ(A[V])| < |Cₐₐₐₐₐ(A)| then
      flips = flips ∪ {V};
    end if;
  end for;
  return flips;
end hillClimb
```

Obviously, in *hillClimb*, all variables can compute $|\mathcal{C}_{un...}(A[V])|$ simultaneously. Furthermore, we can enlarge the possible neighbourhood of each variable assignment: In the sequential case, the assignments reachable in one step of the algorithm, are those assignments differing in only one truth value. A wider neighbourhood then means that in certain cases, we allow the simultaneous flip of more than one variable in such a way, that faulty computations are excluded. This is called a *multi-flip*.

In the following section, we give some technical details and describe under which respects such multiflips are acceptable.

3 SAT and Energy Functions

A SAT-problem given as a propositional formula ϕ with Variables $\mathcal{V} = \{X_1, \ldots, X_n\}$ in CNF can be transformed to an energy function such that the energy of a given variable assignment equals the number of clauses left unsatisfied by this assignment via the following construction [9]: For $\phi = \bigwedge_{i=1}^{l} \phi_i$ with $\phi_i = \bigvee_{j=1}^{m_i} L_{ij}$ we have $E(\mathbf{X}) = \sum_{i=1}^{l} \prod_{j=1}^{m_i} E_{L_{ij}}$ where

$$E_{L_{ij}} = \begin{cases} X_k & \text{if } L_{ij} = \neg X_k \\ 1 - X_k & \text{if } L_{ij} = X_k \end{cases}$$

The energy function for a 3-CNF formula then has the form

$$E(\mathbf{X}) = \sum_{i<j<k} c_{ijk} X_i X_j X_k + \sum_{i<j} c_{ij} X_i X_j + \sum_i c_i X_i + c.$$

where $i, j, k \in \{1, \ldots, n\}$. This function can be directly associated to the energy function describing a Hopfield neural network (HNN) [7] with higher-order connections[3] of order 3. With the equalities $c_{ij} = -w_{ij}$ and $c_{ijk} = -w_{ijk}$, the coefficients describe the negative weights on the (multilateral) connections between units U_i and U_j (and U_k, respectively). X_i is the output of unit U_i being either 0 or 1, and $c_i = \theta_i$ is its threshold. The behaviour of a higher-order hopfield network is determined by local information only, i.e. each unit computes its current activation and output

---

[3] The standard hopfield model has only bilateral connections, i.e. connections of order 2.

depending on its local input at time $t + 1$, which is determined by its connections, their weight and the output of connected units at time t:

$$input_{U_i}(t + 1) = \sum_{j < k} w_{ijk} u_j(t) u_k(t) + \sum_j w_j u_j(t) - \theta_j.$$

with $u_i(t) := output_{U_i}(t) = pos(act_{U_i}(t))$ and $act_{U_i}(t) = sgn(input_{U_i}(t))$ where "sgn" is the signum function and

$$pos(x) = \begin{cases} 0 \text{ if } x \leq 0 \\ 1 \text{ if } x > 0 \end{cases}$$

The re-computation of a unit's output is called an *update*. In the standard Hopfield model, units are updated asynchronously, but sequentially, i.e. at each moment only one unit is updated. The network has reached a *stable state*, if no unit has changed its output value during its last update (marked as time t_i and $t_i + 1$ individually): $\forall i\ u_i(t_i) = u_i(t_i + 1)$. If a stable state is reached, the computation may be stopped as the network will not further change its state as long as there is no interference from "outside". The stable states correspond directly to the local minima of the energy function describing the HNN.

The execution of the update algorithm for Hopfield networks can be seen as a local hill-climbing procedure with a strong relation to GSAT-like algorithms: Whereas HNNs search for *any* minimum of the energy function, GSAT-like algorithms only look for *global* ones. Given a propositional formula ϕ, we can now construct a Hopfield network with $n = |\mathcal{V}|$ units directly from the energy function corresponding to the SAT-problem. The activation of the units in the HNN corresponds to the truth value assignments of the variables of the given formula, i.e. an activation of 0 means "false", 1 means "true". The stable states are equivalent to local minima in the corresponding energy function.

Hence, search for a satisfying assignment of the propositional formula corresponds to finding a stable state with (globally) minimal energy in the Hopfield network, i.e. we can use the HNN directly for the SAT-problem. But although now the GenSAT-algorithm works on a neural network, its parallelism is still rather limited. *hillClimb* can obviously be performed in parallel for each unit, but in every execution of the inner for-loop of the GenSAT-frame only one flip of a unit (or variable) is possible as *pick* usually picks only one variable out of possflips.

A way to further parallelize the algorithm is to allow simultaneous flips of more than one unit at a time—i.e. multi-flips. The problem then is, that "flipping" the activation of one unit U_1 from 0 to 1 (or vice versa) may result in a decrease of energy as well as the flip of unit U_2 does, but flipping both in parallel may *increase* energy. So flipping both simultaneously may lead to a mistake and may even cause oscillation of the network, i.e. it never reaches a stable state [1].

Nevertheless, the problem of false computations can only occur if the units U_1 and U_2 updated in parallel are adjacent, i.e. receive input from each other by a symmetric connection with a non-zero weight. If not, flipping both will result in an energy decrease equal to the sum of decreases achieved by only flipping U_1 or U_2, respectively [5]. Thus, performing a multi-flip of non-adjacent, i.e. *independent* units at the same time results in a faster decrease of energy.

A possibility to avoid simultaneous flips of adjacent units is the use of a multi-flip network (MFN), described in the next section. The MFN can replace every Hopfield network, not only those used for SAT-problems. As we consider SAT-algorithms with *random walk*, we will describe an extension of MFNs that also mirrors the clausal structure of the propositional formula at hand, which is normally lost during transformation via energy functions. This enables the MFN to perform also parallel *random walk* steps.

4 Multi-Flip Networks

A multi-flip network (MFN) is a recurrent network with a layered structure. A basic MFN corresponds to an arbitrary Hopfield network, whose multi-flips it has to compute. Its extended version represents a propositional formula in CNF preserving information about the clause structure. In order to allow multiple flips at the same time, we have to change our algorithm in two aspects: The function *pick* has to be redefined, such that it selects a subset of independent units out of possFlips; and all units left in this independent set have to flip their activation simultaneously. This is done in a two-part computation. First, each virtual HNN-unit announces, whether it wants to flip its value (this will be called a *flip-request* in the sequel). It then waits for allowance to flip. This is determined in the second part by an ensemble of winner-take-all (WTA-)subnetworks, which, for competing adjacent units, select those that will be allowed to flip.

The structure of the MFN is completely determined by the given propositional formula: It consists of four types of units, namely the H-, C-, S-, and M-units. If the C-units are omitted, we obtain a basic MFN which performs multi-flips for an arbitrary HNN (without the relation to a clausal structure).

The H-units have two different states corresponding to the two-part computation described above; they correspond directly to the variables in a given SAT-problem and represent the corresponding Hopfield network (which is why they are called H-units). In the first state, each H-unit determines if it wants to flip. If so, it announces a flip request. In the second state, those flips are actually performed, that were selected by the WTA subnetworks. All other units are single state units. The S- (for *select*), and M-units (for *maximum*) form the WTA-subnetwork. A C-unit for each clause of the propositional formula determines the units participating in a walk step. These can be omitted, if the walk option is not used.

The H-, C-, and S-units sum up their inputs, whereas the M-units compute the maximum of their inputs. Furthermore, all units are assumed to generate an output only once, i.e. in the time step directly after they have received an input. This means, that after having generated the output, units remain inactive until they get a new input. The thresholds $\theta_h(i)$ of H-units and the weights on connections between H-units are determined by the energy function of the HNN or propositional formula, respectively, as given in section 3. The weights wc on connections between H-units and C-units and the thresholds $\theta_c(i)$ of C-units are determined as follows, where ϕ_i is a clause of the propositional formula:

$$wc_{ij} = \begin{cases} 1 & \neg X_j \in \phi_i \\ -1 & X_j \in \phi_i \end{cases} \qquad \theta_c(i) = |\{X_j \mid \neg X_j \in \phi_i\}| - 0.5$$

This results in an activation of a unit C_i in state A of the HNN-part, if $\phi_i \in C_{unact}(A)$. The properties of the different units are summarized in Table 1 with $\text{rnd}(0,1)$ being a random number from $[0,1]$ and:

$$\text{prob}(p) = \begin{cases} 1 & p \le \text{rnd}(0,1) \\ 0 & p > \text{rnd}(0,1) \end{cases}$$

Indexed uppercase letters indicate the units themselves whereas indexed lower case letters mean the appropriate output value; so u_i is the output of unit U_i. The column marked "activation" designates how $act_{U(i)}$ is computed from U_i's input. The activation is then used to compute the output given in the second part. The two states of H_i are given as the first and last row due to the course of the corresponding algorithm. An overview over the connection structure is given in Table 2. This is visualized in a small example of a HNN and its corresponding MFN in Figure 1.

Unit	activation act_{U_i}
$H_i(1)$	$act_{H_i}(t+1) = act_{H_i}(t)$
C_i	$act_{C_i}(t+1) = \sum_j wc_{ij}h_j(t) - \theta_c(i)$
S_i	$act_{S_i}(t+1) = h_i(t) + \text{prob}(p) \cdot \sum_{\{j|wc_{ji}\neq 0\}} c_j(t)$
M_i	$act_{M_i}(t+1) = \max_j\{s_j(t)|w_{ij} \neq 0\} - s_i(t)$
$H_i(2)$	$act_{H_i}(t+1) = m_i(t) \cdot (2act_{H_i}(t-3) - 1)$

Unit	output u_i
$H_i(1)$	$h_i(t+1) = \text{pos}((1 - 2act_{H_i}(t)) \cdot input_{H_i}(t))$
C_i	$c_i(t+1) = \text{pos}(act_{C_i}(t+1))$
S_i	$s_i(t+1) = \text{rnd}(0,1) \cdot \text{pos}(act_{S_i}(t+1))$
M_i	$m_i(t+1) = \text{sgn}(act_{M_i}(t+1))$
$H_i(2)$	$h_i(t+1) = \text{pos}(act_{H_i}(t+1))$

Table 1. The properties of the different units in the MFN

weight	H_i	H_j	C_j	S_i	M_i	M_j
H_i	-	w_{ij}	wc_{ji}	-1	-	-
C_j	-	-	-	1^{**}	-	-
S_i	-	-	-	-	-1	1^*
M_i	1	-	-	-	-	-

Table 2. The connection structure of the different units in the extended HNN. * if $w_{ij} \neq 0$, ** if $wc_{ji} \neq 0$.

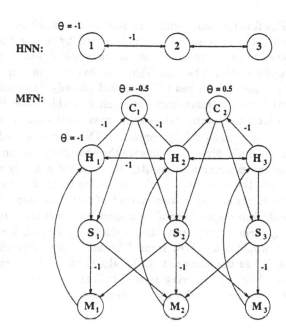

Fig. 1. The HNN and corresponding extended MFN for the formula $(X_1 \vee X_2) \wedge (\neg X_2 \vee X_3)$. Weights are 1 and thresholds are 0 if not specified otherwise.

The network is initialized in the following way: $act_{H_i}(0) := -1$ or 1 with probability 0.5 each. $h_i(0) = \text{pos}(act_{H_i}(0))$, $c_i(0) = s_i(0) := 0$, and $m_i := 1$. The following algorithms describe the functions *hillClimb* and *pick* functions, where $\mathcal{H}$ is the set of H-units and $\mathcal{C}$ is the set of C-units in the MFN.

```
function hillClimb(Units)
    for all U ∈ H ∪ C in parallel do update(U);
    for each Sᵢ in parallel do update(Sᵢ);
    return {i|sᵢ(t) > 0}
end hillClimb

function pick(possFlips)
    for each i ∈ possFlips in parallel do
        update(Mᵢ);
    return {i|mᵢ(t) = −1}
end pick
```

Walk steps are realized by the S-units: The C-units are activated, if the current assignment does not satisfy the corresponding clause. But their output is used by the corresponding S-units only with probability p, the walk probability. The realization of the walk steps can be done in several manners. In our experiments, we used a global walk variant: With walk probability p *all* variables occurring in an unsatisfied clause request a flip. This variant is the direct parallelization of walk as it is used in

GSAT-variants. The function *hillClimb* then returns the variables (i.e. indices of all units) that request a flip. The set of indices returned by *pick* is then independent and identical to the indices of units H_i that actually will flip their activation value in the following update step. The algorithm now has only to stop, if a global energy minimum is reached, which has to be checked globally. Depending on the walk probability p, local energy minima may not result in stable states if a walk step is performed, as in a local minimum always some unsatisfied clauses remain.

In the worst case, e.g. when a fully connected HNN is represented, only one unit will participate in the multi-flip—the one with the absolutely maximal priority of all candidate units. In the experimental results, we compared not only numbers of flips or multi-flips, but also the time steps needed to perfom them. Because the *hillClimb*-function for MFNs is computed in two instead of one time step, the execution of each multi-flip needs four steps. Even if we neglect the effort for variable updates in GSAT by counting them as *one* step, then a single flip in such a straight forward parallelized GSAT would take three steps. The MFN algorithm therefore has the same time complexity as the standard GSAT algorithm in the worst case. But our experiments reported in the following section indicate that in general the MFN is much faster, even if we neglect GSAT's updating cost.

5 Experiments

To relate our approach to other local search algorithms, we used the random 3CNF-formulas commonly used for GSAT-experiments. We also report some preliminary results on experiments with SAT-encodings of graph-colouring problems. The random formulas are generated with $n = 100$, 200, and 300 variables, each with a fixed ratio clauses/variables of 4.3 (which is approximately the crossover point of random formulas [3]). They are generated purely at random and unsatisfiable formulas are filtered out afterwards. We used 100 satisfiable instances for the 100 and 200 variable problem and 50 instances for the 300 variable problems. Each formula was tested 10 times. We tested GSAT with and without walk (the walk probability set to the optimal value 0.5). The parameter *maxLoops*, here denoting the number of single flips, was set to $100 * n$. The experimental results with the sequential algorithms compared to MFN are shown in Table 3. The column labeled "assign" shows the percentage of tries in which an assignment satisfying ϕ was found.[4] and the column labeled "L/A" (loops per assignment) shows the average number of flips or multi-flips, respectively, necessary to find one solution, where *maxTries* $= 1$ (i.e. flips in unsuccessful tries were included)[5]. Because of including unsuccessful tries (which always count as *maxLoops* steps but do not increment the number of solutions found), the average number of loops per assigment may be higher than *maxLoops*. The column "S/A" gives the time steps needed for one solution, where a single flip counts as 27.8 time steps—two steps for the flip plus 25.8 variable updates (see below)—and

---

[4] Each problem instance was solved, but some of them were not solved in each of the 10 tries per instance.

[5] In our opinion, omitting unsuccessful tries dilutes the differences in performance significantly.

a multi-flip counts as 4 time steps. Column "Sp" gives the speedup of the multi-flip algorithm compared to GSAT and I$_2$SAT.

The selection mechanism implemented in the MFN corresponds to a parallel version of I$_2$SAT. For our experiments, we used a walk probability of 0.4, which was found to be optimal in preliminary experiments. The parameter *maxLoops* now denotes the number of *multi-flips*. In order to adjust this with the parameters of the sequential algorithms, we did some preliminary experiments to determine the ratio flips per multi-flip (F/L in Table 4) and then adjusted *maxFlips* appropriately: For 100-variable problems, in a preliminary test the ratio with walk probability 0.4 was found to be 2.78, so *maxFlips* was set to $10,000 : 2.78 \approx 3600$. The parallelity achieved with the MFN algorithm is given in Table 4. The column "F/L" gives the average number of flips per multi-flip, whereas κ gives the theoretically possible number of parallel flips. As was pointed out in [12], in a random 3-CNF formula with a ratio clauses/variables $= 4.3$, each variable shares clauses with approximately 25.8 other variables. So a successful flip request automatically blocks 25.8 other variables in average, resulting in a theoretically possible parallelity of $\kappa = n/25.8$. Consequently, the connection structure in the network is relatively less dense, when the number of variables is higher, which results in a higher number of possible simultaneous flips.

n	no walk	assign	L/A	S/A	Sp
100	GSAT	23.5%	34120	948536	–
	I$_2$SAT	23.9%	33398	918445	1.02
	MFN	24.1%	9708	38832	24.42
200	GSAT	8.4%	223750	6220250	–
	I$_2$SAT	8.7%	216341	6014279.8	1.03
	MFN	9.4%	26363	105452	58.98
300	GSAT	2.7%	1091611	30346786	–
	I$_2$SAT	2.3%	1288396	35817409	0.85
	MFN	2.2%	127889	511556	59.32

n	walk	assign	L/A	S/A	Sp
100	GSAT	82.2%	4776	132773	–
	I$_2$SAT	82.6%	4720	131216	1.01
	MFN	83.2%	1728	6912	19.2
200	GSAT	48.7%	28695	797721	–
	I$_2$SAT	45.7%	31784	883595	0.90
	MFN	39.4%	8853	35412	22.52
300	GSAT	26.3%	98059	2726040	–
	I$_2$SAT	21.3%	125623	3492319	0.78
	MFN	13.5%	33244	132976	20.5

Table 3. GSAT and I$_2$SAT compared to MFN.

The results given in Table 3 show, that the indifferent GenSAT instance I$_2$SAT

n	Variant	F/L	κ
100	MFN no walk	3.77	3.87
	MFN walk	2.65	
200	MFN no walk	7.47	7.75
	MFN walk	4.36	
300	MFN no walk	10.86	11.63
	MFN walk	6.01	

Table 4. Experimental and theoretically possible parallelity for MFN.

Variant	assign	L/A	S/A	F/L	Sp
GSAT	100%	342	2055	1	–
MFN	100%	68	272	2.2	7.55

Table 5. Results on graph colouring with 3 colors, 30 nodes, 54 edges equals 90 Vars, 282 clauses.

has a performance comparable to GSAT, although it is "less greedy". The MFN algorithm has to be compared with the results for I_2SAT. Regarding the results for the parallel algorithm, we found a very low variance from the mean ratio of flips per multi-flip. Table 4 shows, that experimental and theoretical parallelity are very near for MFN without walk. Obviously, this ratio depends on the number of variables in the formula and the walk probability. The higher the walk probability, the more units request a flip per step, this results in more dependencies between requested flips and therefore, in the end less flips are performed. This might explain the phenomenon of a smaller degree of parallelism when the walk option is used. The experiments show that by parallel search a comparable performance can be achieved with a significant speedup. For the 100 variable problems, the MFN performs even slightly better than the sequential algorithms and the amount of single flips is nearly the same.

The results for graph 3-coloring problems are given in Table 5. The graphs were randomly generated with 30 nodes and 54 edges which results in a SAT-encoded formula of 90 variables and 282 clauses. These are very preliminary results, where no parameter fine-tuning for the special problem structure was made. One flip in GSAT equals 6 steps: Two steps for the flip plus 4 variable updates[6]. The energy landscape of these problems has very many very deep local minima, which makes them rather difficult. Although the corresponding MFN is only sparsely connected ($\kappa = 90/4 = 22.5$), the parallelity is very low. This seems to be a result of the steps performed in the local minimum: there are always only very few variables that want to flip. Nevertheless the speedup is still 7.55, which is nearly an order of magnitude.

---

[6] The SAT-encoding results in a formula where each variable shares clauses with four other variables.

6 Further Approaches

MFNs may be used also for some extensions of HNNs. One possible extension would be the use of a probabilistic updating rule, similar to the Boltzmann machine [1], which allows the parallel execution of Simulated Annealing. A similar approach to parallelize updates in Boltzmann machines was developed by [2]. They used an unsupervised update rule, such that every unit requesting a flip participates in the multi-flip. The multi-flip itself is then allowed through a global control mechanism computing the actual energy change caused by this multi-flip. Unfortunately, this algorithm requires a global computation of the overall energy of the whole network, which seems to be rather complex. Then, some implementational "tricks" in the computation of energy changes, which helped to speed up the updating of each unit significantly [2], can no longer be used. Nevertheless, the experiments in [2] have shown a better performance and faster decrease of energy for the parallel algorithm than for the usual sequential Simulated Annealing, which may also indicate for the usefulness of our multi-flip algorithm.

When using a probabilistic updating rule, we can omit the clause units which are needed only for the walk steps. This results in a much smaller network, as the number of clauses is often much higher than the number of variables in a SAT-problem. Another possibility to avoid the clause-units is the use of a tabu list instead of walk. In some preliminary experiments we found that this performs at least as well as the variant with walk.

The usefulness of the MFN is depending on the degree of connectivity in the HNN. In the worst case of a fully connected HNN (e.g. for solving Euclidean traveling salesman problems), all units willing to flip are adjacent. So no multi-flips are possible. But if the HNN is sparsely connected or if we have structured problems which result in a clustering of units (for instance, when crossword puzzles are formulated as SAT-problems [8], or in graph coloring problems [11]), the multi-flips might help to solve problems faster, as rather independent parts of a problem can be solved simultaneously.

7 Discussion

In this paper, we have shown how a feed-forward network equivalent to a symmetric network can be used to parallelize GSAT-like algorithms for SAT-problems. With the MFN, we can simulate a symmetric network performing multiple flips, thus overcoming its sequential updating scheme without doing faulty computations. We have pointed out its applications for SAT-problems and have shown how the MFN can parallelize local search algorithms. The achieved speedup is quite significant. Nevertheless, this method is not a "maximal" solution to the problem of multiple flips, as not always a *maximal* set of possible flips will be selected. Furthermore, the possible number of simultaneous flips remains small, so there is no need to further restrict the amount of parallel flips to a portion of the possible ones. For problems with a very high number of possible parallel flips, the control of the degree of parallelism might be an interesting topic.

The use of multi-flips may have several advantages beyond these experimental results. So there are still many things to do: First experiments using a tabu list instead of walk indicate that this might perform even better – and the C-units would become obsolete. Furthermore, we want to perform more experiments on structured problems to determine optimal parameter settings and the class of problems, where MFNs are best suited for. We expect to achieve an even higher speedup with highly clustered problems due to a higher parallelity.

Acknowledgements: We would like to thank Thomas Stützle, Olaf Steinmann and Christoph Herrmann for many fruitful discussions and anonymous referees for valuable comments on an earlier draft of this paper.

References

1. Emile Aarts and Jan Korst. *Simulated Annealing and Boltzmann Machines.* John Wiley & Sons, 1989.
2. N. Boissin and J.-L. Lutton. A parallel simulated annealing algorithm. *Parallel Computing,* 19:859–872, 1993.
3. J. M. Crawford and L. D. Auton. Experimental results on the crossover point in satisfiability problems. In *Proceedings of the AAAI National Conference on Artificial Intelligence,* pages 21–27. MIT press, 1993.
4. I. P. Gent and T. Walsh. Towards an understanding of hill–climbing procedures for SAT. In *Proceedings of the AAAI National Conference on Artificial Intelligence,* pages 28–33. MIT press, 1993.
5. J. Hertz, A. Krogh, and R. G. Palmer. *Introduction to the Theory of Neural Computation.* Addison-Wesley Publishing Company, 1991.
6. S. Hölldobler, H. Hoos, A. Strohmaier, and A. Weiß. The GSAT/SA-Familiy – Relating greedy satisifability testing to simulated annealing. Technical Report AIDA-94-17, TH Darmstadt, 1994.
7. J. J. Hopfield. Neural networks and physical systems with emergent collective computational abilities. In *Proceedings of the National Academy of Sciences USA,* pages 2554 – 2558, 1982.
8. K. Konolige. Easy to be hard: difficult problems for greedy algorithms. In *Proceedings of the International Conference on Principles of Knowlege Representation and Reasoning,* pages 374–378, 1994.
9. G. Pinkas. The equivalence of energy minimization and propositional calculus satisfiability. Technical Report WUCS-90-03, Washington University, 1990.
10. B. Selman, H. A. Kautz, and B. Cohen. Noise strategies for improving local search. In *Proceedings of the AAAI National Conference on Artificial Intelligence,* volume 1, pages 337–343, 1994.
11. B. Selman, H. Levesque, and D. Mitchell. A new method for solving hard satisfiability problems. In *Proceedings of the AAAI National Conference on Artificial Intelligence,* pages 440–446. MIT press, 1992.
12. W. M. Spears. Simulated annealing for hard satisfiability problems. Technical report, Naval Research Laboratory, Washington D.C., 1993.

Resource-Adaptive Action Planning in a Dialogue System for Repair Support *

Thomas Weis

Fachbereich Informatik, Universität des Saarlandes
Postfach 151150, D-66041 Saarbrücken, Germany
EMail: tweis@cs.uni-sb.de, Phone: +49 681 302-3393, Fax: -4136

Abstract. For reasonable application in critical domains dialogue systems not only have to pay attention to user knowledge and dialogue goals but they also have to adapt their dialogue behaviour to current limitations of the user's cognitive processing capabilities. In case of a help system the point of concern is on the one hand the aspect as to what kind of help is appropriate for the user $\mathcal{P}$ (*What to do?*). This action planning has to take into account $\mathcal{P}$'s resource limitations like time pressure and working memory load. On the other hand the system's utterances should also be adapted to $\mathcal{P}$'s language processing capabilities (*What to say – and how?*). This work presents primarily approaches to adaptive action planning. Its interaction with dialogue planning is outlined.

1 Introduction

1.1 Issues

In the field of human-computer-communication considerable progress has been made since the first approaches to user modelling in adapting system behaviour to individual user knowledge and current dialogue goals. However up to now such systems barely take into account the resource limitations restricting the dialogue partner's cognitive processing.

In the field of planning for example, current systems almost exclusively take into account the resource limitations of the planning process ignoring those of other agents. In addition, such planners have hardly been applied to the modelling of dialogue situations.[1]

This work is concerned with the question of how a dialogue system can adapt its dialogue behaviour to the individual cognitive resource limitations of its dialogue partner $\mathcal{P}$. As a domain for such a system we have chosen the setting of a help system. The System $\mathcal{S}$ is faced with a diagnosis task and a repair task. The diagnosis—to find the cause of $\mathcal{P}$'s problem—has to be found interactively in a dialogue with $\mathcal{P}$. The repair task comprises of instructing $\mathcal{P}$ to take actions to solve the problem. For $\mathcal{S}$ both

---

* This work has been founded by the Deutsche Forschungsgemeinschaft in its Special Research Program SFB 378, "Ressourcenadaptive kognitive Prozesse", Project B2: `READY: Ressourcenadaptive Dialogführung'.

[1] An overview of such planning approaches is given by Wahlster, Jameson, Ndiaye, Schäfer, and Weis (1995).

tasks require information gathering (by questioning P) and P's instructing. This paper mainly focuses on the selection and verbalization of actions in such a way that suits P to probably understand and execute them under his current constitution and the given constraints (e.g., time pressure).

Although actions are rather related to the repair task they are also important to the diagnosis part, e.g., when S instructs P to check a failure hypothesis.[2] When instructing P resource-adaptive dialogue behaviour is relevant in two fields: (a) action selection (action planning), because these actions have to be executed by P; and (b) formulation of system utterances (dialogue planning), since P's understanding constitutes a prerequisite for his successful acting.

Resource-adaptive action and dialogue planning takes place considering estimations about P's *cognitive resource limitations*. Such information is maintained in the partner model of the dialogue system—besides classical aspects as, e.g., P's knowledge. Here the use of this information for adapting the system behaviour is investigated, not however issues of the partner model itself.[3] The following cognitive resource limitations of P are considered:

- **available working memory capacity (AWMC):** The partner model provides an estimate of the cognitive load presently acceptable for P.[4]
- **time pressure:** The user has more or less time to solve his problem, e.g., depending on whether and when he has to meet a deadline.[5] As a simplifying starting point, time pressure is used as an analogue measure. Nevertheless, fixed deadlines can affect the dialogue behaviour of the system due to the fact that the estimation of P's time pressure will be updated during the discourse.

1.2   System Context of READY and Example Scenario

The project READY aims at laying the foundations for a **Re**source-**A**daptive **D**ialog **System**. This system will estimate and explicitly model its user's cognitive resource limitations, which vary individually and from situation to situation, in order to adapt its dialogue behaviour to this limitations.[6] The system READY will exemplarily conduct spontaneous dialogues in a domain in which the dialogue partner's resource limitations play an important role:[7] READY provides repair support by phone to a dialogue partner P, who has to repair the failure on the road; because he cannot make a note of the information offered by READY, and because of time restrictions, distractions and stress he is

---

[2] Many of the aspects depicted here with reference to instructions are also relevant to questions (besides others); but space restrictions do not allow for a detailed description.

[3] Details of acquisition, representation und maintenance of the partner model by means of dynamic Bayesian networks are given by Schäfer and Weyrath (1997). Based on perceived symptoms and causes of resource limitations estimations are build up by diagnostic respectively predictive inference, e.g., about P's working memory load and time pressure.

[4] This estimation is inferred among other things from P's age (cf., e.g., Kemper, Jackson, Cheung, & Anagnopoulos, 1993), emotional strain and distracting factors.

[5] The partner model is able to estimate P's time pressure not only by explicit utterances by P but also based on symptoms as extraordinarily high speech rate.

[6] An overview of the READY project is given by Wahlster et al. (1995).

[7] A first system prototype is planned for autumn 1997.

not always able to make complex inferences. The modelling is based on the assumption that all the communication in the scenario is realized exclusively by speech. Up to now the investigations have been concentrated on the core functionality of the system such as partner modeling, action and dialogue planning. In a later project phase modules for speech recognition, analysis and generation will be integrated.[8]

The following **example situation** serves to illustrate the different aspects of resource-adaptive system behaviour throughout the paper: A car driver P has a failure in the electrically movable sliding roof of his car: It stands open and refuses to close. After heavy (and persistent) rain falls have started P stops under a bridge. Before he has not solved this problem—with the help of the dialogue system S—he cannot continue his ride. The explanation of alternative dialogue behaviours for S in the discourse with P relates to this initial situation.

2 Resource-Adaptive Action Planning

2.1 Discussed Issues

- According to which pragmatic criteria should S select the actions suggested to P?
- How can domain knowledge about appropriate actions to achieve P's goal(s)— here to resolve the breakdown—be modeled? Domain knowledge here means the knowledge about nature and organization of actions, e.g., about how to replace a blown fuse.
- What aspects of actions are relevant to their execution by P with regard to the cognitive load?

2.2 Evaluation Criteria for Action Plans

To optimize its behaviour a dialogue system needs criteria according to which it can evaluate the alternatives at its disposal and select the appropriate ones. In accordance with the global goal of offering a successful breakdown service we use as *pragmatic evaluation criteria* for action plans the (expected) *success* of P's execution of the suggested actions and the (expected) *duration* of this execution. When aggregating the two separated evaluations to an overall one, current preferences about these two dimensions, e.g., based on time pressure and/or the importance of an action, can be taken into account. The estimations influencing the separate evaluations about actions can depend on P's cognitive abilities (modeled by AWMC in the partner model) as well as P's time pressure and knowledge level.

For example, a stressed driver not familiar with car technique will have more difficulties to control and replace a fuse than an expert; he will also need more time than a focused and concentrated driver with background knowledge about electrical connections. The two main criteria are now described in more detail:

---

[8] As a starting point we use semantic representations for user utterances which also reflect some performance-oriented aspects as, e.g., speech rate, hesitations and self corrections. Similar representations are used for system utterance.

Time consumption comprises the total time required until an instruction is executed. On the one hand there is the time the system requires for planning and verbalization (including articulating) of utterances. This aspect is mentioned here, because it is initially a decision on the action planning level with which degree of specificity (with respect to single steps) the suggested actions are described.[9] Thus, for example, instead of the instruction "Please, control the electric fuse of the sliding roof!" a sequence of single step instructions might be more suitable for a technically untalented person, beginning with "Open the fuse box on the top left of the driver's floor space! …". On the other hand the total time consumption also comprises the expected time for P executing the suggested actions. Here differences arise when alternative action plans differ elementarily, i.e. by different single steps. But also in principle equal action plans can individually differ in the time they demand from P: In order to execute an abstract instruction P has to plan the single steps, i.e. the elementary actions (as with the first variant of the example in the last section).

Our consideration of the criterion time consumption simplifying assumes a linear cost measure: The longer the resolving of P's problem lasts, the more unfavourable the evaluation. How "expensive" a certain time unit is depends on the evaluation preferences, and thus among other things on the time pressure.

The **success** of P's action plan execution is determined by the probability of success and the expected quality of the problem solution. The probability of success is affected by P's error rate when planning and executing the actions, but also by the inherent uncertainty of an action plan regarding its applicability (correctness). E.g., this uncertainty can originate from the uncertainty or incompleteness of (S's) knowledge about context conditions, so that a plan can possibly prove as not or badly applicable afterwards (qualification problem). The quality of an action plan can be measured by the quality and reliability of the results of a successful execution. In the field of diagnosis alternative proceedings can supply results of different reliability, e.g., the quick reading of the oil *pressure* lamp as an uncertain indication in relation to controlling the oil *level* by using the dip stick in the engine compartment. An aspect that can affect both quality and success is the robustness of a plan in the sense of *anytime execution* (e.g., see Dean & Boddy, 1988): A plan with a continuous success improvement over the time permits a premature breaking off with a partial success; e.g., the manual closing of an electric sliding roof (a crank procedure) is robuster than the changing the safety device in order to try it again using the motor. Under time pressure or strong uncertainty about its existence robust plans should be preferred.

The described pragmatic evaluation criteria and the factors influencing them form the starting point to situation-adapted handling of conflicting goals by taking trade-offs into account.

---

[9] In principle it would also be possible to assign this system time to the dialogue planning task; but this approach complicates the modeling of goal conflicts and trade-offs within action planning.

2.3 Planning Approach

For the planning of its assistance for P the dialogue system S needs knowledge about domain actions—in our scenario about proceedings for diagnosis and repair of break-downs. It is assumed that the dialogue partner's knowledge forms a subset of S's knowl-edge, on which S can base itself if necessary.[10] The representation chosen for action knowledge is based on formalisms for hierarchical organization of such knowledge as developed so far (for an overview of such approaches see, e.g., Tate, Hendler, & Drum-mond, 1990). The special requirements imposed by resource-adaptive planning were considered; further details on this are described in Section 2.4, while the general ap-proach is first sketched now.

Hierarchical Planning Approach: The organization of action knowledge relates the possible actions to domain goals for whose achievement they are suitable. This is real-ized by means of *plan operators* whose postconditions specify what is valid after their (successful) execution, i.e., which goals they can in principle be used for to reach. The general structure of plan operators is depicted in Figure 1, and an example is given in Figure 2. Abstract actions—meaning complexly composed actions— can be decom-posed into sub-actions by means of *subgoals* in plan operators. By iterating this process over the subgoals one can finally arrive at the level of elementary actions, which are re-garded as being directly executable. The tree-like structures built up this way according to goal-action relations describe structured proceedings for achieving goals.[11] The do-main context necessary for a successful application of an plan operator can be restricted by specifying *applicability conditions* for the operator. The approach of building up ac-tion plans using plan operators for achieving subgoals ensures flexibility of modelling concerning the application by means of adding and modification of operators.

    Relevant Characteristics of the Approach: The decomposition of goals into sub-goals by means of plan operators opens a way of describing alternative proceedings on different levels of an action plan by specifying alternative plan operators. This hierar-chical organization of actions by abstraction permits the variation of the *specificity of action descriptions*: This specificity relates to the choice of an abstraction level up to which an action plan gets expanded (i.e., gets decomposed into subgoals).

    Conditioned subgoals, which are only relevant under certain contextual conditions, allow for dynamic and retarded adjustments of plans to different domain situations dur-ing plan execution (incremental planning / plan executing). E.g., in the current example it is only necessary to open a cover if the mechanical emergency crank of the sliding roof is covered by one.

---

[10] Incorrect knowledge of P is not explicitly modelled, however the probability that P can inde-pendently implement an abstractly described action correctly.

[11] Although the plan structures are built up dynamically they more compare to planning schemes than to HTN (hierarchical task network) planning approaches in respect to expression power and handling of subgoal interactions. The project READY is particularly concerned with ap-propriate applying of planning knowledge; therefore these restrictions can be accepted—and they simplify investigating our main research area.

```
Plan operator: <name>
Postconditions: <domain conditions>;; effects of executing the operator
Applicability conditions: <contextual conditions>
   ;; specify necessary domain conditions for the operator to be applicable
Action description:
- resource-related characteristics: <resource specifications>
   ;; serve to evaluate the action and their decomposition (if any)
- linguistic information: <semantic action representation>
   ;; specification of the abstract action of the operator as basis for dialogue planning
Subgoals: <subgoal specifications>;; only relevant for operators for abstract actions
   ;; decomposition of an abstract action into subgoals
```

Fig. 1. Schematic description of the syntax of plan operators.

Optional subgoals permit adjustments for example to time limits—with consideration of the importance of the pursued goal. Thus, in the example closing the crank cover can be omitted if necessary since it isn't absolutely necessary to continue the ride.

Interrelationship with Dialogue Planning: The actions specified by plan operators get verbalized by dialogue planning for example in the form of instructions. As basis for this process those plan operators for whose actions a (direct) verbalization should be possible, comprise references to *linguistic knowledge* about the actions (cf. the approach in Eugenio, 1993). This knowledge serves in dialogue planning to realize a concrete verbalization; while doing so further information can be taken into account, for example about *how* an action is to be taken (e.g., where to find a cover to open or what it looks like). This aspect will be treated in greater detail in the context of dialogue planning (see Section 3).

```
Plan operator: Close_roof_mechanically
Postconditions: "sliding roof closed" & ...
Applicability conditions: "mechanical emergency device / crank exists" & ...
Action description:
- resource-related characteristics: "time consumption: high"; "execution quality: high, ro-
bust"; "difficulty: high for beginners, low for experts"; ...
- linguistic information: "Close the sliding roof [by means of the mechanical emergency crank
in the luggage compartment]!" (example of a verbalization)
Subgoals: "Open luggage compartment" & "Open crank cover" & "Operate crank" &
   "Close crank cover" & "Close luggage compartments"
```

Fig. 2. Plan operator for mechanically closing of a faulty electric sliding roof (shortened informal description).

Example: For closing the electric sliding roof there are two alternative proceedings: (a) assuming a faulty electric fuse this device can be checked and replaced if necessary to close the roof by motor; (b) the roof could be closed using a mechanical emergency crank located in the luggage compartment of the car. These two alternative action plans are represented in the system on top level by two plan operators which achieve the goal of closing in their respective way. Figure 2 exemplarily shows the operator for alternative (b).

The planning tree for closing the sliding roof is presented in Figure 3. It does not only represent the two general alternatives *Put_electrical_circuit_into_operation* and *Close_roof_mechanically*, but also their variants emerging for example from omitting optional (sub)goals or from a differing expansion depth of abstract goals such as *Check_fuse*. This goal can be verbalized either directly or be described in its single steps in a more time-consuming way (e.g., to be sure to be understood by a technically untalented driver). The evaluation of the alternative action plans will be captured by the next section.

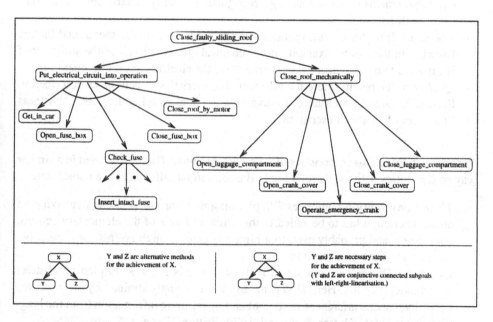

Fig. 3. Scheme of a planning structure for closing a faulty electric sliding roof (excerpt).

2.4 Resource-Related Evaluation of Action Plans

In order to be usable in a resource-adaptive system the presented approach to action planning has to be augmented by information about performance aspects of the represented action knowledge. In the case of READY not only the actual time required by the dialogue partner $\mathcal{P}$ to implement actions is of importance, but also—among other things— the extent to which P will be cognitively strained by this implementation. At first we describe the resource-related characteristics of abstract and elementary actions and then give an explanation on how action plans can be evaluated on this basis.

Resource-Related Characteristics of Elementary Actions:

- **Time Consumption:** How long will it probably take for P to implement an single action? This duration also covers the time P requires to recall the procedural knowledge required to implement an action, e.g., knowledge about course of motion when cranking. In this case some dependencies exist for example on P's AWMC (How good can P focus himself on an action?), on the time pressure (Will P hurry up?), and also of P's knowledge level in the domain. In the example the crank procedure will always be regarded as comparatively time-consuming.
- **Execution Difficulty:** The difficulty of an action for P depends—in addition to the aforementioned factors—on P's motor and sensory skills in relation to the respective requirements of an action. E.g., recognizing a faulty electric fuse *can* sometimes be difficult.
- P's **Error Rate** for executing the actions depends on the aforementioned factors likewise. In the current example the mechanical cranking to close the sliding roof is expected to be less error-prone than putting the electric circuit into operation.
- **Quality** of the results: Here the inherent characteristics of actions as described in Section 2.2 are of importance; for example the quality, reliability, and robustness of success of an action execution.

Resource-Related Characteristics of Abstract Actions: They are defined in a similar way as elementary actions; therefore only the substantial differences are named here.

- **Time Consumption** comprises P's planning time for independently realizing an abstract action; it has to be added to the actual run time of the elementary actions. As before—and probably even to a higher degree—a high AWMC will probably increase P's time consumption.
- **Execution Difficulty:** How cognitively straining is it for P to plan an abstract action independently. Here P is generally more strongly strained by an increased necessity to make inferences in content and by recalling information from the long-term memory (cf. Kintsch & Vipond, 1979; Britton, Glynn, & Smith, 1985).
  In the example, the steps for mechanically closing the sliding roof might be hardly derivable—in particular for a technically untalented driver; thus they will better be explained to him in detail.
- P's **Error Rate** for planning the elementary steps in order to execute an abstract action: Is P able to find a correct plan on his own? This judgment affects the expected success, and it also depends on P's knowledge level, besides his AWMC.
- **Quality** of the results of implementing an abstract action means how well the action will achieve its goal—independent of sub-steps by which it is realized . E.g., the mechanical closing of the sliding roof will reliably and robustly succeed, whereas the success of replacing the electric fuse is questionable.

Resource-Related Characteristics of Subgoals: Certain characteristics of actions cannot be *statically* assigned to them, since they depend on the context in which the actions are placed.

Therefore such characteristics are associated with those subgoals in plan operators for whose achievement the actions are used. In this way the context is given by the superordinate goals of the plan operators in each case.

- **Inferability:** How difficult is it for P to independently recognize a subgoal which is not explicitly addressed, but is to be inferred from the context? For example, P will probably close the fuse box after having replaced an electric fuse even when he is not explicitly told to do so.
- **Importance:** How important is it for the success of the superordinate goal that a subgoal is (correctly) realized? This question is relevant to the decision whether the system should pursue an optional goal at all; and it is also of importance to whether an inferable subgoal is explicitly verbalized or omitted for time reasons. An example of such an optional goal is the closing of the crank cover.

Resource-Related Evaluation of Action Plans: The approach presented so far permits the construction of alternative action plans. Now we will describe how to come up with resource-related evaluations for these plans—on the basis of the characteristics of the actions occurring in the plans. As a first step, the different characteristics of actions (as described in the previous section) are combined separately for each action into an evaluation with respect to the two pragmatic evaluation criteria *Time Consumption* and *Success*.

The derivation of overall evaluations for action *plans* is based on the fact that the plans are constructed through the composition of subplans (which correspond to subgoals in plan operators). Accordingly, when an action in a plan is evaluated, not only the properties of the action itself are taken into account but also the evaluations of its subplans. By contrast, elementary actions can be evaluated directly. Thus there is a flow of information from the elementary actions in the leaves of a planning tree up to the abstract action in the root, for which the overall evaluation of the plan is determined. For the *aggregation* of the evaluations of subplans, different metrics are applicable, depending on the evaluation criterion: For the evaluation of *Time Consumption*, a reasonable approximation is to aggregate additively on the basis of the following assumptions: (a) linear cost function for time (cf. Section 2.2); (b) no parallel execution or other temporal interaction among subtasks. For the evaluation of *Success*, the minimum metric is chosen, the idea being that the failure of part of a plan endangers the entire plan.[12]

---

[12] With respect to the cognitive load imposed by an action plan—an important factor influencing its success—this metric corresponds to the maximum metric, given the following assumptions: no simultaneous demands on working memory by two steps; clearing of working memory at the end of each step.

3 Resource-Adaptive Dialogue Planning

Because of space restrictions, with regard to the related area of dialogue planning we can only sketch briefly, by way of example, our approach to the resource-adaptive formulation of instructions.

3.1 Issues Addressed

- According to what pragmatic criteria should the system design its utterances?
- In connection with the verbalization of instructions, which are the factors that have an impact on P's cognitive processing?
- In what ways can dialogue planning influence action planning, i.e. the planning of the to-be-verbalized actions?

3.2 Evaluation Criteria for Utterance Design

As in the area of action planning, the criteria *Time Consumption* and *Success* can be applied to the evaluation of formulations. *Time Consumption* refers to the time that P will require in order to understand an utterance. The result depends not only on the length of an utterance but also on its difficulty. The *Success* of P's understanding forms the basis for P's execution of the instructions in question.

3.3 Decision Variables in Resource-Adaptive Dialogue Planning

P's comprehension of an utterance can be influenced by a number of properties of the utterance. If the consequences of these properties with respect to the various evaluation criteria are taken into account, the generation of utterances can be resource-adaptive. Since the influence of a given property usually depends on P's cognitive strengths and limitations, an evaluation should always take the current partner model into account. Here are some of the important properties of utterances:[13].

- *Level of detail:* Relatively detailed instructions seldom result in errors of comprehension, but they take a comparatively long time to verbalize and may overload P with information. Example: "Open the square gray cover of the fuse box in the upper right-hand part of the area in front of the driver's seat!".
- *Technical terms:* Such terms can lead to considerably more concise and precise descriptions; but they can also cause cognitive overload—especially if P lacks the relevant knowledge and is suffering from working memory limitations (cf. Clark & Marshall, 1981; Berg & Imhof, 1996). For example, a technically untalented driver will have difficulty in understanding the instruction "Open the fuse box!" unless it is further explained, simply because he does not know this box.
- *Syntactic complexity:* Nested relative clauses and long lists cause special problems for listeners with working memory limitations (cf. Kemper et al., 1993, for relevant research concerning the comprehension of written texts).

---

[13] A more comprehensive overview of research relevant to the problem of taking a dialogue partner's working memory limitations into account is given by Jameson (1997)

3.4 Dependencies Between Action and Dialogue Planning

In order to perform the actions suggested by the system successfully, the dialogue partner P has to accomplish two tasks: (a) understanding the system's utterances; and (b) executing the proposed actions. Trade-offs between these two tasks may arise: For example, a long, easily comprehensible instruction by S is worthless if it leaves P with no time to execute the action. The system can handle such trade-offs by computing an overall evaluation for the pair of tasks with respect to the criteria of *Time Consumption* and *Success*.

4 Conclusions and Future Work

The main contribution of the present paper is a framework for evaluating action plans and utterances to verbalize them. This forms the basis for resource-adaptive action and dialogue planning. Our approaches to action planning and utterance design were presented mainly with reference to the task of generating instructions for the dialogue partner P. The other main task of a help system, diagnosis, involves a higher degree of interactivity, since S can obtain information only by asking P questions. For example, when S is evaluating alternative plans, the problem may arise that the applicability of particular solution steps is unknown, so that S has to invest resources in order to determine the possible actions in the first place. There are also cases in which such information only becomes available during the execution of a plan. For example, if a hidden part of a device has to be checked, several other parts may have to be removed first. One possible approach to this problem is a decision-theoretic approach that makes use of expected values.

Another problem not dealt with in this paper concerns the relationships among different dialogue contributions: Coherence among utterances can influence their comprehensibility strongly. Some of the previous research in this area (see, e.g., Mann & Thompson, 1987; Grosz & Sidner, 1990) offers a good framework within which cognitive resource limitations can be taken into account.

References

Berg, D., & Imhof, M. (1996). Zuhören lernen – lernen durch Zuhören. In H. Sedlak (Ed.), *Ich-Du-Wir: Persönlichkeitsentwicklung und Gemeinschaftsförderung* (p. 39-53). Wien: Bundesministerium für Unterricht und kulturelle Angelegenheiten.

Britton, B. K., Glynn, S. M., & Smith, J. W. (1985). Cognitive demands of processing expository text: A cognitive workbench model. In B. K. Britton & J. B. Black (Eds.), *Understanding expository text: A theoretical and practical manual for analyzing explanatory text* (p. 227-248). Hillsdale, NJ: Erlbaum.

Clark, H. H., & Marshall, C. R. (1981). Definite reference and mutual knowledge. In A. K. Joshi, B. L. Webber, & I. A. Sag (Eds.), *Elements of discourse understanding* (p. 10–63). Cambridge, UK: Cambridge University Press.

Dean, T. L., & Boddy, M. (1988). An analysis of time-dependent planning. In *Proc. of the 7th National Conference on Artificial Intelligence* (p. 49–54). St. Paul, MN.

Eugenio, B. D. (1993). *Understanding natural language instructions: A computational approach to purpose clauses.* Unpublished doctoral dissertation, University of Pennsylvania, Philadelphia, PA. (IRCS Report 93–52)

Grosz, B. J., & Sidner, C. L. (1990). Plans for discourse. In P. R. Cohen, J. Morgan, & M. E. Pollack (Eds.), *Intentions in communication* (p. 417–444). Cambridge, MA: MIT Press.

Jameson, A. (1997). Wie gehen wir mit dem Arbeitsgedächtnis unserer Dialogpartner um? Eine Integration von Ergebnissen aus vier Forschungsrichtungen. In H. Mandl (Ed.), *Bericht über den 40. Kongreß der Deutschen Gesellschaft für Psychologie.* Göttingen, Germany: Hogrefe. (In preparation)

Kemper, S., Jackson, J. D., Cheung, H., & Anagnopoulos, C. A. (1993). Enhancing older adults' reading comprehension. *Discourse Processes, 16,* 405–428.

Kintsch, W., & Vipond, D. (1979). Reading comprehension and readability in educational practice and psychological theory. In L.-G. Nilsson (Ed.), *Perspectives on memory research: Essays in honor of Uppsala University's 500th anniversary* (p. 329–365). Hillsdale, NJ: Erlbaum.

Mann, W. C., & Thompson, S. A. (1987). Rhetorical structure theory: Description and construction of text structures. In G. Kempen (Ed.), *Natural language generation: New results in artificial intelligence, psychology, and linguistics* (p. 85–95). Dordrecht, The Netherlands: Nijhoff.

Schäfer, R., & Weyrath, T. (1997). Assessing temporally variable user properties with dynamic bayesian networks. In A. Jameson, C. Paris, & C. Tasso (Eds.), *User modeling: Proceedings of the sixth international conference, um97.* Vienna, New York: Springer Wien New York. (Available on-line from http://um.org)

Tate, A., Hendler, J., & Drummond, M. (1990). A review of ai planning techniques. In J. Allen, J. Hendler, & A. Tate (Eds.), *Readings in planning* (p. 26–49). San Mateo, CA: Kaufmann.

Wahlster, W., Jameson, A., Ndiaye, A., Schäfer, R., & Weis, T. (1995). Ressourcenadaptive Dialogführung: Ein interdisziplinärer Forschungsansatz. *Künstliche Intelligenz, 9*(6), 17–21. (Available on-line from http://w5.cs.uni-sb.de/Publist/)

A Modal Computational Framework for Default Reasoning

Alberto Artosi[1], Paola Cattabriga[1], and Guido Governatori[2]

[1] Dipartimento di Filosofia, Università di Bologna,
via Zamboni 28, 40126 Bologna, Italy, Fax +39(0)51-258326
[2] Department of Computing, Imperial College
180 Queen's Gate, London SW7 2BZ
E-mail: {artosi,paola,governat}@cirfid.unibo.it

Usually a default rule $A : B/C$ is intended to mean that if A holds in a state of affairs and B is consistent, then C follows by default. However, C is not a necessary conclusion: different states of affairs are possible (conceivable). According to this view, Meyer and van der Hoek [MvH92] developed a multimodal logic, called $S5P_{(n)}$, for treating non-monotonic reasoning in a monotonic setting. In this paper we shall describe a proof search algorithm for $S5P_{(n)}$ which has been implemented as a Prolog Interpreter.

$S5P_{(n)}$ arises as a combination of $S5$ with n distinct $K45$ "preference" modalities P_i $(1 \leq i \leq n)$ characterized by the following axioms:

$$1. \Box P_i A \equiv P_i A \qquad\qquad 3. \neg P_i \bot \rightarrow (P_i \Box A \equiv \Box A)$$
$$2. \neg P_i \bot \rightarrow (P_i P_j A \equiv P_j A) \qquad\qquad 4. \Box A \rightarrow P_i A (1 \leq i \leq n).$$

The semantics for $S5P_{(n)}$ is given in terms of clusters of preferred worlds.

To "simulate" default resoning in $S5P_{(n)}$ we simply have to translate the usual default rules in the $S5P_{(n)}$ language. The $S5P_{(n)}$ version of Reiter's rule is $A \wedge \Diamond B \rightarrow P_i C$ meaning that if A is true and B is (considered) possible then C is preferred. Similarly, normal defaults can be expressed as $A \wedge \Diamond B \rightarrow P_i B$ and multiple defaults as $A_1 \wedge \Diamond B_1 \rightarrow P_1 C_1$, $A_2 \wedge \Diamond B_2 \rightarrow P_2 C_2$... where P_1 and P_2 are preference operators associated with distinct preferred sets.

To compute inferences in $S5P_{(n)}$ we need the following label formalism. Let $\Phi_C^i = \{w_1^i, w_2^i, \ldots\}$ and $\Phi_V^i = \{W_1^i, W_2^i, \ldots\}$ $(0 \leq i \leq n)$ be two (nonempty) sets respectively of constant and variable "world" symbols. An element of the set $\Im$ of "world" labels (henceforth labels) is either (i) an element of Φ_C^i, or (ii) an element of Φ_V^i, or (iii) a path term (k', k) where (iiia) $k' \in \Phi_C^i \cup \Phi_V^i$ and (iiib) $k \in \Phi_C^i$ or $k = (m', m)$ where (m', m) is a label. Intuitively, we may think of a label $i \in \Phi_C^i$ as denoting a world, and a label $i \in \Phi_V^i$ as denoting a set of worlds (any world) in a cluster of preferred i-worlds. A label $i = (k', k)$ may be viewed as representing a path from k to a (set of) world(s) k' accessible from k. From now on we shall use $i, j, k, \ldots$ to denote arbitrary labels. For any label $i = (k', k)$ we call k' the head of i, k the body of i, and denote them by $h(i)$ and $b(i)$ respectively. Notice that these notions are recursive: if $b(i)$ denotes the body of i, then $b(b(i))$ will denote the body of $b(i)$, $b(b(b(i)))$ will denote the body of $b(b(i))$, and so on. We call each of $b(i)$, $b(b(i))$, etc., a segment of i. Let $s(i)$ denote any segment of i (obviously, by definition every segment $s(i)$ of a label i is a label); then $h(s(i))$ will denote the head of $s(i)$. We call a label i restricted if $h(i) \in \Phi_C$, otherwise we call it unrestricted. We shall say that a label k is *i-preferred* iff $k \in \mathfrak{S}^i$ where $\mathfrak{S}^i = \{k \in \mathfrak{S} : h(k) \text{ is either } w_m^i \text{ or } W_m^i, 1 \leq i \leq n\}$, and that a label k is *i-ground* $(1 \leq i \leq n)$ iff: 1) $\forall s(k) : h(s(k)) \notin \Phi_V^i$, and 2) if $\exists s^m(k) : h(s^m(k)) \in \Phi_V^i$, then $\exists s^j(k), j < m : h(s^j(k)) \in \Phi_C^i$.

The formalism just described allows labels to be manipulated in a way closely related to the semantics of modal operators and "matched" using a specialized (logic-dependent) unification algorithm. For two labels i, k and a substitution σ we shall use $(i, k)\sigma$ to denote both that i and k are σ-unifiable and the result of their unification. On this basis we may go on to define the notion of two labels i, k being $\sigma^{S5P(n)}$-unifiable in the following way:

$$\sigma^* : \Phi_V^0 \longrightarrow \mathfrak{S} - \Phi_V^i, (1 \leq i \leq n) \qquad \sigma^{S5P(n)} : \Phi_V \longrightarrow \mathfrak{S}$$
$$: \Phi_V^i \longrightarrow \Phi_C^i, (1 \leq i \leq n) \qquad\qquad : \Phi_V^i \longrightarrow \mathfrak{S}^i, (1 \leq i \leq n).$$

The corresponding PTP ("PROLOG Theorem Prover" [ACG95,Cat95]) clauses are:

```
unifypn(vw(N),vw(N1),vw(N2)):- (N >= N1, N2 = N); N1 =N2.
unifypn(w(N),vw(N1),w(N)).
unifypn(vw(N1),w(N),w(N)).
unifypn(w(N),w(N),w(N)).
unifypn(vw(N1),w(J,N),w(J,N)).
unifypn(w(J,N),vw(N1),w(J,N)).
unifypn(vw(J,N),vw(J,N1),vw(J,N2)):- (N >= N1, N2 = N); N1 =N2.
unifypn(w(J,N),vw(J,N1),w(J,N)).
unifypn(vw(J,N1),w(J,N),w(J,N)).
unifypn(w(J,N),w(J,N),w(J,N)).
unifypn(i(A,B),i(C,D),i(E,G)):- functor(i(A,B),F,N),
      functor(i(C,D),F,N), unifyargspn(N,i(A,B),i(C,D),i(E,G)).
unifyargspn(N,X,Y,T):- N>0, unifyargpn(N,X,Y,AT), N1 is N - 1,
      functor(T,i,2), arg(N,T,AT), unifyargspn(N1,X,Y,T).
unifyargspn(0,X,Y,T).
unifyargpn(N,X,Y,AT):- arg(N,X,AX), arg(N,Y,AY), unifypn(AX,AY,AT).
```

We are now able to define the notion of $\sigma_{S5P_{(n)}}$-unification as follows:

$(i, k)\sigma_{S5P_{(n)}} = (h(i), h(k))\sigma^*$ if

$\qquad i, k$ are *i*-ground, $1 \leq i \leq n$, or

$\qquad \exists s(i), s(k) : h(s(i)), h(s(k)) \in \Phi^i$, and $(h(s(i)), h(s(k)))\sigma^{S5P_{(n)}}$.

PTP clauses:

```
unifydefault(T1,T2,T3):- iground(T1), iground(T2),
      arg(1,T1,H1), arg(1,T2,H2), unifypn(H1,H2,T3), !.
unifydefault(T1,T2,T3):- isegment(T1,i(H1,B1)),
      isegment(T2,i(H2,B2)), unifydefault(H1,H2,T3).
isegment(I,S):- (subterm(i(w(J,N),K),I), i(w(J,N),K)=S;
      subterm(i(vw(D,M),H),I), i(vw(D,M),H)=S),!.
iground(I):- ( compound(I), I =.. [F], not memb(vw(A,B),F); ig(F);
      (subterm(i(vw(H,M),K),I), subterm(w(C,D),K))),! .
ig([]):- !.
ig([T|B]):- (T = w(H); T = vw(G); T = w(A,B)), ig(B).
```

In contrast with the usual branch-expansion rules of the tableau method, all the rules involved in the following proof search algorithm are linear. Their application generates a one-branch refutation tree (thus eliminating redundancy from the search space). Splitting occurs only as a result of applying the "cut rule" in steps 9, 10 below. The algorithm works with formulas of the form X, i called *labelled formulas* (ℓ-formulas). Formulas will be expressed in Smullyan-Fitting's "α, β, ν, π" notation with the following addition: formulas of the forms $P_i A$ and $\neg P_i A$ will be classified, in analogy with ν and π type formulas, as being of type $p_i \nu$ and $p_i \pi$ respectively. As usual X^C will be used to denote the conjugate of X (i.e. $\neg Z$ if $X = Z$, and *viceversa*). The algorithm is displayed in its most general formulation, with "L" to be replaced by "$S5P_{(n)}$" or by any other logic among those treated in [AG94,Gov95] (to which the reader is also referred for all details). The procedure is based on *canonical* trees. A tree is canonical iff it is generated by applying the inference rules in the following fixed order: first the 1-premise rules (see steps 3,4,5,6,7), then the 2-premise rules (see step 8), and finally the 0-premise (cut) rule. An essential property of canonical trees is that they always terminate, thus providing a computable algorithm.

Preliminary definitions. Two ℓ-formulas X, i and X^C, k, such that $(i, k)\sigma_L$ are called σ_L-complementary. An ℓ-formula X, i is said to be *E-analysed in a branch* τ if either (i) X is of type α and both α_1, i and α_2, i occur in τ; or (ii) X is of type β and the following condition is satisfied: if β_1^C, k (resp. β_2^C, k) occurs in τ and $(i, k)\sigma_L$, then also $\beta_2, (i, k)\sigma_L$ (resp. $\beta_1, (i, k)\sigma_L$) occurs in τ; or (iii) X is of type ν and $\nu_0, (i', i)$ occurs in τ for some $i' \in \Phi_V$ not previously occurring in τ, or (iv) X is of type π and $\pi_0, (i', i)$ occurs in τ for some $i' \in \Phi_C$ not previously occurring in τ, similarly if X is of type $p_i \nu$ or $p_i \pi$. A branch τ is said to be *E-completed* if every ℓ-formula in it is E-analysed and there are no complementary ℓ-formulas which are not σ_L-complementary. We say that a branch τ is *completed* if it is E-completed and all the ℓ-formulas of type β in it are either analysed or cannot be analysed. We call a tree *completed* if every branch is completed. Finally, a branch τ is said to be σ_L-closed if it contains a pair of σ_L-complementary ℓ-formulas, and a tree is σ_L-closed if all its branches are σ_L-closed.

Let Λ, Δ denote the sets of analysed and unanalysed ℓ-formulas respectively, and $\mathcal{L}$ denote the set of generated labels. To prove a formula X of L start the following algorithm with X^C, i (where i is an arbitrary constant label) in Δ, and i is in $\mathcal{L}$.

STEP 1. If a pair of σ_L-complementary ℓ-formulas occurs in Δ, then the tree is σ_L-closed. A is a theorem of L.

STEP 2. If Δ is empty, then the tree is completed. Every literal is deleted from Δ and added to Λ.

STEPS 3, 4. For each ℓ-formula ν, i (π, i) in Δ, (i) generate a new unrestricted (restricted) label (i', i) and add it to $\mathcal{L}$; (ii) delete ν, i (π, i) from Δ; (iii) add $\nu_0, (i', i)$ ($\pi_0, (i', i)$) to Δ; and (iv) add ν, i (π, i) to Λ.

STEPS 5, 6. For each ℓ-formula $p_i \nu, k$, $(p_i \pi, k)$ in Δ, (i) generate a new unrestricted (restricted) label (m^i, k) and add it to $\mathcal{L}$; (ii) delete $p_i \nu, k$ ($p_i \pi, k$) from Δ; (iii) add $p_i \nu_0, (m^i, k)$ ($p_i \pi_0, (m^i, k)$) to Δ; and (iv) add $p_i \nu, k$ ($p_i \pi, k$) to Λ.

STEP 7. For each ℓ-formula α, i in Δ, (i) add α_1, i, and α_2, i to Δ; (ii) delete α, i from Δ; and (iii) add α, i to Λ.

STEP 8. For each ℓ-formula β, i in Δ, such that either β_1^C, k or β_2^C, k is in $\Delta \cup \Lambda$ and $(i, k)\sigma_L$ for some k, (i) add $\beta_2(i, k)\sigma_L$ or $\beta_1(i, k)\sigma_L$ to Δ; (ii) delete β, i from Δ; (iii) add the labels resulting from the σ_L-unification to $\mathcal{L}$; and (iv) add β, i to Λ.

STEP 9. For each ℓ-formula β, i in Δ, if $\Delta \cup \Lambda$ does not contain formulas β_1^C, k such that i, k are σ_L-unifiable, then form sets $\Delta_1 = \Delta \cup \beta_1, m$, $\Lambda_1 = \Lambda \cup \beta_i$, $\Delta_2 = \Delta \cup \beta_1^C, m \cup \beta, i$ where $(i, m)\sigma_L$ and m is a given restricted label, and $\Lambda_2 = \Lambda$.

STEP 10. For each ℓ-formula β, i in Δ, if $\Delta \cup \Lambda$ does not contain formulas β_2^C, k so that i, k are σ_L-unifiable, then form sets $\Delta_1 = \Delta \cup \beta_2, m$, $\Lambda_1 = \Lambda \cup \beta_i$, $\Delta_2 = \Delta \cup \beta_2^C, m \cup \beta, i$ where $(i, m)\sigma_L$ and m is a given restricted label, and $\Lambda_2 = \Lambda$.

STEPS 11, 12. If Λ contains two complementary but not σ_L-complementary ℓ-formulas, search in $\mathcal{L}$ for restricted labels which σ_L-unify with both the labels of the complementary formulas; if we find (do not find) such labels then the tree is σ_L-closed (completed). A is (is not) a theorem of L.

In this paper we have presented a proof system for computing default reasoning in a monotonic setting. The above algorithm can be used to verify whether a conclusion C is implied by a (multiple) default D (where D denotes the conjunction of the $S5P_{(n)}$ translation of the default(s)) and, thanks to the distinctive features of the label formalism it uses, it yields a countermodel similar to the state of affairs corresponding to the default(s).

References

[ACG95] Artosi A., P. Cattabriga and G. Governatori. A Prolog implementation of KEM. In M. Alpuente and M. I. Sessa (eds.), *Proceedings of the GULP-PRODE'95 Joint Conference on Declarative Programming. Marina di Vietri, 11–14 september 1995*, Università degli Studi di Salerno, 1995: 395–400.

[AG94] Artosi A. and G. Governatori. Labelled Model Modal Logic. In *Proceedings of the CADE-12 Workshop on Automated Model Building*, 1994: 11–17.

[Cat95] Cattabriga P. *Sistemi algoritmici indicizzati per il ragionamento giuridico.* PhD Thesis, University of Bologna, 1996.

[Gov95] Governatori G. Labelled Tableaux For Multi-Modal Logics. In P. Baumgartner, R. Hähnle, and J. Posegga (eds.), *Theorem Proving with Analytic Tableaux and Related Methods*, Lecture Notes in Computer Science, Springer-Verlag, 1995: 79–84.

[MvH92] Mayer J.-J.Ch and W. van der Hoek. A Modal Logic for Nonmonotonic Reasoning. In W. van der Hoek, J.-J.Ch. Mayer, Y. H. Tan and C. Witteveen (ed.), *Non-Monotonic Reasoning and Partial Semantics*. Ellis Horwood: N.Y., 1992: 37–77.

Planning Diagonalization Proofs

Lassaad Cheikhrouhou

Fachbereich Informatik
Universität des Saarlandes
D-66041 Saarbrücken, Germany
lassaad@cs.uni-sb.de

1 Introduction

Proof planning [Bun91] is the search for a sequence of tactics (a proof plan) which can be applied to construct an object level proof. The used operators (methods) are specifications of tactics represented in a meta-language. A method specifies when the associated tactic can be applied and what its effects are. In our approach, we extend methods that represent well-known proof techniques, such as induction or diagonalization, with control knowledge and call them *strategies*.

The point of proof planning is to analyze proof techniques in order to determine their typical proof steps and to find a suitable control to perform these steps within the proof planning process. This paper [1] is a first attempt of formalizing the diagonalization proof technique. After introducing the diagonalization principle in the next section, we describe how this strategy can be realized in the proof planning environment of ΩMEGA [BCF+97].

2 The Diagonalization Principle

In [DSW94] a proof by diagonalization is described as follows:

> *The diagonalization method turns on the demonstration of two assertions of the following sort:*
> 1. *A certain set E can be enumerated in a suitable fashion.*
> 2. *It is possible, with the help of the enumeration, to define an object d that is different from every object in the enumeration, i.e. $d \notin E$.*

We empirically studied some diagonalization proofs [Che96] to elaborate this proof technique:

- The first task is carried out by searching for a *surjective function f* from some set N into a certain set E, the set to be enumerated. The *indexing property* of f [$\forall x.\, E(x) \rightarrow \exists y.\, N(y) \land x = f(y)$] guarantees for each element of E the existence of an index in N.
- The central point of diagonalization is the construction of the object d, *the diagonal element*. On the one hand, it must be different from every object in the enumeration: For each element z of the set N, the object $f(z)$ must be different from d. As d is a function, we achieve this by enforcing that the application of d to the element z ($d(z)$) differs from *the diagonal term* $f(z)(z)$ in some property. On the other hand, the function d is defined in such a way, that it belongs to the enumerable set E. Consequently, it has an index i ($d = f(i)$) and this leads apparently to a contradiction.

---

[1] This paper is a short version of [Che97].

3 A Diagonalization Proof Strategy

In this section, we give a declarative representation of the diagonalization strategy and explain how it can be applied.

Representation of the Strategy

To represent the diagonalization proof strategy, we use the declarative framework for the representation of proof methods in [HKRS94] with some extensions. These extensions allow the reasoning with metavariables and the representation of some control knowledge within methods, e.g. the ordering of method subgoals. The diagonalization strategy is represented in Figure 1.

Strategy : Diag	
Declarations	—
Goal	8
Precondition	NIL
Postcondition	6, $newconst(\overline{i}, \alpha)$, $< \parallel differs(D, \lambda x_\alpha \bullet x)$ $occurs(x, \overline{D}(x))$ $differs(\underline{D(i), F(i)(i))}$ 5 $inverts(\overline{D}, F(i)(i), \overline{IP}) >$
Proof Schema	1. 1 $\vdash$ $n(i) \wedge D = F(i)$ (Hyp) 2. 1 $\vdash$ $n(i)$ (AndEL 1) 3. 1 $\vdash$ $D = F(i)$ (AndER 1) 4. 1 $\vdash$ $\perp$ (MEC(D, IP) 2 3) 5. $\vdash$ $E(\overline{D})$ (Open) 6. $\vdash$ $\forall x_{\overline{\alpha} \to \overline{\beta}} \bullet \overline{E}(x) \to \exists y_{\overline{\alpha}} \bullet \overline{n}(y) \wedge x = \overline{F}(y)$ (Open) 7. $\vdash$ $\exists y_\alpha \bullet n(y) \wedge D = F(y)$ (6 5) 8. $\vdash$ $\perp$ (ExistsE 7 4)

Fig. 1. The Diag strategy

The *proof schema* consists of ND (natural deduction) lines whose formulae are schematic, i.e. propositions with *metavariables* [2]. Each ND line has a justification which can be either open (annotated by Open) or closed. A closed justification consists of a tactic, e.g. a ND rule, an argument list, and a list of ND lines (the premises). This means, the ND line can be proven from the premises by applying the tactic with the given arguments.

The *goal* of a strategy should match an open ND line at the object level, which is to be proven by the strategy. Before applying the strategy, its *precondition*

---

[2] *Higher order metavariables* (HOV), denoted in capital letters, can be instantiated

must be fulfilled, where a precondition consists of ND lines from the proof schema and constraints. The ND lines have to match *support lines* of the goal and the constraints are evaluated. The support lines of an open ND line consist of its hypotheses and their derived consequences.

The application of the strategy would reduce the goal to new subgoals to be closed and additional constraints to be satisfied. Both subgoals and constraints are given in the *postcondition* list. The ND lines and the constraints should be considered sequentially from the left to the right, if they are separated by commas in the list, and simultaneously by grouping them in a list marked with ∥.

Application of the Strategy

The strategy Diag can be used to prove a contradiction, i.e. ⊥. This strategy can be chosen, among other methods with the same goal ⊥, either by the user or by the control module of the planner which classifies available methods according to additional information about the problem. The precondition list of Diag is empty. Thus, it can directly be applied by considering its postcondition list:

The indexing property is determined by closing the subgoal 6, i.e. proving the formula schema of the ND line 6 by assertion application from the support lines. Hereby, the metavariables α, β, E, n, and F must be fully instantiated. The next postcondition is the constraint $newconst(\overline{i}, \alpha)$ whose evaluation binds the metavariable i to a new constant, the index of the diagonal element D.

The rest of the postcondition list has to be evaluated simultaneously and leads to the construction of D. The function D belongs to the enumerable set E and inverts some property wrt. the diagonal term $F(i)(i)$. The first property can be stated by closing the subgoal 5. The second property can be fulfilled by some propositions which depend on β, the type of $F(i)(i)$, and on the instantiation of D. This is the reason why we represent the inverting property as a constraint. The satisfaction of the *inverts* constraint would deliver the proofs IP to the propositions that guarantee the inverting property of D. To prevent nonsense instantiations of D, we use the restriction constraints: $occurs(x, \overline{D}(x))$, $differs(D, \lambda x_\alpha \cdot x)$, and $differs(D(i), F(i)(i))$.

A vague specification of D can be given by $D = \lambda x_\alpha \cdot \overline{G}(F(x), x)$, and requiring the inverting property $\overline{U}(\overline{G}(F(i), i))) \leftrightarrow \neg \overline{U}(F(i)(i))$. Some alternative instantiations of these schemata, that we obtained by investigating examples in [Che96], would make this task easier, as they provide more control:

1. The diagonal term $F(i)(i)$ denotes a proposition: we consider the formula schema $\neg F(i)(i) \leftrightarrow \overline{D}(i)$ as inverting property.
2. Otherwise: two important possible instantiations of D are distinguished:
   2.1. $D(x)$ can be defined according to some condition $U(F(x), x)$: $D(x)$ equals $Y(x)$, if $U(F(x), x)$ holds, and it is $Z(x)$ otherwise. Thus, D must be instantiated by the schema $\lambda x_\alpha \cdot if(\overline{U}(F(x), x), \overline{Y}(x), \overline{Z}(x))$, where the constraint $differs(Y(x), Z(x))$ must hold.
   The inversion of the term $F(i)(i)$ is obtained, if we prove the subgoals: $\overline{Q}(F(i)(i)) \rightarrow \neg \overline{U}(F(i), i)$, $\overline{Q}(\overline{Y}(i))$, $\overline{R}(F(i)(i)) \rightarrow \overline{U}(F(i), i)$, and $\overline{R}(\overline{Z}(i))$.

2.2. After proving the subgoal 5, D can be instantiated with the function $\lambda x_\alpha \cdot C(F(x), x)$: the inverting property of D can be either the inequality $C(F(i), i) \neq F(i)(i)$ or the formula schema $\overline{U}(C(F(i), i)) \leftrightarrow \neg\overline{U}(F(i)(i))$.

While closing subgoals represented by formula schemata, metavariables are incrementally instantiated. This is done especially for HOVs by middle out reasoning [KBB93].

Execution of the Strategy

The instantiated proof schema of Diag is inserted into the ND proof. Lines, that are not justified by ND rules, can be expanded further by applying their justification tactics. The expansion of line 4 in the proof schema of Diag corresponds to making the implicit contradiction of the diagonal element explicit. The tactic MEC generates a contradiction proof at ND level according to the instantiation of D and of the proven properties that guarantee the inversion of the diagonal term $F(i)(i)$.

References

[BCF⁺97] C. Benzmüller, L. Cheikhrouhou, D. Fehrer, A. Fiedler, X. Huang, M. Kerber, M. Kohlhase, K. Konrad, E. Melis, A. Meier, W. Schaarschmidt, J. Siekmann, and V. Sorge. ΩMEGA: Towards a Mathematical Assistant. In William McCune, editor, *Proceedings of the 14th Conference on Automated Deduction*, LNAI, Townsville, Australia, 1997. Springer Verlag.

[Bun91] Alan Bundy. A Science of Reasoning. In *Computational Logic: Essays in honor of Alan Robinson*. MIT Press, 1991. also presented at the 10th CADE 1990 as extended abstract.

[Che96] Lassaad Cheikhrouhou. The Mechanization of the Diagonalization Proof Strategy. SEKI Report SR-96-14, Fachbereich Informatik, Universität des Saarlandes, Im Stadtwald, Saarbrücken, Germany, 1996.

[Che97] Lassaad Cheikhrouhou. Planning Diagonalization Proofs. SEKI Report SR-97-06, Fachbereich Informatik, Universität des Saarlandes, Im Stadtwald, Saarbrücken, Germany, 1997.

[DSW94] Martin D. Davis, Ron Sigal, and Elaine J. Weyuker. *Computability, Complexity, and Languages: Fundamentals of Theoretical Computer Science*. Academic Press, second edition, 1994.

[HKRS94] Xiaorong Huang, Manfred Kerber, Jörn Richts, and Arthur Sehn. Planning Mathematical Proofs with Methods. *Journal of Information Processing and Cybernetics*, EIK, 30(5-6):277–291, 1994.

[KBB93] I. Kraan, D. Basin, and A. Bundy. Middle-Out Reasoning for Program Synthesis. In P. Szeredi, editor, *Proceedings of the 10-th International Conference on Logic Programming*. MIT Press, 1993.

Suffix Tree Automata in State Space Search

Stefan Edelkamp

Institut für Informatik, Albert-Ludwigs-Universität,
Am Flughafen 17, D-79110 Freiburg
eMail: edelkamp@informatik.uni-freiburg.de

Abstract. An on–line learning algorithm for pruning state space search is described in this paper. The algorithm is based on a finite state machine which is both created and used in the search. The pruning technique is necessary when memory resources in searching huge problem spaces are restricted. A duplicate sequence is a generating path in the search tree that has a counterpart with smaller weight. The automaton provides the dictionary operations *Insert* and *Delete* for the duplicate sequences found in the search and *Search* for pruning the search tree.
The underlying data structure is a multi suffix tree. Given that the alphabet Σ of state transitions is bounded by a constant an optimal worst case bound of $O(|m|)$ for both insertion and deletion of a duplicate sequence $m \in \Sigma^*$ is achieved. Using the structure as a finite state machine we can incrementally accept a given sequence x in time $O(|x|)$.

1 Introduction and Background

State space problems dealing with a huge problem space are actually described implicitly and thus the transition alphabet Σ is bounded. A sequence $\delta_m(u) = \delta(\ldots \delta(\delta(u, m_1), m_2), \ldots, m_n)$ of transitions applied to a given problem state u can be identified with the string $m \in \Sigma^n$. We wish to prune the search tree at all revisited states but the storage of the search tree in a hash table is impossible. The key idea of Taylor and Korf (1993) is to regard the transition sequences instead of the problem states themselves. In the *learning phase* a breadth-first search is invoked to find m and m' in Σ^* with $\delta_m(u) = \delta_{m'}(u)$ and $w(m) > w(m')$ (w is the transition cost function) s.t. m is called *duplicate* sequence and m' *shortcut* sequence. The conflict between m and m' is found using a hash table. In the *search phase* the set of duplicate strings is applied to prune the search tree. Consider an unconstrained search space in which every transition sequence can be applied. If a node with the generating path $x = \alpha m$, $\alpha \in \Sigma^*$, is reached no further expansion is needed since a sequence $\alpha m'$ has been or will be examined in the search. One duplicate found in the learning phase can thus eliminate hundreds of strings in the search phase. We call this an *off–line* learning algorithm since the automaton is only created but not used in the learning phase. Taylor and Korf propose the algorithm of Aho and Coarsic (1975) to recognize the set of duplicate strings $m \in M$ for which there exists a shortcut m'.

A constrained search space, cancellation of the common prefix in m and m', different initial states, a cycle detection search using a heuristic heading back to the start node or a successive repetition of some transition sequences raise the quest of a dictionary D for maintaining the different duplicates. Updating the failure function in the AC-algorithm is not very efficient (cf. Meyer (1985)) so we choose another approach. The dictionary in this paper provides *on–line* learning, since it can be used to detect duplicates parallel to the search.

2 The Algorithm and Multi Suffix Trees

The algorithm combines the function of the hash table H and the dictionary automaton D. The input is a state space problem Π and the output is the solution path for Π. A node u in the search tree consists of the problem state description itself, the automaton state q_u, the last character a_u on the generating path p_u, the heuristic estimate $h(u)$ and the weight $g(u)$ of p_u. The procedure *ccp* cancels the common prefix of the input strings and *findSuperString* returns a superstring in D if there is one. Before a state has to be searched in H the automaton state in D is determined. This might be an accepting state which prunes the search tree immediately. Otherwise suppose that a collision v' with a state v is detected in the hash table and the generating path m of v is inserted in D together with the shortcut generating path m' of v'. The duplicate strings in D are kept substring free with respect to each other since a substring m' of a duplicate m which has a shortcut also provides a shortcut for m. Thus before inserting a new duplicate sequence m in the dictionary all superstrings of m are deleted. The algorithm uses a priority queue PQ and extends the well known A^* algorithm (Hart et al. (1968)) in the lines marked with an asterisk (*).

```
procedure OnLineLearn (Π)
    PQ.Insert(s); H.Insert(s);              // init data structures, s start node
    while PQ ≠ ∅ do                          // if PQ = ∅ then no solution is found
      u ← PQ.Deletemin                       // u not deleted in H for reopening
      for all v ∈ expand(u) do               // for all successors v of u
        if goal(v) return p_v                // a goal is found
(*)     q.v ← D.Search(p_v)       // extract new automaton state, q.v ← δ_{p_v}(q_0)
(*)     Let (m, m') be associated with q_v   // extract duplicate/shortcut string
(*)     if q_v is accepting and δ_{m^{-1}m'}(v) = v continue   // m^{-1}m' applicable
        v' ← H.Search(v)                      // v' is counterpart of v
        if v' = nil then                      // v is not found in H
          PQ.Insert(v); H.Insert(v) continue      // insert v in data structures
        if w(p_v) < w(p_{v'})                 // g(v) + h(v) < g(v') + h(v')
(*)       m' = p_v; m = p_{v'}             // v''s generating path is duplicate
          PQ.Delete(v'); PQ.Insert(v);                              // reopen v
(*)     else m = p_v; m' = p_{v'}            // v's generating path is duplicate
(*)     ccp(m, m')                    // use least common ancestor of v and v'
(*)     if D.Search(m) is accepting continue         // m has substrings in D
(*)     while m'' ←findSuperString(m) do D.Delete(m'')
(*)     D.Insert((m, m'))                 // new duplicate with shortcut inserted
```

In this algorithm the automaton only prevents us from searching a state in the hash table. Although hashing of a state is in general not available in constant time it is quite fast compared to the calculation of $Search(p_v)$ in D. On the one hand we will examine how the calculation of $\delta_{p_v}(q_0)$ (q_0 is the initial automaton state) can be done incrementally by analyzing a procedure that can perform $\delta(q_u, a_v)$ in (amortized) constant time. On the other hand notice that under memory restrictions the information that a state has been revisited may not be encountered in the hash table. Many memory restricted search algorithms that have been analyzed in the last decade can be combined with the on-line pruning method. This is a important topic of further research since searching the tree of generating paths can lead to an exponential blow up of time.

A *Patricia tree* is a compact representation of a trie where all nodes with only one successor are merged to their parents. A *suffix tree* is a Patricia tree corresponding to the suffixes of a given string. Although there are $\Theta(|m|^2)$ characters for the $|m|$ suffixes of a string m the suffix tree only needs space of size $O(|m|)$. The substring information stored at each suffix node is simply given by the indices of first and last character. If an internal node v represents $a\alpha$, $a \in \Sigma$ and $\alpha \in \Sigma^*$ then the *suffix link* points to a node representing α which has to exist in the suffix tree. Using these suffix links McCreight (1976) presents and analyses an optimal linear time algorithm to build a suffix tree ST of a given string $m\$$. His approach can be extended naturally to more than one string for example by building the suffix tree of the string $m_1\$_1 \ldots m_n\$_n$. Amir et al. (1994) proved that the suffix tree ST for $m_1\$_1 \ldots m_n\$_n$ is isomorphic to the compacted trie ST' (cf. Fig. 1) for all suffixes of $m_1\$_1$ up to to all suffixes of $m_n\$_n$. Furthermore, the trees are identical except for the labels of the edges incident to leaves. This fact allows to insert and delete a string into an existing suffix tree. The description and the correctness proof of the linar-time insertion and deletion scheme for multi suffix trees can be found in Amir et al. (1994).

In solving the (100×100) *Maze* with a chance of 35 percent for a square to represent a wall we count the number of pruned nodes in the *OnLineSearch* algorithm. In Fig. 2 we have depicted the first 20 random instances that need more than 1000 expansions. The competitors are two predefined automata as well as two automata learned in a breadth-first-search up to *depth* 5 and 25. In the learning phase of the last two approaches we reconstruct the finite state machine for each increase of search depth. The automata sizes measured in the number of trie nodes are: 10 for the automaton based on predecessor elimination, 14 for the one described in Taylor and Korf (1993), 17 for a learning depth of 5, 43 for a learning depth of 25 and 75 up to 135 for the on-line learning dictionary.

3 Incremental Search using State Transitions

There are two different approaches to find a substring of a given string x in the suffix tree. Amir et al. (1994) determine the longest pattern prefix h of the string stored in the suffix tree that matches x *starting* at position i, $i \in \{1, \ldots, |m|\}$. In contrast to this algorithm we fix the longest substring h of the strings stored

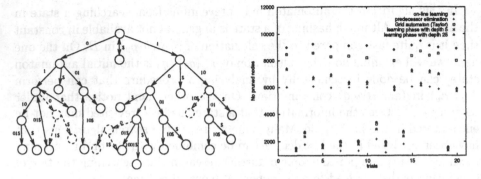

Fig. 1 The multi suffix tree ST' for (1100110), (1011001), (010101) and (11010) to be inserted.

Fig. 2 Experimental results on on-line and off-line pruning the (100×100) *Maze*.

in ST' that matches x *ending* at position i. If the strings m stored in ST' are *substring free*, i.e., no string is a substring of another one, then the only thing to do in both cases is to check if h is maximal ($|h.m| = |h|$). In the general case we have to test the membership of the prefixes of h in M which is called the *dictionary prefix problem (DPP)* introduced by Amir et al. (1994). Our algorithm will be called *incremental* because it doesn't refer to characters x_j with $j < i$. This is crucial, since in the overall *OnLineLearn* algorithm we need an efficient way to determine $\delta_{p_v}(q_0) = \delta(q_u, a_v)$. To find $q_v = \delta(q_u, a_v)$ we search for a new node el and an integer offset at such that a_v corresponds to the transition stored at position *first*+at of the string stored at el. Thus we will use the suffix links until we have achieved this task. The returned value h_j of $\delta(x_j)$ is the substring corresponding to the path from the root to the new location.

Theorem 1. *Let $x \in \Sigma^n$ be read from x_1 up to x_{j-1}. The returned value h_j of procedure δ invoked with x_j is the longest suffix $x(i, j)$ of $x(1, j)$ which is also substring of one $m \in M$ stored in the suffix tree ST'. The amortized time complexity for δ is $O(1)$.*

References

1. A. V. Aho and M. J. Corasick. Efficient string matching: an aid to bibliographic search. *Communications of the ACM*, 18(6):333–340, 1975.
2. A. Amir, M. Farach, Z. Galil, R. Giancarlo, and K. Park. Dynamic dictionary matching. *J. Comput. Syst. Sci.*, 49(2):208–222, 1994.
3. P. E. Hart, N. J. Nilsson, and B. Raphael. A formal basis for heuristic determination of minimum path cost. *IEEE Trans. on SSC*, 4:100, 1968.
4. E. M. McCreight. A space-economical suffix tree construction algorithm. *Journal of the ACM*, 23(2):262–272, 1976.
5. B. Meyer. Incremental string matching. *Inf. Process. Lett.*, 21:219–227, 1985.
6. L. A. Taylor and R. E. Korf. Pruning duplicate nodes in depth-first search. In *AAAI-93*, pages 756–761, 1993.

Connection Cutting for Contraction Free Logic

Bertram Fronhöfer

Institut für Informatik, TU München, D – 80290 München

fronhoef@informatik.tu-muenchen.de

Abstract. The paper is inspired by previous work on proof procedures for the Linear Connection Method; in particular, by a refinement of path checking called Connection Cutting, which is a dynamic handling of 'virtual' tautologies. Since the Linear Connection Method is closely related to Contraction Free Logic, we propose an extension of Connection Cutting to the multiplicative fragment of this logic.

1 Introduction

The *Linear Connection Method* (LCM) [1] was proposed as a logic-oriented approach to plan generation. With its restriction that every literal may be involved in at most one connection (*linearity*) it allowed to cope with destructive effects of actions.

In a previous paper [3] we presented a proof procedure for the LCM by adapting a simple path checking algorithm of the classical Connection Method to the Linear Connection Method, and by enhancing it through a special technique called *Connection Cutting*.

Theoretical investigations showed that the LCM—as proposed for the application to plan generation—can be understood as defining theoremhood in a *multiplicative Horn clause like logic*—the 'Horn clauses' may have conjunctive heads—where contraction has been restricted to implications [2][1].

From 'restricting contraction to implications' to 'abandoning contraction completely' is a relatively small step, which suggests to investigate the applicability of the proof procedures, previously developed for the LCM in [5] and [3], to Contraction Free Logic. Hereby, the challenging aspect is to go beyond the Horn like case and to treat the multiplicative fragment of Contraction Free Logic. For reasons of space we will have to assume knowledge of the main concepts of the Connection Method, especially of matrices in non-normal form. (The symbol $\in$ will denote the reflexive transitive closure of set membership.) For the concepts used in the sequel we refer the reader to [2], where the Connection Method is developed in view of its application to the multiplicative fragments of substructural logics like Contraction Free, Linear or Relevance.

We also proved in [2,Th. 35], that a formula F of the multiplicative fragment of Contraction Free Logic is a theorem iff there is a linear, acyclic[2], complementary

---

[1] See [4] for an overview of alternative answers concerning the logic underlying the LCM, as well as for a general survey of work on the LCM and related approaches.

[2] The somewhat complicated concept of acyclicity will be used as a kind of 'black box' in the following, and we refer to [2] for its definition.

matrix graph $(\mathcal{M}, \mathcal{S})$ (with set of connections $\mathcal{S}$), where the matrix $\mathcal{M}$ has been obtained as translation of the formula F.

Such a matrix graph is given below. (The thin dotted line is just a temporary connection made during proof search and will be explained below.) With a path checking procedure for classical logic, augmented by a linearity check, this proof may be found as follows: Starting with column **4** on the right[3], we first enter column **3** (connection $(J^4, \overline{J}^3)$),

- where A^3 is connected to $\overline{A}^0$,
- with G^3 we enter column **1** (connection $(G^3, \overline{G}^1)$), whose subgoals D^1, F^1 and E^1 are connected to $\overline{D}^0$, $\overline{F}^0$ and $\overline{E}^0$ respectively,
- and C^3 is connected to $\overline{C}^0$.

For the subgoal I^4 we enter column **2** (connection $(I^4, \overline{I}^2)$) and we encounter C^2. *But now we are stuck with ordinary path checking!* The only literal $\overline{C}$ around for making a connection is already connected, and the only way out is backtracking: Instead of connecting C^3 to $\overline{C}^0$ we make a connection $(C^3, \overline{C}^2)$. Now path checking continues successfully without further backtracking.

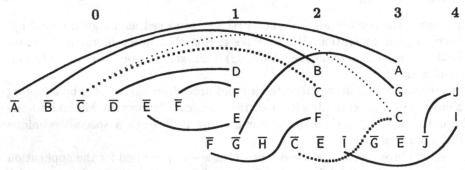

In [3] we proposed an improvement of path checking which avoids backtracking in cases like the one above: We extended the proof procedure by an *additional proof step* and on the other hand imposed a *special restriction on making connections* during the ordinary path checking process. The additional proof step allows to cut the connection $(C^3, \overline{C}^0)$ into the two connections $(C^3, \overline{C}^2)$ and $(C^2, \overline{C}^0)$ (dotted lines in the picture above), and then to continue. The special restriction forbids to make connection $(C^3, \overline{C}^2)$ during ordinary path checking, i.e. we are no more allowed to make a connection to a literal $\overline{L}$, if there is a literal L 'somewhere above' in the same column. Thus we avoid dynamically to connect only a tautological virtual column. To assure completeness every possibility of connection cutting must be tried in principle. The growth of the search space stemming from connection cutting—which depends on the size of the partial proof constructed so far—is generally widely compensated by the search space reduction entailed by forbidding certain connections—which applies to the size of the entire given formula. See [3] for some practical experiments. What we considered in [3] were top-level columns C of a matrix $\mathcal{M}$, i.e. $C \in \mathcal{M}$, of the form: $\{A_1, \ldots, A_n, P_1, \ldots, P_k, \{\overline{B}_1, \ldots, \overline{B}_m, \overline{P}_1, \ldots, \overline{P}_k\}\}$

---

[3] We distinguish the different occurrences of a (logical) literal in the matrix by upper indices, written above the respective columns. All unit columns got the same index 0.

with propositional variables A_i, P_i and B_i. We study in this paper the generalisation of connection cutting to multiplicative Contraction Free Logic, which means practically to deal with the extension from Horn like to general matrices. Not having yet found out the utmost generalisation possible, we will generalize as follows:

$$\mathcal{C} \Subset \mathcal{M}, \qquad K \in \mathcal{C}, \qquad \overline{K} \in \mathcal{R} \in \mathcal{C}, \qquad K \text{ a (positive or negative) literal}$$

2 Path Checking and Connection Cutting

When we are interested whether a given matrix graph $(\mathcal{M}, \mathcal{S})$ is complementary, the standard way to proceed is to check whether all paths in $\mathcal{M}$ are complementary w.r.t. $\mathcal{S}$. Based on the characterisation of contraction free derivable formulae mentioned above, we may now adapt the proof search algorithm existing for the classical Connection Method. The algorithm simplifies, because linearity entails the absence of reduction steps; on the other hand we have to take care not to connect literals twice and we have to check continuously during proof search that we create no cycles. This yields the following path checking procedure:

Definition 1 [CMCF proof procedure]. The two subroutines choose_column(N, SubGoal) and choose_row(C, SubGoal) select a column or row $\mathcal{N}^*$ from $\mathcal{N}$ and $\mathcal{C}$, the respective values of N and C. (If N or C refer to a literal, this literal is chosen.) Moreover, in order to assure linearity, the selections must satisfy the following restrictions. We have the cases:

[1] If SubGoal = NIL, then the selection is unrestricted and constitutes a *backtracking point* of the subroutine choose_column.

[2] Otherwise, SubGoal refers to an occurrence L^1 of a literal.

[2.1] If there is already a connection $(L^1, \overline{L}^1) \in$ ConnSet then we have to choose $\mathcal{N}^*$ such that $\overline{L}^1 \Subset \mathcal{N}^*$. (Since $\Subset$ is transitive, $\mathcal{N}^* = \overline{L}^1$ is included.) *If this is not possible, we backtrack.*

[2.2] If L^1 is still unconnected in ConnSet then we choose $\mathcal{N}^*$ such that there is an unconnected occurrence $\overline{L}^1 \Subset \mathcal{N}^*$. (Again, $\mathcal{N}^* = \overline{L}^1$ is included.)
Different possible choices of $\overline{L}^1$ are a backtracking point. *If there is no such $\mathcal{N}^*$, we backtrack.*

```
 1.  proc CMCF
 2.       N := 'given non-empty matrix M' ;
 3.       SubGoal := NIL ; ConnSet:= ∅ ; push(∅,∅) ;
 4.  col: C := choose_column(N, SubGoal) ; N = N \ C;
 5.  row: R := choose_row(C, SubGoal) ; C := C \ R ;
 6.       if C ≠ ∅ then push(C, N) fi ;
 7.       if R is not a literal then  N := N ∪ R ; goto col fi ;
 8.       if R is a literal ∧ SubGoal ≠ NIL then
 9.            ConnSet:= ConnSet ∪ {(R, SubGoal)} ;
10.            if ConnSet not cycle-free then backtrack fi ; goto pop
11.       fi ;
12.       if R is a literal ∧ SubGoal = NIL then  SubGoal := R; goto col fi ;
13.  pop: (C, N) := pop ;
14.       if C = ∅ then return (ConnSet) else SubGoal := NIL ; goto row fi
15.  endproc
```

We will next augment the proof procedure CMCF with the possibility to cut connections, together with the mentioned restriction on connection making. We define for a matrix graph $(\mathcal{M}, \mathcal{S})$: A **tautological pair** in $\mathcal{M}$ is a vertical pair $K \overset{v}{\sim} \overline{K}$ of literals such that there is a column $\mathcal{C} \in \mathcal{M}$ and a row $\mathcal{R} \in \mathcal{M}$ with $K \in \mathcal{C}$ and $\overline{K} \in \mathcal{R} \in \mathcal{C}$. **Cutting** a connection $(K^1, \overline{K}^1) \in \mathcal{S}$ at a **tautological pair** $K^2 \overset{v}{\sim} \overline{K}^2$ in $\mathcal{M}$ means to create a new set of connections $\mathcal{S}^* := (\mathcal{S} \setminus \{(K^1, \overline{K}^1)\}) \cup \{(K^1, \overline{K}^2), (K^2, \overline{K}^1)\}$.

Definition 2 [CMCF$_{cutting}$ **proof procedure**]. We modify CMCF as follows:

- In the subroutine choose_column(N, SubGoal) we extend the case [2.2]:
  (SubGoal refers to an unconnected literal L^1.)
  Let us assume that we have already chosen a column $\mathcal{C}$. Just before we return $\mathcal{C}$, we insert the following check:
  > if there is an unconnected $L^2 \in \mathcal{C}$ and a $\overline{L}^2 \in \mathcal{R} \in \mathcal{C}$
  > /* I.e. the chosen column $\mathcal{C}$ contains the tautological pair $L^2 \overset{v}{\sim} \overline{L}^2$ */
  > then choose_column $(N \setminus \mathcal{C}, L^1)$ fi

- In the CMCF main procedure line 12 is replaced by:
  if R is a literal $\wedge$ SubGoal = NIL then cut_or_connect(R) fi ;
  where cut_or_connect(R) is a new subroutine which offers the alternative to solve literal R by making an ordinary connection or by connection cutting. It constitutes a *backtracking point*.

```
proc cut_or_connect (R)
        choose with K² the literal referred to by R begin
                if K² ∼ K̄² is a tautological pair
                        with an unconnected K̄² ∈ R ∈ C (and K² ∈ C unconnected)
                and there is a connection (K¹, K̄¹) ∈ ConnSet
                then ConnSet := (ConnSet \ {(K¹, K̄¹)}) ∪ {(K¹, K̄²), (K², K̄¹)}
                        if ConnSet not cycle-free then backtrack fi ;  goto pop
                fi ;
                []
                SubGoal := K² ; goto col ;
        end ;
endproc
```

[1] W. Bibel. A Deductive Solution for Plan Generation. *New Gen. Comp.*, 6:115–132, 1986.

[2] B. Fronhöfer. *The Action-as-Implication Paradigm: Formal Systems and Application*, vol. 1 of *Computer Science Monographs*. CSpress, München, Germany, 1996. (revised version of Habilitationsschrift, TU München 1994).

[3] B. Fronhöfer. Cutting Connections in Linear Connection Proofs. In *Int. Computer Symposium'96*, pp. 109–117, Kaohsiung, Taiwan, 1996. Sun Yat-Sen University.

[4] B. Fronhöfer. Plan Generation with the Linear Connection Method. *INFORMATICA, Lithuanian Academy of Sciences*, 8(1), 1997. (to appear).

[5] B. Fronhöfer. Situational Calculus, Linear Connection Proofs and STRIPS-like Planning: An Experimental Comparison. In *TABLEAUX'96*, pp. 193–209, Terrasini, Palermo, 1996, Springer, LNAI 1071.

Agents in Proactive Environments

Dov Gabbay[1] and Rolf Nossum[2] and Michael Thielscher[3]

[1] Department of Computing
Imperial College
London (UK)
[2] Department of Mathematics
Agder College
Kristiansand (Norway)
[3] Intellectics, Department of Computer Science
University of Technology
Darmstadt (Germany)

Abstract. Agents situated in proactive environments are acting autonomously while the environment is evolving alongside, whether or not the agents carry out any particular actions. A formal framework for simulating and reasoning about this generalized kind of dynamic systems is proposed. The capabilities of the agents are modeled by a set of conditional rules in a temporal-logical format. The environment itself is modeled by an independent transition relation on the state space. The temporal language is given a declarative semantics.

1 Introduction

To motivate what follows, we discuss some aspects of scenarios involving agents and their environment, both capable of changing the state of affairs of the world. The environment in these scenarios is evolving freely, whether or not there is any action on the part of the agents. This seems realistic, many real-world scenarios are like that. This contrasts with the scenario classes that have mainly been studied, where the environment is perceived as a purely reactive mechanism; e.g. in [San94] pp. 16-17 we find: "The definitions in this book will be made in such a way that if no action is invoked by the ego, then the world will advance by one single timestep while keeping all feature-values unchanged." Scenarios like the following go beyond this idealistic view of the world pausing whenever an agent decides not to act:

> An interest-bearing bank deposit accrues interest from time to time, increasing the balance of the account. The owner of the account can meanwhile make deposits and withdrawals, not necessarily synchronized with the times at which interest is added. The rate of interest on such accounts varies with the bank, with the size of the deposit, with inflation, trading balance and other economic parameters in that particular country, and ultimately on the current state of the world economy.

We propose a formal framework for modeling dynamic environments with situated agents whose actions influence the development in the course of time. We start with a brief discussion on inert vs. transient state components in Section 2. In Section 3, we introduce a temporal execution language named TEAL. It allows for the specification of both proactive environments and the effects on it caused by the performance of actions. Section 4 contains a brief discussion on the operational semantics, followed by the sketch of a declarative semantics in Section 5 on the basis of an abstract, general model structure for specifications of dynamic systems developed in [Thi95].

2 Inertia vs. transience

We take the state of affairs in the world to consist of a countable set F of atoms (called *fluents*), some of which are designated as *inert*. These are the fluents that are thought of as stable if not explicitly changed. The agent, as well as the environment, can change them. For example, the lights in a room are inert; when the switch is flicked, the status of the light changes, and remains inert until the bulb burns out, or the switch is flicked again. The lights in the stairways of some buildings are fitted with a time-delay circuit, which turns them off when they have been on for a while; this can be viewed as the environment acting on the fluent, independently of the agent that turned it on.

The non-inert fluents are *transient*, i.e. lasting for a single time unit. This is an approximation to the transient nature of events like the sound of a doorbell, or a flash of lightning.

Some transient fluents are designated as *actions*, and are carried out by agents or their environment. The flicking of a switch is an action, and therefore transient, but the status of the light, which is an effect of the flicking, is inert. Ringing a doorbell is an action, and so is setting off a lightning flash in a thunderstorm, but the latter is an action available only to the environment.

A flash of lightning can have drastic effects, which can greatly influence the further evolution of agent scenarios, for instance by rendering some courses of action impossible for some agents. Flashes of lightning are in general not provoked by any action on the part of an agent, so it would be unnatural to have a model where the environment was restricted to responding directly to actions of an agent. On the other hand, the agent can influence the evolution of the environment, for instance by erecting a lightning rod.

3 TEAL—a Temporal Executable Action Language

We proceed to give a formula language similar to that in [GN95], with an informal interpretation of some formulas as describing the actions of an agent. A precise formal semantical interpretation in terms of the logic of dynamical systems (in the sense of [Thi95]) is sketched in a later section.

The language elements are the following. Propositional fluents, denoted p, q, r, etc; classical connectives with their usual semantics, as well as temporal modalities $\bigcirc$ ("tomorrow"), $\bullet$ ("yesterday"); and actions, which are denoted by atomic terms like *flick_switch*, and ground terms like *make_deposit*(250). There is a distinguished predicate *exec*(...) on actions, generating atomic propositions from action terms.

Fluents and negated fluents are called literals. Literals are combined with connectives and modalities into formulas. Literals with 1 or more ●'s on them are called past literals, and literals with 1 or more ○'s on them are called future literals. Clauses of the form

$$past\ literals \wedge exec(a) \rightarrow future\ literals$$

are called action rules. Action rules are interpreted by evaluating the past literals, and if they are true, recording the action as having been carried out at the present time, and performing the future literals at the appropriate points in time. More precisely, a rule

$$\bigwedge_i \bullet^i c_i \wedge exec(a) \rightarrow \bigwedge_j \bigcirc^j e_j$$

is eligible at time t if $t \models \bigwedge_i \bullet^i c_i$, cfr. the operational semantics below. Whether it is actually carried out depends on constraints, and on possible conflicts with other rules.

4 Operational semantics

For simplicity we take integer time with finite past. Action rules can be executed at points of time, resulting in a change in the future state.

For the moment, we disregard possible conflicts between different rules, and concentrate on the operational semantics of executing a single rule at a certain timepoint t. Issues of competing clauses, and in the case of concurrency, conflicting ones, are dealt with elsewhere.

We rely on an underlying notion of truth of fluents at timepoints. Intuitively, we may visualize the development of the state through time as a two-dimensional matrix, indexed in one direction by fluents and in the other by time. For finite-past integer time, the matrix will be infinite in one direction, that of advancing time.

Thus, operationally speaking, an execution model is a set of fluents together with a mapping $\models$ of timepoints and fluents to truth values. For a fluent f and a timepoint t, $t \models f$ is either true or false. This matrix can be maintained as a temporal database, e.g. using the techniques of [McB93]. Formulas composed by propositional connectives or temporal modalities are interpreted by the usual inductive definitions:

- $t \models \neg\varphi$ iff not $t \models \varphi$
- $t \models \psi \rightarrow \varphi$ iff $t \models \psi$ implies $t \models \varphi$
- $t \models \bullet\varphi$ iff $t - 1 \models \varphi$
- $t \models \bigcirc\varphi$ iff $t + 1 \models \varphi$

To execute a rule at time t, the preconditions are computed against the temporal database. If they are met, the action fluent $exec(a)$ is recorded as true at time t, and the effect fluents are entered into the database at the appropriate times as indicated by their temporal prefixes.

There is no guarantee that these updates of the temporal database can be made consistently. Conflict resolution between rules that have inconsistent effects, can be dealt with along the lines of [BT97].

5 Declarative Semantics

As the basis for a declarative semantics we adopt a general abstract framework proposed in [Thi95], which provides formal means for declarative characterization of a variety of action languages. This framework is commonly referred to as "Logic of Dynamic Systems," abbreviated LoDS.

Like TEAL, LoDS grounds on the paradigm that state transitions in a dynamic system naturally occur while time passes by, and one or more agents have the possibility to direct the development of the system by executing actions. LoDS supports concurrency of actions and events, and allows to formalize nondeterministic actions and delayed effects. The semantics includes the conflict resolution strategy of [BT97].

Domain and scenario specifications in terms of LoDS are given formal notions of interpretations, models, and entailment. The mapping of TEAL programs to LoDS domains thus enables us to precisely characterize what conclusions a specification in TEAL allows. The details on this mapping can be found in [GNT97].

References

[BT97] S.-E. Bornscheuer and M. Thielscher. Explicit and implicit indeterminism: Reasoning about uncertain and contradictory specifications of dynamic systems. *Journal of Logic Programming*, 31(1–3):119–155, 1997.

[GN95] D. Gabbay and R. Nossum. A temporal executable agent language. *Workshop on Executable Temporal Logic at IJCAI'95*, Montreal, 1995.

[GNT97] D. Gabbay, R. Nossum, and M. Thielscher. Agents in Proactive Environments. Imperial College Research Report, 1997.

[McB93] P. J. McBrien. Principles of implementing historical databases in RDBMS. In M. Worboys and A. F. Grundy, editors, *Advances in Databases*, pp. 220–237, Keele, UK, 1993. Springer LNCS 696.

[San94] E. Sandewall. *Features and Fluents. Volume 1: The representation of knowledge about dynamical systems.* Oxford University Press, 1994.

[Thi95] M. Thielscher. The logic of dynamic systems. In C. S. Mellish, editor, *Proceedings of the International Joint Conference on Artificial Intelligence*, pp. 1965–1962, Montreal, 1995. Morgan Kaufmann.

Reducing Lexical Redundancy by Augmenting Conceptual Knowledge

Sven Hartrumpf and Marion Schulz

Applied Computer Science VII, University of Hagen, 58084 Hagen, Germany
{Sven.Hartrumpf,Marion.Schulz}@FernUni-Hagen.De

1 Systematic Ambiguity

Lexical (and structural) ambiguities make language as expressive as it is. Computational lexicons thus have to cope with a large amount of polysemous words. Research in the last decade (e. g., Pustejovsky (1995), Kilgarriff and Gazdar (1995)) has aimed at identifying different types of polysemy in order to capture underlying regularities. This paper deals with a subtype of regular polysemy illustrated by the following sentences:

(1) *Mrs. Richwoman donated a significant amount to the opera* (institution).
(2) *The opera* (building) *was built by a famous architect.*
(3) *The opera* (staff) *was on strike yesterday.*
(4) *The opera* (contents) *features a Russian Tsar.*
(5) *I enjoyed the opera* (performance) *very much.*
(6) *I bought the opera* (recording) *at WOM's.*

As you can see the English word *opera* stands for a range of concepts which are closely interrelated. Bierwisch (1983) introduces the name *Konzeptfamilie* (**concept family**) for this range of possible interpretations of lexemes denoting institutions or cultural performances.[1] We call this kind of polysemy **inherent polysemy** because a single occurrence of a lexeme of this special subtype of regular polysemy can simultaneously be interpreted as different **variants**[2]. A variant then, in contradistinction to a reading of other types of polysemes, need not be the exclusive interpretation of the polysemous word:

(7) *I enjoyed very much the opera* (performance/contents) *featuring a Tsar*
     yesterday in the local opera house.

A member of the concept family may be lexicalized as a separate lexeme, like the building variant of the polyseme *city council*: it is lexicalized as *town hall*. This seems to imply that the members of the family have conceptual status of their own.

The aim of this paper, however, is not to postulate (cognitively adequate) concepts. We have a rather practical goal in view: the construction of a lexicon[3] where knowledge is located at (and inherited from) the most general place in the hierarchy possible. We group concepts into a concept family whenever this family is lexicalized by an inherently polysemous lexeme. In order to minimize redundancy and maximize reuse of information, especially when building language lexicons for several languages, one should maximize the information stored in the concept lexicon and thereby minimize the information in the language lexicon.

Although concept lexicon and language lexicons are distinguished, both are unified in one (inheritance) structure. A combined treatment has been advocated for several reasons:

---

[1] Bierwisch mentions additional interpretations for *Oper* without claiming completeness.

[2] Cruse (1995) uses the term *cooperative readings* (in contrast to *antagonistic readings*).

[3] The lexicon reported here is applied for example in the NatLink subproject, which provides a natural language interface to large distributed multimedia databases in the project *Virtual Knowledge Factory* (*Virtuelle Wissensfabrik*) of the state Nordrhein-Westfalen.

no duplication of information (Cunningham and Veale, 1991, p. 987)

cognitive adequacy (Dahlgren, 1988, p. 18) argues for identifying word meaning with concept. This suggests storing concepts and lexical entries in one structure.

linguistic adequacy Linguistic and nonlinguistic knowledge should be represented on the same level (cf. Jackendoff (1983)).

In addition to these advantages, we see three other advantages:

small redundancy Combined lexicons allow to isolate information in the concept lexicon thereby removing redundancy from several language lexicons.

reuse of knowledge One can reuse the knowledge encoded in a concept lexicon across different grammar theories and across different languages.

relevance for machine translation The concepts defined in the concept lexicon can be thought of as an interlingua.

2 Lexicon Formalism

We use the lexicon formalism **IBL (inheritance-based lexicon formalism)**, which Hartrumpf (1996) has developed and implemented. IBL is heavily inspired by the lexicon formalism of the *Environnement Linguistique d'Unification* (ELU), which uses multiple default inheritance as described by Russell et al. (1992). IBL differs from ELU's formalism in four main ways: feature structures may contain complex disjunctions and complex negations; predicative constraints can use coroutining to wait for arguments to become sufficiently instantiated; a class can decide where in the feature structure to inherit information from a superclass (**locating inheritance**); IBL is strongly typed, i. e., all feature structures must have a type.

An IBL lexicon consists of type, generator and class definitions. Types are defined to type feature structures. A generator is a rule that can be used to generate a new class from another class. The most important concept are classes. A class is defined by its name, a list of direct superclasses (superclass list), a (possibly empty) main feature structure containing definite information, a (possibly empty) default feature structure containing default information, and a set of variant feature structures defining a set of mutually exclusive alternatives.

The default information coming from a superclass can be overwritten in subclasses. Inheritance conflicts are solved by prioritized inheritance which uses the concept of class precedence lists (CPLs) from the Common Lisp Object System. The information of a superclass can be inherited by a subclass at a certain position (locating inheritance); such a position can be a feature path or an element of a set value, list value or a disjunction. The information inherited cannot be restricted or selected because this contradicts the principle of data encapsulation and may lead to unwieldy and poorly structured lexicons. To calculate the extension of a lexical class (a class describing a single lexeme), one adds to it the information from main/variant feature structures of its superclasses by unification and the information from default feature structures of its superclasses by default unification.

3 Combining Concept Lexicon and Language Lexicon(s)

We distinguish the **concept lexicon** and language-specific lexicons (**language lexicons**) and call the combination of a concept lexicon with a language lexicon a **combined lexicon**. Both parts use the inheritance formalism described in section 2. This allows a seamless integration of conceptual and linguistic knowledge. To achieve this integration, lexemes inherit from concepts all the information that is language-independent.

A class describing a single lexeme adds the language-specific information by inheriting from classes higher in the language lexicon hierarchy and by stating the lexeme's idiosyncratic properties like the base form.

The basic categories for describing concepts are taken from the knowledge representation language MESNET (Multi-layered Extended Semantic NETworks, cf. Helbig and Schulz (1997)). A concept is described by an IBL class containing a feature structure of type *concept*. It specifies the concept's semantics, information about semantic argument structure and further compatible semantic relations with the help of MESNET's classificatory means. Using IBL's multiple inheritance with defaults, the concept lexicon is built as an inheritance hierarchy of classes.

A lexeme is described by an HPSG-like feature structure. Morphological (feature MORPH), syntactic (feature SYN), and semantic/subcategorization information (feature SEMSEL) is distinguished. The latter, which is central for the purpose of our paper, is a set-valued feature whose elements have type *semsel*. This type is a subtype of *concept* as a lexeme inherits semantic information from concept classes and might have additional semantic features under the feature SEMSEL. This feature has sets as values in order to allow all readings of a polyseme to be stored with small redundancy; common information under the features MORPH and SYN is shared and only one feature structure is needed to represent a polyseme.

Due to the thorough definition of types for concepts and features, combing concepts and lexemes is straightforward: The concept lexicon is an inheritance hierarchy defining concept classes by feature structures of type *concept*; the language lexicon is an inheritance hierarchy which embeds by locating inheritance information from the concept lexicon as elements of the set-valued feature SEMSEL.

4 Inherent Polysemy in Combined Lexicons

The definition of a concept is a value of type concept: for a concept family, it is a disjunctive one; for all other concepts, a nondisjunctive one. In the language lexicon, an "ordinary" polyseme (one not allowing switching between readings) has more than one element in the set value for feature SEMSEL (Each element can be a disjunctive value introduced for a concept family on the conceptual level.); all other lexemes have just one element under SEMSEL.

Bierwisch (1983) distinguishes two *Unterfamilien* (subfamilies) for the German noun *Oper*. They relate to a subconcept of *institution-f* and a subconcept of *performance-f*, respectively. In our opinion, both subconcepts constitute independent concepts that happen to be lexicalized by the same lexeme in German (and some other languages). This lexeme (an "ordinary" polyseme) has two readings (corresponding to the concepts *opera-institution-f* and *opera-performance-f*) which are an inherent polyseme each.

The concept *opera-performance-f* is defined by locating inheritance forming a disjunctive value with three disjunction elements inherited from *opera-contents*, *opera-recording*, and *opera-performance* (similarly for *opera-institution-f*). In addition, the concept *opera-performance-f* is defined by the superconcept *performance-f*, which has three more general variants, and is refined by locating inheritance from those more specific variants mentioned above, which are all subconcepts of the corresponding variants of *performance-f*.

A lexeme of a language is described by its idiosyncratic properties (base form etc.) and is linked to a concept by inheriting from the corresponding concept class in the concept lexicon hierarchy.

Figure 1 shows the basic structure of the lexicon information for the German noun *Oper* which is derived by inheritance. The feature SEMSEL has two set elements, each consisting of three disjunction elements (only their origin, not their content is shown). The advantage of small redundancy becomes evident if one compares the feature structure in figure 1 (which is much larger if fully shown) with the three-line definition of the lexicon entry for *Oper*:

word "Oper"
    inherit ((opera-institution-f (semsel 1)) (opera-performance-f (semsel 2)) n-f)
    main ((morph base) "Oper"

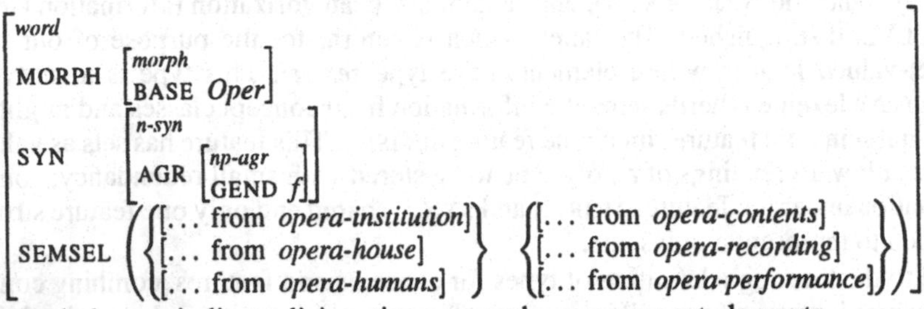

$$
\begin{bmatrix}
word & \\
\text{MORPH} & \begin{bmatrix} morph \\ \text{BASE } Oper \end{bmatrix} \\
\text{SYN} & \begin{bmatrix} n\text{-}syn \\ \text{AGR} \begin{bmatrix} np\text{-}agr \\ \text{GEND } f \end{bmatrix} \end{bmatrix} \\
\text{SEMSEL} & \left(\left\{ \begin{matrix} [\dots \text{ from } opera\text{-}institution] \\ [\dots \text{ from } opera\text{-}house] \\ [\dots \text{ from } opera\text{-}humans] \end{matrix} \right\} \left\{ \begin{matrix} [\dots \text{ from } opera\text{-}contents] \\ [\dots \text{ from } opera\text{-}recording] \\ [\dots \text{ from } opera\text{-}performance] \end{matrix} \right\} \right)
\end{bmatrix}
$$

Note: Curly braces indicate disjunctions, parentheses group set elements.

Fig. 1: Basic Structure of the Lexicon Information for *Oper* Derived by Inheritance

References

Bierwisch, Manfred (1983). Semantische und konzeptuelle Repräsentation lexikalischer Einheiten. In *Untersuchungen zur Semantik* (Edited by Ružička, Rudolf; Motsch, Wolfgang), studia grammatica XXII, pp. 61–99. Akademie-Verlag, Berlin.

Cruse, D. A. (1995). Polysemy and related phenomena from a cognitive linguistic point of view. In *Computational Lexical Semantics* (Edited by Saint-Dizier, Patrick; Viegas, Evelyne), pp. 33–49. Cambridge University Press, Cambridge, England.

Cunningham, Pádraig; Veale, Tony (1991). Organizational issues arising from the integration of the lexicon and concept network in a text understanding system. In *Proceedings of the 12th International Joint Conference on Artificial Intelligence*, volume 2, pp. 986–991.

Dahlgren, Kathleen (1988). *Naive Semantics for Natural Language Understanding*. Kluwer Academic Publishers, Boston.

Hartrumpf, Sven (1996). *Redundanzarme Lexika durch Vererbung*. Master's thesis, Universität Koblenz-Landau, Koblenz.

Helbig, Hermann; Schulz, Marion (1997). Knowledge representation with MESNET: A multi-layered extended semantic network. In *Working Notes of the 1997 AAAI Spring Symposium on Ontological Engineering*, pp. 64–72.

Jackendoff, Ray (1983). *Semantics and Cognition*. MIT Press, Cambridge, Massachusetts.

Kilgarriff, Adam; Gazdar, Gerald (1995). Polysemous relations. In *Grammar and Meaning: Essays in Honour of Sir John Lyons* (Edited by Palmer, F. R.), pp. 1–25. Cambridge University Press, Cambridge, England.

Pustejovsky, James (1995). *The Generative Lexicon*. Number 13 in CSLI Lecture Notes. MIT Press, Cambridge, Massachusetts.

Russell, Graham; Ballim, Afzal; Carroll, John; Warwick-Armstrong, Susan (1992). A practical approach to multiple default inheritance for unification based lexicons. *Computational Linguistics*, 18(3):311–337.

A Graphical User Interface for an ECG Classifier System

Jörg Nilson[1] and Gabriella Kókai[2]

[1] Department of Computer Science, Programming Languages
Friedrich-Alexander-University of Erlangen-Nürnberg
Martensstr. 3, D-91058 Erlangen, Germany
e-mail: nilson@informatik.uni-erlangen.de
[2] Institute of Informatics, József Attila University
Árpád tér 2, H-6720 Szeged, Hungary
e-mail: kokai@inf.u-szeged.hu

Abstract. The PECG system merges an ECG classifier program (implemented in Prolog) with the IDTS algorithmic debugger module. If the ECG classifier cannot analyze the input, the built-in IDTS (Interactive Diagnosis, Testing and Slicing) debugger will help to find the location of the error. This paper presents a prototypical graphical user interface (GUI) of PECG and its merging with the ECG classifier program that gives the user more information about the state of the debugging process. It provides a more user-friendly environment of the system.

1 Introduction

In the papers [2] and [3] a system (called PECG) was presented for the classification of ECG wave-forms. This system is based on an attribute grammar approach of ECG analysis introduced by Skordalakis et al. [8].

Skordalakis's system can classify the recognized ECG waveforms according to certain synthesized attributes. It contains a preprocessing part which produces a linguistic representation from an ECG signal. This linguistic representation is used as the input for the PECG system.

The basic idea of PECG, introduced in [2], is to merge Skordalakis' ECG classifier program (implemented in Prolog) with the IDTS algorithmic debugger module [1]. This integrated tool can recognize the necessity of any modification in the classifier program. If the system cannot analyze the input the built-in IDTS (Interactive Diagnosis, Testing and Slicing) debugger will help to find the false or missing clause.

Initially a simple textual user interface of PECG was given. In this paper we present a Graphical User Interface (GUI) for the ECG system. This GUI assists the user with the identification of buggy clauses in the classifier program. By using this interface the functions of the IDTS can be easily invoked. Furthermore, the user can directly follow the debugging process by following the graphical representation of the proof tree. During the debugging the IDTS system asks the user whether the evaluated clauses are correct. To answer these questions would be very difficult (almost impossible) without an analyzation of the graphical representation of the sub-wave-forms. The GUI of the PECG system contains a drawing tool which offers a display of an analyzation of the corresponding part of the ECG wave-form.

In the remainder of this paper first a brief overview of the PECG will be given. Section 3 contains the description of the function supported by GUI. Finally in Section 4 a summary and comments on future work are given.

2 The PECG system

This is a short overview of the PECG system. A more detailed description can be found in [2]. The structure of the system can be seen in Figure 1.

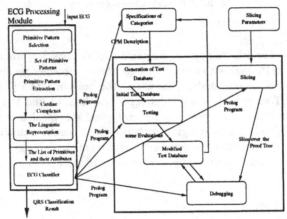

Fig. 1. The structure of the PECG system

The main parts coming from the PECG are the following:

- *the ECG processing module:* this part of the system uses a syntactic approach to recognize an electrocardiographic pattern. In this part Skordalaki's work was used to decompose the waveform, to select the peaks and to present the waveform as a string from an alphabet. The classifier module recognizes the ECG waveforms from their linguistic representation.

- *the IDTS module:* this part is an interactive debugging and testing tool that is based on the Shapiro's Interactive Diagnosis Algorithm [7] , Category Partition Testing Method (CPM) [5] and a slicing technique [6]. It can be divided into three submodules. The *test database* module generates the initial test database from a CPM specification. In the *testing* part a predicate can be chosen and the user can give a representing element of the testframe generated for this predicate. Then he or she can decide whether, for the given input, the output is correct or not. The *debugging* part is based on the idea that if the program has already been tested then the test results can be directly applied without asking the user *difficult* questions. In addition, a slicing method is used, that is based on a *program dependence graph*, to compute which parts of the program are relevant for the search, thus further improving bug localisation.

3   The graphical user interface for PECG: PECG-GUI

In this section the graphical user interface, PECG-GUI will be presented. The New Graphical User Interface Developer's Environment (NGUIDE) was used for programming PECG-GUI. More details about NGUIDE can be found in [4]. The complete PECG-GUI with all trees, browsers and editors can be seen in Fig. 2.

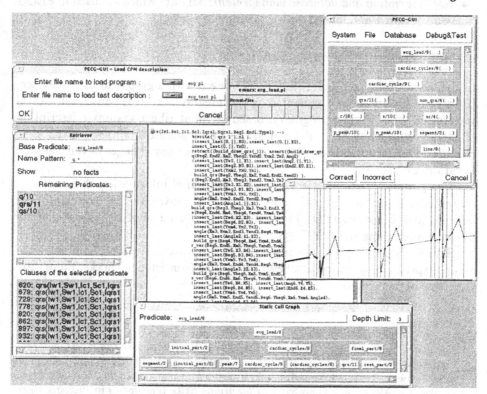

Fig. 2. The complete PECG-GUI with all trees, browsers and an editor

The GUI supports the following activities

- *clickable execution trees:* In each step of the debugging process the GUI labels one node of the proof tree, the intended behaviour of which the debugger needs to know, to go on with the debugging process. Nodes can be hidden and extended, which is a very important feature of the GUI because the ECG classifier uses a lot of parameters. The user can answer by pressing one of the presented buttons *correct*, *incorrect* or *cancel*. To help the user in the decision the currently recognized part of the ECG waveform is displayed in another window as bold outline. This process can be executed repeatedly until the error is located. On the other hand the user can tail the control of the bug location.

- *source code browsing:* The *static call graph* shows which predicates could be invoked by a given procedure. With the help of this window a static program structure can be visualized as a complement to the dynamic proof

tree window. *The information retrieval display* shows the line number and the clauses matching the pattern selected by the user.

- *editor interface:* By pressing a mouse button over a node of the proof tree an editor window opens and displays the part of the Prolog program which corresponds to the node, and the source code can be edited. After saving the changes in the program it can be debugged with PECG again.
- *test description and database management:* All data which are used in PECG can be stored and loaded with a few mouse clicks.

4   Conclusion, Further Work

In this paper the extension of the PECG system with a graphical user interface, the PECG-GUI has been presented. This integrated system can classify ECG waveforms. The classifier program is based on an attribute grammar description of ECG published by Skordalakis et al [8]. The system contains the IDTS algorithmic debugger module which can realize whether any changes in the classifier program are necessary.

The graphical user interface provides additional information that makes it easier for the user to answer the questions and to control the debugging process. We consider a user-friendly graphical interface to be of great importance for (successfully) using the PECG system.

Several implementation details could be improved. We are planning to develop a special support for test description files (consistency checks, more intuitive way of definition).

References

1. Horváth, T., Gyimóthy, T., Alexin, T., Kocsis, F.: *Interactive Diagnosis and Testing Logic Programs* in Proc. of the Third Symposium on Programming Languages and Software Tools, ed. Mati Tombak, Kääriku Estonia August 23-24. (1993) 34–46
2. Kókai, G., Alexin, Z.,Gyimóthy, T.: *Classifying ECG Waveforms in Prolog* in Proc. of the Fourth International Conference on The Practical Application of PROLOG (PAP96) London, United Kingdom April 23-25, (1996) 193–221
3. Kókai, G., Alexin, Z., Gyimóthy, T.: *Analyzing and Learning ECG Waveforms* in Proc. of The Sixth International Workshop on Inductive Logic Programming (ILP'96)Stockholm, Sweden 28-30 August, 1996 152-171
4. Nilson J.: NGUIDE Programmierhandbuch. Department of Computer Science, Programming Languages, University Erlangen Nürnberg, 1997.
5. Ostrand, T. J., Balker, M. J.: *The Category-Partition Method for Specifying and Generating Functional Tests* CACM 31:6 June (1988) 676–686
6. Paakki, J., Gyimóthy, T., Horváth T.: *Effective Algorithmic Debugging for Inductive Logic Programming* in Proc of the Fourth International Workshop on Inductive Logic Programming (ILP-94) Bad Honnef/Bonn Germany September 12-14 (1994) 175-194
7. Shapiro, E. Y.: *Algorithmic Program Debugging* MIT Press (1983)
8. Skordalakis, E.: *ECG Analysis in Syntactic and Structural Pattern Recognition Theory and Applications* ed. Bunke, H. and Sanfeliu, A. World Scientific (1990) 499–533

Expert System in Additional Finishing

N. Stojanović[1], Lj. Stoiljković[1], D. Milenović[1], V. Stoiljković[2]

[1] Faculty of Electronic Engineering, Beogradska 14, 18000 Niš, Yugoslavia
[2] Faculty of Mechanical Engineering, Beogradska 14, 18000 Niš, Yugoslavia

Abstract. Chemical technology, additional finishing, represents a very important phase in textile industry. With a tendency of achieving specific requirements which modern trends demand from textiles (appearance, touch, shine, etc.) as from an input and almost the most important component in the process of getting clothing articles by additional finishing of textiles, such effects can be achieved so as to make the final product of a higher quality and concurrence on the market. In this paper we present a novel approach to solve that problem: simulation of additional textile finishing by using the KB system. Using the shells of expert systems, created by the same group authors, we developed an expert system for the generation of new technology additional finishing of textiles and on the basis of the already existing technologies. The system has been tested on a greater number of famous technologies and it was very successful.

1 Quality Generation in Additional Finishing

The chemical technology of additional finishing represents a very important phase in the textile industry [1]. The additional finishing itself comprises a great number of operations starting from the primary processing (scorching, boiling, bleaching, etc.) by which impurities and other substances added to it in the previous phases are removed from a material, through dyeing and printing by which the material is given a desired color, and up to appurtenance, the phase of the final processing by which the most sophisticated users' requirements are satisfied.

A problem in generating technology for a particular product quality in the additional finishing is that knowledge about complex operation's dependencies is almost always the property of technicians who work on particular machines, while a technological sequence of operations is decided upon by a small number of experts from the development sector. Another problem is in the very complexity of operations so that the planning of new technologies mostly requires a lot of experiments, including wrong steps.

It is for this reason that the problem of generating quality in additional finishing is approached from the standpoint of artificial intelligence and use of experts systems.

2 Basic Characteristics of The System

2.1 Knowledge Base

The central (basic) object of knowledge in the observed field is a technological operation which is described by its name and a set of parameters affecting its flow, as well as by values of these parameters (for instance, what should be defined in the textile dyeing operation is temperature as well as pressure in the dyeing chamber, velocity of the textile's motion, sort of color and concentration of dyeing agents, etc.). The links between two operations can be reduced to defining the operation as well as the conditions under which it is performed after the ongoing operation has been completed (for instance, dyeing can be followed by neutralization or washing or nothing else - this is defined by the rules).

The structure (package) of knowledge shows that the most natural structure for presenting knowledge is a system of frames with two kinds of frames defined, the frames of "operation" and the frames of "relations" which are mutually connected through the slots "relations-operations" within the frame "operations".

The conditions under which two operations are linked are described by the "If-Then Rules" (their format is enlarged with the following attributes: 1.Reliability Factor, 2.Rule Priority, 3.Number of Fulfillments - memorizes the number of times a particular rule has been fulfilled and 4. Previous State Saving - memorizes in unknown rules which parts are correct and which are unknown) stored in the frame "relations" so that they actually describe a procedural knowledge component in the system; declarative knowledge is stored in the attributes' slots of the frame "operations".

An explicit gain from such a way of presenting technological knowledge (uniformity of each technological operation, uniformity of relations' presentation, etc.) is added by implicit improvement provided by the frame system. Namely, thanks to the possibility of inherent slots it is possible to define a certain hierarchy of operations by integrating congenial operations, defined by experts as essentially different, by means of representants at a higher and more abstract level [2, 3].

2.2 Working Memory

Due to system' funcionality, format of the variables making up a working memory is also reduced to the frame structure, with following attributes: 1."MultiValues" denotes the possibility that a variable may have many values at the same time, 2. "User'sInput" states that the value of a variable is directly determined by the user, 3."Determines" determines what variables depend on its values and , 4. The procedure "DetermineValue" represents a procedure by which, on the basis of variables determining it, its value is found.

This structure of the rules requires a backward chaining in determining the values of the derived variables in the working memory, as explained later on. Otherwise, each variable can be found, in the rules or even in the working memory, in an affirmative or negative form.

2.3 Inference Engine

Due to complex relations which exist within the frame systems inference process is realized through combination of backward and forward chaining [4]. Since the aim of this system is to generate a particular technology which consists of an ordered set of operations coming after one another and completing each other and since the user expects such an inference-result, it is not possible to perform inference-making by the backward chaining method (starting from goal parameters and arriving at input values) since there is no goal parameter which should be determined but the inference is done by the forward chaining method (initial values of the input parameters, for example material=cotton, color=white, are introduced and on this basis a choice is made of a technical operation to be performed before proceeding to determination of the subsequent operation, etc.).

Surely, in determining value of some unknown variable (needed for conclusion-making due to examination of accuracy of a certain rule), the goal is known so that an appropriate inference strategy is used, namely, the backward chaining, which is automatically called when a need emerges in the external inference for determining some variable.

Inference Acceleration The presented system is designed for an off-line resolving of the problem of generating a new technology in the additional finishing sector and regarding this aspect, the question of the system reply is of secondary importance. The basic acceleration is achieved by reducing the space for the search of the rules, that is, by limiting a set of rules that can be examined at a moment, grouping them according exsisting textil technologies. In the same way, in order to avoid unnecessary matching of the patterns which have already been examined within the frame of one rule, the saving of the previous state of the rule is done, that is, of accuracy by premises. The inference acceleration is also done by reducing the space of the search for unknown rules in such a way that the user is asked only about the values of those unknown variables which directly affect momentous inference-making and for this he finds the smallest necessary set of inference variables.

Conflict Resolution A problem in the systems like this one, is to solve the situations when inference-making can be continued through a greater number of rules. There are various strategies of the conflict resolution in this system: 1. Rule's priority, 2. Rule's specifity (number of AND parts in premise), 3. Rule's strenght (number (frequency) of the conditions' fulfillment), 4. Rule's reliability factor and 5. Optional choice.

3 System Implementation

The whole system has been developed in the data base MS ACCESS 2.0 while the inference system is realized in the same tool since the operation velocity, as the only critical element in the data base, was not a limiting factor. The data base contains about 700 complex "If-Then" rules. They are divided into three large groups related to the structure of a material being processed such as textiles, knitting and weaving whose inferences go separately. A minimal computer configuration for the system operation is PC 386 with 8 MB RAM and the operational system Windows 3.1.

4 Conclusion

In this paper we gave general overview of expert system for production planning (system generates a list of technologies operations to fulfill user's orders). Even the system is in testing phase, principally knowledge base refinement, the first results pointed justifiableness of such system's development. The most important is system's accuracy, which is in this development phase expected (small database), if consider very long and extensive knowledge acquisition process. As system' accuracy we can observe possibility to refine knowledge base, while system automatically offers knowledge base parts (production rules), which are lacked (by using this KB refinement tool, knowledge engineer is delivered from very long and sometimes boring knowledge base validation process) [5, 6]. As a most significant system possibility we found user's question "What If", which enables experimentation with possible technologies (such manipulation is impossible with conventional approach - experimentation in laboratory). This is realized through the possibility given to the user to go back, in the course of inference, one or more steps backwards and to continue inferring from there (back-tracking). New knowledge extraction possibility is not test in proper way still, while testing phase and phase of extra knowledge acquisition continue (knowledge extracting from current knowledge base is possibility to find solution for previous unseen-untested values of input variables). However, some initial generalizations, like derived inner variables "containing", point their relevance.

Due to approach generality, it is easy to conclude that presented system is universal approach in solving similar problems in each industry.

References

1. Vachtsevanos G., Dorrity, J. L., Kim, S. and Kumer, A.: Advanced Application of Statistical and Fuzzy Control to Textile Processes. IEEE Transactions on Industry Applications Vol **30** (1994) no. 3
2. Jackson, P.: Expert Systems. Addison Wesly Publishing Company (1989)
3. Stojanović, N., Stoiljković, Lj., Stoiljković, V., Mitić, I.: Quality Generation in Finishing by Expert System Knowledge Acquisition and Representation. Proceedings of the First International YOSQ Congress, Belgrade (1996) 543–548
4. Neches, R., MacGregor, R.: CLASP: Integrating Term Subsumption Systems and Production System. IEEE TKDE, Vol. **30** no. 1 25–32
5. Pazzani, M. J., Brunk, C. A.: Detecting and Correcting Rule-Based Expert System. Knowledge Acquisition **3** 157–173
6. Sleemen, D.,Craw, S.: Knowledge-based refinement of Knowledge Based System. Technical Report **95/2** (1995) University of Aberdeen

Reasoning About Exceptions*
(extended abstract)

Leendert W.N. van der Torre[1] and Yao-Hua Tan[2]

[1] Max-Planck-Institut für Informatik
Im Stadtwald, D-66123 Saarbrücken, Deutschland
torre@mpi-sb.mpg.de

[2] EURIDIS, Erasmus University Rotterdam
P.O. Box 1738, 3000 DR Rotterdam, The Netherlands
ytan@euridis.fbk.eur.nl

Abstract. In this paper we analyze the conditional logic approach to default logic, the logic that formalizes reasoning about default assumptions. Conditional logic is a popular framework to formalize defeasible reasoning. The conditional sentence "if β (the *antecedent* or condition) then by default α (the *consequent* or conclusion)" is represented in this framework by the formula $\beta > \alpha$, where '$>$' is some kind of implication of conditional logic. In this paper different usages of preference orderings for defeasible conditional logics are discussed. The different usages, so-called minimizing and ordering, are represented by different modal operators. Each operator validates different inference rules. Hence, the combination of different modal operators imposes restrictions on the proof theory of the logic. The restriction discussed in this paper is that a proof rule can be blocked in a derivation due to the fact that another proof rule has already been used earlier in the derivation. We call this the two-phase approach in the proof theory.

1 Introduction

Consider the following typical example of reasoning about exceptions. At working days I normally leave my home at 8:00. If I do not leave my home at 8:00 (the exception), then normally I am ill. If I do not leave my home at 8:00 and I am not ill, then normally I go to the dentist. Etc etc. This kind of reasoning structures has been ignored in default logic literature, and most default logics do not deal satisfactorily with it. This is a consequence of the fact that they focus on the normal cases neglecting the exceptional cases. For example, consider the defaults $a > p$, $\neg a > \neg p$ and $(\neg a \wedge p) > \neg q$. The popular System Z [Pea90] derives $((a \wedge \neg p) \vee (\neg a \wedge p \wedge q)) > a$. If only the worst states are possible, then a is preferred because if a then only one rule is falsified (rank 1) and if $\neg a$ then two rules are falsified (rank 2). However, this violation-counting is highly counterintuitive, because the violation of the first default may be more exceptional than the violation of the latter two defaults.

* This research was partially supported by the ESPRIT III Basic Research Project No.6156 DRUMS II and the ESPRIT III Basic Research Working Group No.8319 MODELAGE.

We argue that two phases are necessary to formalize reasoning about exceptions, and therefore also to formalize reasoning about default assumptions. A sequencing in derivations is rather unnatural and cumbersome from a proof-theoretic point of view. Surprisingly, the two-phase approach can be obtained very intuitively from a semantic point of view, by combining two usages of a preference ordering in a preference-based semantics. For the two usages we define two different types of conditionals, which we call phase-1 and phase-2 conditionals. Phase-1 conditionals are formalized by strong preferences and evaluated by what we call *Ordering*, a process in which the whole ordering is used to evaluate a formula. Phase-2 conditionals are formalized by weak preferences and evaluated by what we call *Minimizing*, in which the ordering is used to select the minimal elements that satisfy a formula. In semantic terms the two-phase approach simply means that first a preference ordering has to be constructed by ordering worlds, and subsequently the constructed ordering can be used for minimization.

2 Exception logic

Credulous defaults are formalized in the normal modal logic S4. As is well-known, the normal modal system S4 contains the two axioms **T:** $\Box \alpha \to \alpha$ and **4:** $\Box \alpha \to \Box\Box \alpha$, and is characterized by reflexive transitive orderings (partial pre-orderings). We define phase-1 defaults as strong preferences (new) and phase-2 defaults as weak preferences [Bou94]. Intuitively, the formula $\Box p$ can be read as 'it is not more exceptional (at least as normal) that p.'

Definition 1. Credulous phase-1 and phase-2 defaults 'if β then by default α,' written as $\beta >_1 \alpha$ and $\beta >_2 \alpha$ respectively, are defined in S4 as follows.

$$\beta >_1 \alpha =_{def} \Box((\beta \wedge \alpha) \to \Box(\beta \to \alpha)) \wedge \Diamond(\beta \wedge \alpha)$$
$$\beta >_2 \alpha =_{def} \Diamond(\beta \wedge \Box(\beta \to \alpha))$$

Intuitively, a phase-1 default $\beta >_1 \alpha$ expresses a strict preference of all $\beta \wedge \alpha$ over $\beta \wedge \neg\alpha$. However, a preference of all $\beta \wedge \alpha$ worlds to every $\beta \wedge \neg\alpha$ world would be much too strong, because two independent defaults $\top >_1 \alpha_1$ and $\top >_1 \alpha_2$ would not have a model containing $\neg\alpha_1 \wedge \alpha_2$ and $\alpha_1 \wedge \neg\alpha_2$ worlds. The following proposition shows that this preference is represented by the negative condition that no $\beta \wedge \neg\alpha$ is preferred to a $\beta \wedge \alpha$.[1] The phase-2 default $\beta >_2 \alpha$ is true iff α is true in an equivalence class of most preferred β worlds of the model, or it eventually becomes true in an infinite descending chain of β worlds [Bou94].

Proposition 2. *Let $M = \langle W, \leq, V \rangle$ be a Kripke model. We have $M, w \models \beta >_1 \alpha$ iff for all $w_1, w_2 \in W$ such that $w_1 \leq w$, $w_2 \leq w$, $M, w_1 \models \beta \wedge \alpha$ and $M, w_2 \models \beta \wedge \neg\alpha$, it is true that $w_2 \not\leq w_1$, and there is such a world w_1. We have $M, w \models \beta >_2 \alpha$ iff there*

---

[1] In this paper we do not consider facts, we only consider the derivation of conditionals from conditionals. If we also consider facts, then we have to define the conditional in a bimodal logic by $\beta >_1 \alpha =_{def} \Box_2((\beta \wedge \alpha) \to \Box_1(\beta \to \alpha)) \wedge \Diamond_2(\beta \wedge \alpha)$ where the two modal operators are related by $\Box_2\alpha \to \Box_1\alpha$. Due to space limitations, we cannot discuss this kind of complications in this paper.

is a world $w_1 \in W$ with $w_1 \leq w$ and $M, w_1 \models \beta \wedge \alpha$ such that for all worlds $w_2 \in W$ with $w_2 \leq w$ and $M, w_2 \models \beta \wedge \neg \alpha$, it is true that $w_2 \not\leq w_1$.

The following proposition gives several properties of the phase-1 and phase-2 defaults. In this paper we are interested in **RMon**, **OR** and **RW**.

Proposition 3. *The logic S4 has the following theorems.*

> **RMon** $(\beta_1 >_1 \alpha \wedge \Diamond(\beta_1 \wedge \beta_2 \wedge \alpha)) \rightarrow (\beta_1 \wedge \beta_2) >_1 \alpha$
> **RAnd** $(\beta >_1 \alpha_1 \wedge \beta >_1 \alpha_2 \wedge \Diamond(\beta \wedge \alpha_1 \wedge \alpha_2)) \rightarrow \beta >_1 (\alpha_1 \wedge \alpha_2)$
> **COR** $(\beta >_1 \alpha_1 \wedge \beta >_1 \alpha_2) \rightarrow \beta >_1 (\alpha_1 \vee \alpha_2)$
> **Trans'** $(\gamma >_1 \beta \wedge \beta >_1 \alpha \wedge \Diamond(\alpha \wedge \beta \wedge \gamma)) \rightarrow \gamma >_1 (\alpha \wedge \beta)$
> **OR$_\exists$** $(\beta_1 >_2 \alpha \wedge \beta_2 >_2 \alpha) \rightarrow (\beta_1 \vee \beta_2) >_2 \alpha$
> **RW$_\exists$** $\beta >_2 \alpha_1 \rightarrow \beta >_2 (\alpha_1 \vee \alpha_2)$
> **Rel$_\exists$** $\beta >_1 \alpha \rightarrow \beta >_2 \alpha$

The logic S4 does not have the following theorems.

> **OR** $(\beta_1 >_1 \alpha \wedge \beta_2 >_1 \alpha) \rightarrow (\beta_1 \vee \beta_2) >_1 \alpha$
> **RW** $\beta >_1 \alpha_1 \rightarrow \beta >_1 (\alpha_1 \vee \alpha_2)$
> **NC** $\neg(\beta >_1 \alpha \wedge \beta >_1 \neg \alpha)$
> **Mon$_\exists$** $\beta_1 >_2 \alpha \rightarrow (\beta_1 \wedge \beta_2) >_2 \alpha$
> **And$_\exists$** $(\beta >_2 \alpha_1 \wedge \beta >_2 \alpha_2) \rightarrow \beta >_2 (\alpha_1 \wedge \alpha_2)$
> **NC$_\exists$** $\neg(\beta >_2 \alpha \wedge \beta >_2 \neg \alpha)$

We now proceed to explain the two-phase approach to defeasible reasoning. The two phases in a defeasible logic correspond to the two types of defaults $>_1$ and $>_2$. Semantically, the first phase corresponds to ordering ($>_1$) and the second phase to minimizing ($>_2$). From a proof theoretic point of view, the first phase corresponds to applying valid inferences of $>_1$ like RMON, RAND etc, and the second phase corresponds to applying valid inferences of $>_2$ like OR and RW.

3 Examples

The two-phase reasoning is illustrated by the following two examples. They illustrate two causes of the distinction between the two phases: the disjunction rule and right weakening.

Example 4 (Disjunction rule). Let $S = \{a >_1 p, \neg a >_1 p\}$ be an S4 theory. The application of RMON is blocked after OR has been applied. We have $S \not\models \top >_1 p$ and $S \models \top >_2 p$, $S \not\models (a \leftrightarrow p) >_1 p$ and $S \not\models (a \leftrightarrow p) >_2 p$. The derivable $\top >_2 p$ expresses that p is true in the most normal world. It cannot be used to derive the counterintuitive $(a \leftrightarrow p) >_2 p$, because $>_2$ does not have monotony. In fact, the model represented below shows that we can have the opposite $M \models (a \leftrightarrow p) >_1 \neg p$. This figure should be read as follows. Every circle is a nonempty set of worlds, satisfying the propositions written in the circle. The arrows represent strict accessibility. The transitive closure is left implicit.

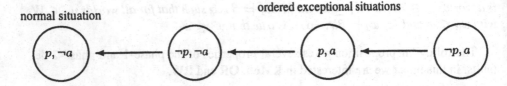

normal situation   ordered exceptional situations

Example 5 (Weakening). Let $S = \{\top >_1 (a \vee p), \top >_1 \neg a\}$ be an S4 theory, where $\neg a$ does not entail $\neg p$. The application of RMON is blocked after RW has been applied. We have $S \models \Diamond(\neg a \wedge p)$, $S \models \top >_1 (\neg a \wedge p)$ and $S \models \top >_2 (\neg a \wedge p)$, $S \not\models \top >_1 p$ and $S \models \top >_2 p$. The crucial observation is that $a >_2 p$ is not entailed by S, as represented by the blocked derivations below. A dashed line represents a blocked derivation step.

$$\cfrac{\cfrac{\top >_1 (a \vee p) \quad \top >_1 \neg a}{\top >_1 (\neg a \wedge p)} \text{ RAND}}{\cfrac{ (\text{RW})}{\cfrac{\top >_1 p}{\cfrac{a >_1 p}{a >_2 p} \text{ REL}} \text{ RMON}}}$$

$$\cfrac{\cfrac{\cfrac{\top >_1 (a \vee p) \quad \top >_1 \neg a}{\top >_1 (\neg a \wedge p)} \text{ RAND}}{\cfrac{\top >_2 (\neg a \wedge p)}{\top >_2 p} \text{ RW}} \text{ REL}}{a >_2 p (\text{RMON})}$$

$$\cfrac{\cfrac{\cfrac{\top >_1 (a \vee p) \quad \top >_1 \neg a}{\top >_1 (\neg a \wedge p)} \text{ RAND}}{\cfrac{ (\text{RMON})}{\cfrac{a >_1 (\neg a \wedge p)}{\cfrac{a >_2 (\neg a \wedge p)}{a >_2 p} \text{ RW}} \text{ REL}}}}{}$$

First of all, $a >_2 p$ is not entailed by S via $\top >_1 p$, because $\top >_1 p$ is not entailed by S. Secondly, $a >_2 p$ is not entailed by S via $\top >_2 p$ either, because $>_2$ does not have monotony at all. Thirdly, it is not entailed by S via $a >_1 (\neg a \wedge p)$, because $a >_1 (\neg a \wedge p)$ is not entailed by $\top >_1 (\neg a \wedge p)$ due to the restriction in RMON. A typical model of S is represented below.

exceptional situations

normal situation

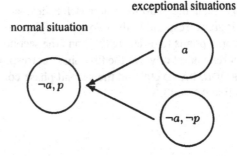

The inference patterns OR and RW are standard properties of the Kraus-Lehmann-Magidor paradigm [KLM90]. However, the last two examples show that they are not as unproblematic as they seem at first sight, because the properties conflict with monotony.

References

[Bou94] C. Boutilier. Conditional logics of normality: a modal approach. *Artificial Intelligence*, 68:87–154, 1994.

[KLM90] S. Kraus, D. Lehmann, and M. Magidor. Nonmonotonic reasoning, preferential models and cumulative logics. *Artificial Intelligence*, 44:167–207, 1990.

[Pea90] J. Pearl. System Z: a natural ordering of defaults with tractable applications to default reasoning. In *Proceedings of the TARK'90*, San Mateo, 1990. Morgan Kaufmann.

Learning and Interpretation of the Layout of Structured Documents

Hanno Walischewski

Daimler Benz, Research and Technology, 89013 Ulm, Germany
walischewski@dbag.ulm.DaimlerBenz.com

Abstract. In this paper, a qualitative representation for the layout of structured documents is presented, which is established by the means of supervised learning from a labeled training set of documents. For this formal representation, an inference algorithm has been developed, adopted from error tolerant subgraph isomorphism, which assigns logic labels to layout objects of a test document.

1 Introduction

In spite of the *paperless office*, nowadays business communication still relys on paper- and faxdocuments. In order to integrate these documents and the information enclosed into the electronic world, systems are under developement extracting this information automatically (see [3, 4, 5]). Most of the documents exhibit a certain geometric structure given by convenience or by norms. Aim of project READ[1] is to develop new concepts for the automatic acquisition of knowledge and to improve the process of interpreting spatial documents.

This paper describes a formal representation used to represent single documents as well as classes of documents. It is also shown how such models can be acquired from labeled examples. An inference mechanism solves the spatial document interpretation.

2 Representation

The representation for single documents as well as for models of document classes is realized as attributed directed graphs $G = (V, E, \mu, \nu)$ where V is the set of vertices, $E \subseteq V \times V$ is the set of edges, $\mu : V \mapsto A_V$ maps vertices to the vertex attributes and $\nu : E \mapsto A_E$ maps edges to the edge attributes.

Starting from the image of a document, preprocessing (layout analysis) generates a set of layout objects $O = \{o_1, \ldots, o_n\}$. The algorithms necessary for this task are described detailed in [2]. Each layout object is characterized by its bounding box and a type label, which is one of the set $L = \{$PAGE, BLOCK, LINE, WORD, CHAR$\}$. Furthermore, the layout objects are organized in form of a tree

---

[1] The project READ is funded by the German Ministry for Education and Research (BMBF) under grant 01IN503C. The author is responsible for the contents of the publication.

where the root is a page object. The function $p : O \mapsto O$ maps a layout object to its parent.

The set of vertices V contains exactly one element for each layout object of the document. For all edges, the following condition must hold for the corresponding layout objects: $o_i = p(o_j) \lor p(o_i) = p(o_j)$. Hence, the edges in the graph describe relative locations between layout objects and their sons and between layout objects having the same father.

The vertex attributes are 3-tuples $A_V = (l, s, c)$, where $l \in L$ denotes the layout type and $s \in I\!N_0$ holds the number of sons of the corresponding layout object. The third attribute $c \in C$ holds the logic label of the layout object. The edge attributes are 2-tuples $A_E = (\mathbf{h}, \mathbf{v})$ describing qualitatively the relative location between two layout objects. The basis is Allen's interval algebra which was originally developed in the area of temporal reasoning (see [1]). He defined a set of 13 relations $\mathcal{A} = \{<, m, o, fi, di, s, =, si, d, f, oi, mi, >\}$ being sufficient to express any qualitative relation that can be held between two intervals.

The intervals needed for this representation can be obtained by projecting the bounding boxes of the layout objects on the bounding box of the page object. The horizontal and vertical component is represented by a 13 dimensional vector. Each dimension represents one qualitative relation: given a relation $a \in \mathcal{A}$ the components of the corresponding vector $\mathbf{r} = (r_<, \ldots, r_>)$ are $r_a = 1.0$ and $r_i = 0.0$ for $i \neq a$. Thus, the edge attributes can be defined: $A_E = (\mathbf{h}, \mathbf{v})$ with $\mathbf{h}, \mathbf{v} \in I\!R^{13}$. The first vector represents the horizontal and the second the vertical component of a qualitative spatial relation.

The representation of document classes is also realized by attributed directed graphs. Such a graph is called a class model $M = (V_M, E_M, \mu_M, \nu_M)$ and is derived automatically from a given set of graphs of labeled documents belonging to a specific domain, called the training set $T_D = \{G_1, G_2, \ldots, G_d\}$.

The set of vertices V_M contains one element for each label $c \in C_D \backslash \{c_0\}$ where C_D is the union over all logic labels used in the document graphs $G_i \in T_D$. Hence, there can be at most as many vertices as there are labels defined for the document class. The set of edges is derived as follows: if there is an edge $(v_j, v_k) \in G_i$ with $\mu(v_i) = (l, p, c) \land c \neq \text{OTHER}$ for $i = j, k$ then there is also an edge in the graph of the class model.

The vertices of the model graph have more attributes as in the document graphs: $A_{V_M} = (l, c, \check{n}, \hat{n}, \check{p}, \hat{p})$. The meaning of the first two attributes is the same as in the case of document graphs: $l \in L$ denotes the layout type and $c \in C$ is the logic label. $\check{n}, \hat{n} \in I\!N_0$ describe the minimal and maximal cardinality of the label and $\check{p}, \hat{p} \in I\!N_0$ the minimal and maximal cardinality of the parts of the label. The edge attributes are again 2-tuples $A_{E_M} = (\mathbf{h}, \mathbf{v})$, which describe the relative location between the labels horizontally and vertically.

3 Learning and Inference

The aim of the learning process is to create class models from labeled training sets of structured documents with a minimum amount of interaction. At the beginning, the class specific set of logic labels $C = \{c_0, c_1, \ldots, c_m\}$ has to be defined by the user. Thereafter, the training set $T_D = \{G_1, G_2, \ldots, G_d\}$ can be created.

The learning algorithm starts with a generic class model $M_0 = (\emptyset, \emptyset, \mu, \nu)$. Then, the class model is extended incrementally by each document of the training set $G_i \in T_D$. Hence, the final model is the combination of all documents of the training set: $M = ((M_0 \circ G_1) \circ \ldots \circ G_d)$.

To update the vertices of the class model graph, the following steps have to be performed for each layout object of the document graph: Get the vertex of the model graph, which corresponds to the father of the current layout object. If this node exists, adapt the cardinality for its parts. If the current layout object is labeled and if there is already a vertex in the model graph which corresponds to the label of the current layout object then adapt its cardinality. Otherwise, create a new vertex for the current labeled layout object.

To update the edges of the graph in the class model, the algorithm runs over all edges in the document graph which connect two labeled vertices. Within this loop, a new spatial relation will be created if necessary. This relation will then be updated in such a way that the resulting weights in the 13-dimensional vectors of the horizontal and vertical components are the arithmetic mean of all seen relations.

The inference mechanism is realized as a search for an error tolerant subgraph isomorphism, i.e. a subgraph isomorphism from a class model M to a document G has to be found while an error function $\rho : (M, G) \mapsto I\!\!R$ has to be minimized. The strongest influence in ρ comes from the comparison of the spatial relations:

$$\delta_e(e_1, e_2) = 2.0 - \frac{\mathbf{h_1} \cdot \mathbf{h_2}}{|\mathbf{h_1}| \cdot |\mathbf{h_2}|} - \frac{\mathbf{v_1} \cdot \mathbf{v_2}}{|\mathbf{v_1}| \cdot |\mathbf{v_2}|}$$

The basis of the implementation of this search is the A*-algorithm, which is described detailed in [6].

4 Experimental Results

The presented system has been applied to a class of enveloped sended from companies. The set of logic labels used here is $C = \{$TA, MVB, MDR, RA$\}$ where TA stands for target address, RA for the receiver address and MVB and MDR are two kinds of stamps. In each run, a learnset of 10 and a testset of 1000 documents were selected randomly from a complete set of 2000 documents. This experiment was repeated 100 times. Results are shown in table 1 which is read as follows: the first column holds the label and the second the number of objects with that label. The next two columns hold the results regarding only the first vote of the inference while for the last two columns the first two votes were taken. The numbers in the *errs* columns show the number of wrong instances and the number of omitted objects, which the columns named *reco* hold the recognition rate in percent. The experiments were run on a Pentium Pro with 200MHz. The running times for learning the representation of envelopes as well as the inference needs about 0.01s per example.

label	objs	1 vote		2 votes	
		errs	reco	errs	reco
all	3613	1046/13	70.7%	221/13	93.5%
TA	936	8/ 1	99.0%	1/ 1	99.8%
MVB	799	395/ 7	49.7%	13/ 7	97.5%
MDR	794	503/ 2	36.4%	67/ 2	91.3%
RA	64	62/ 0	3.1%	62/ 0	3.1%

Table 1. Experimental results on a set of 2000 envelopes.

5 Conclusions

It was shown how structured documents and classes of structured documents can be represented as attributed directed graphs. The class models can be constructed automatically from a labeled training set of documents. By the means of finding subgraph isomorphisms, it is possible to perform a logic labeling of unseen documents of a previously learned class.

This system aims at the semi automatic generation of document models which can be used for the representation language FRESCO for information extraction on structured documents as described in [3]. Currently, it is possible to create skeletons of FRESCO models representing the topology of concepts. These skeletons can then completed manually by the user.

In the future, the learning mechanism should setup representations with more attributes like cardinalities, keyword lists, dictionaries, absolute box sizes, etc, so that the generated FRESCO models are more complete. Furthermore the qualitative spatial relations should be used to create constraint expressions.

References

1. James F. Allen. Maintaining knowledge about temporal intervals. *Communications of the ACM*, 26(11):832–843, November 1983.
2. Thomas Bayer, Ulrich Bohnacker, and Ingrid Renz. *Information Extraction from Paper Documents*. Handbook on Optical Character Recognition and Document Image Analysis. P. Wang and Horst Bunke, to be published.
3. Thomas A. Bayer and Hanno Walischewski. Experiments on extracting structural information from paper documents using syntactic pattern analysis. In *Proceedings of the 3rd International Conference on Document Analysis and Recognition*, volume 1, pages 476–479, 1995.
4. F. Esposito, D. Malerba, and G. Semeraro. Multistrategy Learning for Document Recognition. *Applied Artificial Intelligence*, 8(33–84), 1994.
5. Amitabha Mukerjee and Gene Joe. A qualitative spatial representation based on rangency and alignment. Technical report, Texas A&M University, Department of Computer Science, 1992.
6. J. Pearl. *Heuristics*. Addison Wesley, London, 1984.

Author Index

Springer
and the
environment

At Springer we firmly believe that an international science publisher has a special obligation to the environment, and our corporate policies consistently reflect this conviction.

We also expect our business partners – paper mills, printers, packaging manufacturers, etc. – to commit themselves to using materials and production processes that do not harm the environment. The paper in this book is made from low- or no-chlorine pulp and is acid free, in conformance with international standards for paper permanency.

Springer

Lecture Notes in Artificial Intelligence (LNAI)

Lecture Notes in Computer Science